INDEX TO
FAIRY TALES, 1978-1986

Including
Folklore, Legends, and Myths
in Collections

Fifth Supplement

compiled by
Norma Olin Ireland
and
Joseph W. Sprug

The Scarecrow Press, Inc.
Metuchen, N.J., & London
1989

British Library Cataloguing-in-Publication data available.

Library of Congress Cataloging-in-Publication Data.

Ireland, Norma Olin, 1907–
    Index to fairy tales, 1978–1986, including folklore, legends, and myths in collections : fifth supplement / complied by Norma Olin Ireland and Joseph W. Sprug.
        p.   cm.
    Supplement to Index to the author's fairy tales, 1949–1972 (Faxon, 1973) and to Mary Huse Eastman's Index to fairy tales, myths, and legends (Faxon, 1926).
    ISBN 0-8108-2194-X
    1. Fairy tales—Indexes. 2. Mythology—Indexes. 3. Folklore—Indexes. 4. Folk literature—Indexes. I. Sprug, Joseph W., 1922-   . II. Ireland, Norma Olin, 1907– Index to fairy tales, 1949-1972. III. Eastman, Mary Huse, 1870–1963. Index to fairy tales, myths, and legends. IV. Title.
Z5983.F17I732   1989
[GR550]
016.3982—dc19   89-6042

DEDICATION

To the memory of my late husband, Dave, who was scheduled to be my joint-author for this book. But he passed on, just at retirement, in 1970. He was joint-author for one of my earlier books, *Index to Monologs and Dialogs* (Faxon, 1939), and was accurate and meticulous in his indexing. He was experienced in detailed work of his own profession as an industrial engineer—accountant, cost estimator, purchasing agent, and finally head of cost reduction—in Cal Tech's Jet Propulsion Laboratory, in space work.

He was also a talented man in other fields, versed in the arts: music (voice), wood-carving, and sculpture. But always he encouraged me in my own profession (as a librarian-writer). Dave was a wonderful husband who gave me a lifetime of love and devotion. May the "little people" of our fairy tales (which he enjoyed so much) join God in blessing him always.

—N.O.I.

ACKNOWLEDGMENTS

I wish to thank Mrs. Norma Olin Ireland for giving me this oppor-
tunity to work with her on the fairy-tale-plus project.

I also wish to thank various departments of St. Edward's
University: the Administration for a faculty development grant in
support of this work; my colleagues on the SEU Scarborough-
Phillips Library staff; special thanks to Ray Spinhirne and his staff
for their cooperation in writing a computer program for this index
and for their patient assistance in the course of completing the
work.

Thanks to the ever-friendly and effective interlibrary loan
service of the Austin Public Library. In addition to Austin, the
public libraries of San Antonio, Dallas, and Colorado Springs
(Colorado) supplied a significant number of the titles indexed. A
number of publishers have contacted me in support of the effort
and I am grateful to them.

—J.W.S.

Thanks to Mr. Joseph Sprug for his large contribution, as joint-
author, and long hours putting it on the computer.

I also want to acknowledge the interlibrary loan services of
the Fallbrook and Vista County libraries, and the Carlsbad City
libraries.

—N.O.I.

CONTENTS

Foreword, by Peggy Sullivan vii

Introduction ix

List of Collections Analyzed and
  Key to Symbols Used 1

THE INDEX 23

FOREWORD

Fairy tales can be as elusive as they are universal. The same themes and stereotypical characters, the same plots and problems turn up in many different countries' stories and in many different publications. Since people often store them in their memories of stories as they have been told, there is another dimension to the problem of locating them in print. Anyone who needs to find a fairy tale has reason to applaud and treasure the work of Norma Ireland.

Ireland has been preparing indexes longer than many of her readers have been using them. She has ranged into many subjects, often at a point in time when others had not yet realized the need for organizing the materials available. She has been consistent in her preparation of indexes to fairy tales and has offered to storytellers both real and potential, to librarians, teachers, parents, children, and all those who might consult her several indexes, a valued resource. Like all good indexers, she has many of the characteristics of some favored characters from fairy tales: patience and persistence, skill and resourcefulness, and the ability to begin a long task and conclude it successfully. Her work is welcome.

Peggy Sullivan
Past A.L.A. President
September 1988

INTRODUCTION

This work is a supplement to two previous indexes—*Index to Fairy Tales, 1949–1972,* and *Index to Fairy Tales, 1973–1977*—and covers the period 1978–1987. As indicated in the Dedication, this volume was planned to be co-authored by Norma Ireland and her late husband, Dave, who passed on in 1970. Joseph Sprug, who like Norma Ireland had been a Faxon author, became co-author of this work. It was agreed that compilation would be facilitated by placing the records on computer.

Scope and Arrangement

A total of 261 titles (collections only) have been indexed, selected on the basis of availability and favorable reviews in professional journals. Arrangement is alphabetical, primarily by title and subject; author entries have been included only when an author is specifically listed in a collection. The title entry is the main entry. Author-title abbreviations are used to locate stories as cited in the "List of Collections Analyzed and Key to Symbols Used" at the beginning of the *Index.* The "Key to Symbols Used" consists of abbreviated author-title entries and is as simple and easy-to-use as possible.

If the first word of the title is the same, or similar to the subject entry, then it is omitted under the subject classification as redundant. We have arranged the entries alphabetically by the word following the entry word; personal surnames are arranged before the other entries beginning with the same word; when title and subject headings are identical, the title comes first.

Subject Headings

Many new subject headings are included in this volume, reflecting in part the inclusion of folklore as indicated in this volume's title. More than 2,700 subject headings have been used, not including cross-references. We have consulted children's librarians, who urged as much "subject indexing" as possible, not only to help them quickly locate stories (including those with unusual subjects), but also to please their young readers who request specific types of stories. The

latter consideration accounts for the large number of entries under certain topics that are frequently requested, such as "Princes and Princesses."

In general, the headings used in the previous *Index* are repeated here with some additions and a few changes. Inevitably, new developments and new titlings have been reflected in the choice of headings. However, early names of countries have been used when the stories pertain to the early years of those countries (e.g., Persia). (Cross-references from the countries' present names have been provided.)

We hope that this Supplement will be helpful to all libraries, both large and small (especially in their children's rooms), which contain fairy tales, folklore, legends and myths in their collections.

Norma Olin Ireland
Joseph Sprug

LIST OF COLLECTIONS
ANALYZED AND
KEY TO SYMBOLS USED

ADAMS—IRON
> Adams, Richard. *The iron wolf, and other stories.* Illus. by Yvonne Gilbert and Jennifer Campbell. Allen Lane, 1980. 142 p.

AESOP—FABLES. *See* WATSON—FABLES; WILLIAMS—AESOP.

AFANASEV—RUSSIAN. *See* BILIBIN—RUSSIAN.

AIKEN—MEXICAN
> Aiken, Riley. *Mexican folktales from the borderlands.* Drawings by Dennis Zamora. Dallas: Southern Methodist University Press, c1980. 159 p.

AINSWORTH—BEAR
> Ainsworth, Ruth. *The bear who liked hugging people, and other stories.* Illus. by Antony Maitland. New York: Crane Russak, 1978. 102 p.

AINSWORTH—PHANTOM
> Ainsworth, Ruth. *The phantom carousel, and other ghostly tales.* Illus. by Shirley Hughes. Chicago: Follett Pub. Co., c1977. 176 p.

ALDERSON—PINK. *See* Lang–Pink/K.

AMORE—LUSTFUL GR 305 A46
> Amore, Roy C., and Larry D. Shinn. *Lustful maidens and ascetic kings; Buddhist and Hindu stories of life.* Illus. by Sharon Wallace. New York: Oxford Univ. Press, c1981. 198 p.

ANAYA—CUENTOS. *See* GRIEGO—CUENTOS.

AND EVERY
> *And everywhere, children! An international story festival.* Selected by the Literature Committee, Association for Childhood Education International. New York: Wm Morrow/Greenwillow Books, c1979. 266 p.

ANDERSEN—HAGUE
> Andersen, Hans Christian. *Michael Hague's favourite Hans Christian Andersen fairy tales.* New York: Holt & Winston, c1981. 162 p.

ANDERSON—TRICK.
> Anderson, Bernice G. *Trickster tales from prairie lodgefires.* Illus. by Frank Gee. Nashville: Abingdon, 1979. 94 p.

2

ARROWSMITH—FIELD
Arrowsmith, Nancy, with George Moorse. *A field guide to the little people.* New York: Pocket Books, 1978. 296 p. London : Macmillan 1977

ASIMOV—FANT.
Asimov, Isaac, Martin Greenberg, and Charles Waugh. *Fantastic creatures; an anthology of fantasy and science fiction.* New York: Franklin Watts, 1981. unpaged.

BANG—FIVE
Bang, Betsy, trans. *Five tales from Bengal: the demons of Raipur.* Illus. by Molly Garrett Bang. New York: Greenwillow Books, c1980. 81 p.

BASKIN—IMPS
Baskin, Leonard. *Imps, demons, hobgoblins, witches, fairies & elves.* New York: Pantheon, c1984. 47 unnumbered pages.

BERGER—ANIMALIA
Berger, Barbara. *Animalia; thirteen small tales retold, handwritten, & illuminated by B. B.* Millbrae, CA: Celestial Arts, c1982. 63 unnumbered pages.

BIERHORST—GLASS. *See* PERRAULT—GLASS.

BIERHORST—HUNGRY F 1219.76 F65 H86 1986
Bierhorst, John, ed. *The hungry woman; myths and legends of the Aztecs.* [Illus. by 16th-cent. Aztec artists.] New York: Wm Morrow, c1984. 148 p.

BILIBIN—RUSSIAN f GR202 A42PZ8 A26 RW 1980
Bilibin, Ivan I. *Russian folk tales.* Tr. by Robert Chandler. Boulder: Shambhala, 1980. 77 p.

BLYTON—MY
Blyton, Enid. *My best book of Enid Blyton stories.* Illus. by Rene Cloke. London: Award Publications, n.d. 77 p.

BOOSS—SCAND. GR 205 533
Booss, Claire, ed. *Scandinavian folk & fairy tales; tales from Norway, Sweden, Denmark, Finland, Iceland.* New York: Avenel Books, c1984. 666 p.

BRANSTON—GODS
Branston, Brian. *Gods and heroes from Viking mythology.* Illus. by Giovanni Caselli. New York: Schocken Books, c1978. 156 p.

BRIGGS—VANISH. GR 549 B75
Briggs, Katharine. *The vanishing people; fairy lore and legends.* Illus. by Mary I. French. New York: Pantheon Books, c1978. 218 p.

CAMPOS—MEXICAN GR 115 M45
Campos, Anthony John, ed. & tr. *Mexican folk tales.* Tucson: Univ. of Arizona Press, c1977. 136 p.

CARILLO—ARMADILLO. *See* RITCHIE—ARMADILLO.

CHALK—TALES
Chalk, Gary. *Tales of ancient China*. London: Frederich Muller, c1984. paper, unp.

CHESNUTT—CONJURE. *See* SHEPARD—CONJURE.

CLASSIC CHILD.
Classic children's stories. London: Cavendish House, 1984. 91 p.

COHEN—EVERY.
Cohen, Daniel. *Everything you need to know about monsters and still be able to get to sleep*. Illus. by Jack Stokes. Garden City, NY: Doubleday, c1981. 118 p.

COLOMBO—WIND. E99.A35 W56 1982
Colombo, Robert. *Windigo, an anthology of fact and fantastic fiction*. Saskatoon, Sask.: Western Producer Prairie Books, c1982. 208 p.

CORTES—BYELORUSSIAN
Cortes, L. *Byelorussian folk tales*. Drawings by V. Slawuk. Minsk: Vysheishaya Shkola, c1983. 151 p.

CROSSLEY—FOLK
Crossley-Holland, Kevin. *The Faber book of northern folk-tales*. Illus. by Alan Howard. Boston: Faber & Faber, c1980. 157 p.

CROSSLEY—LEGENDS
Crossley-Holland, Kevin. *The Faber book of northern legends*. Illus. by Alan Howard. Boston: Faber & Faber, 1977. 236 p.

CROSSLEY—MABINOGION. *See* THOMAS—MABINOGION.

CROUCH—WHOLE
Crouch, Marcus. *The whole world storybook*. Illus. by William Stobbs. Oxford: Oxford Univ. Press, c1983. 168 p.

DAY—CASTLES. *See* LEE—CASTLES.

DEPAOLA—FAVORITE PZ8.1 D43 To 1986
dePaola, Tomie. *Favorite nursery tales*. New York: Putnam's, c1986. 127 p.

DE WIT—TALKING
De Wit, Dorothy. *The talking stone; an anthology of Native American tales and legends*. With decorations by Donald Crews. New York: Greenwillow Books, c1979. 213 p.

DUTTON—HOPI
Dutton, Bertha, and Caroline Olin. *Myths & legends of the Indians of the southwest*. Book II: *Hopi, Acoma, Tewa, Zuni*. Santa Barbara: Bellerophon Books, c1984. [48] p.

4

DUTTON—NAVAJO
Dutton, Bertha, and Caroline Olin. *Myths & legends of the Indians of the southwest.* Book I: *Navajo, Pima, Apache.* Santa Barbara: Bellerophon Books, c1979. [48] p.

EELS—BRAZIL PZ8 E27 F 1972
Eels, Elsie Spicer. *Fairy tales from Brazil; how and why tales from Brazilian folk-lore.* New York: Dodd, Mead, 1959 c1917. 210 p.
Kraus Reprint Co., 1972

EHRLICH—RANDOM PZ8.E32 Ran 1985
Ehrlich, Amy. *The Random House book of fairy tales.* Illus. by Diane Goode. Introd. by Bruno Bettelheim. New York: Random House, c1985. 208 p.

ELBAZ—FOLKTALES
Elbaz, Andre E. *Folktales of the Canadian Sephardim.* Illus. by Raphael Benchetrit. Toronto: Fitzhenry & Whiteside, c1982. 192 p.

EWART—LORE
Ewart, Neil. *The lore of flowers.* New York: Bladford Press, 1982. 184 p.

FABER BOOKS. *See* CROSSLEY—FOLK; CROSSLEY—LEGENDS; HAVILAND—N.AMER.

FATTOROSS—SIMPLETON
Fattoross, Camille. *The simpleton of Naples, and other Italian folktales,* by Nonna Maria Scarpato; tr. and retold by her daughter Camille Fattoross. Illus. by Ted Guerin. Toms River, NJ: Capricorn Books, c1982. 82 p.

FAULKNER—DAYS
Faulkner, William J. *The days when the animals talked; Black American folktales and how they came to be.* Illus. by Troy Howell. Chicago: Follett, 1977. 190 p.

FROUD—FAERIES f GR549.F76
Froud, Brian, and Alan Lee, ed. and illus. *Faeries.* Designed by David Larkin. New York: Harry N. Abrams, 1978. unp.

GALLANT—CONSTEL.
Gallant, Roy A. *The Constellations: how they came to be.* New York: Four Winds Press, 1979. 203 p.

GANTZ—EARLY
Gantz, Jeffrey, trans. *Early Irish myths and sagas.* New York: Dorset Press, 1981. 280 p.

GARNER—BRITISH PZ8 G226 Bo1984
Garner, Alan. *Book of British fairy tales.* Illus. by Derek Collard. New York: Delacorte Press, 1984. 159 p.

GIBSON—GODS
Gibson, Michael. *Gods, men & monsters from the Greek myths.* Illus. by Giovanni Caselli. New York: Schocken Books, c1977. 116 p.

GINSBURG—TWELVE
Ginsburg, Mirra. *The twelve clever brothers and other fools.* Illus. by Charles Mikolaycak. New York: Lippincott, c1979. 89 p.

GOROG—TASTE j PZI GG825 +a
Gorog, Judith. *A taste for quiet, and other disquieting tales.* New York: Philomel, c1982, 128 p.

GRIEGO—CUENTOS GR III M49. G74
Griego y Maestas, Jose. *Cuentos; tales from the Hispanic southwest.* Retold in English by Rudolfo A. Anaya; based on stories collected by Juan B. Rael. Illus. by Jaime Valdez. Sante Fa: Museum of New Mexico Press, c1980. 174 p.

GRIMM—ABOUT. *See* SHUB—ABOUT.

HADLEY—LEGENDS
Hadley, Eric, and Tessa Hadley. *Legends of the sun and moon.* Illus. by Jan Nesbitt. New York: Cambridge Univ. Press, c1983. 32 p.

HAINING—LEPRE.
Haining, Peter. *The leprechaun's kingdom.* Designed by Christopher Scott. New York: Harmony, 1980. 128 p.

HARRIS—MOUSE E 78 N78 H33 1977
Harris, Christie. *Mouse woman and the mischief-makers.* Drawings by Douglas Tait. New York: Atheneum, 1977. 115 p.

HAVILAND—N.AMER.
Haviland, Virginia. *The Faber book of North American legends.* Illus. Ann Strugnell, Boston: Faber & Faber, 1979. 214 p.

HAYES—COYOTE
Hayes, Joe. *Coyote & . . . . Native American folk tales retold.* Illus. by Lucy Jelinek-Thompson. Santa Fe: Mariposa, c1983. 77 p.

HESLEWOOD—TALES
Heslewood, Juliet. *Tales of sea and shore.* Illus. by Karen Berry. New York: Oxford Univ. Press, 1983. 151 p.

HIGHWATER—ANPAO E 9 8 FG H58 A77
Highwater, Jamake. *Anpao, an American Indian Odyssey.* Illus. by Fritz Scholder. Philadelphia: Lippincott, 1977. 256 p.

HILL—MORE
Hill, Kay. *More Glooscap stories. Legends of the Wabanaki Indians.* Illus. by John Hamberger. New York: Dodd, Mead, c1970. 179 p.

HOKE—DEMONIC
Hoke, Helen. *Demonic, dangerous & deadly.* New York: Dutton, c1983. 143 p.

HOKE—HORRORS
Hoke, Helen. *Horrors, horrors, horrors.* Illus. by Bill Prosser. New York: Franklin Watts, 1978. 177 p.

HOKE—SPIRITS
Hoke, Helen. *Spirits, spooks, and other sinister creatures.* New York: Franklin Watts, c1984. 136 p.

HOKE—UNCANNY
Hoke, Helen. *Uncanny tales and unexpected horrors.* New York: Dutton, c1983. 126 p.

HYDE-CHAMBERS—TIBET.
Hyde-Chambers, Frederick and Audrey. *Tibetan folk tales.* Boulder, CO: Shambhala, 1981. 186 p.

JACOBS—CELTIC
Jacobs, Joseph. *Celtic fairy tales (being the two collections: Celtic fairy tales & More Celtic fairy tales).* Illus. by Victor Ambrus. New York: World Publ. Co., New ed. 1971. 330 p.

JAGENDORF—FIRST
Jagendorf, Mortiz A. *Tales from the first Americans.* Illus. by Jack Endewelt. Morristown, NJ: Silver Burdett, 1979. 96 p.

JAGENDORF—MAGIC
Jagendorf, M. A., and Virginia Weng. *The magic boat, and other Chinese folk stories.* New York: Vanguard Press, c1980. 236 p.

KEIGHTLEY—WORLD
Keightley, Thomas. *The world guide to gnomes, fairies, elves and other little people.* New York: Avenel Books, 1978. 560 p.

KENDALL—HAUNTING
Kendall, Carol. *Haunting tales from Japan.* Lawrence: Spencer Museum of Art, the University of Kansas, c1985. 39 p.

KENDALL—SWEET PZ 8.1 K36 Sw 1980
Kendall, Carol, and Yao-Wen Li. *Sweet and sour; tales from China.* Drawings by Shirley Fetts. New York: ~~Seabury Press, c1978~~. 112 p. *Houghton-Mifflin/Clarion Books 1980*

KUDIAN—MORE PR 6061.U3 M67 1983
Kudian, Mischa. *More apples fell from heaven; a selection of Armenian folk and fairy.* London: Mashtots Press, 1983. 82 p.

KUDIAN—THREE. *See* SHEOHMELIAN—THREE.

LANG—BLUE
Lang, Andrew. *Blue fairy book.* Ed. by Brian Alderson. Illus. by John Lawrence. Harmondsworth: Kestrel Books, c1975. 373 p.

LANG—GREEN
Lang, Andrew. *Green fairy book.* Ed. by Brian Alderson. Illus. by Antony Maitland. New York: Viking Press, c1978. 408 p.

LANG—PINK/D
Lang, Andrew. *The pink fairy book.* Illus. by H. J. Ford. New York: Dover,

[n.d.]. 360 p. [Note: The contents of this edition are not exactly identical with the following ed.]

LANG—PINK/K

Lang, Andrew. *The pink fairy book.* Ed. by Brian Alderson. Illus. by Colin McNaughton. London: Kestrel; New York: Viking Press, c1982. 331 p. [Note: The contents of this edition are not exactly identical with the Dover ed.]

LANIER—KING. *See* MALORY—KING.

LEE—CASTLES

Lee, Alan. *Castles.* Written by David Day. New York: Bantam Books, c1984. 190 p.

LEE—FAERIES. *See* FROUD—FAERIES.

LEETE—GOLDEN

Leete-Hodge, Lornie. *The big Golden book of fairy tales.* Illus. by Beverlie Manson. New York: Golden Press, c1981. 157 p.

LEHANE—LEGENDS

Lehane, Brendan. *Legends of valor (The enchanted world).* Chicago: Time-Life Books, c1984. 143 p.

LEHANE—WIZARDS

Lehane, Brendan. *Wizards and witches (The enchanted world).* Chicago: Time-Life Books, c1984. 142 p.

LESTER—BLACK GR 350. L47 1970

Lester, Julius. *Black folktales.* Illus. by Tom Feelings. New York: Grove Press, c1969. 159 p.

LEWIS—ANIMAL

Lewis, Shari. *One-minute animal stories.* Illus. by Kelly Oechsli. Garden City, NY: Doubleday, c1986. 48 p.

LEWIS—BEDTIME

Lewis, Shari, with Lan O'Kun. *One-minute bedtime stories.* Illus. by Art Cumings. Garden City, NY: Doubleday, c1982. 48 p.

LEWIS—FUN. *See* MANLEY—FUN.

LEWIS—MINUTE

Lewis, Shari. *One-minute favorite fairy tales.* Illus. by Benton Mahan. Garden City, NY: Doubleday, c1985. 48 p.

LINDOW—MYTHS

Lindow, John. *Myths & legends of the Vikings.* Art by N. Conkle, R. Costa, R. Zydycrn. Santa Barbara: Bellerophon Books, c1979. 48 p.

LINDOW—SWEDISH GR 225. S85

Lindow, John. *Swedish legends and folktales.* Berkeley: Univ. of California Press, c1978. 219 p.

LINES—GREEK
> Lines, Kathleen, ed. *The Faber book of Greek legends.* Illus. by Faith Jaques. London: Faber & Faber, 1983, c1973. 268 p.

LISKER—TALL
> Lisker, Tom. *Tall tales; American myths.* Milwaukee: Contemporary Perspectives, Inc., c1977. 48 p.

LLOYD—MYTHICAL
> Lloyd-Jones, Hugh. *Mythical beasts.* Sculptures by Marcelle Quinton. London: Duckworth, c1980. 70 p.

LOBEL—FABLES jE PZ Z L7835 fa
> Lobel, Arnold. *Fables.* [Illus. by the author.] New York: Harper & Row, 1980. 40 p.

LOCHHEAD—BATTLE
> Lochhead, Marion. *The battle of the birds, and other Celtic tales.* Illus. by Pat Hannah. Edinburgh: James Thin, 1981. 148 p.

LOFGREN—BOY
> Lofgren, Ulf. *The boy who ate the giant, and other Swedish folktales.* Tr. by Sheila LaFarge. New York: Collins/World, c1978. 32 p.

LOGAN—OLD
> Logan, Patrick. *The old gods; facts about Irish fairies.* Belfast: Appletree Press, c1981. 152 p.

LOW—GREEK BL782 L68 1985 c.2
> Low, Alice. *The Macmillan book of Greek gods and heroes.* Illus. by Arvis Stewart. New York: Macmillan, c1985. 184 p.

LURIE—CLEVER PZ 8.1 L974 C1 1980
> Lurie, Alison. *Clever Gretchen, and other forgotten folktales.* Illus. by Margot Tomes. New York: Crowell, c1980. 113 p.

LURIE—HEAVENLY PZ 8.1 L974 He 1974
> Lurie, Alison. *The heavenly zoo; legends and tales of the stars.* Illus. by Monika Beisner. New York: Farrar Straus Giroux, c1979. 58 p.

LUZZATTO—LONG
> Luzzatto, Paola Caboara. *Long ago when the earth was flat; three tales from Africa.* Illus. by Aimone Sambuy. New York: Collins, c1979. 44 p.

MCCARTHY—RACCOON
> McCarthy, Eugene J. *Mr. Raccoon and his friends.* Illus. by James Ecklund. Chicago: Academy Press Ltd., c1977. 119 p.

MCCARTY—SKULL
> McCarty, Toni. *The skull in the snow, and other folktales.* Illus. by Katherine Coville. New York: Delacorte Press, c1981. 87 p.

MACDONALD—GOLDEN
> MacDonald, George. *The golden key, and other stories.* Illus. by Craig Yoe. Grand Rapids, MI: Eerdman's, c1980. 165 p.

MACDONALD–GRAY
> MacDonald, George. *The gray wolf, and other stories.* Illus. by Craig Yoe. Grand Rapids, MI: Eerdman's, c1980. 186 p.

MACDONALD—TWENTY Z 675.53 M16 1986
> Macdonald, Margaret Read. *Twenty tellable tales; audience participation folktales for the beginning storyteller.* Drawings by Roxane Murphy. New York: H. W. Wilson Co., c1986. 220 p.

MACDONALD—WISE
> MacDonald, George. *The wise woman, and other stories.* Illus. by Craig Yoe, Grand Rapids, MI: Eerdman's, c1980. 172 p.

MACE—HOME
> Mace, Jean. *Home fairy tales* (*Contes du petit-chateau*). Tr. by Mary L. Booth. Great Neck, NY: Core Collection, 1979. 304 p.

MCGARRY—FOLK
> McGarry, Mary. *Great folk tales of Ireland.* Illus. by Richard Hook. London: F. Muller, 1980 c1972. 112 p.

MCKEE—SCOTTISH
> Mckee, Christian M. *Scottish folklore, legend, and superstition.* Illus. by Charles Logan. Baltimore: Gateway Press, c1983. 43 p.

MCKINLEY—DOOR P Z 8 M1793 Do 1981
> McKinley, Robin. *The door in the hedge.* New York: Greenwillow Books, c1981. 216 p.

MACLEAN—CUENTOS wdwrd / GR 110. C2 M32
> MacLean, Angus. *Cuentos; based on the folk tales of the* Spanish Californians. Illus. by Ione MacLean Bowman. Fresno: Pioneer Publ. Co., c1979. 205 p.

MACMILLAN—CANADIAN
> Macmillan, Cyrus. *Canadian wonder tales.* Illus. by Elizabeth Cleaver. London: The Bodley Head, 1980 c1974. 276 p.

MCNEIL—CHARM
> McNeil, W. K. *The charm is broken; readings in Arkansas and Missouri folklore.* Little Rock: August House, c1984. 201 p.

MAGEL—GAMBIA
> Magel, Emil A. *Folktales from the Gambia: Wolof fictional narratives.* Tr. and annotated by E. A. M. Washington: Three Continents Press, c1984. 208 p.

MAGIC KNIFE
> *The magic knife; folk tales from China* (Fifth series). Beijing: Foreign Language Press, 1982. 142 p.

MAGICAL BEASTS
> *Magical beasts,* by the editors of Time-Life Books. (The enchanted world) Chicago: Time-Life Books, c1985. 143 p.

MALORY—KING

Malory, Thomas. *King Arthur and his knights of the Round Table;* from *Le morte d'Arthur.* Ed. by Sidney Lanier. Illus. by Florian. New York: Grosset & Dunlap, 1986, c1950. 282 p.

MANLEY—FUN

Manley, Seon, & Gogo Lewis. *Fun phantoms; tales of ghostly entertainment.* New York: Lothrop, Lee & Shepard, c1979. 186 p.

MANNING—CATS

Manning-Sanders, Ruth. *A book of cats and creatures.* Illus. by Robin Jacques. New York: Dutton, c1981. 127 p.

MANNING—KINGS

Manning-Sanders, Ruth. *A book of kings and queens.* Illus. by Robin Jacques. New York: Dutton, c1977. 126 p.

MANNING—MARVELS

Manning-Sanders, Ruth. *A book of marvels and magic.* Illus. by Robin Jacques. New York: Dutton, c1978. 123 p.

MANNING—SPOOKS

Manning-Sanders, Ruth. *A book of spooks and spectres.* Illus. by Robin Jacques. New York: Dutton, c1979. 128 p.

MARSHALL—EVERY

Marshall, Sybil. *Everyman's book of English folk tales.* Illus. by John Lawrence. London: J. M. Dent, c1981. 384 p.

MARTIN—HUNGRY BQ 1462 E5 M37 1984

Martin, Rafe. *The hungry tigress, and other traditional Asian tales.* Illus. by Richard Wehrman. Boulder: Shambhala, c1984. 152 p.

MAYNE—BLUE

Mayne, William. *The blue book of Hob stories.* Illus. by Patrick Benson. New York: Philomel Books, c1984. 26 p.

MAYNE—GREEN

Mayne, William. *The green book of Hob stories.* Illus. by Patrick Benson. New York: Philomel Books, c1984. 25 p.

MAYNE—RED

Mayne, William. *The red book of Hob stories.* Illus. by Patrick Benson. New York: Philomel Books, c1984. 26 p.

MAYNE—YELLOW

Mayne, William. *The yellow book of Hob stories.* Illus. by Patrick Benson. New York: Philomel Books, c1984. 27 p.

MAYO—BOOK

Mayo, Margaret. *The book of magical horses.* Illus. by Victor Ambrus. New York: Hastings House, c1976. 119 p.

MINFORD—FAV.
Minford, John, tr. *Favourite folktales of China*. Illus. by He Youzhi et al.
Beijing, New World Press, 1983. 202 p.

MITCHNIK—EGYPTIAN
Mitchnik, Helen. *Egyptian and Sudanese folk-tales*. Illus. by Eric Fraser.
New York: Oxford Univ. Press, c1978. 115 p.

MULHERIN—FAVORITE
Mulherin, Jennifer, ed. *Favorite fairy tales*. Editorial and picture research:
Patrick Rudd, Leila Kooros. New York: Grosset & Dunlap, c1982.
[96] p.

MULLETT—SPIDER E99 H7 M86
Mullett, G. M. *Spider Woman stories; legends of the Hopi Indians*. Tucson:
Univ. of Arizona Press, c1979. 142 p.

MYLES—BUTTERFLIES
Myles, Colette Gauthier. *The butterflies carried him home, and other Indian tales*. Illus. by Aaron Yava. Berkeley: Artman's Press, c1981. 73 p.

NAGISHKIN—FOLKTALES
Nagishkin, Dmitri. *Folktales of the Amur; stories from the Russian far east*.
Illus. by Gennady Pavlishin. Tr. by Emily Lehrman. New York: H. N.
Abrams, c1980. 224 p.

NAHMAN—TALES BM 532 N 33 1978
Nahman of Bratslav. *The tales*. Tr., introd. and commentaries by Arnold J.
Band. Preface by Joseph Dan. Series: The classics of western spirituality. New York: Paulist Press, c1978. 340 p.

NICHOLSON—MEXICAN f F 1219.3 R38 N5
Nicholson, Irene. *Mexican and Central American mythology*. (Library of
the world's myths and legends) New York: Peter Bedrick Books, 1985.
144 p. London, Hamlyn 1967

NIGHT CREATURES
Night creatures, by the editors of Time-Life Books. (The enchanted world)
Chicago: Time-Life Books, c1985. 143 p.

NYE—OUT
Nye, Robert. *Out of this world and back again; three stories*. Illus. by Bill
Tinker. Indianapolis: Bobbs-Merrill, c1977. 59 p.

O'CONNOR—TIBET
O'Connor, Wm F. *Folk tales from Tibet; with illus. by a Tibetan artist*.
Folcroft, PA: Folcroft Library Editions, 1980. [Reprint of 1906 ed.]
176 p.

ONASSIS—FIREBIRD. *See* ZVORYKIN—FIREBIRD.

O'SULLIVAN—LEGENDS
O'Sullivan, Sean. *Legends from Ireland*. Drawings by John Skelton. London: Batsford, c1977. 176 p.

12

OXENBURY—NURSERY
Oxenbury, Helen. *The Helen Oxenbury nursery story book.* New York: Knopf, c1985. 72 p.

OZAKI—JAPANESE
Ozaki, Yei Theodora. *The Japanese fairy book.* Rutland, VT: Tuttle, 1985 c1970. 296 p.

PARKER—AUSTRALIAN GR 365 P18
Parker, K. Langloh. *Australian legendary tales.* Introds. by Andrew Lang and Wandjuk Marika. Illus. by Rex Backhaus-Smith. London: The Bodley Head, c1978. 190 p.

PATAI—GATES BM 530 G37 1981
Patai, Raphael. *Gates to the old city; a book of Jewish legends.* ~~New York~~: Detroit ~~Avon, c1980. 807 p.~~
Wayne State University Press, 1981

PEACOCK MAID
The Peacock maid—folk tales from China (third series). Beijing: Foreign Language Press [distrib. by China Books], 1981. 141 p.

PERRAULT—GLASS
Perrault, Charles. *The glass slipper; tales of times past.* Tr. by John Bierhorst. Illus. by Mitchell Miller. New York: Four Winds Press, c1981. 114 p.

PHELPS—MAID
Phelps, Ethel Johnston. *The maid of the north; feminist folk tales from around the world.* Illus. by Lloyd Bloom. New York: Holt, Rinehart and Winston, c1981. 176 p.

PHELPS—TATTERHOOD PZ8.1 T162 1978
Phelps, Ethel Johnston. *Tatterhood, and other tales.* Illus. by Pamela Baldwin Ford. Old Westbury, NY: The Feminist Press, 1978. 165 p.

PHILLIPS—HOITY
Phillips, Charles Fox. *The hoity-toity mouse, and other Bayou tales.* Garden City, NY: Doubleday, c1979. 48 p.

PIERCE—LAROUSSE
Pierce, Patricia, comp. *The Larousse book of fairy tales.* New York: Larousse, c1985. 176 p.

PIGGOTT—JAPANESE f BL 2202 P5 1983
Piggott, Juliet. *Japanese mythology.* New York: Peter Bedrick Books, c1982. (Library of the world's myths and legends) 144 p.

PIGGOTT—MEXICAN
Piggott, Juliet. *Mexican folk tales.* Illus. by John Spencer. New York: Crane Russak, 1976. 128 p.

PINSENT—GREEK f BL 782 P53 1983
Pinsent, John. *Greek mythology.* New York: Peter Bedrick Books, c1982. (Library of the world's myths and legends) 144 p.

PITCHER—TOKOL.
Pitcher, Diana. *Tokoloshi; African folk-tales adapted and re-told.* Illus. by Meg Rutherford. Millbrae: Celestial Arts, c1981. 64 p.

POLAND—MANTIS
Poland, Marguerite. *The mantis and the moon; stories for the children of Africa.* Illus. by Leigh Voigt. Johannesburg: Raven Press, c1979. 120 p.

POLLACK—MOONBEAM
Pollack, Pamela. *Moonbeam fairy tales.* New York: Hart Publ. Co., c1977. 47 p.

POTTER—PETER
Potter, Beatrix. *Peter Rabbit giant treasury.* Ed. and with an Introd. by Cary Wilkins. New York: Derrydale Books, c1980. 92 p.

PUSHKIN—FAIRY f P63347 A15 1978
Pushkin, Aleksandr. *Pushkin's fairy tales.* Tr. by Janet Dalley; Introd. by John Bayley; lithographs by Arthur Boyd. New York: Mayflower Books, c1978. 95 p.

QUILLER—SLEEPING
Quiller-Couch, Arthur. *The Sleeping Beauty, and other tales from the Old French.* Illus. by Edmund Dulac. New York: Abaris Books, c1980. 175 p.

RACKHAM—FAIRY
Rackham, Arthur. *The Arthur Rackham fairy book.* New York: Weathervane Books [Crown], c1978. 271 p.

RADIN—AFRICAN
Radin, Paul. *African folktales.* New York: Schocken Books, 1983. 322 p.

RANSOME—WAR
Ransome, Arthur. *The war of the birds and the beasts, and other Russian tales.* Ed. and introd. by Hugh Brogan. Illus. by Faith Jaques. London: J. Cape, c1984. 112 p.

RATCLIFF—SCOTTISH
Ratcliff, Ruth. *Scottish folk tales.* London: F. Muller, c1976. 144 p.

RAYCHAUDHURI—STUPID
Raychaudhuri, Upendrakishore. *The stupid tiger, and other tales.* Tr. from the Bengali by William Radice. Illus. by William Rushton. London: A. Deutsch [New York: Dutton], c1981. 86 p.

REED—ABORIGINAL
Reed, A. W. *Aboriginal legends; animal tales.* Sydney: The Author, c1978. 141 p.

REID—MYTHS
Reid, Martine J. *Myths & legends of the Haida Indians of the northwest,*

14

the children of the raven. Drawings by Nancy Conkle. Santa Barbara: Bellerophon Books, c1985. [48] p.

REID—RAVEN $f \ E \ 99 \ H2 \ R45 \ 1984$
Reid, Bill, and Robert Bringhurst. *The raven steals the light.* Seattle: Univ. of Washington Press, c1984. 91 p.   *Vancouver:*
Douglas & MacIntyre
RIORDAN—ARTHUR
Riordan, James. *Tales of King Arthur.* Illus. by Victor Ambrus. Chicago: Rand McNally, c1982. 124 p.

RIORDAN—RUSSIA
Riordan, James. *Tales from central Russia.* Illus. by Krystyna Turska. Middlesex: Kestrel Books, c1976. 286 p.

RIORDAN—TARTARY
Riordan, James. *Tales from Tartary,* retold by James Riordan. Illus. by Anthony Colbert. New York: Viking, c1978. 171 p.

RIORDAN—WOMAN o.P.
Riordan, James. *The woman in the moon, and other tales of forgotten heroines.* Illus. by Angela Barrett. New York: Dial, c1984. 86 p.

RITCHIE—ARMADILLO
Ritchie, Michael James, and David L. Carrillo. *The armadillo and twelve others.* [Illus. by Bud Breen.] Austin: Eakin Press, c1982. 60 p.

ROBE—HISPANIC
Robe, Stanley L. *Hispanic legends from New Mexico.* Berkeley: Univ. of California Press, c1980. 548 p.

ROBERTS—CHINESE PL 2658.E8 C48
Roberts, Moss. *Chinese fairy tales and fantasies.* [Tr. & ed. with the assistance of C. N. Tay.] New York: Pantheon Books, c1979. 258 p.

ROBERTS—JUNG
Roberts, Richard. *Tales for Jung folk; original fairytales dramatizing Jung's archetypes.* San Anselmo, CA: Vernal Equinox Press, c1983. 107 p.

ROBERTSON—HIGHLAND
Robertson, R. Macdonald. *Selected Highland folk tales.* Ed. by Jeremy Bruce-Watt. North Pomfret, VT: David & Charles, 1977. 212 p.

ROBINSON—RAVEN
Robinson, Gail. *Raven the trickster; legends of the North American Indians.* Introd. by Douglas Hill. Illus. by Joanna Troughton. New York: Atheneum, c1981. 125 p.

ROBINSON—THREE
Robinson, Adjai. *Three African tales.* Illus. by Carole Byard. New York: Putnam's, c1979. 47 p.

ROCKWELL—OLD PZ 8.1 O46 1979
Rockwell, Anne. *The old woman and her pig, & 10 other stories.* Told & illus. by A. R. New York: Crowell, c1979. 87 p.

ROSS—DRUIDS
Ross, Anne. *Druids, gods & heroes from Celtic mythology.* New York: Schocken Books, c1986. 132 p.

ROYDS—ANIMAL
Royds, Caroline, ed. *The animal tale treasury.* Illus. by Annabel Spenceley. New York: Putnam's, c1986. 92 p.

RUNGACHARY—TALES
Rungachary, Santha. *Tales for all times.* Illus. by P. Khemraj. New Delhi: National Book Trust [distrib. by Auromere, 1979], c1971. 64 p.

SADLER—HEAVEN
Sadler, Catherine Edwards. *Heaven's reward; fairy tales from China.* Illus. by Cheng Mung Yun. New York: Atheneum, 1985. 37 p.

SADLER—TREASURE
Sadler, Catherine Edwards. *Treasure mountain: folktales from Southern China.* Illus. by Cheng Mung Yun. New York: Atheneum, 1982. 66 p.

SAMPSON—GYPSY
Sampson, John. *Gypsy folk tales.* Engravings by Agnes Miller Parker. Salem: Salem House, 1984. 108 p.

SANDERS—DRAGONS *BL 1802 S26 1983*
Sanders, Tao Tao Liu. *Dragons, gods & spirits from Chinese mythology.* Illus. by Johnny Pau. New York: Schocken Books, c1980. 132 p.

SANDERS—HEAR *PZ81 S23 Hb 1985*
Sanders, Scott R. *Hear the wind blow: American folk songs retold.* Illus. by Ponder Goembel. New York: Bradbury Press, c1985. 202 p.

SCARPATO—SIMPLETON. *See* FATTOROSS—SIMPLETON.

SCHINDLER—GOLDEN
Schindler, S. D., illus. *The golden goose, and other tales of good fortune.* [Ed. by Eric Suben.] New York: Golden Book, c1986. 44 unnumbered pages.

SCHWARTZ—DARK *JE PZ2 Sch 956 in*
Schwartz, Alvin. *In a dark, dark room, and other scary stories.* Illus. by Dirk Zimmer. New York: Harper & Row, c1984. 63 p. *HarperCollins*

SCHWARTZ—ELIJAH'S
Schwartz, Howard. *Elijah's violin, & other Jewish fairy tales.* Illus. by Linda Heiler. Calligraphy by Tsila Schwartz. New York: Harper & Row, 1983. 302 p.

SCHWARTZ—GREAT
Schwartz, Betty Ann. *Great ghost stories.* Illus. by Paul Geiger. New York: Simon & Schuster, c1985. 177 p.

SCHWARTZ—TALES
Schwartz, Alvin. *Tales of trickery from the land of spoof.* Pictures by David Christiana. New York: Farrar, Straus and Giroux, c1985. 87 p.

SCOTT—FANTASTIC
Scott, Allan, and Michael Scott Rohan. *Fantastic people.* New York: Galahad Books, c1980. 194 p.

SEEKERS SAVIORS
Seekers and saviors; the enchanted world, by the editors of Time-Life Books. Chicago: Time-Life Books, c1986. 143 p.

SEGOVIA—SPANISH
Segovia, Gertrudis. *The Spanish fairy book.* Tr. by Elisabeth Vernon Quinn. Great Neck, NY: Core Collection Books, 1979. 321 p.

SERGEANT—WITCHES
Sergeant, Philip W. *Witches and warlocks.* Detroit: Gale, 1974, 290 p.

SEROS—SUN
Seros, Kathleen. *Sun & moon; fairy tales from Korea.* Illus. by Norman Sibley & Robert Krause. Elizabeth, NJ: Hollym Int'l Corp., 1986 c1982. 61 p.

SEVEN SISTERS
The Seven Sisters—folk tales from China (sixth series). 2nd ed. Beijing: Foreign Languages Press, 1982. 122 p.

SHAH—AFGHANISTAN
Shah, Amina. *Tales of Afghanistan.* London: Octagon Press, c1982. 115 p.

SHAH—DERVISHES
Shah, Amina. *The tale of the four dervishes, and other Sufi tales.* San Francisco: Harper & Row, c1981. 258 p.

SHAH—WORLD
Shah, Idries. *World tales; the extraordinary coincidence of stories told in all times, in all places.* New York: Harcourt Brace Jovanovich, 1979. 258 p.

SHANNON—SOLVE
Shannon, George. *Stories to solve; folktales from around the world.* Illus. by Peter Sis. New York: Greenwillow Books, c1985. 55 p.

SHAW—PIMA
Shaw, Anna Moore. *Pima Indian legends.* Tucson: Univ. of Arizona Press, 1983 c1968. 111 p.

SHELLEY—LEGENDS
Shelley, Noreen. *Legends of the gods; strange and fascinating tales from around the world.* Illus. by Astra Lacis Dick. New York: Crane Russak, c1976. 96 p.

SHEOHMELIAN—THREE
Sheohmelian, O. *Three apples from heaven: Armenian folktales.* Saddle Brook, NJ: Agbu Ararat Press, c1982. 133 p.

SHEPARD—CONJURE *PZ1 Sh 474 co*
> Shepard, Ray Anthony. *Conjure tales,* by Charles W. Chesnutt; retold. . . . Illus. by John Ross and Clare Romano. New York: Dutton, 1973. 99 p.

SHUB—ABOUT *PZ 8. 6882 Ab 1971*
> Shub, Elizabeth, tr. *About wise men and simpletons; twelve tales from Grimm.* Etchings by Nonny Hogrogian. New York: Macmillan, 1986 c1971. 118 p.

SHUB—SEEING *jE PZ2 Sh 914 Se*
> Shub, Elizabeth. *Seeing is believing.* Illus. by Rachel Isadora. New York: Greenwillow Books, c1979. 63 p.

SINGER—POWER *J PZ1, S1645 Po*
> Singer, Isaac Bashevis. *The power of light; eight stories for Hanukkah.* New York: Avon Books, c1980. 71 p.

SKURZYNSKI—FOOLS
> Skurzynski, Gloria. *Two fools and a faker; three Lebanese folk tales.* Illus. by William Papas. New York: Lothrop, Lee & Shepard, c1977. 39 p.

SMITH—MANACHAR
> Smith, Riley K. *Manachar and Munachar;* two Celtic tales retold and illus. by Riley K. Smith. Garden City, NY: Doubleday, c1977. 64 unnumbered pages.

SOYER—ADVENTURES
> Soyer, Abraham. *The adventures of Yemima, and other stories.* Tr. by Rebecca S. Beagle and Rebecca Soyer. Introd. by Peter S. Beagle. Illus. by Raphael Soyer. New York: Viking Press, c1979. 70 p.

SPELLS & BIND
> *Spells and bindings,* by the editors of Time-Life Books. (The enchanted world) New York: Time-Life Books, c1985. 143 p.

SPERRY—WHERE
> Sperry, Margaret. *Where stories grow; tales from Finland.* By Zacharias Topelius; tr. and adapted by Margaret Sperry. Illus. by Maija Karma. New York: Crane Russak, c1977. 94 p.

STALLMAN—DRAGONS
> Stallman, Birdie. *Learning about dragons.* Illus. by Lydia Halverson. Chicago: Childrens Press, c1981. 46 p.

STALLMAN—WITCHES
> Stallman, Birdie, with Laura Alden. *Learning about witches.* Illus. by Lydia Halverson. Chicago: Childrens Press, c1981. 46 p.

STAPLETON—DICTIONARY
> Stapleton, Michael. *The illustrated dictionary of Greek and Roman mythology.* New York: Peter Bedrick Books, 1986. 224 p.

STEELE—OZARK
> Steele, Phillip W. *Ozark tales and superstitions.* Illus. by Donna Chapman and Erwin Doege. Gretna, LA: Pelican Publ. Co., 1985. 96 p.

STOKES—TURTLE
Stokes, Donald S. *The turtle and the island; folk tales from Papua New Guinea.* Retold by Barbara Ker Wilson. Illus. by Tony Oliver. Sydney: Hodder and Stoughton, c1978. 143 p.

STOVICEK—AROUND
Stovicek, Vratislav. *Around the world fairy tales.* Tr. by Vera Gissing. Illus. by Zdenka Krejcova. London: Octopus, 1981. 207 p.

STUCHL—AMERICAN
Stuchl, Vladimir. *American fairy tales.* Illus. by Ludek Manasek. London: Octopus, c1979. 254 p.

SYNGE—LAND
Synge, Ursula. *Land of heroes; a retelling of the Kalevala.* New York: Atheneum, c1977. 222 p.

TARRANT—FAIRY
Tarrant, Margaret. *Fairy tales.* New York: Crowell, c1978. 96 p.

THOMAS—IT'S GR 111 F73 I86
Thomas, Rosemary Hyde. *It's good to tell you; French folktales from Missouri.* Illus. by Ronald W. Thomas. [Includes texts of the French versions compiled by Joseph Medard Carriere.] Columbia: Univ. of Missouri Press, 1981. 246 p.

THOMAS—MABINOGION f PB2273. M3 1985
Thomas, Gwyn, and Kevin Crossley-Holland. *Tales from the Mabinogion.* Illus. by Margaret Jones. Woodstock, NY: Overlook Press, c1984. 88 p.

THOMPSON—HAWAIIAN
Thompson, Vivian L. *Hawaiian tales of heroes and champions.* Illus. by Herbert Kawainui Kane. Honolulu: Univ. of Hawaii Press, 1986 c1971. 128 p.

TIMPANELLI—TALES
Timpanelli, Gioia. *Tales from the roof of the world: folktales of Tibet.* Illus. by Elizabeth Kelly Lockwood. New York: Viking Press, c1984. 53 p.

TITIEV—MOOLAH
Titiev, Estelle. *How the moolah was taught a lesson, & other tales from Russia.* Tr. and adapted by Estelle Titiev and Lila Pargment. Pictures by Ray Cruz. New York: Dial Press, c1976. 53 p.

TODD—SOME GR 351 T59
Todd, Loreto. *Some day been dey; West African Pidgin folktales.* [English and Pidgin on opposite pages.] London: Routledge & Kegan Paul, c1979. 186 p.

TODD—TORTOISE
Todd, Loreto. *Tortoise the trickster, and other folktales from Cameroon.*

With drawings by Geoffrey Whittam. New York: Schocken Books, 1979. 121 p.

TOMPERT—THREE

Tompert, Ann. *Three foolish tales.* Illus. by Diane Dawson. New York: Crown, c1979. 48 p.

TOPELIUS—WHERE. *See* SPERRY—WHERE.

TOTH—TALES

Toth, Marian Davies. *Tales from Thailand: folklore, culture, and history.* Illus. by Supee Pasutanavin. Rutland, VT: C. E. Tuttle, 1982 c1971. 183 p.

TUDOR—BEDTIME

Tudor, Tasha. *Tasha Tudor's bedtime book.* Ed. by Kate Klimo. New York: Platt & Munk, c1977. 41 unnumbered pages.

UTTLEY—FOXGLOVE

Uttley, Alison. *Foxglove tales.* Chosen by Lucy Meredith. Illus. by Shirley Felts. Boston: Faber & Faber, c1984. 107 p.

VILLA—ARMENIAN GR 280 V54

Villa, Susie Hoogasian. *100 Armenian tales.* Detroit: Wayne State University Press, 1982 c1966. 602 p.

VUONG—BROCADED PZ 8 V889 Br 1985

Vuong, Lynette Dyer. *The brocaded slipper, and other Vietnamese tales.* Illus. by Vo-Dihn Mai. Reading, ~~MA: Addison-Wesley~~, c1982. 111 p.

NY: Lippincott

WADE—INDIAN

Wade, Mary Hazelton. *Indian fairy tales, as told to little children of the wigwam.* Pen and ink drawings by Sears Gallagher. Great Neck, NY: Core Collection, 1979. 240 p.

WAHL—NEEDLE

Wahl, Jan. *Needle and Noodle, and other silly stories.* Illus. by Stan Mack. New York: Pantheon Books, c1979. 56 p.

WALKING—SONG

Walking Night Bear. *Song of the seven herbs.* Stan Padilla, illustrator. Nevada City, CA: Gold Circle Productions, c1983. 60 p.

WATER SPIRITS

Water spirits, by the editors of Time-Life Books. (The enchanted world) Chicago: Time-Life Books, c1985. 143 p.

WATSON—AESOP

Watson, Carol. *Aesop's fables retold.* Illus. by Nick Price. London: Usborne, c1982. 24 p.

WATSON—THAILAND

Watson, Jenny. *Favourite stories from Thailand.* Illus. by Samart Suksatu. Hong Kong: Heinemann Asia, c1976. 47 p.

WEEKS—PACHEE
Weeks, Rupert. *Pachee Goyo; history and legends from the Shoshone.* Laramie, WY: Jelm Mountain Press, c1981. 110 p.

WEISS—RUSSIAN
Weiss, Pola. *Russian legends.* Tr. by Alice Sachs. New York: Crescent Books, c1980. 202 p.

WENG—MAGIC. *See* JAGENDORF—MAGIC.

WESTERVELT—HAWAIIAN GR 385 H3 W32 1978
Westervelt, William D. *Hawaiian historical legends.* ~~New ed. Rutland, VT: Tuttle, c1977.~~ 218 p.   NY: AMS Press

WHEELER—FOX
Wheeler, M. J. *Fox tales.* Pictures by Dana Gustafson. Minneapolis: Carolrhoda Books, Inc., c1984. 56 p.

WILBERT—BORORO F 2520.1 B75 F64 1983
Wilbert, Johannes, and Karin Simoneau, eds. *Folk literature of the Bororo Indians.* Los Angeles: UCLA Latin American Center Publications, c1983. 339 p.

WILDE—FAIRY
Wilde, Oscar. *The fairy stories of Oscar Wilde.* Illus. by Harold Jones. Introd. by Naomi Lewis. New York: Peter Bedrick Books, 1986. 223 p.

WILLIAMS—AESOP
Williams, Alexander. *Aesop's fables retold.* Illus. by Robin Moffett. New York: Dandelion Press, c1979. [32] p.

WILLIAMS—PRACTICAL
Williams, Jay. *The practical princess, and other liberating fairy tales.* Illus. by Rick Schreiter. New York: Parents' Magazine Press, c1978. 99 p.

WILLIAMS—WICKED
Williams, Jay. *The wicked tricks of Tyl Uilenspiegel.* Illus. by Friso Henstra. New York: Four Winds Press, c1978. 51 p.

WILSON—TURTLE. *See* STOKES—TURTLE.

WISE—MONSTER
Wise, William. *Monster myths of ancient Greece.* Illus. by Jerry Pinkney. New York: Putnam's, c1981. 48 p.

WOLKSTEIN—INANNA BL 1616 I5 W64 1983
Wolkstein, Diane, and Samuel Noah Kramer. *Inanna, queen of heaven and earth; her stories and hymns from Sumer.* Art comp. by Elizabeth Williams-Forte. New York: Harper & Row, c1983. 227 p.

WOLKSTEIN—MAGIC PZ 8.1 W84 Mag 1978
Wolkstein, Diane. *The magic orange tree, and other Haitian folktales.* Drawings by Elsa Henriquez. New York: Knopf, c1978. 212 p.

WOOD—KALILA PN989. I5 B4
Wood, Ramsay. *Kalila and Dimna; selected fables of Bidpai.* Illus. by Margaret Kilrenny. New York: Knopf, 1980. 262 p.

WOOD—PALACE
Wood, Ruzena. *The palace of the moon, and other tales from Czechoslovakia.* Illus. by Krystyna Turska. London: Andre Deutsch, c1981. 128 p.

WOOD—SPIRITS E98 F6 W83 1992
Wood, Marion. *Spirits, heroes & hunters from North American Indian mythology.* Illus. by John Sibbick. New York: Schocken Books, c1981. 132 p.

WRIGHT—GOLD
Wright, David Glen. *Gold of the gods, and other fascinating tales of old Mexico.* Provo, UT: ARO Publ. Co., c1981. 47 p.

WRIGHT—PIGEON
Wright, Glen. *The pigeon with nine heads, and other fascinating legendary tales of Samoa.* Provo, UT: ARO Publ. Co., c1981. 48 p.

WYATT—PRINCESS
Wyatt, Isabel. *The book of fairy princes.* Illus. by Daniel Brandon Gilbert. San Rafael: Dawne-Leigh, c1978. 187 p.

XENOPHONTOVNA—FOLK
Xenophontovna, Verra. *Folk tales from the Russian.* Illus. by Lucy Fitch Perkins. Great Neck, NY: Core Collection Books, 1979. 151 p.

YEATS—FAIRY
Yeats, W. B., ed. *Fairy and folk tales of Ireland.* New York: Macmillan, c1983. 387 p.

YELLOW ROBE—TONWEYA
Yellow Robe, Rosebud. *Tonweya and the eagles, and other Lakota Indian tales.* Pictures by Jerry Pinkney. New York: Dial Press, c1979. 118 p.

YOLEN—FAVORITE
Yolen, Jane, ed. *Favorite folktales from around the world.* New York: Pantheon Books, c1986. 498 p.

YOLEN—HUNDREDTH PZ1 Y785 hu
Yolen, Jane. *The hundredth dove, and other tales.* Illus. by David Palladini. New York: Crowell, c1977. 64 p.

YOURCENAR—ORIENTAL PQ2649 08 N7413
Yourcenar, Marguerite. *Oriental tales.* Tr. by Alberto Manguel. New York: Farrar Straus Giroux, c1985. 147 p.

ZITKALA—OLD E99 D1258
Zitkala-Sa. *Old Indian legends retold.* Illus. by Angel de Cora. Lincoln: Univ. of Nebraska Press, c1985. 165 p.

ZONG—KOREA GR 342 C45   NY: Grove Press
    Zong, In-Sob. *Folk tales from Korea.* 3rd ed. Elizabeth, ~~NJ: Hollym Interna-~~
    ~~tional Corp., c1982.~~ 257 p.
ZVORYKIN—FIREBIRD J GR 202 0313
    Zvorykin, Boris. *The firebird, and other Russian fairy tales.* Illus. by Boris
    Zvorykin. Ed. by Jacqueline Onassis. New York: Viking Press, c1978.
    78 p.

THE INDEX

Aaltawheel Bridge
  O'Sullivan-*Legends,* 150
AARON (biblical)
  The ten plagues of Egypt
Abandoned babies
  See BABIES—abandoned
ABANDONMENT
  Tibet's first king
ABBOTS AND ABBEYS
  Thurnley Abbey
ABDUCTION(S)
  See also KIDNAPPING
  The antelope maid
  The black geese
  A bride kidnapped by the jnun
  Clever woman
  Faithful John
  The fire plume
  Girl who stayed in fork of a
    tree
  Guleesh
  How three serpents carried
    princesses. . .
  The hunter who threw stars
  Immortal mountains [Magnolia]
  Jamie Freel and the young
    lady
  Kwi-na the eagle: animal-god
    persons
  The legend of Eagleman
  Lost sister
  The magic bonnet
  Man-Eagle conquered by
    youth
  Meamei the seven sisters
  Mountain of jade
  Nanasimgat [wife abducted by
    killer whale]

Nanasimgit and his [abducted]
    wife
  The practical princess
  Prince Feroz-Shah and the fly-
    ing horse
  Rising rock [Chiricahua]
  Ruslan and Chernomor
  Sheena and the water-horse
  Shepherd's dream
  The silkworm [origin: marriage
    of horse & maid]
  Sister Lace
  Stretching kupua [taller than
    40 feet]
  Thumbelina
  To-Dola
  The treachery of Lelewaga
  Wastewin and the beaver
  The young girl and the moon
—bear takes woman; child is
    born
  Ivan Bear's Ear
—of blackbirds
  How the blackbird went to war
—by dragon
  Golden reed pipe
—by fairies
  Weardale fairies [dislike being
    observed]
—Great Spirit destroys
    village
  How Hoof Lake got its name
—planned
  Master and man
—plotted by geni
  Farmer's son and the geni
ABDUCTION(S) (subject)
—by fairies
  Briggs-*Vanish.,* 215 (index)

Abductions to the fairy palace
    [condensed]
    Logan-*Old,* 111–117
ABISHAI (biblical)
    King David and the giant
Abo Beckeer
    Villa-*Armenian,* 119–124, 452–
    454
"ABOMINABLE SNOWMEN"
    The field of Boliauns
    Wild men
ABORTION
    Two sisters, Rose and Lotus
About Abner the tinker
    Gorog-*Taste,* 105–111
ABRAHAM (biblical) (subject)
    Patai-*Gates,* 767 (index)
ABSALOM
    King Solomon and the winds
ABSURDITY
    See also FOOLS AND
    FOOLISHNESS
    The imaginary babouche and
    the scorpion
    Jha sells beans to the sultan
—foolish lie
    The iron-eating mice
Abuelita's bell
    Ritchie-*Armadillo,* 15–19
ABUNDANT HOUSE, THE
    Halibut Man and the house on
    the waves
Abuse. *See* CRUELTY
Abzelil and the Master of the
    Lake
    Riordan-*Tartary,* 100–103
Acacia
    Ewart-*Lore,* 150–152
ACACIA TREES
    Anpu and Bata
Accidental knowledge. *See*
    KNOWLEDGE—accidental
    possession
Accidental success. *See* LUCK—
    good; SUCCESS—
    accidental

ACCIDENTS
    From bad to good to bad to
    good
—automobile
    The crowd
Accomplishment. *See*
    ACHIEVEMENT
ACCOUNTANTS
    Murder and lonely hearts
Accumulative stories. *See* REPETI-
    TIVE RHYMES AND
    STORIES
ACHIEVEMENT
—when heart is in it
    Great Joy, the self-respecting
    ox
ACHILLES
    The childhood of Achilles
    The fall of Troy
    Peleus and Thetis [marriage]
Achilles and the death of Hector
    Lines-*Greek,* 169–200
ACHILLES (subject)
    Pinsent-*Greek,* 142 (index)
ACORNS
    The end of the world
An act of truth
    Amore-*Lustful,* 132–134
Act of truth: The eye restored
    Amore-*Lustful,* 136–137
Activity: demon of energy
    Baskin-*Imps,* 30–31
ACTORS AND ACTRESSES
    Jerry Bundler
ADAM AND EVE (biblical)
    See also MAN—first
    Atam and Im
    The genesis of the Hid-folk
ADAM AND EVE (biblical) (subject)
    Briggs-*Vanish.,* 30–31
    Patai-*Gates,* 768 (index)
Adam's wedding [Midrash]
    Patai-*Gates,* 283–285
Addlers and menters
    Keightley-*World,* 308–310
Admiral Yi

Zong-*Korea*, 77
Adugo the jaguar and Buke the
    anteater
    Wilbert-*Bororo*, 161–164
Adugo the jaguar and Ruwo the
    snail
    Wilbert-*Bororo*, 164–165
ADULTERY
    See also FIDELITY;
        MARRIAGE
    Aphrodissia, the widow
    Beware of hypocrites!
    The carpenter's wife
    The dervish and the thief
    El Diablo, el chivo, y Senor
        Bonifacio
    Her lover's heart
    How women got an excuse
    Magic mirror of Rabbi Adam
    Search for a friend
    Story of a gentleman['s wife]
    Touch not a married woman
    Two lovers punished
—boy and stepmother
    Toribugu: legend of the hero
—multiple infidelities
    The last love of Prince Genji
Adultery with the "demon"
    Elbaz-*Folktales*, 113–114
ADVENTURE(S)
    Don Cacahuate
    Miss Peggy Top
—risk-taking
    The lobster and the crab
Adventure of the German student
    [Irving]
    Schwartz-*Great*, 93–101
The adventures of Iktomi
    Wood-*Spirits*, 97–101
Adventures of John Dietrich
    Keightley-*World*, 178–194
Adventures of Mrile
    Radin-*African*, 237–242
Adventures of Ntini, the small
    otter
    Poland-*Mantis*, 6–40

The adventures of Perseus
    Gibson-*Gods*, 73–79
Adventures of Sikku
    Sperry-*Where*, 6–16
Adventures of Sir Galahad
    Riordan-*Arthur*, 80–89
Adventures of the first dervish
    Shah-*Dervishes*, 9–24, 29–30
Adventures of the third dervish [a]
    Shah-*Dervishes*, 100–115
Adventures of the third dervish [b]
    Shah-*Dervishes*, 116–139
The adventures of Yemima
    Soyer-*Adventures*, 1–13
ADVERSITY
    Minnie
ADVICE
    Dumplings in the river
    King and the poor man
    The tale of Ivan
    The three counsels
—by spear
    The talking spear
—choice of advisers
    The carpenter's monkey
—some good/some bad
    The baboon's umbrella
ADVISING
—biggest fool of all
    The six fools
ADZE
—devil tries to use
    The devil's cloven foot
AENEAS
    The wanderings of Aeneas
AEOLUS
    The children of Aeolus
Aeranth: the golden key
    Macdonald-*Golden*, 1–35
Aesop
    Belling the cat
    The country maid and her
        milkpail
    The dog and his shadow
    The fox and the grapes
    The fox and the hedgehog

Aesop (continued)
  The fox and the stork
  Hare and the tortoise [the true
    story]
  The lion and the mouse
  Lioness and the mouse
  The miller, his son, and their
    donkey
  Raven and the fox
  The shepherd who cried "wolf"
  The tortoise and the hare
Aesop's dog [chasing rabbit]
  Lewis-*Animal*, 8–9
Aetiological legends [six]
  Robe-*Hispanic*, 45–50
AFANASIEV, Alexander, 1826–
    1871 [Biographical sketch]
  Riordan-*Russia*, 274–279
Affection. *See* FRIENDSHIP; KIND-
    NESS; LOVE
AFRICA
  How spider obtained the sky
    god's stories (Ashanti)
—east
  The bushbabies
  Zamani goes to market
—Ethiopia
  The leopard
  Moses King of Ethiopia
—Ghana
  The maid who chose a hus-
    band [Ghana]
—native chants
  The king's rival
—Sierra Leone
  The hunter's dilemma
  The king's rival
—South Africa-wedding customs
  The enchanted buck
—tribes-Ashanti
  How contradiction came to the
    Ashanti
  How diseases came to the
    Ashanti
—tribes-Zulu
  Frog and Umdhlubu

  The tall maiden, Untombinde
AFRICAN TALES (subject)
  Radin-*African*, 1–19
—Beginnings of mankind; 17 Ban-
    tu/Zulu tales
  Pitcher-*Tokol.*, 1–64
—Friendship between the earthly
    and the heavens
  Luzzatto-*Long*, 44
AFRICANS (subject)
  Keightley-*World*, 495–496
Afterlife. *See* FUTURE LIFE;
    OTHERWORLD
AGADA (subject)
—Legend and myth
  Patai-*Gates*, xvii–li
AGAMEMNON
  The fall of Troy
  The homecoming of
    Agamemnon
AGAMEMNON (subject)
  Pinsent-*Greek*, 142 (index)
Age, or Aging. *See* GROWTH;
    OLD AGE; TIME; YOUTH
The aged father
  Zong-*Korea*, 186–187
Agelessness. *See* TIME
AGNES, Saint
  Bolster and Jecholiah
AGNI (God of Fire)
  Burning of the Khandava forest
AGREEMENTS (bargaining)
  See also DEVIL(S)—pact with
  Barter
  Brer wolf's second pinder
    patch
  The building of the wall of
    Asgard
  Exchange [barter]
  The fairy chapman
  [Hameln: punishment for
    not keeping bargain with
    piper]
  The iron wolf
  Jack and his master
  King O'Toole and his goose

Old Nick and the girl
Old Nick and the pedlar
A rare bargain
The skipper and old Nick
The walls of Asgard
AGRICULTURE
See also FARMS AND FARM-
ING; PLOUGHS AND
PLOUGHING
Houji, the child abandoned on
the ice
El Aguaje de las Yeguas [legend]
MacLean-*Cuentos,* 46–47
AGUANE
Salvani and Aguane
Aguila (the Eagle)
Gallant-*Constel.,* 91–95
AGUILAR, Senor Bonifacio
El Diablo, el chivo, y Senor
Bonifacio
Ahmad and the nagging wife
Shah-*Dervishes,* 242–245
Aid and punishment
Keightley-*World,* 277
AIFA (a warrior-queen)
A champion's schooling in an-
other world
Aiken, Joan
Lodging for the night
Aina-kizz and the black-bearded
bai
Riordan-*Woman,* 42–46
Aine in Irish sagas
Logan-*Old,* 53–56
Ainsel
Keightley-*World,* 313–314
AIR (subject)
—fairy hosts of
Briggs-*Vanish.,* 215 (index)
AIR TRAVEL
—basket-car
Daughter of the stars
Air-demons and Fergus O'Mara
Yeats-*Fairy,* 341–344
Aisha Kandisha and the drunkard
Elbaz-*Folktales,* 39

AJAX (subject)
Pinsent-*Greek,* 142 (index)
ALABAMA
Wiley and the hairy man
ALADDIN
Summoning a spirit servant
Aladdin and his magic [wonderful]
lamp
Lang-*Blue,* 75–91 (notes, 352,
366)
Pollack-*Moonbeam,* 30–39
Rackham-*Fairy,* 143–171
Stovicek-*Around,* 88–92
ALADDIN (subject)
Shah-*World,* 172
ALASKA
Julie of the wolves
ALBAN, Saint
England's first martyr
ALBANIA
Goat people
The milk of death
Moerae
Nereides
ALBERICH the Dwarf
Oberon: castles of
Alberich
ALCOHOLISM
El borracho del bahio
The monk and the drunk
El que canta sus males
espanta
Three wishes [of Billy
Dawson]
The trolls of Skurugata
Aldar-Kose and Shigai-Bai
Riordan-*Tartary,* 25–32
Alder
Froud-*Faeries,* unp
ALDER TREES
—stumps
Leppa Polkry and the blue
cross
Alex and Avery [dogs exercised by
telephone]
Schwartz-*Tales,* 40–41

ALEXANDER the Great
> Unicorn: peerless mount for
> Alexander

The Algonquin Cinderella
> Shah-*World*, 152–154

ALI BABA
> Slave maiden's eye for evil

Ali Baba and the forty thieves
> Lang-*Blue*, 248–258 (notes,
> 370–371)
> Rackham-*Fairy*, 192–208
> Stovicek-*Around*, 188–191

ALI ISLAND
—origin
> The great flood

[Alien races older than humankind]
> Seekers Saviors, 56

Alison Gross (condensed)
> Briggs-*Vanish.*, 44

All I possess!
> Booss-*Scand.*, 221–223

All that happened must happen
> again
> Highwater-*Anpao*, 79–
> 83

All the dogs in the world
> Stokes-*Turtle*, 143

ALLAH
> The food of Paradise
> Hare seeks endowments from
> Allah

[Allah helps those who help
> themselves]
> Riordan-*Tartary*, 125–128

All-Devourer and the mantis
> Radin-*African*, 93–99

ALLEGORIES
> Burgher and the pauper

ALLEGORIES (subject)
> Nahman-*Tales*, 329

Allen, Woody
> Count Dracula [by Woody
> Allen]

Allerleirauh; or, The many-furred
> creature
> Lang-*Green*, 316–323

ALLIGATORS AND CROCODILES
> Beginning of the Narran Lake
> Elephant's child [from Kipling]
> The hoity-toity mouse
> King Crocodile
> Lake Espantosa, the
> alligators?
> Monkey and the crocodile
> (India)
> The monkey's heart
> Origin of the Narran Lake
> Pikuwa and his wives
> The prince and his fate
> Run brer gator, run!
> The stupid crocodile
> White hare and the crocodiles

—captures girl
> Oh Mister Crocodile

—no tongue
> The rabbit's tale

—origin of lump on fore-
> head
> Sad fate of Pikuwa

—skin-origin
> Lizard and crocodile

—speaks, but not to "master"
> 'Morning, alligator!

—stupidity
> The scholar jackal

—why men hate
> The treachery of Lelewaga

Allingham, William
> A dream [poem]
> Yeats-*Fairy*, 119
> The fairies [poem]
> Yeats-*Fairy*, 13–14
> Lepracaun; or Fairy shoemak-
> er [poem]

ALMONDS
> The magic almond

ALMS
> Charity can change a man's
> fate

ALMS (subject)
—Buddhist stories
> Amore-*Lustful*, 115–116

ALNKAOUA, Ephraim, Rabbi, d.
   1442.
   Flying lion of the Rab of
      Tlemcen
ALPS (mountains)
   Salvanelli
   Salvani and Aguane
The altar-cup in Angerup
   Keightley-*World*, 109–111
Altynchech and the padishah's wife
   Riordan-*Tartary*, 106–114
Alven
   Arrowsmith-*Field*, 19
Always say, "God willing"
   Patai-*Gates*, 522–524
The Amadan Mor and the
      Gruagach
   Haining-*Lepre.*, 62–65
Amadis and the castle of Apollidon
      on . . . island
   Lee-*Castles*, 150–151
Amaranth, Weigela
   Ewart-*Lore*, 162–163
AMATERASU (subject)
   Piggott-*Japanese*, 142 (index)
AMAZONS (subject)
   Pinsent-*Greek*, 142 (index)
Ambrus, Victor, illus.
   Jacobs-*Celtic*
   Riordan-*Arthur*
AMENDMENT OF LIFE
   Master James' nightmare
American Revolution. *See* UNITED
   STATES—history—
   Revolution
AMERICAN TALES (subject)
—[Based on 20 historical
   folksongs]
   Sanders-*Hear*, xi–xvi
—The green prairie
   Stuchl-*American*, 9–10
AMIR
—place taken by angel until Amir
   gains wisdom
   The Amir who was a beggar
The Amir who became a weaver

Shah-*Afghanistan*, 10–14
The Amir who was a beggar
   Shah-*Afghanistan*, 108–113
AMPHIBALUS
   England's first martyr
AMPHISBAENA (subject)
—[Snake with head at both ends]
   Lloyd—*Mythical*, 9–11
AMPUTATIONS
   The old smith
AMRAM BEN DIOUANE, Rabbi
   Pilgrimages to tomb of Rabbi
      Amram Ben Diouane
AMULETS
   The disrespectful son
   The golden tree [queen and
      amulet]
AMUR REGION (Russia) (subject)
—Folktale world
   Nagishkin-*Folktales*, 8–12
AMUSEMENTS
   Flying pole dance
Ananse: origin, big hinder part;
   small head
   Radin-*African*, 139–140
Anansi: Getting common sense [by
   all]
   Yolen-*Favorite*, 405
ANANSI STORIES
   Being greedy chokes Anansi
      (Jamaica)
   Cat lying on velvet cushion,
      while dog sleeps
   How diseases came to the
      Ashanti
   How Kwaku Ananse got Aso in
      marriage
   How spider obtained the sky-
      god's stories
   How spider read the sky-god's
      thoughts
   Separation of god from man
   Sleeping-mat confidences not
      to be repeated
   Whipping children: how it
      came about

Anansi's six sons
Hadley-*Legends,* 26–27
Anaya, R. A.
Storytelling
Griego-*Cuentos,* 7–9
ANCESTORS (subject)
—spirits of
Briggs-*Vanish.,* 31, 35–37, 66
ANCESTRY
Drill, ye tarriers, drill [song and
story]
The ancient spirits of the coast
Haining-*Lepre.,* 15–19
And they wondered
MacLean-*Cuentos,* 184–189
Andersen, Hans Christian
The bottle-neck
The elf of the rose
The emperor's new clothes
The flying trunk
The girl who trod on the loaf
The goblin and the huckster
Little Claus and Big Claus
The little mermaid
Little Tuk
The marsh king's daughter
The nightingale
The old house
The princess and the pea
She was good for nothing
The snow queen
Soup from a sausage skewer
The steadfast tin soldier
The swine herd
Thumbelina
The tinder-box
The travelling companion
The ugly duckling
The wild swans
Andrew and King Solomon [in 2
parts]
Fattoross-*Simpleton,* 31–36
Andrew Coffey
Jacobs-*Celtic,* 129–132
ANDROMEDA
The adventures of Perseus

Andromeda dances
Manning-*Marvels,* 37–39
Andromeda (the Chained Woman)
Gallant-*Constel.,* 101–102
ANDVAER
The Cormorants of Andvaer
Anemone and pasque flower
Ewart-*Lore,* 50–53
ANEMONE (flower)
Blood-begotten anemone
Butterfly love
Angakok and Mother of Seals [sea
petrel]
De Wit-*Talking,* 168–174
The Angekkok, Oolak, and the
Moon-God
Shelley-*Legends,* 63–69
Angel of death
Patai-*Gates,* 179–184, 588–
593
ANGEL OF DEATH
The fox and the angel of death
King David matches wits with
Angel of Death
[Little bird singing]
Pious bride and the angel of
death
Story of the robbers [master
thief]
The young seamstress
ANGELS
Fairies: how it all began
Flight of the eagle
Flying money
Foretelling the future [written
on forehead]
Moses faces the angels
The word the devil made up
("Uhn hunh")
—at birth of child
The fairy child
—bad angels
The fairies [war in heaven]
—guardian
"If I had the wings of an angel"
Tummeldink

—in form of hermit
  The hermit [paradoxical
    behavior]
—takes role of Amir
  The Amir who was a beggar
ANGELS (subject)
—fallen
  Briggs-*Vanish.*, 215 (index)
  Patai-*Gates*, 769 (index)
ANGER
  See also TEMPER
  A ghost's vengeance
  The master and the worker
  Prince Bellerophon and
    Pegasus
  Rumpelstiltskin
—strength lost by
  The first mosquito
The anglers of Arz
  Asimov-*Fant.*, 131–139
The angry merwife of Nordstrand
  Heslewood-*Tales*, 60–63
ANGUISH, King
  Sir Tristram and La Belle
    Isolde
"Anima" and "animal"
  Berger-*Animalia* [7]
Animal characteristics [motif index]
  Wilbert-*Bororo*, 238–240, 282
[Animal children]: school days
  McCarthy-*Raccoon*, 83–95
ANIMAL FOOD
—taboo
  Kelfala's secret something
ANIMAL-HUMAN COMMUNICA-
  TION
  See also BIRDS—language
    understood
  Ahmad and the nagging wife
  The enchanted forest
  The farmer who listened to his
    livestock
  Farmer's son and the geni
  The golden man and the finger
    men
  Hailibu the hunter

Man and the snake
Man or beast
The man who knew the lan-
  guage of animals
The princess in the ivory tower
Rooster's advice [beat your
  wife]
A taste for quiet
The white snake
The animal master
  Magical Beasts, 17
Animal people [five tales]
  Reed-*Aboriginal*, 50–62
Animal sacrifice. *See*
    SACRIFICE—of animals
ANIMALS
  See also CRUELTY—to
    animals
  *See also names of individual
    animals*
  Anizu's magic wonder flute
  Anpao and the animals
  Anpao brings the corn
  The bat [war of birds and
    animals]
  The blessed gift of joy be-
    stowed upon man
  Bremen town musicians
  Coming of spring
  Creation of the Mayas
  The dawn of the world
  Fabulous beasts
  Glooscap, the great chief
  How Jack went to seek his
    fortune
  How long will you live?
  How the animals stopped the
    freeway
  Jack and the robbers
  Little John and his animals
  Magic birds and enchanted
    animals
  The magic boat
  Melampus—physician and
    prophet
  Men and animals

32

ANIMAL (continued)
    The moon walk
    Old woman who stole milk
    The party
    Pecos Bill becomes a coyote
    Pepito Conejo: prepare for
        winter
    Rainbow and the autumn
        leaves
    Seligen Fraulein
    Tale of a she-bear
    Unusual animals [14 legends]
    Vaino and the swan princess
    The war of the birds and the
        beasts
    The white pet
    Why the hare runs away
    The year summer was stolen
    The youth and the dog-dance
—all but three leave house
    The faithful trio [shelter in
        house]
—all corralled to deprive hunters
    The great hunters [animals]
—beauty
    The peacock's tail
—bow's size, animal's fierceness
    Coyote and his bow
—changing of
    The man from P.I.G.
—characteristics
    The jaguar and the lizard
        [qualities]
    Master rabbit [tries to do what
        other species do]
    Scarface
—devotion of mates
    The jackal, Mpungutye,
        searches for lost mate
—digging a well
    Why a rabbit hides in a burrow
—domestic
    How some wild animals be-
        came tame ones
    Why some animals are
        domesticated

—farm
    Vazili, Bagany and Banniki
—food
    Rabbit and the Indian chief
—fur
    The vain bear
—gifts (from Creator)
    Pervasive perfume of Las Zor-
        rillas the skunk
—in house
    It could always be worse
        (Jewish)
—killing
    Why apes look like people
    The young man who refused
        to kill
—language
    The language of animals
    See also ANIMAL-HUMAN
        COMMUNICATION
—long-tailed
    Brer rabbit's protest meeting
—man and
    Why apes look like people
—meetings
    The umbrella tree
—mythical
    Egypt's divine menagerie
—naked
    "A nude horse is a rude horse"
—origin of characteristics
    How the lizard got its hat
—origin of fish, snakes, tortoises,
    etc.
    The sky-god: Ratu and the
        Dyaks
—protector of
    Brown man of the Muirs
—races
    The fleetest of foot
—self-protection
    The rattlesnake receives his
        fangs
—short-tailed
    Brer rabbit's protest meeting
—spirits

The girl who married a bear
The piper and the puca
Sable souls
The theft of fire
—suitable parts (limbs)
How the fox and the elk ex-
changed legs
—tails
Snubby's tail
—talking. *See* ANIMAL-HUMAN
COMMUNICATION
—training
Davy Crockett, king of the old
wild west
—who is the oldest
The deer, the hare, and the
toad
—wild
How some wild animals be-
came tame ones
ANIMALS (subject)
—Fairyland
Briggs-*Vanish.*, 16–17, 22, 76,
172–174
—Motif index
Wilbert-*Bororo*, 227–228, 242–
244, 276–277
Animals in different parts of
Australia
Reed-*Aboriginal*, 50–51
Animals in winter
Riordan-*Russia*, 222–226
Animals transformed into humans
Piggott-*Japanese*, 72–74
Aniz the shepherd
Minford-*Fav.*, 95–100
Anizu's magic wonder flute
Jagendorf-*Magic*, 149–155
Annie Norn and the fin folk
Crossley-*Folk*, 85–89
Another being
Colombo-*Wind.*, 9
Anpao and coyote
Highwater-*Anpao*, 151–158
Anpao and the animals
Highwater-*Anpao*, 125–139

Anpao and the magic dogs
Highwater-*Anpao*, 194–205
Anpao brings the corn
Highwater-*Anpao*, 140–150
Anpao is born
Highwater-*Anpao*, 58–78
Anpu and Bata
Shah-*World*, 87–92
Answers. *See* QUESTIONS AND
ANSWERS
Ant and lizard [origin of enmity]
Stokes-*Turtle*, 49–51
Ant and the dove
Watson-*Aesop*, 6–7
The ant, the elephant, and the
brahmin's servant
Raychaudhuri-*Stupid*, 77–84
ANTEATERS
Echidna's spines
—origin of thin back legs
Adugo the jaguar and Buke
the anteater
The antelope maid
Mullett-*Spider*, 118–126
ANTELOPES
Boy-who-snared-the-wind and
shaman's daughter
The lion's treasured goat
Turtle feeds his children
ANTHONY, Saint
The cripple and Senor San
Antonio
The Holy Child
Senor San Antonio retrieves
an axe
ANTHROPOLOGY
Flight over XP-637
Anticipation. *See* EXPECTATIONS
Antigone
Stapleton-*Dictionary*, 26–28
ANTIGONE
The tragic story of Antigone
ANTIQUE SHOPS
A most unusual murder
ANTIQUES
Draw the curtains

ANTISEMITISM
    The community that was saved
        by a jinn
    The enchanted journey [time
        warp]
    The king's dream
    The prince who was made of
        precious gems
    The rabbi and the inquisitor
    Sidna Mussa
ANTI-SOCIAL BEHAVIOR
    Dog and monkey build a town
    Kumba the orphan girl
—rewarded
    Samba the Satan and Omadi
        the Righteous
ANTS
    Bokodori Ecerae chief and
        clan customs
    Boots and the beasts
    Boy-who-snared-the-wind and
        shaman's daughter
    El caballero porfiado
    Educated frogs and martial
        ants
    Eros and Psyche
    Fox and the ant [race]
    Grasshopper and the ant
    The grasshopper and the ant
    The great flood [deluge]
    The heavenly song of the
        green-spotted dove
    How the blackbird went to war
    The magic boat
    The meat ants and the fire
    A Navajo story of creation
    The new people and their food
    Pixies
    Queen bee
    The season of the stubby
        caterpillar
    The son of Tata Juan
        Pescador
    Soup from a sausage skewer
    Stepmother's head
    The white snake

—origin of characteristics
    Locust, ant, and the kingfisher
—as workers; origin
    The ants and the hare
The ants and the hare
    Zong-*Korea*, 33
Ants [creation of earth, light, sun,
        &]
    Stuchl-*American*, 22
Antti and the wizard's prophecy
    Booss-*Scand.*, 547–553
Aoibheal
    Logan-*Old*, 44–49
AOIFE
    [Swan-children of Lir]
Ape [why it has no tail]
    Pitcher-*Tokol.*, 43–46
APES
    See also MONKEYS
    Why apes look like people
—origin of characteristics
    Ape [why it has no tail]
The apes and the busybody bird
    Wood-*Kalila*, 160–163
Aphrodissia, the widow
    Yourcenar-*Oriental*, 101–115
Aphrodite
    Stapleton-*Dictionary*, 29–30
APHRODITE
    The apple of discord
    Atalanta [and Hippomenes]
    Blood-begotten anemone
    Cupid and Psyche
    Eros and Psyche
    In the beginning: the Greek
        panoply
    Pygmalion
    Pygmalion's statue
Aphrodite, goddess of love
    Gibson-*Gods*, 37–40
APHRODITE (subject)
    Pinsent-*Greek*, 142 (index)
Apocrypha [O.T., introd. and
        selections]
    Patai-*Gates*, 121–157
APOLLO

Artemis and Apollo
Hermes, messenger of the
    gods
Hermes, the messenger of the
    gods
Apollo
    Stapleton-*Dictionary*, 31–32
Apollo and Hyacinthus
    Lines-*Greek*, 89–92
Apollo and the Oracle at Delphi
    Lines-*Greek*, 50–55
APOLLO (subject)
—Myths
    Lines-*Greek*, 263 (index)
    Pinsent-*Greek*, 142 (index)
APOLOGIZING
    Quevedo and the king
        (Mexico)
APPALACHIAN MTS.
    Old fire dragaman
APPARITIONS
    See also BANSHEES
    King O'Toole and his goose
    Two neighbors
    Two sisters, Rose and Lotus
    The white butterfly
—first wife
    The cruel stepmother
The appeal of bells
    Ewart-*Lore*, 16–17
APPEARANCE
    The fox and the drum
—deceiving
    Beautiful girl who had no teeth
    Beauty and the beast
    Cap o' Rushes
    Cat in the box
    The fox who went to heaven
    Princess on the glass hill
—vs person
    Djuha's sleeve (Syria)
Appearance of the spirits Meri and
    Ari
    Wilbert-*Bororo*, 97–101
Apple blossom, Forsythia, Aubrietia
    Ewart-*Lore*, 45–49

The apple of discord
    Lines-*Greek*, 146–150
The apple on the boy's head [Wm
    Tell]
    Shah-*World*, 222
Apple pie
    Wahl-*Needle*, 47–53
Apple trees
    Froud-*Faeries*, unp.
APPLE TREES
    The big turtle
    The enchanted apple tree
    Johnny Appleseed
    The old witch
    Olga and the brown cow
    Selim and the snake queen
—branches
    Cormac MacArt went to Faery
APPLES
    The black bull of Norroway
    Disappearing apples [of
        immortality]
    The juniper tree
    The nine-seeded apple
    Rosy apple and the golden
        bowl
    Son of the Knight of the Green
        Vesture
—golden
    The apples of eternal life
    The battle of the birds
    The castle of Melvales
    Conn-eda; or The golden ap-
        ples of Lough Erne
    Connla and the fairy maiden
    East of the sun and west of
        the moon
    The firebird
    The fisher-prince with the sil-
        ver apple
    Golden mermaid [theft of gold-
        en apples]
    The Greek princess and the
        young gardener
    The new gods-Zeus and Hera
    Princess on the glass hill

APPLES (continued)
   The princess on the glass
      hill
—golden-stolen
   Ivan Tsarevich, the wolf, and
      the firebird
—rotten
   What the old man does is al-
      ways right
—of truth
   True Thomas [Thomas the
      Rhymer]
The apples of eternal life
   Branston-*Gods,* 65–71
The apples of Iduna
   Crossley-*Legends,* 57–61
APPLESEED, JOHNNY
   Johnny Appleseed
   Johnny Appleseed, the ap-
      pleseed planter
Appointment at Ticonderoga
   Robertson-*Highland,* 32–33
APPRECIATION
   See also GRATITUDE
   Three wishes
The apprentice [rabbit as
      painter]
   Poland-*Mantis,* 58–65
APPRENTICES
   Sorcerer's apprentice
   The spirit of the spring
   Vanooshka
   Wise man and the apprentice
APRICOT TREES
   Bagged wolf
APRIL FOOL'S DAY
   The box marked secret
   Jean Sotte
APRONS
   The rejected gift
APULEIUS, Lucius (Madaurensis)
   The golden ass
Aquarius (the Water-Carrier)
   Gallant-*Constel.,* 91–95
AQUATIC LIFE
—origin

   Glooskap and the monster
      bullfrog
ARABIANS
   The bushbabies
Arachne
   Low-*Greek,* 45–48
ARACHNE
   Athene, goddess of wisdom
   Arachne: price of a weaver's pride
   Spells & Bind, 42–43
The Aran Islands and Lough Corrib
   O'Sullivan-*Legends,* 154
ARAWN, King
   Pwyll, Prince of Dyfed
Arbitration. *See* JUDGES AND
      JUSTICE
Arbitration: monkey and the cheese
   Lewis-*Animal,* 46–47
ARBUTUS
   Clematis and Arbutus (the
      strawberry tree)
ARCHAEOLOGY
   Monkeys
ARCHBISHOPS
   The enchanted mule
   The three old men
   The wild swans
The archer who went I know not
      where to fetch I know not
      what
   Riordan-*Russia,* 243–261
ARCHERS
   Chang'o and the elixir of
      immortality
   The early heroes: Yi, the ten
      suns, the monsters
   Shooting the moon; a Yao
      folktale
ARCHERY
   Anpao and coyote
   The apple on the boy's head
   Four magic arrows
   Gesar of Ling
   Kitpouseagunow
   Sagittarius (the Archer)
   The twins of Paikala Mountain

—the contest for tsar's daughter
Green lizard, gray squirrel and
the eagle
ARCHITECTURE
See also BUILDERS AND
BUILDING
Theseus, king of Athens
ARCTIC
Jack of Sjoholm and the Gan-
Finn
Ares, god of war
Gibson-*Gods,* 41–43
ARES (subject)
Pinsent-*Greek,* 142 (index)
ARGENTINA
Roam the wild country
ARGONAUTS
Jason and the golden fleece
The sea gods' realm
ARGONAUTS (subject)
—Apollonius, books I–IV
Stapleton-*Dictionary,* 33–38
Argumentativeness: Room Bacha &
Baki
O'Connor-*Tibet,* 147–157
Arguments. See QUARRELING
ARI (moon as person)
Appearance of the spirits Meri
and Ari
First death of Ari and his
resurrection
Meri and Ari, sun and moon:
death of Meri
Meri and Ari take revenge
Second death of Ari and his
new resurrection
Ari, his third death and his
resurrection
Wilbert-*Bororo,* 28–30
ARIANROD
Welsh enchanter's fosterling
Ariel and Caliban
Baskin-*Imps,* 34–35
Aries (the Ram)
Gallant-*Constel.,* 103–105
ARION

Orpheus and Eurdice
The arising of Bodhi
Martin-*Hungry,* 1–4
Aristocratic fairies [condensed]
Logan-*Old,* 7–12
Aristotle and the bees
O'Sullivan-*Legends,* 131–132
ARIZONA
—Wilcox
Billy the milkmaid
ARJUNA (god)
Burning of the Khandava forest
Arjuna's penance
Amore-*Lustful,* 157–159
ARK OF THE COVENANT
The witch and the boy Israel
ARKANSAS
French place names in
Arkansas
Speech of the pioneers
ARKANSAS (subject)
—Jonesboro-Tornado: folklore,
popular religion, grass-roots
history
McNeil-*Charm,* 126–138
Arkansas folk-ballads and back-
ground of history
McNeil-*Charm,* 101–110
The armadillo
Ritchie-*Armadillo,* 56–60
ARMADILLOS
Encounter with the armadillo
How the tiger got his stripes
Origin of the name "Bokodori
Exerae"
Why the monkey still has a
tail
ARMENIA
Eight donkeys
The soul-taking angel [Gabriel]
ARMENIA (subject)
—Armenia's past: a brief survey
Villa-*Armenian,* 29–36
ARMENIAN TALES (subject)
—The Detroit collection
Villa-*Armenian,* 47–73

ARMENIAN TALES (subject)
  (continued)
—[National character, collections,
    translations; 25 tales]
  Sheohmelian-*Three,* v–ix
—The oral tradition
  Villa-*Armenian,* 36–40
—Published folktales
  Villa-*Armenian,* 43–46
ARMIES
  See also BATTLES; SOL-
    DIERS; WARRIORS
  Momotaro, or the son of a
    peach
  Phantom army of Flowers
    Barrow
ARMOUR
  The widow's son
ARMOURERS
  The unanswerable
ARMS
  A true money tree
—severed
  Ogre of Rashomon
ARNOLD, John
  Link chains as folk art
Arrogance. *See* PRIDE
ARROWHEADS
  Obsidian arrow points
  Tepoztecatl [swallowed by
    giant; escapes]
ARROWS
  See also BOWS
  Prince Meerzat Istvan and the
    horse of dust . . .
  Shooting the moon; a Yao
    folktale
  The summer birds of K'yakime
  Why stems of arrows have
    joints
—feathered
  Stompe Pilt
—first
  Baitogogo and the arrows
  Butoreagaddu legend
—magic

Four magic arrows
  Iktomi and the fawn
  Magic mirror of Rabbi Adam
  The magic rattle
  The tree-bound
—poisoned
  The lovers
—speaks
  Tiyo rejoins his clan
ARROWS (subject)
  Briggs-*Vanish.,* 127–128
ARSON
  Let the fire burn, you cannot
    put it out
ART
—drawing
  Odd jobs
Art of Ireland fights for Delvcaem
  Lehane-*Legends,* 80
The art of killing fleas
  Elbaz-*Folktales,* 149
Artemis and Apollo
  Gibson-*Gods,* 44–49
Artemis, Orion and the Seven
    Sisters
  Lines-*Greek,* 77–80
ARTEMIS (subject)
  Pinsent-*Greek,* 142 (index)
The artful lad
  Booss-*Scand.,* 208–220
ARTHUR, King
  Balin and Balan
  Castle [Chariot] of Morgan le
    Fay
  The coming of Arthur
  Coming of King Arthur
  Death of King Arthur
  Dream of King Arthur
  [Gawain and Dame Ragnell]
  Gawain and the Lady Ragnell
  The great king's last battle
  Lancelot and Guenevere
  Marriage of Sir Gawaine
  Noblest quest of all
  The passing of Arthur
  Quest of the Fair Unknown

Quest to the castle of the
cauldron
The Round Table
Siege of Joyous Garde
Sir Lancelot of the Lake
Tom Thumb
The Wooing of Olwen
—sword (Excalibur)
The coming of Arthur
Coming of King Arthur
The sword Excalibur
The sword in the stone
ARTHUR, King (subject)
—Legend of King Arthur
Ross-*Druids*, 82–97
Arthur, R.
The haunted trailer [by R.
Arthur]
Arthur, Robert, 1909–1969.
My displaced ghosts
To starch a spook [de-ghosting
a house]
Artifacts. *See* HANDICRAFTS
ARTIFICIAL MEN
Mummies, zombies, and artifi-
cial men
ARTISTS. *See* PAINTERS AND
PAINTING
Aryeh-Ben-Gadi and Fox-of-the-
Burnt-Tail
Soyer-*Adventures*, 21–36
As the king, so the kingdom
Amore-*Lustful*, 63–65
Asbjornsen, P. C.
Chicken Licken
The pig builds the house on
the hill
The three billy goats Gruff
The ascetic and the deer
Amore-*Lustful*, 174–176
The ascetic who visited home
Amore-*Lustful*, 161–163
ASCETICISM
Arjuna's penance
The destruction of love
Enlightenment

—generates heat
A boon of immortality
—worldly gain
A boon of immortality
ASCETICISM (subject)
—Buddhist stories
Amore-*Lustful*, 86
—Hindu stories
Amore-*Lustful*, 81–82,
155
Asceticism now, nymphs later
Amore-*Lustful*, 159–161
ASCETICS
The seven-day vigil
ASGARD
The golden age in Asgard
Loki and his evil children
The Norns
The walls of Asgard
War in heaven
Yggdrasill, the world ash
Asgard: war of the gods and
giants
Lee-*Castles*, 38–43
Ash
Froud-*Faeries*, unp.
Ash lad who had an eating match
with the troll
Yolen-*Favorite*, 348–350
Ash lad who made princess say
"You're a liar!"
Yolen-*Favorite*, 28–29
ASH TREES
The first humans
Yggdrasill, the world ash
Ashanti. *See under* AFRICA—
tribes
ASHES
Bad Indian's ashes [flies tor-
ment people]
The warlike seven
Ashiepattle who made the princess
tell the truth at last
Booss-*Scand.*, 71–72
The ashman's money
Villa-*Armenian*, 369–371

ASMODEUS (devil-king)
  The beggar king [Solomon and
    Asmodeus]
  The demon princess
  King Solomon and Asmodeus
  Magic flute of Asmodeus
  Partnership with Asmodeus
ASMODEUS (devil-king) (subject)
  Patai-*Gates*, 770 (index)
ASPEN TREES
  The death of Chanticleer
  Old woman's faith overcomes
    devil
—why leaves always tremble
  The Indian Cinderella
Asrai
  Arrowsmith-*Field*, 246–247
  Froud-*Faeries*, unp.
The ass in pantherskin
  Shah-*World*, 162
Assaraf baths closed
  Elbaz-*Folktales*, 104
Asses. *See* DONKEYS
ASSESSORS
  Why the executioner is called
    assessor
[Assipattle vs Stoorworm the sea-
    serpent]
  Ratcliff-*Scottish*, 129–136
Assorted monsters
  Cohen-*Every.*, 101–111
ASSYRIA
  Dividing the axe
  The wolf cub
Astaroth (demon)
  Lehane-*Wizards*, 78
ASTOLFO (palladin)
  Castle of Earthly Paradise
The astonishing brush
  Blyton-*My*, 73–77
ASTROLOGY
  The cobbler who became an
    astrologer
  Luck in a strange place
  The outlaw
  Tidings of the heavens

ASTRONOMY (subject)
  See also CONSTELLATIONS;
    MOON; STARS; SUN
—history
  Hadley-*Legends*, [30–32]
At the wrong post
  Roberts-*Chinese*, 56
Atalanta [and Hippomenes]
  Low-*Greek*, 79–83
[Atalanta vs Calydon]
  Wise-*Monster*, 24–25
Atam and Im
  Stuchl-*American*, 45–46
ATHAMAS, King
  Helle and Phrixus
ATHENA (or Athene; goddess)
  The apple of discord
  Poseidon's ocean kingdom
ATHENA (subject)
  Pinsent-*Greek*, 142 (index)
Athene, goddess of wisdom
  Gibson-*Gods*, 53–57
Athens
  Pinsent-*Greek*, 100–105
ATHENS
  Theseus, king of Athens
ATHLETIC CONTESTS
  See also RACES—athletic
  The adventures of Perseus
  Fairy hurling game: Ireland vs
    Scotland
ATHLETICS
  See also SPORTS
  Hulama, the royal ball game
Ati-tia bird; Boy-who-snared-the
    wind and . . .
  De Wit-*Talking*, 161–168
ATLAS (subject)
  Pinsent-*Greek*, 142 (index)
ATONEMENT
  See also PENITENCE
  The tinker and the ghost
ATTACHMENT
  The well of life
ATTICA
—Greece

Poseidon's ocean kingdom
ATTICS
  The secret ones
ATTILA the Hun
  Walter and Hildegund
Attitudes toward Missouri speech
  McNeil-*Charm,* 36–47
Aturuarodo and the monster
  Butoriku
  Wilbert-*Bororo,* 138–142
The Aturuarodo legend
  Wilbert-*Bororo,* 142–144
AUBRIETIA
  Apple blossom, Forsythia,
  Aubrietia
Auden, W. H., jt. author
  The lay of Thrym
AUKELE
  The water of life
Aultsigh Inn
  Robertson-*Highland,* 73–74
Aunascaul Lake
  O'Sullivan-*Legends,* 155–157
Auriga (the Charioteer)
  Gallant-*Constel.,* 135–137
AURORA BOREALIS
  The strongest boy in the
  world
AUSTRALIA
  Animals in different parts of
  Australia
  Baiame: in the beginning
  February dragon
  That wicked crow
—Goomade
  Oongnairwah and Guinarey
—the first aboriginals
  Koala and the rainbow
AUSTRALIAN ABORIGINAL
  TALES (subject)
  Parker-*Austral.,* 101–109
—Glossary
  Parker-*Austral.,* 183–186
—Native
  Parker-*Austral.,* 187–189
AUSTRALIAN ABORIGINES

Bahloo the moon, and the
  Daens
Beginning of the Narran Lake
Crane, kangaroo rat, fire
  makers
Goomblegubbon, Beeargah,
  and Ouyan
The mirage maker Beereeun
The rain bird
  Bougoodoogahdah
The sacred island, Nar-oong-
  owie
Sturt's desert pea, the blood
  flower
Wayambeh the turtle
—initiation: boys into manhood
  The borah of Byamee
—killed by Weedah
  The mocking bird, Weedah
—marriage
  Coral creeper [origin]
—Munkan tribe
  Red and black flying foxes
AUSTRALIAN ABORIGINES
  (subject)
—Animal tales
  Reed-*Aboriginal,* 7–8
—[Culture: past]
  Parker-*Austral.,* 7
—[Narran tribe]
  Parker-*Austral.,* 11–13
Australian legendary tales
  Parker-*Australian,* 14–16
AUSTRIA
  Seligen Fraulein
  Witchtln
AUTHORITIES
  The Amir who became a
  weaver
Autumn and the bear
  Crossley-*Legends,* 184–
  191
The autumn sky
  Gallant-*Constel.,* 98–116
"AVARICE"
  The young king

Avarice. *See* GREED
AVENGERS
    The badger and the bear
    Shooting of the red eagle
—tricked by Iktomi
    The tree-bound
Axad Bakht meets the dervishes
    Shah-*Dervishes,* 4–8
Axe porridge
    Riordan-*Russia,* 56–58
AXES
    The archer who went I know
        not where to . . .
    The death of Chanticleer
    Dividing the axe
    How they got Hairlock home
    Meri steals an ax
    The missing axe
    Mouse Woman and the mon-
        ster killer whale
    Munachar and Manachar
    Munachar and the raspber-
        ries
    The Paddo
    Senor San Antonio retrieves
        an axe
    Terror
—ice
    The cunning Lapp
—magic
    Wooing of Pumei; and Orogen
        story
AXSUQ (source of evil)
    Why raven is no longer
'Aye, we're flitting'
    Marshall-*Every.,* 58–64
Ayoga
    Nagishkin-*Folktales,* 61-64
Azad Bakht's tale
    Shah-*Dervishes,* 55–99
AZTEC LEGENDS
    Creation myths [8 tales]
AZTEC LEGENDS (subject)
—The dangerous woman
    Bierhorst-*Hungry,* 9–12
—[Myths and legends]

Bierhorst-*Hungry,* 3–18
—Quetzalcoatl and Tezcatli-
    poca
    Bierhorst-*Hungry,* 7–9
Aztec sun goddess
    Riordan-*Woman,* 80–83
Aztec's journey to Anahuac
    Nicholson-*Mexican,* 132–141
Aztecs. *See under* INDIANS OF
    LATIN AMERICA (tribes)

BA'AL SHEM TOV, Israel, 1699?–
    1760
    Patai-*Gates,* 667–701
Baba Yaga
    Xenophontovna-*Folk,* 118–127
BABA YAGA
    The archer who went I know
        not where to . . .
    The black geese
    The blacksmith
    Chavalai: taboos and
        deception
    Fenist the bright-eyed falcon
    Fenist the Falcon
    The frog princess
    Haunter of the birch forest
    Ivan and Nastasia [scrubbing
        off sin]
    Ivan Bear's ear
    Ivan Byelarasseiski [sucks
        blood]
    Ivan young in years, old in
        wisdom
    Marya Morevna
    A pool of bright water
    The swan geese
    Vanooshka
    Vasilisa the Beautiful
    Vassilisa [Fair] and Baba Yaga
BABA YAGA (subject)
—[Characteristics]

Riordan-*Russia,* 279–280
Baba Yaga and the hedgehog
  Lewis-*Minute,* 18–19
Babe the blue ox
  Haviland-*N. Amer.,* 175–183
Babes in the wood
  Pierce-*Larousse,* 113–115
  Tarrant-*Fairy,* 89–96
  Tudor-*Bedtime,* [22–23]
BABIES
  See also CHILDREN
  Antti and the wizard's
    prophecy
  The crow and the daylight
  Glooscap and the baby: Wasis
  Hello, Aurora
  How Ableegumooch tracked a
    fox
  King Eagle
  Kitpouseagunow
  The man/whale
  The piebald calf
  Rock-a-bye baby
  A story about death
  The two pickpockets
  The witch
—abandoned
  See also CHILDREN—
    abandoned
  Bird of truth
  The Bunbundoolooeys
  Fairest of all others
—cries for two years
  Tushcoon Eigna
—killed during famine
  The blacksmith
—lost
  Stars in the snow
—newborn
  Unborn child avenged its
    mother's death
  Wild Darrell [infant murdered]
—seven-day old tells story to
    Sultan
  Bead-seller and the jinn's
    sister

—speaks
  Half a blanket (Ireland)
—switching of
  King's/servant's sons switched
BABIES (subject)
—Scottish superstitions
  McKee-*Scottish,* 1–3
The baboon's umbrella
  Lobel-*Fables,* 12–13
Baboushka, the Wise Men and the
    Prince of Peace
  Shelley-*Legends,* 60–62
BABY CLOTHES
  The blood stain
A baby kidnapped by the jnun
  Elbaz-*Folktales,* 108
BABY SITTERS
  Dilly-dilly-doh!
The baby with the fangs [13
    legends]
  Robe-*Hispanic,* 158–171
BABYLON
  Seven days and nights
Babylonia: Tiamat
  Stallman-*Dragons,* 12–13
BABY-MAKER
  The moon god [how moon got
    up in sky]
BACABS
  Creation of the Mayas
Bacchae (Euripides)
  Stapleton-*Dictionary,* 44–47
Back for Christmas
  Hoke-*Uncanny,* 120–126
Back of the moon
  Adams-*Iron,* 120–125
Backhaus-Smith, Rex, illus.
  Parker-*Australian*
BACKS
—made crooked
  Crookened back [pooka]
BACON, Roger, 1214?–1294
    (subject)
—Masters of forbidden arts
  Lehane-*Wizards,* 56–63
—[Resolve to abjure magic]

44

BACON, Roger (continued)
    Lehane-*Wizards*, 87
—[Roger Bacon foils Satan]
    Lehane-*Wizards*, 74
The bad fairy of Strathardle
    Robertson-*Highland*, 17–18
Bad Indian's ashes [flies torment
    people]
    Macmillan-*Canadian*, 17–19
The bad kangaroo
    Lobel-*Fables*, 28–29
Bad luck omens
    Steele-*Ozark*, 81–82
Bad luck. *See* LUCK—bad
[Bad news keeps building]
    Cortes-*Byelorussian*, 137–
    139
The bad wife [in bottomless pit]
    (Russia)
    Yolen-*Favorite*, 367–368
The badger and the bear
    Zitkala-*Old*, 61–74
Badger and the fox cub
    Piggott-*Japanese*, 119–123
Badger and the green giant
    De Wit-*Talking*, 197–203
The badger and the rabbit
    Piggott-*Japanese*, 117
BADGER IN THE BAG
—origin
    Powel and Rhiannon
    Pwyll, Prince of Dyfed
Badger rents a house
    McCarthy-*Raccoon*, 43–55
BADGERS
    Farmer and the badger
    Honey bird [joins in hunt for
        wild honey]
    Mister Raccoon realizes that
        winter is coming
    Pots for hire [Dankuro]
    The rogue of Kachi Kachi
        Mountain
    The year summer was stolen
BADGERS (subject)
    Piggott-*Japanese*, 142 (index)

The bag of money
    Magel-*Gambia*, 109–115
BAGANY
    Vazili, Bagany and Banniki
Bagged wolf
    Kendall-*Sweet*, 49–59
BAGPIPE MUSIC
    Lure of the pipes [Big John
        Clach-na-Harnich and Black
        Simon]
BAGPIPES
    The sunset call
Bags. *See* SACKS
Bahloo the moon and Mooregoo
    the mopoke
    Parker-*Australian*, 61
Bahloo the moon, and the Daens
    Parker-*Australian*, 22–23
BAHUKA RIVER
    The brahman and the sacred
        river [purification]
BAIAME
    Leaving home
Baiame: in the beginning
    Shelley-*Legends*, 7–10
The Baiporo legend
    Wilbert-*Bororo*, 148–149
Baitogogo and Akaruio Boroge go
    to rule land of the dead
    Wilbert-*Bororo*, 62–67
Baitogogo and Akaruio Boroge re-
    nounce their powers
    Wilbert-*Bororo*, 90–92
Baitogogo and Aroia Kurireu fight
    the Kaiamo-Doge
    Wilbert-*Bororo*, 218–221
Baitogogo and the arrows
    Wilbert-*Bororo*, 106
The Baitogogo legend
    Wilbert-*Bororo*, 58–62
Baitogogo names the hill Kudorori
    Wilbert-*Bororo*, 67–69
Baitogogo takes possession of Aije
    spirit
    Wilbert-*Bororo*, 118–119
BAKERS

Fairy peel (condensed)
How the rhinoceros got his
saggy, baby skin
Magic knife [Uygur]
The baker's daughter
Lewis-*Bedtime*, 32–33
Lurie-*Clever*, 30–34
The baker's magic wand
Macmillan-*Canadian*, 1–6
The Bakororo and Itubore legend
Wilbert-*Bororo*, 180–187
Balan and Balin
Riordan-*Arthur*, 34–42
The bald old man
Zong-*Korea*, 191
BALDER THE GOOD
The death of Balder
Balder's doom
Crossley-*Legends*, 215–223
Baldheads
Aiken-*Mexican*, 51–52
BALDNESS
When one man has two wives
BALIN
Noblest quest of all
Balin and Balan
Riordan-*Arthur*, 34–42
The ball game
Nicholson-*Mexican*, 120–122
BALL GAMES
[Finn] Fan Mac Cuil and the
Scotch giant
Sky high went the sun
The ball of gold
Villa-*Armenian*, 350–351
Ballad of the boll weevil [song and
story]
Sanders-*Hear*, 150–158
BALLADS
Alison Gross (condensed)
Duke Magnus and the
mermaid
Lai D'Ywenee
Lord Nann and the Korrigans
Tam Lin
Thomas the rhymer

Ballet: The camel dances
Lobel-*Fables*, 22–23
BALLOONS
The bottle-neck
BALLS
The piebald calf
—golden
The companion
The golden ball
Prince Mahsud and King Rat
Tale of Elidurus
The unbroken web
BALLS (dances)
Cinderella
The nightingale and the rose
"BALLYRAM"
The tiger-eating jackal cubs
BALOR (giant and hero)
The evil eye
Balor of the Strong Blows
Magical Beasts, 38–39
Baluan: origin of the island
Shelley-*Legends*, 11–16
BAMBOO
Baitogogo and the arrows
The magic bamboo
—dancing
The promise of the three
sisters
—origin of joints
Origin of sun shield and joints
of bamboo
Bamboo-cutter and the moon-child
Ozaki-*Japanese*, 98–118
BANANA TREES
Why the bananas belong to
the monkey
—origin
The turtle wife
BANANAS
The gold harvest
How the monkey and goat
earned their reputations
The magician and the bananas
Why the bananas belong to
the monkey

Banca Flor
  Aiken-*Mexican*, 66–73
BANDITS
  See also THIEVES AND
    THIEVERY
  A boom in guarache leather
  El borracho del bahio
  Coffin cash
  The faithful lion
  A fiendish compadre gets
    caught
  Hong Gil-Dong
  How Jack went to seek his
    fortune
  Juan Oso
  Maid of the mill
  Pulga
  The snow queen
  The three counsels
  Willie Brennan [highwayman]
—soul saved
  The priest goes down to hell
Bang, Molly Garrett, illus.
  Bang-*Five*
Bangs, John Kendrick, 1862–
  1922
  The water ghost: Harrowby
    Hall
BANNIKI
  Vazili, Bagany and Banniki
BANQUETS
  See also DINNERS
  Djuha's sleeve (Syria)
  The tongue-cut sparrow
  What melody is the sweetest?
The banshee
  Logan-*Old*, 73–81
Banshee cases [list]
  Logan-*Old*, 137
Banshee of the MacCarthys
  Yeats-*Fairy*, 104–115
BANSHEES
  The bean-nighe
  The face at the window
  How Thomas Connolly met the
    banshee

The wailing messenger of
    death
BANSHEES (subject)
  Yeats-*Fairy*, 99, 289
The Bantam phantom
  Hoke-*Spirits*, 33–39
The banyan deer [the Buddha]
  Martin-*Hungry*, 105–114
Bao Luotuo the sage
  Minford-*Fav.*, 133–142
BAPTISM(S)
  See also CHRISTENINGS
  Cat's baptism
  The changeling speaks on the
    way to baptism
  Conor mac Nessa
  The devil in guise of the
    Blessed Virgin
  How the slaves worshipped
  Juan de Toluca
  Little Lapp and the Ice King
  With her godmother to
    Josefsdal
  The young lady of Hellerup
Barabao
  Arrowsmith-*Field*, 149–150
BARBARIAN INVASIONS
  A great misfortune
BARBERS
  The tailor-bird and the barber
  There is no such thing as a
    secret
  Three brothers [craft contest]
BARDIC ASSOCIATION
  Seanchan the Bard and the
    king of the cats
The bare mountains
  Stuchl-*American*, 113–116
Bargains. *See* AGREEMENTS
The bark lizard, Walloobahl
  Parker-*Australian*, 150–151
BARLEY CORN
  Thumbelina
The barmecide's feast
  Rackham-*Fairy*, 178–183
The barn is burning

Yolen-*Favorite,* 195–197
BARNS
    Drakes [house spirits]
    Linchetti
    The tomts
    Whose horse is it?
BARRELS
    Peik
Barrenness. *See*
    CHILDLESSNESS
Barrett, Angela, illus.
    Riordan-*Woman*
Barrett, Mary
    Death out of season
BARRETT, Peggy
    Crookened back [pooka]
Barter
    Ginsburg-*Twelve,* 72–81
Barter. *See* AGREEMENTS
BARTON, Andrew, d.1511.
    Sir Andrew Barton [ballad]
The bashful bride
    Patai-*Gates,* 743–745
Basilisk
    Magical Beasts, 94–95
BASILISKS
    Land monsters
    Roosters, snakes and basiliscs
    The white doe
BASKET MAKERS
    The man who had no story
Basket of Ngomba
    Radin-*African,* 266–268
BASKETS AND BASKET-
    WEAVERS
    The heavenly flute player; a Li
        story
    How the rabbit lost his tail
    How the speckled hen got her
        speckles
    I won't forgive you
    Lam Ku, the basket lady
    Only a dream
    Star Maiden
    A stepchild that was treated
        mighty bad

Bastard son: Ivan, the Windfall
    Cortes-*Byelorussian,* 16–30
The bat Narahdarn
    Parker-*Australian,* 54–56
The bat [war of birds and animals]
    Lewis-*Animal,* 44–45
Bata and Anpu
    Shah-*World,* 87–92
BATH HOUSES
    Vazili, Bagany and Banniki
Bathwater becomes gold: Vartiter
    Sheohmelian-*Three,* 104–115
BATS
    Anpao and the animals
    How the rat lost his wings
    Vampires
—origin
    The children with one eye
—origin: hanging upside down
    The bat [war of birds and
        animals]
—why they fly at night
    The bat-women of Koitabu
Battle [Cheyennes attack
        Shoshones]
    Weeks-*Pachee,* 33–34
The battle of Stamford Bridge
    Crossley-*Legends,* 192–198
The battle of the birds
    Garner-*British,* 63–75
    Jacobs-*Celtic,* 133–142
    Lochhead-*Battle,* 3–16
Battle of the bulls: the Donn of
        Cuailnge
    Ross-*Druids,* 52
The battle with the birds
    Highwater-*Anpao,* 206–215
Battle with the katsina
    Dutton-*Hopi,* 33–35
BATTLES
    See also NAVAL BATTLES
    Ant and lizard [origin of enmity]
    Baitogogo and Aroia Kurireu
        fight the Kaiamo-Doge
    Burning of the Khandava forest
    The castle in the lake

BATTLES (continued)
  The cat Johann
  Elstorps Woods
  From bad to good to bad to
    good
  The great battle between the
    grasshoppers and the
    monkeys
  The king's daughter and the
    pepper man
  Koroge tribe defeated by Jerigi
    Otojiwu
  Llyr: children of the sea-god
  Mice in the corn
  Naddi
  Phya Paan and the Golden
    Chedi
  Son of the Knight of the Green
    Vesture
  Stones of five colours and the
    Empress Jokwa
  Strategy
  Teigneux
  Thor fights the giant Krangnir
  The widow's son
—animals vs birds
  Elephant and blackbird court
    the same girl
—of the books
  Saints Colmkille and Edna
The bat-women of Koitabu
  Stokes-*Turtle,* 62–64
Baucis and Philemon
  Lines-*Greek,* 122–128
BAY TREES
  Wiley and the hairy man
BAYBERRY
—causes pregnancy
  Golden reed pipes
Bayou tales [five]
  Phillips-*Hoity,* 6–46
BEACHES
  Annie Norn and the fin folk
Bead chant myth
  Dutton-*Navajo,* 36–45
Bead-seller and the jinn's sister

  Shah-*Dervishes,* 185–190
BEAKS
  Raven with the broken beak
The bean-nighe
  Froud-*Faeries,* unp
BEANS
  Jha sells beans to the sultan
—magic
  Jack and the beanstalk
  The magic of the katsinas
The bear and the crow
  Lobel-*Fables,* 16–17
Bear cub [and six companions]
  Kudian-*More,* 14–22
The bear husband
  Villa-*Armenian,* 409–411, 529
Bear Mother and her husband
  Reid-*Raven,* 49–59
The bear mother [human] and
    father
  Reid-*Myths,* 40–48
"BEAR OF THE STRONG HEART"
  Ermine and the hunter
The bear trainer and the trolls
  Lindow-*Swedish,* 90–91
The bear who liked hugging peo-
    ple
  Ainsworth-*Bear,* 7–11
The bearded rock
  Magel-*Gambia,* 137–138
BEARDS
  Ednoth's relics, and Thurkill's
    beard
  Gods of the stars: ancient
    China
  Stupid Peikko
  Ten jugs of wine
  Three musicians [princess un-
    der spell]
BEARS
  See also POLAR BEARS
  See also titles beginning with
    "Bear . . ."
  Animals in winter
  Autumn and the bear
  The big shaggy dog

Brer bear gets a taste of man
Brer rabbit goes a courting
Bruin and Reynard partners
The castle of Melvales
Choril and Cholchinay
The clever little tailor
Coyote retrieves his brother's
    scalp
East of the sun and west of
    the moon
The end of the world
Farmers three
The fox who went to heaven
Frightened wolves [wolf head]
The gipsy baron
The girl who married a bear
Goldilocks and the three bears
How bear and chipmunk
    stopped . . . friends
How raven brought the salmon
How the cow went under the
    ground
How they got Hairlock home
Ivan Bear's Ear
Juan Oso
King's son goes bear hunting
    (Finland)
Kintaro, the golden boy
Little Masha and Misha the
    bear
The lodge of the bear [the
    Great Mystery]
Lox, the mischief maker
Master rabbit [tries to do what
    other species do]
Mighty bear has problems
Moonflower
[The old, vagrant woman and]
    The three bears
Peter Gynt
Pookong kills a bear
A pool of bright water
Pork and honey
The prayer that was answered
Rabbit and the grain buyers
The rabbit and the well

Severi and Vappu
Snow White and Rose Red
Sody sallytytus
The straw ox
The summer birds of K'yakime
Tale of a she-bear
The tar baby
The three bears
The three bears [the first
    printed version]
True and untrue
Two weak ones against one
    strong one
Ua-pa-chi (Kickapoo titles)
The umbrella tree
Ursa Major (the Great Bear)
Ursa Minor (the Lesser Bear)
Ursulo, hijo del oso
The vain bear
The valiant chanticleer
The war of the birds and the
    beasts
The water nick
The water sprite and the bear
Wayland Smith
Who got brer Gilyard's
    treasure?
Zan and the Dactyls in early
    Crete
—battle with
    Grasshopper [Indian
    superman]
—becomes human, then Queen,
    mother of Dan-Gun
    Dan-Gun, first king of Korea
—fights deer
    Rainbow and the autumn
    leaves
—frightened by goat
    The farmer and the bear
—harnessed to cart
    Old man Zackery and the
    cranes
—in den for winter; not killed
    The Blackfoot and the bear
—monster

BEARS (continued)
The Seneca chief's adventures
—origin of characteristics-short tail
Rabbit and the Indian chief
—prince under spell
Brown Bear of Norway
Charcoal burner and the bear
East of the sun, west of the
moon
Snow-White and Rose-Red
—reward for kindness to
The blacksmith
—squashes smaller animals
The squeaking mouse
—stupidity
The fox and the bear
How a bear kept reindeer
—taboo: kill only one a year
Girls and bears [Musquakie]
—tails
How the bear lost his tail and
the bees gained a friend
—takes badger's food & home by
force
The badger and the bear
—trapped
The Catholic fox
—why bears fear fire
Fire [personified]
Bearskin (Germany)
Yolen-*Favorite*, 389–393
Beast-human relationships
Nicholson-*Mexican*, 36–41
The beastly creature and the magi-
cal flower
Piggott-*Mexican*, 84–100
Beast-men: Pari Ao
Wilbert-*Bororo*, 212–213
Beasts. *See* ANIMALS;
MONSTERS
Beating the changeling
Lindow-*Swedish*, 91–92
BEATINGS
The widow's son
BEAUMAINS, Sir
Sir Gareth of Orkney

Beausoleil
Thomas-*It's*, 170–176
Beautiful girl who had no teeth
Radin-*African*, 269–271
Beautiful lady whose name was
Ruth
Marshall-*Every.*, 228–230
The beautiful maidens of the
sea
Haining-*Lepre.*, 77–79
BEAUTY
Echo and Narcissus
Eros and Psyche
The god of faces
Gold-tree and Silver-tree
The hunting of the hind
The king's favorite [beauty
fades]
Lai D'Ywenee
Maiden Bright-Eye
Nourie Hadig [a "Snow White"
type]
The prostitute who lost her
charm
Pygmalion's statue
Rickety Topknot
Riquet with the Tuft
Snow White and the seven
dwarfs
The ugly duckling
The young king
—disfiguration by potion
The vengeance of Oiwa
—evil
Waxworks
—fades
The king's favorite
—kindheartedness superior to
Cinderella
—passion's effect on
The monk and Lady Kiyo
—pursuit of
Why the crow is black
—vain; spoiled
Ayoga
—of women

Fabiano and Reyes
BEAUTY (subject)
   Keightley-*World*, 22–23
Beauty and the Beast
   Ehrlich-*Random*, 82–93
   Lang-*Blue*, 108–129 (notes,
     367)
   Quiller-*Sleeping*, 113–175
   Rackham-*Fairy*, 45–59
   Tarrant-*Fairy*, 68–88
BEAUTY CONTESTS
   How the polar bear became
Beaver Tail and the Indians
   Shaw-*Pima*, 97–103
BEAVERS
   Glooskap's country
   Grasshopper [Indian
     superman]
   Rabbit and the Indian chief
   Raccoon's tale
   Raven and the beavers
   The raven and the salmon
   Raven steals the salmon from
     the beaver house
   The snail and the beaver
—origin of characteristics
   How beaver got his flat tail
—saves Indian maiden
   Wastewin and the beaver
Becoming a werewolf
   Lindow-*Swedish*, 179–180
BED SHEETS
   The master thief
The bedbug and the flea
   Wood-*Kalila*, 109–126
Bedbug, the louse, and the
    flea
   Zong-*Korea*, 36
BEDS
   [The old, vagrant woman and]
    The three bears
—feather
   The bear who liked hugging
    people
—four-posted
   Draw the curtains

The beduin's gazelle (Saudi
    Arabia)
   Yolen-*Favorite*, 415–416
Beebyeebyee and the water-god
   Todd-*Tortoise*, 100–105
BEER
   Death and the doctor
   The fairies' christening
   The field of Boliauns
   King Brian Boru the Danish
    heather ale
   The parson and the clerk [II]
   Skotte in the fire
   Tom Hickathrift and the old
    giant
—heath
   The field of Boliauns
BEER BARRELS
   The spook and the beer barrel
BEES
   The blacksmith
   The elf of the rose
   The flies and the bees
   The flowers' forever land
   The grateful bee
   Jack and his cudgel
   The jackal, the dove, and the
    panther
   Johnny and the three goats [in
    turnip field]
   Little rooster and the Turkish
    sultan
   The lost hum
   The magic boat
   Marya Morevna
   Old Man La Feve
    [bumblebees]
   Queen bee
   Rabbit and the grain buyers
   The sacred honey bees
   The season of the stubby
    caterpillar
   The tale of the magic green
    water-pearl
   The three daughters
   The Tibetan envoy's mission

BEES (continued)
   Two weak ones against one
     strong one
   The unwilling magician
   Which flower?
   Zan and the Dactyls in early
     Crete
—how they make honey
   Aristotle and the bees
—protected by man
   How the bear lost his tail
     and the bees gained a
     friend
The bees from Borneo
   Asimov-*Fant.*, 117–130
BEETLES
   The ducks and the fox
   Thumbelina
   Tomorrow's child
—colors
   How the Brazilian beetles got
     their . . . coats
The beggar and the gazelle
   Shah-*World*, 218–221
The beggar king [Solomon and
     Asmodeus]
   Schwartz-*Elijah*, 59–66
The beggar, the lion and the dog
   Shah-*Afghanistan*, 76–82
BEGGARS
   The barmecide's feast
   The blind boy and his dog
   The boy, his sisters, and the
     magic horse
   Day of the dead
   Eye will see what it is destined
     to see
   The faithful gazelle
   The great misfortune of Lay
     Tee-Kwai
   Juan Soldado
   Lake of Zangze
   Legends of the mill
   Little Freddy with his fiddle
   Master Tobacco
   One who deserved the money

   The seven beggars
   Simmer Water
   The star child
   The story-teller at fault
   A stranger comes to Leon
   The test [beggar; love]
   Today's laughter, tomorrow's
     sadness
   Wicked John and the devil
—fakirs
   Kupti and Imani
—removes his ears
   Donkeys of Jolof
—royal inspector in disguise
   The young widow
The beggar's bridge
   O'Sullivan-*Legends*, 150–151
BEGGARS (subject)
   Lindow-*Swedish*, 7–8
BEGGEY
   Sleigh Beggey and Tylwyth
     Teg
The beginning: Father Sky, Mother
     Earth
   Jagendorf-*First*, 59–61
Beginning of the Narran Lake
   Yolen-*Favorite*, 231–233
The beginning of the world
   Dutton-*Hopi*, 6–7
BEGINNINGS
   See also CREATION
   See also titles under
     "How . . ." "Origin . . ."
     "Where" & "Why . . ."
   Baiame: in the beginning
   The Crab [and He-Who-Made-
     All-Things]
   How thunder and lightning
     came to be
   Pervasive perfume of las zor-
     rillas the skunk
   The prince who had two eyes
   Sea, sun and moon [visiting;
     sun and moon. . .]
   Universe and its beginnings
     [21 tales]

Begonia
  Ewart-*Lore,* 121
BEHAVIOR [problems]
  The hermit [paradoxical
    behavior]
  Prince Featherhead and Prin-
    cess Celandine
  The wise woman, or The lost
    princess
—children reflect parents
  The bad kangaroo
—contrarian
  Dimian the peasant
—reversal: totally negative to total-
    ly positive
  The traveller and the
    innkeeper
BEHEADED [-ING]
  See also HEADS—severed
  Sharp sword
—head and life restored
  Uath the Stranger [a giant]
—head of goddess attached to
    prostitute
  Kali beheaded
Behind the waterfall
  Wood-*Spirits,* 90–91
Being greedy chokes Anansi
    (Jamaica)
  Yolen-*Favorite,* 130–131
Bek, William G. 1873–1948.
  Marriage customs among Mis-
    souri Low Germans
Bel Inconnu. *See* GINGALIN
Le Bel Inconnu and the castle of
    Senaudon
  Lee-*Castles,* 154–155
BELCHING
  Graduation
BELDYS, The
  How the Beldys stopped
    fighting
Belfield House, Perth
  Robertson-*Highland,* 60–62
BELGIUM
  Follets

—Antwerp
  The bold soldier of Antwerp
Belief
  Robe-*Hispanic,* 454–469
BELIEF AND DOUBT
  Clever man and ordinary
    Priest's soul
Beliefs and dieties of Japan
  Piggott-*Japanese,* 38–60
Believe it or not
  Cortes-*Byelorussian,* 123–124
A bell for the cat
  Lewis-*Bedtime,* 28–29
BELL RINGERS
  Legend of the old bell-ringer
Bellerophon
  Low-*Greek,* 75–79
BELLEROPHON
  Prince Bellerophon and
    Pegasus
Bellerophon, the Valiant
  Magical Beasts, 57–65
[Bellerophon vs Chimera]
  Wise-*Monster,* 18–23
Belling the cat
  dePaola-*Favorite,* 62
  Marshall-*Every.,* 365–367
BELLOWS
—magic
  The disrespectful son
BELLS
  Abuelita's bell
  Chisos ghosts
  Death comes at a trot
  The herd-boy
  The lost bell
  The pheasants and the bell
  The thief who kept his hands
    clean
  The three billy goats Gruff
  The trolls in Resslared
—broken by boy's prank
  Ednoth's relics, and Thurkill's
    beard
—bronze
  The ugly son-in-law

BELLS (continued)
—church
 Delsbo's churchbell [Sweden]
 The giant puke
 The silver mountain
 Toller's neighbors
 Troll's stone
 The Ulfgryt stones
 The wow o'Rivven; the bell
—church-"Great Harry"
 Devil's armful [Canterbury]
—monastic
 The monk and Lady Kiyo
—of police
 Why wolves fear the bell
—towers
 Church grims
BELLS (flowers)
 The appeal of bells
BELLS (subject)
—fairies and
 Briggs-*Vanish.*, 50–51
The bell-shaped pendant
 Sanders-*Dragons,* 95
BELTS
 The giant of Skalunda
 The grateful elfwoman
 Jack and his magic aids [dish,
 belt, flute]
—golden
 Little cinder girl
—magic
 The first mosquito
 The giants who moved
BELVEDERE, Sir
 Death of King Arthur
Ben Vair dragons
 Robertson-*Highland,* 140–141
BENAIAH (biblical)
 The eternal light [Solomon &
 Benaiah]
BENARES
—India
 The blossom tree
Bending Willow [Indian maid]
 Phelps-*Maid,* 149–153

Benedict, Andrew (pseud. of
 Robert Arthur)
 To starch a spook [deghosting
 a house]
BENGALI TALES (subject)
—[classic themes, five demon
 tales]
 Bang-*Five,* ix–xi
Benson, E. F.
 The confession of Charles
 Linkworth
 Monkeys
Benson, Patrick, illus.
 Mayne-*Red*
Benten, bringer of happiness
 Piggott-*Japanese,* 134–138
BEOWULF
 Heorot, the haunted hall
[Beowulf and Heorot]
 Night Creatures, 7–10
Beowulf fights the dragon
 Crossley-*Legends,* 98–107
B'er [*sic*] rabbit is an uncle
 Crouch-*Whole,* 109–112
BERG-PEOPLE (subject)
 Briggs-*Vanish.,* 116, 195
Bergtagen
 Lindow-*Swedish,* 96–97
Bergtagen: The silver mountain
 Lindow-*Swedish,* 97–98
BERRIES
 Mouse Woman and the Snee-
 nee-iq
Berry, Karen, illus.
 Heslewood-*Tales*
"BERSERKS"
 Odin prepares for the
 Ragnarok
Berton, Pierre
 Supernatural creatures
BERTRAND du Guesclin (subject)
 Briggs-*Vanish.,* 145–146
The best coon and possum dog
 Yolen-*Favorite,* 294
Best liar in the land
 Kudian-*More,* 58–59

BESTIARIES
An enchanted bestiary
Beth Gellert
Jacobs-*Celtic*, 123–124
BETRAYAL
See also TREACHERY
Altynchech and the padishah's
wife
The bedbug and the flea
Curiosity punished
A fiendish compadre gets
caught
John the Bear
Kertong
King's son goes bear hunting
(Finland)
Magic knife [Uygur]
The poor rich man's son gets
a second chance
The tailor (Mikhei) and the
shoemaker
The three talismans
Wicked girl and her
punishment
Wise sayings for a thousand
dinars each
—of benefactors
The north country wolf
The betrothal
Kendall-*Sweet*, 80–85
BETROTHAL
Bearskin (Germany)
Bobburr the giant brown and
yellow snake
The butcher's mitzva
Dead couple marry after
death
Hans my Hedgehog
The pirate princess
The promise
Pwyll, Prince of Dyfed
Rainbow bridge: Buck Ante-
lope and Evening Breeze
The twelve huntsmen
The weasel and the well
—broken

The death waltz
—girl promised in marriage to evil
dwarf
Parselina [marriage to evil
dwarf]
—saved by non-human witnesses
The two brothers [fire and
water]
—unfaithfulness
Mysterious cannon ball
Bets. *See* WAGERS
Bettelheim, Bruno
—[Fairy tales and child
psychology]
Ehrlich-*Random*, x–xi
Betty Booker's bridle
McCarty-*Skull*, 25–30
Beware of hypocrites!
Elbaz-*Folktales*, 147–
148
Beware of the bull
Ainsworth-*Bear*, 26–33
Bewitched butter [Donegal]
Yeats-*Fairy*, 137–138
Bewitched butter [Queen's County]
Yeats-*Fairy*, 142–150
Bewitched cow
O'Sullivan-*Legends*, 88
Bewitchery. *See* ENCHANTMENT;
TRANSFORMATIONS;
WITCHCRAFT
Bewitching by sympathetic
magic
Robe-*Hispanic*, 272–274
Bhima slays the demon [giant,
man-eating cannibal]
Rungachary-*Tales*, 43–51
BIBLE
*See also names of biblical
persons, e.g.* MOSES
—defense against spooks
The owl
—wards off spectre
The spectre wolf
BIBLE. New Testament
Where love is, God is

Bible. Old Testament. Introd. &
  selections
  Patai-*Gates*, 1–120
BIBLE (subject)
—fairies and
  Briggs-*Vanish.*, 103
Biblical heroes [Midrash]
  Patai-*Gates*, 282–349
Biblical heroes [Talmud]
  Patai-*Gates*, 190–209
BIDPAI TALES (subject)
—[Introd. by Doris Lessing]
  Wood-*Kalila*, ix–xix
Bierce, Ambrose
  The boarded window [by
    Bierce]
  A resumed identity
Big Bear. *See* GREAT BEAR
  (constellation)
The big bird Katchka
  Manning-*Cats*, 118–123
Big bird of south Texas
  Ritchie-*Armadillo*, 46–49
Big boulder north of Torstuna
  church
  Lindow-*Swedish*, 84–85
Big brother: man; Little brother:
  rabbit
  Jagendorf-*Magic*, 63–67
Big city folk tales
  McNeil-*Charm*, 82–87
BIG DIPPER
  Gods of the stars: ancient
    China
—origin
  The star dipper [Ursa major]
Big family in the little house
  Lewis-*Bedtime*, 36–37
BIG FISH UNLIMITED
  Water monsters
"BIG KNIVES"
  Anpao and the magic dogs
Big long man's corn patch
  Haviland-*N. Amer.*, 71–75
The big shaggy dog
  Stuchl-*American*, 193–195

The big turtle
  Wood-*Spirits*, 68–72
BIGAMY
  Taken [wife taken by fairies]
"BIGFOOT"
  Wild men
Biggle, Lloyd, Jr.
  The Botticelli horror
BI-HYONG
  The goblin bride
Bilak Pokis
  Stokes-*Turtle*, 86–87
Bilber and Mayrah
  Parker-*Australian*, 124–125
Billy the milkmaid
  Schwartz-*Tales*, 42–45
Billy-goat and the handkerchief
  Stuchl-*American*, 131–132
"Binding" and driving off a sjora
  Lindow-*Swedish*, 128–130
BINDWEED
  Sea bindweed, sea holly, sea
    pea, samphire
BIOLOGISTS
  Mouse
The birch boy
  Nagishkin-*Folktales*, 89–98
BIRCH TREES
  Elstrops Woods
  The fool and the birch
  Stupid Peikko
The bird and the sea: Jingwei
  Sanders-*Dragons*, 22
The bird-bride
  Synge-*Land*, 170–175
BIRD CAGES
  The bottle-neck
Bird from the golden land
  Stuchl-*American*, 175–182
The bird 'Grip'
  Lang-*Pink/D*, 132–142
  Lang-*Pink/K*, 86–95
"BIRD IN THE HAND" (proverb)
  The hawk and the nightingale
["A bird in the hand . . ."] Two
  badgers

Riordan-*Tartary*, 115
The bird maiden
Shah-*World*, 238–251
"BIRD MAIDEN"
The talking spear
BIRD-MEN
The hummingbird brothers
The bird of happiness
Jagendorf-*Magic*, 53–56
Minford-*Fav.*, 81–86
Bird of truth
Manning-*Marvels*, 65–78
Bird that made milk
Radin-*African*, 146–149
The bird wife
Manning-*Cats*, 75–82
BIRDS
See also ANIMAL-HUMAN
COMMUNICATION
See also names of particular
species, e.g. PARROTS
The battle of the birds
The big bird Katchka
The birth of Cu Chulaind
The black colt
The bride from Bird Island
The chao ku bird
The destruction of Da Derga's
hostel
The enchanted forest
Foolish coyote
Gesar of Ling
The girl who trod on the loaf
The golden legend
(condensed)
The happy prince
How three serpents carried
princesses. . .
Jorinde and Joringel
Juan and the bony one
Kate Crackernuts
[Little bird singing: angel of
death]
The lost bell
Mabinogion (condensed)
Magic bird [tells stories]

Magic birds and enchanted
animals
Man without a heart
Marya Morevna
Meri and Ari ascend to the sky
Princess on the glass
mountain
The sleepy one: Senor
Opossum and the rattler
Tomik and the magic mat
Vaino and the swan princess
Wasting sickness of Cu
Chulaine . . .
Wejosis and the wind giant
The youth and the dog-dance
—artificial
The nightingale
—beaks
Meri improves beaks of birds &
gives Bororo teeth
—colors
The nightingale
—eat garden bugs
The rabbits go hunting
—evil
The sun journey
—featherless
The sad end of Wu-Lung-Tru
—giant
The bare mountains
The greedy brother
—giant, wind-maker
Gluska'be, the Penobscot hero
—golden
Golden mermaid [theft of
golden apples]
The Greek princess and the
young gardener
—killer
Scarface
—language understood
Language of the birds
Two brothers and the
magistrate
Water lily: the gold spinners
The witch and the boy Israel

BIRDS (continued)
—magic
  A wonderful bird
—magical transformations
  Jorinde and Joringel: Castle of
    the Birds
—maiden bewitched as
  The brothers and the singing
    toad
—migration
  Raven and the north lands
—monsters (-strous)
  The battle with the birds
  The wampum bird
—origin
  How Glooskap made the birds
—origin of characteristics
  The Weeoombeens and the
    Piggiebillah
—origin of characteristics-
    featherless heads
  Meri and Ari take revenge
—origin of small
  The singing birds
—ransoming caged birds
  His compassion is over all his
    works
—singing/song(s)
  The golden bird
  The juniper tree
  The monk and the bird
  The nightingale
  The rose tree
—talking
  The jackdaw
—Thekwane
  Adventures of Ntini, the small
    otter
—trapped
  The dove and the mouse
—war over one grain of corn
  The war of the birds and the
    beasts
—wounded, turns into fairy
  Tobacco fairy from the Blue
    Hills

—yellow
  The battle with the birds
  The competitive tiger
BIRDS (subject)
—magical
  Briggs-*Vanish.*, 12, 40, 79–80
—Motif index
  Wilbert-*Bororo*, 279–280
BIRTH
  See also MULTIPLE BIRTHS
  Anpao is born
  B'er rabbit is an uncle
  Labor pains of the Ulaid, and
    twins of Macha
  Moerae
  The pixy-labour
  The troll labour
—gives birth to egg
  Go Zu-Mong, king of Goguryo
—magic
  Room Bacha and Baki
—magic: queen, horse,
    dog
  Prince and the ogre's castle
—marvelous
  Golden reed pipe
—monstrous
  Hans my Hedgehog
  Pilar's indiscretion
  Prince Nocha
  The providential pot
  Retribution
—woman inside body of whale
  Yeghnig Aghpar
BIRTH (subject)
—Newborn babies; Scottish
    superstitions
  McKee-*Scottish*, 1–3
Birth, dreaming, death: school-
    master's story
  Macdonald-*Gray*, 173–186
The birth of Cu Chulaind
  Gantz-*Early*, 130–133
Birth of Finn MacCumhail
  Yolen-*Favorite*, 202–210
The birth of Huitzilopochtli

Bierhorst-*Hungry*, 65–70, 137–138
The birthday of the Infanta
  Wilde-*Fairy*, 119–146
The bishop and the elves
  Booss-*Scand.*, 604–605
Bishop Svedberg and the devil
  Booss-*Scand.*, 283–284
BISHOPS
  See also ARCHBISHOPS
  Hodeken
  King and the bishop
    [Clonmacnoise]
  Mice in the corn
  The skeleton in Holar church
  The troll in the Skrudur
—form of address (humor)
  The new bishop
—parson's ambition to succeed
  Parson and the clerk [island in
    Devon]
BISON SKULL
  Spirit of the bison skull
The biter bit
  Lang-*Green*, 198–206
Black and white
  Roberts-*Chinese*, 94
Black Annis
  Froud-*Faeries*, unp
The Black Bull of Norroway
  Crossley-*Folk*, 102–105
  Garner-*British*, 41–46
  Lang-*Blue*, 334–348 (notes, 373)
  Phelps-*Tatterhood*, 49–54
The black colt
  Mayo-*Book*, 29–41
BLACK DEATH
  Greedy Kanchuga
  The survivors
  The wizards of the Vestmanna
    Isles
The Black Dog [death to touch]
  Baskin-*Imps*, 20–21
The black dog of Creag an Ordain
  Robertson-*Highland*, 86

The black dragon of the Sea of
  Dunting
  Heslewood-*Tales*, 42–50
The black dwarfs of Granita
  Keightley-*World*, 204–205
"BLACK ENCHANTERS"
  The wonderful plough
The black fox
  Ransome-*War*, 54–63
The black geese
  Lurie-*Clever*, 17–22
The Black General
  Roberts-*Chinese*, 132–136
The black horse
  Garner-*British*, 127–134
  Jacobs-*Celtic*, 189–194
"Black Horse," the third Brother
  Zhang (Tu)
  Seven Sisters, 80–81
The black king, or Fair Ferentine
  Thomas-*It's*, 91–100
The black lady
  Sampson-*Gypsy*, 100–101
Black magic. See MAGIC—black
The black mare
  Griego-*Cuentos*, 57–61
Black monk's curse
  Marshall-*Every.*, 90–96
The Black Officer of Ballachroan
  Robertson-*Highland*, 201–204
The black pearl
  And Every., 175–181
[Black school (Satan's) for wizards]
  Lehane-*Wizards*, 70–73
The black spectre
  Manning-*Spooks*, 43–50
The black swans
  Reed-*Aboriginal*, 134–137
The black umbrella
  Stuchl-*American*, 158–160
Blackberry tart
  Blyton-*My*, 33–37
BLACKBIRDS
  Elephant and blackbird court
    the same girl
  Golden blackbird

60

BLACKBIRDS (continued)
—color, song, eyes
    Why blackbird has white eyes
—dancing
    Coyote and the blackbirds
—enchanter
    Prince Vivien and the Princess
        Placida
—mate abducted
    How the blackbird went to war
The Blackfoot and the bear
    Macmillan-*Canadian,* 130–133
A Blackfoot legend
    Gallant-*Constel.,* 17
BLACKMAIL
    Ednoth's relics, and Thurkill's
        beard
BLACKS
    Brer rabbit and his riding horse
    Brer rabbit dances for a wife
    Brer rabbit goes a courting
    Brer rabbit keeps his word
    Brer rabbit rescues his children
    Brer rabbit's protest meeting
    Brer tiger and the big wind
    Brer wolf and brer fox get a
        big surprise
    Brer wolf plants pinders
    Brer wolf wants the honey
    Brer wolf's magic gate
    Brer wolf's second pinder patch
    Fishing with bare hands
    How ole woodpecker got ole
        rabbit's conjure bag
    How the cow went under the
        ground
    How the slaves helped each
        other
    How the slaves worshipped
    One for you, one for me
    A riddle for freedom
    Run brer gator, run!
    Simon and the pater-rollers
    Simon challenges the
        McCrackens
    Simon marries Ellen
Simon sees a ghost
A slave's dangerous courtship
A slave's escape
Stagolee
The tar baby
The tar baby tricks brer rabbit
The ways of a witch
Who got brer Gilyard's
    treasure?
Who stole brer Gilyard's
    sheep?
Wiley and the hairy man
The blacksmith
    Cortes-*Byelorussian,* 50–61
The blacksmith in heaven
    Ransome-*War,* 81–84
BLACKSMITHS
    Aphrodite, goddess of love
    The bride from Bird Island
        [abducted]
    The choosy maid of Yen-Pien
    An evening in the squire's
        kitchen
    The herd boy and the dragons
    The hill-smith
    How Thor got his hammer
    The lad and the devil
    The lad and the devil (Norway)
    The laird's lass and the
        gobha's son
    The leopard
    The magician earl
    On top of Old Smoky [song
        and story]
    The red czar and the golden-
        haired Tihota
    Singard the dragon-slayer
    The smith and the devil
    Smith Riechert
    Swarthy Smith of the Socks
    Three brothers [craft contest]
    The troll's hammer
    The water smith
    Wayland Smith
    The white doe
    The white pony

Wicked John and the devil
Wooden horse [mechanical flight]
The wooing of Seppo Hmarinen
The blacksmith's wife of Yarrowfoot (Scotland)
Yolen-*Favorite*, 308–310
BLACKTHORN
Unantishee
Blackwood, Algernon
The Wendigo (I–IX)
BLADDERS
The warlike seven
Blair, Walter
Johnny Appleseed
Blake, W. H.
A tale of the Grand Jardin
BLANKET WEAVING
End of the world (Sioux tale)
BLANKETS
—dancing
Mouse Woman and the wooden wife
—given to Great Spirit, then taken back
Iktomi's blanket
—magic
The white fox
BLASPHEMY
Tummeldink
—punished
The old woman and El Senor
"BLESS YOU" [origin]
Plague victims dig their own graves
The blessed gift of joy bestowed upon man
Haviland-*N. Amer.*, 101–106
BLESSINGS
Departure of the giants (Africa)
The dwarfs' banquet
The lost horse [blessings and disasters as interchangeable]

Mally Whuppy
The robin
The son of the goblin
—turn to disasters
The lost horse
BLIND
The bird 'Grip'
The bird of happiness
The eye restored
The fairy child
The gizzard [riches for the one who eats it]
Good and evil
The haunted well
How a king learned to care for parents
Ivan and Nastasia [scrubbing off sin]
The last love of Prince Genji
Lox and the chief's wife
Lox, the mischief maker
Menashe and Rachel [children in love]
The old man wouldn't take advice [young wife]
Old woman and the doctor
Shun, the wise emperor
Sprig of rosemary
Supparaka
Tobias goes on a journey
True and untrue
The two blind men [thieves]
The wonderful Chuang brocade
Wonderful healing leaves
—blinded
Owney and Owney-na-peak
Rapunzel
—blindness as punishment
The blind sea captain
The two travellers [evil man blinded]
—one eye shared by brother/sister
The children with one eye
—origin of blindness

BLIND (continued)
Separation of god from man
—sight restored
Adugo the jaguar and Buke
the anteater
—trades home and magic food bag
for . . .
Manstin, the rabbit
The blind boy and his dog
Adams-*Iron*, 69–75
The blind man and the devils
Zong-*Korea*, 59–62
The blind ones and the matter of
the elephant
Shah-*World*, 84
The blind sea captain
Lindow-*Swedish*, 132–136
BLOB the Whale
How the Summer Queen came
to Canada
Bloch, Robert
A most unusual murder
Waxworks
BLOCKS
Peik
BLODEUWEDD
Welsh enchanter's fosterling
BLOMIDON (island)
Why Bootup, the whale,
smokes a pipe
BLOOD
—drops
The goose girl
—fairies are bloodless
Why the fairies are vindictive
—shedding
Saint Martin's Eve [a]
Blood feasts of the damned
Night Creatures, 73–97
The blood stain
Ainsworth-*Phantom*, 47–63
Blood-begotten anemone
Spells & Bind, 36–37
BLOODTHIRSTINESS
Red caps
Bloody Bones

Baskin-*Imps*, 14–15
Bloody castle of Altaripa
Lee-*Castles*, 148–149
The blossom tree
Hyde-Chambers-*Tibet*, 7–13
The blown away rabbit
Blyton-*My*, 25–32
Blue Beard. *See* BLUEBEARD
Blue bird [King Charming]
Lang-*Green*, 23–54
"BLUE EGG"
The prince who had two eyes
The blue lake
Segovia-*Spanish*, 1–51
Blue Men of the Minch
Robertson-*Highland*, 169–170
BLUE TITS (birds)
The lost hum
BLUEBEARD
Lang-*Blue*, 290–296 (notes,
372)
Mulherin-*Favorite*, 32–39, in-
trod., 30–31
Perrault-*Glass*, 25–35
Quiller-*Sleeping*, 53–77
Rackham-*Fairy*, 135–142
[Bluebeard, Isabelle, the bleeding
key]
Spells & Bind, 94–102
Bluebell
Froud-*Faeries*, unp
Bluebells-hyacinths
Ewart-*Lore*, 41–42
BLUEBIRDS
Bird from the golden land
Why coyote's coat is the color
of sand
—color
Coyote and bluebird
Bluejay and woodpecker: a sad
tale
Macmillan-*Canadian*, 123–
125
Blue-jay who married daughter of
god
Radin-*African*, 79–80

The blue-tail fly [song and story]
  Sanders-*Hear,* 71–81
BLUFFING
  The herd-boy and the giant
Boa constrictors. *See under*
  SNAKES
Boar of Eskdale
  Marshall-*Every.,* 327–331
The boarded window [by Bierce]
  Schwartz-*Great,* 127–133
BOARHOUNDS
  Yorkshire giant [Penhill]
Boars. *See* HOGS
The boaster no man could kill
  Thompson-*Hawaiian,* 66–71
Boasting. *See* BRAGGARTS
BOAT BUILDERS
  The partridge and his
    drum
BOATS
  See also CANOES; SHIPS
    AND SHIPBUILDING
  The enchanted princess
  The fisherman and the draug
  Little boat that could sail on
    land and sea
  The lobster and the crab
  Seven days and nights
  Stupid Peikko
  Thor's holiday
  Vainamoinen's boat building
—building
  Jack of Sjoholm and the Gan-
    Finn
—fairies turn boat back into tree
  Fly together, chips and
    shavings!
—of feathers
  The water palace [boat of
    feathers]
—paper
  The steadfast tin soldier
—paper (magic)
  The magic boat
—sinking
  The sjora in Helgasjon

Bobburr the giant brown and yellow
    snake
  Parker-*Australian,* 166–167
BOBCATS
  The great hunters [animals]
  Why the bob-cat stays in the
    woods
BODY, HUMAN
—assembled, part by part
  Knock! knock!
—headless human, pursues
    husband
  The cruel stepmother
BOERBOON TREES
  If the boerboon flowers fall
BOGATYRS (supermen)
  Kile Bamba and the Loche
    bogatyr
BOGEY-BEASTS (subject)
  Briggs-*Vanish.,* 16, 22, 68, 76,
    122, 172, 195
The boggart
  Keightley-*World,* 307–
    308
BOGGARTS
  The golden ball
  The green mist
  Yallery Brown
BOGIES
  Shellycoat
Bogles
  Froud-*Faeries,* unp
BOGLES (little people)
  Farmer and the bogle
  Jeanie, the bogle of Mulgrave
    Wood
Boguet, Henri, *fl.* 1603
—Short way with witches
  Sergeant-*Witches,* 44–51
BOHEMIANS
  Hey-hey men
  Hinzelmann
Bohrah the kangaroo and Dinewan
    the emu
  Parker-*Australian,* 119–
    120

Bokodori Ecerae chief and clan
  customs
  Wilbert-*Bororo*, 109–110
The bold soldier of Antwerp
  Crossley-*Folk*, 106–108
BOLDNESS
  Mister Fox [suitor/murderer]
BOLIAUNS
  The field of Boliauns
Boliauns (grass-covered boulders):
  Manachar and leprechauns
  Smith-*Manachar*, 43–63
BOLL WEEVILS
  Ballad of the boll weevil [song
  and story]
Bolster and Jecholiah
  Marshall-*Every.*, 151–154
Bolstre Castle
  Booss-*Scand.*, 305
Bond, Ruskin
  Tigers forever
The bone garden
  Wheeler-*Fox*, 27–34
BONES
  Dog and the bone
  Give me my bone
  The singing bone
  The story of trembling hood
  Up from the Dead Land
—of goats: burn, and set spirits
  free
  The feast of the mountain
  goats
—magic
  Magic moccasins: the Wearer
  of the Ball
The bonfire
  Hadley-*Legends*, 6–7
BONFIRES
  Saint John's Eve bonfires
BONG FIRE FESTIVAL
  How the fire festival came to
  be
Bonnie Prince Charlie
  O'Sullivan-*Legends*, 124–125
Booker, Cech

The leopard
BOOKS AND READING
  The goblin and the grocer
  The goblin and the huckster
  Horace the horse
  Master and pupil
  Odd jobs
  The skeleton in Holar church
  The story of Jon Asmundsson
—constant
  Billy-goat and the handkerchief
A boom in guarache leather
  Aiken-*Mexican*, 11–16
BOOMERANGS
  The Galah, and Oolah the
  lizard
  Koala and the rainbow
  The mopoke, and the mosquito
  bird
—used to make first woman
  Moon and Morning Star
A boon of immortality
  Amore-*Lustful*, 155–157
Bootes (the Herdsman)
  Gallant-*Constel.*, 151–154
Bootmakers. See SHOEMAKERS
Boots. See SHOES—boots
Boots and the beasts
  Booss-*Scand.*, 152–157
The boots of Hunain
  Shah-*World*, 224
BORA BORA (island)
  The giant eel
The borah of Byamee
  Parker-*Australian*, 79–85
BOREDOM
  The cows who came to tea
[Bormus and the water spirits]
  Water Spirits, 100–102
BORNEO
  The bees from Borneo
  The sky-god: Ratu and the
  Dyaks
El borracho del bahio
  Aiken-*Mexican*, 64–66
BORROWING

See also LOANS
The dwarfs borrowing bread
The fairy borrowing oatmeal
The friendly dwarfs
The Hodja and the cauldron
(Turkey)
BORS, Sir
Castle of an enchantress
Elaine the Fair Maid of Astolat
Knights' tales
Noblest quest of all
Quest for the Holy Grail
Boss. See SUPERVISORS
BOSTON
The ghost rider
The Botticelli horror
Asimov-*Fant.*, 20–61
The bottle-neck
Booss-*Scand.*, 460–468
BOTTLES
Occasion [death trapped in
bottle]
—messages
The bottle-neck
—vinegar
The old woman who lived in a
vinegar bottle
—wine; never empty
Gift of Elijah
Bouki dances the kokioko
Wolkstein-*Magic*, 80–86
Bow and arrow. See
ARROWS; BOWS
Bowering, George
Windigo [II]
BOWLS
The poor man's bowl
Rosy apple and the golden
bowl
—golden
The disrespectful son
—magic
The man who wanted to bury
his son
—silver
Lisalill

Bowman, James Cloyd
Pecos Bill becomes a coyote
BOWS
See also ARROWS
Meri steals a bow
Shooting the moon; a Yao
folktale
The summer birds of K'yakime
—magic
The three talismans
The box marked secret
Schwartz-*Tales*, 71–72
The box with the funny thing in it
Booss-*Scand.*, 56
BOXERS
Kid Cardula
BOXES
The castle in the lake
The giant puke
Katrineholm Manor
Boy abducted by fairies
O'Sullivan-*Legends*, 71–72
A boy and his dog
Griego-*Cuentos*, 77–81
The boy and his grandfather
Griego-*Cuentos*, 115–117
The boy and his three helpers
Macmillan-*Canadian*, 79–81
The boy and the dancing fairy
Macmillan-*Canadian*, 24–29
The boy and the dragon
Macmillan-*Canadian*, 209–213
The boy and the filberts
Williams-*Aesop*, [16]
The boy and the robbers' magical
booty
Macmillan-*Canadian*, 91–96
The boy, his sisters, and the magic
horse
Timpanelli-*Tales*, 1–13
The boy in the donkey skin
Stuchl-*American*, 236–242
The boy in the Land of Shadows
Macmillan-*Canadian*, 268–272
Boy-man
Wade-*Indian*, 101–109

Boy of great strength and the
 giants
  Macmillan-*Canadian,* 112–114
The boy of the red twilight sky
  Heslewood-*Tales,* 141–145
Boy of the red twilight sky
  Macmillan-*Canadian,* 184–187
The boy, the crow and the sesame
 seeds
  Watson-*Thailand,* 25–27
The boy who ate more than the
 giant
  Lofgren-*Boy,* 5–24
The boy who cried wolf
  Lewis-*Bedtime,* 12–13
The boy who did not know what
 fear was
  Booss-*Scand.,* 646–651
The boy who drew cats [by Hearn]
  Schwartz-*Great,* 61–66
The boy who laughed at death
  Amore-*Lustful,* 164–166
Boy who overcame the giants
  Macmillan-*Canadian,* 253–257
Boy-who-snared-the-wind and
 shaman's daughter
  De Wit-*Talking,* 161–168
The boy who told lies
  MacLean-*Cuentos,* 154–155
The boy who was called Thickhead
  De Wit-*Talking,* 183–187
  Macmillan-*Canadian,* 166–170
Boy who was saved by his
 thoughts
  Macmillan-*Canadian,* 246–249
The boy who wore turtle shell
 moccasins
  Yellow Robe-*Tonweya,* 59–65
Boy with the deformed head
  O'Connor-*Tibet,* 92–102
The boy with the knucklebones
  Riordan-*Tartary,* 70–78
The boyhood dreams of Cu
 Chulaind
  Gantz-*Early,* 134–146
BOYS
 Ainsel
 The box with the funny thing in it
 The boyhood dreams of Cu
  Chulaind
 The drowned boys
 The fly (as witness)
 The flying kite
 George's picnic
 Juan Pelon
 Logic
 Mister Miacca
 The nis and the boy
 The nis stealing corn
 The old house
 The old troll of Big Mountain
 Settlement out of court
 Shurik: A story of the siege of
  Leningrad
 The strongest boy in the world
—black
 How black became white
—steals food
 The bark lizard, Walloobahl
The boys and the giant
  Macmillan-*Canadian,* 134–135
Bradbury, Ray
 The crowd
 The illustrated man
The braggart
  Nagishkin-*Folktales,* 77–79
BRAGGARTS
 The cock who wanted to be
  shah
 Coyote and the water serpent
 El gallo braggadocio
 The girl who was already queen
 Glooscap and the baby: Wasis
 The hare and the magpie
 Helping to lie
 Koala and the rainbow
 The lad and the fox
 Magic moccasins: The Wearer
  of the Ball
 Rumpelstiltskin
 The sad end of Wu-Lung-Tru
 The shirt collar

Stupid Peikko
The two old women and the
  boastful fish
—farmer expects to be king
  Brave Bear, Snake, and Croco-
    dile Killer
The brahman and the demons
  Amore-*Lustful,* 71–73
The brahman and the sacred river
  [purification]
  Amore-*Lustful,* 111–112
The brahman in the graveyard
  Amore-*Lustful,* 16–18
BRAHMANS
  The curse of a brahman
  A mistaken gift
  The brahmin's wife and the
    mongoose
  Shah-*World,* 106
Bran and the monster of Achanalt
  Robertson-*Highland,* 136–137
Bran: Birth of Finn MacCumhail
  Yolen-*Favorite,* 202–210
BRAN Mac FEBAL (subject)
  Briggs-*Vanish.,* 22–23, 89, 93
BRAN the Blessed (subject)
  Briggs-*Vanish.,* 12–13
BRAN the Brave
  Llyr: children of the sea-god
BRANCHES
—fairy
  How Cormac MacArt went to
    Faery
Branner, John Casper, 1850–1922.
  French place names in
    Arkansas
Branstock: the hall of the Volsungs
  Lee-*Castles,* 30–31
Branston, Brian
  Thor goes fishing with Hymir
BRANTS (geese)
  Grasshopper [Indian
    superman]
Branwen, daughter of Llyr
  Ross-*Druids,* 69–72
  Thomas-*Mabinogion,* 29–44

BRANWEN the Beautiful
  Llyr: children of the sea-god
Bratkowski, Joann
  Wesolego Alleluja = Happy
    Easter
The brave Azmun
  Nagishkin-*Folktales,* 13–26
Brave Bear, Snake, and Crocodile
  Killer
  Toth-*Tales,* 57–65
The brave clever tailor
  Stovicek-*Around,* 24–27
The brave lion and the foolish rabbit
  Martin-*Hungry,* 5–14
Brave little parrot and the eagle's
  tears
  Martin-*Hungry,* 73–78
Brave little tailor (seven at one
  blow)
  Lang-*Blue,* 306–316, 372
Brave warrior, Malietoa!
  Wright-*Pigeon,* 30–31
Bravery. See COURAGE
BRAZIL
  How black became white
  How night came
  How the Brazilian beetles got
    their . . . coats
  How the monkey and goat
    earned their reputations
  How the monkey became a
    trickster
  How the monkey escaped
    being eaten
  How the monkey got a drink
    when he was thirsty
  How the monkey got food when
    he was hungry
  How the pigeon became a
    tame bird
  How the rabbit lost his tail
  How the speckled hen got her
    speckles
  How the tiger got his stripes
  How the toad got his bruises
  The Tsantsa

BRAZIL (continued)
  Why the bananas belong to
    the monkey
  Why the lamb is meek
  Why the monkey still has a tail
  Why the sea moans
  Why the tiger and the stag fear
    each other
BREAD
  Boots and the beasts
  The dwarfs borrowing bread
  The girl who trod on the loaf
  Water of life
—crumbs
  Hansel and Gretel
—magic
  Girl with the golden hair
—rye
  The mouse bride
Breakfast party [witch]
  Marshall-*Every.*, 288–291
BREAST
  Papaya [origin]
BREATHING
  Draw the curtains
BREEN, Bud
—Biographical note
  Ritchie-*Armadillo*, vi
The Bremen town musicians
  Crossley-*Folk.*, 29–33
  Lewis-*Animal*, 26–27
  Ross-*Druids*, 52–61
  Shub-*About*, 110–115
  Tudor-*Bedtime*, [30–31]
Bremen Town musicians [variant]
  Macdonald-*Twenty*, 101
Bremen Transcript: In the
    beginning
  Scott-*Fantastic*, 23–36
BRENNAN, Willie
  Willie Brennan [highwayman]
Brer bear gets a taste of man
  Faulkner-*Tales*, 85–88
Brer fox meets Mister Trouble
  Faulkner-*Tales*, 137–138
Brer fox tries farming, too

Faulkner-*Tales*, 110–114
Brer possum and brer snake
  Faulkner-*Tales*, 99–101
Brer rabbit and brer cooter race
  Faulkner-*Tales*, 132–136
Brer rabbit and his riding horse
  Faulkner-*Tales*, 146–151
Brer rabbit dances for a wife
  Faulkner-*Tales*, 141–145
Brer rabbit goes a courting
  Faulkner-*Tales*, 75–79
Brer rabbit keeps his word
  Faulkner-*Tales*, 95–98
Brer rabbit rescues his children
  Faulkner-*Tales*, 168–177
Brer rabbit's protest meeting
  Faulkner-*Tales*, 115–121
Brer tiger and the big wind
  Faulkner-*Tales*, 89–94
Brer wolf and brer fox get a big
    surprise
  Faulkner-*Tales*, 164–167
Brer wolf plants pinders
  Faulkner-*Tales*, 102–105
Brer wolf wants the honey
  Faulkner-*Tales*, 139–140
Brer wolf's magic gate
  Faulkner-*Tales*, 80–84
Brer wolf's second pinder patch
  Faulkner-*Tales*, 106–109
BREVIARY
  One member of a family fated
    to die
BREWERIES
  The girl who trod on the loaf
Brewery of eggshells
  Haining-*Lepre.*, 22–23
  Jacobs-*Celtic*, 143–144
  McGarry-*Folk*, 39–42
  Yeats-*Fairy*, 49–51
  Yolen-*Favorite*, 50–52
BRIAN BORU, King, d.1014.
  King Brian Boru the Danish
    heather ale
BRIAR PATCH
  The rabbit and the well

Briar-Rose [princess]
  Lee-*Castles*, 158–159
BRIARS
  The Wooing of Olwen
Bricriu's feast
  Gantz-*Early*, 219–255
The bridal present
  Booss-*Scand.*, 276
The bride from Bird Island
  Stovicek-*Around*, 94–97
A bride from the lake
  Crouch-*Whole*, 75–81
Bride from the sea: the mermaid's
    cap
  Lochhead-*Battle*, 84–87
A bride kidnapped by the jnun
  Elbaz-*Folktales*, 109
The bride of gold and silver
  Synge-*Land*, 166–169
The bride of heaven
  Stovicek-*Around*, 124–125
The bride who would not speak
  Zong-*Korea*, 189–190
BRIDEGROOMS
  The Cormorants of Andvaer
  The dead bridegroom
  Ebbe Skamelson
  The giant maiden in Boraserod
    mountain
  The girl clad in mouseskin
  The noodle
  Only a dream
  The troll ride
Bride-price: a woman for a hundred
    cattle
  Radin-*African*, 298–303
BRIDES
  The bashful bride
  Big brother: man; Little brother:
    rabbit
  The Chinese bride
  The deacon of Myrka
  Death to the giant snake
  The doll in the grass
  Ebbe Skamelson
  The frog

  The giant maiden in Boraserod
    mountain
  The girl clad in mouseskin
  Give me something you
    have . . . unawares
  Guleesh
  The hundredth dove
  The iron wolf
  Man without a heart
  The mouse bride
  Origin of the house of Haro
  Pious bride and the angel of
    death
  The prize bull
  Pygmalion's statue
  The red stream
  The sea nymph
  The squire's bride [a horse]
  The stealing of Thor's hammer
  The swan maiden
  Three foolish brides
  Tobias goes on a journey
—horse as
  The squire's bride
—instruction to
  The wedding feast at Pohja
—South Africa
  The enchanted buck
—to-be
  The fate of Aino
—true and false
  Far have I sought ye: Red Bull
    of Norroway
  Wolfskin's bride
—wooden
  The giant's bride
Bridge of One Hair: Molly
    Whuppie
  Lurie-*Clever*, 45–52
The bridge over Kalmarsound
  Booss-*Scand.*, 270
BRIDGES
  The beggar's bridge
  The giant maiden in Boraserod
    mountain
  The greedy youngster

BRIDGES (continued)
  The pulque vendor tricks the
    devil
  Stubbornness does not pay
  The three billy goats Gruff
  The three billy-goats who
    went . . . to get fat
—Bendigeidfran, the river Shannon
  Branwen, daughter of Llyr
—built with help of spirit
  Zo Han-Zun who became a
    stone Buddha
contest: Lu Ban vs Lu Jiang
  Zhaozhou Bridge [Han]
—created by devil
  Old Nick is a gentleman
—golden
  The winding-horn village
—the "Gizzen Briggs"
  The golden bridge of Dornoch
Bridget and the Lurikeen
  Yolen-*Favorite*, 342–343
BRIDLES AND BITS
  Betty Booker's bridle
  Guleesh
  Hildur, the queen of the elves
  Sheena and the water-horse
  The widow's son
Brier Rose
  Shub-*About*, 23–27
Bright Light
  Walking-*Song*, 53–58
BRIGID, Saint
  Saint Brigid's cloak
BRIGID, Saint (subject)
—Celtic magic
  Lochhead-*Battle*, x
[Brindled cat and the miller's son]
  Seekers Saviors, 7–12
BRITAIN. *See* ENGLAND; GREAT
    BRITAIN
BRITANNIA
  Dream of Macsen
Brittany. *See under* FRANCE
BROCADE
  The Chuang brocade

  The wonderful Chuang
    brocade
—beautiful estate becomes reality
  Piece of Zhuang brocade
The brocaded slipper
  Vrong-*Brocaded*, 1–26
The broken oaths
  Keightley-*World*, 498–506
The broken swords
  Macdonald-*Gray*, 54–81
The bronze ring
  Lang-*Blue*, 14–26 (notes, 354,
    364–365)
The brook's secret
  Uttley-*Foxglove*, 87–93
Broom-binder: Ha! Ha! Ha!
  Manning-*Spooks*, 126–128
BROOMS
  Plague omens
A broomstick trick [make glass of
    water stick to ceiling]
  Schwartz-*Tales*, 58–59
BROOMSTICKS
  Pix! Pax! Pox!
  The witch's cat
Brother and sister: Golden reed
    pipe
  Minford-*Fav.*, 161–167
"BROTHER NOBODY"
  The archer who went I know
    not where to . . .
Brotherhood of the Round Table
  Lehane-*Legends*, 74–99
BROTHERS
  See also FRATRICIDE; SONS
  All that happened must hap-
    pen again
  Anpao is born
  Anpu and Bata
  Azad Bakht's tale
  "Black Horse," the third
  Brother Zhang (Tu)
  The blacksmith's wife of Yar-
    rowfoot (Scotland)
  The candy man; a Han folktale
  The castle: a parable

BROTHERS (continued)
 The twelve clever brothers go
  to town
 Twilight, Midnight, and Dawn
 Two brothers
 The two brothers
 Two brothers [and seven-
  headed monster]
 The two hunchbacks (Italy)
 Twopence Halfpenny
 Water of life
 Wayland Smith
 When rocks rolled crackling
  wisdom
 Why the sea is salt
 The wicked sister-in-law
 The wild swans
 Woe [personified]
 The world below
 The year summer was stolen
—one evil, one good
 Glooskap's country
 The princess and the frog
—one rich, one poor
 Enchanted castle
 The wise little girl
 Woe Bogotir
—save their sister
 Zilyan
—searches for dead sister
 The boy in the Land of
  Shadows
—sun and moon
 First death of Ari and his
  resurrection
—trans. into doves
 Ten white doves
—two mountains, once brothers
 Manam Island and the Sepik
  River
The brothers and the singing toad
 Piggott-Mexican, 107–117
The brothers Samba
 Magel-Gambia, 96–99
Brothers (Sun and Moon) and the
 pretty girl

 Radin-African, 45–48
Brown Bear of Norway
 Lochhead-Battle, 61–72
Brown, Fredric
 Mouse
Brown man of the Muirs
 Froud-Faeries, unp.
"BROWN ONES"
 The lost bell
The Browney at the grocer's
 Lang-Pink/K, 33–38
The brownie
 Froud-Faeries, unp.
The BROWNIE (subject)
 Keightley-World, 357–361
The brownies
 Arrowsmith-Field, 193–196
 Keightley-World, 395–396
BROWNIES
 The Bwca (booka)
 Bwciod
 The cauld lad of Hilton
 An evening in the squire's
  kitchen
 The fenoderee
 Fincastle mill
 Killmoulis
 Susie and her shadow
BROWNIES (subject)
 Briggs-Vanish., 195, 215
  (index)
 Mckee-Scottish, 18–19
Bruin and Reynard partners
 Booss-Scand., 140
BRUSH [vegetation]
 Farmers three
BRUSHES
 The astonishing brush
 Something for nothin (a Hui
  story)
—paint: things painted become
 real
 Magic brush; a Han folktale
BRYNHILD
 Treachery of the Nibelungs
Bubbly's trick

Blyton-*My,* 18–24
Bucca Dhu and Bucca Gwidden
  Phelps-*Tatterhood,* 139–142
BUCKS
  Mally Whuppy
BUDDHA AND BUDDHISM
  See also JATAKA TALES;
    MONKS—Buddhist
  The banyan deer [the Buddha]
  Beliefs and dieties of Japan
  The blossom tree
  A deer king offers his life
  The destruction of the world
  The dying Buddha's
    compassion
  Enlightenment
  Fearless lion, brave elephant,
    merchant's cries
  The footprint of Buddha
  The god of faces
  The great bronze Buddha and
    the whale
  Havoc in heaven: Monkey and
    the Jade Emperor
  How a king learned to care for
    parents
  How Asanga came to see the
    future Buddha
  Mahosoth [Buddha as wise
    man]
  A mansion in heaven
  The merchant's walk
  Miaoshan-Guanyin, protectress
    of mortals
  Prayer that was answered
    (Tibet)
  Supparaka
  The three stars
  Tripitaka: quest of the Buddhist
    scriptures
  The young man and the priest
  —monasticism. *See* MONKS—
    Buddhist.
—Rishi (holy man)
  Gazelle horn
—statues

  The emerald Buddha
  Zo Han-Zun who became a
    stone Buddha
BUDDHA AND BUDDHISM
  (subject)
  Piggott-*Japanese,* 142 (index)
—Symbols (eight)
  Timpanelli-*Tales,* 52–53
Buddha finds a middle path
  Amore-*Lustful,* 86–87
Buddha sets the wheel in motion
  Amore-*Lustful,* 76–77
The Buddhist Job
  Amore-*Lustful,* 119–120
BUDDHIST TALES (subject)
—Chinese thought: goddess of
    mercy
  Sanders-*Dragons,* 60
—[Stories of life]
  Amore-*Lustful,* 183–198
Buddhur Bap
  Raychaudhuri-*Stupid,* 47–52
BUFFALO
  Anpao and the animals
  Behind the waterfall
  Boy-who-snared-the-wind and
    shaman's daughter
  Chano's first buffalo
    hunt
  Good faith
  How Sainday brought the
    buffalo
  How the seven brothers saved
    their sister
  The poor lame horse
  The search for the buffalo
  Water buffaloes
  Why crows are black
  Wonder-worker of the plains
—all stolen by giant
  Giant with the grey feathers
—monster
  In the days of the great buffalo
BUFFALO HUNTING
  Buffalo skinners [song and
    story]

Buffalo skinners [song and
story]
Sanders-*Hear,* 169–180
Bugle of life, sweet dung, and the
cake tree
Zong-*Korea,* 178–180
Bugs. *See* INSECTS
BUILDERS AND BUILDINGS
Who built Reynir church?
—skeleton in wall as support
The milk of death
BUILDERS AND BUILDINGS
(subject)
—moved by fairies
Briggs-*Vanish.,* 129–130
The building of the wall of Asgard
Crossley-*Legends,* 36–47
Building the ceremonial
house; . . . rain dance
Dutton-*Navajo,* 20–23
BULBUL, Princess
Aladdin, or The wonderful
lamp
Bull-calf goes to school
Riordan-*Russia,* 262–263
The Bull [Europa and Minos]
Lurie-*Heavenly,* 50–52
The bull in the china shop
Uttley-*Foxglove,* 102–107
[Bull, Schanzabeh, fights to his
death]
Wood-*Kalila,* 172–176
Bullfrogs. *See* FROGS
BULLIES
The parson and the clerk [I]
"BULL-MAN"
Pilar's indiscretion
Bullock: The tiger and the man
O'Connor-*Tibet,* 6–11
BULLS
Anpu and Bata
The Black Bull of Norroway
The camel, lion, leopard, crow,
& jackal
Far have I sought ye: Red Bull
of Norroway
The fisher-prince with the sil-
ver apple
The flying bull
Jack and the robbers
Kalila and Dimna
The labours of Hercules
Peter Bull
Saga of Santiago Sanchez
The small, small cat
Taurus (the Bull)
Three heroes [and the 3-head-
ed boa]
The valiant chanticleer
Ygnacio y el toro gigantesco
—branded
And they wondered
—calves
The little bull calf
Peter Bull
The treasure in Saby Creek
—cannot have calves
Mahosoth [Buddah as wise
man]
—carries bride to her true love
The prize bull
—enchanter in form of
Crystal coffin
—hyena, an "Indian-giver"
Hyena and hare search for
wealth
—killed by lice
[Tyrannical bull with discon-
tented lice]
—protects orphan
The brothers Samba
—saves stepson from death
The jealous co-wife
—white
Beware of the bull
The bun [personified]
Riordan-*Russia,* 31–33
The Bunbundoolooeys
Parker-*Australian,* 51–52
The bundle of straw
O'Sullivan-*Legends,* 92–93
BUNOLA (island)

How the turtle got her shell
BUNYAN, PAUL
Babe the blue ox
Paul Bunyan, the giant logger
BURD ELLEN
Childe Rowland
[Burd Helen, Childe Rowland, and
Elf King]
Seekers Saviors, 49–77
Burgess, Gelett, 1866–
1951.
The ghost extinguisher
[humorous]
Burgher and the pauper
Nahman-*Tales,* 163–187
[notes: 165, 311–313]
Burglars. *See* THIEVES AND
THIEVERY
BURGUNDIANS
Siegfried and the Rhine
castles
BURIAL(S)
Aphrodissia, the widow
Buried alive to stop the plague
The death of Abraham Azulai
The Milky Way [Wahn (crow) &
Baripa (cat)]
The story of Bergthor
Teig O'Kane and the corpse
—in Ireland
Saints Colmkille and Edna
The burial cave [Sinbad]
Rackham-*Fairy,* 83–88
BURIED-ALIVE
The boy, his sisters, and the
magic horse
Three snake-leaves
Buried alive to stop the plague
Lindow-*Swedish,* 72–73
BURMA
Tall tales (Burma)
The burning of Bergthorsknoll
Crossley-*Legends,* 135–145
BURNING (subject)
—as exorcism
Briggs-*Vanish.,* 101–103

Burning of the Khandava forest
Rungachary-*Tales,* 43–51
Burrage, A. M.
The waxwork [Murderers' Den,
by Burrage]
Burros. *See* DONKEYS
Bury me in England [fake-dying
wish; humor]
Marshall-*Every.,* 221–228
BUSCO, BEAST OF
Assorted monsters
BUSH CATS
How hunter obtained money
from friends [not repaid]
BUSH PIGS
Why one does not reveal the
origin of another
The bushbabies
And Every., 183–204
BUSHMEN
The apprentice [rabbit as
painter]
Son of the wind [was once a
man]
Sun and the children
BUSTARD (bird)
—why it only lays two eggs
Dinewan the emu, and the
bustard
BUTCHERS
Saint Nicholas and the children
The butcher's bills
Macdonald-*Gray,* 131–172
The butcher's mitzva
Patai-*Gates,* 650–652
Butler, Sir William Francis
He's a Windigo
Butoreagaddu legend
Wilbert-*Bororo,* 107
BUTTER
B'er [*sic*] rabbit is an uncle
Don't beat your children before
they're born
Fairies: taking the butter
The missing butter
Munachar and Manachar

BUTTER (continued)
    Munachar and the raspberries
    The penitent nis
    Wise frog and foolish frog
Butterflies
    Zong-*Korea,* 39
BUTTERFLIES
    Dream: the philosopher and
       the butterfly
    Filial piety [souls of parents in
       butterflies]
    How the turtle got her shell
    Priest's soul
    Thumbelina
    Ua-pa-chi (Kickapoo titles)
    The white butterfly
    The woman and the butter-
       flies
—"flutter-byes"
    How God made the butterflies
—origin of
    Butterflies
—self centered
    Butterfly love
The butterflies carried him home
    [Tewa]
    Myles-*Butterflies,* 15–19
The butterfly
    Roberts-*Chinese,* 19
Butterfly love
    Sperry-*Where,* 45–48
BUTTES
—origin
    The lodge of the bear [the
       Great Mystery]
Buying loyalty
    Roberts-*Chinese,* 209–211
Buying shoes
    Roberts-*Chinese,* 57
BUZZARDS
    Coyote's trip to the Land
       Above
    The creation
    Creation story [Pima]
    The great hunters [animals]
    How the toad got his bruises

    Klis-to E-eki Ta-u-ue-a
    Little Yellow Bird
    Why the buzzard's head is
       bald
Buzz-buzz aunty
    Villa-*Armenian,* 296–299, 511
BWACA
    Bwciod
The Bwca (booka)
    Froud-*Faeries,* unp
Bwciod
    Arrowsmith-*Field,* 196—198
"Bye-bye"
    Wolkstein-*Magic,* 190–193
"Bye-bye" (Haiti)
    Yolen-*Favorite,* 194–195
The Byse
    Booss-*Scand.,* 269–270

Cabal of the red hand
    O'Sullivan-*Legends,* 118–121
El caballero porfiado
    Aiken-*Mexican,* 148–153
El caballo negro muy magnifico
    MacLean-*Cuentos,* 47–49
CABIN BOYS
    The kobold and the pirate
    Master Tobacco
[The Cabinet des Fees, of M.
    Cuchet]
    Quiller-*Sleeping,* 9–14
CABINS
    The captain's cabin
Cadmus
    Pinsent-*Greek,* 46–48
CAELITE
    Love of Credhe for Cael
CAGES
    Brer rabbit rescues his children
    Silbado
—golden
    The Greek princess and the
       young gardener

CAILLEACH BHEUR (subject)
  Briggs-*Vanish.*, 66, 195
CAKES
  Munachar and the raspberries
  The sparrows and the tiger
  The tale of Ivan
  —pine-nut
  Mouse Woman and the tooth
  Cake-tree, bugle of life, and sweet
    dung
  Zong-*Korea*, 178–180
  Calabash child [born to First
    Woman]
  Pitcher-*Tokol.*, 14–17
CALABASHES
  —gourd
  Tokoloshi [origin of herds and
    flocks]
  Caladrius: powers of foretelling
    Magical Beasts, 80
CALAKO (Hopi god)
  The youth who brought the
    corn
CALDRONS
  The beduin's gazelle (Saudi
    Arabia)
  The father of eighteen elves
  Quest to the castle of the
    cauldron
  —fairy
  The fairies' caldron
  —"gives birth"
  The Hodja and the cauldron
    (Turkey)
  —power to restore life
  Llyr: children of the sea-god
  —of rebirth
  Branwen, daughter of Llyr
  The calendar
  Nicholson-*Mexican*, 43–52
  Caliban and Ariel
  Baskin-*Imps*, 34–35
CALIFORNIA
  The devil's herd
  Sweet Betsy from Pike [song
    and story]

—Paso Robles
  Mighty bear has problems
CALIFORNIA (subject)
  —Spanish tales
  MacLean-*Cuentos*, ix–
    xiii
  Caliph Stork
  Lang-*Green*, 1–15
  Callicantzaroi
  Arrowsmith-*Field*, 125–
    128
  Calling the ghost of Montezuma
  Bierhorst-*Hungry*, 117–118
CALMNESS
  How the Thai learned to be
    calm
CALVES
  Bull-calf goes to school
  Following the witch
  The pregnant priest
  [Calydon vs Atalanta]
  Wise-*Monster*, 24–25
CAMBRIC
  The white cat
  The camel dances
  Lobel-*Fables*, 22–23
  The camel, lion, leopard, crow, &
    jackal
  Wood-*Kalila*, 132–146
CAMELLIAS
  Tea and camellias
CAMELOT
  Siege of Joyous Garde
  Camelot [illus.]
  Lee-*Castles*, 73–77
  The Camelot of T. H. White
  Lee-*Castles*, 183
CAMELS
  The lost camel
  The three brothers [camel
    stolen & butchered]
  —six-humped
  Water carrier's fabulous sons
CAMEROON PIDGIN TALES
    (subject)
  Todd-*Some*, 1–186

78

CAMEROON TALES (subject)
—[Themes: 27 tales]
  Todd-*Tortoise,* xi–xii
CAMPBELL, Duncan
  Appointment at Ticonderoga
Campbell, Marie
  A stepchild that was treated
    mighty bad
CAMPFIRES
  The Milky Way [Wahn (crow) &
    Baripa (cat)]
CANADA
  How summer [personified]
    came to Canada
  Wolfskin's bride
—Hudson's Bay
  Another being
  Cannibals
  The devil
  An evil being
  He's a Windigo
  A tale of the Windego
  A Weetigo in the woods
—Manitoba
  Windagoos! Cannibals!
—Nova Scotia
  The Chenoo who stayed to
    dinner
  Coolnajoo, the foolish one
  Glooscap and the wishes
  Glooscap, the great chief
  Glooscap, the peacemaker
  The great Penobscot raid
  How Ableegumooch tracked a fox
  Kespak and the caribou
  Kitpouseagunow
  Lox and the chief's wife
  The magic snowshoes
  Pulowech, the partridge
  The rabbit makes a match
  The strongest boy in the world
  Tomik and the magic mat
  Wasek and the red giants
  Wejosis and the wind giant
  The year summer was stolen
—Ontario

Stories of the Windigo
The walker of the snow
The Wendigo (I–IX)
—Quebec
  Giant cannibals
  The immortal cannibal
  Red-headed Windego
  A tale of the Grand Jardin
  To kill Windigo
  Veritable werewolves
  The Windigo [I]
—Saskatchewan
  Guilty of murder
—summer/winter seasons
  How the Summer Queen came
    to Canada
CANADA (subject)
—Canadian wonder tales
  Macmillan-*Canadian,* ix–xi
CANADIAN TALES (subject)
—prehistory
  Macmillan-*Canadian,* 140
CANALS
  Far out the long canal
  Hohokam: the people who are
    gone
Cancer (the Crab)
  Gallant-*Constel.,* 144–146
CANDELABRA
  The magic candelabra
Candida
  Aiken-*Mexican,* 115–119
CANDLES
  Godfather death (Germany)
  The white rooster
  Why do Jews rock when
    studying?
—blowing out; humor
  The crooked-mouthed family
—miracle weight
  Rabbi David Ben Baruk, can-
    dle-salesman
CANDY
  The pig at the candy store
The candy man; a Han folktale
  Sadler-*Treasure,* 30–38

CANES
Genie of the mountains
The golden cradle
—power of life and death
How Aisu found the happy land
Canis major (the Big Dog)
Gallant-*Constel.*, 141–146
Canis minor (the Little Dog)
Gallant-*Constel.*, 141–146
Cannibal
Robinson-*Raven*, 21–35
CANNIBAL DEMON
The hunter maiden
Cannibal Lake
Colombo-*Wind.*, 29–30
A cannibal spirit
Colombo-*Wind.*, 44
Cannibals
Colombo-*Wind.*, 12–13
CANNIBALS
See also OGRES AND
OGRESSES; WENDIGO
Bhima slays the demon [giant,
man-eating cannibal]
The Chenoo who stayed to
dinner
Cinderella [sisters kill/eat
mother]
Count Dracula [by Woody
Allen]
Gheeger Gheeger the cold
west wing
Giant of the great water
Goblin of Adachigahara
The immortal cannibal
The island of beautiful women
Kenkebe
Kitpouseagunow
Konyek and his father [Masai]
Manyi's escape [wife eaten by
mistake]
The rain bird
Bougoodoogahdah
The shark and the turtle
To-Dola
Veritable werewolves

Windagoos! Cannibals!
—onions as cure for
Onions
—ToKonokonomlor
Five strange plants
CANNON BALLS
—Ashe House
Mysterious cannon ball
Canobie Dick and Thomas of
Ercildoun
Ratcliff-*Scottish*, 49–52
CANOES
The boy in the Land of
Shadows
The bushbabies
The giant sturgeon
Glooscap, the peacemaker
Goanna makes a canoe
How Ableegumooch tracked a
fox
A taste for quiet
Wasek and the red giants
—magic
Hiawatha
CANS
The lost treasure
The Canterville ghost
Manley-*Fun*, 63–99
CANYONS
The sun journey
[Caoilte rescues Finn MacCumal]
Seekers Saviors, 65–73
Caoilte the swift
O'Sullivan-*Legends*, 118
Cap o' Rushes
Lurie-*Clever*, 84–91
CAPITAL PUNISHMENT
The Groom's Crimes
Capricornus (the Sea-goat)
Gallant-*Constel.*, 113–115
Caps. *See under* HATS
Captain Eli
Lindow-*Swedish*, 172–174
Captain Murderer and the devil's
bargain [by Dickens]
Schwartz-*Great*, 45–60

The captain's cabin
  Ainsworth-*Phantom*, 77–94
Captains, Sea. *See* SEA
  CAPTAINS
CAPTIVES
—escapes
  The boys and the giant
—fairy
  Working for the Bergfolk
  (condensed)
Captives and fugitives [motif index]
  Wilbert-*Bororo*, 269–270
Carambot
  Thomas-*It's*, 189–196
CARAVANS
  The blossom tree
  Dream of Habeeb-son-of-
  Habeeb
  Something for nothin (a Hui
  story)
Carbonek: castle of the Holy Grail
  Lee-*Castles*, 110–111
The card player
  Robe-*Hispanic*, 155–156
CARD PLAYERS
  Saint Martin's Eve [b]
Cardiff Giant: A ghost story [by
  Mark Twain]
  Schwartz-*Great*, 11–19
CARDINALS
  Coyote's vanity
CARDING COMBS
—golden
  East of the sun and west of
  the moon
Cardplayers and the devil
  Lindow-*Swedish*, 152–154
CARDS, PLAYING
  The devil's bargain
—magic
  Pedro de Ordimalas
  The soldier and death
CARELESSNESS
  Milkmaid and the bucket of
  milk
  The tortoise and the hare

CARIBOU
  Kespak and the caribou
—personified
  Strange tale of caribou and
  moose
CARING
  The banyan deer [the Buddha]
Carleton, William
  Fairies and Frank Martin
  Knockmany legend
  Paddy Corcoran's wife
  Pudding bewitched
  Rival kempers
  Three wishes [of Billy Dawson]
Carlotta the Italian cat
  Fattoross-*Simpleton*, 37–39
CARNATIONS
  Pinks and carnations
Carnivals. *See* FAIRS
CAROUSELS
  The phantom carousel
CARPENTERS
  Genjias [three with same
  name]
  Wooden horse [mechanical
  flight]
The carpenter's monkey
  Wood-*Kalila*, 49–53
The carpenter's wife
  Amore-*Lustful*, 27–28
CARPENTRY
—devil tries to learn
  The devil's cloven foot
CARPET MAKERS
  Dream of Habeeb-son-of-
  Habeeb
CARPET WEAVING
  A craft is worth more than gold
CARPETS
—magic
  Magic carpet: on the wings of
  wishes
—magic rug
  The magic bird-heart
—rag
  Jack and the green lady

CARRIAGES
 The magic horn [flying
  carriage]
CARRIER, Martha
 Sergeant-*Witches*, 285 (index)
Carter, Albert Howard
 Big city folk tales
CARTS
 —"gives birth" to
  foal
 The wise little girl
 —lights after dark
  John Brodison and the police-
  man (Ireland)
CARVING
 —animal from ice
  The day Tuk became a hunter
CASA GRANDE, Az.
 Hohokam: the people who are
  gone
CASAUBON, Meric
 Sergeant-*Witches*, 285 (index)
The case of the royal Arabian
 jewels
 Schwartz-*Tales*, 23–24
The case of the uncooked eggs
 Wolkstein-*magic*, 50–55
Caselli, Giovanni, illus.
 Gibson-*Gods*
Casey Jones [song and story]
 Sanders-*Hear*, 99–109
CASKETS
 Bolstre Castle
 Eros and Psyche
CASKS
 The goblin and the huckster
CASSANDRA, prophetess
 The homecoming of
  Agamemnon
Cassiopeia (the Queen)
 Gallant-*Constel.*, 39–47
Cassley: Cnoc na Cnoimn
 Robertson-*Highland*, 130–132
Cassowary [bird] and Kokomo [abil-
 ity to fly]
 Stokes-*Turtle*, 82–83

Cast thy bread upon the waters
 [satire]
 Patai-*Gates*, 598–600
The castle: a parable
 Macdonald-*Wise*, 155–172
The castle and the dragons
 Lee-*Castles*, 20–21
Castle: Caer Arianrod
 Lee-*Castles*, 63
Castle [Chariot] of Morgan le Fay
 Lee-*Castles*, 98–103
The castle [five live in empty horse-
 skull]
 Riordan-*Russia*, 76–77
Castle in the air: Odainsaker
 Lee-*Castles*, 34–35
The castle in the lake
 Hyde-Chambers-*Tibet*, 71–75
Castle of an enchantress
 Lee-*Castles*, 96–97
Castle of Balor
 Lee-*Castles*, 52–53
Castle of Earthly Paradise
 Lee-*Castles*, 142–143
The castle of Melvales
 Garner-*British*, 146–159
 Lee-*Castles*, 160
The castle of Seoul
 Zong-*Korea*, 68–69
Castle of the crow
 Lee-*Castles*, 164
Castle of the Maimed King
 Lee-*Castles*, 108–109
Castle of the serpent
 Lee-*Castles*, 164–165
CASTLES
 Aaltawheel Bridge
 The cauld lad of Hilton
 Curse at Lochgarry
 East of the sun and west of
  the moon
 The giant who had no heart
 The green lady of Barrogil
 The green lady of Newton
 Hinzelmann
 Jack and the green lady

CASTLES (continued)
  Jorinde and Joringel
  Katla's dream
  Little Ida's flowers
  Lord of the rings
  The magician earl
  The marsh king's daughter
  Mice in the corn
  Mister Fox
  The Moddey Dhoo
  The mouse bride
  The seawife and the crone
  The tale of Ivan
  Three musicians [princess
    under spell]
  Tibble Castle and Klinta Spring
  The white cat
—copper
  Severi and Vappu
—haunted
  The tinker and the ghost
  A youth set out to learn what
    fear was
—legends
  The wolves of Cernogratz
—of weeping maidens
  Adventures of Sir Galahad
—sieges
  Tyl on a tightrope
Castles in fantastical literature
  Lee-*Castles*, 137–139
Castles in modern fantasy
  Lee-*Castles*, 176
Castles in the Inferno
  Lee-*Castles*, 156–157
Castles of Faerie
  Lee-*Castles*, 52–71
Castles of fairy-tale giants
  Lee-*Castles*, 171–173
Castles of the wizard and the
    hippogriff
  Lee-*Castles*, 140–141
CASTLES (subject)
—age of romance
  Lee-*Castles*, 72–136
—fairy tale castles

  Lee-*Castles*, 158–165
—history
  Lee-*Castles*, 12–13
—names
  Lee-*Castles*, 84
—origins
  Lee-*Castles*, 14–18
—variety in fairy tales
  Lee-*Castles*, 168–169
Castles: the age of myths
  Lee-*Castles*, 14–71
[Castles vanished beneath the sea]
  Lee-*Castles*, 64–71
Caswell, Helen R.
  Sedna the sea goddess
Cat and dog and return of the dead
  Wolkstein-*Magic*, 66–68
The cat and his visions
  Lobel-*Fables*, 18–19
The cat and mouse in partnership
  Classic Child., 60–67
The cat and the dog
  O'Sullivan-*Legends*, 38–39
  Zong-*Korea*, 25–29
The cat and the mice
  O'Connor-*Tibet*, 26–29
The cat and the mouse
  dePaola-*Favorite*, 114–116
Cat in the box
  Stuchl-*American*, 26–28
The cat in the sea
  Adams-*Iron*, 12–17
The cat Johann
  Manning-*Cats*, 111–117
Cat lying on velvet cushion, while
    dog sleeps
  Radin-*African*, 133–138
Cat of Catton [princess and pea
    story]
  Lewis-*Minute*, 34–35
The cat palace
  Stovicek-*Around*, 112–113
The cat, the cock and the scythe
  Wood-*Palace*, 72–79
The cat woman (France)
  Yolen-*Favorite*, 313–314

CATA
  Needle and Noodle
Catafay the cat and Liza the fox
  Riordan-*Russia*, 91–95
Caterina the Wise (Sicily)
  Riordan-*Woman*, 27–34
Caterpillar and the wild animals
  Radin-*African*, 113–114
CATERPILLARS
  The giant caterpillar
  The season of the stubby
    caterpillar
  Twins Akaruio Bokodori and
    Mamuiawuge Eceba
Cathedrals. *See* CHURCHES AND
  CATHEDRALS
Catherine and her destiny
  Lang-*Pink/D*, 167–173
Catherine, sly country lass (Italy)
  Yolen-*Favorite*, 33–37
Catherine's fate
  Shah-*World*, 110–113
The Catholic fox
  Cortes-*Byelorussian*, 15
CATHOLICISM
  Gellivor
—Mass
  The parrot tale-teller
Catoblepas and Gulon
  Magical Beasts, 96–97
CATS
  A bell for the cat
  Belling the cat
  The Bremen town musicians
  [Brindled cat and the miller's
    son]
  Cat and dog return of the dead
  Celtic cats
  Conall Yellowclaw
  The cow who tried to act like a
    kitten
  Dance in a buffalo skull
  Demon cat
  Dick Whittington and his cat
  The foolish young Mussulman
  The game of rat and dragon

  The honest penny
  How the rabbit lost his tail
  How they got Hairlock home
  How they went to Jotunheim
  Jack and his comrades
  Jack and the robbers
  The king o' the cats
  The leeshy cat
  Liza the fox and Catafay the
    cat
  Magic bird [tells stories]
  The magic mirror
  Majantali Sarkar
  Malicious cats
  A message for the cat
  Mister Velvet's bad deeds
  Monkey and the cheese
  Munachar and Manachar
  Munachar and the raspberries
  The owl and the pussycat
    [poem]
  Owney and Owney-na-peak
  The parrot who bought
    firewood
  Periquito, wood dealer
  Pix! Pax! Pox!
  Puss in Boots
  The scabby child
  Seanchan the Bard and the
    king of the cats
  The secret ones
  Seven families of Lake Pipple-
    Popple
  The small, small cat
  The tailor-bird and the cat
  A taste for quiet
  Thor in the giant's stronghold
  Town mouse and country
    mouse
  The troll turned cat
  War of the wolf and the fox
  The white cat
  Why the monkey still has a
    tail
  Wicked girl and her
    punishment

84

CATS(continued)

CATS (continued)

—aged
  The cat and the mice
—banished
  The country of the mice
—black
  Legends of the mill
  The witch's cat
—enormous appetite
  Pussy-Greedyguts
—girl under spell
  Katchen the cat
—imp in form of
  The imp cat
—kill monster rat
  The boy who drew cats [by
    Hearn]
—killed
  Pan is dead
—"kind of human nature"
  The cat and the dog
—kittens
  Rock-a-bye baby
—Kot Boltun
  The archer who went I know
    not where to fetch I know
    not what
—livers
  The cat in the sea
—man with face of cat
  Prince Miaow
—origin
  The prince who had two eyes
—origin of characteristics
  Why the cat washes after
    meals
—origin of hostility to dogs
  The cat and the dog
—sells skin to witch
  Pussy Cat Twinkle
—Siamese
  Mouse
—Simpkin
  The tailor of Gloucester
—tails
  Why women are like cats

—talking, tricks devil
  The tailor and the deev
—why cats eat mice
  Carlotta the Italian cat
Cat's baptism
  Wolkstein-*Magic*, 124–126
The cat's elopement
  Lang-*Pink/D*, 1–5
Cats: sinuous helpers of witches
  Lehane-*Wizards*, 115
CATS (subject)
  Briggs-*Vanish.*, 79, 109–110
  Piggott-*Japanese*, 143 (index)
CATTLE
  See also BULLS; COWS
  Bride-price: a woman for a
    hundred cattle
  Fairies and the cattle
    [condensed]
  The old witch
  The rival twins
—hoofs removed to keep from get-
    ting wet
  Devil's tale
—rustling
  The devil's herd
Cattle and the evil eye
  Logan-*Old*, 127–128
CATTLE DRIVERS
  Little Claus and Big Claus
CATTLE PENS
  The iron wolf
Cattle raid of Cooley
  Ross-*Druids*, 32–52
The cattle raid of Froech
  Gantz-*Early*, 113–126
CATTLE (subject)
—and fairies
  Briggs-*Vanish.*, 63, 74, 76, 126
The cauld lad of Hilton
  Keightley-*World*, 296–301
CAULD LAD OF HILTON (subject)
  Briggs-*Vanish.*, 56, 195
Cauldrons. *See* CALDRONS
"CAULS"
  Fylgiar

CAUSE AND EFFECT
   The chain
   Needle and Noodle
Cause of the seasons
   Gallant-*Constel.*, 14–16
Causes celebres, high and low: C.
   Radcliffe
   Marshall-*Every.*, 250–257
CAVALCADES (subject)
—fairy rades
   Briggs-*Vanish.*, 216 (index)
The cave of emeralds
   Segovia-*Spanish*, 223–247
Caverns. *See* CAVES
CAVES
   Ali Baba and the forty thieves
   The bear who liked hugging
      people
   The black pearl
   The boy who did not know
      what fear was
   The city of Luz [blue dye:
      Tekhelet]
   Curse of the devil's gold
   Dietrich of Bern
   Fate
   Gold of the gods
   The gray wolf
   The green children
   In a dim room [by Dunsany]
   The inheritance
   The kind man
   Klabautermannikins and
      Kaboutermannikins
   Salvanelli
   Seligen Fraulein
   Stan Bolovan and the dragon
   Toller's neighbors
   Troll's stone
   Wejosis and the wind giant
   The white rooster
   Who got brer Gilyard's
      treasure?
   Why the executioner is called
      assessor
   The wild swans

   Yggdrasill, the world ash
   The young man who refused
      to kill
—mountain
   Katrineholm Manor
   Snipp, Snapp, Snorium
Cecino the tiny
   Shah-*World*, 21–26
CELIBACY
   How a king learned to care for
      parents
CELLARS
   Piskies in the cellar
      (condensed)
Celtic cats
   Ross-*Druids*, 113–116
CELTIC MYTHS
   See also ARTHUR, King
   Cattle raid of Cooley
   Gods of the pagan Celts
   Luch and the sons of Tuirenn
   The Mabinogion: four branches
   Royal pillow-talk: Medb and
      Ailill
CELTIC MYTHS (subject)
—Arrival of the gods
   Ross-*Druids*, 14–16
—Celtic magic
   Lochhead-*Battle*, vii–x
—Symbols in Celtic myths and
     legends
   Ross-*Druids*, 130
CELTS
   Andrew Coffey
   The battle of the birds
   Beth Gellert
   The black horse
   Brewery of eggshells
   Conall Yellowclaw
   Connla and the fairy maiden
   Cu Chulainn: the wooing of
      Emer
   Dream of Owen O'Mulready
   Elidore
   Fair, brown, and trembling
   The farmer of Liddesdale

CELTS (continued)
The fate of the children of Lir
The field of Boliauns
Gold-tree and Silver-tree
The Greek princess and the
young gardener Guleesh
The horned woman
How Cormac MacArt went to
Faery
How Fin went to the kingdom
of the big men
Hudden and Dudden and Do-
nald O'Neary
Jack and his comrades
Jack and his master
Jack the cunning thief
King O'Toole and his goose
The lad with the goat-skin
The leeching of Kayn's leg
The legend of Knockgrafton
A legend of Knockmany
Morraha
Moytura: the second battle
Munachar and Manachar
Paddy O'Kelly and the weasel
[Pwyll] Powel, Prince of Dyfed
The ridere of riddles
The russet dog
The sea maiden
The Shee and Gannon and the
Gruagach Gaire
The shepherd of Myddvai
Smallhead and the king's son
The sprightly tailor
The story of Deirdre
The story of the McAndrew
family
The story-teller at fault
The tail
The tale of Ivan
The vision of MacConglinney
The Wooing of Olwen
CELTS (subject)
Keightley-*World*, 361–442
—The ancient Celtic world
Ross-*Druids*, 11–13

—[Celts through the centuries]
Smith-*Manachar*, 5
—chess; fairies
Briggs-*Vanish.*, 174–175
CEMETERIES
See also BURIAL(S)
The death coach
Ebbe Skamelson
Ketill, the priest of Husavik
One for you, one for me
Simon sees a ghost
The skeleton in Holar church
The son of the goblin
The story of Bergthor of Blafell
White cap
The wild swans
—desecrated
The dead defend their
cemetery
—hallowed ground
Strand-ghosts
La cenicienta huasteca
Aiken-*Mexican*, 96–98
The censor and the tiger
Roberts-*Chinese*, 183–187
CENSORSHIP (subject)
—Russia
Riordan-*Russia*, 273, 277
Centaurs
Magical Beasts, 26–31
CENTAURS (subject)
Pinsent-*Greek*, 142 (index)
Scott-*Fantastic*, 111–120
—[Ixion, Nessus, Chiron]
Lloyd-*Mythical*, 13–16
The centipede girl
Zong-*Korea*, 97–100
CENTIPEDES
—monster
My lord bag of rice
Cepheus (the King)
Gallant-*Constel.*, 39–47
[Cerberus vs Hercules]
Wise-*Monster*, 34–37
CEREMONIALS
The smallest dragonboy

Ceridwen and Taliesin
  Lehane-*Wizards*, 13–20
Cerunnos
  Magical Beasts, 17–18, 23
Cetus (the Whale)
  Gallant-*Constel.*, 108–110
CEYLON
  The footprint of Buddha
The chain
  Roberts-*Chinese*, 214
[Chain: the harmonious order of
  creation]
  Lehane-*Wizards*, 65
CHAINS
  Ebbe Skamelson
  The legend of Bodedys
  Leppa Polkry and the blue
    cross
—golden
  The juniper tree
  True and untrue
  Vaino and the swan princess
CHAIRS
  The death of Chanticleer
  [The old, vagrant woman and]
    The three bears
CHALICES. *See* HOLY GRAIL
CHAMELEONS
  The blossom tree
  Origin of death: chameleon
The chamois-hunter
  Keightley-*World*, 271–272
Champion spearsman
  Thompson-*Hawaiian*, 58–65
A champion's schooling in another
    world
  Lehand-*Legends*, 34–41
CHANCE
  See also LUCK
  The Mauritanian and his
    wealth
  The pig at the candy store
CHANGE
  The seed's secret
The changeling [a]
  Keightley-*World*, 125–126

The changeling [b]
  Keightley-*World*, 227–231
The changeling [c]
  Keightley-*World*, 393
The changeling [d]
  Keightley-*World*, 355–356
Changeling elf and the woman
  Shub-*About*, 34–35
Changeling [exposed with help of
    magician]
  Manning-*Marvels*, 118–123
Changeling of Yesnaby
  Robertson-*Highland*, 23–24
The changeling speaks on the way
    to baptism
  Lindow-*Swedish*, 92–93
The changelings
  Booss-*Scand.*, 306–307
  Yeats-*Fairy*, 48–59
CHANGELINGS
  Abductions to the fairy palace
    [condensed]
  Beating the changeling
  Brewery of eggshells
  Changing a housewife
  Fair exchange
  The fairy changeling
    [condensed]
  The father of eighteen elves
  The greedy youngster
  Hob and the strange lady
  Johnnie in the cradle
    (condensed)
  Quiet folk changelings
  The smith and the fairies
    (condensed)
  The smith and the fairies
    [MacEachern]
  Taken [wife taken by fairies]
  Twelve children on a platter
  The witch
—puppies put in place of newborn
    children
  Little cinder girl
Changelings [brew of eggshells]
  Lochhead-*Battle*, 80–81

CHANGELINGS (subject)
—midwives and fairies
Briggs-*Vanish.*, 93–103, 153
Changing a housewife
Lindow-*Swedish*, 93–94
Chang'o and the elixir of
immortality
Sanders-*Dragons*, 29–32
Chano
Yellow Robe-*Tonweya*, 21–23
Chano's first buffalo hunt
Yellow Robe-*Tonweya*, 31–41
CHANTS
Groundhog dance
The chao ku bird
Jagendorf-*Magic*, 7–10
CHAPLAINS
The confession of Charles
Linkworth
CHAPMAN, John
Peddler of Swaffham
(England)
CHARACTER
Little shepherdess and English
prince
The three fish [wise; clever;
stupid]
—defects changed by love
Prince Vivien and the Princess
Placida
Character and culture of the Mis-
souri French
Thomas-*It's*, 221–228
The charcoal burner
Booss-*Scand.*, 106–111
Charcoal burner and the bear
Shah-*Dervishes*, 212–220
CHARCOAL BURNERS
The man with the wen
Olafur and the trolls
The polite coal burner
CHARCOAL MAKERS
The maiden made of fire
Charge this to the cap
Aiken-*Mexican*, 47–50
The chariot of the sun

Gibson-*Gods*, 50–52
CHARIOTS AND CHARIOTEERS
Auriga (The Charioteer)
CHARITY
See also COMPASSION
Bagged wolf
The exiled princess
Glooscap and the wishes
Gray Arrow learns a lesson
A Hanukkah evening in my
parents' house
Heaven and hell [cooperation]
Jesse James [song and story]
Pablito prays for El Senor
Diablo
Pedro de Ordimalas
The reward of charity
Waves save the saintly
Where love is, God is
—heavenly reward for
Cian of the golden ears
—holy person sells soul to devil
Countess Kathleen O'Shea
Charity can change a man's fate
Elbaz-*Folktales*, 67
Charity saves from death
Elbaz-*Folktales*, 128–129
Charlemagne: Aix-la-Chapelle
Lee-*Castles*, 118–119
Charlemagne and Ogier, the
Dane
Lee-*Castles*, 124–125
Charlemagne and Pamplona
Lee-*Castles*, 122–123
CHARLES EDWARD, Prince,
1720–1788.
Bonnie Prince Charlie
"CHARMING," King
Blue bird [King Charming]
"CHARMING" [person]
Pretty Goldilocks
CHARMS
Goophered grapevine
Hot-foot Hannibal
Talismans: a cache of charms
—makes fire

The mischief maker, Lox, and
the three fires
CHARMS (subject)
—Double-edged power
Spells & Bind, 6–33
Charting the kingdom of dreams
Night Creatures, 62–71
CHARYBDIS (whirlpool)
The wanderings of Odysseus
Chase, Richard
Old fire dragaman
CHASTITY
—of wife
Mud-snail fairy
Chavalai: taboos and deception
Cortes-*Byelorussian*, 31–35
CHEATING
See also CONFIDENCE MEN;
DECEPTION; IMPOSTERS
The building of the wall of Asgard
Cardplayers and the devil
Ten jugs of wine
Tyl on a tightrope
—cheater-cheated
Aina-kizz and the black-
bearded bai
The gizzard [riches for the one
who eats it]
How a poor man made a
swindler cough up
The master and the worker
Outwitting the landlord
Rabbi Mordekhai Benjio ren-
ders justice to an Arab
The two blind men [thieves]
—gypsy vocation
The gypsy and Saint George
Cheats, rogues, and Tricksters
Yolen-*Favorite*, 125–166
CHEESE
The artful lad
Back of the moon
The frog
The herd-boy and the giant
Monkey and the cheese
Chelm justice (Jewish)

Yolen-*Favorite*, 176
CHENOO
The dreaded chenoo
The Chenoo who stayed to dinner
Hill-*More*, 120–130
Cherokees fight king of
rattlesnakes
Stallman-*Dragons*, 20–21
Cherry of Zennor (condensed)
Briggs-*Vanish.*, 85–86
Cherry pickers
Radin-*African*, 262–265
Cherry trees and cucumbers
Piggott-*Japanese*, 131–133
CHESNUTT, Charles, 1858–1932
—Conjure tales
Shepard-*Conjure*, vii–ix
CHESS (subject)
—and Celtic fairies
Briggs-*Vanish.*, 174–175
Chestnut grey
Riordan-*Russia*, 184–189
CHESTS
The artful lad
The boy who did not know
what fear was
"Lars, my lad!"
Little Claus and Big Claus
Saxe of Saxeholm
—sea
Jurma and the sea god
Chetwynd-Hayes, E.
The elemental
CHICKADEE (truthteller)
Spearfinger, the witch
Chicken Licken
dePaola-*Favorite*, 105–111
CHICKENS
*See also stories beginning
with* Cock. . . Hen. . .
Rooster. . . *etc.*
Don't count your chickens . . .
Half-chick [Medio Pollito]
How Samoa was named
The little chicken Kluk and his
companions

CHICKENS (continued)
Little crop-tailed hen
The man who knew how to
divide a chicken
Rabbi Haim Pinto revives the
dead
Who stole brer Gilyard's
sheep?
—hens
The cock and the crested hen
The end of the world
The fox who went to heaven
House in the wood
How the blackbird went to war
How the monkey got food
when he was hungry
The little red hen
The little white hen and the
three fox-cubs
Revenge of Joaquina
Three sisters were entrapped
into a mountain
The ugly duckling
—hens-lays 24 eggs a day
Jack and his wonderful hen
—hens-scratching; looking for
house key
Hen and hawk [once married,
now enemies]
—hens-speckled
How the speckled hen got her
speckles
—rooster tricks fox
House of ice and house of
wood
Mother confessor fox
—roosters
Animals in winter
The Bremen town musicians
Brer rabbit keeps his word
The cat, the cock and the
scythe
The cock and the crested hen
Cock with the golden feathers
The death of Chanticleer
The guardian cock

Half-Rooster
Hans my Hedgehog
The hare's hut [fox chased
out]
House in the wood
How hunter obtained money
from friends & avoided
repaying
It started with a thorn
Jack and his comrades
Jack and the robbers
The little chicken Kluk and his
companions
The little red hen
March cock banishes the devil
The mouse and the rooster
Owl [ashamed of his face]
The pig builds the house on
the hill
Reynard and Chanticleer
The russet dog
The valiant chanticleer
A well-deserved punishment
The young rooster
—roosters-boasting while being
cooked
The shah who wanted to be
shah
—roosters-crowing
Andromeda dances
Gumiya; a Blang story: origins
of characteristics
Why the sun rises when the
rooster crows
—roosters-crowing: position
Woodcutter and the heavenly
maiden
—roosters-magic stomach
Little rooster and the Turkish
sultan
—roosters-pin in throat
The cock and the hen
—roosters-skins
The white rooster
Chicoria [invited to eat at rancher's
table]

91

Griego-*Cuentos,* 29–31
CHICORY
The flowers from the sky
Chief Akaruio Bokodori and the
jaguars
Wilbert-*Bororo,* 110–111
The chief and the black dog
Mckee-*Scottish,* 37–38
CHIEFS
Glooscap, the great chief
Chiefs make the rivers beautiful
Wilbert-*Bororo,* 56–58
CHIEFTAINS
Mice in the corn
Chilbik and the greedy czar
Titiev-*Moolah,* 9–26
CHILD ABUSE
Babes in the wood
Beating the changeling
The magic orange tree [child
abuse]
The child and the eagle
Radin-*African,* 258–259
Child in the silk-cotton tree
Magel-*Gambia,* 28–32
CHILD PSYCHOLOGY (subject)
—[B. Bettelheim]
Ehrlich-*Random,* x–xii
Childbirth. *See* BIRTH
Childbirth: Ndhlovu
Pitcher-*Tokol.,* 47–49
Childe Rowland
Shah-*World,* 126–129
Childe Rowland and Burd Ellen
Lee-*Castles,* 166–167
Childe Rowland, Burd Helen, and
Elf King
Seekers Saviors, 49–77
The childhood of Achilles
Lines-*Greek,* 151–156
CHILDLESSNESS
The boy in the donkey skin
Bamboo-cutter and the moon-
child
The bashful bride
Boy of the red twilight sky

Child in the silk-cotton tree
A cure for jealousy
Daughter of the moon
An eventful pilgrimage
The fortune teller
The golden tree [queen and
amulet]
Hershele and Hanukkah
The imprisoned princess
King who had no children
Leppa Polkry and the blue
cross
The magic box
Momotaro, or the son of a
peach
The mute prince [kingship
rejected]
The origin of the winds
The priest goes down to hell
[pact with devil]
The prince who was made of
precious gems
The Santa Lucias [demon-
foundling; legend]
The snow maiden
Snowflake [snowchild comes
to life]
Stumpy
The talking nightingale
Thumbelina
Tom Thumb
Triplets [Light Foot, Skilful
Hand, Keen Eye]
The valiant chanticleer
The woman and the children of
the sycamore tree
Youth without age and life
without death (Turkey)
CHILDREN
See also BABIES; BOYS;
GIRLS; PARENTS;
SCHOOL CHILDREN;
TWINS
Don't beat your children before
they're born
Draw the curtains

CHILDREN (continued)
    The fate of the children of Lir
    The golden comb [witch claims
      first-born]
    The green children
    In the middle of the night
    A little love story
    Mouse's three children [tiger,
      peacock, boy]
    The pancake
    The pied piper of Hamelin
    Pix! Pax! Pox!
    Powdered blondie and three-
      haired blondie
    The secret ones
    The selfish giant
    The trolls of Skurugata
    Wejosis and the wind giant
    Whipping children: how it
      came about
    Wisdom belongs to everyone
—abandoned
    See also BABIES-Abandoned
    Babes in the wood
    Hansel and Gretel
    Houji, the child abandoned on
      the ice
    Little Thumb
    Man and woman with too
      many children
    Molly Whuppie (England)
    The promise of the three
      sisters
—born of animal/human marriage
    The bear mother [human] and
      father
—cruelty
    The woman from the sea
—deformed
    Legend of Melusina
—freed by cat under spell
    Katchen the cat
—green
    Green children (condensed)
—helping with home chores
    The youth and the eagles

—killed by witch
    The black lady
—mother often absent
    The children with one eye
—neglected child
    Gifts of the child Christ
—one gold, one silver
    Creator Nyame and his four
      wives
—stolen
    Morraha
    The toad and the boy
—stump comes to life, via devil
    Stumpy
—training
    The fairy and the prince
    The wise woman, or The lost
      princess
—wise
    The twins
[Children and fruit trees in Haiti]
    Wolkstein-*Magic*, 14
The children and the hummingbird
    Mullett-*Spider*, 108–117
The children of Aeolus
    Pinsent-*Greek*, 56–60
The children of Io
    Pinsent-*Greek*, 42–55
Children of the fairies
    Haining-*Lepre.*, 21–24
The children of the Omokoy tribe
    Stokes-*Turtle*, 26–28
The children with one eye
    Macmillan-*Canadian*, 233–236
Child's soul in a tree
    O'Sullivan-*Legends*, 97–99
Chimaera. See CHIMERAS
Chimera
    Magical Beasts, 61–64
CHIMERAS
    [Bellerophon vs Chimera]
    The death of the Chimaera
    Land monsters
    Prince Bellerophon and
      Pegasus
CHIMNEYS

—smoking
   Hob and Sootkin
CHINA
   Bagged wolf
   The betrothal
   The blind boy and his dog
   The clever sewing-maid
   The clever wife
   Clod's comb
   Coffin cash
   Door gods
   The dragon who cried
   Drinking companions
   Dumplings in the river
   The festival of the seven
     maidens
   From bad to good to bad to
     good
   Golden life
   The great misfortune of Lay
     Tee-Kwai
   Havoc in heaven: Monkey and
     the Jade Emperor
   Houji, the child abandoned on
     the ice
   How salt was discovered
   How the world was made
   Imperial left-overs
   Isles of the blest
   The kitchen god
   Lam Ku, the basket lady
   Liu Yi and the dragon king
   The living kuan-yin
   Logic
   Lord Guan: god of martial
     arts
   Luck in a strange place
   Maiden's silky winding sheet
   Meng Chiang and the Great
     Wall of China
   The monk and the drunk
   The Monkey spirit
   The nightingale
   The noodle
   Old fuddlement
   One hairball

   The piebald calf
   The pointing finger
   A princess on a swing
   Prophecy: Wan and the Great
     Wall of China
   The rain-makers, the dragon-
     palace, and the Ling
     mountains
   A rare bargain
   The serpent-slayer
   The shepherd and the em-
     peror's daughter
   The silkworm [origin: marriage
     of horse & maid]
   Stewed, roasted, or live?
   The swordmaker's son: King-
     don of Chu
   Tale of the golden vase and
     the bright monkeys
   The tears of blood
   Ten jugs of wine
   The thief who kept his hands
     clean
   Thievery
   The Tibetan envoy's mission
   Tripitaka: quest of the Buddhist
     scriptures
   The ugly son-in-law
   The unanswerable
   Underworld god of marriage
   Wagging my tail in the mud
   Why the flat fish is flat
   The wine bibber
   The Yellow Emperor: war
     against Chitou
   The young head of the family
—Ch'iang
   Big brother: man; Little brother:
     rabbit
—Chinese tyrants
   Kile Bamba and the Loche
     bogatyr
—Chuang
   The wonderful Chuang
     brocade
—Han

94

The chao ku bird

Erh-lang and the suns

The great deeds of King Yu

The magic boat

The red stream

The sad end of Wu-Lung-Tru

The sad tale of the rabbit's tail

Tale of the shrimp and the
earthworm

A true money tree

Why the sun rises when the
rooster crows

—history

Unofficial history of the Confucian Academy

—history-invasions

Mambu the orphan [tyrants'
tribute]

The twins

—Kawa

The competitive tiger

—Kazakh

Smart head better than sharp
teeth

—Korean

The choosy maid of Yen-Pien

—Lisu

The heavenly song of the
green-spotted dove

—Miao

How panpipes came to be
played (Miao)

The peacock's tail

—Middle Kingdom

Civilization

—Mongol

Hunter Hailibu's great sacrifice

A merry prank of Pa-leng-ts'
ang

—Nung

The tale of the magic green
water-pearl

—Oronchon

The twins of Paikala Mountain

—Pai

The winding-horn village

—Peking: water supply stolen

Gaoliang bridge [Peking]; water supply

—Puyi

The great battle between the
grasshoppers and the
monkeys

—Shui

The story of the house

—Tai

The god of faces

—Tibet. *See* TIBET

—Tuchia

T'ien the brave, hero of the
Hsia River

—Tung

The white-hair waterfall

—Uighur

Anizu's magic wonder flute

—Yi

A well-deserved punishment

When rocks rolled crackling
wisdom

CHINA (subject)

—The Chinese world: myth, re-
ligon, dynasties

Sanders-*Dragons*, 11–12

—Minority nationalities

Minford-*Fav.*, 195–202

China: dragons on parade

Stallman-*Dragons*, 34–35

China poblana, the Chinese girl
from Puebla

Wright-*Gold*, 42–47

CHINA SHOPS

The bull in the china shop

China: the black dragon

Stallman-*Dragons*, 32–33

CHINESE

—in Mexico

China poblana, the Chinese
girl from Puebla

The Chinese bride

Nagishkin-*Folktales*, 109–116

CHINESE MYTHS (subject)

—Where the stories come from
  Sanders-*Dragons,* 130
CHINESE TALES (subject)
—[Han folktales; characteristics]
  Sadler-*Treasure,* ix–xii
—Introduction
  Roberts-*Chinese,* xv–xx
—Introduction by Zhong Jingwen
  Minford-*Fav.,* 5–16
—[Six tales, spanning 2,000 years
  of history and philosophy]
  Sadler-*Heaven,* vii–ix
CHIPMUNKS
  How bear and chipmunk
    stopped . . . friends
  How coyote stole fire
—origin of stripes
  The antelope maid
CHIRON
  Centaurs
  Peleus and Thetis [marriage]
Chisos ghosts
  Aiken-*Mexican,* 103–106
Chit-chat [African tale]
  Lewis-*Minute,* 10–11
Chitchat turtle and the geese
  Wood-*Kalila,* 148–159
CHITONS
  Raven and the first men
Chittum, Ida
  The monster of Poot Holler
A choir [of croaks]
  Berger-*Animalia* [21–23]
The choosy maid of Yen-Pien
  Jagendorf-*Magic,* 177–181
Choril and Cholchinay
  Nagishkin-*Folktales,* 46–56
CHRISTENINGS
  See also BAPTISM
  The fairies' christening
  The hill folk
  The hill men invited to the
    christening
  Sleeping Beauty in the wood
—presents
  The old man from Haberg

CHRISTIAN LIFE
  The three brothers
CHRISTIANITY
  The marsh king's daughter
—coming of (parody)
  Marjatt
—giant's fear of
  The giants who moved
—trolls
  Trolls take over the farm
CHRISTIANITY (subject)
—Belief in fairies
  Briggs-*Vanish.,* 8, 20–22, 30,
    72–73, 152, 167–168
CHRISTIANSEN, R. TH. (subject)
  Briggs-*Vanish.,* 27–31
CHRISTMAS
  The altar-cup in Angerup
  Baboushka, the Wise Men and
    the Prince of Peace
  Callicantzaroi
  The crossways
  The deacon of Myrka
  Dilly-dilly-doh!
  The dwarfs' banquet
  The elf maiden
  The expedition of Thorfin
    Karisefni
  The fiddler and the fairy
  The fiddler and the sea nymph
  The fir tree
  Gellivor
  The giant and Johannes
    Blossom
  Gifts of the child Christ
  The girl who trod on the loaf
  Hildur, the queen of the elves
  Hob and the Sad
  Jerry Bundler
  The lake monster
  Ljungby horn and pipe
  The man-servant and the
    water-elves
  The shepherd of Silfrun-
    Arstadir
  The story of trembling hood

CHRISTMAS (continued)
  The sword in the stone
  The tailor of Gloucester
  Thornstein staff-struck
  The tomts
  Troll's stone
  Trolls take over the farm
  The two fiddlers
  Una the elfwoman
  Valbjorg the Unelfed
  Why the sea is salt
  The wizards of the Vestmanna
    Isles
—Jesus' invitation
  The straight road: Christmas in
    heaven
CHRISTMAS EVE
  Peter Gynt
  The Urko of North Wij
Christmas service of the
    dead
  Lindow-*Swedish*, 193–194
The Christmas thief
  Williams-*Wicked*, 39–51
Chrysanthemum
  Ewart-*Lore*, 134–135
CHU KUAN
  The kitchen god
The Chuang brocade
  Sadler-*Treasure*, 16–29
CHURCH
—gifts to the
  The Indian and the hundred
    cows
—offense against, punished
  The man turned into a mule
—worldliness
  Devil's armful [Canterbury]
Church attendance: the devil
  Lindow-*Swedish*, 159–161
Church bells. See BELLS—church
Church grims
  Arrowsmith-*Field*, 53
CHURCHES AND CATHEDRALS
  Big boulder north of Torstuna
    church

The boy who did not know
    what fear was
  Church grims
  The crossways
  Fair, brown, and trembling
  Gellivor
  A giant builds a church [the
    Finn legend]
  The giant who had no heart
  Hildur, the queen of the
    elves
  The man-servant and the
    water-elves
  The man/whale
  The skeleton in Holar church
  The trolls in Resslared
  Una the elfwoman
—building of
  Kallundborg church
  Who built Reynir church?
—haunted
  The sprightly tailor
Churchill, Winston
  "Man overboard"
CHURCHING OF WOMEN
  Changing a housewife
Churchyards. See CEMETERIES
CHUVASH TALES
  How grandpa moved the
    Lord's meadow
  How two brothers improved
    their luck
Cian of the golden ears
  O'Sullivan-*Legends*, 100–
    101
Cibairago and her husband Jure
    [snake]
  Wilbert-*Bororo*, 196–198
CIGARETTES
  [Origin of tobacco] The
    Kuddogo fish
Cinderella
  Classic Child., 85–91
  Ehrlich-*Random*, 130–137
  Lang-*Blue*, 66–74 (notes, 366)
  Leete-*Golden*, 108–123

Mulherin-*Favorite*, 62–71, introd., 9, 60–61
Perrault-*Glass*, 51–65
Pierce-*Larousse*, 85–100
Pollack-*Moonbeam*, 5–13
Quiller-*Sleeping*, 79–112
Rackham-*Fairy*, 209–216
Stovicek-*Around*, 60–65
Cinderella [sisters kill/eat mother]
Villa-*Armenian*, 240–244, 489–491
"CINDERELLAS"
The Algonquin Cinderella
The brocaded slipper
Cap o' Rushes
Fair, brown, and trembling
The Indian Cinderella
Liisa and the prince
Little burnt face
Little cinder girl
The little white hen and the three fox-cubs
Mossycoat
Poor turkey girl
The red cow [a Cinderella-type story]
Undying guardianship: Rashin Coatie
CINDERS
Ainsel
CIRCE (goddess)
Odysseus and Circe
Voyage of Odysseus
The wanderings of Odysseus
Circe: the island enchantress
Lehane-*Wizards*, 13
CIRCUMCISION
The ruse of Rabbi Reuben Estrogli
CIRCUS
The illustrated man
CITIES
Clod's comb
—destruction of
Simmer Water
—underground

The anglers of Ar
City mouse and country mouse
Lewis-*Animal*, 12–13
The city of Luz [blue dye: Tekhelet]
Schwartz-*Elijah*, 279–293
City of the Not-Dead
Lee-*Castles*, 50–51
City where men are mended
Radin-*African*, 250–253
Civilization
Roberts-*Chinese*, 249–250
CIVILIZATION
—development of
Bao Luotuo the sage
CLAIRVOYANCE
See also SECOND SIGHT
The dream house (Ireland)
—specious
The unwilling magician
—the "ring is here"
The ruby ring
CLAMSHELLS
Raven and the first man
CLANS (ancestors)
The Iparexeba legend
CLAPPING MOUNTAINS
Raven and the north lands
CLAUS, BIG
Little Claus and Big Claus
CLAUS, LITTLE
Little Claus and Big Claus
CLEANING-WOMEN
The astonishing brush
CLEER, Saint
The hurlers
Clematis and Arbutus (the strawberry tree)
Ewart-*Lore*, 114–117
Clemens, Samuel L. See TWAIN, Mark
Clements, William M.
Jonesboro tornado: folklore . . . religion . . . history
CLERGYMEN
See also BISHOPS; DERVISHES; PRIESTS

CLERGYMEN (continued)
    The artful lad
    Bishop Svedberg and the devil
    The charcoal burner
    The fairy's inquiry
    A false ghost
    Isaac and the Parson of Brono
    The master thief
    The mistake
    The parson and the clerk [I]
    The parson and the clerk [II]
    The stone statue
    The triumph of death
—and money
    Goat's funeral [religious satire]
—pastors
    Little Genius
Clerical curse of Duthil
    Robertson-*Highland*, 99–100
CLERKS
    The parson and the clerk [I]
    The parson and the clerk [II]
    Peter Bull
Clever answers (Russia)
    Yolen-*Favorite*, 41–42
Clever boy
    Villa-*Armenian*, 372–374
The clever bride [theft of chick
    peas]
    Shannon-*Solve*, 23–25
The clever brothers
    Riordan-*Tartary*, 116–121
Clever Daniel
    Villa-*Armenian*, 96–102, 446–
    448
The clever fool
    Ginsburg-*Twelve*, 48–51
Clever Gretchen
    Lurie-*Clever*, 1–8
A clever judge
    Roberts-*Chinese*, 224
The clever little tailor
    Lang-*Green*, 366–370
Clever man and ordinary
    Nahman-*Tales*, 139–161
    [notes: 141, 309–310]

Clever Manka
    Phelps-*Tatterhood*, 109–114
The clever mice
    Hyde-Chambers-*Tibet*, 94–95
The clever Nikorima
    Stovicek-*Around*, 192–193
The clever old bride [and child-groom]
    Zong-*Korea*, 190
The clever sewing-maid
    Chalk-*Tales*, unp.
Clever Tom and the leprechauns
    Keightley-*World*, 373–375
The clever wife
    Kendall-*Sweet*, 14–17
Clever woman
    Peacock Maid, 83–105
Clever Yaro
    Sheohmelian-*Three*, 29–34
The cleverest son [task: fill a room]
    Shannon-*Solve*, 34–36
CLEVERNESS
    See also DECEPTION; DE-
    DUCTION (logic); INGE-
    NUITY; RIDDLES;
    TRICKERY
    Abzelil and the Master of the
    Lake
    Admiral Yi
    Aina-kizz and the black-
    bearded bai
    Aldar-Kose and Shigai-Bai
    Aryen-Ben-Gadi and Fox-of-
    the-Burnt-Tail
    Believe it or not
    Best liar in the land
    Carambot
    Catherine, sly country lass
    (Italy)
    Coyote and his bow
    Coyote and rabbit
    Coyote and turtle
    Daniel O'Connell [justice]
    The day Tuk became a hunter
    The devil and the old hag
    The devil's hide [temper]
    Dividing the goose

A drink for a crow
An expensive hide
The falcon and the quail
The farmer and the bear
Farmer and the bogle
The farmer who listened to his
  livestock
The fly (as witness)
Genius deserves his name
Genius [more intelligent than
  the king]
The ghoul and the youth of
  Ispahan
The gingerbread house
  [Hansel and Gretel]
The gold harvest
Hansel and Gretel
Hare and hyena in the well
Hare seeks endowments from
  Allah
High John the conqueror
How Abosom, the lesser gods,
  came into the world
How El Bizarron fooled the
  devil
How sly-fox was fooled
How the moolah was taught a
  lesson
A hundred times
Impossible judgement
It happened in a bath
Jack the cunning thief
The jewel of the fox's tongue
Jha and Jewish cleverness
John Brodison and the police-
  man (Ireland)
Kamala and the seven thieves
King and the poor man
The king, the coin, and the
  clown
The Knockmany legend
Lambikin [drumikin]
A legend of Knockmany
The liar
Logic
Magic flute of Asmodeus

Man and woman with too
  many children
The man who buried his
  money
Marriage of two masters of
  Wolof. [A]
Marriage of two masters of
  Wolof. [B]
The master thief
Molly Whuppie
The monk and the drunk
Mountain of jade
Mulha
Narahari Das
Nasr-ed-Din Hodja in the pulpit
  (Turkey)
The noodle
The north country wolf
Old Nick and the girl
Old Tommy and the spectre
The old woman and the tramp
Oonagh and the giants
Outwitting giants
Outwitting the landlord
Owney and Owney-na-peak
The parson and the clerk [I]
Passover soup
Poisonous persimmons
A priest and his servant Balda
Puss in Boots
Quick-witted [boy outsmarts
  evil dervish]
The rabbi and the inquisitor
Redmond O'Hanlon
The royal detectives
The ruse of Rabbi Reuben
  Estrogli
Sagacious monkey and the
  boar
The scholar jackal
Search for a friend
The serpent [trust betrayed]
Sidna Mussa
Sinbad and the genie
Sleeping-mat confidences not
  to be repeated

CLEVERNESS (continued)
  Smart head better than sharp
    teeth
  Smartest man in the
    countryside
  Stan Bolovan and the dragon
  The sticks of truth
  The story of the McAndrew
    family
  Story of the robbers [master
    thief]
  Stupid Peikko
  The stupid rich man
  The sultan and the cobbler
  The sun and the moon
  The tailor-bird and the cat
  The theft of fire
  There'll always be a tomor-
    row
  The three fish [wise; clever;
    stupid]
  The three little pigs
  The tiger behind the fox
  Tight-fisted farmer and clever
    farmhand
  Tom Thumb
  The wager: clever slave wins
    freedom
  When they gave out wisdom,
    H. queued up twice
  Whose horse is it?
  Why the tiger is striped
  Why tigers have stripes
  The wicked tiger
  Willie Brennan [highwayman]
  The wolf and the tailor
  The wooden sword
  The woodsman's riddle
  Working the field
  Yankee Doodle [song and
    story]
—adapting to obstacles
  The wooden sword
—evading death
  Donald of the Burthens
—outwitting the king

  Sri of Siam
—saves life
  Pussy Cat Twinkle
—test
  Sri Thanonchai
—wit superior to wealth
  Puss in Boots
CLIFFS
  The captain's cabin
  Johan and the trolls
  The man/whale
  Severi and Vappu
Cliona
  Logan-*Old,* 49–53
Cloaks. *See under* CLOTHES
Clod's comb
  Kendall-*Sweet,* 86–88
Cloke, Rene, illus.
  Blyton-*My*
CLONES
  A little love story
CLONMACNOISE (monastery)
  King and the bishop
    [Clonmacnoise]
CLOTH
  See also BROCADE;
    TABLECLOTHS
  The dwarf's feast
  The mouse bride
—invisible
  The three imposters
—magic-gives food and drink
  The three talismans
—measuring of
  Saint Peter and the two
    women
—stealing of
  False witnesses
CLOTHES
  See also FASHION; HATS;
    SHOES
  Big brother: man; Little brother:
    rabbit
  Djuha's sleeve (Syria)
  The emperor's new clothes
  New clothes for the tomte

Why the sea moans
—cloak indefinitely expanding
  Saint Brigid's cloak
—cloaks
  Performing stick
—cloaks-strand of golden
  hair
  Elsa and the evil wizard
—coat: saves Shun
  Shun, the wise emperor
—coats
  Mossycoat
  Susie and her shadow
  The wild swans
—dresses
  Madame rhinoceros and her
  dress
—dresses, Mexican
  China poblana, the Chinese
  girl from Puebla
—for elves
  The elves and the shoemaker
—jackets
  Thievery
—new
  The working waterman
—pegs (pins)
  Miss Peggy Top
—robes
  The peri-wife
—shirts
  East of the sun and west of
  the moon
  Gold colt and the fire dragon
  shirt
  The happy man's shirt (Italy)
—shirts-having none
  The happiest man in the world
—shirts-of nettles
  [Sister saves six brothers cast
  into swan-form]
—shirts-shirttails
  Keeping the shirttail in
—suits
  Charge this to the cap
  The vain lord

—suits: naked husband persuaded
  that he has one on
  The two old women's bet
CLOTHES (subject)
—given to fairies
  Briggs-*Vanish.*, 55–57, 167–
  168
"CLOUD MOUNTAIN"
  The kingdom of beautiful
  colors
Cloud-maidens: Helle and Phrixus
  Lines-*Greek*, 70–76
CLOUDS
  The creation
  How three serpents carried
  princesses . . .
  Kespak and the caribou
  Nanasimgit and his [abducted]
  wife
  The sky belongs
  Vaino and the swan princess
—storm
  Thunderbird
Clover
  Froud-*Faeries*, unp.
CLOVER (subject)
—four-leafed
  Briggs-*Vanish.*, 7, 82, 119–120
CLOWNS
  The king, the coin, and the
  clown
—toy
  Pom-Pom the clown
CLUBS
  See also STICKS
  The archer who went I know
  not where to fetch I know
  not what
  The flying war club
CLUMSINESS
  Wayland Smith
Cluricaun
  Froud-*Faeries*, unp.
CLURICAUNS
  The mischievous little drinker
  Wildbeam's pranks

CLURICAUNS (subject)
  Briggs-*Vanish.*, 49, 195
The clutching hand
  Robertson-*Highland*, 65–67
CLYTEMNESTRA, Queen
  The homecoming of
  Agamemnon
CLYTEMNESTRA, Queen (subject)
  Pinsent-*Greek*, 142 (index)
[Clytie the water nymph & the
  Greek sunflower]
  Spells & Bind, 34–35
COACHES
  The death coach
  Phantom coach
  The ride of the headless
  phantom
COAL
  The rejected gift
The coal burner and the troll
  Booss-*Scand.*, 302–305
Coals on the devil's hearth
  (Ireland)
  Yolen-*Favorite*, 376–377
Coats. *See under* CLOTHES
The cobbler and the devil
  Wood-*Palace*, 24–30
The cobbler who became an
  astrologer
  Shah-*World*, 192–197
Cobblers. *See* SHOEMAKERS
Cobbler's son and the serpent
  Shah-*Dervishes*, 227–234
Coblynau
  Froud-*Faeries*, unp.
Cobras. *See under* SNAKES
COBWEBS
  Son of Kimanaueze and
  daughter of sun and
  moon
Cochran, Robert
  The game of washers
The cock and the crested hen
  Booss-*Scand.*, 223–224
The cock and the hen
  Cortes-*Byelorussian*, 12–13

The cock who wanted to be shah
  Riordan-*Tartary*, 50–53
Cock with the golden feathers
  Manning-*Marvels*, 86–101
COCKATOOS
  The gift of the white cockatoo
  —yellow crest, origin
  The proper way to make sago
The cockatoo's head-dress [origin]
  Stokes-*Turtle*, 100–102
COCKATRICE
  Philbert the Fearful
COCKERELS
  The golden cockerel
COCK-FIGHTING
  El gallo braggadocio
  The talking spear
COCKLEBURRS
  Fleas and cockleburrs
Cocks. *See* CHICKENS—roosters
COCONUT PALMS
  Bilak Pokis
COCONUTS AND COCONUT
  TREES
  The giant eel
  The magic coconuts
  —origin
  Tokanao: the first coconut
COCOONS
  All that happened must hap-
  pen again
CODICES, MEXICAN (subject)
  Nicholson-*Mexican*, 143
  (index)
Coffin cash
  Kendall-*Sweet*, 108–112
COFFINS
  Foolish men and scolding
  wives
  Ketill, the priest of Husavik
  The men who wouldn't stay
  dead (France)
  The mistake
  —glass
  A stepchild that was treated
  mighty bad

—sleeping spell
  Crystal coffin
COINS
  Flying money
  The hill man at the dance
COLD
  See also WIND—north
  Abuelita's bell
  The frozen logger [song and
    story]
  Gluska'be, the Penobscot hero
  Graduation
  Miraculous flower [stolen by
    prince of ice]
  Sad marriage of North
  The star child
—magic
  Frost
The cold iron spurs
  O'Sullivan-*Legends,* 70–71
COLEMAN GREY (subject)
  Briggs-*Vanish.,* 118
The collar
  Lang-*Pink/K,* 46–49
COLLECTORS AND COLLECTING
  Give me my bone
COLLEGE LIFE
  Graduation
COLLEN, Saint (subject)
  Briggs-*Vanish.,* 90
Collier, John
  Back for Christmas
  Green thoughts
COLMKILLE, Saint
  Saint Colmkille's well
  Saints Colmkille and Edna
COLOGNE
  Heinzelmanchen
COLOMBIA
—Bogata
  Pulga
—mountains
  Pulga
COLONIAL LIFE (U.S. history)
  Yankee Doodle [song and
    story]

COLOR (subject)
  Zong-*Korea,* 255 (index)
COLORADO
  When they gave out wisdom,
    H. queued up twice
COLORS
  How black became white
Colts. *See* HORSES—colts
Colum, Padraic
  Balder's doom
COLUMBA, Saint (subject)
—Celtic magic
  Lochhead-*Battle,* ix–x
[Colville and the water nymph]
  Water Spirits, 111–115
Coma Berenices (Berenice's hair)
  Gallant-*Constel.,* 161–162
Comatas: The sacred honey bees
  Lines-*Greek,* 107–110
COMBS
  Clod's comb
—gold & silver
  Molly Whuppy
—reminder of chastity (women)
  Mud-snail fairy
COMEDY
—of errors
  The nagging husband [Estonia]
Comedy of errors: Brave Nazar
  Kudian-*More,* 41–48
The coming of Arthur
  Malory-*King,* 1–18
Coming of King Arthur
  Riordan-*Arthur,* 9–23
The coming of Raven
  Wood-*Spirits,* 16–20
Coming of spring
  McCarthy-*Raccoon,* 23–33
Coming of the corn
  Macmillan-*Canadian,* 97–99
Commandments, Ten. *See* TEN
    COMMANDMENTS
COMMERCE
  Rabbit and the grain buyers
  Something for nothin (a Hui
    story)

COMMON SENSE
Andrew and King Solomon [in 2 parts]
Getting common sense [Anansi]
The mendacious child
The practical princess
The six fools
Stretch your legs according to your quilt
Wisdom belongs to everyone
—lack of
Simpleton of Naples [in two parts]
Three wishes [of Billy Dawson]
Communicating with the gods
Nicholson-*Mexican*, 66–71
Communication with animals. *See* ANIMAL-HUMAN COMMUNICATION
Communion cup. *See* LORD'S SUPPER
Communion, Holy. *See* LORD'S SUPPER
Communion wine in the troll food
Lindow-*Swedish*, 94–95
COMMUNISM
How a poor muzhik looked for truth . . .
COMMUNISM (subject)
—Values-China
Phelps-*Tatterhood*, 161
COMMUNITY LIFE
Badger rents a house
The community that was saved by a jinn
Elbaz-*Folktales*, 73—74
Compact with the devil. *See under* DEVIL(S)
The companion
Booss-*Scand.*, 125–134
COMPASSES
Shinansha, or the south-pointing carriage
—origin

The Yellow Emperor: war against Chitou
COMPASSION
See also CHARITY; MERCY; SELF-SACRIFICE
A deer king offers his life
The dove and the mouse
The dying Buddha's compassion
Fearless lion, brave elephant, and the merchant's cries
The hare's sacrifice
How Asanga came to see the future Buddha
The kind man
The monkey's heart
Opame, Chenrezik, and Dolma
Supparaka
Tend the sick
The young man who refused to kill
—excessive
The ascetic and the deer
The competitive tiger
Jagendorf-*Magic*, 185–188
Complacency: Prince Dorus
Lang-*Blue*, 227–235 (notes, 369–370)
The complacent one; sheep to be slaughtered
MacLean-*Cuentos*, 93–101
COMPLAINING
See also GRUMBLING
The magic coconuts
Oxen and the creaky wheels
—never satisfied
The girl who always cried
Complaining: The seed's secret
Roberts-*Jung*, 45–47
COMPROMISING
The great bronze Buddha and the whale
COMPUTERS
Haunting of [computer] Y-12 [Sarrantonio]

The comyn and the witch of
Badenoch
Robertson-*Highland*, 111–112
CONALL, Saint
Saint Conall's stone
Conall Yellowclaw
Jacobs-*Celtic*, 27–34
Conceit. *See* PRIDE; VANITY
The conceited prince
Mayo-*Book*, 110–118
CONCEPTION
See also IMPREGNATION
—by walking in giant's footprints
Houji, the child abandoned on
the ice
—miraculous
How a king learned to care for
parents
Concerning the poor man covetous
Ransome-*War*, 64–69
Conch. *See* SHELLS
CONCHOBAR, King
Deirdre and Naoise
Lords of the chariot and the
spear
CONCUBINES
A cure for jealousy
The master and the serving
maid
The scholar's concubine
The waiting maid's parrot
(China)
Conditions. *See* STIPULATIONS
CONDORS
The bride of heaven
CONDUCT OF LIFE
See also AMENDMENT OF
LIFE; MAXIMS
Mind your own business:
Words of wisdom
Words of wisdom
—a fruitful life
Three former lives
The confession of Charles
Linkworth
Hoke-*Horrors*, 30–48

Confessions of Tom Bourke
Yeats-*Fairy*, 154–166
CONFIDENCE (CON GAMES or
CON MEN)
Peter Bull
The pilgrim from paradise
Confidence game: The old hag
Sheohmelian-*Three*, 7–10
Confidence in God. *See* TRUST IN
GOD
Confidences (sleeping-mat) not to
be repeated
Radin-*African*, 212–214
Conflict of the magicians
Shah-*World*, 186–187
CONJURE BAGS
How ole woodpecker got ole
rabbit's conjure bag
The conjure wives
Haviland-*N. Amer.*, 122–125
Conjurers. *See* MAGICIANS;
WIZARDS
Conjurer's revenge [slave changed
into mule]
Shepard-*Conjure*, 15–25
CONJURING
Wiley and the hairy man
Conkle, Nancy, illus.
Reid-*Myths*
CONLA (son of Cuchulain)
Cuchulain's death
CONNACHAR, King
Deirdre and Naoise
Conn-eda; or The golden apples of
Lough Erne
Yeats-*Fairy*, 275–285
Connla and the fairy maiden
Jacobs-*Celtic*, 6–8
Conor mac Nessa
O'Sullivan-*Legends*, 104–
105
CONQUISTADORES
Curse of the devil's gold
CONSCIENCE
Bird of truth
The broken swords

CONSCIENCE (continued)
—professor chides king for his
  faults
  Doctor Bidpai
CONSCIOUSNESS
  Travels with Mozart
CONSERVATISM
  Two badgers
CONSIDERATION
  Kinsman accompany you when
  he asks to go along
CONSPIRACY
  The camel, lion, leopard, crow,
  & jackal
  The lion and the hare
CONSTELLATIONS
  *See also names of particular
  constellations, e.g.,* BIG
  DIPPER; GREAT BEAR;
  ORION; PLEIADES
  Aguila (the Eagle)
  Andromeda (the Chained
  Woman)
  Aquarius (the Water-Carrier)
  Aries (the Ram)
  Auriga (the Charioteer)
  Bootes (the Herdsman)
  The Bull [Europa and Minos]
  Cancer (the Crab)
  Canis major (the Big Dog)
  Canis minor (the Little Dog)
  Capricornus (the Sea-goat)
  Cassiopeia (the Queen)
  Cepheus (the King)
  Cetus (the Whale)
  Coma Berenices (Berenice's
  hair)
  Corona Australis (the Southern
  Crown)
  Corona Borealis (the Northern
  Crown)
  Corvus (the raven)
  The Crab [and He-Who-Made-
  All-Things]
  Crater (the Cup)
  Cygnus (the Swan)

Delphinus (the Dolphin)
The Dove [Noah and the
  Flood]
Draco (the Dragon)
The Dragon [Marduk and
  Tiamat]
The eagle [Aquila vs
  Aesculapius]
Eridanus (the River)
The Fishes [Odschig, the chief]
From pinpoints to pollywogs
Gemini (the Twins)
Great Bear and her Cub: star-
  bound beasts
The Great Bear [Callisto and
  Arcas]
The Great Dog [Yudistira and
  Svana]
Heracles (Hercules)
The Hyades
Hydra (the many-headed
  monster)
Leo (the Lion)
Libra (the Scales)
The Lion [Heracles]
Lyra (the Lyre)
Ophiuchus (the Serpent
  Holder)
Orion (the Hunter)
Patterns in the sky
Pegasus (the Winged Horse)
Perseus
Pisces (the Fishes)
Piscis Australis (the Southern
  Fish)
The Pleiades
Sagittarius (the Archer)
The Scorpion [Orion, the
  Hunter]
Scorpius (the Scorpion)
The Sea Goat [Pan vs Typhon]
Serpens (the Serpent)
The Swan [Phaethon and
  Cygnus]
Taurus (the Bull)
Triangulum (the Triangle)

CONSTELLATIONS (continued)
    Ursa Major (the Great Bear)
    Ursa Minor (the Lesser Bear)
    Virgo (the virgin)
    The Water Serpent [Heracles
      vs the Hydra]
    The Whale [and Jonah]
    The Wolf [Noah's Ark]
—Big Bear: origin
    The seven stars of the
      north
—origin
    Zan and the Dactyls in early
      Crete
—Vega: origin
    The three stars
—Wagoner, Procyon, Virgo
    Erigone and her dog
Constellations: Orion, Cassiopeia,
    Castor/Pollux
    Low-*Greek,* 170–177
Contagious diseases. *See*
    DISEASES—communicable
CONTEMPLATIVE LIFE
    The broken swords
CONTEMPT
    The rock and the weasel
CONTENTMENT
    See also DISCONTENT
    The dog and his shadow
    Dog and the bone
    Dog and the wolf [dog chained
      by-day]
    The fir tree
    The happy man's shirt
      (Italy)
    Manstin, the rabbit
    The steadfast parrot and
      his tree
    Stonemason: a T'ung folktale
      [be content with what you
      are]
    Tobacco fairy from the Blue
      Hills
The contest
    Synge-*Land,* 13–23

CONTESTS
    See also ATHLETIC CON-
      TESTS; RACES—Athletic;
      TESTS
    Champion spearsman
    Foolish Vanya and Princess
      Helena the Fair
    Foot racers of Payupki
    Four magic arrows
    Four sworn brothers
    [The fox with the purple
      umbrella]
    Glass mountain
    The herd boy and the dragons
    Ice castle of Utgard-Loke
    Knight of the riddles
    The liar
    The magic mirror of Rabbi
      Adam
    Matching wits [two robbers
      have same wife]
    The merry wives
    One particular small, smart
      boy
    The princess on the glass
      hill
    Rival magicians
    Selfish husband
    The sparrow and the crow
    The storytellers
    Swarthy Smith of the Socks
    Tall tales (Burma)
    Triplets [Light Foot, Skilful
      Hand, Keen Eye]
    Two lies
    Vassilissa the valiant
—archery; tsar's daughter
    Green lizard, gray squirrel and
      the eagle
—craftsmen
    The turner and the goldsmith
—harvesting
    Farmer and the bogle
—man vs. machine
    John Henry [song and story]
—masterpiece of a trade

CONTESTS (continued)
  Three brothers [craft contest]
—to win princess
  Chestnut grey
—winner gets a husband
  Rival kempers
—won by cleverness
  Abzelil and the Master of the
    Lake
—words/wit/wisdom
  The mill spirit
CONTRACTS
  Impossible judgement
CONTRADICTION
  How contradiction came to the
    Ashanti
Contrarianism: traveller and
    innkeeper
  Stuchl-*American,* 50–54
CONTRARINESS
  The hermit [paradoxical
    behavior]
Contrariness: The headstrong
    woman
  Griego-*Cuentos,* 157–159
CONUNDRUMS
  How to win a prince
CONVENTS
  The little goddess
  The promise
CONVERSION
  King who decreed conversion
—moral
  Value of a Pater and a Creed
Conversion of King Laoghair's
    daughters
  Yeats-*Fairy,* 202
Conversion of manners. *See*
  AMENDMENT OF LIFE
CONVERTS
  Saint Patrick and Crom Dubh
—Catholic
  The devil as a cat
—Jewish
  Flight of the eagle
COOK, Capt. James

—[called "O Lono"]
  Westervelt-*Hawaiian,* 100–113
Cook, pot, cook!
  Stovicek-*Around,* 173
Cooking. *See* COOKS AND
  COOKERY
Cookooburrahs and the Goolahgool
  Parker-*Australian,* 48–49
COOKS AND COOKERY
  See also names of food, e.g.,
    CORN
  How raven brought the salmon
  Imperial left-overs
  Mossycoat
  The pie and the patty-pan
  Son of the Knight of the Green
    Vesture
  A story about death
  The three lemons
  The unwilling magician
  Vhy, vhy, vhy [humor]
  The witch's cat
—banished for s. in Amir's
    soup
  The unforgetable sneeze
Coolnajoo, the foolish one
  Hill-*More,* 96–104
COOMARA (sea creature)
  The merrow and the soul
    cages
COOPERATION
  See also TEAMWORK
  Animals in winter
  Heaven and hell
  Hiawatha
  Lion tamer [Tibetan]
  Mastermaid
  The pig builds the house on
    the hill
  Seven sisters; a Miao story
  The squeaking mouse
  The white pet
  Wise pigeon
—fire brought to earth
  Gift from a star
—freedom a result of

The wise quail and the foolish
  quail
COOTS (birds)
  The dawn of the world
Copil's heart
  Bierhorst-*Hungry*, 71–75,
  138
COPPER
  The tinder-box
  Twilight, Midnight, and Dawn
Coral creeper [origin]
  Reed-*Aboriginal*, 64–67
Coranieid: Llud and Llefelys
  Lochhead-*Battle*, 91–95
CORBET, Bishop (subject)
  Briggs-*Vanish.*, 7, 50
CORMAC, King
  Land of promise
CORMAC Mac ART
  Reckoning with the Fianna's
  ancient bane
Cormac Mac Art and Mananan
  Mac Lir
  Lehane-*Wizards*, 30–34
Cormac Mac Art, Finn, and
  Grainne . . .
  Lehane-*Legends*, 56–63
Cormac MacArt went to Faery
  McGarry-*Folk*, 33–37
The cormorant and the star
  Wood-*Kalila*, 127–131
The Cormorants of Andvaer
  Heslewood-*Tales*, 18–25
CORN
  Anpao brings the corn
  The Aturuarodo legend
  Behind the waterfall
  Big long man's corn patch
  Coming of the corn
  Dwarfs stealing corn
  The fairy gift
  Mice in the corn
  The new people and their food
  The nis stealing corn
  Puukonhoya wins a bride
  Rabbit and the grain buyers

Spirit Burekoibo (Meri) pun-
  ishes the Bororo
The thief: neighbor steals
  farmer's corn
True corn [origin of plant life]
The Veracruz maize legend
Wise pigeon
—jewels in ears of
  Two neighbors
—maize crop poisoned
  How Jiculi served his tribe
—maize crop ravaged
  The brothers and the singing
  toad
—man made from
  Trial and error creation
—origin
  How corn came to the Indians
—origin of four types
  The Iwaguddudogue myth
—shucking
  Simon challenges the
  McCrackens
The corn maidens
  Wood-*Spirits*, 107–110
CORN (subject)
—Wild corn; modern Indian corn
  Dutton-*Navajo*, 4–5
Corona Australis (the Southern
  Crown)
  Gallant-*Constel.*, 91
Corona Borealis (the Northern
  Crown)
  Gallant-*Constel.*, 75–78
Corpse of the cat
  McNeil-*Charm*, 85–86
CORPSE(S)
  See also DEAD; DEATH
  El borracho del bahio
  The boy who did not know
  what fear was
  The deacon of Myrka
  Far Darrig in Donegal
  The flying childer
  A ghost's vengeance
  In the graveyard

CORPSE(S) (continued)
  The ostler and the grave
    robbers (Scotland)
  Teig O'Kane and the corpse
  The two Sigurdurs
—comes to life
  The cuckoo: its origin and its
    call
—evil man in coffin; set afire
  Wrecker of Sennen Cove
—on spit
  A fairy enchantment
CORPUS CHRISTI (feast)
  Rain for Bongi
Corrigans. See KORRIGANS
CORROBOREES
  The borah of Byamee
  Crane, kangaroo rat, fire
    makers
CORTES, Hernando, 1485–1547.
  The weeping woman: Cortes
    and Malinzin
Corvus (the raven)
  Gallant-Constel., 169–170
Cosmogony and cosmology [motif
    index]
  Wilbert-Bororo, 234–235
Cosmogony and the origin of man
  [18 narratives]
  Wilbert-Bororo, 55–59
COSMOLOGY
  Baiame: in the beginning
The costly ring
  Ransome-War, 40–50
La Cote Mal Taile
  Malory-King, 99–120
The cottage garden
  Ewart-Lore, 33–41
COTTAGES
—lakeside
  Terror
COTTON
  The Aturuarodo legend
—fields
  Ballad of the boll weevil [song
    and story]

Cottontail plays a trick on coyote
  De Wit-Talking, 127–130
COUGH(ING)
  The frog
  Hob and the cough
  Manabozho and the squirrels
  One hairball
Counselor to the wolves
  Roberts-Chinese, 119
COUNSELORS
  Dumplings in the river
Count Dracula [by Woody Allen]
  Schwartz-Great, 171–177
[Count Dracula's castle]
  Lee-Castles, 176–179
Countess Kathleen O'Shea
  Yeats-Fairy, 211–214
The countess of Hojentorp
  Booss-Scand., 279
COUNTING
—chickens before hatched
  Milkmaid and the pail
Country dance in the Ozarks in
    1874
  McNeil-Charm, 173–176
The country maid and her milkpail
  dePaola-Favorite, 53
Country mouse and city mouse
  Tudor-Bedtime, [28–29]
The country of the beautiful
    gardens
  Villa-Armenian, 180–189, 470–
    473
The country of the mice
  O'Connor-Tibet, 133–140
Country of thieves
  Roberts-Chinese, 206
COURAGE
  See also HEROES AND
    HEROINES; QUESTS
  The apple on the boy's head
    [Wm Tell]
  The black spectre
  The boyhood dreams of Cu
    Chulaind
  The broken swords

The brothers Samba
Gawain: test of valor
Genie of the mountains
The ghost at Fjelkinge
The giant caterpillar
Glooscap and the wishes
Hassan the brave
The hunter maiden [and
  Cannibal Demon]
Kalele the Bold Wisher
Kespak and the caribou
A legend of Knockmany
Lord Guan: god of martial arts
The man who never knew fear
Marko's [Kraljevic] smile
My lord bag of rice
Patience overcomes fate [piast]
Photogen and Nycteris; a
  day/night mahrchen
Prince Five-Weapons
Samba the Satan and Omadi
  the Righteous
Seven fears
The steadfast tin soldier
Stillson's leap: a jataka
Stompe Pilt
The story of trembling hood
Strange visitors
The strongest boy in the world
Tangletop: the cave at the
  world's end
T'ien the brave, hero of the
  Hsia River
Tiyo meets Spider Woman
Tonweya and the eagles
Tumani and his mother's
  promise
The valiant chanticleer
The warrior's death
Why raven is no longer
Wonderful healing leaves
—test: steal skull from graveyard
  March cock banishes the devil
COURIERS
  Snipp, Snapp, Snorium
Courlander, Harold

Foot racers of Payupki
Court jester. *See* CLOWNS
COURTESY
  Chicoria [invited to eat at
    rancher's table]
  Diamonds and toads
  A horse called Terror
  The water of life
—accepted mores not followed
  Dimian the peasant
COURTSHIP
  See also LOVE; MARRIAGE;
    SUITORS
  Adventures of John Dietrich
  Brer rabbit and his riding horse
  Brer rabbit goes a courting
  The cattle raid of Froech
  The choosy maid of Yen-Pien
  Crane woos the heron
  Elephant and blackbird court
    the same girl
  Frog went a-courting [song
    and story]
  The girl with the silver voice
  The great flood
  Hot-foot Hannibal
  Kelfala's secret something
  Monkey and dog court the
    same girl
  Princess Minon-Minette
  Puukonhoya wins a bride
  The rabbit makes a match
  The shepherd of Silfrun-
    Arstadir
  The shirt collar
  A slave's dangerous court-
    ship
  Son of Kimanaueze and
    daughter of sun and moon
  The wagtail Deereeree, and
    the rainbow
  The Wooing of Etain
  The Wooing of Olwen
  Wooing of Pumei; and Oroqen
    story
  Wooing of Seppo Hmarinen

Courtship of Inanna and Dumuzi
  Wolkstein-*Inanna,* 29–49
The courtship of Yasin
  Magel-*Gambia,* 144–148
Convergence
  Wood-*Kalila,* 33–44
COVETING
  See also LUST
  Eagle Woman comes to The
    People
  Fisherman and the prince
—has 99 wives; wants son's too
  The seven penitential psalms
—wife of another
  Bead-seller and the jinn's
    sister
  How the moolah was taught a
    lesson
  Oskus-ool and his wise wife
Covetousness. *See* COVETING;
  GREED
Cow doomed to the slaughter-
    house
  Elbaz–*Folktales,* 36
The cow who tried to act like a
    kitten
  MacLean-*Cuentos,* 143–145
COWARDICE
  Brave Bear, Snake, and Croc-
    odile Killer
  Canobie Dick and Thomas of
    Ercildoun
  Comedy of errors: Brave
    Nazar
  The guardian cock
  House of ice and house of
    wood
  Nazar the Brave ["kills a thou-
    sand at a single blow"]
  Philbert the Fearful
  Seven fears
Cowboy Billy Coyote
  Stuchl-*American,* 11–19
COWBOYS
  Buffalo skinners [song and
    story]

Dream of Owen O'Mulready
The dying cowboy [song and
    story]
Fair, brown, and trembling
Pecos Bill becomes a coyote
The Shee and Gannon and the
    Gruagach Gaire
—last request
The parting song
COWHERDS
  Adventures of Sikku
  The fiery dragon
  Finn MacCumhail and the son
    of the king of Alba
  Truthful John
COWS
  Bagged wolf
  Beware of the bull
  Bewitched butter [Donegal]
  Bewitched cow
  A boom in guarache leather
  Dame Soasan
  Departure of the giants (Africa)
  The elf maiden
  The harvesters
  Hermes, the messenger of the
    gods
  House in the wood
  The house of Thebes
  How the cow went under the
    ground
  Hudden and Dudden and Do-
    nald O'Neary
  The iron wolf
  [King Shivi] The gift of cows
  The leopard
  A lesson from a lovelorn cow
  Milking others' cows
  Munachar and Manachar
  The nis stealing corn
  Olga and the brown cow
  Piglet and the cow
  The red cow [a Cinderella-type
    story]
  The Shee and Gannon and the
    Gruagach Gaire

The shepherd of Myddvai
The three daughters and the
lost cow
Twingmuntus, Cowbelliantus,
Perchnosius
Wine and the devil
The world of ice and fire
—calves
The nisses in Vosborg
—calves-piebald
The piebald calf
—calves-tails
The box with the funny thing in it
—gifts to the church
The Indian and the hundred
cows
—grey
The merman
—monster
The Urko of North Wij
—origin
The prince who had two eyes
—stolen by ganconers
Loughleagh [lake of healing]
—sucked by hare/witch
Bewitched butter [Queen's
County]
—"woman" only can milk them
Billy the milkmaid
The cows who came to tea
Phillips-*Hoity*, 38–46
Cowslips
Froud-*Faeries*, unp.
COWSLIPS
The green mist
—wreath of, makes invisible
The fox and the little white hen
Coyote and bluebird
Hayes-*Coyote*, 48–51
Coyote and his bow
Hayes-*Coyote*, 9–13
Coyote and horned toad
Hayes-*Coyote*, 72–75
Coyote and Iitoi: the flood
Dutton-*Navajo*, 15–16
Coyote and locust

Hayes-*Coyote*, 36–41
Coyote and rabbit
Hayes-*Coyote*, 25–29
Coyote and skunk
Hayes-*Coyote*, 14–20
Coyote and the blackbirds
Hayes-*Coyote*, 52–56
Coyote and the mice
Hayes-*Coyote*, 30–35
Coyote and the quail
Hayes-*Coyote*, 65–71
Coyote and the rattlesnake
Hayes-*Coyote*, 57–60
Coyote and the rock
Hayes-*Coyote*, 42–47
Coyote and the swallowing monster
De Wit-*Talking*, 122–126
Coyote and the water serpent
Mullett-*Spider*, 132–140
Coyote and turkey
Hayes-*Coyote*, 21–24
Coyote and turtle
Hayes-*Coyote*, 61–64
Coyote brings fire to The People
MacLean-*Cuentos*, 172–176
Coyote Bun and the turkey
Shaw-*Pima*, 84–89
Coyote eats his own fat
Shaw-*Pima*, 90–94
Coyote fights a lump of pitch
Yolen-*Favorite*, 134–136
Coyote retrieves his brother's scalp
Shaw-*Pima*, 56–62
COYOTES
Anpao and coyote
Big long man's corn patch
Cottontail plays a trick on
coyote
The creation
The great hunters [animals]
How coyote stole fire
How rabbit got the best of
coyote
Iktomi and the coyote
Juan fetches the devil
Little frog repays coyote

COYOTES (continued)
Masquerading trickster
Moonflower
Obsidian arrow points
Pecos Bill and the cyclone
Pecos Bill becomes a coyote
The quail clan punishes coyote
Rabbit and the gum-baby
The rabbit and the two coyote
Repaying good with evil
Sister Fox and Brother Coyote
Skinkoots steals the springtime
The theft of fire
The twisting tree [Kiowa]
The well-baked man
—adds feathers; flies; crashes
Coyote and the blackbirds
—blinded
Foolish coyote
—brown color
Coyote and bluebird
—called "Yellow-Behind-the-Ears"
Coyote and the mice
—color
Why coyote's coat is the color
of sand
—origin of black nose & paws
Coyote and rabbit
—raise baby boy
Cowboy Billy Coyote
—smallest bow given to
Coyote and his bow
—tail
Coyote and the water serpent
—tricked into biting rock
Coyote and locust
—tricks turtle
Turtle feeds his children
Coyote's crying song
Macdonald-*Twenty*, 10–19
Coyote's rain song
Macdonald-*Twenty*, 20–23
Coyote's trip to the Land Above
Shaw-*Pima*, 63–69
Coyote's vanity
Shaw-*Pima*, 82–83

Crab
Adams-*Iron*, 47–51
The Crab [and He-Who-Made-All-
Things]
Lurie-*Heavenly*, 31–34
CRABS
Cancer (the Crab)
The crane and the crab
The crocodile's tail
Enmity between monkeys and
crabs
Little crab and his magic
eyes
The lobster and the crab
The name [girl must learn em-
ployer's name or not eat]
Quarrel of the monkey and the
crab
Crack and crook (Italy)
Yolen-*Favorite*, 136–138
CRADLES
A legend of Knockmany
Leppa Polkry and the blue
cross
The man/whale
Rock-a-bye baby
—golden
The golden cradle
A craft is worth more than gold
Kudian-*More*, 22–25
Craftiness: The fox and the bear
Nagishkin-*Folktales*, 146–150
CRAFTSMANSHIP
A craft is worth more than gold
The crane and the crab
Wood-*Kalila*, 80–89
Crane and the crow
Parker-*Australian*, 111
Crane, kangaroo rat, fire makers
Parker-*Australian*, 33–36
The crane maiden
Sanders-*Dragons*, 39–41
Crane woos the heron
Riordan-*Russia*, 144–145
CRANES
The pelican and the crane

Scar Face and the sun dance
Story of a gentleman['s wife]
—lose plumage, turn white
The golden cranes
—origin of its call
Crane and the crow
—pull cart into sky
Old man Zackery and the
    cranes
Cranes of the Great Lakes
Jagendorf-*First,* 43–45
Crater (the Cup)
Gallant-*Constel.,* 170–172
CRAYFISH
—tricks crow
The crow's call
The creation
Hyde-Chambers-*Tibet,* 1–4
Shaw-*Pima,* 4–7
CREATION
    See also BEGINNINGS;
        GLOOSKAP; GOD
    See also subhead "creation"
        or "origin" *under topics, e.g.*
        CORN; PLEIADES; RAIN-
        BOWS; WOMEN
    Ants [creation of earth, light,
        sun, &]
    Atam and Im
    Baiame: in the beginning
    The beginning: Father Sky,
        Mother Earth
    The beginning of the world
    The big turtle
    The bonfire
    The coming of Raven [Eskimo
        myth]
    The Crab [and He-Who-Made-
        All-Things]
    The dawn of the world
    The Dragon [Marduk and
        Tiamat]
    Duration of life (Germany)
    Eagle Woman comes to The
        People
    The fifth and final sun

The first humans
First Man and First Woman
First tale: In the beginning . . .
Footsteps of the god
Glooscap, the great chief
Glooskap and the whale
Glooskap's country
The golden man and the finger
    men [life, language,
    reason—of man]
A goddess is born [peopling
    the earth]
Good and evil: Buri vs Ymir
Gumiya; a Blang story: origins
    of characteristics
How God made the butterflies
How the snake got his rattles
How the world began
How the world was made
The hungry woman [earth]
In the beginning
Ladder of grass [six races of
    men]
Man, the burro, and the dog
The man who sat on the tide
Men in the world of light
    [human development]
Meri, the creator-traveler
Monkeys, turkeys, and fish
    [creation]
The Morning Star
Mother Earth and her children
A Navajo story of creation
The new people and their
    food
Origins of the world
People and other creatures
    formed [Sun-father]
The Ram [devil as creator]
Sila [human female born to be
    a sea-being]
Trial and error creation [of
    man]
Up from the Dead Land
The village beneath the water
The well-baked man

CREATION (continued)
  [White man created by Juko,
    the monkey]
  Why apes look like people
  Why raven isn't perfect
  Woman chooses death
  Zan and the Dactyls in early
    Crete
  A Zuni creation legend
CREATION (subject)
  Nahman-*Tales*, 330
—Beginnings of mankind [17 Ban-
    tu/Zulu tales]
  Pitcher-*Tokol.*, 1–64
—Friendship between the earthly
    and the heavens
  Luzzatto-*Long*, 44
—Stories of transubstantiation
  Nicholson-*Mexican*, 27–31
Creation and ordering of human life
  [motif index]
  Wilbert-*Bororo*, 236–238, 284
CREATION (literary, artistic)
  Where stories grow
Creation myths [8 tales]
  Bierhorst-*Hungry*, 21–41, 133–
    136
The creation of Samoa
  Wright-*Pigeon*, 12–14
Creation of the Mayas
  Shelley-*Legends*, 72–74
The creation of the world
  Branston-*Gods*, 20–23
Creation story [Pima]
  Dutton-*Navajo*, 12–15
CREATOR
  Why Bootup, the whale,
    smokes a pipe
  Why there is death [Nikoduma]
Creator Nyame and his four wives
  Radin-*African*, 33–35
Creatures and spirits
  Piggott-*Japanese*, 61–87
The creatures of magic
  Haining-*Lepre.*, 61–65
Credulousness. *See* GULLIBILITY

CREEK WOMEN
  Eagle and the frog
CREEKS
  In the beginning
  The treasure in Saby Creek
—crossing
  Parley Garfield and the frogs
CREOLES
—songs (words and score)
  Songs in English and Creole
CREON
  The tragic story of Antigone
CRESTS (totems)
  The girl who married a bear
Crete
  Magical Beasts, 7–8
CRETE
  Nereides
  Zan and the Dactyls in early
    Crete
The cricket
  Roberts-*Chinese*, 3–8
CRICKET-FIGHTING
  The crickets
CRICKETS
  Hob and the Cough
  The jaguar and the cricket
  Why the opossum's tail is bare
CRIME AND CRIMINALS
  See also THIEVES AND
    THIEVERY
  Baldheads
  Pedro de Urdemalas
  The police marshall [mass
    murder]
  So you won't talk
  Waxworks
Crimes. *See* CRIMES AND
    CRIMINALS
The crimson parrot
  Adams-*Iron*, 52–61
The cripple
  Nahman-*Tales*, 79–93 [notes:
    81, 293–295]
The cripple and Senor San Antonio
  Campos-*Mexican*, 69–72

A crippled hero
  Cortes-*Byelorussian*, 96–99
CRIPPLES
—daughter
  Two brothers
Critch
  Gorog-*Taste*, 113–128
CRITICISM
  Finn blood
CROATIA
  Fate
CROCKETT, DAVY
  Davy Crockett, king of the old
    wild west
  Strong but Quirky
Crocodile and hare
  Pitcher-*Tokol.*, 24–26
The crocodile in the bedroom
  Lobel-*Fables*, 2
Crocodile people [three tales]
  Reed-*Aboriginal*, 69–86
Crocodiles. *See* ALLIGATORS
    AND CROCODILES
The crocodile's tail
  Classic Child., 18–25
CROCUSES
  Snowdrops and crocuses
Croker, T. Crofton
  Banshee of the MacCarthys
  Brewery of eggshells
  Confessions of Tom Bourke
  Crookened back [pooka]
  Daniel O'Rourke
  Funeral of Flory Cantillon
  Giant's stairs [Mahon Mac-
    Mahon; Ronayne's Court]
  Knockgrafton legend
  Lady of Gollerus
  [Little bird singing: angel of
    death]
  Master and man
  Priest's supper
  Soul cages
  Teigue of the Lee
  The young piper
Crom Dubh [convert] and St Patrick

O'Sullivan-*Legends*, 109–112
Crones. *See* WITCHES
CRONUS
  In the beginning: the Greek
    panoply
  Mother Earth and her children
CRONUS (subject)
  Pinsent-*Greek*, 142 (index)
The crooked pine
  Ginsburg-*Twelve*, 44–47
The crooked-mouthed family
  Stuchl-*American*, 190–192
Crookened back [pooka]
  McGarry-*Folk*, 107–112
CROPS
  Bruin and Reynard partners
  Gazelle and the leopard
  Wamundo
—destroyed by cockatoo
  The cockatoo's head-dress
    [origin]
–hay
  Princess on the glass hill
Cross purposes
  Macdonald-*Wise*, 131–154
CROSS (subject)
—sign of
  Briggs-*Vanish.*, 20, 152
CROSSES
  The boy who did not know
    what fear was
  Ebbe Skamelson
  Hinzelmann
  The marsh king's daughter
  The tinder-box
  The wonderful plough
—blue
  Leppa Polkry and the blue
    cross
Crossing the river [man, wolf, goat,
    cabbage]
  Shannon-*Solve*, 11–13
Crossley-Holland, Kevin
  Beowulf fights the dragon
The crossways
  Booss-*Scand.*, 625–626

CROTTY, William (subject)
  O'Sullivan-*Legends*, 138–139
The crow and the daylight
  Adams-*Iron*, 86–92
Crow and the jug
  Watson-*Aesop*, 4–5
The crow and the parrot
  eggs
  Dutton-*Hopi*, 36
The crow and the peacock
  Watson-*Thailand*, 11–13
Crow and the pitcher
  Williams-*Aesop*, [20–21]
Crow people [ten tales]
  Reed-*Aboriginal*, 108–141
The crow, the snake, and the
  jackal
  Wood-*Kalila*, 79–89
The crowd
  Hoke-*Uncanny*, 45–55
CROWING
  The young rooster
CROWNS
  Dead snake and young wife
CROWS
  Artemis and Apollo
  The bear and the crow
  The black swans
  The camel, lion, leopard, crow,
    & jackal
  The crane and the crab
  A drink for a crow
  Fox and the crow
  Gheeger Gheeger the cold
    west wing
  Gift of fire
  The heavenly song of the
    green-spotted dove
  How mussels were brought to
    the creeks
  How Wahn became a star
  Libor and the swan princess
  The medicine-man
  The Milky Way [Wahn (crow) &
    Baripa (cat)]
  Miss Peggy Top
  The moon god [how moon got
    up in sky]
  Munachar and the raspberries
  The snow queen: an adventure
    in seven stories
  The tale of the magic green
    water-pearl
  That wicked crow
  Why crows are black
  Zirac and friends
—black feathers, origin
  Crane and the crow
  The crow and the peacock
  The proper way to make sago
  Why the crow is black
  Yawayawa and crow
—brown
  Eagle hawk again
—fooled by frog
  The frog and the crow
—foolish
  The sparrow and the crow
—prince under spell
  Castle of the crow
—skins
  The crow and the daylight
—smoky white
  The eagle hawk
—steals grain from garden
  The boy, the crow and the
    sesame seeds
—war with owls
  The wise old crow
—why they don't sing
  The fox and the crow
The crow's call
  Cortes-*Byelorussian*, 14–15
CRUCIFIX
  The woman who was saved by
    a miracle
CRUCIFIXION
  The robin
The cruel painter
  Macdonald-*Gray*, 11–53
The cruel stepmother
  Macmillan-*Canadian*, 242–245

Cruel words: Diarmuid, son of
  Donn
Spells & Bind, 125–129
CRUELTY
  See also CHILD ABUSE;
    "CINDERELLAS"; KIND-
    NESS; STEPMOTHERS
  Aniz the shepherd
  Azad Bakht's tale
  The bag of money
  Blue bird [King Charming]
  Boy who overcame the giants
  The cat palace
  Cinderella
  The cruel painter
  The devoted son
  Dinewan the emu, and Wahn
    the crow
  The fairy and the prince
  Fomushka the village idiot
  The forbidden apple
  Galo and Vasiri
  The giant maiden in Boraserod
    mountain
  The girl who trod on the loaf
  Gold colt and the fire dragon
    shirt
  The golden fish, wicked sis-
    ters, and good Forgetta
  The golden haired twins
  Golden reed pipe
  Good and evil
  Grandfather Frost
  Greedy Kanchuga
  The greedy youngster
  A Hani story: Queen forbids
    servant to eat rice
  How the first rain came
  How Wang-Fo was saved
  The Indian Cinderella
  John and Mary; girl with
    chopped-off hands
  Jora the troll
  Lake of Zangze
  Lam Ku, the basket lady
  The lampstand princess

A lesson for the landlord
Little Elga
Littel One-Eye, . . . Two-Eyes,
  and . . . Three-Eyes
The Lord of Rosendal
Lynching a witch [folk-hysteria]
Master James' nightmare
Meng Chaing and the Great
  Wall of China
Mongolian story of a serf: Ulan
  Bator
Orphan Yan Ran [Kawa]
Owney and Owney-na-peak
Papaya [origin]
Rent-day
[Servant forces princess into
  servitude]
Slave girl tried to kill her
  mistress
The sparrow with the slit-
  tongue
The squirrel wife
The star child
Story of Miriam
Stretch out your legs to length
  of your quilt
The stupid boy and the wand
Those three wishes
Two sisters, Rose and Lotus
Vartiter (Rose-Petal)
Wings
The woman and the giant
The wow o'Rivven; the bell
Yorkshire giant [Penhill]
—by animals
  The rattlesnake receives his
    fangs
—to animals
  Cow doomed to the slaughter-
    house
  Pamarindo
—of children
  The woman from the sea
—to children
  See CHILD ABUSE;
    CHILDREN—abandoned

CRUELTY (continued)
—merchant leaves laborer on mt.
  top to die
  The golden mountain
—punished
  The name [girl must learn employer's name or not eat]
—of sisters
  Little burnt face
—to stepdaughter
  Kate Crackernuts
Crunar the cruel
  Robertson-*Highland*, 200–201
CRUSADES
  Black monk's curse
  Ebbe Skamelson
  The quest for the Star of the
    Sea
CRYING
  See also TEARS
  Johnny and the three goats [in
    turnip field]
  The remarkable rocket
—over imagined future evil
  The three sillies [imagined future evils]
Cryptic speech: Marriage of masters of Wolof
  Magel-*Gambia*, 163–167
Crystal coffin
  Lang-*Green*, 333–338
The crystal people
  Roberts-*Jung*, 63–66
The crystal sisters
  Stovicek-*Around*, 82–85
Crystal-gazing
  Sergeant-*Witches*, 286 (index)
CU CHULAIN
  Aunascaul Lake
  A champion's schooling in another world
  Knighting of Cuculain
  The Knockmany legend
  Lords of the chariot and the
    spear
  Oona and the giant Cuchulain

Oonagh and the giants
Cu Chulainn and Ferdiad
  Ross-*Druids*, 47–49
Cu Chulainn, Hound of Culann
  Ross-*Druids*, 32–37
Cu Chulainn: the wooing of
  Emer
  Ross-*Druids*, 37–41
Cuchulain vs Calatin and his sons
  Lehane-*Legends*, 30–31
Cuchulainn's boyhood
  McGarry-*Folk*, 25–28
Cuchulain's death
  Lehane-*Legends*, 42–50
CUAUHCOATL
  The eagle on the prickly pear
La cucaracha
  Aiken-*Mexican*, 29–32
CUCHET, M. (subject)
—The Cabinet des Fees
  Quiller-*Sleeping*, 9–14
CUCKOLDS
  El Diablo, el chivo, y Senor
    Bonifacio
  Raven and the big fisherman
The cuckoo
  McCarty-*Skull*, 14–17
The cuckoo: its origin and its call
  Sanders-*Dragons*, 24
The cuckoo's riches
  Nagishkin-*Folktales*, 39–45
CUCULAIN. *See* CU CHULAIN
Cucumbers and cherry trees
  Piggott-*Japanese*, 131–133
Cudgels. *See* CLUBS; STICKS
Cumings, Art, illus.
  Lewis-*Bedtime*
CUMULATIVE TALES
  See also REPETITIVE
    RHYMES AND STORIES
  The boy, the crow and the
    sesame seeds
  The boy who was called
    Thickhead
  The bull in the china shop

The castle [five live in empty horse-skull]
The cat and the mouse
Cherry pickers
Chicken Licken
The cock and the hen
Drop of honey
Esben and the witch
Exchange [barter]
A fisherman and his wife
The fox without a tail
From bad to worse
God is stronger
A grain of millet
Half-Rooster
How Jack went to seek his fortune
How the Thai learned to be calm
The husband who stayed at home
It started with a thorn
Johnny and the three goats [in turnip field]
Johnny Cake
Kinsman accompany you when he asks to go along
The landlord and the muzhik
The little girl who wanted everything back
The little red hen
Mac Iain Direach
Master tailor
Mosquito [origin of its buzz]
The mouse and the rooster
Munachar and Manachar
Munuck
Needle and Noodle
Old Dry Fryge (rogue preacher)
The old woman and her pig
Rabbit and the berries
Rat's bridegroom [who is most powerful?]
Sam Pig seeks his fortune
Seventh father of the house

Simpleton of Naples [in two parts]
Smallboy and his halfpenny wife
The sparrow and the crow
A speckled hen
The squeaking mouse
The straw ox
The strongest in the world
Stumpy
The tailor-bird and the barber
The tailor-bird and the king
Talk; everything Ashanti farmer contacts starts to talk
Titty Mouse and Tatty Mouse
The turnip [huge; many help in pulling]
What the old man does is always right
The white pet
Who is the mightiest in the world?
The young gentleman and the tiger
Cunning. See CLEVERNESS; TRICKERY
The cunning Lapp
  Booss-*Scand.*, 334
Cunning mouth
  Todd-*Some*, 94–100
  Todd-*Tortoise*, 109–112
The cunning shoemaker
  Lang-*Pink/D*, 154–163
  Lang-*Pink/K*, 106–113
Cupid and Psyche
  Shah-*World*, 178–183
CUPIDITY
  The pointing finger
CUPS
  The altar-cup in Angerup
  The black horse
  Crater (the Cup)
  Ljungby horn and pipe
—fairy
  The fairy banquet [a]
  The fairy banquet [b]

CURANDEROS
—breaks command given by Death
  Dona Sebastiana
CURANDEROS (subject)
—Black magic
  MacLean-*Cuentos*, 70
A cure for jealousy
  Roberts-*Chinese*, 140–145
A cure for the "Evil Eye"
  Robertson-*Highland*, 89–90
Cured by a viper!
  Elbaz-*Folktales*, 121
Cures. *See* HEALING (cures)
Cures and remedies
  Steele-*Ozark*, 94–96
CURIOSITY
  The blue lake
  Bluebeard
  The duck with red feet
  Elephant's child
  Heinzelmanchen
  King Goldemar
  The other Celia
  Pandora
  The three counsels
  The ugly son-in-law
—feminine vice
  Blue Beard
Curiosity punished
  Keightley-*World*, 273–275
CURLEWS (bird)
—origin of long red legs
  Ouyan the curlew
Curse: an embowered sleep [one
  hundred years]
  Spells & Bind, 74–87
Curse at Lochgarry
  Robertson-*Highland*, 49–50
The curse [elk takes liver of new
  mother]
  Villa-*Armenian*, 352–354
The curse of a brahman
  Amore-*Lustful*, 74–75
The curse of Andvari's ring
  Crossley-*Legends*, 92–97
Curse of the devil's gold

MacLean-*Cuentos*, 62–66
Curse on the only son
  Zong-*Korea*, 51–54
Curses
  Robe-*Hispanic*, 54–56
CURSES
  Black monk's curse
  Brier Rose
  The day the sun did not rise
  Echo and Narcissus
  Fate of Frank M'Kenna
  Gesar of Ling
  Hildur, the queen of the elves
  How Sigourd awoke Brynhild
    upon Hindfell
  [Impregnation by earrings] Ara-
    ruga Paru
  King and the bishop
    [Clonmacnoise]
  Monkeys
  Poor Sandy [conjure woman]
  The Red Etin
  Saint Conall's stone
  Saint Patrick curses Ireland
  The seven-day vigil
  Simmer Water
  The skeleton in Holar church
  Sleeping Beauty in the woods
  The two wagoners
  Wedding feast of the little
    people
  A widow's curse
  The woman who cursed
    herself
—choice
  Eighteen rabbits
—king, knights, etc. turned to
    stone
  The rollright stones
—long nose
  Prince Dorus
—Sunday not kept holy
  The hurlers
—tigers to eat general's mother
  General Gim Dog-Nyong
Curtain, Jeremiah

Finn MacCumhail and the son
of the king of Alba
CURUPIRAS
Jack and the green lady
Wiley and the hairy man
CUSCUS
In the land of the dead
How a man found his wife in
Land of the Dead
Cusheen Loo [song]
Yeats-*Fairy*, 37–38
Cyclamen, Delphinium, Virginia
creeper
Ewart-*Lore*, 140–141
CYCLONES
Pecos Bill and the cyclone
CYCLOPES (giants)
Voyage of Odysseus
Cygnus (the Swan)
Gallant-*Constel.*, 52–
58
CYMRY (subject)
Keightley-*World*, 361–442
CYNICISM
The sadness of Cornelius Berg
Czarina frog
Stovicek-*Around*, 72–75
Czars. *See* TSARS
CZECHOSLOVAKIA
Domoviye
Leshiye and Lisunki
Moss people
Roosters, snakes and basiliscs

DA DERGA (god)
The destruction of Da Derga's
hostel
DACTYLS
Zan and the Dactyls in early
Crete
Daedalus
Low-*Greek*, 139–146

Stapleton-*Dictionary*, 60–62
DADELUS
Theseus, king of Athens
Daedalus: a fatal ascent
Magical Beasts, 64
Daffodils
Ewart-*Lore*, 13–15
[Dagda, Giant God of the Earth]
Lee-*Castles*, 54–55
DAGGERS
—seed of the
The fisher-prince with the sil-
ver apple
Dahl, Roald
Lamb to the slaughter
DAHLIAS
Sunflower, Michaelmas, daisy,
dahlia
The dahut [hunting prohibited]
Schwartz-*Tales*, 34–37
DAISIES
Sunflower, Michaelmas, daisy,
dahlia
The daisy
Ewart-*Lore*, 128–129
DAKSHA (creator god)
A goddess is born
Dale, Edward Everett, 1879–
1972.
Speech of the pioneers
Dame Soasan
Booss-*Scand.*, 252–256
DAMER, Joseph, 1630–1720.
O'Sullivan-*Legends*, 125–126
Dames vertes
Arrowsmith-*Field*, 32–33
DAMS
Adventures of Ntini, the small
otter
DANA, PEOPLE OF
Aristocratic fairies (condensed)
The magic people
Sidhe
DANA, PEOPLE OF (subject)
Logan-*Old*, 150 (index)
Danby, Mary

124

The secret ones
The dance and the song of the
    Korred
    Keightley-*World*, 438–442
The dance at Frisagard
    Lindow-*Swedish*, 151–152
Dance in a buffalo skull
    Zitkala-*Old*, 113–116
Dance of death
    Macmillan-*Canadian*, 100–102
Dance of the dead
    O'Sullivan-*Legends*, 60–62
Dance of the dead (condensed)
    Briggs-*Vanish.*, 164–165
Dance of the esqueletons
    MacLean-*Cuentos*, 66–70
The dance of the owls
    Griego-*Cuentos*, 143–151
The dance of the spectres
    Manning-*Spooks*, 118–122
The dance of the thirteen skeletons
    Hoke-*Spirits*, 63–66
The dancer of Etive
    Robertson-*Highland*, 14–15
DANCERS AND DANCING
    See also INDIANS OF NORTH
        AMERICA—dances; RAIN
        DANCES
    Andromeda dances
    Basket of Ngomba
    The blessed gift of joy
        bestowed upon man
    Bouki dances the kokioko
    Brer rabbit dances for a
        wife
    Country dance in the Ozarks in
        1874
    Coyote and the blackbirds
    The dance at Frisagard
        [unceasing]
    Dance of the dead
        (condensed)
    The dance of the spectres
    The dance of the thirteen
        skeletons
    The dancing bird Bralgah

Daughter of the stars
The devil goes to a dance [35
    legends]
The dwarfs' banquet
The elle-maids
Fairies of Corrie Chaorachain
    (condensed)
The fisherman and his soul
The girl at the troll-dance
Gitto Bach
Golden pears
Golden reed pipe [compelling
    dance]
The harga-dance [religious
    aspects]
The hill man at the dance
How an old man lost his wen
How the monkey escaped
    being eaten
King of the pipers and the
    wonderful tune
The lamb with the golden
    fleece
Little Ida's flowers
The man with the wen
Mossycoat
The nack's reel
Old Nick and the girl
Owl [ashamed of his face]
Poor turkey girl
Rhys at the fairy-dance
Scarface
Seven Simeons [brothers]
The Shrove Tuesday visitor
    [stop at midnight]
The sorcerer's dance
The sorceress
Star Maiden
The steadfast tin soldier [bal-
    let; paper]
Strangers (condensed)
Sunday and Whirlway maiden
Twelve dancing daughters
The twelve dancing princesses
The twelve princesses
The white gander

Why all prairie dogs are brown
Why dogs sniff each other's
   tails
The woman of the sea
The young man in the shian
—elves
   The elves' dance
   Sir Olof in the elve-dance
—"scalp dance"
   Deer woman
DANCERS AND DANCING
   (subject)
—fairies
   Briggs-*Vanish.*, 215 (index)
The dancing bird Bralgah
   Parker-*Australian*, 126–
   130
Dancing in Dalarna
   Lindow-*Swedish*, 150–151
The dancing princess
   Crouch-*Whole*, 93–100
The dandelion [beloved of the
   South Wind]
   Stovicek-*Around*, 157
DANDELIONS
   Kosi, the eagle, and the moun-
    tain lion
   Odd jobs
   South Wind and his golden-
    haired love
DANES
   Edmund the holy
   Ednoth's relics, and Thurkill's
    beard
DANGER
   Adventures of Ntini, the small
    otter
   Belling the cat
   The chain
   Country mouse and city
    mouse
   The rocks of Korsan
—fool doesn't see
   The sky is falling
—overcoming
   The eight-forked serpent

Dan-Gun, first king of Korea
   Zong-*Korea*, 3–4
Daniel O'Connell [justice,
   cleverness]
   O'Sullivan-*Legends*, 127–128
Daniel O'Connell [trickery]
   O'Sullivan-*Legends*, 128–131
Daniel O'Rourke
   Yeats-*Fairy*, 90–96
DANTE Alighieri
   Castles in the Inferno
"DAOINE SHI"
   The fairy's inquiry
Daoine Shi
   Mckee-*Scottish*, 12–17
DAOINE SIDHE
   Hurling
   The immortal fairy folk
   Jemmy Doyle in the fairy
    palace
   Tuatha de Danann
Darakhvei, the great oak
   Cortes-*Byelorussian*, 91–95
Daring the sea-gods' realm
   Water Spirits, 36–59
The dark of the sea
   Haining-*Lepre.*, 35–37
DARKNESS
   The crow and the daylight
   Knockers
   Leppa Polkry and the blue
    cross
   Raven steals the light
   The red czar and the golden-
    haired Tihota
DARRELL, John, 1562–1602.
   The "Kissing witch"
Date stone; a Han story
   Seven Sisters, 1–5
The daughter and the helper
   Timpanelli-*Tales*, 15–27
The daughter of Peter de Cabinam
   Keightley-*World*, 456–
   457
Daughter of the moon
   McCarty-*Skull*, 47–51

Daughter of the stars
    Wade-*Indian,* 11–20
DAUGHTERS
    The beastly creature and the
        magical flower
    The black bull of Norroway
    The eight-forked serpent
    Fair, brown, and trembling
    Fenist the bright-eyed falcon
    Gertrude and Rosy
    Gold-tree and Silver-
        tree
    Gulnara the Tartar warrior
    Mally Whuppy
    A mother's yarn
    "O luck of the ugly . . ."
    On top of Old Smoky [song
        and story]
    Rosy apple and the golden
        bowl
    Snow White and Rose Red
    The story of Deirdre
    The story of Jon Asmundsson
    The three daughters
    The three daughters and the
        lost cow
    The twins of Paikala Mountain
    What shall baby's name
        be?
    The white rooster
—craves father's love
    The lady and the merman
—disrespectful
    Owl with the face of a woman
—kept isolated from men
    Nature's ways
—left in cold to die
    Grandfather Frost
—made pregnant by monk
    The three stars
—pledged as bride to ogre
    The enchanted orchard
—sacrificed
    King Crocodile
—sold, to support father's evil
        ways

    The boy and the robbers' mag-
        ical booty
DAUGHTERS-IN-LAW
    The bride who would not
        speak
    The chao ku bird
    The devoted son
    [Daughters nightly go to Under-
        world . . . dance of death]
        Spells & Bind, 109–117
"DAUGHTERS OF THE AIR"
    The little mermaid
DAVID, King
    King David and the giant
    King David matches wits with
        Angel of Death
    Ways of providence are
        inscrutable
DAVID, King (subject)
    Patai-*Gates,* 775 (index)
DAVID Ben Baruk, d.1760.
    Cured by a viper!
    Rabbi David Ben Baruk,
        candle-salesman
Davidson, D. S.
    To kill Windigo
Davy Crockett, king of the old wild
        west
        Lister-*Tall,* 38–45
DAWN
    Anpao is born
    Leppa Polkry and the blue
        cross
    Night and day
    The dawn of the world
        Highwater-*Anpao,* 45–83
DAY
    See also DAYLIGHT
    Gumiya; a Blang story: origins
        of characteristics
    Night and day
Day dreaming. *See*
        DAYDREAMING
The day El Diablo ripped the earth
        asunder
        MacLean-*Cuentos,* 39–44

Day of the dead
 Wright-*Gold*, 36–41
The day the sun did not rise
 Amore-*Lustful*, 68–70
Day the sun rose in the west
 Kudian-*More*, 32–40
The day Tuk became a hunter
 De Wit-*Talking*, 174–
 177
DAYDREAMING
 See also ABSENT-
 MINDEDNESS; FANTASY
 The country maid and her
 milkpail
 Don't beat your children before
 they're born
 Milkmaid and the bucket of
 milk
 Milkmaid and the pail
DAYLIGHT
 The crow and the daylight
 How raven brought fire to the
 Indians
 Photogen and Nycteris; a
 day/night mahrchen
 Raven lets out the daylight
 Sun and the children
Daylight saving time
 McCarthy-*Raccoon*, 35–41
De Jong, Meindert
 Far out the long canal
De la Potherie, Bacqueville
 Onaouientagos
The deacon of Myrka
 Booss-*Scand.*, 653–655
DEAD
 See also CORPSES; DEATH;
 GHOSTS; RESUSCITATION
 Baitogogo and Akaruio Boroge
 go to rule land of the dead
 The bird 'Grip'
 Cat and dog and return of the
 dead
 The crowd
 Dance of the dead
 (condensed)

Hades, lord of the underworld
How a man found his wife in
 the Land of the Dead
In the graveyard
Old Dry Frye (rogue preacher)
Persephone among the dead
Rendezvous with a death ship
Sluagh (condensed)
Soul cages (condensed)
The soul-eater
The stone statue
The story of Deirdre
Wife who ate the wrong
 porridge
A youth set out to learn what
 fear was
—child restored to life
 Saint Martin's Eve [b]
—choice of life
 The skull
—could be revived . . .
 Sleeping warrior [fear: to return
 to life]
—"dead" man as companion
 The travelling companion
—father rewards dutiful son
 Glass mountain
—footprints
 Only a dream
—forgiveness of
 Finn blood
—husband persuaded that he is
 dead
 The two old women's bet
—land of; no living person
 enters
 In the land of the dead
—Land of the Dead Departed
 Coyote brings fire to The
 People
—man to dog to man
 Servant in the monastery
—mourning for
 Origin of gourd trumpet,
 memento of the dead
—no dead in Land of Shadows

128

DEAD (continued)
The boy in the Land of
Shadows
—prayers for the
The bundle of straw
—protection against threat of
Christmas service of the dead
—reduced to dust by spectre
The little old man in the tree
—restored to life
The descent of Inanna
The feast of the mountain
goats
Flight of the eagle
Giant of the great water
Herb of life
Lochman Hehkeem, the great
healer
Only One, the great shaman
The singing bone
The swan of Tuonela
—sorcerer
Master Log
—unregenerate sinners
Dance of the esqueletons
—visit to dead brother in grave
The two brothers
—visitor gives warning
The San Francisco earthquake
DEAD (subject)
—fairies and
Briggs-*Vanish.*, 215 (index)
The dead bridegroom
Lindow-*Swedish*, 191–193
Dead couple marry after death
O'Sullivan-*Legends*, 62–64
The dead defend their cemetery
Elbaz-*Folktales*, 43
The dead man's debt
O'Sullivan-*Legends*, 67–69
The dead man's nightcap
Crossley-*Folk*, 90–91
Dead mother/children come for
dying father
O'Sullivan-*Legends*, 93–95
A dead princess and seven giants

Pushkin-*Fairy*, 54–81
Dead snake and young wife
Villa-*Armenian*, 374–375
The dead soldier
Haining-*Lepre.*, 78–79
A dead son
Roberts-*Chinese*, 149
DEAF
The orphan boy and the elk
dog
—fairies make woman
deaf
Jamie Freel and the young
lady
DEANS
The charcoal burner
DEARG-DUA
The terror of the red blood
sucker
DEATH
See also ANGEL OF DEATH;
BANSHEES; BURIALS;
CEMETERIES; CORPSES;
DEAD; FUNERALS;
MURDER; RESUSCITA-
TION; VIOLENT DEATH;
WAKES; WATER OF
DEATH
Abuelita's bell
The apprentice [rabbit as
painter]
The bearded rock
The Black Dog [death to touch]
The boarded window [by
Bierce]
The boy who laughed at death
Caladrius: powers of foretelling
Charity can change a man's
fate
The city of Luz [blue dye:
Tekhelet]
The cuckoo
The curse of a brahman
[Daughters nightly go to under-
world: dance of death]
The dawn of the world

Day of the dead
Dead mother/children come for
dying father
Deer Hunter and White Corn
Maiden
Deer woman
The devoted bride
Dona Sebastiana
The enchanted apple tree
The end of Marko Kraljevic
Fairies and Frank Martin
The fairy fetch [apparition]
Foretelling the future [written
on forehead]
The god of faces
Godfather death (Germany)
Goha on the deathbed (Egypt)
Golden lads
The happy prince
He comes from the east
His just reward
How Abosom, the lesser gods,
came into the world
How evil produces evil
The hungry peasant, God, and
death (Mexico)
Hyena engages a strange-
farmer
Julio
Jump into my sack (Italy)
Kalele the Bold Wisher
The land where time stood still
The last love of Prince Genji
Leaving home
The lure of the marsh lights
La madrina muerte
Maui seeking immortality
The mortal lord
Mysterious palace [Solomon
and Ramirat]
The nightingale
Occasion [death trapped in
bottle]
Okiku and the saucers
Origin of the poari
Pedro de Ordimalas

The Pleiades
Prince Meerzat Istvan and the
horse of dust . . .
Prophecy: Wan and the Great
Wall of China
Rabbi Haim Pinto predicts a
man's death
The ride of the headless
phantom
The secret ones
The selfish giant
The skull
Snowflake [snowchild comes
to life]
The spirit-wife
Stagolee
A story about death
The straight road: Christmas in
heaven
A tale of love
Tearless woman cries on
seeing the devil
Tia Miseria's pear tree
A time for everything
The triumph of death
Tungustapi
Twin brothers
Two sisters and a harlot
The wailing messenger of
death
The wolves of Cernogratz
The wow o'Rivven; the
bell
The young king
Youth without age and life
without death (Turkey)
—accidental; appointed
time
Banshee of the MacCarthys
—all equally subject to
Papa God and General Death
—apparent
Anpu and Bata
Banshee of the MacCarthys
The merchant's fortune
Princess in the chest [coffin]

130

DEATH (continued)
    Snow White and the seven
      dwarfs
    Sulphur water: El Paso de los
      Robles
—cause
    Glooskap and Malsum, the
      wolf
—cowboy's last request
    The parting song
—devil bears news of impending
    Wild huntsman
—devil summons priest
    The devil does a good deed
—escape from witch
    Vulnerable spot
—excessive mourning
    The power of sorrow
—foretold
    The geomancer's three sons
    The prince and the three
      fates
—humor
    The illiterate priest
—inevitable
    Donald of the Burthens
—of mermaids
    The little mermaid
—of newborn child
    Birth, dreaming, death: school-
      master's story
—origin
    How sickness came
    Kintu tested before he could
      marry
    Origin of death: chameleon
    Origin of death [Hottentot]
    Origin of death: Krachi
    Snake [steals skin of everlast-
      ing life]
    Up from the Dead Land
    Why there is death [Nikoduma]
    Woman chooses death
—prayers for priest answered
    The Spanish sailor
—pretense

The biter bit
Bury me in England [fake-
    dying wish; humor]
The dilemma [corpse]
Giufo's debts
Gohc Amu and the matzoon
The greedy father
The hemp smoker, Zimwam-
    banje
The King's favourite and the
    beautiful slave
Story of Campriano (Italy)
Young man who was carred
    off by a lion
—prophecy: husband to die in one
    year
    Savatri and the god of death
—returning to state of
    Bahloo the moon, and the
      Daens
—in snowstorm
    Fate of Frank M'Kenna
—trapped in sack
    The soldier and death
—wife outwits God of Death
    Dialogue with death
DEATH (subject)
    Zong-*Korea,* 249 (index)
—caused by fairies
    Briggs-*Vanish.,* 215 (index)
—Celtic beliefs
    McKee-*Scottish,* 38–43
—Highland vision
    Robertson-*Highland,* 172–177
—Omens, warnings and fetches
    Marshall-*Every.,* 40, 104
—personified
    Briggs-*Vanish.,* 24
—[Whispering about mortality]
    Yolen-*Favorite,* 447
Death and punishment [Kabbala]
    Patai-*Gates,* 439–450
Death and revival of Meri
    Wilbert-*Bororo,* 34–36
Death and the dead
    Robe-*Hispanic,* 57–79

Death and the doctor
   Booss-*Scand.*, 134–136
Death and the soldier
   Riordan-*Russia*, 115–126
[Death chooses the best (humor)]
   Yolen-*Favorite*, 465
The death coach
   Haining-*Lepre.*, 40–41
Death comes at a trot
   Aiken-*Mexican*, 156–159
Death of a miser (Russia)
   Yolen-*Favorite*, 466
The death of Abraham Azulai
   Patai-*Gates*, 643–645
The death of Alfe's only son
   Gantz-*Early*, 147–152
The death of Balder
   Branston-*Gods*, 134–140
The death of Chanticleer
   Booss-*Scand.*, 121–124
Death of King Arthur
   Riordan-*Arthur*, 114–123
The death of little Kiko
   Sheohmelian-*Three*, 11–14
Death of Moses
   Patai-*Gates*, 321–326
The death of the Chimaera
   Gibson-*Gods*, 129–132
The death of Windigo
   Colombo-*Wind.*, 204–207
Death omens
   Steele-*Ozark*, 84
Death out of season
   Hoke-*Horrors*, 164–171
Death penalty. *See* CAPITAL
   PUNISHMENT
Death rides a black horse
   MacLean-*Cuentos*, 56–58
Death to the giant snake
   Reed-*Aboriginal*, 15–19
The death waltz
   Stuchl-*American*, 95–97
Death's substitute
   Amore-*Lustful*, 123–125
DEBTORS
   The fly (as witness)

DEBTS
—personal
   The dead man's debt
   Gohc Amu and the toot
   The poor man Monokto
—prepaid
   Giufo's debts
Deceit. *See* DECEPTION;
   DISLOYALTY; HYPOCRISY
DECEPTION
   See also IMPOSTERS;
   TRICKERY
   Ant and lizard [origin of
      enmity]
   The bad wife [in bottomless
      pit] (Russia)
   Badger and the green giant
   The bag of money
   The Bakororo and Itubore leg-
      end [pretended-betrothed]
   The biter bit
   Blue bird [King Charming]
   Bouki dances the kokioko
   The boy who ate more than
      the giant
   The cat and mouse in
      partnership
   Chavalai: taboos and decep-
      tion [servant claims credit]
   The clever bride [theft of chick
      peas]
   Clever Yaro
   Coyote fights a lump of pitch
   A crippled hero [false friend
      takes tsar's daughter]
   Daniel O'Rourke
   Darakhvei, the great oak
      [tsar's children]
   The dervish and the thief
   The devil and the female
   Devil's tale
   Dinewan the emu, and the
      bustard
   The donkey who hit his mother
      [thieves]
   Double-headed phoenix

132

DECEPTION (continued)
The everlasting frogs [daughters turned to]
The eye can deceive
Farmer and the badger
The fleetest of foot
Flying horse [wooden; deceiver foiled]
The foolish weaver and the jackal
The foolish young Mussulman
The fox and the little white hen
Frightened wolves [wolf head]
Genjias [three with same name]
The girl with the silver voice [evil brother substituted]
The glass diamond
Gold colt and the fire dragon shirt
Goonur, the woman-doctor
Goophered grapevine
Halibut Man and the house on the waves
The hare, Nwashisisana
Helle and Phrixus
Horse and toad
How a bear kept reindeer
How a peasant cured his wife of telling tales
How a youth lost his virtue
How Donald Solomon became state deputy
How the moolah was taught a lesson
The illiterate priest
Ivan and Nastasia [scrubbing off sin]
Jack the Giant Killer
Jackals and the tiger
The jaguar and the cricket
Jha's nail
Kenkebe
King of the pomegranate tree

The King's favourite and the beautiful slave [death pretended]
King's son goes bear hunting (Finland)
The landlord and the muzhik
Lazarus and the dragons
The lazy husband, Ngurmi [II]
The lion and the hare
Lion tamer [Tibetan]
Lizard and crocodile
Lox, the mischief maker
Magic figs
The magic mirror
Maiden Bright-Eye
Majantali Sarkar
The man who sold his goat
The men who wouldn't stay dead (France)
The miller and the fox
The miller's three sons
"Of course!"
The open window [by Saki]
The ostler and the grave robbers (Scotland)
Ouyan the curlew
The peasant and his goat [cumulative; humor]
Pelican babies
The prayer that was answered
Prince of nettles
Pursuit of Numeuk the hunter
Puss in Boots
Rabbit and the berries
Redbreasts: The Gwineeboos
Roast duckling [to cover guilt]
Sedna, the witch under the sea
Sheep, lamb, wolf, and the hare
The shrew
Sidna Mussa
Slave girl tried to kill her mistress
Sneaky, straight, and the tree
The sorcerer's dance

Story of a gentleman['s wife]
Story of Campriano (Italy)
The story of Zibong
The strong man
Sun and moon
The sun and the moon [tiger
  pretends to be mother]
The three brothers [camel
  stolen & butchered]
The topknot pigeons,
  Goolahwilleel
The tortoise and the monkey
Triplets [Light Foot, Skilful
  Hand, Keen Eye]
Truth and falsehood
  [personified]
Turtle feeds his children
The two old women's bet
The ugly son
Ukrainian tale [grief: imagined
  future woes]
Unwelcome neighbour [broth-
  ers frighten him off]
What happened to Ivan
Why Bootup, the whale,
  smokes a pipe
Why the hare runs away
The wise old crow
Wolf and the seven kids
Yeghnig Aghpar [pretense of
  prince's wife]
Yesterday's witch [Miss
  Marble]
DECEPTION (subject)
—Motif index
  Wilbert-*Bororo*, 230, 260–264,
  287
DEDUCTION (logic)
  The clever brothers
  The deer thief
  Judgements of a magistrate
  King's/servant's sons switched
  The lost camel
  One word solves a mystery
DEE, John, *d.* 1608.
—Magician in spite of himself

Sergeant-*Witches*, 185–227
Dee, Roger
  The anglers of Arz
Deeg: One way to catch a fish
  Villa-*Armenian*, 354–355
DEER
  See also FAWNS
  Adventures of the third dervish
    [a]
  Anpao and the animals
  The banyan deer [the Buddha]
  The doe, the hunter, and the
    great stag
  Good faith
  Her lover's heart
  How Saynday got the sun
  Katchen the cat
  Kintaro, the golden boy
  Maidens (condensed)
  Munachar and Manachar
  Munachar and the raspberries
  The princess in the ivory tower
  Quest of the white hart
  Shooting the moon; a Yao
    folktale
  Sky high went the sun
  The sure shot
  The white doe
  Why the tiger and the stag fear
    each other
  Woodcutter and the heavenly
    maiden
—brother transformed to stag
  Crystal coffin
—bucks
  The enchanted buck
—dancing
  Raven brings fire
—goes to live in sky
  Rainbow and the autumn
    leaves
—Golden Hind
  The hunting of the hind
—grows cherry tree instead of
  antlers
  Munchausen and the buck

134

DEER (continued)
—race with lizard
How the lizard got its hat
—saved, gives useful information
Heavenly maiden and the
wood cutter
—steals bag of money
The Mauritanian and his
wealth
The deer and the snake
Zong-*Korea,* 94–95
Deer and Vila
Keightley-*World,* 493–494
Deer Hunter and White Corn
Maiden
Yolen-*Favorite,* 121–123
The deer in the dream
Roberts-*Chinese,* 83–84
A deer king offers his life
Amore-*Lustful,* 65–68
The deer, the hare, and the toad
Zong-*Korea,* 33–34
The deer thief
Griego-*Cuentos,* 127–129
Deer woman
Highwater-*Anpao,* 159–167
DEFEAT
—in battle
The haughty chief
DEFECATION
The young man and the talking
skull
DeFord, Miriam Allen
Not snow nor rain
DEFORMITIES
Boy with the deformed head
The crooked-mouthed family
Prince Dorus
—club foot; no marriage
How Hoof Lake got its name
—origin
Crookened back [pooka]
—putative
The two pickpockets
Defrauding. *See* CHEATING
Degei and his sons

Shelley-*Legends,* 78–81
Deirdre
Lochhead-*Battle,* 17–29
Deirdre and Naoise
Lehane-*Legends,* 51–56
McGarry-*Folk,* 43–55
DEIS-IUIL (subject)
Mckee-*Scottish,* 32
Deities. *See* GODS AND
GODDESSES
Deliverance. *See* RESCUES
Deliverance from magic's coils
Spells & Bind, 88–123
DELPHI
Artemis and Apollo
DELPHIAN ORACLE
Apollo and the Oracle at
Delphi
DELPHIAN ORACLE (subject)
Pinsent-*Greek,* 142 (in-
dex)
Delphic oracle
Stapleton-*Dictionary,* 64–
65
DELPHINIUM
Cyclamen, Delphinium, Virginia
creeper
Delphinus (the Dolphin)
Gallant-*Constel.,* 95–97
Delsbo's churchbell [Sweden]
Lindow-*Swedish,* 61–63
Deluge (Biblical) *See* FLOOD
(Biblical)
DELUSION
Coyote and the blackbirds
The little soldier
The Wasgo and three killer
whales
DEMETER
Persephone
Persephone among the dead
Demon cat
Yeats-*Fairy,* 209–210, 293
Demon of energy
Baskin-*Imps,* 30–31
The demon princess

Schwartz-*Elijah*, 107–117
DEMONIC POSSESSION
See also EXORCISM
The haunted well
Partnership with Asmodeus
Possessed by devil [daughters
of J Baldwin]
Princess in the chest [coffin]
DEMONS
See also DEVIL(S); INCUBUS;
JINN; LILITH (female de-
mon); RAKHOSES (demons)
Adultery with the "demon"
Air-demons and Fergus
O'Mara
The Black General
The brahman and the demons
Buried alive to stop the plague
Callicantzaroi
Choril and Cholchinay
The cripple
Curse of the devil's gold
The dark of the sea
The daughter of Peter de
Cabinam
Death and the soldier
The descent of Inanna
Disappearing apples [of
immortality]
The disrespectful son
The emerald Buddha
The enchanted fountain
The evil eye
The goddess who drank blood
Gods and demons
The grant
A great misfortune
The haunted pavilion
How an old man lost his wen
The hunchback's hump
The hunted hare
The island of beautiful women
The Jerusalemite's story cop-
ied by R. Abraham
King Solomon and Asmodeus
Konyek and his father [Masai]

Lady White and Shushuan
Legions of the night
Magic flute of Asmodeus
The man who never knew
fear
The man with the wen
The night bird
The ogre's soul
Portunes
Puck
The Santa Lucias [demon-
foundling; legend]
Shuralee the wood demon
The talking fish
Tobias goes on a journey
The sparrow with the slit-
tongue
Tripitaka: quest of the Buddhist
scriptures
The ugly son
The white rooster
—chatter unbearable to
Talkative wife
—Hiranyakashipu
A boon of immortality
—horned
Momotaro, or the son of a
peach
—in form of baby
The baby with the fangs [13
legends]
—passion turns lady into mon-
strous serpent
The monk and Lady Kiyo
DEMONS (subject)
Patai-*Gates*, 775 (index)
Scott-*Fantastic*, 191–192
Denham tracts (condensed)
Briggs-*Vanish.*, 119–120
Denizens of faerie
Froud-*Faeries*, unp.
DENMARK
The bottle-neck
Church grims
The elf of the rose
Ellefolk

DENMARK (continued)
    The flying trunk
    The girl clad in mouseskin
    The girl who trod on the loaf
    The goblin and the huckster
    Heinzelmannchen and
        Hutchen
    The little chicken Kluk and his
        companions
    Little Claus and Big Claus
    The little mermaid
    Little Tuk
    The magician's pupil
    The marsh king's daughter
    The master of Ugerup
    The nightingale
    The old house
    The outlaw
    Peter Bull
    The Pleiades
    The rocks of Korsan
    She was good for nothing
    Singard the dragon-slayer
    Soup from a sausage skewer
    A stork is not always a stork
    The story of trembling hood
    The swine herd
    Temptations
    The tinder-box
    Toller's neighbors
    The troll's hammer
    The ugly duckling
    The wild swans
DENMARK (subject)
—fairies and
    Briggs-*Vanish.*, 215 (index)
"DEO GRATIAS"
    Saint Patrick and Crom Dubh
Departure of the fairies
    Keightley-*World*, 356−357
Departure of the giants (Africa)
    Yolen-*Favorite*, 352−353
Departure of the trolls from
        Vendsyssel
    Keightley-*World*, 127−
        128

DEPENDENCE
    Frost, Sun, and Wind
Derleth, August
    Ithaqua
    The Metronome
    The thing that walked on the
        wind
The Dervish and the fakir
    Shah-*Dervishes*, 35−46
The dervish and the thief
    Wood-*Kalila*, 63−78
DERVISHES
    Axad Bakht meets the
        dervishes
    Azad Bakht's tale
    Halva-maker
    The magic candelabra
    Quick-witted [boy outsmarts
        evil dervish]
    Wisely spent
—takes 7-year-old son
    The nine-seeded apple
The descent of Inanna
    Wolkstein-*Inanna*, 51−89
Desecrators of Rabbi Haim Mes-
        sas' tomb
    Elbaz-*Folktales*, 42
DESERTS
    The drowned boys
DESIRE(S)
    See also COVETING
    Kali beheaded
    The monk and Lady Kiyo
    Saga of Santiago Sanchez
    Samba the Satan and Omadi
        the Righteous
    The wind cap
—foolish
    Iktomi and the fawn
—object turns out to be right at
        hand
    Rat's bridegroom
The desolate island
    Shah-*World*, 114−115
DESPOTISM
    The tragic story of Antigone

Destiny
Aiken-*Mexican,* 138–141
Mitchnik-*Egyptian,* 1–13
Destiny [subject]. *See* FATE
DESTRUCTION
Curiosity punished
—of household goods
The cows who came to tea
The destruction of Da Derga's
hostel
Gantz-*Early,* 60–106
The destruction of love
Amore-*Lustful,* 84–86
The destruction of the world
Amore-*Lustful,* 170–171
DETACHMENT
The ascetic and the deer
The ascetic who visited home
The destruction of the world
The dying Buddha's
compassion
The man who didn't notice
women
DETACHMENT (subject)
—Buddhist stories
Amore-*Lustful,* 169
—Hindu Stories
Amore-*Lustful,* 163–164
DETECTIVES
Lamb to the slaughter
Detroit. *See under* MICHIGAN
Deucalion and Pyrrha and the
great flood
Low-*Greek,* 26–29
DEVI
The goddess who drank blood
The devil
Colombo-*Wind.,* 8–9
Robe-*Hispanic,* 145–219
DEVIL(S)
See also DEMONS; EXOR-
CISM; SATANISM
The bad wife [in bottomless
pit] (Russia)
Banca Flor
Bishop Svedberg and the devil

The black bull of Norroway
The black dog of Creag an
Ordain
The black lady
Black monk's curse
[Black school (Satan's) for
wizards]
The brave clever tailor
El caballo negro muy
magnifico
Captain Murderer and the de-
vil's bargain [by Dickens]
The card player
Cardplayers and the devil
Clever man and ordinary
The day El Diablo ripped the
earth asunder
Death and the doctor
Death of a miser (Russia)
Devil with the three golden
hairs
Downfall of the mighty hunter
The fiddler and the fairy
The fiddler and the sea nymph
Four hairs from the beard of
the devil
The genesis of the Hid-folk
Girls at parsonage get help
sewing crinoline
Giving the devil a ride
The greedy youngster
The hakham and the tam
How El Bizarron fooled the
devil
Is much land needed for a
man?
Juan fetches the devil
Jump into my sack (Italy)
Katrineholm Manor
Kile Bamba and the Loche
bogatyr
The lad and the devil
Lox and the chief's wife
Lure of the pipes [Big John
Clach-na-Harnich and Black
Simon]

DEVIL(S) (continued)
  March cock banishes the devil
  The old crone who was more
    wily than Iblees
  Old Erik in the mill
  Old Nick and the girl
  Old Nick and the pedlar
  Old Nick is a gentleman
  Old woman's faith overcomes
    devil
  "One, my darling, come to
    mama"
  Outwitting the devil
  Parson and the clerk [island in
    Devon]
  The peasant and the fiend
  Pierre, Prince of Murom
  Pilar's indiscretion
  A priest and his servant Balda
  Puck
  The Ram [devil as creator]
  The rich ranchero's maguey
    fence
  Saint Michael wins a soul from
    devil
  Satan and the boy
  Shaitan the devil and his forty
    daughters
  The Shrove Tuesday visitor
  The skilful brothers
  The sly devil
  The smith and the devil
  The snow queen
  Tearless woman cries on
    seeing the devil
  The tooth of gold
  The ways of a witch
  Why the sea is salt
  Wicked John and the devil
  Wiley and the hairy man
  Wine and the devil
  The word the devil made up
    ("Unh hunh")
  The young man and the talking
    skull
—Barkantz
  The fox and the Barkantz
—buys souls
  Countess Kathleen O'Shea
—can't stand shrew
  The shrew
—castrated
  Paleschuk and the devil
—cheating the
  The peasant and the devil
—compact with. *See below*—pact
    with
—contract with
  King Lindorm [a snake]
—demands
  Banca Flor
—female
  A sort of werewolf
—in form of greyhound
  Fairy greyhound
—godfather
  Godfather death (Germany)
—guess his name
  Duffy and the devil
—humor
  One for you, one for me
—informer of baby son's death
  Wild huntsman
—loses at cards
  The soldier and death
—Lucifer
  The fairies [war in heaven]
—origin of cloven foot
  The devil's cloven foot
—outsmarted
  The cobbler and the devil
  Jack and the devil's daugh-
    ter
  The old smith
  The tailor and the deev
—pact with
  And they wondered
  Bearskin (Germany)
  The boy who laughed at death
  Coals on the devil's hearth
    (Ireland)
  The devil's hide [temper]

Don Giovanni de la Fortuna
Herne the hunter
King Eagle
Lawyer and the devil (Ireland)
The priest goes down to hell
Partnership with Asmodeus
Revenge of Joaquina
That her children might be fed
Three wishes [of Billy Dawson]
—as piper; dancers unable to stop
Wedding at Stanton Drew
—prayed to, for a child
Stumpy
—praying for
Pablito prays for El Senor
Diablo
—refuses to keep shrewish wife
The devil and the farmer's wife
—Samael
King who fought many wars
The rabbi's son [in disguise]
—selling soul to
Countess Kathleen O'Shea
Devil's mill
El Diablo, el chivo, y Senor
Bonifacio
The general and the devil
The pulque vendor tricks the
devil
The rich rancher's maguey
fence
[Roger Bacon foils Satan]
—souls won from, in card
game
Saint Martin's Eve [b]
—takes over village well
The well-digger and the deev
—trapped in sack
The soldier and death
—trapped inside nut
The lad and the devil (Norway)
—tricked
Head devil in Texas [satire]
Paleschuk and the devil
—"troublemaker"
Atam and Im

—whirlwind
The devil and his
entanglements
—as wild stallion
Give me something you
have . . . unawares
—woman outsmarts the
Clever Gretchen
DEVIL(S) (subject)
Briggs-*Vanish.*, 215 (index)
Lindow-*Swedish*, 43–48, 217
Marshall-*Every.*, 39–40, 87
O'Sullivan-*Legends*, 21
Patai-*Gates*, 797 (index)
—Fooling the devil
Yolen-*Favorite*, 447
—Rogue
McKee-*Scottish*, 29–30
The devil advises suicide
Lindow-*Swedish*, 154
The devil and his agents
Robertson-*Highland*, 113–115
The devil and his entanglements
Ritchie-*Armadillo*, 11–14
The devil and Kitta Gra
Lindow-*Swedish*, 174–176
The devil and the farmer's wife
Sanders-*Hear*, 110–119
The devil and the female
Cortes-*Byelorussian*, 107–
110
The devil and the old hag
Stovicek-*Around*, 52–53
The devil as a black dog
Lindow-*Swedish*, 147–148
The devil as a cat
O'Sullivan-*Legends*, 23–25
The devil as the fourth wheel
Lindow-*Swedish*, 157–158
The devil described
Robertson-*Highland*, 115–
116
The devil does a good deed
Campos-*Mexican*, 28–30
Devil fish: a tentacled invader
Water Spirits, 66–67

The devil goes to a dance [35
  legends]
  Robe-*Hispanic*, 175–201
The devil in guise of the Blessed
  Virgin
  O'Sullivan-*Legends*, 22–23
The devil in the church
  Lindow-*Swedish*, 159–161
The devil invented alcoholic drink
  O'Sullivan-*Legends*, 31–32
"DEVIL KING"
  Magic knife [Uygur]
Devil: the long spoon
  Yeats-*Fairy*, 210–211
Devil with the three golden hairs
  Yolen-*Favorite*, 212–217
DEVIL WORSHIP
  Worship of the devil
Devil's armful [Canterbury]
  Marshall-*Every.*, 96–99
The devil's bargain
  Fattoross-*Simpleton*, 25–29
The devil's cloven foot
  O'Sullivan-*Legends*, 34–35
DEVIL'S DANDY DOGS (subject)
  Briggs-*Vanish.*, 76, 151, 195
The devil's dark legions
  Haining-*Lepre.*, 119–123
DEVIL'S DAUGHTER(S)
  Banca Flor
  The fern girl
  Give me something you
    have . . . unawares
  Lion tamer [Tibetan]
  Little old women with five cows
"DEVIL'S FROTH"
  The devil invented alcoholic
    drink
The devil's herd
  MacLean-*Cuentos*, 58–62
The devil's hide [temper]
  Yolen-*Favorite*, 378–386
Devil's jewels; the devil's Teakettle
  Steele-*Ozark*, 56–58
DEVIL'S MANUAL
  The story of Jon Asmundsson

Devil's mill
  Yeats-*Fairy*, 335–340
DEVIL'S MOTHER
  The cat and the dog
  Lough Derg
The devil's own [dragon]
  Marshall-*Every.*, 335–340
The devil's supper: Taghairm
  Robertson-*Highland*, 119–120
Devil's tale
  Sampson-*Gypsy*, 13–15
The devil's yellehr [sic]
  Villa-*Armenian*, 392–393
The devoted bride
  Patai-*Gates*, 565–568
The devoted friend
  Wilde-*Fairy*, 42–59
The devoted son
  Villa-*Armenian*, 315–321
Devotion. *See* LOVE
The dewdrop tiara
  Stovicek-*Around*, 92–93
DEW-DROPS
  —blue-breaks spell
  The enchanted forest
DHARMA
  Buddha sets the wheel in motion
DHARMA (subject)
  —Buddhist stories
    Amore-*Lustful*, 76
  —Five duties
    Amore-*Lustful*, 93–94
El Diablo, el chivo, y Senor
    Bonifacio
  MacLean-*Cuentos*, 3–36
Dialogue with death
  Rungachary-*Tales*, 3–17
The diamond
  Perrault-*Glass*, 46–50
  Soyer-*Adventures*, 37–
    41
"DIAMOND BUTTON"
  Little rooster and the Turkish
    sultan
DIAMONDS
  The glass diamond

Supparaka
Diarmid and Grania
Lochhead-*Battle,* 45–48
Diarmuid and Grainne
McGarry-*Folk,* 81–85
Ross-*Druids,* 57–59
Diarmuid, son of Donn: a spell-
shackled devotion
Spells & Bind, 125–139
Dick o' Tunstead
Marshall-*Every.,* 136–
138
Dick Whittington and his cat
Lang-*Blue,* 217–226 (notes,
369)
Pierce-*Larousse,* 131–143
Rackham-*Fairy,* 26–36
Shah-*World,* 12–17
Dickens, Charles
Captain Murderer and the de-
vil's bargain
DIEGO, Juan, *fl.* 1531
The virgin of Guadalupe
Dietrich and the dwarf-king's castle
Lee-*Castles,* 134–136
Dietrich of Bern
Crossley-*Legends,* 69–77
Dietrich [of Verona]; castle of the
Ice Queen
Lee-*Castles,* 131–133
Different times have different
'adans'
Mitchnik-*Egyptian,* 21–22
DIFFICULTIES
Bird of happiness
The black bull of Norroway
Mushkil Gusha: remover of all
difficulties
The two elephants
—as good experiences
The mouse at the seashore
—psychological reaction
Woe Bogotir
DIJUN (god)
Chang'o and the elixir of
immortality

The early heroes: Yi, ten suns,
monsters
The dilemma [corpse-pretense]
Villa-*Armenian,* 375–376
DILEMMAS
Best liar in the land
On naming a son [Joseph]
Tall tales (Burma)
Dilly-dilly-doh!
Manning-*Spooks,* 36–38
Dimian the peasant
Xenophontovna-*Folk,* 118
DINADAN, Sir
Sir Tristram and La Belle
Isolde
Dinewan the emu, and the bustard
Parker-*Australian,* 17–20
Dinewan the emu, and Wahn the
crow
Parker-*Australian,* 64
DINGOES
Mice women who turned into
dingoes
The rain bird
Bougoodoogahdah
DINNERS
See also BANQUETS
The Chenoo who stayed to
dinner
—harvest
The fairies banished
DINOSAURS
Land monsters
Dinosaurs of the sky
Reed-*Aboriginal,* 89–90
DIOMEDE (subject)
Pinsent-*Greek,* 142 (index)
Dionysus
Magical Beasts, 32–33
DIONYSIUS
Erigone and her dog
Pan and Dionysus, the wild
gods
The youngest god [Dionysius]
DIONYSIUS (subject)
Pinsent-*Greek,* 142 (index)

DIRT
   See also DUST
   The crow and the daylight
Disabled veterans. *See* VET-
   ERANS—disabled
DISAPPEARANCE(S)
   And they wondered
   Annie Norn and the fin folk
   The bridal present
   Erikur rescues a woman from
     the otherworld
   The fairies banished
   The fairy chapman
   The festival of the seven
     maidens
   The hand and the whirlpool
   Journey of dwarfs over the
     mountain
   Lake Espantosa, the
     alligators?
   The sea nymph
Disappearing apples [of
   immortality]
   Kudian-*More*, 67–74
DISASTERS
   See also EARTHQUAKES;
     FLOODS
   Ballad of the boll weevil [song
     and story]
   Beauty and the beast
   Drop of honey
   The lost horse [blessings and
     disasters interchangeable]
   The man who did not believe
     in luck
   Minnie
   The plague of Moscow
     [Varvarka]
—turn to blessings
   The lost horse
Disbelief. *See* BELIEF AND
   DOUBT
Discension: wise/foolish quails
   Martin-*Hungry*, 45–52
A discerning old 'faki'
   Mitchnik-*Egyptian*, 37–39

Discharged soldiers: broken swords
   Macdonald-*Gray*, 54–81
DISCIPLINE
   The governor and the Buddhist
   Upamanyu learns a lesson
     [hermitage school]
DISCONTENT
   See also CONTENTMENT
   The enchanted mule
Discontented Lado
   Nagishkin-*Folktales*, 122–127
DISCOURTESY
   The fox and the stork
   The giant caterpillar [rudeness]
   Goggle eyes
DISCOVERY
—voyages of
   Viking of the Pacific
Discovery and decipherment of
   "The descent of Inanna"
   Wolkstein-*Inanna*, 127–135
DISCRETION
   Little Red Riding Hood
DISCUS
   Apollo and Hyacinthus
DISEASE(S)
   The vision of MacConglinney
—communicable
   Plague omens
—origin
   How diseases came to the
     Ashanti
   Origin of sickness
DISGUISES
   See also SHAPE SHIFTERS;
     TRANSFORMATIONS
   Allerleirauh; or, The many-
     furred creature
   The ass in pantherskin
   The black colt
   The Christmas thief
   Clever Gretchen
   Clever woman
   The fiery dragon
   Hare and otter
   Hassan the physician

Heimdall in Midgard
The hen and the apple tree
The jealous shoemaker
King Josef
King Thrushbeard
Lambikin [drumikin]
The lute player [as minstrel]
Mizilca [woman disguised as
   knight]
The monster's hairs
The old flea-bag
Prince Vamato Take
Separation of god from man
Twelve huntsmen [test of
   feminity]
Two lovers punished
The young widow
DISHES
Jack and his magic aids [dish,
   belt, flute]
Whipping children: how it
   came about
DISHONESTY
  See also CHEATING; FRAUD;
   HONESTY;
   UNTRUSTWORTHINESS
The emperor's new clothes
A fine phoenix
Pistoleer Mike Fink
The royal jewel
Social connections
The stupid rich man
Tale of the golden vase and
   the . . .
The two compadres
Dismembered body: The peach
   thief
  Roberts-*Chinese*, 45–48
DISOBEDIENCE
  See also OBEDIENCE
Abuelita's bell
The antelope maid
Battle of the birds
The bird 'Grip'
Bird that made milk
Bluebeard

The children with one eye
Clever Daniel
Cock with the golden feathers
Coyote's trip to the Land
  Above
The crane maiden
Eagle and the frog
East o' sun and west o' the
  moon
East of the sun, west of the
  moon [loss of husband]
The Eskimo Indian and his fox
  wife
Faithful John
Fate of Frank M'Kenna
The fire bird and Ryska and
  vixen
The firebird
The giant-slayer
The golden cranes
The green frog
The gunny wolf
Holecek and the water nymph
  [loss of wife]
How Aisu found the happy
  land
Ivan Tsarevich, the wolf, and
  the firebird
The Jerusalemite's story cop-
  ied by R. Abraham
King Eagle
King Kojata
King Lindorm [a snake]
King of the herrings
The last tiger in Haiti
Li Ching and the rain god
  [good intentions]
Little Yellow Bird
The magic box
Magic moneybag
The magic rattle [limits
  disregarded]
Maria Morevna
The mastermaid
Meamei the seven sisters
The Morning Star

DISOBEDIENCE (continued)
  Mother of the Waters
    [punishment]
  My mother warned me . . .
  Orpheus and Eurydice
  The pigeon with nine heads
  The poor lame horse
  The porpoises of Koromira
    [children transformed]
  Powdered blondie and three-
    haired blondie
  Prince Fickle and fair Helena
  The princess, the horse, and
    the she-devil
  The rain-makers, dragon-
    palace, Ling mountains
  Red Riding Hood
  Seven families of Lake Pipple-
    Popple
  Shaitan the devil and his forty
    daughters
  Silbado
  Simangolo and the akara
  Sister Alyonushka and Brother
    Ivanushka [turns into goat]
  The sky-god: Ratu and the
    Dyaks
  The spectre wolf
  Sprig of rosemary
  Star-Boy and the sun dance
  Sun and sago [punishment]
  The swan geese
  The tale of Peter Rabbit
  Tremsin and the maid of the sea
  Tushcoon Eigna
  Urashima Taro, the fisher lad
  Urashima the fisherman
    (Japan)
  Vanooshka
  The water of life
  Why the gibbon says "pua"
  Why there is death [Nikoduma]
  Woodcutter and the heavenly
    maiden
  Woodpecker and bluejay: a
    sad tale

  The youth and the eagles
  The disobedient sun-child
    Hadley-*Legends*, 24–25
  A dispute in sign language
    Yolen-*Favorite*, 42–44
DISRESPECT
  The tale of Squirrel Nutkin
  The disrespectful son
    Hyde-Chambers-*Tibet*, 112–
    122
  Ditch-digger falls into his own ditch
    Villa-*Armenian*, 321–322
"DITTO"
  Princess Minon-Minette
DIVER DUCKS
  —origin of characteristics
    Manabozho and how the diver
    [duck] got a flat back
DIVERS AND DIVING
  The black pearl
  The divided daughter
    Roberts-*Chinese*, 152–154
  Dividing the axe
    Ginsburg-*Twelve*, 60–63
  Dividing the goose
    Yolen-*Favorite*, 160–161
  Dividing the horses
    Shannon-*Solve*, 45–47
DIVINATION
  The ruby ring
  The sabio sees a sow
DIVORCE
  The tailor's sleeve
DIVS (Persian evil spirits)
  Girl who had seven divs for
    brothers
  Mountain of jade
  Princess and the donkey
  Djuha's sleeve (Syria)
    Yolen-*Favorite*, 411
Do unto others. . . *See* GOLDEN
    RULE
DOBIES
  Fincastle mill
  The doctor and his pupil
    Yolen-*Favorite*, 300–303

Doctor Bidpai
  Wood-*Kalila,* 21–32
Doctor Tyl
  Williams-*Wicked,* 14–25
Doctors. *See* PHYSICIANS
The doe, the hunter, and the great
    stag
  Martin-*Hungry,* 85–90
The dog and his shadow
  dePaola-*Favorite,* 63
Dog and monkey build a town
  Magel-*Gambia,* 141–143
Dog and the bone
  Watson-*Aesop,* 18–19
The dog and the possum [origin of
    enmity]
  Stokes-*Turtle,* 29–30
Dog and the wolf [dog chained by-
    day]
  Lewis-*Animal,* 22–23
Dog [becomes man's slave]
  Pitcher-*Tokol.,* 21–22
Dog captures the hyena
  Magel-*Gambia,* 139–140
DOG DANCE
  The youth and the dog-dance
The dog goes to court
  Roberts-*Chinese,* 95–96
The dog got them
  Manley-*Fun,* 51–61
DOG-HEADED MEN
  The ugly son-in-law
Dog in the manger
  Watson-*Aesop,* 8–9
  Williams-*Aesop,* [5–7]
Dog people tribe: children of the
    Omokoy
  Stokes-*Turtle,* 26–28
The dog that ran to the
    moon
  Aiken-*Mexican,* 79–82
Dogfish woman
  Reid-*Raven,* 87–91
Dog-men of the Andaman Isles
  Magical Beasts, 42
DOGS

Aesop's dog [chasing rabbit]
Alex and Avery [dogs ex-
    ercised by telephone]
The best coon and possum
    dog
Black and white
The blind boy and his dog
The boy with the knucklebones
The Bremen town musicians
Cat and dog and return of the
    dead
Cat lying on velvet cushion,
    while dog sleeps
The chief and the black dog
The cunning shoemaker
The devil as a black dog
Duration of life (Germany)
End of the world (Sioux tale)
Erigone and her dog
The first mosquito
Fleas and cockleburrs
Foolish wife
George's picnic
Glooskap and the witch
    maidens
Grateful dog
The Great Dog [Yudistira and
    Svana]
Hob and the black dog
Hound-dog stories (four tall
    tales)
How Asanga came to see the
    future Buddha
How the monkey got food
    when he was hungry
The hunchbacked old woman
The iron wolf
Jack and his comrades
Jack and the robbers
The language of animals
Leppa Polkry and the blue
    cross
The loyal dog
Lure of the pipes [Big John
    Clach-na-Harnich & Black
    Simon]

DOGS (continued)
Magic bird [tells stories]
The magician's pupil
Man, the burro, and the dog
Man's best friend
Momotaro, or the son of a peach
Monkey and dog court the same girl
The nis and the boy
Panhu, the marvellous dog
The poor old dog
The prince and his fate
The russet dog
Scabby: beauty is only skin deep
The scabby child
The serpent-slayer
Snipp, Snapp, Snorium
The snow-man [the dog and the sun]
The split dog
Tametomo and his dog
The three daughters and the lost cow
Three dogs [named Salt, Pepper, Mustard]
The tinder-box
The ugly son-in-law
War of the wolf and the fox
The white cat
The wicked stepmother
The witches' fire
The wolves of Cernogratz
—big
Canis major (the Big Dog)
—black
Assorted monsters
The Moddey Dhoo
—bull dogs
The wow o'Rivven; the bell
—cocker spaniels
Murder and lonely hearts
—collar with 12 rubies
Azad Bakht's tale
—deer-hounds
The story of Jon Asmundsson
—eight-legged
Golden apple and his stepmother
—enemies of wallabies; origin
The greedy dogs
—French poodles
Murder and lonely hearts
—greyhounds
Beth Gellert
Fairy greyhound
—heroic
Stone memorial to a dog
—hounds
Artemis and Apollo
The blood stain
Brer fox meets Mister Trouble
The labours of Hercules
Mice in the corn
Munachar and Manachar
Munachar and the raspberries
A slave's escape
A stepchild that was treated mighty bad
The way of the world
Wiley and the hairy man
—inside acorn
The white cat
—Jinn in shape of
The beggar, the lion and the dog
—kangaroo mix
February dragon
—killed by envious neighbor
Old man who made withered trees to flower
—killed; eaten; bones turn to stone
Two hunting dogs [Burrajahnee and Inneroogun]
—"kind of human nature"
The cat and the dog
—little
Canis minor (the Little Dog)
—lost; leads to marriage
The ugly dog

—magic
  Anpao and the magic dogs
    —magic picture of
  The cat palace
—nine-headed
  How Aisu found the happy
    land
—origin
  Origin of dogs
  The prince who had two eyes
—origin of hostility to cats
  The cat and the dog
—poodles
  The trolls of Skurugata
—reflection in water
  Greed can cause one's
    downfall
—skins
  The castle in the lake
—spaniels
  Heart of ice [Prince Littleboots]
—tails
  Why dogs sniff each other's
    tails
—tails lost in fire
  All the dogs in the world
DOGS (subject)
  Piggott-*Japanese*, 143 (index)
—Dando's dogs
  Briggs-*Vanish.*, 17, 195
—Devil's Dandy Dogs
  Briggs-*Vanish.*, 76, 151, 195
The dog's fiancee [jinn]
  Elbaz-*Folktales*, 82
DOGWOOD
  Hazel and dogwood
DOLL HOUSES
  Two bad mice
Doll in the grass
  Lewis-*Minute*, 26–27
  Stovicek-*Around*, 78–79
DOLLS
  The lost hum
  The origin of the winds
  Pom-Pom the clown
—comes to life, for a frog

The brook's secret
—helps Vassilisa
  Vassilisa [Fair] and Baba
    Yaga
  Vasilisa the Beautiful
—magic
  Haunter of the birch forest
—wax
  Little Ida's flowers
The doll's house
  Uttley-*Foxglove*, 73–80
DOLPHINS
  Delphinus (the Dolphin)
  Pedorus Jack
—origin
  Lizard and crocodile
Domoviye
  Arrowsmith-*Field*, 77–81
Don Cacahuate
  Aiken-*Mexican*, 153–156
Don Giovanni de la Fortuna
  Lang-*Pink/D*, 356–360
  Lang-*Pink/K*, 269–274
Don Juan Zurumbete
  Aiken-*Mexican*, 106–111
Dona Sebastiana
  Griego-*Cuentos*, 15–21
Donald and his neighbours
    [Hudden & Dudden]
  Yeats-*Fairy*, 270–273
Donald of the Burthens
  Ratcliff-*Scottish*, 53–56
The donkey who hit his mother
  Skurynski-*Fools*, 16–27
Donkey Wonkey
  Wahl-*Needle*, 29–33
DONKEYS
  The ass in pantherskin
  The boy in the donkey skin
  The boy who told lies
  The Bremen town musicians
  The cow who tried to act like
    a kitten
  The cunning shoemaker
  Date stone; a Han story
  Duration of life (Germany)

DONKEYS (continued)
  Eight donkeys
  The farmer who listened to his
    livestock
  Jack and his comrades
  Man, the burro, and the dog
  The miller, his son, and their
    donkey
  El que canta sus males
    espanta
  Race between toad and
    donkey
  That's no way to do it!
  The two donkeys
  A very happy donkey
—kyang = wild ass
  Kyang, the fox, the wolf and
    the hare
—Lucius Apuleius trans. into
  The golden ass
—man under spell
  Princess and the donkey
—stupidity
  The monkey's heart
Donkeys of Jolof
  Magel-*Gambia,* 154–158
Donkey's shadow
  Lewis-*Animal,* 42–43
Donn of Knockfierna
  Logan-*Old,* 33–41
Don't beat your children before
    they're born
  Skurzynski-*Fools,* 4–14
Don't count your chickens . . .
  Lewis-*Bedtime,* 46–47
  Shah-*World,* 18
Door gods
  Sanders-*Dragons,* 121
Door in the cliff
  O'Sullivan-*Legends,* 59–
    60
The door in the hedge
  McKinley-*Door,* 1–77
Door prayer at evening
  Crossley-*Folk,* 154
DOORS

  The death of Chanticleer
  Through the door
DORMITORIES
  Graduation
Double bodies: the divided
    daughter
  Roberts-*Chinese,* 152–154
DOUBLE STANDARD (morals)
  [Woman with the head of a horse]
Double-headed phoenix
  Minford-*Fav.,* 173–179
DOUBLES
  Nails [anatomy]
Doubt. *See* BELIEF AND DOUBT
DOUGH
  The conjure wives
DOULTON, Royal
  The tile pictures
  Pierce-*Larousse,* 12–14, 176
The dove and the mouse
  Amore-*Lustful,* 172–174
"DOVE MAIDEN"
  The archer who went I know
    not where to . . .
The Dove [Noah and the Flood]
  Lurie-*Heavenly,* 59–61
DOVES
  See also TURTLEDOVES
  Ant and the dove
  Banca Flor
  El caballero porfiado
  Coyote's crying song
  The giantess leader
  The hundredth dove
  The jackal, the dove, and the
    panther
  The peri-wife
  Piglet and the cow
  Ten white doves
  The white dove [princess
    under spell]
  The wooden horse and the
    painted jug
—feathers
  Suit of white feathers
    (Dongxiang)

—green-spotted-song
Downfall of the mighty hunter
  MacLean-*Cuentos,* 162–164
Draco (the Dragon)
  Gallant-*Constel.,* 33–38
DRACS (subject)
  Briggs-*Vanish.,* 73, 93–94, 195
DRACULA
  [Count Dracula's castle]
—humor
  Count Dracula [by Woody
    Allen]
DRAGON KING(S)
  The little talking animal and
    the shining blue fish
  Liu Yi and the dragon king
  My lord bag of rice
  Posting the dragon tablet
  Wild Goose Lake
—under sea
  The cat and the dog
  Prince Nocha
DRAGON KING OF THE SEA
  Happy hunter and the skilful
    fisher
  The heavenly flute player; a Li
    story
  Jelly fish and the monkey
Dragon kingdom: Urashima Taro
  Nye-*Out,* 45–59
Dragon King's Third Daughter: Wild
    goose lake
  Sadler-*Heaven,* 31–37
The Dragon [Marduk and Tiamat]
  Lurie-*Heavenly,* 24–27
The dragon who cried
  Chalk-*Tales,* unp.
DRAGONFLIES
  The warlike seven
The dragon-king's palace:
    Urashima Taro
  Crouch-*Whole,* 136–142
"DRAGONRIDERS"
  The smallest dragonboy
DRAGONS
  Beowulf fights the dragon

Boots and the beasts
The boy and the dragon
Boy with the deformed head
The devil's own [dragon]
The eight-forked serpent
The fiery dragon
Friendly dragons
The game of rat and dragon
Gaoliang bridge [Peking]; wa-
    ter supply
Glooskap and the magic gifts
Golden reed pipe
The great deeds of King Yu
The guardian dragon's magic
    pearl
The herd boy and the dragons
How the dragon was tricked
Hunter Hailibu's great sacri-
    fice
Jason and the golden fleece
Kingdoms of copper, silver,
    and gold
Laidley worm of Spindlestone
    Heugh
Lazarus and the dragons
Learning about dragons
The little bull calf
Lludd and Llefelys
The Longwitton dragon
The practical princess
The rain-makers, dragon-
    palace, Ling mountains
Roly Poly
Scary dragons
Seeing is believing
Singard the dragon-slayer
Sister Lace
The smallest dragonboy
Stan Bolovan and the dragon
The story of the house
The story of trembling hood
Thorston and the dwarf
Tokarsberget's treasure
The treasure in Saby Creek
Tripitaka: quest of the Buddhist
    scriptures

DRAGONS (continued)
  Twilight, Midnight, and Dawn
  Victory over Butoriku, the
    dragon
  The way of the world
  The white doe
  Wooing of Pumei; and Oroqen
    story
  Yu controls the flood
—Baba Yaga's nephew
  Ivan young in years, old in
    wisdom
—blood
  Singard the dragon-slayer
—Chudo Yudo
  Ivan the peasant's son and the
    three dragons
—eats King's daughters
  The fisher-prince with the sil-
    ver apple
—flying
  Land monsters
—komodo
  Land monsters
—sea
  The black dragon of the Sea of
    Dunting
—steal sun and moon
  The red czar and the golden-
    haired Tihota
—takes Emperor to hereafter
  Shinansha, or the south-point-
    ing carriage
—tears
  The dragon who cried
DRAGONS (subject)
  Scott-Fantastic, 39–60
—The chinese dragons
  Sanders-Dragons, 48–49
Dragon's eye; jewel as reward
  Berger-Animalia, [17–19]
Drakes [house spirits]
  Arrowsmith-Field, 245–246
Drakestail [and the king]
  Schindler-Golden, 29–43
DRAUGS (demons)

Finn blood
  The fisherman and the draug
  Jack of Sjoholm and the Gan-
    Finn
Draw the curtains
  Ainsworth-Phantom, 105–124
Drawer 14
  Hoke-Horrors, 11–23
DRAWERS
  Little Ida's flowers
DRAWING
  Turkey tale [drawing while
    telling]
  The dreaded chenoo
  McCarty-Skull, 52–60
Dream bread
  Schwartz-Tales, 56–57
The dream castle
  Roberts-Jung, 13–14
The dream house (Ireland)
  Yolen-Favorite, 432–433
The dream of Dumuzi
  Wolkstein-Inanna, 74–84
Dream of Habeeb-son-of-Habeeb
  Shah-Dervishes, 180–184
Dream of King Arthur
  Lehane-Legends, 83
Dream of Macsen
  Lochhead-Battle, 107–110
The dream of Oengus
  Gantz-Early, 107–112
Dream of Owen O'Mulready
  Jacobs-Celtic, 200–202
Dream: the philosopher and the
    butterfly
  Berger-Animalia, [37–39]
The dreamer and his dream
  Villa-Armenian, 167–175, 468
Dreams
  Roberts-Chinese, 216–217
DREAMS AND DREAMING
  The blind boy and his dog
  The butterfly
  El caballero porfiado
  Charting the kingdom of
    dreams

Daniel O'Rourke
The deer in the dream
The golden bird
Jorinde and Joringel
Katla's dream
King Dabschelim [rules for
  governing]
King who fought many wars
The little match girl
Little Tuk
Mice in the corn
The moon walk
The one who would not listen
  to his own dream
Only a dream
Peddler of Swaffham
  (England)
The phantom carousel
Pygmalion's statue
The rich farmer and the poor
  farmer
Tushcoon Eigna
The unbroken web
The waiting maid's parrot
  (China)
The wanderer's dream
The world in a pillow
The young king
The young man and the priest
—advice received in
  Rabbi David Bussidan pre-
  vented sale of synagogue
—interpretation of
  A sure sign
—Nartu, keeper
  The crystal sisters
DREIDEL
—Jewish game
  The parakeet named Dreidel
Dresses. *See under* CLOTHES
Drill, ye tarriers, drill [song and
  story]
  Sanders-*Hear,* 82–87
A drink for a crow
  Shannon-*Solve,* 17–19
DRINKING

Daniel O'Rourke
The devil invented alcoholic drink
The elle-maids
Great Heart and the three
  tests
Jemmy Doyle in the fairy
  palace
Master and man
The mischievous little drinker
Noah and Satan [wine: proper
  amount]
Woe [personified]
—contests
  Thor in the giant's strong-hold
Drinking companions
  Roberts-*Chinese,* 178–182
  Yolen-*Favorite,* 440–444
DRINKS
—magic
  The little mermaid
DRIPPINGS
  The cat and mouse in
  partnership
Drolmakyid the fairy [Tibetan]
  Magic Knife, 1–27
DRONA (warrior)
  The power of a lie
Drop of honey
  Kudian-*More,* 75–77
DROUGHT
  The children and the
  hummingbird
  Gazelle horn
  The girl with the large eyes
  If the boerboon flowers fall
  The jackal, Mpungutye,
  searches for lost mate
  Posting the dragon tablet
  Princess Hase
  Rabbit and the gum-baby
  Rainbow [Nvelingange relieves
  drought]
  Roam the wild country
  Snake with an ear for music
  The tale of the magic green
  water-pearl

DROUGHT (continued)
Why a rabbit hides in a bur-
row
Why koala has no tail
Wild Goose Lake
The witch and the boy Israel
Drovers: The phantom herd
MacLean-*Cuentos*, 53–56
The drovers who lost their feet
(Mexico)
Yolen-*Favorite*, 177–180
The drowned boys
Highwater-*Anpao*, 168–179
DROWNING
The bird and the sea: Jing-
wei
Boy abducted by fairies
The deacon of Myrka
"Man overboard"
The man who drowned in a
washbasin
The Metronome
Nennir, or the one who feels
inclined
The peasant and the
waterman
The pig-headed wife
River claims a victim
Vodyaniye
—in bowl of cream
Wise frog and foolish frog
DRUDGERY
Husband and wife should
share equally
DRUG ADDICTS
Tomorrow's child
DRUIDS
Connla and the fairy maiden
The destruction of Da Derga's
hostel
The intoxication of the Ulaid
The story of Deirdre
DRUIDS (subject)
—The ancient Celtic world
Ross-*Druids*, 11–13
The drum of Timpenni

Stokes-*Turtle*, 136–137
Drummer-boy: Truth and murder
will out
Marshall-*Every.*, 257–262
Drummond, William Henry
The Windigo [I]
DRUMS
The candy man; a Han folk-
tale
Coals on the devil's hearth
(Ireland)
The hill men invited to the
christening
The Yellow Emperor: war
against Chitou
—noisy but empty
The fox and the drum
—sticking to
Pedro de Ordimalas
—tells king's secret
There is no such thing as a
secret
The drunkard in hell
Cortes-*Byelorussian*, 95–96
The drunkard saint [Hershele]
Patai-*Gates*, 698–701
DRUNKENNESS
Erigone and her dog
DRYADS
Orpheus and Eurdice
Dryads: The green people
Scott-*Fantastic*, 151–161
DUBHLACHANS
The death coach
The duck with red feet
Macmillan-*Canadian*, 82–84
DUCKS
Boy-who-snared-the-wind and
shaman's daughter
Drakestail [and the king]
The duck with the red feet
Five million ducks
Hansel and Gretel
Iktomi and the ducks
Iktomi and the red-eyed
ducks

The lazy ducks
The little chicken Kluk and his
   companions
Mandarin ducks
The platypus Gayardaree
Queen bee
Rabbit and the grain buyers
Shingebiss: the wild duck
The ugly duckling
—ducklings
The blown away rabbit
The ugly duckling
—rescues/raises human infant
Child in the silk-cotton tree
—transformation into woman
Give me something you
   have . . . unawares
—trapped
Iktomi and the ducks
—wild
The wooing of Seppo
   Hmarinen
The ducks and the fox
Lobel-*Fables*, 5
DUDDEN
Donald and his neighbours
   [Hudden & Dudden]
The duel in Pohja
Synge-*Land*, 132–139
DUELS
Onions [keg of "powder"]
Duende
Arrowsmith-*Field*, 210–212
A duergal story
Froud-*Faeries*, unp.
"DUERGAR, THE"
The dwarf-sword tirfing
Loki and the dwarf
Thorston and the dwarf
DUERGAR, The (subject)
Keightley-*World*, 66–68
Duet: song
Berger-*Animalia*, [9–11]
Duffy and the devil
Phelps-*Maid*, 119–127
Duke Magnus and the mermaid

Heslewood-*Tales*, 104–107
Keightley-*World*, 154–155
Duke Pishposh of Pash
Williams-*Wicked*, 26–37
DUKES AND DUCHESSES
"Lars, my lad!
Duktuthl: The strong man
Wood-*Spirits*, 64–67
Dulac, Edmund, illus.
Quiller-*Sleeping*
DULCIMERS
The dwarfs' banquet
DULCINDA (fairy)
The enchanted forest
DULLAHANS
The death coach
The ride of the headless
   phantom
DUMB
—can't speak
Sikulume and the seven
   brothers
Dumling and the golden goose
Lewis-*Bedtime*, 18–19
"DUMMLING"
The golden goose
Dumplings in the river
Chalk-*Tales*, unp.
DUMUZI (husband of Inanna)
The dream of Dumuzi
Duncan Fraser and the fairies
Robertson-*Highland*, 10–
   12
DUNG
Sweet dung, cake-tree, and
   the bugle of life
DUNLOP, Bessie (subject)
Briggs-*Vanish.*, 163
Dunsany, Lord
In a dim room
DUNSANY, Lord (subject)
The fantasy land of Lord
   Dunsany
Duntulm Castle, Skye
Robertson-*Highland*, 43–
   45

DUPES
  See also GULLIBILITY
  Sister Fox and Brother Coyote
DUPLICITY
  The camel, lion, leopard, crow,
    & jackal
  The Catholic fox
  The cormorant and the star
Duration of life (Germany)
  Yolen-*Favorite*, 448–449
DURESS
  The yellow dwarf
DUST BOWL
  The Johnson boys [song and
    story]
DUST (subject)
—crumbling to
  Briggs, *Vanish.*, 12, 14, 16–17,
    19, 21–23, 25
A dutiful son
  Zong-*Korea*, 44–45
DUTY
  Axad Bakht meets the
    dervishes
  The kingdom of beautiful
    colors
DUTY (subject)
—family roles
  Amore-*Lustful*, 49–50
The dwarf husband
  Keightley-*World*, 232
The dwarf in search of lodging
  Keightley-*World*, 278–279
The dwarf who wanted to grow
  Stuchl-*American*, 104–106
Dwarfs
  Froud-*Faeries*, unp.
DWARFS
  See also PYGMIES
  Aid and punishment
  The birthday of the Infanta
  The black dwarfs of Granita
  Brewery of eggshells
  The chamois-hunter
  The changeling [b]
  The creation of the world

Curiosity punished
The curse of Andvari's ring
Dietrich of Bern
The dwarf in search of lodging
The dwarfs on the tree
The dwarf-sword tirfing
Fenrir the wolf is bound
The fiery dragon
The friendly dwarfs
Gawain: test of valor
Gertrude and Rosy
The hill man at the dance
How Thor got his hammer
Inge of Rantum
Journey of dwarfs over the
  mountain
Korred
Loki and the dwarf
Loki makes mischief
The magic gifts [dwarf-
  sorcerer]
The ogre's soul
Parselina [marriage to evil
  dwarf]
The rejected gift
Singard the dragon-slayer
Sir Thynne
Smith Riechert
Snow White and Rose Red
Snow White and the seven
  dwarfs
A stepchild that was treated
  mighty bad
Thorston and the dwarf
Three musicians [princess un-
  der spell]
The tiger and the dwarf
Water of life
Wedding feast of the little
  people
The wonderful little pouch
The yellow dwarf
Young boy and the dwarf
—big-eared
  Erdluitle
—elks; try to take liver

The woman in blue
—King of the Forest
Goggle eyes
Dwarfs and goblins
Robe-*Hispanic*, 414–418
The dwarfs' banquet
Keightley-*World*, 130–139
The dwarfs borrowing bread
Keightley-*World*, 226–227
The dwarf's feast
Keightley-*World*, 218–219
The dwarfs on the tree
Keightley-*World*, 273
Dwarfs stealing corn
Keightley-*World*, 222–223
DWARFS (subject)
Briggs-*Vanish.*, 215 (index)
Keightley-*World*, 94–96, 216–
233, 264–279
Scott-*Fantastic*, 77–92
The dwarf-sword tirfing
Keightley-*World*, 72–75
[Dyfed: under spell because mor-
tals trespass on Faerie]
Seekers Saviors, 107–121
Dying. *See* DEATH
The dying Buddha's compassion
Amore-*Lustful*, 177–178
The dying cowboy [song and story]
Sanders-*Hear*, 181–191

EA (god)
Seven days and nights
Eagle and the frog
Reid-*Raven*, 75–86
The eagle [Aquila vs Aesculapius]
Lurie-*Heavenly*, 8–10
The eagle hawk
Reed-*Aboriginal*, 119–122
Eagle hawk again
Reed-*Aboriginal*, 131–134
The eagle on the prickly pear

Bierhorst-*Hungry*, 80–83, 139
EAGLE PRINCE
Eagle and the frog
Eagle Woman comes to The
People
MacLean-*Cuentos*, 113–117
EAGLE-HAWKS
The mocking bird, Weedah
EAGLES
Aguila (the Eagle)
The apples of eternal life
The apples of Iduna
Bead chant myth
The black fox
The blessed gift of joy be-
stowed upon man
Boy who was saved by his
thoughts
The child and the eagle
The fisher-prince with the sil-
ver apple
Flight of the eagle
The four rings
Glooscap, the peacemaker
Good done to you, do good in
return
Green lizard, gray squirrel and
the eagle
The heavenly song of the
green-spotted dove
Joukahainen's revenge
Juan and the bony one
King Eagle
King of Lochlann's three
daughters
Kingdoms of copper, silver,
and gold
Kosi, the eagle, and the moun-
tain lion
Kwi-na the eagle: animal-god
persons
Montezuma's wound
Mysterious palace [Solomon &
Ramirat]
Shooting of the red eagle
Silbado

EAGLES (continued)
    The son of Tata Juan
      Pescador
    Tonweya and the eagles
    Upon Jewel Mountain
    Wicked girl and her punish-
      ment
    The Wooing of Olwen
    The world below
    The youth and the eagles
—as bridegroom
    Marya Morevna
—as pets
    Beaver Tail and the Indians
—carries baby away
    Tremsin and the maid of the
      sea
—deceit; takes D. to moon
    Daniel O'Rourke
—a god
    Brave little parrot and the
      eagle's tears
—magic
    The tree-bound
EARACHE
    Panhu, the marvellous dog
EARLS
    The magician earl
The early heroes: Yi, ten suns,
    monsters
    Sanders-*Dragons,* 25–28
Early man
    Pinsent-*Greek,* 37–41
EARRINGS
    Liisa and the prince
    Treasure Mountain; a Yao
      folktale
EARS
    Anpao brings the corn
    The lazy husband, Ngurmi. [I]
—mule
    Midas, the golden king
EARTH
    The creation of the world
    The dawn of the world
    How salt was discovered

    The lessons of heaven and
      earth
    Nature
    Night and day
—creation
    The big turtle
—mouths, never sated
    The hungry woman [earth]
—visits sky
    Long ago when the earth was
      flat
—world supported by Duktuthl
    The strong man
EARTH (subject)
    Pinsent-*Greek,* 142 (index)
—Motif index
    Wilbert-*Bororo,* 289
"EARTH FOLK"
    Erdluitle
Earth goddess: A story of a flood
    Piggott-*Mexican,* 74–83
Earthmaker: creation story
    Dutton-*Navajo,* 12–15
Earthmaker: how sickness came
    Dutton-*Navajo,* 17
EARTHQUAKES
    The day El Diablo ripped the
      earth asunder
    The fifth sun [Nanahuatl]
    The giant without a head
    The princess on the glass
      hill
    The San Francisco earthquake
    The tricking of King Gilfi
EARTHQUAKES (subject)
—California: the San Andreas
      Fault
    MacLean-*Cuentos,* 43–44
Earthworms. *See* WORMS
Earwig in sickle
    O'Sullivan-*Legends,* 85–86
EAST
    He comes from the east
East of the sun and west of the
    moon [title varies]
    Booss-*Scand.,* 63–71

Lang-*Blue,* 1–13 (notes, 349,
  353, 364)
Phelps-*Maid,* 69–78
Stovicek-*Around,* 7–9, 58,
  108, 158–159, 206–207
EASTER
  The troll shoes
  Tungustapi
  Wesolego Alleluja = Happy
    Easter
Easter-hag put a water-trough in
  her place
  Lindow-*Swedish,* 163–164
EATING
  See also OVEREATING
  Ash lad who had an eating
    match with the troll
  The end of the world
  The fox and the stork
  Great Heart and the three
    tests
  The greedy youngster
  —tall tales
  A whale of a tale
EAVESDROPPING
  Periquita
Ebbe Skamelson
  Booss-*Scand.,* 260–262
ECCENTRICS
  Death out of season
Echidna's spines
  Reed-*Aboriginal,* 60–62
Echo and Narcissus
  Gibson-*Gods,* 124–125
  Lines-*Greek,* 56–61
Echo [nymph]
  Low-*Greek,* 54–57
ECHOES
  Kwi-na the eagle: animal-god
    persons
ECLIPSES
  —dog trying to steal sun or moon
  The fire dogs
  —origin
  Rahou [origin of eclipses]
EDDAS (subject)

Keightley-*World,* 60–75
Eden, Garden of. *See* GARDEN
  OF EDEN
Edgell, John
  Just married
EDITORS
  —children's books
  The Mother Goose madman
Edmund the holy
  Marshall-*Every.,* 182–189
EDNA, Saint
  Saints Colmkille and Edna
Ednoth's relics, and Thurkill's beard
  Marshall-*Every.,* 191–200
Educated frogs and martial ants
  Roberts-*Chinese,* 106
EDUCATION
  [Animal children]: school days
  Caterina the Wise (Sicily)
  "If I had the wings of an angel"
  Mary's little lamb: further ad-
    ventures [verse]
  —college
  Twist-mouth family
  —humor
  The crooked-mouthed family
EEL (river god)
  —killed; punishes
  The great flood
Eels. *See under* FISH
Eerin, the small grey owl
  Parker-*Australian,* 177–180
EFFIGIES
  Why the bananas belong to
    the monkey
EFRIT (bird)
  The bird maiden
EGGS
  The battle of the birds
  El caballero porfiado
  The case of the uncooked eggs
  The family's fortune
  Hob and Eggy Palmer
  How the world was made
  Snake boy
  The valiant chanticleer

EGGS (continued)
—duck
    The giant who had no heart
—golden
    The goose and the golden
        eggs
    Goose that laid the golden
        eggs
—the Golden Egg of life
    Lini the lost prince
—goose eggs
    The greedy youngster
—lord hidden in
    Enchanted castle
—magic
    The iron wolf
    Kumba the orphan girl
EGGSHELLS
    The brewer of eggshells
    Brewery of eggshells
    Changeling elf and the woman
    The fairies banished
EGYPT
    The extra days: Ra, Thoth,
        and Nut
    The happy prince
    Monkeys
    Mummies, zombies, and artifi-
        cial men
    The prince and his fate
    The ten plagues of Egypt
EGYPT (subject)
    Patai-*Gates*, 776 (index)
Egypt: Apep
    Stallman-*Dragons*, 14–15
Egypt's divine menagerie
    Magical Beasts, 19–22
Eight donkeys
    Ginsburg-*Twelve*, 32–35
Eight omens
    Bierhorst-*Hungry*, 96–99
Eighteen rabbits
    Sampson-*Gypsy*, 66–71
The eight-forked serpent
    Kendall-*Haunting*, 17–21
Eilean-nan-Sithean

Robertson-*Highland*, 168–
    169
ELAINE
    Sir Lancelot of the Lake
Elaine the Fair Maid of Astolat
    Malory-*King*, 203–241
Elaine, the lily maid of Astolat
    Lehane-*Legends*, 94
ELANDS (a kind of antelope)
    Mantis creates an eland
Elder
    Ewart-*Lore*, 142–144
ELDER BROTHER (Se-eh-ha)
    The creation
Elder (trees)
    Froud-*Faeries*, unp.
ELDER TREES
    The marsh king's daughter
ELDER TREES (subject)
    Briggs-*Vanish.*, 74–75
Electra
    Stapleton-*Dictionary*, 71–76
The elemental
    Hoke-*Uncanny*, 15–35
ELEMENTALS (subject)
    See also IMMORTALS
—in mines
    Briggs-*Vanish.*, 37, 82–84
Elementals: In the beginning
    Scott-*Fantastic*, 2023–36
ELEMENTS
    The four elements
Elephant and blackbird court the
    same girl
    Magel-*Gambia*, 70–74
The elephant and his son
    Lobel-*Fables*, 32–33
Elephant and the tortoise
    Radin-*African*, 104–105
The elephant girls
    Manning-*Marvels*, 107–108
The elephant hunt [Sinbad]
    Rackham-*Fairy*, 97–102
ELEPHANTS
    The ant, the elephant, and the
    brahmin's servant

Fearless lion, brave elephant,
  merchant's cries
The hares and the elephants
How the blackbird went to war
The jackal inside the elephant
The magic mirror
The peacock's tail
Sidi Ngali and his traveling
  companions
The tiger and the man
Tortoise and elephant: small-
  ness not an illness
Tortoise and the elephants:
  fine goods often . . .
—defeated by mouse
  Mouse's three children [tiger,
  peacock, boy]
—formerly a man-eater
  First Woman and Elephant
—knowing about
  The blind ones and the matter
  of the elephant
—origin of long trunk
  Elephant's child [from Kipling]
—origin of trunk
  Elephant's child
—people &, in stomach of
  Unanana and the elephant
Elephant's child
  Royds-*Animal*, 60–71
Elephant's child [from Kipling]
  Lewis-*Animal*, 16–17
Elf King, Burd Helen, and Childe
  Rowland
  Seekers Saviors, 49–77
Elf King's Dark Tower
  Lee-*Castles*, 166–167
The elf maiden
  Crossley-*Folk*, 67–71
The elf of the rose
  Booss-*Scand.*, 362–366
The elfin hill
  Andersen-*Hague*, 83–94
ELFLAND
  Father of eighteen elves
  Janet and Tamlin

Tomlin [elf-knight]
ELF-SHOT (subject)
  Briggs-*Vanish.*, 25, 127–128
The elf-woman and Sir Olof
  Keightley-*World*, 84–86
ELIDOR (Eliderus) (subject)
  Briggs-*Vanish.*, 157–159
Elidore
  Jacobs-*Celtic*, 252–254
ELIJAH, the prophet
  Hershele and Hanukkah
  The two brothers [fire and
  water]
Elijah's violin
  Schwartz-*Elijah*, 19–24
The elixir of immortality [Chang'o]
  Sanders-*Dragons*, 29–32
ELIZABETH, Queen
  Sergeant-*Witches*, 286 (index)
ELK
  The curse [elk takes liver of
  new mother]
  Grasshopper [Indian
  superman]
  How the fox and the elk ex-
  changed legs
  The hunting of the elk
  Sky Elk, the ghost of White-
  face Mountain
—hunter transformed; fights
  Downfall of the mighty hunter
ELK DOGS
  The orphan boy and the elk
  dog
Ellefolk
  Arrowsmith-*Field*, 25–28
The elle-maid near Ebeltoft
  Keightley-*World*, 90–91
The elle-maids
  Keightley-*World*, 89
Ellis, Ella Thorp
  Roam the wild country
Ellis, Henry
  Another being
ELM TREES
  The first humans

ELM TREES (subject)
  Briggs-*Vanish.*, 74
ELOPEMENT
  Coral creeper [origin]
Elphame: True Thomas
  Nye-*Out,* 13–29
Elsa and the evil wizard
  Phelps-*Maid,* 97–105
Elstorps Woods
  Booss-*Scand.*, 272–273
ELVES
  Addlers and menters
  The bishop and the elves
  Brewery of eggshells
  The crossways
  Diarmuid, son of Donn: a spell-
    shackled devotion
  The elf of the rose
  The elfin hill
  The elf-woman and Sir Olof
  The elle-maid near Ebeltoft
  The elle-maids
  The fairy thieves
  The father of eighteen elves
  The fisherman of Gotur
  Gellivor
  The genesis of the Hid-folk
  Girl at the shieling [elf]
    (Iceland)
  The grateful elfwoman
  Grimsborg
  Hans Puntleder
  The herd-boy
  Katla's dream
  Maid Vae
  The man/whale
  Shoemaker and the elves
  Sir Olof in the elve-dance
  Soup from a sausage skewer
  The strongest boy in the world
  Svend Faelling and the elle-
    maid
  Thordur of Thrastastadir
  Tungustapi
  Una the elfwoman
  Valbjorg the Unelfed
  Who built Reynir church?
  The young swain and the
    elves
—dark
  Church grims
  Erdluitle
  Knockers
  Korred
  Quiet folk
  Quiet folk changelings
  Red caps
  Witchtln
—dusky
  Asrai
  Barabao
  The brownies
  Bwciod
  Callicantzaroi
  Domoviye
  Drakes [house spirits]
  Duende
  Elves, night
  Elves, tree
  Fairies, English
  Fate
  Fees
  Fir Bolg
  Follets
  Folletti and Incubi
  Fountain women
  Giane
  Glashans and Shopiltees
  Goat people
  The Gwagedd Annwyn
  Heinzelmannchen and
    Hutchen
  Hey-hey men
  Hobgoblins
  Klabautermannikins and
    Kaboutermannikins
  Kobolde
  Kombocke and Hausbocke
  Lauru
  Leprechauns
  Leshiye and Lisunki
  Linchetti

Lutins
Massarioli
Mer-men
Mer-women
Moerae
Monacielli
Moss people
Mound folk
Nereides
Nissen and Tomtra
Nixen and river men
Norggen, Orculli and
    Fankenmannikins
Pamarindo
People of peace
Pixies
Poleviki and Poludnitsy
Poltersprites
Portunes
River women
Roosters, snakes and basiliscs
Rusalky
Salvanelli
Salvani and Aguane
Seal people: Sea trows and
    Roane
Seligen Fraulein
Servan
Sirens
Skogsra or wood trolls
Sleigh Beggey and Tylwyth
    Teg
Vazili, Bagany and Banniki
Vily
Vodyaniye
—Dutch
    Alven
—house
    Domoviye
    Drakes [house spirits]
    Duende
    Hobgoblins
—light
    Alven
    Dames vertes
    Ellefolk

Fylgiar
Sidhe
White ladies
Will-o'-the-wisp
Wind folletti
—night
    Duende
—queens
    Hildur, the queen of the elves
—red eyes
    Korred
—small
    Portunes
—standing-stone
    Korred
—water
    The man-servant and the wa-
        ter-elves
ELVES (subject)
    Briggs-*Vanish.*, 195, 215
        (index)
    Keightley-*World*, 78–82
    Scott-*Fantastic*, 179–188
—night
    Arrowsmith-*Field*, 122–125
—tree
    Arrowsmith-*Field*, 180–183
The elves and the shoemaker
    Baskin-*Imps*, 22–23
    dePaola-*Favorite*, 100–104
    Ehrlich-*Random*, 22–25
    Oxenbury-*Nursery*, 47–53
Elves and the shoemaker whose
        work they did
    Shub-*About*, 31–32
Elves ask a servant girl to be
        godmother
    Shub-*About*, 33–34
The elves' dance
    Booss-*Scand.*, 298–299
ELYSIUM
    Hades, lord of the underworld
EMBROIDERY
    Giane
    Shooting the moon; a Yao
        folktale

The emerald Buddha
  Toth-*Tales*, 121–126
EMERALDS
  The cat in the sea
EMOTIONS
  The little mermaid
—uncontrolled
  The passion of the gewel
EMPEROR, JADE
  Havoc in heaven: Monkey and
    the Jade Emperor
  Master Frog
EMPEROR OF HEAVEN
  The shepherd and the em-
    peror's daughter
EMPERORS
  Burgher and the pauper
  Dietrich of Bern
  Dream of Macsen
  Dumplings in the river
  The fisherman and his soul
  Frog who became an em-
    peror
  Golden life
  How Wang-Fo was saved
  The magic boat
  Magic brush; a Han folktale
  Meng Chiang and the Great
    Wall of China
  The nightingale
  Sister Lace
  The swine herd
  The swordmaker's son: King-
    don of Chu
  Three thieves [eggs, shoe
    soles, food]
  The Tibetan envoy's mission
  The ugly son-in-law
  The Yellow Emperor: war
    against Chitou
  Youth without age and life
    without death (Turkey)
—daughter refuses to become
    empress
  The little goddess
Emperor's lesson

Villa-*Armenian*, 328–331, 516–
    518
The emperor's new clothes
  Andersen-*Hague*, 106–112
  dePaola-*Favorite*, 86–95
  Ehrlich-*Random*, 2–9
  Leete-*Golden*, 8–15
  Lewis-*Bedtime*, 30–31
  Rackham-*Fairy*, 224–229
  Stovicek-*Around*, 76–78
EMPLOYEES
  The bull in the china shop
  Cunning mouth
—why some are upper-level
  The king's boatman
An empty head
  Nagishkin-*Folktales*, 128–133
The empty sea
  Thompson-*Hawaiian*, 93–102
EMUS (bird)
  The medicine-man
  The soldier-bird
    Deegeenboyah
—eggs
  How the sun was made
—origin of short wings
  Dinewan the emu, and the
    bustard
The enchanted apple tree
  Crossley-*Folk*, 58–60
An enchanted bestiary
  Magical Beasts, 88–89
The enchanted buck
  Phelps-*Tatterhood*, 143–
    148
Enchanted castle
  Sampson-*Gypsy*, 72–75
The enchanted fisherman
  Heslewood-*Tales*, 122–127
The enchanted forest
  Segovia-*Spanish*, 97–136
  Stuchl-*American*, 33–37
The enchanted fountain
  Schwartz-*Elijah*, 118–121
Enchanted guinea-fowl
  Radin-*African*, 235–236

The enchanted island
  Haining-*Lepre.*, 96–97
The enchanted journey [time
    warp]
  Schwartz-*Elijah*, 181–186
The enchanted mule
  Mayo-*Book*, 90–97
The enchanted orchard
  Fattoross-*Simpleton*, 41–45
The enchanted princess
  Bang-*Five*, 1–20
Enchanted ring
  Lang-*Green*, 62–71
Enchanted snake
  Lang-*Green*, 188–197
Enchanted watch
  Lang-*Green*, 55–61
Enchanted youth: Osseo and
    Oweenee
  Wade-*Indian*, 43–51
ENCHANTMENT
  See also MAGIC; SLEEPING
    SPELLS; TRANSFORMA-
    TIONS
  The Black Bull of Norroway
  [Bluebeard, Isabelle, the bleed-
    ing key]
  The brothers and the singing
    toad
  Castle of the crow
  The cat in the sea
  Charcoal burner and the bear
  Deliverance from magic's coils
  The food of Paradise
  [Gawain and Dame Ragnell]
  Hans Puntleder
  Jorinde and Joringel: Castle of
    the Birds
  Katchen the cat
  King Lindorm [a snake]
  Little Daylight
  Master Frog
  The mastermaid
  Princess on the glass
    mountain
  Snow white and Rose red

[Swan-children of Lir]
The Tsarevna frog
Webs of enchantment
The white cat
The witch and the boy Israel
Witches of Ashkelon
—bestial spells
  Ricky of the Tuft
—girl struck dumb
  Guleesh
—girl with sheep's head
  Kate Crackernuts
—husband in form of horse
  The princess, the horse, and
    the she-devil
laugh/cry at same time
  The enchanted forest
—maidens changed to birds
  Jorinde and Joringel
—prince in form of monster
  Beauty and the beast
—prince under spell
  East of the sun, west of the
    moon
—prince with pig's head
  Love: queen and foundling
—princess in stone
  Elijah's violin
—queen & subjects as mice
  The juniper bush
—spells broken
  Castle of the serpent
  [Daughters nightly go to under-
    world; dance of death]
  Doll in the grass
  Far have I sought ye: Red bull
    of Norroway
  The frog prince
  House in the wood
  The hunted hare
  The princess and the frog
  Princess in the chest [coffin]
  Queen bee
  Six swans
  Sleeping Beauty in the wood
  Snow White and Rose Red

ENCHANTMENT—spells broken
  (continued)
  The sun princess
  Three sisters
  The toad bridegroom
  Water of life
  [Well at the World's End]
  The white cat
  White dove
  The widow's son and the fig-
    pecker
ENCHANTMENT (subject)
—fairies
  Briggs-*Vanish.*, 47–49, 126,
    128–130
Enchantment of Earl Gerald
  Yeats-*Fairy*, 265–267
The enchantress Medusa
  Stovicek-*Around*, 30–33
[Enchantress more dangerous than
    dragons]
  Lee-*Castles*, 96–107
Encounter with the armadillo
  Wilbert-*Bororo*, 93–95
ENCOUNTERS
—fairy
  Faerie encounters
Encounters with the skogsra
  Lindow-*Swedish*, 105–107
Encounters with tomtar
  Lindow-*Swedish*, 136–138
ENCOURAGEMENT
  Great Joy, the self-respecting
    ox
The end of Marko Kraljevic
  Yourcenar-*Oriental*, 127–134
End of the Golem
  Patai-*Gates*, 639–642
End of the heroes
  Pinsent-*Greek*, 131–140
The end of the world
  Booss-*Scand.*, 589–590
END OF THE WORLD
  Ragnarok
  The Ragnarok, doom of the gods
—Buddhism

The destruction of the world
End of the world (Sioux tale)
  Yolen-*Favorite*, 474–475
Endewelt, Jack, illus.
  Jagendorf-*First*
Endless story (Japan)
  Yolen-*Favorite*, 45
ENEMIES
  Glooskap and the turtle
  Lizard and crocodile
—killing of
  Scar Face and the sun dance
—tricked by one warrior
  The clever Nikorima
ENGLAND
  See also GREAT BRITAIN
  Addlers and menters
  Ainsel
  Asrai
  The boggart
  The brownies
  The cauld lad of Hilton
  Drakes [house spirits]
  Elidore
  The fairies' cauldron
  Fairies, English
  The fairy banquet [a]
  The fairy fair
  The fairy horn
  The fairy thieves
  The fary-labour
  A fary-nurseling
  The grant
  The green children
  Hobgoblins
  The king o' the cats
  Lady witches [England, history]
  The Longwitton dragon
  The luck of Eden Hall
  Mice in the corn
  Mister Fox
  Mister Miacca
  The old witch
  Paddy O'Kelly and the weasel
  Pixies
  Pixy-gratitude

The pixy-labour
Pixy-vengeance
Portunes
Puck
The rose tree
The Tale of Ivan
The three heads of the
   well
Tom Tit Tot
Yallery Brown
—Canterbury
Devil's armful [Canterbury]
—Cornwall
Fairy dwelling on Selena Moor
   (condensed)
[Mermaid rewards Cornishman
   with magic powers]
—Craddock Moor
The hurlers
—vs France
God on our side
—history
The rollright stones
William Wake of Wareham
—history-Danish invasion
Edmund the holy
—history-18th century
Causes celebres, high and
   low: C. Radcliffe
—Lancashire
The enchanted fisherman
—Leicester
Llyr: children of the sea-god
—Lincolnshire
Yallery Brown
—Norfolk
Peddler of Swaffham
   (England)
—Yorkshire
Church grims
ENGLAND (subject)
Ross-*Druids,* 131 (index)
—Cornwall
Briggs-*Vanish.,* 215 (index, un-
   der Cornwall)
—Devon

Briggs-*Vanish.,* 8
—Exmoor
Briggs-*Vanish.,* 25–26
Keightley-*World,* 285–349
—Herefordshire
Briggs-*Vanish.,* 48–49, 103,
   129, 138–139
—Lincolnshire
Briggs-*Vanish.,* 55, 75, 154–156
—Oxfordshire
Briggs-*Vanish.,* 7, 87–88
—Pembrokeshire
Briggs-*Vanish.,* 11, 159–160
—Ross-shire
Briggs-*Vanish.,* 68, 70
—Selkirkshire
Briggs-*Vanish.,* 49
—Shropshire
Briggs-*Vanish.,* 145
—Somerset
Briggs-*Vanish.,* 45–46, 74, 81–
   82, 90, 120, 122
—Suffolk
Briggs-*Vanish.,* 85, 100
—Witch hunters: Lancashire and
   Essex
Sergeant-*Witches,* 55–114
England's first martyr
Marshall-*Every.,* 177–182
English colonists. *See* COLONIAL
   LIFE (U.S. history)
ENJOYMENT
The camel dances
ENLIGHTENMENT
The kind man
The magic bamboo
Enlightenment
Martin-*Hungry,* 137–145
Enmity between monkeys and
   crabs
Piggott-*Japanese,* 124–125
Enter the Sumerians
Gallant-*Constel.,* 8–10
Entertainment. *See* AMUSEMENTS
ENTOMOLOGISTS
Little Genius

ENTRAPMENT
  Why the hare runs away
ENVIRONMENT
  How the animals stopped the
    freeway
  Why apes look like people
ENVY
  See also JEALOUSY
  Altynchech and the padishah's
    wife
  The cat palace
  Glass mountain
  The good girl and the bad girl
  Hassan the physician
  The little talking animal and
    the shining blue fish
  The poor man's bowl
  Two visits to the jnun
  —frog bursts; wanted to be big as
    ox
  The frog and the ox
Envy punished
  Elbaz-*Folktales,* 34–35
Eodain the poetess
  Haining-*Lepre.,* 92–93
EPICS
  Gesar of Ling
EPILEPSY
  The wow o'Rivven; the bell
EQUALITY
  Caterina the Wise (Sicily)
  Chicoria [invited to eat at
    rancher's table]
  Dona Sebastiana
  Godfather death (Germany)
  —each his own lord
  The tailor (Mikhei) and the
    shoemaker
  —housework
  The husband who stayed at
    home
EQUINOXES
  The Zodiac, precession of the
    Equinoxes
ERCELDOUNE, Thomas of, 13th
  cent.

Canobie Dick and Thomas of
  Ercildoun
True Thomas [Thomas the
  Rhymer]
ERCILDOUNE, Thomas of
  (subject)
  Briggs-*Vanish.,* 86–87, 200
Erdluitle
  Arrowsmith-*Field,* 42–46
Erec challenges Yder
  Lehane-*Legends,* 74–79
ERESHKIGAL, Queen of the
  Underworld
  The descent of Inanna
Erh-lang and the suns
  Jagendorf-*Magic,* 3–6
Eridanus (the River)
  Gallant-*Constel.,* 146–147
Erigone and her dog
  Lines-*Greek,* 101–106
Erikur rescues a woman from the
  otherworld
  Crossley-*Folk,* 118–120
ERMINE
  —origin of white fur
  Ermine and the hunter
Ermine and the hunter
  Macmillan-*Canadian,* 199–202
Eros and Psyche
  Gibson-*Gods,* 119–121
  Spells & Bind, 103–108
ERRORS
  —in diagnosis
  The pregnant priest
  —false presumption
  Iktomi and the coyote
  —second wife
  Manyi's escape [wife eaten by
    mistake]
  —wrong son murdered
  The guardian sheep
Esben and the witch
  Lang-*Pink/D,* 258–273
  Lang-*Pink/K,* 191–205
Esben [meets a witch]
  Stallman-*Witches,* 36–37

Escape at bedtime [poem]
    Tudor-*Bedtime,* [38–39]
ESCAPES
    Baba Yaga
    Basket of Ngomba
    The cockatoo's head-dress
      [origin]
    Curse on the only son
    The dove and the mouse
    The falcon and the quail
      [cleverness]
    The frog and the crow
    Frog went a-courting [song
      and story]
    Girl who had seven divs for
      brothers
    Groundhog dance
    The gunny wolf
    The handsome suitor [A]
    Hansel and Gretel
    The hawk and the rattlesnake
    Little Lapp and the Ice King
    Little Masha and Misha the bear
    The little wise woman
    Manabozho's fishing: the king
      of fishes
    The mastermaid
    The practical princess
    The rabbi and the inquisitor
    Shun, the wise emperor
    A slave's escape
    Sody sallytytus
    Stepmother's head
    The stupid boy and the wand
    Traveller, the fox, and the tiger
    The turner and the goldsmith
    Wings
—gullible snake
    Snake and goat: tomorrow is
      another day
—magic pebble
    The hunter and his greedy wife
—painting becomes reality
    How Wang-Fo was saved
Escaping ghosts
    Roberts-*Chinese,* 175

The Eskimo Indian and his fox
    wife
    Jagendorf-*First,* 55–57
ESKIMO TALES (subject)
—[Storytelling]
    De Wit-*Talking,* 159–160
ESKIMOS
    Angakok and Mother of Seals
      [sea petrel]
    The Angekkok, Oolak, and the
      Moon-God
    The blessed gift of joy be-
      stowed upon man
    The coming of Raven
    The crow and the daylight
    The day Tuk became a hunter
    Julie of the wolves
    Sedna (Eskimo)
    Sedna the sea goddess
    A whale of a tale
Esplandian and the forbidden
    mountain
    Lee-*Castles,* 152–153
ETERNAL LIFE
    See also HEAVEN
    Princess and the slave
The eternal light [Solomon &
    Benaiah]
    Schwartz-*Elijah,* 67–75
The eternal lovers
    Magel-*Gambia,* 151–153
Eternal punishment. *See*
    PUNISHMENT—eternal
ETERNITY
    The wanderer's dream
Ethiopia. *See under* AFRICA
Ethiopia: The big mouth dragons
    Stallman-*Dragons,* 24–25
EULENSPIEGEL, Till
    The Christmas thief
    Doctor Tyl
    Duke Pishposh of Pash
    Tyl on a tightrope
    Tyll Ulenspiegel's merry prank
EURIDICE
    Orpheus and Eurydice

EUROPA
    The Bull [Europa and Minos]
Europa and Io
    Low-*Greek,* 33–37
EUROPE
    Elves, night
    Elves, tree
    Kombocke and Hausbocke
    Poltersprites
    Sirens
—Eastern
    Vily
—Northern
    Kobolde
    Mer-women
    Nixen and river men
    White ladies
EUROPE (subject)
—Eastern
    Keightley-*World,* 487–494
—Southern
    Keightley-*World,* 443–486
EURYDICE
    Orpheus and Eurydice
EURYSTHEUS, King
    The labours of Hercules
EUSTACE, Saint
    Saint Eustace's well
EUTHANASIA
    Babes in the wood
    Hansel and Gretel
Eve. *See* ADAM AND EVE
"EVEN TROT"
    Rival kempers
An evening in the squire's kit-
    chen
    Booss-*Scand.,* 72–84
EVENING STAR
    Enchanted youth: Osseo and
        Oweenee
    Powdered blondie and three-
        haired blondie
"EVENING STAR LADY"
    Thunderbird
An eventful pilgrimage
    Elbaz-*Folktales,* 136–137

The everlasting frogs [daughters
    turned to]
    Reed-*Aboriginal,* 33–36
EVIL
    The Angekkok, Oolak, and the
        Moon-God
    The bird 'Grip'
    Catherine's fate
    The creation
    Enchanted ring
    Father Frost
    [Glooskap] Gluscap, lord of the
        north
    Good and evil: Buri vs Ymir
    Graduation
    A Hani story: Queen forbids
        servant to eat rice
    How an old man lost his wen
    How evil produces evil
    How Jiculi served his tribe
    How the fire festival came to
        be
    How the Thai learned to be
        calm
    The inheritance
    Juan Pelon
    The juniper tree
    The Koranic teacher
    The little soldier
    Llyr: children of the sea-god
    Loki and his evil children
    Loss of memory
    The magic bag
    Magic pumpkins
    Maiden Bright-Eye
    The merchant's fortune
    The mouse at the seashore
    Munuck
    Old man who made withered
        trees to flower
    Owl with the face of a woman
    The pearl that shone by night
    Pint of flax seeds
    Prometheus and Pandora
    Ragnarok
    Repaying good with evil

The rogue of Kachi Kachi
Mountain
The selfish giant
Sister Alyonushka and Brother
Ivanushka
The sky beings
The snow queen
Sorcerer's apprentice
The sparrow with the slit-
tongue
Spirits and demons
The stone lion [vomits gold]
The stone statue
Suit of white feathers
(Dongxiang)
The three sillies [imagined fu-
ture evils]
Toads and diamonds
The triumph of death
The two brothers
Two enemy kings
Two neighbors
The two travellers [evil man
blinded]
Why raven is no longer
Why raven isn't perfect
The wisdom of a child
Witches on the lake
—appearances are deceiving
Two sisters and a harlot
—heartless
The fisherman and his soul
—magic drum
The drum of Timpenni
—origin
Why there is death [Nikoduma]
—returning evil for good
Good done to you, do good in
return
Herb of life
—rewarded
Samba the Satan and Omadi
the Righteous
—seeing all, is unbearable
The blacksmith in heaven
—seeing into other people

The girl with the silver voice
—tests
A boy and his dog
—three causes of harm
Bewitched cow
—to prevent a greater evil
The power of a lie
—tolerated, to avoid greater evil
The fox and the hedgehog
—vices result in non-recognition
Prince Featherhead and Prin-
cess Celandine
An evil being
Colombo-*Wind.*, 10
The evil eye
Haining-*Lepre.*, 37
Logan-*Old*, 100–101
EVIL EYE
Cattle and the evil eye
A cure for the "Evil Eye"
The evil eye
Harmful power of the evil eye
—gossiper changed to parakeet
Periquita
Evil for good: The wicked tiger
Raychaudhuri-*Stupid*, 40–43
Evil spirit of stream: Dance of
death
Macmillan-*Canadian*, 100–102
Evil spirits. *See* SPIRITS—evil
Evil tongue. *See under* TALK
Evil tongue: The devil and the old
hag
Stovicek-*Around*, 52–53
EVOLUTION
—old couple into monkeys
A pair of skinnies
Evolution, Cultural. *See* SOCIAL
EVOLUTION
EXAGGERATION(S)
See also TALL TALES
Sidi Ngali and his traveling
companions
EXAMINATIONS
Gods of the stars: ancient
China

Excalibur. *See* ARTHUR, King—
sword (Excalibur)
EXCESS
The dreamer and his dream
Sidi Ngali and his traveling
companions
The wolf who wished to hoard
[absurd]
—orderliness
The crocodile in the bedroom
Excessive conservation: The wolf
who wished to hoard
Wood-*Kalila*, 220–222
Exchange [barter]
Riordan-*Russia*, 181–183
EX-CONVICTS
A sharp loss of weight
EXCREMENT
See also DUNG
How the turtle got her shell
Hyena eats the ostrich's
eggs
The Koranic teacher
Monkey and dog court the
same girl
The monkey who asked for
misery
The young man and the talking
skull
—becomes mountain range
The mountain and the rivers
—of gods = gold
Gold of the gods
EXECUTIONERS
Why the executioner is called
assessor
EXECUTION(S)
Chelm justice (Jewish)
The confession of Charles
Linkworth
The sacred honey bees
The sacred sheet [at
execution]
—avoided
Beware of hypocrites!
Halva-maker

Saint Michael wins a soul from
devil
Scabby: beauty is only skin deep
The talking goat
Ten white doves
—avoided at last minute
Twelve wild geese
—by fairies
White cap
—saving from
The woman who chose her
brother
—tsar's daughter saves hero
A crippled hero
EXERCISE
Alex and Avery [dogs ex-
ercised by telephone]
EXILE
Gesar of Ling
The king and the emperor
The loss of the princess
The exile of the sons of Uisliu
Gantz-*Early*,20256–267
The exiled princess
Schwartz-*Elijah*, 263–269
The existence of the Witigo
Colombo-*Wind.*, 162–163
Exorcising the tomte
Lindow-*Swedish*, 143–
144
EXORCISM
The blind man and the devils
The devil as a black dog
The devil as a cat
The elemental
The "Kissing witch"
EXORCISM (subject)
—burning
Briggs-*Vanish.*, 101–103
EXOTICAS
Nereides
EXPECTATIONS
The cat and his visions
—count chickens before they hatch
The country maid and her
milkpail

—fanciful
  Milkmaid and the pail
—foolish worry
  The death of little Kiko
The expedition of Thorfin Kari-
  sefni
  Crossley-*Legends,* 172–183
An expensive hide
  Cortes-*Byelorussian,* 125–
  127
EXPERIENCE
  Something for nothin (a Hui
  story)
—Buddhism
  The world in a pillow
—learn by
  Wise man and the apprentice
Expiation. *See* ATONEMENT
EXPLOITATION
  The golden mountain
—of female servant
  The giant's daughter
The extinguished light
  Singer-*Power,* 9–16
EXTORTION
  King Crocodile
  The poor man Monokto
—tribute demanded by Chinese
  Kile Bamba and the Loche
  bogatyr
The extra days: Ra, Thoth, and Nut
  Shelley-*Legends,* 45–47
EXTRATERRESTRIAL BEINGS
  Not snow nor rain
EXTREME UNCTION
  The devil does a good deed
The eye can deceive
  Todd-*Tortoise,* 45–46
EYE-OINTMENT
  A fary-nurseling
The eye restored
  Amore-*Lustful,* 136–137
The eye transplant
  Amore-*Lustful,* 130–131
Eye will see what it is destined to
  see

Mitchnik-*Egyptian,* 71–79
EYES
  See also BLIND
  The apples of eternal life
  Foolish Vanya and Princess
  Helena the Fair
  Little crab and his magic eyes
  Little One-Eye, . . . Two-Eyes,
  and . . . Three-Eyes
  The pixy-labour
  The prince who had two eyes
  Tale of the shrimp and the
  earthworm
  The terrible head
  The trolls in Hedale Wood
  Vartiter (Rose-Petal)
—nightstalker
  Dance in a buffalo skull
—origin of stars
  How the stars came: Iku's
  eyes
—removed and restored
  Fair Margaret
—sold to brother, for food
  Squirrel and the fox
—traded for food
  Good and evil
EYESIGHT
  Glooscap and the wishes
—no eyes, see through nose!
  Meamei the seven sisters
EYNISSYEN the Evil
  Llyr: children of the sea-god

Fabiano and Reyes
  Griego-*Cuentos,* 131–141
FABLES (subject)
  Shah-*World,* 170
Fabulous beasts
  Marshall-*Every.,* 335–348
The face at the window
  Haining-*Lepre.,* 13

FACES
    The crowd
—god of
    The god of faces
The fachan
    Froud-*Faeries*, unp.
[Faerie abductions]
    Seekers Saviors, 56–57
Faerie encounters
    Froud-*Faeries*, unp.
Faerie flora
    Froud-*Faeries*, unp.
Faerie islands
    Froud-*Faeries*, unp.
Faerie, or Faerieland. *See*
    FAIRYLAND
Faerie queene
    Keightley-*World*, 54–59
Faerie rades
    Froud-*Faeries*, unp.
Faerie rings
    Froud-*Faeries*, unp.
Faerie trees
    Froud-*Faeries*, unp.
Faerie ways
    Froud-*Faeries*, unp.
Faeries on the eastern green
    Froud-*Faeries*, unp.
FAILURE
    See also SUCCESS
    The camel dances
    The fox and the grapes
    Imp of the perverse
    Johnny and the three goats [in
        turnip field]
—social
    The pelican and the crane
Fair, brown, and trembling
    Jacobs-*Celtic*, 109–116
Fair exchange
    Phelps-*Maid*, 25–33
"FAIR FAMILY"
    The tylwyth teg
Fair Magdelon, or the Knight of the
    Keys
    Thomas-*It's*, 162–166

Fair Margaret
    Thomas-*It's*, 143–148
Fairest of all others
    Heslewood-*Tales*, 88–97
Fairie ring mushroom
    Froud-*Faeries*, unp.
Fairies [twenty-eight tales]
    Robertson-*Highland*, 1–27
FAIRIES
    Addlers and menters
    Adventures of John Dietrich
    Ainsel
    Alder
    Apple Trees
    Aristocratic fairies [condensed]
    Ash
    Asrai
    The baker's magic wand
    The bean-nighe
    Beauty and the beast
    Black Annis
    "Black Horse," the third Broth-
        er Zhang (Tu)
    Bluebell
    Bogles
    Boy abducted by fairies
    Bridget and the Lurikeen
    Brier Rose
    Brown man of the Muirs
    The brownie
    Buzz-buzz aunty
    The bwca (booka)
    Castles of Faerie
    La cenicienta huasteca
    The changeling [c]
    The changeling [d]
    The Chuang brocade
    Clover
    Cluricaun
    Coblynau
    Confessions of Tom Bourke
    Connla and the fairy maiden
    Cowslips
    Cross purposes
    Denizens of faerie
    Diamonds and toads

FAIRIES (continued)
    Pudding bewitched
    Ragwort
    Rapunzel
    The realm of faerie
    The Red Etin
    Redcap
    Rhys at the fairy-dance
    Rowan
    Rustam and Tahmina
    Saint John's wort
    Selkies
    The shadows
    Shellycoat
    Shepherd of Myddvai and the
      lake maiden
    Sleeping Beauty in the wood
    The smith and the Fairies
      [MacEachern]
    Solitary fairies
    The son of Tata Juan
      Pescador
    Spriggans
    The stolen lady
    The stolen ox
    Stonemason: a T'ung folk-
      tale
    Story of Ciccu
    Stray sod
    Taken [wife taken by fairies]
    Tam Lin
    Teapot spout: Mother Han-
      nah's story
    Teig O'Kane and the corpse
    The terrible head
    Thomas the rhymer
    The three wishes
    Thumbelina
    Toadstools
    The treasure seekers
    Trows
    Tuatha de Danann
    The two fiddlers
    Unantishee
    The unseelie court
    Urisk

    Visions of fairies [sightings, fu-
      neral, etc.]
    The water leaper
    Weardale fairies [dislike being
      observed]
    The wee folk [17 tales]
    White cap
    The white cat
    Whitethorn
    Why a girl should marry him to
      whom she is given
    Wichtlein
    Wild thyme
    Will-o'-the-wisp
    Willow trees
    The wonderful Chuang
      brocade
    The young lady of Hellerup
    The young man in the shian
    The young piper
—cave
    The ancient spirits of the coast
—Celtic
    The laird's lass and the
      gobha's son
—claims child
    Whuppity Stoorie
—customs
    Faerie ways
—departure
    Departure of the fairies
—disguise
    The baker's daughter
—English
    Fairies, English
—evil
    Sleeping Beauty in the woods
—excluded from heaven
    Why the fairies are vindictive
—food
    Ghillie Dhu
—free salmon from net
    Priest's supper
—gifts at christening
    Heart of ice [Prince Littleboots]
—gifts to princesses

The sleeping beauty
—good-*Melinette*
    Prince Narcissus and the Princess Potentilla
—grants wishes
    The boy and the dancing fairy
—hairstrings
    Pulowech, the partridge
—Irish
    Sidhe
—Italian
    Fate
—kidnappers
    The stolen princess
—live beneath waves
    The wave of Toime
—Mazilla
    Blue bird [King Charming]
—mountain
    Gwyllion
—music
    Jamie Freel and the young lady (condensed)
    Jemmy Doyle in the fairy palace
    The legend of Knockgrafton
—nurses & nursing
    Fairy nurse (condensed)
—origin
    Fairies: how it all began
    The fairies [war in heaven]
    Tobacco fairy from the Blue Hills
—palaces
    Jemmy Doyle in the fairy palace
—powers
    Denham tracts (condensed)
—protection against
    Protection against faeries
—queens
    Alison Gross (condensed)
—sea
    The woman of the sea
—sickly child for healthy one
    Fair exchange

—solitary
    Eodain the poetess
    The spell of the fairy mistress
—staring at, dangerous
    Fairy bride
—tears become pearls
    The fairy in a cage
—trooping
    Piskies in the cellar (condensed)
—water
    The glaistig
    The Gwagedd Annwyn
    Jenny Greenteeth
    The kelpie
    Pulowech, the partridge
    Water faeries
—wicked
    How black became white
FAIRIES (subject)
—abduction of humans
    Briggs-*Vanish.*, 215 (index)
—classification: sociable; solitary
    Yeats-*Fairy*, 381–385
—dealing with mortals
    Briggs-*Vanish.*, 133–140
—gifts
    Briggs-*Vanish.*, 216 (index)
—glamour
    Briggs-*Vanish.*, 216 (index)
—glossary
    Briggs-*Vanish.*, 195–201
—habitations
    Briggs-*Vanish.*, 81–91
—Irish fairies
    Logan-*Old*, 1–2
—lake
    Briggs-*Vanish.*, 39, 74, 89, 143–145
—midwives and changelings
    Briggs-*Vanish.*, 93–103
—morality
    Briggs-*Vanish.*, 151–161
—nature
    Briggs-*Vanish.*, 66–80

FAIRIES (subject) (continued)
—Newborn babies; superstitions
    McKee-*Scottish*
—origins of, beliefs and legends
    Briggs-*Vanish.*, 27–38
—origin of the word
    Keightley-*World*, 4–13
—origins of belief in
    Keightley-*World*, 1–4
—patrons, and wives
    Briggs-*Vanish.*, 141–150
—powers
    Briggs-*Vanish.*, 118–131
—queens
    Briggs-*Vanish.*, 217 (index,
        under Queens)
—rings
    Briggs-*Vanish.*, 11, 18–19, 49,
        82, 165
—size
    Briggs-*Vanish.*, 218 (index)
—skills taught by
    Briggs-*Vanish.*, 71–72, 74, 87,
        133–136
—solitary: terms; types
    Yeats-*Fairy*, 75–76
—sports
    Briggs-*Vanish.*, 39–40, 162–
        180
—trooping
    Briggs-*Vanish.*, 39–51
    Yeats-*Fairy*, 11–12
—virtuous
    Briggs-*Vanish.*, 157–160
Fairies and Frank Martin
    Yeats-*Fairy*, 14–17
Fairies and other supernaturals
    (condensed)
    Mckee-*Scottish*, 9–24
Fairies and the cattle [condensed]
    Logan-*Old*, 119–131
The fairies banished
    Keightley-*World*, 417–419
The fairies' caldron
    Keightley-*World*, 295–296
The fairies' christening

Keightley-*World*, 400
Fairies' dancing place [man builds
    house on]
    Yeats-*Fairy*, 307–308
Fairies, English
    Arrowsmith-*Field*, 159–162
Fairies: how it all began
    Logan-*Old*, 5–6
Fairies in the twentieth century
    Logan-*Old*, 133–135
The fairies [jewels or frogs . . .]
    Lewis-*Minute*, 24–25
The fairies' nurse
    Keightley-*World*, 353–354
Fairies of Corrie Chaorachain
    (condensed)
    Briggs-*Vanish.*, 166
The fairies of Seely Howe
    Robertson-*Highland*, 13–14
The fairies social life
    Logan-*Old*, 86–87
Fairies: taking the butter
    Logan-*Old*, 125–126
The fairies [war in heaven]
    O'Sullivan-*Legends*, 44–45
FAIRS
    The Botticelli horror
    Looking is free [State Fair]
    The phantom carousel
    Wasting sickness of Cu
        Chulaind . . .
—fairy
    The fairy fair
The fairy and the prince
    Segovia-*Spanish*, 249–274
The fairy banquet [a]
    Keightley-*World*, 283–284
The fairy banquet [b]
    Keightley-*World*, 399
FAIRY BLUE MOUNTAIN
    Ermine and the hunter
The fairy borrowing oatmeal
    Keightley-*World*, 389
Fairy bride
    Sampson-*Gypsy*, 95–99
The fairy changeling [condensed]

Logan-*Old*, 105–117
The fairy chapman
Keightley-*World*, 398–399
The fairy child
Villa-*Armenian*, 91–96, 445
Fairy doctors, witches
Yeats-*Fairy*, 133–135, 290
Fairy dwelling on Selena Moor
(condensed)
Briggs-*Vanish.*, 79–80
A fairy enchantment
Yeats-*Fairy*, 319–320
The fairy fair
Keightley-*World*, 294–295
The fairy fetch [apparition]
Marshall-*Every.*, 112–115
The fairy flag
Robertson-*Highland*, 16–17
Fairy frog (condensed)
Briggs-*Vanish.*, 99–100
The fairy gift
Keightley-*World*, 389–390
FAIRY GODMOTHERS
The blue lake
Cinderella
The kingdom of beautiful
colors
Salt above gold
FAIRY GODMOTHERS (subject)
Briggs-*Vanish.*, 37, 142
Fairy greyhound
Yeats-*Fairy*, 325–327
The fairy grotto
Vuong-*Brocaded*, 45–63
Fairy herbs
Logan-*Old*, 102–104
The fairy horn
Keightley-*World*, 284–285
Fairy horses
Logan-*Old*, 128–131
The fairy hunt
Keightley-*World*, 401–402
Fairy hurling game: Ireland vs
Scotland
O'Sullivan-*Legends*, 73–75
The fairy in a cage

Uttley-*Foxglove*, 59–66
FAIRY KINGS
The herd-boy
—takes form of drake
Boy with the deformed head
Fairy kings [condensed]
Logan-*Old*, 27–41
The fairy lalour
Keightley-*World*, 388
Fairy medicine [condensed]
Logan-*Old*, 89–104
Fairy music
Logan-*Old*. 84–85
Robertson-*Highland*, 3–4
Fairy nurse (condensed)
Briggs-*Vanish.*, 94–97
Fairy of Happiness: The tinkling
laugh
Segovia-*Spanish*, 137–187
Fairy of Hope: Genie of the
mountains
Segovia-*Spanish*, 223–247
Fairy of Hope: The cave of
emeralds
Segovia-*Spanish*, 223–247
Fairy of Kindness: Fairy and the
prince
Segovia-*Spanish*, 223–247
"FAIRY OF THE DESERT"
The yellow dwarf
"FAIRY OF THE PALACE"
Youth without age and life
without death (Turkey)
Fairy of the wandering star:
Merchant's . . .
Segovia-*Spanish*, 223–247
Fairy of the woods: The merchant's
fortune
Segovia-*Spanish*, 223–247
Fairy peel (condensed)
Briggs-*Vanish.*, 138–139
Fairy people [Irish; condensed]
Logan-*Old*, 63–87
Fairy queens and mistresses
[condensed]
Logan-*Old*, 43–62

The fairy rade
    Keightley-*World*, 354–355
FAIRY RADE (CAVALCADE)
    (subject)
    Briggs-*Vanish.*, 216 (index)
Fairy religion
    Logan-*Old*, 15–21
Fairy revels on Gump of St Just
    (condensed)
    Briggs-*Vanish.*, 84, 122
FAIRY RINGS
    Faerie rings
    Poor man of Peatlaw
        (condensed)
    Rhys at the fairy-dance
Fairy seals and seal maidens
    [condensed]
    Mckee-*Scottish*, 21–23
FAIRY TALES (subject)
—[Bettleheim on child psychology]
    Ehrlich-*Random*, x–xii
—[Collectors and tile pictures]
    Pierce-*Larousse*, 6–14
—history-the 1930's
    Thomas-*It's*, 229–236
—Lang: The "Blue" collection
    Lang-*Blue*, 349–358
—[Origins, by Andrew Lang]
    Lang-*Green*, 390–392
—symbolism
    Stuchl-*American*, 253–254
—Why tell one-minute tales?
    Lewis-*Minute*, 6–7
—[Worldwide usage; moral; truth]
    Lang-*Pink/D*, vii–viii
The fairy thieves
    Keightley-*World*, 305–306
Fairy thieves (condensed)
    Briggs-*Vanish.*, 45
The fairy whipping
    Keightley-*World*, 400–401
The fairy wind [fairy blast]
    Logan-*Old*, 97–98
FAIRY WIVES
    Boy with the deformed head
    The Northern Lights

FAIRYLAND
    See also ELFLAND
    Cherry of Zennor (condensed)
    [Dyfed: under spell because
        mortals trespass on Faerie]
    Fairy dwelling on Selena Moor
        (condensed)
    The realm of faerie
    The stolen princess
—underground
    Fairy revels on Gump of St
        Just (condensed)
FAIRYLAND (subject)
    Keightley-*World*, 44–54
—animals from
    Briggs-*Vanish.*, 16–17, 22, 76,
        172–174
—captives in
    Briggs-*Vanish.*, 104–117
—description
    Briggs-*Vanish.*, 216 (index)
—names of
    Logan-*Old*, 149–150 (index)
—time, supernatural passage of
    Briggs-*Vanish.*, 11–26
—underground
    Briggs-*Vanish.*, 218 (index:
        Under . . .)
—underwater
    Briggs-*Vanish.*, 218 (index:
        Under . . .)
—visits to
    Briggs-*Vanish.*, 218 (index:
        Visits . . .)
The fairy's inquiry
    Keightley-*World*, 385–386
FAITH
    Great Joy, the self-respecting
        ox
    Orpheus and Eurydice
The faithful gazelle
    Shah-*Afghanistan*, 90–95
Faithful John
    Yolen-*Favorite*, 287–293
The faithful lion
    Aiken-*Mexican*, 43–44

A faithful mouse
  Roberts-*Chinese*, 91
Faithful servant: The hundredth
  dove
  Yolen-*Hundredth*, 1–9
The faithful son, Dong Yong
  Sanders-*Dragons*, 114–115
The faithful trio [shelter in
  house]
  Stuchl-*American*, 61–62
Fakers. *See* IMPOSTERS
Fakirs. *See* BEGGARS; HOLY
  MEN—fakirs
The falcon and the quail
  [cleverness]
  Martin-*Hungry*, 19–23
FALCONS
  The apples of Iduna
  Boots and the beasts
  Fenist the bright-eyed falcon
  Gestumblindi's riddles
  Grateful animals and the un-
    grateful man
  How the toad got his bruises
  The kindly ghost [Joseph and
    his brothers]
  —as bridegroom
  Marya Morevna
  —its call: sign of bad luck
  Stingray: legend of the Meru
Fall of the spider man
  Macmillan-*Canadian*, 160–165
The fall of Troy
  Gibson-*Gods*, 133–143
The fall of tula
  Bierhorst-*Hungry*, 43–61
FALLACIES (logic)
  The cormorant and the star
Falling stars. *See* METEORS
FALSE ACCUSATIONS
  The cuckoo: its origin and its
    call
  The deer and the snake
  Esben and the witch
  The golden toothpick
  How a youth lost his virtue

Lanval and the Lady Triamor
Magic bird [tells stories]
Merchant's daughter and the
  slanderer
Mirror of Matsuyama
Nobleman and the slave
Okiku and the saucers
The old crone who was more
  wily than Iblees
Powel and Rhiannon
Prince Bellerophon and
  Pegasus
Pwyll, Prince of Dyfed
The queen who cried rape
The seven giant brothers
The talking nightingale [mon-
  strous birth]
Ten white doves
Three unmarried ministers
Treasurer under suspicion
Two sisters, Rose and Lotus
The vengeance of Oiwa
The wife from heaven
Wise sayings for a thousand
  dinars each
The world in a pillow
False friends. *See* BETRAYAL
A false ghost
  Lindow-*Swedish*, 195–196
False impressions: Lazarus and the
  dragons
  Crouch-*Whole*, 1–6
False pretenses. *See* PRETENSES
The false schoolmaster
  Skurynski-*Fools*, 28–39
False witnesses
  Shah-*World*, 190
FALSEHOOD
  See also DUPLICITY; LIARS
  Truth and falsehood
    [personified]
  —debases the liar
  The power of a lie
Falsehood and truth [personi-
  fied]
  Yolen-*Favorite*, 403–404

FAMILY
The ball of gold
Hop o' My Thumb
The only child who left home
Search for the magic lake
Seventh father of the house
The tax officials and Gohc
Amu
The wooden horse and the
painted jug
—king wants his brothers, even if
in hell
A journey into hell
FAMILY (subject)
—Buddhist stories
Amore-*Lustful,* 23
Family of the gods
Pinsent-*Greek,* 19–36
The family's fortune
Roberts-*Chinese,* 64–65
FAMINE(S)
Brer tiger and the big wind
Fall of the spider man
Giant with the grey feathers
Grimsborg
Hansel and Gretel
Leopard, the squirrel, and the
tortoise
Miracle of the sailing ship
Tortoise and his mother: wise
man dies, . . . buries him
The troll's hammer
—animals eat their mothers
O no, not my mother!
—babies killed
The blacksmith
Fancy. *See* IMAGINATION
FANKENMANNIKINS
Norggen, Orculli and
Fankenmannikins
FANS
The clever sewing-maid
Princess Minon-Minette
—magic
Kupti and Imani
Search for the magic lake

FANTASY
See also DAY DREAMS
The Botticelli horror
Flight over XP-637
The game of rat and dragon
Kid Cardula
The man from P.I.G.
The smallest dragonboy
The fantasy land of Lord Dunsany
Haining-*Lepre.,* 125–127
Far Darrig in Donegal
Haining-*Lepre.,* 44–45
Yeats-*Fairy,* 84–86
FAR DARRIGS
The red man's pranks
Far have I sought ye: Red Bull of
Norroway
Crouch-*Whole,* 113–120
Far out the long canal
And Every., 101–123
FARM GIRLS
—wiser than king
Catherine, sly country lass
(Italy)
Farm hand tied scythes over
horse's back
Lindow-*Swedish,* 182–183
Farmer, Penelope
Wayland Smith
Farmer and the badger
Ozaki-*Japanese,* 43–53
The farmer and the bear
Stovicek-*Around,* 186–187
Farmer and the bogle
Marshall-*Every.,* 64–68
A farmer learns a lesson
Campos-*Mexican,* 55–57
The farmer of Liddesdale
Jacobs-*Celtic,* 219–221
A farmer tricks a troll
Keightley-*World,* 113
Farmer who found his match in
daughter-in-law
Mitchnik-*Egyptian,* 62–71
The farmer who listened to his
livestock

Campos-*Mexican,* 104–110
FARMERS AND FARMING
All I possess!
Antti and the wizard's
  prophecy
The artful lad
The boggart
Brer fox tries farming, too
The brothers and the singing
  toad
The fairy gift
From bad to good to bad to
  good
Gellivor
The ghost and the moneychest
Grimsborg
The harvesters
The heavenly song of the
  green-spotted dove
Hildur, the queen of the elves
The hill men invited to the
  christening
How the tiger got his stripes
Hudden and Dudden and Do-
  nald O'Neary
Husband and wife should
  share equally
Jack and his master
Jack the cunning thief
Johan and the trolls
Johnnie in the cradle
Jurma and the sea god
Kertong
Little Claus and Big Claus
The little glass shoe
Llewellyn and Rhys
  (condensed)
Mally Whuppy
The man-servant and the wa-
  ter-elves
Massarioli
The merman
The nis and the mare
Opele-of-the-Long-Sleeps
Queen Pig
Snake with an ear for music

The snipe
Social connections
Stan Bolovan and the dragon
The story of Bergthor of Blafell
The stupid crocodile
The tiger and the jackal
Tight-fisted farmer and clever
  farmhand
The treasure in Saby Creek
Twigmuntus, Cowbelliantus,
  Perchnosius
Una the elfwoman
Valbjorg the Unelfed
Who built Reynir church?
Who was the stupidest
The wind cap
Witches on the lake
The wonderful plough
The young man in the shian
—farm work done by ghost
  'Aye, we're flitting'
—man changes role with wife
  Gone is gone
—poor
  The rich farmer and the poor
  farmer
—rich
  The rich farmer and the poor
  farmer
Farmer's son and the geni
  Shah-*Dervishes,* 159–170
Farmers three
  Booss-*Scand.,* 590–591
FARMHOUSES
  Portunes
The fary-labour
  Keightley-*World,* 311–312
A fary-nurseling
  Keightley-*World,* 310–311
FASHION
  The bear and the crow
  The hauntings at Frodriver
FASTING
  Buddha finds a middle path
  The hare's sacrifice
—contests

FASTING—contests (continued)
The jaguar and the cricket
FAT
Mouse Woman and the monster killer whale
The fat moon
Hadley-*Legends*, 16–17
Fat woman who melted away
Radin-*African*, 260–261
Fate
Arrowsmith-*Field*, 252–255
FATE
See also PROPHETS AND PROPHECY
Azad Bakht's tale
Catherine and her destiny
Catherine's fate
Charity can change a man's fate
The complacent one; sheep to be slaughtered
Curse on the only son
Destiny
Devil with the three golden hairs
Dialogue with death
Emperor's lesson
The extra days: Ra, Thoth, and Nut
Eye will see what it is destined to see
Fairest of all others
The flying bull
The imprisoned princess
The man who drowned in a washbasin
The meatballs' leader
Patience overcomes fate [piast]
The piece of straw
Princess with the golden hair
River claims a victim
The three golden hairs of Old Man Almanack
Twelve children on a platter
Underworld god of marriage

—curse, or prophecy?
The seven-day vigil
—death of wife avoided
The young man and the priest
—faced and defeated
The prince and his fate
—fickle
The two hunchbacks (Italy)
—wife stronger than
The prince and the three fates
The fate of Aino
Synge-*Land*, 24–34
Fate of Frank M'Kenna
Yeats-*Fairy*, 127–131
The fate of the children of Lir
Jacobs-*Celtic*, 144–161
Fate of the children of Lir
McGarry-*Folk*, 11–16
Fated animal does not see the hunter
Todd-*Some*, 72–76
FATES, THREE (subject)
Briggs-*Vanish.*, 37, 141
Father Frost
Xenophontovna-*Folk*, 141–147
The father of eighteen elves
Booss-*Scand.*, 602–603
Father of eighteen elves
Yolen-*Favorite*, 53–54
Father Wren and King Tiger
Manning-*Cats*, 124–125
FATHERS
The beastly creature and the magical flower
The blind boy and his dog
The brahman in the graveyard
The brothers and the singing toad
The castle: a parable
The daughter and the helper
Dead mother/children come for dying father
The forbidden apple
The girl who was already queen

Haunting of [computer] Y-12
[Sarrantonio]
The legend of Bodedys
Lion tamer [Tibetan]
The poor rich man's son gets
a second chance
Rashness of the young and
wisdom of the old
Settlement out of court
The seven fathers in the house
Seventh father of the house
What happened to Ivan
The young man who refused
to kill
—after death, returns as goose
The goose with the golden
feathers
—arranges marriage for widowed
daughter (tabu)
The young widow
—cowardly
The brothers Samba
—cruelty
Sedna, the witch under the
sea
Springfield Mountain [song and
story]
—forced to abandon children
Yeghnig Aghpar
—negative role model
The lion's treasured goat
—one eye weeps; the other laughs
Prince Mirko
—rejects daughter's suitors
Kuma and Aua
—rejects ugly daughter
The lady and the merman
—well-treated; bad motive
The bag of money
—would marry his daughter
Girl swallowed up by the stone
The golden box
Fatima and the tiger
McCarty-*Skull,* 61–65
FAULTS
—personal

Ruckus in the well
FAUN (wood god)
The merchant's fortune
FAUST (subject)
—[Tarot reading]
Lehane-*Wizards,* 68–69
Faustus and Mephistopheles
Lehane-*Wizards,* 79–86
Favorite verses, proverbs, and
riddles
Hyde-Chambers-*Tibet,* 97–100
FAVORITISM
The king's favorite [beauty
fades]
FAVORS
How the speckled hen got her
speckles
The young lady of Hellerup
—impositions
The devoted friend
FAWNS
Hershele and Hanukkah
Iktomi and the fawn
FAYS
Legend of Melusina
FAYS (subject)
Briggs-*Vanish.,* 37, 141–145
FEAR
See also COURAGE;
COWARDICE
Anpao and the animals
The brave lion and the foolish
rabbit [mass fright]
The butcher's bills
Chestnut grey
Coyote and turkey
Degei and his sons
Enchantment of Earl Gerald
[permanent transformation]
The hill folk
The lobster and the crab
The man who couldn't catch a
ghost
Outwitting giants
Pyoli and Lord Krishna
The red room [by Wells]

FEAR (continued)
    Seven fears
    Shingebiss: the wild duck
    The sky-god: Ratu and the
      Dyaks
    Taufatahi and Fakapatu or
      Why sharks . . . Moungone
    The teeth
    Terror
    Why raven is no longer
    Why the tiger and the stag fear
      each other
    A youth set out to learn what
      fear was
    The youth who went forth to
      learn what fear was
  Fearless lion, brave elephant, mer-
    chant's cries
    Martin-*Hungry,* 99–103
The feast of the mountain goats
    De Wit-*Talking,* 137–142
FEASTS
    See also names of feasts:
      CHRISTMAS; HANUKKAH;
      etc.
    Bricriu's feast
    The dwarfs' banquet
    The dwarf's feast
    The fairy banquet [a]
    The fairy banquet [b]
    How Cormac MacArt went to
      Faery
    The pig-headed wife
    The tale of Macc Da Tho's pig
—wedding
    Stupid Peikko
    Wedding feast of the little
      people
FEATHER WOMAN
    The Morning Star
FEATHERS
    The apples of Iduna
    King of the herrings
    The magic horse
    Marya Morevna
    El pajaro cu

    Rustam and the iron fortress
    Soup from a sausage skewer
    The three feathers
—colored, origin
    Origin of certain necklaces and
      plants
—golden
    The golden bird
    The golden feather [talking
      colt]
—magic
    Cock with the golden feathers
—raven
    The battle with the birds
    The village beneath the water
—turns into young man
    Fenist the bright-eyed fal-
      con
February dragon
    And Every., 125–152
Feelings, Muriel L.
    Zamani goes to market
Feelings. *See* EMOTIONS
Fees
    Arrowsmith-*Field,* 73–76
FEES (subject)
    Briggs-*Vanish.,* 37, 141–145,
      156–157, 195
FEET
    The apples of eternal life
    Curiosity punished
    The drovers who lost their feet
      (Mexico)
    How twelve clever brothers got
      feet mixed up
—goat-like
    Origin of the house of Haro
—hidden
    Erdluitle
—hoofs
    Deer woman
—wooden spike stuck in foot
    John and Mary; girl with
      chopped-off hands
FEMINISM
—anti-feminist tales

The honorable wife
FEMINISM (subject)
—[Women in fairy tales]
Phelps-*Maid,* ix–xvi
FENCERS AND FENCING
—fencing-masters
Three brothers [craft contest]
FENCES
The rich ranchero's maguey
fence
Feng-huang, the Chinese phoenix
Magical Beasts, 62–63
Fenist the bright-eyed falcon
Riordan-*Russia,* 63–72
FENNIANS
Oisin
—the first
Birth of Finn MacCumhail
The fenoderee
Froud-*Faeries,* unp.
Fenoderee. *See*
PHYNNODHEREE.
Fenrir the wolf is bound
Branston-*Gods,* 97–100
FERAL CHILDREN
Little Brother of the Winds
Ferguson, Samuel
Fairy thorn; an Ulster ballad
Yeats-*Fairy,* 41–43, 288
Fairy well of Lagnanay [poem]
Yeats-*Fairy,* 21–23
The fern girl
Riordan-*Tartary,* 37–43
FEROES (subject)
Keightley-*World,* 162–163
FERRIES AND FERRYMEN
Coffin cash
Departure of the trolls from
Vendsyssel
Devil with the three golden
hairs
The three golden hairs of Old
Man Almanack
FERTILITY
White ladies
—white ladies (pagan dieties)

the hunted hare
FERTILITY (subject)
—fairies and
Briggs-*Vanish.,* 216 (index)
FERTILIZER
Sand as fertiliser
The festival of the seven maidens
Chalk-*Tales,* unp.
FESTIVALS
The blessed gift of joy be-
stowed upon man
The fiddler and the sea nymph
The frog
The white rooster
FETCH (apparition)
The fairy fetch
FETTERS
Fenrir the wolf is bound
FETUS
—monster leaves and reenters
woman's body
Aturuarodo and the monster
Butoriku
FEUDS
The burning of Bergthorsknoll
Finn magic
How the Beldys stopped
fighting
—over eggs
Let the fire burn, you cannot
put it out
FIANCEES
—reminds prince of his promise
The twelve huntsmen
FIANNA (ancient Irish warriors)
Diarmuid, son of Donn: a spell-
shackled devotion
[Iollan and his fairy mistress]
Reckoning with the Fianna's
ancient bane
Fianna [conditions for admission]
McGarry-*Folk,* 77–79
FIANNA FINN (subject)
Briggs-*Vanish.,* 21–22
The Fianna: the god in disguise
Logan-*Old,* 23–26

FICKLENESS
  Prince Featherhead and Princess Celandine
Fiddle playing: The stromkarl . . .
  Lindow-*Swedish*, 121–122
The fiddler and the fairy
  Keightley-*World*, 402
The fiddler and the sea nymph
  Booss-*Scand.*, 299–300
The fiddlers of Tomnahurich
  Robertson-*Highland*, 9–10
FIDELITY
  See also INFIDELITY; MARRIAGE—fidelity
  Honor [fidelity]
  Princess with the golden hair
  A test of fire
  Three unmarried ministers
  Trusty John
Field, Eugene, 1850–1895
  Sugar-plum tree [poem]
FIELD MICE
  The doll's house
  Thumbelina
The field of Boliauns
  Haining-*Lepre.*, 72–75
  Jacobs-*Celtic*, 21–23
FIELDS AND STREAMS
  Bruin and Reynard partners
  Goat people
  The great battle between the grasshoppers and the monkeys
  Kombocke and Hausbocke
  Pixies
  Poleviki and Poludnitsy
A fiendish compadre gets caught
  Campos-*Mexican*, 119–121
The fiery dragon
  Sampson-*Gypsy*, 1–8
Fiery horse
  Kudian-*More*, 59–65
FIFES
  Nippy and the Yankee Doodle
The fifth and final sun
  Hadley-*Legends*, 8–9

  Piggott-*Mexican*, 22–31
The fifth sun
  Nicholson-*Mexican*, 72–76
The fifth sun [Nanahuatl]
  Bierhorst-*Hungry*, 34–36, 135
FIG TREES AND FIGS
  Magic figs
  Occasion [death trapped in bottle]
  Story of Ciccu
  The tumarang's revenge
FIGHTS AND FIGHTING
  Donkey's shadow
  A slave's dangerous courtship
The fig-pecker and the widow's son
  Shah-*Afghanistan*, 30–41
FIGURINES
  Kobolde
FIJI
—origin
  Degei and his sons
FILIAL PIETY
  Chestnut grey
  The cuckoo
  A dutiful son
  The faithful son, Dong Yong
  Foolish Vanya and Princess Helena the Fair
  Golden blackbird
  Half a blanket (Ireland)
  How a king learned to care for parents
  Ivanovoushka the simpleton
  Language of the birds
  The magic gifts [dwarf-sorcerer]
  Magic knife [Uygur]
  The man who wanted to bury his son
  Mirror of Matsuyama
  Mulien rescues his mother
  The old man and his grandson
  On top of Old Smoky [song and story]

"One, my darling, come to
mama"
The seven stars of the north
The three daughters
The tiger and the dwarf
The tiger's grave
Underworld justice
Urashima Taro, the fisher lad
The wisdom of a child
Filial piety [souls of parents in
butterflies]
Piggott-*Japanese*, 115–116
FILICIDE
Shun, the wise emperor
FIN FOLK
Annie Norn and the fin folk
FINBAR, Saint
Saint Finbar and the River Lee
Fincastle mill
Froud-*Faeries*, unp.
FINCHES
—red head feathers
Meri seizes the Iakomea
ornament
A fine phoenix
Roberts-*Chinese*, 225
Finger lock (condensed)
Briggs-*Vanish.*, 133–134
FINGERS
The golden finger
The pointing finger
—broken
The knight of Ellenholm
Finist the Falcon
Bilibin-*Russian*, 25–36
FINLAND
Adventures of Sikku
Antti and the wizard's
prophecy
Church grims
The devil's hide [temper]
The end of the world
Farmers three
Finn blood
Jack of Sjoholm and the Gan-
Finn

Jurma and the sea god
Leppa Polkry and the blue
cross
Liisa and the prince
Lippo and Tapio
The maid of the north
[Kalevala]
The mouse bride
Olli the terrible
The pig-headed wife
Severi and Vappu
The snow queen
Stupid Peikko
The vain bear
Vaino and the swan princess
The wisdom of the rabbit
The wooing of Seppo
Hmarinen
Finn blood
Booss-*Scand.*, 518–527
[Finn] Fann Mac Cuil and the
Scotch giant
Haining-*Lepre.*, 56–59
[Finn] Fionn Mac Cumhall
Ross-*Druids*, 53–64
[Finn] Fionn MacCumhaill and
Doireann
Logan-*Old*, 58–59
The Finn legend: a giant builds a
church
Lindow-*Swedish*, 86–88
FINN Mac COOL
The Aran Islands and Lough
Corrib
Birth of Finn MacCumhail
[Caoilte rescues Finn
MacCumal]
Fann Mac Cuil and the Scotch
giant
[Goll, the Morrigan, and Finn
MacCumal]
Grania and Diarmid
The great heroes of old
Knockmany legend
Oisin in Tir Nan Og, or last of
the Fena

FINN Mac COOL (continued)
    Oona and the giant Cuchulain
    Oonagh and the giants
    Reckoning with the Fianna's
      ancient bane
Finn Mac Cumal: Lineage of
    enchantment
    Lehane-*Legends,* 17–20
Finn MacCumal, Cormac, and
    Grainne . . .
    Lehane-*Legends,* 56–63
Finn MacCumhail and the son of
    the king of Alba
    McGarry-*Folk,* 69–76
Finn MacCumhail: Diarmuid and
    Grainne
    McGarry-*Folk,* 81–85
Finn magic
    Phelps-*Maid,* 155–162
The Finn messenger (Norway)
    Yolen-*Favorite,* 333–334
Finnbheara of Cnoc Meadha
    Logan-*Old,* 27–33
Finney, Jack
    The third level
Finnfolk: The water folk
    Scott-*Fantastic,* 148
[Finnish chanters/enchanters]
    Lehane-*Wizards,* 6–8
FINNISH FOLKLORE (subject)
—Kalevala
    Synge-*Land,* 7–8
FINNS
    The snow queen
FINNS (subject)
    Keightley-*World,* 487–490
FINVARA (subject)
    Briggs-*Vanish.,* 190, 216
    (index)
Fionn. See FINN Mac COOL
Fior Usga [origin of Lough of Cork]
    McGarry-*Folk,* 17–20
FIORDELISA, Princess
    Blue bird [King Charming]
Fir Bolg
    Arrowsmith-*Field,* 83–88

The fir darrig
    Froud-*Faeries,* unp.
The fir tree
    Lang-*Pink/D,* 102–111
    Lang-*Pink/K,* 311–321
FIR TREES
    How they got Hairlock home
FIRE
    The apples of eternal life
    Bishop Svedberg and the devil
    The bonfire
    The clever sewing-maid
    Coyote brings fire to The
      People
    Crane, kangaroo rat, fire
      makers
    Dog [becomes man's slave]
    February dragon
    First death of Ari and his
      resurrection
    The four elements
    The frog
    Gift from a star
    Gift of fire
    The gift of the white cockatoo
    The goblin and the huckster
    Graduation
    How coyote stole fire
    How rabbit got the best of
      coyote
    How raven brought fire to the
      Indians
    How the clever father saved
      his sons
    How the fire festival came to
      be
    How the mason-wasp fetched
      fire from god
    How the speckled hen got her
      speckles
    How they got Hairlock home
    Legend of the roadrunner
    The maiden made of fire
    Ma'nabus [earth god brings
      fire]
    The meat ants and the fire

Meri and Ari take revenge
Meri avenges his brother Ari
Mice in the corn
The monster of Poot Holler
Old man and the sun
The palace of the moon
Pestilence, darkness and fire
Prometheus and Pandora
Run brer gator, run!
Sister Fox and Brother Coyote
Stones of five colours and the
    Empress Jokwa
The theft of fire
The toad and the fire
The vain bear
The walking shadow
The warlike seven
The world of ice and fire
—discovery
    Maui the Polynesian
    Water-rat and fire
—human
    The other Celia
—jumping over
    The Iwaguddudogue myth
—making
    The mischief maker, Lox, and
        the three fires
—mystery
    Chisos ghosts
—origin
    Monkey, the cavy, and the
        jaguar
    Raven brings fire
—saved from, by dog
    Stone memorial to a dog
—stolen
    Maui, son of the sun
    The witches' fire
—to get rid of giant birds
    The bare mountains
FIRE (subject)
—exorcism
    Briggs-*Vanish.,* 101–103
FIRE-BEINGS
    How coyote stole fire

The fire dogs
    Zong-*Korea,* 11
Fire [good friend, bad enemy]
    Pitcher-*Tokol.,* 30–32
"FIRE-IMP"
    Piglet and the cow
Fire [personified]
    Stuchl-*American,* 80
The fire plume
    Wade-*Indian,* 183–205
The firebird
    Riordan-*Russia,* 34–44
    Zvorykin-*Firebird,* 11–28
The firebird and Tyska and vixen
    Wood-*Palace,* 111–128
FIREBIRDS
    Ivan Tsarevich, the wolf, and
        the firebird
    Tremsin and the maid of the sea
    The war of the birds and the
        beasts
Firebird's powers
    Magical Beasts, 84–87
FIREBOATS
    Anpao and the magic dogs
FIREFLIES
    Daughter of the moon
    Fall of the spider man
    Photogen and Nycteris; a
        day/night mahrchen
    Weardale fairies [dislike being
        observed]
—attempt to make fire from
    The apes and the busybody bird
FIREPLACES
    The young lady of Hellerup
Firewood. *See* WOOD—firewood
FIREWORKS
    The box marked secret
    The remarkable rocket
FIRST COMMUNION
    Girls at parsonage get help
        sewing crinoline
First death of Ari and his
        resurrection
    Wilbert-*Bororo,* 17–23

The first humans
  Branston-*Gods,* 29–50
The first Inca: marriage of sun and
  moon
  Shelley-*Legends,* 75–77
The first kantele
  Synge-*Land,* 176–186
First Man and First Woman
  Pitcher-*Tokol.,* 7–9
The first mosquito
  Macmillan-*Canadian,* 59–63
First pig and porcupine
  Macmillan-*Canadian,* 103–107
The first rain [war of two villages in
  Papua]
  Stokes-*Turtle,* 59–61
The first sun
  Bierhorst-*Hungry,* 25–27
First tale: In the beginning . . .
  Mullett-*Spider,* 1–6
First Woman and Elephant
  Pitcher-*Tokol.,* 50–53
FISH
  The anglers of Arz
  The big bird Katchka
  The brave Azmun
  La cenicienta huasteca
  A fisherman and a golden fish
  The giant sturgeon
  How sly-fox was fooled
  Juan and the bony one
  Lake Goldring
  Old One Eye [robbers foiled]
  Origin of certain fish [from
    flowers, palm-leaf, etc.]
  [Origin of tobacco] The Kud-
    dogo fish
  The Papa-Water and
    Bibaiyibaiyi
  Pedorus Jack
  Pisces (the Fishes)
  Seven families of Lake Pipple-
    Popple
  The steadfast tin soldier
  Suited to be a fish [eaten by
    colleagues]

The talking fish
Tall tales (Burma)
Tayzanne [fish killed, joined by
  girl who loves him]
The three fish [wise; clever;
  stupid]
Thumbelina
Tobias goes on a journey
The troll's daughter
Two brothers [and seven-
  headed monster]
The two old woman and the
  boastful fish
The warlike seven
The water sprite and the bear
The white snake
—air fish
  The golden key
—brother trans. into
  Galo and Vasiri
—by will of the fish. . .
  The fool and the magic fish
—carp
  The golden fish, wicked sis-
    ters, and good Forgetta
  Pretty Goldilocks
—deceived by crane
  The crane and the crab
—dinner
  The water nick
—eels
  The bushbabies
  The giant eel
—eels-fishing
  Hare and otter
—feet lacking
  The stars in the sky
—flatness
  Why the flat fish is flat
—flounders
  The fisherman and his wife
—golden-colored
  The dragon who cried
  The fisher-prince with the sil-
    ver apple
  Golden lads

—goldfish
    Happy goldfish; the sage
—herring
    King of the herrings
—jellyfish
    The cat in the sea
—jellyfish-origin of bone-
    lessness
    How the jelly-fish lost its bones
    Rin Jin: The jelly fish and the
      monkey
—jellyfish-stupidity
    Rin Jin: The jelly fish and the
      monkey
—large; unite to punish men for
    eating sardines
    Mermaid of the Magdalenes
—laughs and queen's question
    Clever boy
—made by throwing branches into
    river
    The Baiporo legend
—married to girl
    The girl with the large eyes
—perch
    Twigmuntus, Cowbelliantus,
      Perchnosius
—pike
    The black fox
    Omelya and the pike
    Singard the dragon-slayer
—plaice-origin of twisted
    neck
    The plaice and the salmon
—salmon
    The giant who had no heart
    How raven brought the salmon
    Raven and the beavers
    The raven and the salmon
    Raven steals the salmon from
      the beaver house
—salmon freed
    Priest's supper
—salmon: knowledge from eating
    How the Shannon got its name
—salmon-origin of its jumping

    The plaice and the salmon
—saved by commoner
    A princess on a swing
—southern
    Piscis Australis (the Southern
      Fish)
—spared, gives fortune
    The little old man in the tree
—tr'd into man, answers monster's
    questions
    The talking fish
—trout-lives on land; chokes in
    water
    Tommy the faithful trout
—trout not hurt by fire
    The white trout; a legend of
      Cong
—trout-origin of white mark
    White trout: a legend of
      Cong
—woman in form of
    The little talking animal and
      the shining blue fish
FISH HAWKS
    The girl who always cried
Fish hooks. See FISHHOOKS
FISH NETS
    Huia's dream
    The pelican Goolayyahlee
The fish rejoice
    Roberts-*Chinese,* 125
FISHERFOLK
    Fisherman's dream
A fisherman and a golden fish
    Pushkin-*Fairy,* 87–95
The fisherman and his soul
    Wilde-*Fairy,* 175–223
The fisherman and his wife
    Crouch-*Whole,* 156–165
    Lang-*Green,* 371–381
    Shah-*World,* 200–202
    Shub-*About,* 5–14
The fisherman and the draug
    Booss-*Scand.,* 111–118
Fisherman and the prince
    Mitchnik-*Egyptian,* 79–84

The fisherman of Gotur
  Booss-*Scand.*, 599–600
Fisherman's benefactor
  Seekers Saviors, 22–23
Fisherman's dream
  Sperry-*Where*, 57–68
The fisherman's wife. *See* The fisherman and his wife
FISHERMEN AND FISHING
  Beebyeebyee and the water-god
  Betty Booker's bridle [cured of being mean]
  "Binding" and driving off a sjora
  The black dragon of the Sea of Dunting
  Boy-man
  Boy of the red twilight sky
  The cat and his visions
  The dead soldier
  Drinking companions
  The empty sea
  The enchanted fisherman
  Finn blood
  Finn magic
  The giant eel
  The giant from Klasahall
  The gods' revenge
  Great roving uhu
  Halibut Man and the house on the waves
  Happy hunter and the skilful fisher
  The herd-boy
  The inheritance
  Isaac and the Parson of Brono
  Jack of Sjoholm and the Gan-Finn
  Kitpouseagunow
  Legends of the mill
  Manabozho's fishing: the king of fishes
  The merman
  The merrow and the soul cages
  The miraculous catch
  Mister Jeremy Fisher
  Pergrin and the mermaid (Wales)
  The quest for the Star of the Sea
  The rabbit makes a match
  Raven and the big fisherman
  Raven and the nose of the Gonaqadet [r. steals bait]
  Raven lets out the daylight
  Raven with the broken beak
  The sea maiden
  The sea nymph
  The seal fisher and the Roane
  The seawife and the crone
  The snake bridegroom
  The son of Tata Juan Pescador
  A tale of the Grand Jardin
  Thor goes fishing
  Thor goes fishing with Hymir
  The toad-bridegroom
  Tokanao: the first coconut
  The troll in the Skrudur
  The twins Urashima
  Urashima Taro
  Urashima Taro, the fisher lad
  The water leaper
  What a fish!
  The white seal maid
The fisher-prince with the silver apple
  Wyatt-*Princes*, 110–113
The Fishes [Odschig, the chief]
  Lurie-*Heavenly*, 45–49
FISHHOOKS
  The pearl fish-hook
  The wondrous fish-hook
Fishing of the women [adultery with otters]
  Wilbert-*Bororo*, 192–196
Fishing on the Arkansas: Earl Ott
  McNeil-*Charm*, 111–125
Fishing [two fathers, two sons]
  Shannon-*Solve*, 9–10

Fishing with bare hands
  Faulkner-*Tales*, 26–28
FISTA
  Three heroes [and the 3-
    headed boa]
Five million ducks
  Lewis-*Animal*, 28–29
Five strange plants
  Stokes-*Turtle*, 31–33
FLAGS
  Munachar and Manachar
—Brazil
  How the Brazilian beetles got
    their . . . coats
FLAGSTONES
  Munachar and the raspberries
FLAILS
  The lad with the goat-skin
FLANDERS
  The bold soldier of Antwerp
  The enchanted apple tree
FLATHEAD LAKE MONSTERS
  Water monsters
FLATTERY
  The crow's call
  The fox and the crow
  Fox, the crow, and the cheese
  Honeyed words can't sweeten
    evil
  Madame rhinoceros and her
    dress
FLAX
  Pint of flax seeds
  Tim Tit Tot
  The wild swans
FLEAS
  The art of killing fleas
  The bedbug and the flea
  How raven brought fire to the
    Indians
  How the world was made
—origin of characteristics
  Bedbug, the louse, and the
    flea
Fleas and cockleburrs
  Phillips-*Hoity*, 18–22

Fleece, golden. *See* GOLDEN
  FLEECE
The fleetest of foot
  Nagishkin-*Folktales*, 134–136
Fletcher, John Gould, 1886–
    1950
  Arkansas folk-ballads and
    background of history
FLIES
  Don Juan Zurumbete
  The faithful trio [shelter in
    house]
  In the middle of the night
—black
  Bad Indian's ashes [flies tor-
    ment people]
—forty at one blow
  Lazarus and the dragons
The flies and the bees
  Parker-*Australian*, 86
The flight of Quetzalcoatl
  Bierhorst-*Hungry*, 55–61
Flight of the eagle
  Schwartz-*Elijah*, 82–88
Flight over XP-637
  Asimov-*Fant.*, 106–116
FLINT
—origin
  Esben and the witch
FLINTSTONE(S)
  The golden mountain
  How raven brought fire to the
    Indians
FLOCKS
—origin
  Tokoloshi (origin of herds and
    flocks)
The flood
  Reid-*Myths*, 11-17
FLOOD (biblical)
  The Dove [Noah and the flood]
  The Lapp genesis, or the first
    of mankind
  The Wolf [Noah's ark]
FLOOD CONTROL
  The cuckoo: its origin and its call

FLOODS
Adventures of Ntini, the small
otter
Coyote and Iitoi: the flood
The deer and the snake
The devil invented alcoholic
drink
The frog
Frog heralds of the flood
The giant eel
The great deeds of King Yu
The great flood
The great flood [deluge]
How Akaruio Bokodori repopu-
lated the earth
Hunter Hailibu's great sacrifice
Li Ching and the rain god
The magic boat
A Navajo story of creation
Raven lets out the daylight
[World-devastating flood in-
flicted by Zeus]
Yu controls the flood
—five years of rain
Story of a flood
—gods would destroy all mankind
for wickedness
Seven days and nights
—kills all, save one
The great flood; Jokurugwa or
Meriri Poro
—one family saved
The great flood
—as punishment
Liu Yi and the dragon king
The rain-makers, the dragon-
palace, and the Ling
mountains
Flora, Fletcher
Settlement out of court
The flower child
Reed-*Aboriginal*, 67–68
FLOWER GARDENS
The crocodile in the bedroom
The selfish giant
Flower people [two tales]

Reed-*Aboriginal*, 63–68
FLOWERS
Baiame: in the beginning
The beastly creature and the
magical flower
The birthday of the Infanta
Bluebell
Clover
Cowslips
Echo and Narcissus
Faerie flora
Golden stick, silver stick
Little Ida's flowers
Miraculous flower [stolen by
prince of ice]
Pansy
Phoenix fairy flower [Han]
Primroses
Ragwort
Saint John's wort
The snow queen
The snow queen: an adventure
in seven stories
The two compadres
The tylwyth teg
Wild thyme
—gold turned into
Sam Pig seeks his fortune
—of immortality
Vartiter (Rose-Petal)
—language of
The language of flowers
—magic
Jovita and Mamuelito
—names
Flowers by any other name
—one real, among many artificial
Which flower?
—red
Jorinde and Joringel
—scents of
The little white hen and the
three fox-cubs
—sentiments of
Flowers and the sentiments
they represent

—a small person lives in each
  Thumbelina
—spirits of
  Thumbelina
—spring
  Spring flowers
—state
  State flowers of the
    U.S.A.
FLOWERS (subject)
  Piggott-*Japanese*, 143 (index)
The flowers: a legend
  Parker-*Australian*, 171–174
Flowers and the sentiments they
    represent
  Ewart-*Lore*, 176–180
Flowers by any other name
  Ewart-*Lore*, 172–175
The flowers' forever land
  Anderson-*Trick.*, 76–78
The flowers from the sky
  Walking-*Song*, 39–42
FLUTES AND FLUTISTS
  Aniz the shepherd
  The archer who went I know
    not where to fetch . . .
  Artemis and Apollo
  Forgetful Fred
  Golden pears
  The heavenly flute player; a Li
    story
  Hyena and hare search for
    wealth
  Jack and his magic aids [dish,
    belt, flute]
  The lad with the goat-skin
  Magic flute of Asmodeus
  A Navajo story of creation
  Odd jobs
  Selim and the snake queen
  The two Sigurdurs
  The Yom Kippur flutist
—"gone to play the
    flute"
  Three musicians [princess
    under spell]

—magic
  Anizu's magic wonder flute
  The merchant's fortune
The fly (as witness)
  Yolen-*Favorite*, 55–57
The fly [falls into teacup]
  Berger-*Animalia*, [25–27]
Fly together, chips and shavings!
  Wright-*Pigeon*, 26–26
FLYING
  Cassowary [bird] and Kokomo
    [ability to fly]
  Drakes [house spirits]
  The magic horn [flying
    carriage]
  Princess Minon-Minette
  What happened to six wives
    who ate onions
  Witches: secret of flight
—inside eagle skin
  Boy who was saved by his
    thoughts
—man makes wings
  Bilak Pokis
—man uses swan's wings
  The travelling companion
FLYING (subject)
—magical
  Briggs-*Vanish.*, 216 (index)
The flying bull
  Roberts-*Chinese*, 69
FLYING CARPETS
  Cobbler's son and the serpent
  Dream of Habeeb-son-of-
    Habeeb
  Mysterious palace [Solomon &
    Ramirat]
The flying childer
  Garner-*British*, 140–145
Flying creatures
  Magical Beasts, 57–87
[The Flying Dutchman]
  Water Spirits, 87–91
FLYING FOXES
  Red and black flying foxes
—origin

FLYING FOXES—origin
(continued)
Bilak Pokis
The flying head
Yolen-*Favorite,* 233–234
Flying horse [wooden]
Lewis-*Minute,* 32–33
The flying kite
Blyton-*My,* 13–17
Flying lion of the Rab of Tlemcen
Elbaz-*Folktales,* 106–107
Flying money
Soyer-*Adventures,* 47–70
Flying pole dance
Wright-*Gold,* 28–31
FLYING SAUCERS
Not snow nor rain
Flying ship
Riordan-*Russia,* 78–85
The flying trunk
Booss-*Scand.,* 410–415
Lang-*Pink/D,* 40–46
Lang-*Pink/K,* 1–8
The flying war club
Thompson-*Hawaiian,* 19–28
FOG
How the hermit helped to win
the king's . . .
Shinansha, or the south-point-
ing carriage
Sila [human female born to be
a sea-being]
Stormalong fights the Kraken
Waxworks
FOG MAN
The man who sat on the tide
FOLETTOS
Linchetti
FOLK ART
Link chains as folk art
Folk beliefs about portents
Lindow-*Swedish,* 68–70
Folk religion. *See* RELIGION
FOLK SONGS (subject)
—[Original stories based on 20 his-
torical American songs]

Sanders-*Hear,* xi–xvi
FOLK TALES (subject)
Marshall-*Every.,* 11–50
Thomas-*It's,* 208–211
FOLKLORE (subject)
—[Fieldwork research methods]
McNeil-*Charm,* 11–22
Folklore from the campus
McNeil-*Charm,* 25–29
Folklore in Arkansas
McNeil-*Charm,* 30–35
[Folktales are almost always "true"]
Jagendorf-*First,* 5
Follets
Arrowsmith-*Field,* 217–220
Folletti and Incubi
Arrowsmith-*Field,* 104–109
Following the witch
Lindow-*Swedish,* 169–170
Folly. *See* FOOLS AND
FOOLISHNESS
Fomorians
Magical Beasts, 36–43
FOMORIANS
The dark of the sea
Moytura: the second battle
Fomors: castle of Balor
Lee-*Castles,* 52–53
Fomushka the village idiot
Weiss-*Russian,* 9–19
FOOD
Big brother: man; Little brother:
rabbit
The greedy youngster
How the monkey got food
when he was hungry
How the turtle got her shell
The lake monster
Starkad and Bale
Stupid Peikko
The troll in the Skrudur
The wonderful little pouch
—"Chop-Choy"
Imperial left-overs
—cooked
Maui, son of the sun

—demanded; must be eaten
Door in the cliff
—magic supply (never grows less)
Badger and the green giant
—personified
The meatballs' leader
—provided by Allah
The food of Paradise
—turns to ashes
Manabozho and the squirrels
—unusual
Journey of Nonogo Pori
[Search for parents] Pari Ao
FOOD (subject)
—fairies offer
Briggs-*Vanish.*, 216 (index)
The food balls [Kiowa]
Myles-*Butterflies*, 31–35
Food Mountain: True corn
Bierhorst-*Hungry*, 32–33, 135
The food of Paradise
Shah-*World*, 135–140
FOOD RELIEF
The magic shawl and the enchanted trumpet
FOOD SUPPLY
Coming of the corn
—winter
The fox and the bear
The fool and the birch
Ginsburg-*Twelve*, 24–31
The fool and the magic fish
Riordan-*Russia*, 165–174
The fool: numbskulls and noodleheads
Yolen-*Favorite*, 167–197
Foolish coyote
Weeks-*Pachee*, 9–23
Foolish expenditures: The hoity-toity mouse
Phillips-*Hoity*, 6–17
The foolish jackal
Amore-*Lustful*, 147–148
Foolish men and scolding wives
Booss-*Scand.*, 49–52
A foolish mourner

Zong-*Korea*, 193–194
Foolish sympathy: a speckled hen
Cortes-*Byelorussian*, 5–11
Foolish Vanya and Princess Helena the Fair
Mayo-*Book*, 21–28
The foolish weaver and the jackal
Raychaudhuri-*Stupid*, 19–25
Foolish wife
Riordan-*Russia*, 207–210
Foolish wish: The frog and the ox
Ross-*Druids*, 79–81
The foolish young Mussulman
O'Connor-*Tibet*, 30–42
FOOLS AND FOOLISHNESS
See also DELUSION; IM-PROVIDENCE; IMPRU-DENCE; STUPIDITY
The Amadan Mor and the Gruagach
Beausoleil
B'er rabbit is an uncle
The biter bit
The boy who was called Thickhead
The brave lion and the foolish rabbit
Bride-price: a woman for a hundred cattle
Chestnut grey
The clever fool
Comedy of errors: Brave Nazar
The complacent one; sheep to be slaughtered
Coolnajoo, the foolish one
Coyote Bun and the turkey
Coyote's vanity
The crooked pine
The death of little Kiko
Dividing the axe
Dog and the bone
Donkey Wonkey
Donkey's shadow
The drovers who lost their feet (Mexico)
Eight donkeys

What the old man does is
    always right
White dove
Why the tiger is striped
Wise Ma Zai
Wise men three
The witty joker
The wow o'Rivven; the bell
A youth set out to learn what
    fear was
—attempt to capture moon
The mantis and the moon
—believes man turned into
    donkey
The donkey who hit his mother
—believes word of thief
Jha and the copper bowl
—copper to gold
The gold harvest
—deceived by adulterous wife
The carpenter's wife
—does all/only what he is told
A mother's yarn
—foolish disclosure
The cat and the dog
—good wife a cure for
A pottle o' brains
—humor
A good thing he wasn't wear-
    ing it!
—imagines trouble that may never
    happen
Don't beat your children before
    they're born
—literal
Petty bargaining
—making a fool of someone
The barn is burning
—pride
The haughty chief
—shows magic tablecloth
The spirit of the spring
—wife, livestock eaten up
Jaguar Petronius, a friend of
    the family
—wife tricked into being judged as

A stroke of luck
FOOLS AND FOOLISHNESS
    (subject)
—[How wise humans might be]
    Yolen-*Favorite*, 169–170
Fool's luck
    Villa-*Armenian*, 357–359, 521
Foot racers of Payupki
    De Wit-*Talking*, 63–75
FOOTBALL
    Johnny Chung and the Flying
        Figments
Football on a lake
    Manning-*Spooks*, 17–21
The footprint of Buddha
    Toth-*Tales*, 127–132
Footprints on the ceiling
    Schwartz-*Tales*, 25
Footsteps of the god
    Nicholson-*Mexican*, 49–52
For domestic peace
    Elbaz-*Folktales*, 66
The forbidden apple
    Wolkstein-*Magic*, 172–175
The force of luck
    Griego-*Cuentos*, 33–51
Force. *See* POWER
Forced marriage. *See* MAR-
    RIAGE—forced
FORCIBLE ENTRY
    A mother's yarn
FOREKNOWLEDGE
    See also SECOND SIGHT
    The barn is burning
    Holecek and the water nymph
Foreman: Drill, ye tarriers . . .
    Sanders-*Hear*, 82–87
Foresight. *See* PRUDENCE
FOREST FIRES
    Brave little parrot and the ea-
        gle's tears
    Burning of the Khandava forest
    Fire [good friend, bad enemy]
    Rabbit shoots the sun
Forest people: A great misfortune
    Nagishkin-*Folktales*, 32–38

Foresters. *See* WOODSMEN
FORESTS
    Bremen town musicians
    The bushbabies
    The coal burner and the troll
    Dames vertes
    Elstorps Woods
    The festival of the seven
      maidens
    Goat people
    The gunny wolf [danger]
    Hansel and Gretel
    Hey-hey men
    Jorinde and Joringel
    Kombocke and Hausbocke
    "Lars, my lad!
    Leshiye and Lisunki
    Lisalill
    Moss people
    The princess in the ivory
      tower
    Salvanelli
    Seligen Fraulein
    Skogsra or wood trolls
    A summer night in a Nor-
      wegian forest
    Thor in the giant's strong-hold
    The troll ride
    The trolls in Hedale Wood
    True and untrue
    The umbrella tree
    A Weetigo in the woods
    The Wendigo (I–IX)
    The werewolf
    Why the executioner is called
      assessor
Foretelling the future [written on
    forehead]
    Villa-*Armenian,* 322–323
Forgetful Fred
    Williams-*Practical,* 53–64
Forget-me-not
    Ewart-*Lore,* 156–157
"FORGETTA"
    The golden fish, the wicked
      sisters, and good Forgetta

FORGETTING
    The Northern Lights
    Yvon and Finette
The forging of the sampo
    Synge-*Land,* 55–56
FORGIVENESS
    See also PENITENCE;
      UNFORGIVENESS
    The dance of the spectres
    Flying money
    The golden fish, the wicked
      sisters, and good Forgetta
    Let the fire burn, you cannot
      put it out
    Where love is, God is
FORSYTHIA
    Apple blossom, Forysthia,
      Aubrietia
Fortifications. *See* STOCKADES
FORTS (subject)
—Cusheen Loo
    Yeats-*Fairy,* 288
FORTUNE
    See also LUCK; WEALTH
    Dick Whittington and his cat
    Sam Pig seeks his fortune
    Triplets [Light Foot, Skilful
      Hand, Keen Eye]
    Wisely spent
—reversal of
    Ditch-digger falls into his own
      ditch
    Toads and diamonds
The fortune teller
    Roberts-*Chinese,* 146–148
Fortune-teller recognizes King
    Saul
    Elbaz-*Folktales,* 78
FORTUNETELLERS
    The blind man and the devils
    How Fin went to the kingdom
      of the big men
    Lam Ku, the basket lady
    Luck in a strange place
    Moerae
    The mouse bride

The story of Deirdre
The founding of Mexico [myths]
  Bierhorst-*Hungry*, 63–83
The founding of Rome
  Lines-*Greek*, 232–236
FOUNDLINGS
  The brewer of egg-shells
  The cat Johann
  Children of the fairies
  Devil with the three golden
    hairs
  The giant with three golden
    hairs
  The golden haired twins
  Love: queen and foundling
  The Santa Lucias [demon-
    foundling; legend]
  The star child
—giant in disguise
  Iya, the camp-eater
—prince's exact image
  Ivan Byelarasseiski
FOUNTAIN OF YOUTH
  Woodcutter and the fountain of
    youth
Fountain women
  Arrowsmith-*Field*, 220–222
FOUNTAINS
  Draw the curtains
—sacred
  The trolls of Skurugata
Four ages of thought
  Ewart-*Lore*, 132–138
The four elements
  Griego-*Cuentos*, 23
Four hairs from the beard of the
    devil
  Wolkstein-*Magic*, 44–48
FOUR-LEAFED CLOVER
  Clover
Four-leafed shamrock
  O'Sullivan-*Legends*, 86–87
Four magic arrows
  Thompson-*Hawaiian*, 72–85
The four rings
  Roberts-*Jung*, 71–102

Four sworn brothers
  Zong-*Korea*, 162–166
FOWL
—origin: raising head when
    drinking
  Creator Nyame and his four
    wives
FOWLERS
  The hundredth dove
The fox and the angel of death
  Patai-*Gates*, 598
Fox and the ant [race]
  Lewis-*Animal*, 10–11
The fox and the Barkantz
  Ransome-*War*, 52–54
The fox and the bear
  Nagishkin-*Folktales*, 146–150
The fox and the crow
  Ross-*Druids*, 62–64
  Watson-*Aesop*, 14–15
  Williams-*Aesop*, [10–11]
The fox and the drum
  Wood-*Kalila*, 54–62
The fox and the grapes
  dePaola-*Favorite*, 99
  Williams-*Aesop*, [12–13]
The fox and the hedgehog
  Shah-*World*, 236
The fox and the jackal
  Ransome-*War*, 51–52
The fox and the little white hen
  Uttley-*Foxglove*, 33–43
Fox and the pitcher
  Riordan-*Russia*, 194
The fox and the stork
  dePaola-*Favorite*, 83
Fox and the stork
  Watson-*Aesop*, 22–24
Fox and the wolf
  Radin-*African*, 100–103
FOX HUNTING
  Lady Ren: fox spirit
Fox maiden
  Night Creatures, 132–139
Fox, the crow, and the cheese
  Lewis-*Animal*, 30–31

The fox who went to heaven
  Wyatt-*Princes,* 30–55
[The fox with the purple
  umbrella]
  Tompert-*Three,* 4–14
The fox without a tail
  Sheohmelian-*Three,* 35–
  38
FOXES
  The adventures of Yemima
  Aryeh-Ben-Gadi and Fox-of-
  the-Burnt-Tail
  Badger and the fox cub
  Big long man's corn patch
  The bird 'Grip'
  The black fox
  The bone garden
  The boy with the knucklebones
  Brer fox meets Mister Trouble
  Brer fox tries farming, too
  Brer rabbit keeps his word
  Brer wolf and brer fox get a
    big surprise
  Bruin and Reynard partners
  The Catholic fox
  Coolnajoo, the foolish one
  Drakestail [and the king]
  The ducks and the fox
  The end of the world
  The Eskimo Indian and his fox
    wife
  Farmers three
  The firebird and Ryska and
    vixen
  First pig and porcupine
  [The fox with the purple
    umbrella]
  The gingerbread boy
  The Greek princess and the
    young gardener
  His just reward
  House of ice and house of
    wood
  How a bear kept reindeer
  How Ableegumooch tracked a
    fox
How bear and chipmunk
  stopped being friends
How Saynday got the sun
How sly-fox was fooled
How the fox and the elk ex-
  changed legs
How the hare made a fool of
  the wolf
How the monkey got food
  when he was hungry
How the speckled hen got her
  speckles
How they got Hairlock home
Ivan Bear's ear
The jewel of the fox's tongue
Johnny Cake
King of the pomegranate tree
King's son goes bear hunting
  (Finland)
Kyang, the fox, the wolf and
  the hare
The lad and the fox
Lady Ren: fox spirit
Lazarus and the dragons
The little chicken Kluk and his
  companions
The little fox
The little red hen
Little Sister Fox and Brother
  Wolf
The little white hen and the
  three fox-cubs
Liza the fox and Catafay the
  cat
Mac Iain Direach
The magic fox
Midwife fox [steals honey]
The miller and the fox
Mister Fox [suitor/murderer]
Mother confessor fox
The muzhik, the wolf, and the
  fox
Obdurman the clever
  huntsman
One hairball
The party

A pool of bright water
Pork and honey
Prince of nettles
Rabbit and the grain buyers
The rabbit and the well
Raven and the fox
Reynard and Chanticleer
The russet dog
Sister Fox and Brother Coyote
Skunk's tale
Sky high went the sun
The sky is falling
Slip root, catch Reynard's foot
Smart head better than sharp
    teeth
Song-bird and the healing
    waters
Spirits and demons
The straw ox
The tiger behind the fox
Traveller, the fox, and the tiger
True and untrue
The vain bear
The valiant chanticleer
War of the wolf and the fox
The way of the world
The weathermaker
The white fox
Who stole brer Gilyard's
    sheep?
Wisdom of Senor Zorro
—as judge
    Whose horse is it?
—clever
    The wolf and the fox
—in form of girl
    Fox-girl and her brother
—luck runs out
    Travels of a fox
—old
    The fox and the bear
—origin: color of eyes and coat
    How rabbit deceived fox
—outsmarts tiger
    The stupid fox [and trapped
    tiger]

—rabbit's hut taken over
    The hare's hut [fox chased out]
—steals ducks
    Iktomi and the red-eyed ducks
—transformed from horse
    The golden knucklebone
—tricked into leaving rabbits alone
    Jean Lapin and the foxes
—tricks the bun
    The bun [personified]
—witch
    Mountain witch and the Drag-
    on-King
FOXES (subject)
    Piggott-*Japanese*, 143 (index)
FOXFIRE
    The devil and the farmer's wife
Fox-girl and her brother
    Zong-*Korea*, 171–174
Foxglove
    Ewart-*Lore*, 76–78
FOXGLOVE
    Death out of season
    Faerie flora
FRANCE
    Cinderella
    Drakes [house spirits]
    Follets
    Guleesh
    Legend of Melusina
    Lutins
    The men who wouldn't stay
    dead (France)
    Onaouientagos
    River women
—Brittany
    The dance and the song of the
    Korred
    Fountain women
    Korred
    Lai D'Ywenee
    Lord Nann and the Korrigans
—history-revolution
    Adventure of the German stu-
    dent [Irving]
—vs England

FRANCE—vs England (continued)
   God on our side
FRANCE (subject)
   Keightley-*World*, 465–486
—Brittany
   Briggs-*Vanish.*, 17, 32, 156–
      157
   Keightley-*World*, 419–442
—fairies
   Briggs-*Vanish.*, 73–74, 93–94,
      141–148, 151
—[Magic, in an earlier age]
   Seekers Saviors, 7
Francis and the gaint
   Fattoross-*Simpleton*, 63–66
FRANCIS OF ASSISI, Saint
   Little brothers: insects, etc.
Frankie and Johnny [song and
      story]
   Sanders-*Hear*, 120–130
FRATRICIDE
   Balin and Balan
   Glooskap and Malsum, the
      wolf
   The rose of Peppermette
—attempted
   Clever Daniel
—planned
   The wondrous fish-hook
FRAUD
   See also DISHONESTY
   The golden neckband
   Kile Bamba and the Loche
      bogatyr
   Pint of flax seeds
—selling worthless product
   The art of killing fleas
FREE WILL
—what women want most
   Gawain and the Lady Ragnell
"FREEBOOTERS"
   The outlaw
FREEDOM
   Dog and the wolf [dog chained
      by-day]
   Keep on stepping

A riddle for freedom
A slave's escape
Wolf who traded his freedom
   for security
FREEWAYS
   How the animals stopped the
      freeway
FREEZING
   Kitpouseagunow
   The mischief maker, Lox, and
      the three fires
—to death
   The snow storm
FRENCH PEOPLE
—Missouri
   Character and culture of the
      Missouri French
French place names in Arkansas
   McNeil-*Charm*, 69–81
FRENEY, JAMES, 18th cent.
   O'Sullivan-*Legends*, 143–145
FREYA
   The walls of Asgard
Friendlessness: The pelican and
      the crane
   Lobel-*Fables*, 34–35
Friendly dragons
   Stallman-*Dragons*, 28–37
The friendly dwarfs
   Keightley-*World*, 220
FRIENDSHIP
   The censor and the tiger
   The devoted friend
   Double-headed phoenix
   Drinking companions
   Golden stick, silver stick
   Heaven's reward
   Helpful spirit
   Ludwig and Iskander
   Rooting out bad feelings
   Search for a friend
   The strongest boy in the world
   There is righteousnes
   The two friends [die for each
      other]
   Zirac and friends

—become enemies
   The proper way to make sago
—offer to die for each other
   Two true friends
—tests
   A boy and his dog
FRIGG
   The golden age in Asgard
Frightened wolves [wolf head]
   Riordan-*Russia*, 161–164
Frivolous life: Passion of the gewel
   Magel-*Gambia*, 50–52
The frog
   Hyde-Chambers-*Tibet*, 169–
   186
The frog and the crow
   O'Connor-*Tibet*, 48–50
The frog and the ox
   Ross-*Druids*, 79–81
Frog and Umdhlubu
   Radin-*African*, 106–112
Frog heralds of the flood
   Parker-*Australian*, 175–176
Frog people [two tales]
   Reed-*Aboriginal*, 29–36
The frog prince
   dePaola-*Favorite*, 21–31
   Ehrlich-*Random*, 94–101
   Lewis-*Minute*, 14–15
   Tudor-*Bedtime*, [6–7]
The frog princess
   Bilibin-*Russian*, 69–77
Frog princess: Vassilisa the Wise
   Riordan-*Russia*, 129–137
Frog went a-courting [song and
   story]
   Sanders-*Hear*, 47–58
Frog who became an emperor
   Peacock Maid, 74–82
FROGS
   A choir [of croaks]
   Coming of spring
   Eagle and the frog
   Educated frogs and martial ants
   The everlasting frogs [daugh-
   ters turned to]

Fairy frog (condensed)
How coyote stole fire
Little frog repays coyote
The marsh king's daughter
Mister Jeremy Fisher
The moon and his frog-wife
One hairball
Parley Garfield and the frogs
The singing frog
The skunk and the frogs
Son of Kimanaueze and
   daughter of sun and moon
Thumbelina
The umbrella tree
Wise frog and foolish frog
—a lord under a spell
   [Well at the World's End]
—as bride of youngest son
   The frog princess
—Babushka Lagushka Skakushka
   The archer who went I know
   not where to . . .
—croaking
   The green frog
—escapes from crow
   The frog and the crow
—finds doll, which comes to life
   The brook's secret
—form all-male community
   The timid frogs
—origin of characteristics
   Glooskap and the monster
   bullfrog
   Glooskap's country [bullfrog's
   croak, skin, etc.]
—prince under spell
   Master Frog
   The princess and the frog
—princess under spell
   Czarina frog
   The Tsarevna frog
—skins
   The frog
—transformed into beautiful girl
   The three feathers
—water guard

FROGS—water guard (continued)
  Gluska'be, the Penobscot hero
—why no tail
  The witches' fire
  The frogs at the rainbow end
    Lobel-*Fables,* 14–15
  From bad to good to bad to good
    Kendall-*Sweet,* 39–41
  From bad to worse
    Villa-*Armenian,* 422–423
  From pinpoints to pollywogs
    Gallant-*Constel.,* 19–20
FRONTIERSMEN
  Strong but Quirky
Frost
  Synge-*Land,* 147–153
FROST
  Father Frost
  Grandfather Frost
  How Glooskap found the
    summer
  Ivan the rich and Ivan the poor
  Jack Frost
  Where the frost comes from
FROST GIANTS
  The creation of the world
  How Glooskap made the birds
Frost, Sun, and Wind
  Riordan-*Russia,* 106
Frosty [and five with superhuman
    powers]
  Sampson-*Gypsy,* 55–57
Froud, Brian, illus.
  Froud-*Faeries*
—(letter from reader)
  Froud-Faeries
The frozen logger [song and
    story]
  Sanders-*Hear,* 131–138
FRUIT
  Wooden horse [mechanical
    flight]
—taste poor when king rules
    unjustly
  As the king, so the kingdom
Fruit bat. *See* FLYING FOX

FRUIT TREES
  [Children and fruit trees in
    Haiti]
—attacked by flying foxes
  The children of the Omokoy
    tribe
  Fudo and the prickly pear thieves
    Poland-*Mantis,* 89–114
FUJI, Mountain
  Bamboo-cutter and the moon-
    child
FULLERS' FIELD
  The fisherman and his soul
Funeral of Flory Cantillon
  Yeats-*Fairy,* 71–74
FUNERAL PYRES
  The lovers
FUNERAL SHIPS
  The death of Balder
FUNERALS
  The artful lad
  The black umbrella
  Eerin, the small grey owl
  Goat's funeral [religious satire]
  How the slaves helped each
    other
  How the stars came: Iku's
    eyes
—magic transportation
  Midnight funeral from
    America
—songs
  Merirodo and her husband
  Kuieje Kuri
FUNERALS (subject)
—myths
  Lines-*Greek,* 265 (index)
FURIES (subject)
  Pinsent-*Greek,* 143 (index)
FURNITURE
  Who knows?
Fusang (giant tree): The early
    heroes: Yi . . .
  Sanders-*Dragons,* 25–28
FUTURE
  A little love story

—foolish worry
Ukrainian tale [grief: imagined
future woes]
—imagined evils; crying
The three sillies [imagined
future evils]
—visions of
Spirit of the Van
FUTURE LIFE (life after death)
The boy in the Land of
Shadows
—preparation for
The desolate island
Fylgiar
Arrowsmith-*Field*, 24–25

The Gabilan Mountains [legend]
MacLean-*Cuentos*, 169–172
GABRIEL (angel)
The godfather
The nightingale
The soul-taking angel [Gabriel]
Gad [a rod]: Munachar and the
raspberries
Smith-*Manachar*, 6–42
GADFLIES
Loki makes mischief
"GADS" (scaffolds)
Munachar and Manachar
The Galah, and Oolah the lizard
Parker-*Australian*, 21
GALAHAD, Sir
Adventures of Sir Galahad
Noblest quest of all
Quest for the Holy Grail
Sir Galahad and the quest of
the Holy Grail
Sir Lancelot of the Lake
Galahad and the Grail
Lee-*Castles*, 112–113
Galahad: the castle of maidens
Lee-*Castles*, 78–79

GALAHS
—origin of characteristics
The Galah, and Oolah the
lizard
GALIGANTUS
Jack [the giant-killer] . . . castle
of Galigantus
El gallo braggadocio
MacLean-*Cuentos*, 150–152
Galo and Vasiri
Stokes-*Turtle*, 45–48
Galveston Island: the treasure
Stuchl-*American*, 107–110
GAMBIAN WOLOF TALES
(subject)
—[Thematic patternings]
Magel-*Gambia*, vii–x, 1–22
GAMBLERS AND GAMBLING
See also WAGERS
Banca Flor
The extra days: Ra, Thoth,
and Nut
Foot racers of Payupki
Green Man of No Man's Land
The story-teller at fault
—king possessed by Kali loses all
Good King Nala's downfall
The game of rat and dragon
Asimov-*Fant.*, 140/–end
The game of washers
McNeil-*Charm*, 177–186
GAMES
The ball game
Ganconers steal cow: Loughleagh
Yeats-*Fairy*, 185–189, 292
Gander. See GEESE
GAN-FINN
Jack of Sjoholm and the Gan-
Finn
GAN-FLIES
Jack of Sjoholm and the Gan-
Finn
Gaoliang bridge [Peking]; water supply
Sanders-*Dragons*, 49–53
GARDEN OF EDEN
The mysteries of Eden

GARDEN OF EDEN (subject)
    Patai-*Gates,* 780 (index)
GARDEN PESTS
—bugs
    The rabbits go hunting
GARDENS AND GARDENING
    The boy, the crow and the
        sesame seeds [guard fails]
    The bronze ring
    The cottage garden
    Death out of season
    The Greek princess and the
        young gardener
    The Gwagedd Annwyn [II]
    The large gardens and estates
    The leprechaun in the garden
    The nightingale
    Pom-Pom the clown
    Sprig of rosemary
    Teigneux
    The troll's garden at
        Stallsbacke
    The twelve princesses
    The tylwyth teg
    The widow's son
    Witch's garden
Gareth and Linet: Castle Perilous
    Lee-*Castles,* 86–91
GARETH, Sir
    Knights' tales
    Sir Gareth of Orkney
Garlic and tar [Tibastsagnen]
    Lindow-*Swedish,* 111
GARLON, Sir
    Balin and Balan
Garrulousness: Hyena wrestles
        konderong
    Magel-*Gambia,* 128–131
GARTERS
—red
    The field of Boliauns
GARUDA (magical bird)
    The slowest may win the race
GATES
    Brer wolf's magic gate
—giant's

The giant and Johannes Blessom
Gathorne-Hardy, G. M.
    The expedition of Thorfin
        Karisefni
GAWAIN, Sir
    Death of King Arthur
    The great king's last battle
    Knights' tales
    Marriage of Sir Gawaine
    The passing of Arthur
    Quest of the white hart
[Gawain and Dame Ragnell]
    Spells & Bind, 117–123
Gawain and the Green Knight
    Riordan-*Arthur,* 54–67
Gawain and the Lady Ragnell
    Phelps-*Maid,* 35–44
Gawain: test of valor
    Seekers Saviors, 96–103
Gawain: the castle of wonders
    Lee-*Castles,* 80–82
Gazelle and the leopard
    Radin-*African,* 115–116
Gazelle horn
    Shah-*World,* 116–118
GAZELLES
    The beduin's gazelle (Saudi
        Arabia)
    The beggar and the gazelle
    The faithful gazelle
    The pet of a prince
    Zirac and friends
GEESE
    See also titles beginning with
        "goose"
    Animals in winter
    Baucis and Philemon
    Chitchat turtle and the
        geese
    The dawn of the world
    Dividing the goose
    The golden goose
    King O'Toole and his goose
    Little Annie the goose girl
    The little chicken Kluk and his
        companions

Mouse Woman and the monster killer whale
The pig builds the house on the hill
Raven and the north lands
Seven families of Lake Pipple-Popple
Spooks a-hunting
Stewed, roasted, or live?
Story of the end of trickster Wihio
The swan geese
A taste for quiet
Twelve wild geese
Ua-pa-chi (Kickapoo titles)
The valiant chanticleer
The white gander
Wisdom of Senor Zorro
—the call "Ay-oga-ga-ga"
Ayoga
—golden
Dumling and the golden goose
Hans, who made the princess laugh
—goose & gander as servants
Goosey Goosey, Gander
—old goose's youth restored by Saint
King O'Toole and his goose
—pluck feather from
Clever answers (Russia)
—transformed spook, cooked, sings, etc.
La-lee-lu
—would take D. to Arabia
Daniel O'Rourke
GEESE WOMEN
Pursuit of Numeuk the hunter
GEHENNA
The sinner and his wife
Two Hasidim visit Hell
GEHENNA (subject)
Patai-*Gates*, 780 (index)
Gehenna and its princes [Midrash]
Patai-*Gates*, 277–282
Geiger, Paul, illus.

Schwartz-*Great*
GEIRRID
[Katla protects Odd by 'sight blinding']
Gellivor
Booss-*Scand.*, 630–633
Gemini (the Twins)
Gallant-*Constel.*, 137–141
Gems. *See* JEWELS.
The general and the devil
Stuchl-*American*, 55–58
General Gim Dog-Nyong
Zong-*Korea*, 58–59
General Pumpkin
Zong-*Korea*, 66–68
GENERALS
The iron wolf
The ugly son-in-law
GENERATIONS
Seventh father of the house
GENEROSITY
See also KINDNESS
The Buddhist Job
Cormac MacArt went to Faery
The Dervish and the fakir
The devoted friend
The eye transplant
A handful of rice
[King Shivi] The gift of cows
Knock, knock, who's there?
The living kuan-yin
Ludwig and Iskander
The Moohel
Quiet folk
Who was most generous?
—extreme
The king who gave away his kingdom
—gift of straw; "wild" husband
Saint Michael wins a soul from devil
—reward
A mansion in heaven
GENEROSITY (subject)
—Hindu stories
Amore-*Lustful*, 113

Generosity of Hatim Tai
    Shah-*Dervishes,* 32–33
GENESIS
    The Lapp genesis, or the first
        of mankind
The genesis of the Hid-folk
    Booss-*Scand.,* 598–599
GENESTA (a fairy)
    Heart of ice [Prince Littleboots]
GENETICS
    The bees from Borneo
    The man from P.I.G.
Genie of the mountains
    Segovia-*Spanish,* 189–221
Genie of the waters: The mer-
        chant's fortune
    Segovia-*Spanish,* 223–247
GENIES
    See also JINN
    Aladdin and his magic lamp
    Aladdin and the wonderful
        lamp
    Aladdin, or The wonderful lamp
    Farmer's son and the geni
    The magic mirror
    Sinbad and the genie
    Work of the genii
—evil
    The haunted well
—steals girl, rescued by brothers
    Zilyan
Genius deserves his name
    Todd-*Tortoise,* 37–43
Genius [more intelligent than the
        king]
    Todd-*Some,* 128–137
Genjias [three with same name]
    Minford-*Fav.,* 87–94
GENTLEMEN
    Fees
Genuine. *See* RIGHT . . .
Genuineness: The daughter and
        the helper
    Timpanelli-*Tales,* 15–27
The geomancer's three sons
    Zong-*Korea,* 48–51

GEOMANCY
    Gaoliang bridge [Peking]; wa-
        ter supply
GEORGE, Jean Craighead
    Julie of the wolves
GEORGE, Saint
    The gypsy and Saint George
    Saint George
George's picnic
    Ainsworth-*Bear,* 47–52
Gerald, Earl of Desmond
    Spells & Bind, 61–62
Geriguiguiatugo or Toribugo
    Wilbert-*Bororo,* 204–210
GERMANY
    Beowulf fights the dragon
    Bremen town musicians
    The changeling [b]
    The curse of Andvari's ring
    Domoviye
    Drakes [house spirits]
    The dwarf husband
    The dwarfs borrowing bread
    The dwarf's feast
    Dwarfs stealing corn
    The fisherman and his wife
    The friendly dwarfs
    The Gwagedd Annwyn
    Hansel and Gretel
    Heinzelmanchen
    Heinzelmannchen and
        Hutchen
    Hey-hey men
    The hill man at the dance
    Hinzelmann
    Hodeken
    How Sigourd awoke Brynhild
        upon Hindfell
    Inge of Rantum
    Jorinde and Joringel
    Journey of dwarfs over the
        mountain
    The juniper tree
    King Goldemar
    Moss people
    Nissen and Tomtra

The nix-labour
The Oldenburg horn
The peasant and the
   waterman
River women
Seligen Fraulein
Smith Riechert
Walter and Hildegund
The water smith
The water sprite and the bear
Wayland Smith
Wedding feast of the little
   people
Wichtlein
The working waterman
—Bern
Dietrich of Bern
—Hamburg
The wolves of Cernogratz
—Hamelin
The pied piper of Hamelin
GERMANY
—fairies
   Briggs-*Vanish.*, 12, 57–60, 73,
      76, 100–101
—the wild-woman
   Keightley-*World*, 234–238
   Keightley-*World*, 205–216
Germany: Fafnir
   Stallman-*Dragons*, 18–19
Gertrude and Rosy
   Keightley-*World*, 266–271
GERVASE of Tilbury, 13th century
   Knight to knight [the Gog-
      magog hills]
GERVASE of Tilbury (subject)
   Briggs-*Vanish.*, 73, 93–94,
      146
Gesar of Ling
   Hyde-Chambers-*Tibet*, 27–70
GESTA ROMANORUM (subject)
   Shah-*World*, 226
Gestumblindi's riddles
   Crossley-*Legends*, 146–154
GESTURES
—misinterpreted

Gods of the stars: ancient
   China
'Get up and bar the door'
   Marshall-*Every*, 353–354
Getting common sense [Anansi]
   Yolen-*Favorite*, 405
Getting older and older faster and
   faster
   Schwartz-*Tales*, 33
GEVAUDAN, WILD BEAST OF
   Werewolves
The gewel (hare) and the
   hyena
   Magel-*Gambia*, 53–57
GEWELS
   The monkey who claimed to
      be a gewel
   The passion of the gewel
Ghana. *See* AFRICA—Ghana
Gheeger the cold west wind
   Parker-*Australian*, 121–123
Ghena: The mendacious child
   Magel-*Gambia*, 172–174
GHETTOS
   The secret ones
Ghillie Dhu
   Froud-*Faeries*, unp
The ghost and the moneychest
   Crossley-*Folk*, 109–111
The ghost at Fjelkinge
   Booss-*Scand.*, 244–246
The ghost extinguisher [humorous]
   Manley-*Fun*, 145–157
A ghost gets a free ride
   Lindow-*Swedish*, 184–185
Ghost: Grace Connor
   Yeats-*Fairy*, 120–121
The ghost of John
   Schwartz-*Dark*, 60
Ghost of Lady Hobby
   Marshall-*Every.*, 116–119
[Ghost of mother protects her
   children]
   Seekers Saviors, 21–22
Ghost of the radar base
   Ritchie-*Armadillo*, 34–37

The ghost rider
   Stuchl-*American*, 23–25
"GHOST RIDERS"
   The phantom herd
The ghost ship
   Manley-*Fun*, 109–121
A ghost story [by Mark Twain]
   Schwartz-*Great*, 11–19
Ghost: the black lamb
   Yeats-*Fairy*, 122–123
Ghost: the radiant boy
   Yeats-*Fairy*, 125–126
GHOSTLY
   The sunset call
Ghostly apparitions
   Robe-*Hispanic*, 79–144
Ghosts
   Yeats-*Fairy*, 117–131
GHOSTS
   See also APPARITIONS;
      BOGLES; DEAD; HAUNTED
      HOUSES
   The Bantam phantom
   The beggar's bridge
   The black umbrella
   The blood stain
   The boarded window [by
      Bierce]
   The bold soldier of Antwerp
   The Canterville ghost
   Causes celebres, high and
      low: C. Radcliffe
   Chisos ghosts
   The clutching hand
   The confession of Charles
      Linkworth
   Dance of the dead
   The dance of the spectres
   The deacon of Myrka
   The dead bridegroom
   Dead couple marry after death
   The dead defend their cemetery
   The dead man's debt
   The dead man's nightcap
   The death coach
   The death waltz

The dog got them
Draw the curtains
Drawer 14
The dream house (Ireland)
Drinking companions
Escaping ghosts
Fairy hurling game: Ireland vs
   Scotland
A false ghost
Fate of Frank M'Kenna
Give me my bone
'Gold, Ezekiel! Gold'
Goralasi and the spectres
The green mist
The hanged man seeks his
   pine tree
The haunted mill: or, The
   ruined home
The haunted realm
The haunted trailer [by R.
   Arthur]
A haunting
Haunting of [computer] Y-12
   [Sarrantonio]
The hauntings at Frodriver
The herd boy and the dragons
Herne the hunter
The hitchhiker
In a dark, dark room
In a dim room [by Dunsany]
Jack of Sjoholm and the Gan-
   Finn
Jerry Bundler
Just married
Kate of Ysatter
Ketill, the priest of Husavik
The kindly ghost [Joseph and
   his brothers]
Knight to knight [the Gog-
   magog hills]
Lake Espantosa, the
   alligators?
The Lakota woman
Lay them straight
Legend of the Virgin Arang
Lodging for the night

GHOSTS—specters once human,
  now ghosts (continued)
  Football on a lake
—spectre becomes evil
  giant
  The little old man in the
  tree
—spectre punished
  The Inn of the Stone and
  Spectre
—spectre rejected by heaven &
  hell
  Tummeldink
—spirit of mother protects daughter
  Undying guardianship: Rashin
  Coatie
—spitting on
  The truth about ghosts
—testifies at trial
  John Tregeagle
—weight
  Sung Ting-po catches a ghost
GHOSTS (subject)
  Briggs-Vanish., 216 (index)
  Lindow-Swedish, 52–54, 215
  Marshall-Every., 40–42, 116
  Piggott-Japanese, 143 (index)
  Scott-Fantastic, 123–132
—[Rebirth as, because of evil
  deeds]
  Amore-Lustful, 137
—[Varieties infinite]
  Yolen-Favorite, 421
Ghosts and other revenants [motif
  index]
  Wilbert-Bororo, 251–252
Ghosts of Ashintully
  Robertson-Highland, 30–32
A ghost's vengeance
  Booss-Scand., 645–646
GHOST-WRITERS
  The Bantam phantom
The ghoul and the youth of
  Ispahan
  Shah-World, 78–80
GHOULS

Assorted monsters
  The riddles
  The wild swans
—eats beduin's son
  The beduin's gazelle (Saudi
  Arabia)
GHOULS (subject)
  Scott-Fantastic, 123–132
GIANE
  Arrowsmith-Field, 169–170,
  171
The giant and Johannes Blessom
  Booss-Scand., 53–56
A giant builds a church [the Finn
  legend]
  Lindow-Swedish, 86–88
Giant cannibals
  Colombo-Wind., 30–31
The giant caterpillar
  McCarty-Skull, 31–34
  Phelps-Tatterhood, 61–64
The giant eel
  Adams-Iron, 18–25
  Stokes-Turtle, 69–72
The giant elk [monster]
  Mullett-Spider, 127–131
The giant from Klasahall
  Lindow-Swedish, 79–80
The giant maiden in Boraserod
  mountain
  Booss-Scand., 274–275
The giant of Skalunda
  Booss-Scand., 280–282
Giant of the great water
  Radin-African, 296–297
The giant puke
  Booss-Scand., 256
The giant-slayer
  Villa-Armenian, 102–109, 448
The giant sturgeon
  Haviland-N. Amer., 21–32
The giant who had no heart
  Booss-Scand., 4–10
Giant with the grey feathers
  Macmillan-Canadian 273–241
The giant with three golden hairs

Stovicek-*Around,* 146–151
The giant without a head
Sanders-*Dragons,* 20
The giantess leader
Villa-*Armenian,* 124–127, 454
Giants
Robe-*Hispanic,* 413–414
GIANTS
See also BUNYAN, Paul
Antti and the wizard's
prophecy
The apples of eternal life
The apples of Iduna
Ares, god of war
Asgard: war of the gods and
giants
The battle of the birds
Bhima slays the demon [giant,
man-eating cannibal]
Boy of great strength and the
giants
The boy who ate more than
the giant
The boy who did not know
what fear was
Boy who overcame the giants
The boys and the giant
Brave little tailor (seven at one
blow)
The bridge over Kalmarsound
The building of the wall of
Asgard
Castle of Balor
Castles of fairy-tale giants
City of the Not-Dead
Clever Daniel
Conall Yellowclaw
The costly ring
Coyote brings fire to The
People
The dancing princess
A dead princess and seven
giants
Departure of the giants (Africa)
Devil's tale
Dietrich of Bern

Dietrich [of Verona]; castle of
the Ice Queen
Don Juan Zurumbete
The dwarf in search of lodging
The dwarfs' banquet
The enchanted forest
The fiery dragon
First pig and porcupine
Gellivor
The ghoul and the youth of
Ispahan
Glooscap, the great chief
Glooskap and the giant's frolic
The golden ball
The great heroes of old
Halde hat
Heaven's reward
The herd-boy
The herd-boy and the giant
How Fin went to the kingdom
of the big men
How mosquitoes came to be
How the world was made
How they went to Jotunheim
Human bait
Isles of the blest
Jack and his cudgel
Jack and the beanstalk
Jack and the green lady
Jack-in-irons
Jack o'Legs
Jack the Giant Killer
Jason and the golden fleece
King David and the giant
The King of Ireland's son (Art)
King of Lochlann's three
daughters
King of the herrings
King Zargand's daughter
Kitpouseagunow
The knight of Ellenholm
Knight of the riddles
The Knockmany legend
Kuafu chases the sun
The lad with the goat-skin
The lay of Thrym

The world of ice and fire
The wounded lion
Yorkshire giant [Penhill]
Yvon and Finette
—abducts all new brides
    The boy and the robbers'
        magical booty
—church building
    Big boulder north of Torstuna
        church
—creation
    The first sun
—Double-Face
    Manstin, the rabbit
—enchanter
    Prince Vivien and the Princess
        Placida
—fear of Christianity
    The giants who moved
—Galifron
    Pretty Goldilocks
—gullible
    Francis and the giant
—hearts
    The giant who had no
        heart
—humans as toys for
    A toy for the giant
—Irish
    [Finn] Fann Mac Cuil and the
        Scotch giant
—kills & marries a new wife each
        year
    Bolster and Jecholiah
—Kinak, super!giant
    The woman and the giant
—lightning
    The old man from Haberg
—Mahon MacMahon
    Giant's stairs [Ronayne's
        Court]
—Manabozno
    Grasshopper [Indian
        superman]
—Nasan
    Thunderbird

—Olomano
    The flying war club
—Scottish
    [Finn] Fann Mac Cuil and the
        Scotch giant
—seven-headed
    Hassan the brave
—stupidity
    It's a long way to Gamla
        Uppsala
    Obdurman the clever
        huntsman
    Save it for tomorrow
—swallows entire camp at one
        gulp
    Iya, the camp-eater
—takes first-born son of prince
    The hawk and the rattlesnake
—Wolf-Wind (winter)
    How Glooskap made the birds
GIANTS (subject)
    Lindow-*Swedish,* 32–33, 80,
        215
    Marshall-*Every.,* 42–43, 143
The giant's bride
    Booss-*Scand.,* 333–334
The giant's daughter
    Phelps-*Maid,* 85–90
The giants Jack killed
    Baskin-*Imps,* 24–25
Giants of Morvah
    Ross-*Druids,* 117–120
Giant's stairs [Mahon MacMahon]
    Yeats-*Fairy,* 237–241
Giant's stairs [Ronayne's Court]
    McGarry-*Folk,* 99–105
The giants who moved
    Lindow-*Swedish,* 82–84
GIBBONS
    The baboon's umbrella
—wife transformed into
    Why the gibbon says "pua"
Gift from a star
    Luzzatto-*Long,* 36–43
Gift of Elijah
    Patai-*Gates,* 745–747

Gift of fire
Reed-*Aboriginal,* 114–116
The gift of the jnun
Elbaz-*Folktales,* 79
The gift of the white
cockatoo
Stokes-*Turtle,* 138–142
GIFTS
The fairy gift
[Glooskap] Gluscap, lord of the
north
Hinzelmann
Loki makes mischief
Mossycoat
New clothes for the tomte
The prince who had two eyes
Sleeping Beauty in the wood
Story of Ciccu
Thorston and the dwarf
The three heads of the well
Zamani goes to market
Gifts of the child Christ
Macdonald-*Golden,* 125–165
GIL DONG
—robs the corrupt, gives to the
poor
Hong Gil-Dong
GILFI, King
The tricking of King Gilfi
GILGAMESH
The Huluppu-tree
[Gilgamesh and ut-napishtim]
Water Spirits, 20–27
GILLIES
Mally Whuppy
GINGALIN (Bel Inconnu)
—frees Welsh Queen from spell
Quest of the Fair Unknown
The gingerbread boy
Oxenbury-*Nursery,* 32–39
The gingerbread house [Hansel
and Gretel]
Stovicek-*Around,* 180–183
Gingko trees
Pigott-*Japanese,* 129–131
GINSENG (plant)

A dutiful son
Human bait
The nine-headed giant
The white-eared tiger
Gioga's son
Keightley-*World,* 167–169
Gipsies. *See* GYPSIES
The gipsy baron
Stovicek-*Around,* 14–15
GIRALDUS CAMBRENSIS
(subject)
Briggs-*Vanish.,* 157–158
GIRDLES (armor)
—golden
The labours of Hercules
Girl at the shieling [elf] (Iceland)
Yolen-*Favorite,* 117–120
The girl at the troll-dance
Keightley-*World,* 124–125
The girl clad in mouseskin
Booss-*Scand.,* 493–496
A girl in green
Roberts-*Chinese,* 17–18
Girl swallowed up by the stone
Patai-*Gates,* 605–607
The girl who always cried
Macmillan-*Canadian* 194–198
Girl who had seven divs for
brothers
Shah-*Dervishes,* 144–148
The girl who married a bear
Wood-*Spirits,* 48–52
Girl who stayed in fork of a tree
Radin-*African,* 181–185
The girl who trod on the loaf
Booss-*Scand.,* 393–398
The girl who was already queen
Timpanelli-*Tales,* 43–51
Girl with the golden hair
Thomas-*It's,* 108–113
The girl with the large eyes
Lester-*Black,* 57–61
The girl with the silver
voice
Titiev-*Moolah,* 27–35
GIRL(S)

The fairy whipping
The gunny wolf
Li Chi slays the serpent
The little girl on the moon
Sprig of rosemary
Susie and her shadow
Those three wishes
The witch's cat
—faces
The god of faces
—family murdered, commits
    suicide
The tiger priest
—given head of sheep
Kate Crackernuts
—kidnapped by trolls
Stealing for the trolls
—married to fish
The girl with the large eyes
—servant girl thwarts thieves
Hand of glory [severed hand of
    hanged man]
—seven-year old, wiser than tsar
The wise little girl
—snow figure comes to life
The snow maiden
—thief; loses sight, hearing, etc.
God's court, no appeal
—wants to touch the stars
The stars in the sky
Girls and bears [Musquakie]
Myles-*Butterflies*, 1–6
Girls at parsonage get help sewing
    crinoline
Lindow-*Swedish*, 155–156
Gitto Bach
Keightley-*World*, 416–417
Gitutu [animal unfit to eat]
Robinson-*Three*, 17–31
Giufo's debt
Stovicek-*Around*, 98–99
Give me my bone
Ainsworth-*Phantom*, 36–46
Give me something you
    have . . . unawares
Cortes-*Byelorussian*, 44–50

GIVING
See also CHARITY; GENER-
    OSITY; KINDNESS
Cast thy bread upon the wa-
    ters [satire]
Giving the devil a ride
Lindow-*Swedish*, 156–157
Giving up: Wise frog and foolish
    frog
Riordan-*Russia*, 241–242
The gizzard [riches for the one who
    eats it]
Wolkstein-*Magic*, 100–112
The glaistig
Froud-*Faeries*, unp
The glaistig at Sron-Charmaig
Robertson-*Highland*, 20
Glashans and Shopiltees
Arrowsmith-*Field*, 247–248
GLASS
The snow queen
The glass diamond
Watson-*Thailand*, 39–41
Glass mountain
Weiss-*Russian*, 53 59
GLASSES
The luck of Eden Hall
GLASSES (eye)
Critch
GLASTONBURY TOR (subject)
Briggs-*Vanish.*, 90
The globe flower
Ewart-*Lore*, 159–161
Glooscap and the baby: Wasis
Yolan-*Favorite*, 49–50
Glooscap and the wishes
Hill-*More*, 168–178
Glooscap, the great chief
Hill-*More*, 1–9
Glooscap, the peacemaker
Hill-*More*, 131–139
GLOOSKAP (spirit)
Badger and the green giant
The Chenoo who stayed to
    dinner
Coolnajoo, the foolish one

GLOOSKAP (spirit) (continued)
    The dreaded chenoo
    The first mosquito
    The great Penobscot raid
    How Ableegumooch tracked a fox
    How Glooskap made the birds
    How summer [personified]
      came to Canada
    How the Summer Queen came
      to Canada
    How turtle came
    Kespak and the caribou
    Kitpouseagunow
    Lox and the chief's wife
    The magic snowshoes
    The moon and his frog-wife
    The passing of Glooskap
    [whites vs Indians]
    Fulowech, the partridge
    The rabbit makes a match
    The strongest boy in the world
    Tomik and the magic mat
    Wasek and the red giants
    Wejosis and the wind giant
    Why Bootup, the whale,
      smokes a pipe
    The year summer was stolen
GLOOSKAP (subject)
—[Canada]
    De Wit-*Talking*, 181–182
Glooskap and Malsum, the wolf
    Wade-*Indian*, 125–128
Glooskap and the fairy
    Macmillan-*Canadian*, 67–68
Glooskap and the giant's frolic
    Wade-*Indian*, 129–133
Glooskap and the magic gifts
    Wade-*Indian*, 151–162
Glooskap and the monster bullfrog
    Wade-*Indian*, 135–142
Glooskap and the three seekers
    Wade-*Indian*, 163–169
Glooskap and the turtle
    Wade-*Indian*, 143–150
Glooskap and the whale
    Wade-*Indian*, 111–117

Glooskap and the witch maidens
    Wade-*Indian*, 119–124
[Glooskap] Gluscap, lord of the
    north
    Wood-*Spirits*, 44–47
Glooskap's country
    Macmillan-*Canadian*, 34–39
GLOVES
—leathern
    Hinzelmann
Glow worms. See FIREFLIES
Gluska'be, the Penobscot
    hero
    Jagendorf-*First*, 47–53
GLUTTONY
    The blue lake
    The vision of MacConglinney
—eats only pumpkins
    General Pumpkin
GNOMES
    The field of Boliauns
    The kingdom of beautiful
      colors
    The little gnome
    Stupid Peikko
GNOMES (subject)
    Briggs-*Vanish.*, 84, 1196
"GO AWAYS" (birds)
    The bushbabies
Go Zu-Mong, king of Goguryo
    Zong-*Korea*, 4–7
Goanna makes a canoe
    Reed-*Aboriginal*, 19–20
Goanna: The treachery of
    Lelewaga
    Stokes-*Turtle*, 73–75
Goannas and porcupines
    Reed-*Aboriginal*, 20–23
The goat in the sky
    Manning-*Cats*, 107–110
Goat people
    Arrowsmith-*Field*, 264–266
The goat who laughed and cried
    Amore-*Lustful*, 100–101
GOATHERDS
    Stompe Pilt

The goblin and the grocer
Lang-*Pink/D*, 12–17
The goblin and the huckster
Booss-*Scand.*, 422–426
The goblin bride
Zong-*Korea*, 126–128
Goblin of Adachigahara
Ozaki-*Japanese*, 140–147
Goblins
Froud-*Faeries*, unp
GOBLINS
Bogles
The boy who did not know
what fear was
The boy who drew cats [by
Hearn]
Bucca Dhu and Bucca
Gwidden
The cany man; a Han folktale
Coblynau
Cross purposes
The elfin hill
The magic cap
Magic mallet
The mallet of wealth
Phooka
Redcap
The son of the goblin
The steadfast tin soldier
The three sons
—conversation overheard
How foolish men are!
—mill
Legends of the mill
GOBLINS (subject)
Briggs-*Vanish.*, 8, 82–84, 196
GOD
See also CREATION;
PROVIDENCE—divine; RE-
LIGION; TRUST IN GOD
Blue-jay who married daughter
of god
The castle: a parable
Clever man and ordinary
Day of the dead
Departure of the giants (Africa)
The fisherman and his wife
How long will you live?
The hungry peasant, God, and
death (Mexico)
I won't forgive you
Jonah and the whale
The nightingale
Origin of death: chameleon
—as godfather
Godfather death (Germany)
—desire to be like
A fisherman and his wife
—portrait: blank
King and the wise man
GOD (subject)
Nahman-*Tales*, 330
Zong-*Korea*, 249 (index)
The god behind the curtain
Sanders-*Dragons*, 95
"GOD BLESS US" (said when
sneezing)
Master and man
God is stronger
Shah-*World*, 94
The god of faces
Jagendorf-*Magic*, 131–133
God of Fate: Headman and the
magician
Peacock Maid, 44–53
God of the Mountain: Long Haired
Girl
Minford-*Fav.*, 148–160
God on our side
Marshall-*Every.*, 295–303
"GOD WILLING" (expression)
Always say, "God willing"
Those stubborn souls, the
Biellese
A goddess is born
Amore-*Lustful*, 41–43
The goddess who drank blood
Amore-*Lustful*, 96–99
The godfather
Kudian-*More*, 30–31
Godfather death (Germany)
Yolen-*Favorite*, 466–469

GODMOTHERS
  Cinderella
  Elves ask a servant girl to be
    godmother
  Fees
—fairy. *See* FAIRY
  GODMOTHERS
GODPARENTS
  The hill folk
  Juan de Toluca
GODRIC, Saint
  The stag [saved from the
    hunters]
Gods and demons
  Gallant-*Constel.*, 3–8
GODS AND GODDESSES
  See also DEMONS
  *See also names of individual
    gods, e.g.:* SKY HOLDER;
    ZEUS
  The apples of eternal life
  Asgard: war of the gods and
    giants
  Beliefs and dieties of Japan
  Bricriu's feast
  The building of the wall of
    Asgard
  Chang'o and the elixir of
    immortality
  The crane maiden
  Creation of the Mayas
  The creation
  The death of Alfe's only son
  Degei and his sons
  The eight-forked serpent
  Fenrir the wolf is bound
  The fifth and final sun
  First tale: in the beginning . . .
  The fisherman and his soul
  Gods and demons
  The gods return
  The gods' revenge
  Gold of the gods
  The golden age in Asgard
  The golden man and the finger
    men

Good and evil: Buri vs Ymir
Headman and the magician
The herd boy and the weaving
  girl
How Abosom, the lesser gods,
  came into the world
How Thor got his hammer
Juan Soldado
Kali beheaded
The kitchen god
Llyr: children of the sea-god
Loki makes mischief
The making of the worlds
Maya parallels with the Nahua
  gods
Opame, Chenrezik, and Dolma
The Ragnarok, doom of the
  gods
The rain that came too late
Seven days and nights
The sky-god: Ratu and the
  Dyaks
Sun and moon
The temple ghost and Ai Tzu
The trlcking of King Gilfi
Underworld god of marriage
The walls of Asgard
The world of ice and fire
The Yellow Emperor: war
  against Chitou
The youngest god [Dionysius]
—Aumakua
  Champion spearsman
—China
  Tripitaka: quest of the Buddhist
    scriptures
  Yu controls the flood
—China: Nocha
  Gaoliang bridge [Peking];
    water supply
—eating earthly food; effects
  How the fire festival came to
    be
—fade away; Christianity
  Marjatt
—"family tree"

GODS . . . (continued)
The new gods-*Zeus and Hera*
—Greece
The adventures of Perseus
Aphrodite, goddess of love
Ares, god of war
Artemis and Apollo
Athene, goddess of wisdom
The chariot of the sun
The death of the Chimaera
Echo and Narcissus
End of the heroes
Eros and Psyche
The fall of Troy
Family of the gods
Gods and goddesses of Mount
Olympus
Hades, lord of the underworld
Hermes, the messenger of the
gods
The house of Thebes
In the beginning: the Greek
panoply
Jason and the golden fleece
The labours of Hercules
Midas, the golden king
The new gods-*Zeus and Hera*
Orpheus and Eurydice
Pan and Dionysus, the wild gods
Peleus and Thetis [marriage]
Persephone among the dead
Poseidon's ocean kingdom
Prometheus and Pandora
Pygmalion's statue
The rival twins
Symbols in the Greek myths
Thesus, king of Athens
The wanderings of Aeneas
The wanderings of Odysseus
The world of the gods
—India
Burning of the Khandava forest
—Ireland
The birth of Cu Chulaind
The boyhood dreams of Cu
Chulaind
The cattle raid of Froech
The destruction of Da Derga's
hostel
The dream of Oengus
The exile of the sons of Uisliu
The intoxication of the Ulaid
Labor pains of the Ulaid, and
twins of Macha
The tale of Macc Da Tho's pig
Wasting sickness of Cu
Chulaind, and . . . Emer
The Wooing of Etain
—land of the
Boy with the deformed head
—Mekhala teases Ramasura
How thunder and lightning
came to be
—Mexico
Trial and error creation
—mission: steal sun or moon
The fire dogs
—Ngroondoorie
The sacred island, Nar-oong-
owie
—Okuni-nushi-no-Mikoto
White hare and the crocodiles
—queen mother of the west
Chang'o and the elixir of
immortality
—Yellow River
Golden chisel and the stone
ram
GODS AND GODDESSES
(subject)
Briggs-*Vanish.*, 216 (index)
—China: Gods from the dawn of
time
Sanders-*Dragons,* 13–17, 60
—Greece
Low-*Greek,* 181–184 (index)
—Greece-Dictionaries
Stapleton-*Dictionary,* 1–224
—[Greek myths; Roman
equivalents]
Low-*Greek,* 179–180
—Myths & legends of the Vikings

Lindow-*Myths*, 1–48
—Some female dieties
Nicholson-*Mexican*, 112–115
Gods and goddesses, Greek and
    Roman
    Gallant-*Constel.*, 182
Gods and goddesses of Mount
    Olympus
    Low-*Greek*, 11–21
Gods and superstitions in early
    China
    Sanders-*Dragons*, 120–121
God's court, no appeal
    Todd-*Some*, 118–122
Gods from the dawn of time: China
    Sanders-*Dragons*, 13–17
Gods of the elements
    Sanders-*Dragons*, 121–124
Gods of the landscape
    Ross-*Druids*, 121–123
Gods of the pagan Celts
    Ross-*Druids*, 98–103
Gods of the stars: ancient China
    Sanders-*Dragons*, 124–125
The gods return
    Branston-*Gods*, 149–150
The gods' revenge
    Branston-*Gods*, 141–143
Gods, titans, and dragons
    Scott-*Fantastic*, 39–60
Godsell, Philip H.
    A Weetigo in the woods
GODSONS
    La madrina muerte
GODZILLA
    Assorted monsters
Goggle eyes
    Sampson-*Gypsy*, 84–88
Goha on the deathbed (Egypt)
    Yolen-*Favorite*, 465
Gohc Amu and the matzoon
    Villa-*Armenian*, 408–409
Gohc Amu and the running water
    Villa-*Armenian*, 408
Gohc Amu and the toot
    Villa-*Armenian*, 407

The Gojmati
    Bang-*Five*, 50–63
GOLD
    Aid and punishment
    The ball of gold
    Big brother: man; Little brother;
        rabbit
    The black bull of Norroway
    The bridal present
    Coffin cash
    Connall Yellowclaw
    The crimson parrot
    The curse of Andvari's ring
    The dwarfs' banquet
    Dwarfs stealing corn
    Fairies' dancing place [man
        builds house on]
    The field of Boliauns
    The frog
    The general and the devil
    Golden lads
    Golden stick, silver stick
    The greedy brother
    The happy prince
    Heaven forbid!
    The heavenly flute player; a Li
        story
    How a peasant cured his wife
        of telling tales
    The lad and the north wind
    The lake [personified]
    Little Claus and Big Claus
    The little glass shoe
    The living kuan-yin
    Manachar and the leprechaun
    Midas, the golden king
    The missing treasure
    The mountain kitchen
    Odd jobs
    Paddy O'Kelly and the weasel
    The pointing finger
    Rumpelstiltskin
    The seawife and the crone
    Soul-taker
    Stan Bolovan and the dragon
    The star child

GOLD (continued)
Story of Ivan the Imbecile
The story of Jon Asmundsson
Supparaka
Three sisters were entrapped
into a mountain
The tinder-box
Twilight, Midnight, and Dawn
The Vatters
Walter and Hildegund
When rocks rolled crackling
wisdom
The winding-horn village
—found at foot of rainbow
Sam Pig seeks his fortune
—golden bucket
The daughter and the helper
—magic touch turns to gold
Fair Margaret
—profit from raising bananas
The magician and the bananas
—stolen
The old fort [door will not
open]
—turned to sand; conditions not
fulfilled
Treasure hunt
GOLD (subject)
Zong-*Korea*, 256 (index)
The gold and the honey
Patai-*Gates*, 524–526
Gold colt and the fire dragon shirt
Minford-*Fav.*, 39–48
'Gold, Ezekiel! Gold'
Marshall-*Every.*, 125–128
Gold, gold
Roberts-*Chinese*, 55
The gold harvest
Toth-*Tales*, 49–56
GOLD MINERS
—humor
Noseful of gold
Gold of the gods
Wright-*Gold*, 18–22
The gold piece
Villa-*Armenian*, 327–328

GOLD RUSH
Sweet Betsy from Pike [song
and story]
The gold spinners: water-lily
Lang-*Blue*, 180–189 (notes, 368)
Gold treasure of Mississippi
Stuchl-*American*, 162–168
Gold Tree and Silver Tree
Garner-*British*, 135–139
The golden age in Asgard
Branston-*Gods*, 37–43
Golden apple and his stepmother
Stuchl-*American*, 133–137
Golden apples of Lough Erne
Yeats-*Fairy*, 275–285
The golden ass
Lines-*Greek*, 237–250
The golden ball
Garner-*British*, 123–126
The golden bird
Schwartz-*Elijah*, 247–253
Golden blackbird
Lang-*Green*, 152–159
The golden box
Villa-*Armenian*, 216–217, 483–
484
The golden bridge of Dornoch
Robertson-*Highland*, 5–6
Golden chisel and the stone
ram
Minford-*Fav.*, 17–26
The golden cockerel
Pushkin-*Fairy*, 16–29
The golden comb [witch claims
first-born]
Stuchl-*American*, 87–92
The golden cradle
Booss-*Scand.*, 277–279
The golden cranes
Stovicek-*Around*, 156
The golden feather [talking colt]
Schwartz-*Elijah*, 137–147
The golden finger
Stuchl-*American*, 117–124
The golden fish, the wicked sisters,
and good Forgetta

Stovicek-*Around*, 132–135
The golden fleece
  Low-*Greek*, 116–127
GOLDEN FLEECE
  Helle and Phrixus
  Jason and the golden fleece
The golden goose
  Leete-*Golden*, 124–143
  Pierce-*Larousse*, 79–82
  Schindler-*Golden*, 5–14
  Shub-*About*, 46–51
Golden goose [as subject] *See*
  GEESE—golden
The golden haired twins
  Villa-*Armenian*, 245–253, 491–495
Golden Hind. *See under* DEER
GOLDEN HORDE (Mongols)
  Gulnara the Tartar warrior
The golden idol
  Ross-*Druids*, 124
The golden key
  Macdonald-*Golden*, 1–35
The golden knucklebone
  Manning-*Cats*, 29–36
Golden lads
  Lang-*Green*, 352–359
The golden legend (condensed)
  Briggs-*Vanish.*, 12
Golden life
  Kendall-*Sweet*, 89–91
The golden lion
  Lang-*Pink/D*, 223–229
The golden man and the finger
  men
  Piggott-*Mexican*, 46–57
Golden mermaid [theft of golden
  apples]
  Lang-*Green*, 269–279
The golden mountain
  Schwarts-*Elijah*, 29–35
  Xenophontovna-*Folk*, 132–140
GOLDEN MOUNTAIN
  The loss of the princess
The golden neckband
  Nagishkin-*Folktales*, 205–209

Golden pears
  Lochhead-*Battle*, 113–119
Golden rain
  Stuchl-*American*, 65–69
Golden reed pipe
  Minford-*Fav.*, 161–167
GOLDEN RULE
  Kinsman accompany you when
  he asks to go along
Golden stick, silver stick
  Ban-*Five*, 35–49
The golden toothpick
  Roberts-*Chinese*, 150
The golden tree [queen and
  amulet]
  Schwartz-Elijah, 127–135
The golden vase
  Riordan-*Tartary*, 144–149
GOLDILOCKS
  Pretty Goldilocks
  The three bears
Goldilocks and the three bears
  dePaola-*Favorite*, 55–61
  Laete-*Golden*, 74–79
  Oxenbury-*Nursery*, 6–12
  Pierce-*Larousse*, 157–160
  Pollack-*Moonbeam*, 14–21
  Tarrant-*Fairy*, 9–19
  Tudor-*Bedtime*, [4–5]
Goldilocks [in verse]
  Lewis-*Animal*, 32–33
GOLDSMITHS
  Loki makes mischief
  The turner and the goldsmith
  The wise goldsmith
Gold-tree and Silver-tree
  Jacob-*Celtic*, 60–62
GOLEM(S)
  End of the Golem
  Mummies, zombies, and artificial men
  Rabbi Loew and the Golem
Golem: a brute born of clay
  (Joseph of Prague)
  Spells & Bind, 56–57

[Goll, the Morrigan, and Finn
    MacCumal]
    Seekers Saviors, 73–77
Gone is gone
    Lurie-*Clever*, 92–96
GONZALITO
    The enchanted forest
"Goo, Goo"
    Glooscap and the baby: Wasis
Good and evil
    Riordan-*Russia*, 45–52
Good and evil. *See* EVIL;
    GOODNESS
Good and Evil: Buri vs Ymir
    Shelley-*Legends*, 58–59
Good angel. *See* ANGELS
GOOD DEEDS
    Bearskin (Germany)
    The cave of emeralds
    Genie of the mountains
    The happy prince
    Three former lives
    Tobacco fairy from the Blue
      Hills
    Witch of secret good deeds
      [unloved = sad]
  —god's throne grows hot . . .
    The hare's sacrifice
  —live forever
    Stillson's leap: a jataka
  —repaid
    Eye will see what it is destined
      to see
Good done to you, do good in
    return
    Radin-*African*, 218–220
GOOD EXAMPLE
    Kumba the orphan girl
Good faith
    O'Connor-*Tibet*, 12–19
GOOD FRIDAY
    The robin
The good girl and the bad girl
    Stovicek-*Around*, 114–117
Good King Nala's downfall
    Amore-*Lustful*, 19–23

Good luck. *See* FORTUNE;
    LUCK—good
Good name. *See* REPUTATION
The good sons
    Soyer-*Adventures*, 42–46
"GOOD SPIRIT"
    Woman in the moon
A good thing he wasn't wearing it!
    Elbaz-*Folktales*, 86
Good will: The tailor and the
    shoemaker
    Cortes-*Byelorussian*, 110–114
Good-luck omens
    Steele-*Ozark*, 83–84
GOODNESS
    See also EVIL; GENEROSITY;
      KINDNESS; VIRTUE(S)
    Beauty and the beast
    The bird 'Grip'
    Bird of happiness
    The blind boy and his dog
    Cinderella
    Enchanted ring
    Father Frost
    The girl who was already
      queen
    Glooscap and the three
      seekers
    [Glooskap] Gluscap, lord of the
      north
    Jump into my sack (Italy)
    The little soldier
    Magic pumpkins
    The mouse at the seashore
    Old man who made withered
      trees to flower
    The old troll of Big Mountain
    Patient Griselda
    The pearl that shone by night
    Pint of flax seeds
    Repaying good with evil
    The rich boy and the poor boy
    Rosy apple and the golden
      bowl
    The selfish giant
    The snow queen

Snow-white and Rose-red
Solomon the wise
Sparrow with the slit-tongue
The stone statue
Toads and diamonds
The travelling companion
[rewarded]
The two brothers [people won't listen]
Two enemy kings
Two sisters and a harlot [appearances are deceiving]
GOODNESS (subject)
—[Factors in victory of the good]
Cortes-*Byelorussian*, 4
Goodwife of Laggan: enemy of the sisterhood
Lehane-*Wizards*, 115–121
Gooloo the magpie, and the Wahroogah
Parker-*Australian*, 27–29
Goomblegubbon, Beeargah, and Ouyan
Parker-*Australian*, 59–60
Goonur, the woman-doctor
Parker-*Australian*, 67–70
Goopher: Poor Sandy [conjure woman]
Shepard-*Conjure*, 1–12
Goophered grapevine
Shepard-*Conjure*, 61–72
The goose and the golden eggs
Lewis-*Minute*, 12–13
The goose girl
Lang-*Blue*, 278–285 (notes, 371)
Yolen-*Favorite*, 254–259
Goose that laid the golden eggs
Williams-*Aesop*, [24–26]
The goose with the golden feathers
Martin-*Hungry*, 63–71
Goosey Goosey Gander
Uttley-*Foxglove*, 20–32
GOPHERS
—holes
How the seven brothers saved their sister

Goralasi and the spectres
Manning-*Spooks*, 107–111
GORGON(S)
The monster-killers
GORGON(S) (subject)
Scott-*Fantastic*, 111–120
—Perseus
Lloyd-*Mythical*, 17–23
The gorgon's head
Shah-*World*, 98–105
Gormenghast
Lee-*Castles*, 190
GORONWY
Welsh enchanter's fosterling
Gorse
Ewart-*Lore*, 150–151
GOSSIP
Periquita
GOTHAM
How porridge was cooked in Gotham
How the citizens of Gotham paid their taxes
GOURDS
The magic rattle
Origin of gourd trumpet, memento of the dead
GOVERNING
King Dabschelim [rules for governing]
The governor and the Buddhist
Zong-*Korea*, 71–73
Grace O'Malley [a & b]
O'Sullivan-*Legends*, 122–123
Graduation
Hoke-*Uncanny*, 87–102
Grail. *See* HOLY GRAIL
GRAIN
Eros and Psyche
The harvesters
—golden
Golden life
A grain of millet
Zong-*Korea*, 196–197

Grainne of Ireland, Cormac, and
Finn . . .
Lehane-*Legends,* 56–63
GRAND CANYON
—origin
Five million ducks
GRANDCHILDREN
The wisdom of a child
Grandfather Frost
Riordan-*Russia,* 86–90
GRANDFATHERS
Andrew Coffey
Billy-goat and the handkerchief
The boy and his grandfather
Draw the curtains
Half a blanket (Ireland)
How grandpa mowed the
Lord's meadow
Lisalill
The old man and his grandson
—salty
The two little cottages
—voice from hollow
trees
The centipede girl
GRANDMOTHERS
Abuelita's bell
Anpao is born
The giant sturgeon
Leopard, the squirrel, and the
tortoise
Little Claus and Big Claus
The little match girl
The little mermaid
Little Red Riding Hood
Mouse Woman and the daugh-
ter of the sun
Mouse Woman and the mon-
ster killer whale
Mouse Woman and the por-
cupine hunter
Mouse Woman and the Snee-
nee-iq
Mouse Woman and the tooth
Mouse Woman and the van-
ished princes

Mouse woman and the wood-
en wife
Pulowech, the partridge
Red Riding Hood
The snow queen
A tale of the Windego
—a "fairy godmother"
The red cow [a Cinderella-type
story]
—hunter hides in skin of
The hunter and his greedy wife
—skull
The skull in the snow
—sugary
The two little cottages
Grania and Diarmid
Lochhead-*Battle,* 45–
48
The grant
Keightley-*World,* 286–
292
GRAPES AND GRAPEVINES
The fox and the grapes
Goophered grapevine
Simon and the pater-rollers
Wine and the devil
GRASS
Pixy-led
Stray sod
—Kusha
The blossom tree
The grasshopper and the
ant
Patai-*Gates,* 594–595
Grasshopper and the ant
Watson-*Aesop,* 20–21
Williams-*Aesop,* [30–32]
Grasshopper [Indian superman]
Wade-*Indian,* 207–240
GRASSHOPPERS
The great battle between the
grasshoppers and the
monkeys
The warlike seven
Grateful animals and the ungrateful
man

Shah-*World*, 68–69
The grateful bee
  Piggott-*Japanese*, 111–112
Grateful dog
  Piggott-*Japanese*, 110–111
The grateful elfwoman
  Booss-*Scand.*, 600
GRATITUDE
  See also INGRATITUDE
  Beauty and the beast
  Elves and the shoemaker
    whose work they did
  From bad to good to bad to
    good
  The golden man and the finger
    men
  Pixy-gratitude
  The pointing finger
  A small favor
  Stepmother's head
  Yallery Brown
Grave of a faithful dog
  Zong-*Korea*, 92–93
GRAVE-ROBBERS
—punished
  Desecrators of Rabbi Haim
    Messas' tomb
GRAVES
  The king o' the cats
  A mother saved by her son's
    grave
  Plague victims dig their own
    graves
  The sprightly tailor
—grave-earth used as a charm
  Finn magic
—Korea
  The unmarried girl's grave
—opens; widow joins betrothed
  Butterflies
Graves, Alfred Percival
  Songs of the ghost [poem]
  Yeats-*Fairy*, 123–124
The grave-yard mule
  Elbaz-*Folktales*, 139
Graveyards. *See* CEMETERIES

Gray, Will H.
  The bees from Borneo
Gray Arrow learns a lesson
  Shaw-*Pima*, 104–106
GRAY FOX
  Coyote fights a lump of pitch
The gray wolf
  Macdonald-*Gray*, 1–10
Gray wolf's haint
  Shepard-*Conjure*, 27–40
The great battle between the
    grasshoppers and the
    monkeys
  Jagendorf-*Magic*, 127–129
Great Bear and her Cub: starbound
    beasts
  Spells & Bind, 48–49
The Great Bear [Callisto and
    Arcas]
  Lurie-*Heavenly*, 11–13
GREAT BEAR (constellation)
  See also Ursa Major
—origin
  Zan and the Dactyls in early
    Crete
GREAT BRITAIN
  See also ENGLAND
  The battle of the birds
  The black horse
  The castle of Melvales
  Fairest of all others
  The flying childer
  The golden ball
  The green mist
  Jack and the green lady
  Kate Crackernuts
  The little bull calf
  The little fox
  Mally Whuppy
  Mossycoat
  The Paddo
  The seawife and the crone
  The sword in the stone
  Tom Thumb
GREAT BRITAIN (subject)
  Keightley-*World*, 280–361

The great bronze Buddha and the whale
  Shelley-*Legends*, 20–23
The great deeds of King Yu
  Jagendorf-*Magic*, 11–14
The Great Dog [Yudistira and Svana]
  Lurie-*Heavenly*, 14–17
The great Dreadnought hoax
  Schwartz-*Tales*, 60–67
Great exploits
  Pinsent-*Greek*, 68–81
Great father mosquito [larger than a bear]
  Jagendorf-*First*, 23–25
The great flood
  Shaw-*Pima*, 1–3
  Stokes-*Turtle*, 119–122
  Thompson-*Hawaiian*, 86–92
The great flood [deluge]
  Zong-*Korea*, 16–18
The great flood; Jokurugwa or Meriri Poro
  Wilbert-*Bororo*, 71–75
Great Heart and the three tests
  Macmillan-*Canadian* 178–183
The great heroes of old
  Haining-*Lepre.*, 55–59
The great hunters [animals]
  Shaw-*Pima*, 43–55
Great Joy, the self-respecting ox
  Martin-*Hungry*, 25–35
The great king's last battle
  Lehane-*Legends*, 132–139
GREAT LAKES
  Cranes of the Great Lakes
A great misfortune
  Nagishkin-*Folktales*, 32–38
The great misfortune of Lay Tee-Kwai
  Chalk-*Tales*, unp.
The great Penobscot raid
  Hill-*More*, 105–112
Great roving uhu
  Thompson-*Hawaiian*, 109–121

Great Spirit. *See* SPIRITS—"Great Spirit".
GREAT WALL OF CHINA
  Meng Chiang and the Great Wall of China
  Prophecy: Wan and the Great Wall of China
GREATNESS
  Minnie
GREECE
  See also GODS AND GODDESSES—Greece
  Callicantzaroi
  Goat people
  Gods and goddesses, Greek and Roman
  The Greek princess and the young gardener
  Moerae
  Monacielli
  Nereides
  Roosters, snakes and basiliscs
  The youngest god [Dionysius]
GREECE (subject)
  Keightley-*World*, 443–447
Greece: the baby dragon
  Stallman-*Dragons*, 26–27
GREED
  Babes in the wood
  Baucis and Philemon
  Being greedy chokes Anansi (Jamaica)
  The biter bit
  A boom in guarache leather
  The boy and the filberts
  The candy man; a Han folktale
  The Chinese bride
  The cobbler who became an astrologer
  Concerning the poor man covetous
  The creation
  Day the sun rose in the west
  The dervish and the thief
  Devil's armful [Canterbury]
  The dog and his shadow

Donald and his neighbours
  [Hudden & Dudden]
Duke Pishposh of Pash
The empty sea
An expensive hide
The family's fortune
A fisherman and a golden fish
A fisherman and his wife
The fisherman and his wife
Fisherman's dream
[The fox with the purple
  umbrella]
Genie of the mountains
Gold colt and the fire dragon
  shirt
The golden neckband
The good girl and the bad girl
The goose and the golden
  eggs
Goose that laid the golden
  eggs
The goose with the golden
  feathers
Hudden and Dudden and Do-
  nald O'Neary
The hunter and his greedy wife
Hyena eats the ostrich's eggs
Is much land needed for a
  man?
Judge true
King Josef
Kumba the orphan girl
The lazy husband, Ngurmi. [I]
Liza the fox and Catafay the
  cat
The magic bag
Magic brush; a Han folktale
The magic candelabra
Magic mallet
The magic pear tree
The magic rattle
The mallet of wealth
The man who knew how to di-
  vide a chicken
The Mauritanian and his
  wealth

The Moohel
Mother of the Waters
My godmother's story of buried
  treasure
"Of course!"
The old woman and the tramp
The old woman who lived in a
  vinegar bottle
The patient suitor
The pig who made a hog of
  himself
The pointing finger
Roly poly rice ball
Saran and Yumart
The silver swindle
Soul-taker
Sparrow with the slit-tongue
The stone lion [vomits gold]
Stupid Peikko
Three billy goats Bruse [sic]
The three billy goats Gruff
The three sons
Tismila wanders through the
  forest
The sparrow with the slit-
  tongue
Treasure Mountain; a Yao
  folktale
Wali and the magic saddle-bag
When rocks rolled crackling
  wisdom
White cap
Why the sea is salt
The wine well
Woe [personified]
—avarice
  Dame Soasan
—insatiable
  The fisherman and his wife
—punished
  The baker's daughter
  Golden rain
  Mother Holle
—rejected
  A wonderful bird
—"takes away brains"

GREED—"takes away brains"
  (continued)
  The stupid rich man
—wife keeps demanding more
  Fisherman's benefactor
Greed can cause one's downfall
  Todd-*Tortoise*, 107
Greed of the old man and his wife
  Radin-*African*, 199–200
Greed will be your downfall
  Todd-*Some*, 60–61
The greedy boy
  Wilbert-*Bororo*, 150–151
The greedy brother
  Sadler-*Heaven*, 21–25
The greedy dogs
  Stokes-*Turtle*, 57–58
The greedy father
  Magel-*Gambia*, 123–125
Greedy Kanchuga
  Nagishkin-*Folktales*, 167–173
The greedy youngster
  Booss-*Scand.*, 14–22
Greek gods/myths. *See* GODS
  AND GODDESSES—
  Greece
GREEK MYTHS (subject)
—dictionaries
  Stapleton-*Dictionary*, 1-224
—Monster myths; six tales
  Wise-*Monster*, 7–48
—renditions
  Lines-*Greek*, 17–26
—retellings
  Lines-*Greek*, 251–261
The Greek princess and the young
  gardener
  Jacobs-*Celtic*, 222–229
Greeks: descent from sacred
  animals
  Magical Beasts, 23–25
Green, Roger Lancelyn
  The curse of Andvari's ring
  Loki makes mischief
  Ragnarok
The green children

Keightley-*World*, 281–283
Green children (condensed)
  Briggs-*Vanish.*, 85
The green frog
  Zong-*Korea*, 34–35
"GREEN KNIGHT"
  Gawain and the Green Knight
The green lady of Barrogil
  Robertson-*Highland*, 55–56
The green lady of Caerphilly
  Froud-*Faeries*, unp
The green lady of Newton
  Robertson-*Highland*, 35–37
"GREEN LAND OF
  ENCHANTMENT'
  Briggs-*Vanish.*, 159–160
Green lizard, gray squirrel and the
  eagle
  Weiss-*Russian*, 41–48
Green Man of No Man's Land
  Sampson-*Gypsy*, 17–23
"GREEN MEN"
  Addlers and menters
The green mist
  Garner-*British*, 76–81
The green people
  Scott-*Fantastic*, 151–164
Green people: The squirrel wife
  Royds-*Animal*, 80–92
The green prairie
  Stuchl-*American*, 9–10
The green ribbon
  Schwartz-*Dark*, 24–33
Green thoughts
  Hoke-*Demonic*, 125–143
GREENLAND
  The expedition of Thorfin
  Karisefni
Greenland whale fishery [song and
  story]
  Sanders-*Hear*, 28–36
GREETINGS
  Padmasambhava and the
  felicity scarf
A gremlin: causing mischief
  Baskin-*Imps*, 18–19

GRENDEL (cannibal spirit)
  Heorot, the haunted hall
Grettir, the troll
  Night Creatures, 22–28
The grey selchie of Sule Skerrie
  Robertson-*Highland,* 166–167
The grey stone [fossil personified]
  Uttley-*Foxglove,* 53–58
The grey wolf and the orphan
  [Musquakie]
  Myles-*Butterflies,* 37–38
GRIDDLE CAKES
  [Finn] Fann Mac Cuil and the
  Scotch giant
GRIEF
  See also SORROW
  A dead son
  Proud Margaret
  Ukrainian tale [grief: imagined
  future woes]
—excessive
  The power of sorrow
Griffin, Gerald
  Hy-Brasail: the isle of the blest
  [poem]
  Yeats-*Fairy,* 1
Griffin, Gerald
  Owney and Owney-na-peak
Griffins
  Magical Beasts, 71–74
GRIFFINS
  Boy with the deformed head
  Man without a heart
GRIFFINS (subject)
  Lloyd-*Mythical,* 25–29
GRIMM, Jacob and Wilhelm
  (subject)
—tales; editions; biographical
  note
  Shub-*About,* vii–ix, 117–118
Grimsborg
  Booss-*Scand.,* 601–602
GRINDING STONES
  Treasure Mountain; a Yao
  folktale
—gnaw

Tortoise and pig: good acts not
  always rewarded
Grinnell, George B.
  Scarface
"GRIP"
  The bird 'Grip'
GRISELDA
  Patient Griselda
GRIZZLY BEARS
  Munchausen and the bear
  Skinkoots steals the springtime
—black snout
  Coyote and the swallowing
  monster
GROCERS
  The goblin and the grocer
The groom's crimes
  Roberts-*Chinese,* 212–213
GROOMS (for animals)
—trades places with mule
  The enchanted mule
GROSS, Alison (subject)
—[Scottish witch]
  Lee-*Castles,* 167
Groundhog dance
  Macdonald-*Twenty,* 35–42
Groundhogs. *See* WOODCHUCKS
GROWTH
—abnormally fast
  Ivan, the Windfall
—sudden aging
  The monk and the bird
GRUAGACH
  The Amadan Mor and the
  Gruagach
  The creatures of magic
GRUFFNESS
  The three billy goats Gruff
Gryla
  Booss-*Scand.,* 643
Gryphons. *See* GRIFFINS
GUADALUPE (shrine)
  The virgin of Guadalupe
GUAIRE, King
  Seanchan the Bard and the
  king of the cats

GUAN YU
Lord Guan: god of martial arts
The guardian angel
Baskin-*Imps*, 44–45
Guardian angels. *See* ANGELS—
guardian
The guardian cock
Heslewood-*Tales*, 26–30
The guardian dragon's magic pearl
Sanders-*Dragons*, 58–59
The guardian sheep
Magel-*Gambia*, 37–39
Guardian spirit: corn comes to the
Ojibwa
Jagendorf-*First*, 9–11
GUARDS
Golden life
The Moddey Dhoo
The monk and the drunk
Princess in the chest [coffin]
GUENEVERE, Queen
The great king's last battle
Lancelot and Guenevere
Lancelot, the finest of Arthur's
knights
The passing of Arthur
Sir Lancelot of the Lake
GUESSES (-ING)
See also NAMES—guessing
Inge of Rantum
—accidentally correct
Cat in the box
La Guillonnee: French holidays in
Miss. Valley
McNeil-*Charm*, 150–158
GUILT
The missing axe
—assumed invalidly
The seven giant brothers
—false assumption
Old Dry Frye (rogue preacher)
Guilty of murder
Colombo-*Wind.*, 9
The guilty stone
Shannon-*Solve*, 41–44
GUINEA FOWL

Being greedy chokes Anansi
(Jamaica)
Enchanted guinea-fowl
GUINEA PIGS
Seven families of Lake Pipple-
Popple
Snubby's tail
Guinevere, Queen. *See*
GUENEVERE, Queen
GUINGLAIN, son of Gwain
Le Bei Inconnu and the castle
of Senaudon
GUITARS
The cunning shoemaker
How the monkey became a
trickster
How the monkey escaped
being eaten
How the monkey got a drink
when he was thirsty
Guleesh
Jacobs-*Celtic*, 9–20
Lochhead-*Battle*, 73–79
GULLAH LANGUAGE
The one that got away
GULLIBILITY
The bear and the crow
Bull-calf goes to school
Caterpillar and the wild
animals
Dinewan the emu, and the
bustard
The horsetrader
Ivan the rich and Ivan the
poor
The jackal, the dove, and the
panther
The leaf
Magic figs
The man turned into a mule
Mule lore: "mule eggs"
Nazar the Brave ["kills a thou-
sand with a single blow"]
A reward for honesty
Snake and goat: tomorrow is
another day

Squirrel, leopard, and goat: do
  it again, then
Tiger and the rabbit
The tiger-eating jackal cubs
Wisdom of Senor Zorro
Gulls. *See* SEA GULLS
Gulnara the Tartar warrior
  Riordan-*Woman,* 20–26
The gum-baby and rabbit
  Crouch-*Whole,* 32–35
Gumiya; a Blang story: origins of
  characteristics
  Seven Sisters, 108–118
The gunny wolf
  Macdonald-*Twenty,* 68–74
GUNS AND GUNNERY
  Brer bear gets a taste of man
  The sultan and the psalms
Gushtap and the princess of Roum
  Shah-*Dervishes,* 199–202
The Gwagedd Annwyn
  Arrowsmith-*Field,* 261–264
  Froud-*Faeries,* unp
The Gwagedd Annwyn [II]
  Froud-*Faeries,* unp
GWARWYN-A-THROT
  Briggs-*Vanish.,* 61, 196
GWAWL
  Pwyll, Prince of Dyfed
GWYDION
  Math, son of Mathonwy
  Welsh enchanter's fosterling
Gwydion and Pryderi
  Lehane-*Wizards,* 25–27
Gwyllion
  Froud-*Faeries,* unp
GWYN ap Nudd
  Briggs-*Vanish.,* 90–196
GYLFI, King
  The death of Balder
  The gods return
  King Gylfi is tricked again
  Night and day
  Odin prepares for the
    Ragnarok
GYNT, Peter

Peter Gynt
GYPSIES
  Jack and the green lady
  Liisa and the prince
  The little fox
  Nourie Hadig [a "Snow White"
    type]
  Time to think [crossroads: fatal
    accidents]
  The gypsy and Saint George
  Ransome-*War,* 75–80
GYPSY TALES (subject)
  —[Welsh; 21 tales]
  Sampson-*Gypsy,* 1–108

Ha! Ha! Ha!
  Manning-*Spooks,* 126–128
Ha, ha, Jack-in-the-box!
  Blyton-*My,* 59–65
Habetrot [name of fairy]
  Ratcliff-*Scottish,* 84–88
HABIT(S)
  The boy who told lies
  —bad
  The wise woman, or The lost
    princess
  —change in routines, helpful
  The ducks and the fox
  —twitching and scratching
  How to break a bad habit
Hades. *See* HELL
HADES (god)
  Persephone
Hades, lord of the underworld
  Gibson-*Gods,* 21–24
Haggard, Henry Rider
  Only a dream
Hagop's wish
  Villa-*Armenian,* 197–202,
    477
Hags
  Froud-*Faeries,* unp

HAGS
See also WITCHES
Tale of the Princess of
Damascus
HAIDA ISLANDS
Bear Mother and her husband
Hailibu the hunter
Minford-*Fav.*, 74–80
HAIR
Coma Berenices (Berenice's
hair)
Devil with the three golden
hairs
Genie of the mountains
How Thor got his hammer
Loki makes mischief
Long Haired Girl
Rapunzel
—blonde
Powdered blondie and three-
haired blondie
—golden
Loki and the dwarf
The princess in the ivory tower
The three golden hairs of Old
Man Almanack
—golden; controls wizard
Elsa and the evil wizard
—lock made into cloak
The wounded lion
—long
Kate of Ysatter
The white-hair waterfall
—magic
Maui slows down the sun
The monster's hairs
—red
Connla and the fairy maiden
—yellow
Yallery Brown
HAIRPINS
—magic
The twins of Paikala Mountain
"HAIRY-ONES"
The phynnodderee
HAITI

"Bye-bye" (Haiti)
[Children and fruit trees in
Haiti]
[Haitian storytelling (commentary)]
Wolkstein-*Magic*, 2–12
HAITIAN TALES
[Haitian storytelling
(commentary)]
The hakham and the tam
Nahman-*Tales*, 139–161
Halcyone: a second life for love
Spells & Bind, 46–47
Halde hat
Booss-*Scand.*, 276–277
Half a blanket (Ireland)
Yolen-*Favorite*, 63–64
Half-chick [Medio Pollito]
Lang-*Green*, 16–22
Half-ram leaves home
Crouch-*Whole*, 7–10
Half-Rooster
Thomas-*It's*, 152–154
Halibut Man and the house on the
waves
De Wit-*Talking*, 149–154
HALLOWE'EN
Alison Gross (condensed)
Fairies of Corrie Chaorachain
(condensed)
Janet and Tamlin
Tamlane (condensed)
Tomlin [elf-knight]
Yesterday's witch [Miss
Marble]
HALLOWE'EN (subject)
Briggs-*Vanish.*, 43–45, 105–
106, 113, 164
HALLUCINOGENS
Communicating with the gods
Halva-maker
Villa-*Armenian*, 299–302
Halverson, Lydia, illus.
Stallman-*Dragons*
Hamberger, John, illus.
Hill-*More*
HAMBURG HYDRA

Water monsters
Hamelin. *See under* GERMANY
[Hameln: punishment for not keep-
   ing bargain with piper]
   Spells & Bind, 69–73
HAMMERS
   The lay of Thrym
   Loki and the dwarf
   Loki makes mischief
   Stupid Peikko
   The troll's hammer
—magic
   The disrespectful son
   Roly poly rice ball
—Thor's
   How Thor got his hammer
   The stealing of Thor's hammer
   Thor in the giant's strong-hold
   The walls of Asgard
The hand and the whirlpool
   Ritchie-*Armadillo*, 43–45
Hand of glory [severed hand of
   hanged man]
   Lurie-*Clever*, 53–56
   Marshall-*Every.*, 235–239
A handful of rice
   Amore-*Lustful*, 126–128
HANDICAPPED
   Minnie
—cripple cured by fairy
   Jump into my sack (Italy)
HANDICRAFTS
—creatures made; come to life
   Sister Lace
Handout for the merman
   Lindow-*Swedish*, 130–131
HANDS
   John and Mary; girl with
      chopped-off hands
   Mister Fox
   The sea nymph
   The ten fairy servants
   The white cat
—clean
   The thief who kept his hands
      clean

—severed
   The cat woman (France)
   Golden pears
   Mister Fox [suitor/murderer]
—work
   A true money tree
Handsome ogre-girl of the pool
   Radin-*African*, 243–246
The handsome suitor [A]
   Magel-*Gambia*, 40–44
The handsome suitor [B]
   Magel-*Gambia*, 45–49
Hang the money! I know what I've
   earned
   Lang-*Pink/K*, 101–105
The hanged man seeks his pine
   tree
   Lindow-*Swedish*, 189–190
HANGING(S)
   The golden ball
   "Lars, my lad!"
   Munachar and the raspberries
—hand of hanged-man
   The hand of glory
A Hani story: Queen forbids ser-
   vant to eat rice
   Seven Sisters, 65–70
Hans my Hedgehog
   Lang-*Green*, 382–389
Hans Puntleder
   Keightley-*World*, 91–93
Hans, the mermaid's son
   Lang-*Pink/D*, 112–125
   Lang-*Pink/K*, 66–79
Hans, who made the princess
   laugh
   Booss-*Scand.*, 84–88
Hansel and Gretel
   Classic Child., 5–11
   Ehrlich-*Random*, 150–165
   Lang-*Blue*, 259–268 (notes,
      371)
   Leete-*Golden*, 32–47
   Pierce-*Larousse*, 55–64
   Rackham-*Fairy*, 253–261
   Shub-*About*, 99–107

Hansel and Gretel (continued)
  Stallman-*Witches*, 31–32
  Tudor-*Bedtime*, [26–27]
"HANSEL AND GRETEL"
  STORIES
  The gingerbread house [Hansel and Gretel]
HANUKKAH
  The extinguished lights
  The power of light
A Hanukkah evening in my parents' house
  Singer-*Power*, 3–7
Hanukkah in the poorhouse
  Singer-*Power*, 59–71
HANUMAN
  Monkey god: epic battle for earthly supremacy
The happiest man in the world
  Shah-*World*, 96
HAPPINESS
  See also JOY
  Antti and the wizard's prophecy
  The ball of gold
  The bird of happiness
  Clever man and ordinary
  The golden finger [not lasting because of lie]
  The happiest man in the world
  The happy man's shirt (Italy)
  The haunted well
  Headman and the magician
  The kingdom of beautiful colors
  Legend of the old bell-ringer
  The little soldier
  The poor man's bowl
  Stonemason: a T'ung folktale
  The tale of the magic green water-pearl
  Treasurer under suspicion
  Wagging my tail in the mud
Happy goldfish; the sage
  Berger-*Animalia* [29–31]
Happy hunter and the skilful fisher

Ozaki-*Japanese*, 153–176
The happy man's shirt (Italy)
  Yolen-*Favorite*, 417–418
The happy prince
  Wilde-*Fairy*, 13–28
HARDHEARTEDNESS
  The birthday of the Infanta
  The fox who went to heaven
  The spook and the pigs
Hare: a soft-footed servant of witches
  Lehane-*Wizards*, 100
Hare and hyena in the well
  Magel-*Gambia*, 185–188
Hare and otter
  Wood-*Spirits*, 34–38
Hare and the lions
  O'Connor-*Tibet*, 51–55
The hare and the magpie
  Nagishkin-*Folktales*, 87–88
Hare and the tortoise [the true story]
  Royds-*Animal*, 8–14
The hare in the moon
  Amore-*Lustful*, 128–130
Hare makes hyena his riding horse
  Magel-*Gambia*, 189–191
The hare, Nwashisisana
  Radin-*African*, 123–128
Hare saves the hippopotamus
  Magel-*Gambia*, 182–184
Hare seeks endowments from Allah
  Magel-*Gambia*, 179–181
Hare, the hyena, and the lioness's cave
  Radin-*African*, 120–122
Harebell
  Ewart-*Lore*, 125
HAREBELLS
  Faerie flora
Hares. *See* RABBITS
The hares and the elephants
  Hadley-*Legends*, 28–29
The hare's hut [fox chased out]
  Cortes-*Byelorussian*, 11–12
The hare's sacrifice

Martin-*Hungry*, 91–97
The harga-dance
    Lindow-*Swedish*, 148–150
HARI-KIRI (subject)
    Piggott-*Japanese*, 143 (index)
Harlots. *See* PROSTITUTES
Harmful power of the evil eye
    Elbaz-*Folktales*, 155
The harp [origin]
    O'Sullivan-*Legends*, 41
Harpies
    Magical Beasts, 65–71
HARPIES
    The Bakororo and Itubore
      legend
HARPIES (subject)
    Scott-*Fantastic*, 111–120
HARPS AND HARPISTS
    The boy in the donkey skin
    Gitto Bach
    The harp [origin]
    King Goldemar
    Lyra (the Lyre)
    Power of the harp
    Rhys at the fairy-dance
    The story-teller at fault
—magic
    The first kantele
Harrison, Harry
    The man from P.I.G.
Hart, Michael
    A fairy enchantment
HARTLEY, Edmund, 16th century
    The "Kissing witch"
The harvesters
    Booss-*Scand.*, 293–294
HARVESTS AND HARVESTERS
    Farmers three
    Kate of Ysatter
—saved
    Holecek and the water nymph
HASE, Princess
    Princess Hase
HASEN of Basra
    The bird maiden
HASIDIC TALES (subject)

—Kabbalah
    Nahman-*Tales*, xiii–xix
Hasidism
    Nahman-*Tales*, 331
Hasidism [Introd. & selections]
    Patai-*Gates*, 667–747
Hasjelti's dance
    Wood-*Spirits*, 102–106
Hassan the brave
    Mitchnik-*Egyptian*, 100–108
Hassan the physician
    Mitchnik-*Egyptian*, 93–100
HASSINE, David, 1721–1781.
    The miracle of Rabbi David
      Hassine
    Rabbi David Hassine feasted
      his family
HATE
    Diarmuid and Grainne
    Jose and Princess Florabella
    The mistake
    Sturt's desert pea, the blood
      flower
HATS
    Halde hat
    The shrinking hat
    The stolen lady
    Stupid Peikko
—cap of invisibility
    The magic cap
    The terrible head
—caps
    Adventures of John Dietrich
    Bride from the sea: the mer-
      maid's cap
    Charge this to the cap
    La cucaracha
    Dwarfs stealing corn
    The herd-boy
    White cap
    The wind cap
HATS (subject)
—caps-magic
    Briggs-*Vanish.*, 215 (index)
Hauff, Wilhelm
    Caliph Stork

Haughtiness. *See* PRIDE
The haughty chief
  Shaw-*Pima*, 36–42
Haughty princess
  Yeats-*Fairy*, 263–265
HAUNTED HOUSES
  The bold soldier of Antwerp
  Death and the soldier
  The dream house (Ireland)
  Hold him, Tabb
  Hold on, Jim!
  Teigue of the Lee
  Thurnley Abbey
  The triumph of death
  Yi Chang and the spectres
—Breccles Hall
  Phantom coach
Haunted houses [tales]
  Robertson-*Highland*, 29–86
The haunted mill: or, The ruined
  home
  Manley-*Fun*, 35–39
The haunted pavilion
  Sanders-*Dragons*, 85
The haunted realm
  Haining-*Lepre.*, 47–53
The haunted trailer [by R. Arthur]
  Schwartz-*Great*, 103–126
The haunted well
  Stovicek-*Around*, 66–69
Haunter of the birch forest
  Lehane-*Wizards*, 122–139
A haunting
  Lindow-*Swedish*, 183–184
Haunting of [computer] Y-12
  [Sarrantonio]
  Schwartz-*Great*, 159–169
The hauntings at Frodriver
  Crossley-*Legends*, 164–
  171
Hauntings. *See* GHOSTS
HAUSBOCKE
  Kombocke and Hausbocke
Haviland, Virginia
  Poor turkey girl
  Star Maiden

Havoc in heaven: Monkey and the
  Jade Emperor
  Sanders-*Dragons*, 97–99
HAWAII
  Punia and the King of the
  Sharks
HAWAII (subject)
—Alapa regiment, 1776 [destruc-
  tion at Kakanilua]
  Westervelt-*Hawaiian*, 125–142
—Capt. Cook [called "O Lono"]
  Westervelt-*Hawaiian*, 100–113
—Eight of Oahu [Maui invasion,
  1783]
  Westervelt-*Hawaiian*, 149–154
—First constitution
  Westervelt-*Hawaiian*, 189–199
—First foreigners [history]
  Westervelt-*Hawaiian*, 93–99
—First Hawaiian printing
  Westervelt-*Hawaiian*, 183–188
—The Hawaiian flag
  Westervelt-*Hawaiian*, 200–215
—Kupua tales
  Thompson-*Hawaiian*, 9
—Last of the tabu
  Westervelt-*Hawaiian*, 176–182
—Last prophet of Oahu [Ka-
  hahana, 1782]
  Westervelt-*Hawaiian*, 143–148
—Law of the splintered paddle
  [1783, plunder of the weak]
  Westervelt-*Hawaiian*, 162–175
—Legendary home of the
  Polynesians
  Westervelt-*Hawaiian*, 41–46
—Red Mouth Gun [canoe battle,
  1791]
  Westervelt-*Hawaiian*, 155–161
HAWAIIAN LANGUAGE (subject)
—Glossary
  Thompson-*Hawaiian*, 122–126
HAWAIIAN LEGENDS (subject)
  Westervelt-*Hawaiian*, 3–10
HAWAII-LOA
  Viking of the Pacific

The hawk and the nightingale
Shah-*World,* 20
The hawk and the rattlesnake
Stuchl-*American,* 208–222
HAWKEYE (character)
Long, Wide and Hawkeye
HAWKS
The apples of eternal life
El caballero porfiado
The cock and the crested hen
Crane, kangaroo rat, fire
makers
The nightingale and the hawk
Smallhead and the king's son
The stealing of Thor's hammer
Tortoise and hawk: never
laugh at friends
Ua-pa-chi (Kickapoo titles)
—claims dove from king
A king and a dove
—fed king's own flesh
King Sivi
—skins
Thor's holiday
—white
Star Maiden
—why it eats chicks
Hen and hawk [once married,
now enemies]
Hawthorn
Ewart-*Lore,* 61–66
HAWTHORNS (subject)
Briggs-*Vanish.,* 114–115, 137
HAY AND HAYMAKERS
The princess on the glass hill
Una the elfwoman
HAYSTACKS
The spook and the pigs
Stupid Peikko
Tangletop: the haystacks
The vain bear
Hazel
Froud-*Faeries,* unp
Hazel and dogwood
Ewart-*Lore,* 168–169
He comes from the east

Highwater-*Anpao,* 216–226
He walked upon the water
MacLean-*Cuentos,* 117–120
He who laughs last, laughs
best
Sheohmelian-*Three,* 25–28
Head devil in Texas [satire]
Stuchl-*American,* 196–202
HEADACHES
Hob and Sleepyhead
—pregnancy results
Clever boy
HEADLESS PHANTOMS
The death coach
Headman and the magician
Peacock Maid, 44–53
HEADS
The elf of the rose
The terrible head
The ugly son-in-law
The wonderful head: Celtic
myths
—becomes evil spirit
Metugoe doves and the Indian
Magurereu
—golden
The three heads of the
well
—mummified
The Tsanta
—removeable
Tokanao: the first coconut
—severed
Gawain and the Green Knight
Stepmother's head
—severed head follows Bororo
Metugoe doves and the Indian
Magurereu
—severed, pursues children
The cruel stepmother
The headstrong woman
Griego-*Cuentos,* 157–159
HEALING (cures)
See also MIRACLES;
RESUSCITATION
Aid and punishment

244

HEALING (cures) (continued)
  The bad wife [in bottomless
    pit] (Russia)
  The big bird Katchka
  The black colt
  The bronze ring
  Cock with the golden feathers
  Confessions of Tom Bourke
  The cripple
  Dance of death
  Death and the doctor
  The deer and the snake
  The devil and the old hag
  Diarmuid, son of Donn: a spell-
    shackled devotion
  Doctor Tyl
  February dragon
  Fiery horse
  The godfather
  Godfather death (Germany)
  Golden pears
  Guleesh
  Hassan the physician
  Home-bred boy dislodges spider
  Hong Do-Ryong, the filial tiger
  [Hunchback cured by fairies]
  Kate Crackernuts
  King and the poor man
  King who had no children
  Kupti and Imani
  The lamb with the golden
    fleece
  Lochman Hehkeem, the great
    healer
  MacGovern of Giangevlin;
    Ighne
  La madrina muerte
  Master Tobacco
  Melampus—physician and
    prophet
  [Mermaid rewards Cornishman
    with magic powers]
  Miaoshan-Guanyin, protectress
    of mortals
  Old man who made withered
    trees to flower

  The old smith
  One member of a family fated
    to die
  Owney and Owney-na-peak
  Pepito el corcovado
  Pierre, Prince of Murom
  Pixy-vengeance
  The Prince of Nimroz
  Princess and the slave
  Rabbi Haim Pinto orders jinn
    to cure disciple
  The rocks of Korsan
  Saran and Yumart
  Search for the magic lake
  The seven-day vigil
  The seventh son
  Shepherd of Myddvai and the
    lake maiden
  The snake of Rabbi Daoud
  Sody sallytytus
  Song-bird and the healing waters
  The soul-taking angel [Gabriel]
  Squirrel and the fox
  Sulphur water: El Paso de los
    Robles
  Tales of a parrot
  The tiger's grave
  The tooth of gold
  Truth and falsehood
    [personified]
  The two travellers [evil man
    blinded]
  The umbrella tree
  Upamanyu learns a lesson
    [hermitage school]
  Vainamoinen's wound
  The water of life
  Why the flat fish is flat
  The woman in blue
  Wonderful healing leaves
  Young boy and the dwarf
—daughter made lame by fairy
  Teapot spout: Mother
    Hannah's story
—demon helps
  Talkative wife

HEAVEN—"highest in" (continued)
Tiger boys
—new
The gods return
HEAVEN (subject)
—Steps to heaven and hell
Nicholson-*Mexican*, 24–26
Heaven and hell [cooperation]
Shannon-*Solve*, 51–53
Heaven forbid!
Manning-*Spooks*, 123–125
The heavenly flute player; a Li
story
Seven Sisters, 119–122
Heavenly maiden and the wood
cutter
Zong-*Korea*, 21–25
The heavenly song of the green-
spotted dove
Jagendorf-*Magic*, 93–97
Heaven's reward
Sadler-*Heaven*, 3–8
Hecate, the moon-goddess
Night Creatures, 20
HECTOR
Achilles and the death of
Hector
Helen of Troy
The hedgehog and the fox [Aesop]
Shah-*World*, 236
HEDGEHOGS
Baba Yaga and the hedgehog
George's picnic
Half-ram leaves home
Hans by Hedgehog
The tale of Mrs Tiggy-Winkle
Hedgerows
Ewart-*Lore*, 66–73
The Hedley Kow
Phelps-*Tatterhood*, 13–16
HEDLEY KOW (subject)
Briggs-*Vanish.*, 123, 196
Heifer and the ox
Williams-*Aesop*, [18–19]
HEIGHT
Glooscap and the wishes

HEIMDALL
The golden age in Asgard
Heimdall in Midgard
Branston-*Gods*, 44–45
Heinzelmanchen
Keightley-*World*, 257–258
HEINZELMANCHEN (subject)
Briggs-*Vanish.*, 60, 196
Heinzelmannchen and Hutchen
Arrowsmith-*Field*, 248–252
HEIRS AND HEIRESSES
Gifts of the child Christ
Helen of the Hosts: Dream of
Macsen
Lochhead-*Battle*, 107–110
Helen of Troy
Lines-*Greek*, 157–168
HELEN of Troy
The fall of Troy
HELEN of Troy (subject)
Pinsent-*Greek*, 143 (index)
HELIE (Welsh Queen)
Quest of the Fair Unknown
HELIOS
Phaethon and the sun-horses
HELIUS
The chariot of the sun
HELL
See also GEHENNA;
UNDERWORLD
Castles in the Inferno
The devil and the farmer's wife
The devil and the old hag
Hades, lord of the underworld
Heaven and hell [cooperation]
John Tregeagle
A journey into hell
The magic bag
The merchant's walk
The monk's sins
Pedro de Ordimalas
Persephone among the dead
Prospectors in Paradise
The soldier and death
Stagolee
Tummeldink

Why the sea is salt
Wicked John and the devil
—Hades
Eros and Psyche
Mother Earth and her children
—lord of
Witches on the lake
—selfishness
Once a good man [eat with
arms chained]
—thrown out
The drunkard in hell
HELL (subject)
—Hades
Pinsent-*Greek,* 143 (index)
—Steps to heaven and hell
Nicholson-*Mexican,* 24–26
Helle and Phrixus
Lines-*Greek,* 70–76
Hello, Aurora
And Every., 43–56
Help for a mule caravan
Campos-*Mexican,* 66–68
Helpful animals [motif index]
Wilbert-*Bororo,* 296
Helpful spirit
Villa-*Armenian,* 290–293, 507–
509
HELPFULNESS
The little red hen
Yallery Brown
Helping the sjora [vantevannen]
Lindow-*Swedish,* 126–127
Helping to lie
Yolen-*Favorite,* 27
Heming, Arthur
The Snow-Wetigo
The hemp smoker, Zimwa-mbanje
Radin-*African,* 171–173
Hen and hawk [once married, now
enemies]
Stokes-*Turtle,* 91–92
The hen and the apple tree
Lobel-*Fables,* 11
Henny-Penny
Oxenbury-*Nursery,* 40–46

Pierce-*Larousse,* 51–54
Rackham-*Fairy,* 60–64
HENNY PENNY
The fox and the little white hen
The sky is falling
Hens. *See under* CHICKENS
HENWIVES
Fair, brown, and trembling
Song of the Knight of the
Green Vesture
[Heorot and Beowulf]
Night Creatures, 7–10
Heorot, the haunted hall
Lee-*Castles,* 26–29
HEPHAESTUS (god of fire)
Aphrodite, goddess of love
Mummies, zombies, and artifi-
cial men
HEPHAESTUS (subject)
Pinsent-*Greek,* 143 (index)
Her lover's heart
Shah-*World,* 28–30
HERA (goddess)
The apple of discord
Echo and Narcissus
—jealousy
The youngest god [Dionysius]
Jason and the golden fleece
The new gods-Zeus and Hera
HERA (goddess) (subject)
Pinsent-*Greek,* 143 (index)
Heracles
Pinsent-*Greek,* 85–99
Stapleton-*Dictionary,* 95–98
Heracles (Hercules)
Gallant-*Constel.,* 62–75
HERACLES
The labours of Hercules
The Lion [Heracles]
HERACLES (subject)
—labors of (I–XII)
Stapleton-*Dictionary,* 99–
100
Pinsent-*Greek,* 143 (index)
Heracles: the crime; the labors
Low-*Greek,* 93–109

Herb of life
  Patal-*Gates,* 601–602
HERBS
  Aid and punishment
  Ari, his third death and his
    resurrection
  Death out of season
  Fairy herbs
  Guleesh
  Kosi, the eagle, and the moun-
    tain lion
  Song of the seven herbs [7
    legends]
  Tibast and vandelrot
—medicinal
  The leeching of Kayn's leg
  The plant of gold
Hercules. *See* HERACLES
[Hercules vs Cerberus]
  Wise-*Monster,* 34–37
The herd-boy
  Booss-*Scand.,* 316–323
The herd boy and the dragons
  Manning-*Marvels,* 40–57
The herd-boy and the giant
  Crossley-*Folk,* 92–96
The herd boy and the weaving girl
  Sanders-*Dragons,* 41–45
HERDS
—origin
  Tokoloshi [origin of herds and
    flocks]
HERDSMEN
  Bootes (the Herdsman)
  The castle in the lake
  Hildur, the queen of the elves
  Katla
  The kingdom of beautiful
    colors
  The lovers
  The Nomad
  The phantom herd
HERDSWOMEN
  Gesar of Ling
HEREDITY
  The two pickpockets

"HERE'S OFF"
  White cap
HERLA, King (subject)
  Briggs-*Vanish.,* 15–17, 87
Herman the milk bottle
  McCarthy-*Raccoon,* 107–119
HERMES (god)
  Ares, god of war
HERMES (subject)
  Pinsent-*Greek,* 143 (index)
Hermes, messenger of the gods
  Gibson-*Gods,* 58–59
  Lines-*Greek,* 62–69
The hermit [paradoxical behavior]
  Shah-*World,* 46–48
HERMITS
  Banca Flor
  Destiny
  The disrespectful son
  Gesar of Ling
  How the hermit helped to win
    the king's . . .
  The quest for the Star of the
    Sea
  The serpent-woman (Spain)
  The wicked stepmother
—teach magic to prince
  Why the gibbon says "pua"
—wise man
  The master pupil
Herne the hunter
  Marshall-*Every.,* 119–124
Heroes and heroines
  Piggott-*Japanese,* 88–108
HEROES AND HEROINES
  A crippled hero
  Deirdre and Naoise
  The flying head
  Li Chi slays the serpent
  Maid of the mill
  Marko's [Kraljevic] smile
  The mastermaid
  Slave maiden's eye for evil
  The story of Deirdre
  T'ien the brave, hero of the
    Hsia River

Tom Hickathrift and the old
  giant
The wounded lion
—accidental
  See SUCCESS—accidental
—giant's daughter saves prince
  Battle of the birds
—girl rescues her brothers
  The water of life
HEROES AND HEROINES
  (subject)
—[Heroes and hero types]
  Yolen-*Favorite*, 201
—Notes on heroines
  Phelps-*Tatterhood*, 157–164
—[Plucky women and atypical he-
  roes; six tales]
  Williams-*Practical*, 1–99
Heroic tales
  Patai-*Gates*, 608–615
Heron gives Meri power over the
  night
  Wilbert-*Bororo*, 38–41
HERONS
  Crane woos the heron
  Gheeger Gheeger the cold
    west wind
  The jackal, the dove, and the
    panther
  Little frog repays coyote
  The magic snowshoes
—as bridge
  Honeyed words can't sweeten
    evil
—red and black
  The Iparexeba legend
HERRINGS
—pickled
  Stormalong fights the Kraken
Hershele and Hanukkah
  Singer-*Power*, 49–58
HERTA, King
  Wild huntsman
He's a Windigo
  Colombo-*Wind.*, 31–32
Hesiod

The hawk and the nightingale
HESPERIDES (subject)
  Pinsent-*Greek*, 143 (index)
Hey-hey men
  Arrowsmith-*Field*, 255–258
Hiawatha
  Wade-*Indian*, 83–88
HIBERNATION
  The squirrel and the pixie
Hic! Hic! Hic!
  Macdonald-*Twenty*, 142–153
HICCUPS
  Stupid Marco
"HIDDEN FOLK"
  Girl at the shieling [elf]
    (Iceland)
HIDES AND SKINS
  The devil's hide [temper]
HID-FOLK
  The genesis of the Hid-folk
HIDING
  Severi and Vappu
—task: find the giant
  The King of Ireland's son (Art)
—as test
  Vanooshka
HIGGINS, RACHEL (a witch)
  Bewitched butter [Queen's
    County]
High John the conqueror
  Lester-*Black*, 93–112
The Highland vision [23 tales]
  Robertson-*Highland*, 171–
    194
Highsmith, Patricia
  The snail-watcher
Highways. *See* ROADS
HIISI (evil spirit)
  The hunting of the elk
  Little Lapp and the Ice King
Hiisi's horse
  Synge-*Land*, 87–90
Hildur, the queen of the elves
  Booss-*Scand.*, 619–624
Hill, Douglas, jt. auth.
  How coyote stole fire

The hill folk
    Manning-*Marvels*, 79–85
HILL FOLK
    A farmer tricks a troll
    Kirsten's-hill
Hill, Kay
    The magic snowshoes
The hill-man at the dance
    Keightley-*World*, 217–218
Hill-men. *See* BERG-PEOPLE
The hill-men invited to the
        christening
    Keightley-*World*, 118–120
HILL OGRES
    Boots and the beasts
The hill-smith
    Keightley-*World*, 123–124
HILLEL
    Patience of Hillel
HILLS
    Adventures of John Dietrich
    Hollow hills
    The legend of Bodedys
    The miser on the faerie gump
    Mound folk
    Skotte in the fire
—glass
    The princess on the glass hill
HILLS (subject)
—fairies in
    Briggs-*Vanish.*, 216 (index)
—underground Fairyland
    Briggs-*Vanish.*, 218 (index)
Hind, Henry Youle
    Cannibal Lake
    Giant cannibals
HINDU TALES (subject)
—[Stories of life: content; sources;
        bibliog.]
    Amore-*Lustful*, 183–198
Hinzelmann
    Keightley-*World*, 240–254
HIPPOGRIFFS
    Castles of the wizard and the
        hippogriff
Hippolytus (Euripides)

Stapleton-*Dictionary*, 105–107
HIPPOPOTAMI
    Hare saves the hippopotamus
    The hippopotamus at dinner
    Lobel-*Fables*, 38–39
HIRED MEN
    The ghost and the moneychest
    His compassion is over all his
        works
    Patai-*Gates*, 738–739
His just reward
    Yolen-*Favorite*, 409–411
HISPANIC LITERATURE (subject)
    Griego-*Cuentos*, 3–5
The history of Tom Thumb. *See*
        Tom Thumb
The hitchhiker
    Stuchl-*American*, 249–250
Hitting. *See* STRIKING
HOARDING
    Story-spirits [confined in bag;
        plan revenge]
    The wolf who wished to hoard
HOAXES
    Johnny Chung and the Flying
        Figments
    Snouters
    Who? [Joseph David Oznot]
Hob and Boggart
    Mayne-*Red*, [3–8]
Hob and Eggy Palmer
    Mayne-*Yellow*, 4–9
Hob and Hinky Punk
    Mayne-*Yellow*, 14–19
Hob and Mump
    Mayne-*Green*, 8–11
Hob and Nobody
    Mayne-*Red*, [9–12]
Hob and Sleepyhead
    Mayne-*Yellow*, 20–23
Hob and Sootkin
    Mayne-*Yellow*, 10–13
Hob and the black dog
    Mayne-*Red*, [23–26]
Hob and the black hole
    Mayne-*Red*, [13–16]

Hob and the Cough
  Mayne-*Green*, 16–19
Hob and the Sad
  Mayne-*Red*, [18–22]
Hob and the storm
  Mayne-*Green*, 20–25
Hob and the strange lady
  Mayne-*Green*, 2–7
Hob and the Temper
  Mayne-*Green*, 12–15
Hob and Tooth Fairy
  Mayne-*Yellow*, 24–27
Hob stories [five]
  Mayne-*Red*, [3–26]
The Hobbit's dragon
  Stallman-*Dragons*, 38–39
HOBBY, Lady
  Ghost of Lady Hobby
Hobgoblins
  Arrowsmith-*Field*, 120–122
HOBGOBLINS
  See also ROBIN
    GOODFELLOWS
  Bloody Bones
  The Hedley Kow
  The snow queen
HOBGOBLINS (subject)
  Briggs-*Vanish.*, 8, 53–54, 66,
    123, 196
HOBS (house fairies)
  'Aye, we're flitting'
Hodeken
  Keightley-*World*, 255–256
HODI, Raja
  Her lover's heart
The Hodja and the cauldron
    (Turkey)
  Yolen-*Favorite*, 129–130
HOES
  Something for nothin (a Hui
    story)
Hogmanay [condensed]
  Mckee-*Scottish*, 32–33
Hogner, Dorothy
  Big long man's corn patch
Hogrogian, Nonny, illus.

Shub-*About*
HOGS
  Animals in winter
  Brave little tailor (seven at one
    blow)
  The charcoal burner
  The destruction of Da Derga's
    hostel
  The end of the world
  Foolish wife
  Loki makes mischief
  The magician's pupil
  The man from P.I.G.
  Man without a heart
  Math, son of Mathonwy
  Mice in the corn
  O horrid dede! [monk mur-
    dered: stealing]
  The pancake
  Prince White Hog
  Rooting out bad feelings
  Sam Pig seeks his fortune
  The tale of Macc Da Tho's pig
  The three little pigs
  Three little pigs [houses: mud,
    cabbage, brick]
  Tortoise and pig: good acts not
    always rewarded
  The witches' fire
  Wrecker of Sennen Cove
—boars
  Sagacious monkey and the
    boar
—boars, wild
  The labours of Hercules
—bones
  Queen Pig
—golden
  How Thor got his hammer
—haystacks turned into pigs
  The spook and the pigs
—hunting boars a taboo
  Diarmuid and Grainne
—origin: grunting with snout to ground
  Tortoise and pig: good acts not
    always rewarded

HOGS (continued)
—origin of pigs
First pig and porcupine
—pig would not jump over stile
The old woman and her pig
—skins
Queen Pig
Hohokam: the people who are
gone
Shaw-*Pima,* 27–28
[Hoichi the earless]
Water Spirits, 82–83
The hoity-toity mouse
Phillips-*Hoity,* 6–17
Hold him, Tabb
Yolen-*Favorite,* 439–440
Hold on, Jim!
Stuchl-*American,* 147–150
Holecek and the water nymph
Wood-*Palace,* 57–58
HOLIDAYS
Thor's holiday
Holland. *See* NETHERLANDS
Hollow hills
Froud-*Faeries,* unp
HOLLY
Sea bindweed, sea holly, sea
pea, samphire
The Holy Child
Griego-*Cuentos,* 55
HOLY DAYS
The Shrove Tuesday visitor
HOLY GRAIL
Adventures of Sir Galahad
Carbonek: castle of the Holy
Grail
Castle of the Maimed King
Galahad and the Grail
Noblest quest of all
Quest for the Holy Grail
Sir Galahad and the quest of
the Holy Grail
HOLY MEN
The sorceress
—fakirs
The Dervish and the fakir

HOLY NAMES
Origin of the house of Haro
HOLY WATER
Demon cat
HOME
The wow o'Rivven; the bell
HOME ECONOMICS
The butcher's bills
Dead snake and young wife
—accounts
Uncle Cornelius, his story
—domestic prosperity
The young head of the family
Home-bred boy defeats the enemy
O'Connor-*Tibet,* 172–174
Home-bred boy dislodges spider
O'Connor-*Tibet,* 166–171
Home-bred boy finds lost turquoise
O'Connor-*Tibet,* 158–165
The homecoming of Agamemnon
Lines-*Greek,* 201–209
HOMELINESS
—plain girl
The silver whistle
HOMEMAKERS
The giant's daughter
HOMER (subject)
—Iliad
Pinsent-*Greek,* 143 (index)
—Iliad, Books I–XXIV (summary)
Stapleton-*Dictionary,* 110–119
—Odyssey
Pinsent-*Greek,* 143 (index)
—Odyssey, Books I–XXIV
(summary)
Stapleton-*Dictionary,* 148–158
HOMICIDE
—husband executed for
The bat Narahdarn
The honest penny
Booss-*Scand.,* 118–121
HONESTY
See also DISHONESTY
Adventures of Sikku
Coals on the devil's hearth
(Ireland)

Don Cacahuate
The emperor's new clothes
The force of luck
The merman
The simpleton makes rain fall
The tale of Ivan
Temptations
A wise judge
The wise king and the honest
    thief
—exile
The talking goat
—foolish
A reward for honesty
HONEY
Brer wolf wants the honey
Drop of honey
The flowers: a legend
The fox who sent to heaven
How honey-guide came to
    have authority
How the bear lost his tail and
    the bees gained a friend
How the monkey got a drink
    when he was thirsty
The Johnson boys [song and
    story]
Midwife fox [steals honey]
Pork and honey
The sacred honey bees
—search for
The bat Narahdarn
—thick and sticky, origin
Origin of certain necklaces and
    plants
Honey bird [joins in hunt for wild
    honey]
Pitcher-*Tokol.*, 58–60
Honeyed words can't sweeten evil
Jagendorf-*First*, 13–15
Hong Do-Ryong, the filial tiger
Zong-*Korea*, 84–86
Hong Gil-Dong
Zong-*Korea*, 207–223
Honi the rainmaker
Patai-*Gates*, 224–227

HONOR
The four elements
Prince Asraf and the king of
    the spirits
Search for a friend
—lost
The broken swords
Honor [fidelity]
Villa-*Armenian*, 331–338, 518
The honorable wife
Villa-*Armenian*, 396–401
Honor's cruel demands
Lehane-*Legends*, 42–64
Honpain the star-girl
Stokes-*Turtle*, 40–43
Hoodoo [voodoo]
Sergeant-*Witches*, 270–276
HOODS
—red
Monacielli
HOOF LAKE
How Hoof Lake got its name
Hook, Richard, illus.
McGarry-*Folk*
HOOPS
Anpao is born
HOOTERS
Hey-hey men
Hop o' My Thumb
Perrault-*Glass*, 80–96
Pollack-*Moonbeam*, 40–47
Rackham-*Fairy*, 13–25
HOPE
Genie of the mountains
Fulga
—disappointed
The frogs at the rainbow's end
HOPE CHESTS
The wooing of Seppo
    Hmarinen
Horace the horse
McCarthy-*Raccoon*, 97–
    105
HORN
—drinking
The fairy horn

HORNED TOADS
—swallowed by coyote; survives
  Coyote and horned toad
The horned woman
  Jacobs-*Celtic*, 24–26
The horned women
  Yeats-*Fairy*, 150–152
HORNETS
  Brer wold and brer fox get a
    big surprise
  How spider obtained the sky
    god's stories (Ashanti)
  The hummingbird brothers
  Kamala and the seven thieves
HORNS
  Little bull with the golden horns
  Ljungby horn and pipe
  The magic horn [flying
    carriage]
  Mouse Woman and the Snee-
    nee-iq
  Svend Faelling and the elle-
    maid
—brings 100,000 soldiers
  The miller's three sons
—drinking
  The Oldenburg horn
  Thor in the giant's strong-hold
—on the kahn
  Tale of the kurai
—ram's
  Peik
HORROR
  The Botticelli horror
  The confession of Charles
    Linkworth
  Death out of season
  Drawer 14
  The illustrated man
  In a dim room
  Man's best friend
  The Metronome
  The Mother Goose madman
  The other Celia
  The secret ones
  Settlement out of court

  A sharp loss of weight
  The snail-watcher
  Tomorrow's child
  Who knows?
Horse and toad
  Wolkstein-*Magic*, 144–150
A horse called Terror
  Mayo-*Book*, 60–71
HORSE MEAT
  The stromkarl at Garphytte
HORSE-RACES
  The dog that ran to the moon
  The white rooster
HORSEMEN AND
    HORSEMANSHIP
  Death rides a black horse
  A pretty girl in the road
  A resumed identity
  The troll ride
  Vassilisa [Fair] and Baba Yaga
—daybreak, sun, and night
  Haunter of the birch forest
—white, red, and black
  Vassilisa the Beautiful
HORSES
  The black king, or Fair
    Ferentine
  The building of the wall of
    Asgard
  Changeling [exposed with help
    of magician]
  The chariot of the sun
  Conn-eda; or The golden ap-
    ples of Lough Erne
  Death comes at a trot
  Dividing the horses
  Faerie rades
  The fairy chapman
  Fairy horses
  Farm hand tied scythes over
    horse's back
  Fiery horse
  Foolish Vanya and Princess
    Helena the Fair
  From bad to good to bad to
    good

HORSES (continued)
—excrement
  Gold colt and the fire dragon
    shirt
—Falada
  The goose girl
—Feroz and h. speak to each other
  Farmer's son and the geni
—flying
  The island of beautiful
    women
—ghosts of forefathers
  The herd boy and the dragons
—golden
  Golden mermaid [theft of
    golden apples]
—grey
  Nennir, or the one who feels
    inclined
—heads
  The disrespectful son
—heroic
  Prince Mirko
  Tremsin and the maid of the
    sea
—"Horse with the Golden
    Hair"
  Ivan young in years, old in
    wisdom
—husband under spell
  The princess, the horse, and
    the she-devil
—magic
  The golden knucklebone
  Ivanovoushka the simpleton
  Jose and Princess Florabella
  Maria Morevna
  Prince Meerzat Istvan and the
    horse of dust . . .
  The twins of Paikala Mountain
  The wooden horse and the
    painted jug
—magic, kills itself
  The boy, his sisters, and the
    magic horse
—mare gives birth to man

"Black Horse," the third Broth-
    er Zhang (Tu)
—mares
  The black mare
  The blacksmith
  The labours of Hercules
  The nis and the mare
—mythical
  The knights of Allaberg
—ponies
  Small Star and the mud pony
—ponies-white
  The white pony
—senses presence of spirits
  Time to think [crossroads: fatal
    accidents]
—skins
  Little Claus and Big Claus
  The young man who refused
    to kill
—speaks
  The goose girl
—stallion advises prince
  The King of Ireland's son (Art)
—stallions
  The betrothal
  Thor fights the giant Krangnir
  The walls of Asgard
  The white stallion
—tailless
  Judge true
—talking
  The golden feather [talking
    colt]
  Horace the horse
  Little old women with five cows
  Mountain of jade [man
    bewitched]
  Youth without age and life
    without death (Turkey)
—Teetgong
  [Assipattle vs Stoorworm the
    sea-serpent]
—understands; brings father
  The silkworm [origin: marriage
    of horse & maid]

—water
  See KELPIES
—wild
  El caballo negro muy
    magnifico
  Roam the wild country
—winged
  Pegasus (the Winged Horse)
  See also PEGASUS
—wooden
  Flying horse [wooden]
  Guleesh
HORSES (subject)
—fairies'
  Briggs-Vanish., 216 (index)
—water
  Briggs-Vanish., 200
Horseshoe's magic power
  McKee-Scottish, 29
"HORSE-STATIONS"
  The bird of happiness
The horsetrader
  Roberts-Chinese, 60
HORSE-TRADING
  Canobie Dick and Thomas of
    Ercildoun
Hosford, Dorothy
  The apples of Iduna
HOSPITALITY
  Aldar-Kose and Shigai-Bai
  A small favor
HOSPITALS
  Shurik: A story of the siege of
    Leningrad
HOSTAGES
  Walter and Hildegund
HOSTELS
  The destruction of Da Derga's
    hostel
HOSTS (subject)
—fairy
  Briggs-Vanish., 216 (index)
Hot-foot Hannibal
  Shepard-Conjure, 75–85
HOT SPRINGS
  Mighty bear has problems

HOTTENTOTS
  Elephant and the tortoise
  The little wise woman
  [Houaru and the nix's spell]
    Water Spirits, 119–125
Houji, the child abandoned on the
    ice
  Sanders-Dragons, 34
HOUKOUX
  Hey-hey men
Hound-dog stories (four tall tales)
  Yolen-Favorite, 294–295
Hour is come but not the man
    (condensed)
  Briggs-Vanish., 68–69
House in the wood
  Lang-Pink/D, 18–24
  Lang-Pink/K, 25–32
"HOUSE ISLAND"
  The dwarfs' banquet
House of ice and house of wood
  Riordan-Russia, 112–114
The house of Thebes
  Gibson-Gods, 97–102
House (or Household) spirits. See
    SPIRITS—household
House repairs: The hoity-toity
    mouse
  Phillips-Hoity, 6–17
HOUSEKEEPERS
  The fox and the little white hen
  Goosey Goosey Gander
  Hildur, the queen of the elves
  Una the elfwoman
HOUSES
  The faithful trio [shelter in
    house]
  The maze, or Se-eh-ha's
    house
  Raccoon's tale
  The story of the house
  The three little pigs
  Why the tiger and the stag fear
    each other
—gingerbread
  Hansel and Gretel

HOUSES (continued)
—iron
   The disrespectful son
—old
   The old house
HOUSEWIVES
   Gone is gone
   The man who was going to
     mind the house
   The pancake
HOUSEWORK
   See also HOMEMAKERS
   The man who was going to
     mind the house
   The nagging husband [Estonia]
   The old man and woman who
     switched jobs
   The ten fairy servants
How a bear kept reindeer
   Nagishkin-Folktales, 117–121
How a king learned to care for
   parents
   Amore-Lustful, 46–48
How a man found his wife in the
   Land of the Dead
   Yolen-Favorite, 472–474
How a peasant cured his wife of
   telling tales
   Riordan-Russia, 233–237
How a poor man made a swindler
   cough up
   Elbaz-Folktales, 40–41
How a poor muzhik looked for
   truth . . .
   Cortes-Byelorussian, 150–151
How a youth lost his virtue
   Amore-Lustful, 109–111
How Ableegumooch tracked a fox
   Hill-More, 86–95
How Abosom, the lesser gods,
   came into the world
   Radin-African, 36–40
How Aisu found the happy land
   Seven Sisters, 48–64
How Akaruio Bokodori repopulated
   the earth

   Wilbert-Bororo, 75–76
How an old man lost his wen
   Ozaki-Japanese, 273–282
How Asanga came to see the fu-
   ture Buddha
   Hyde-Chambers-Tibet, 24–26
How bear and chipmunk
   stopped . . . friends
   Nagishkin-Folktales, 27–31
How beaver got his flat tail
   McCarthy-Raccoon, 57–61
How black became white
   Eels-Brazil, 155–162
How contradiction came to the
   Ashanti
   Radin-African, 201–203
How Cormac MacArt went to Faery
   Jacobs-Celtic, 276–278
How corn came to the Indians
   Jagendorf-First, 9–11
How coyote stole fire
   Haviland-N. Amer., 52–56
How diseases came to the Ashanti
   Radin-African, 64–66
How Donald Solomon became
   state deputy
   Stuchl-American, 223–226
How El Bizarron fooled the
   devil
   Yolen-Favorite, 386–389
How elephant married a Nama
   woman and was deceived
   by her
   Radin-African, 153–154
How evil produces evil
   Shah-World, 76
How Fin went to the kingdom of
   the big men
   Jacobs-Celtic, 270–275
How foolish men are!
   Zong-Korea, 149–152
How Glooskap found the summer
   Haviland-N. Amer., 57–59
How Glooskap made the birds
   Macmillan-Canadian 141–146
How God made the butterflies

Lester-*Black*, 15–20

How grandpa mowed the Lord's meadow
Ginsburg-*Twelve*, 20–23

How honey-guide came to have authority
Radin-*African*, 144–145

How Hoof Lake got its name
Stuchl-*American*, 185–189

How hunter obtained money from friends and avoided repaying
Radin-*African*, 165–167

How Ivan frightened away the robbers . . . priest . . . deacon
Cortes-*Byelorussian*, 139–147

How Ivanka freed muzhiks from landlord
Cortes-*Byelorussian*, 129–130

How Jack went to seek his fortune
dePaola-*Favorite*, 118–121
Haviland-*N. Amer.*, 141–143

How Jiculi served his tribe
Piggott-*Mexican*, 32–45

How Kwaku Ananse got Aso in marriage
Radin-*African*, 155–158

How long will you live?
Adams-*Iron*, 116–119

How men and women got together
Yolen-*Favorite*, 68–72

How mosquitoes came to be
Yolen-*Favorite*, 350–351

How mussels were brought to the creeks
Parker-*Australian*, 143–145

How night came
Eels-*Brazil*, 3–11

How ole woodpecker got ole rabbit's conjure bag
Haviland-*N. Amer.*, 115–121

How panpipes came to be played (Miao)
Seven Sisters, 38–47

How porridge was cooked in Gotham
Stovicek-*Around*, 199

How rabbit deceived fox
Macmillan-*Canadian* 203–208

How rabbit got the best of coyote
Jagendorf-*First*, 69–71

How rabbit lost his tail
Macmillan-*Canadian* 40–43

How raven brought fire to the Indians
Macmillan-*Canadian* 188–193

How raven brought the salmon
Robinson-*Raven*, 71–85

How Sainday brought the buffalo
Anderson-*Trick.*, 39–46

How Saint Joseph helped to win the king's daughter
Lang-*Pink/K*, 124–132

How salt was discovered
Chalk-*Tales*, unp.

How Somoa was named
Wright-*Pigeon*, 16–19

How Saynday got the sun
Haviland-*N. Amer.*, 65–70

How sickness came
Dutton-*Navajo*, 17

How Sigourd awoke Brynhild upon Hindfell
Crossley-*Legends*, 121–134

How sly-fox was fooled
Soyer-*Adventures*, 14–20

How some wild animals became tame ones
Crossley-*Folk.*, 16–19

How spider obtained the sky god's stories (Ashanti)
Radin-*African*, 25–27
Yolen-*Favorite*, 24–27

How spider read the sky-god's thoughts
Radin-*African*, 87–89

How summer [personified] came to Canada
Macmillan-*Canadian* 50–54

How the animals stopped the
freeway
McCarthy-*Raccoon*, 63–81
How the Bay of Siam came to be
Toth-*Tales*, 17–24
How the bear lost his tail and the
bees gained a friend
Riordan-*Tartary*, 44–45
How the Beldys stopped fighting
Nagishkin-*Folktales*, 193–198
How the blackbird went to war
Crouch-*Whole*, 66–71
How the Brazilian beetles got
their . . . coats
Eels-*Brazil*, 201–210
How the citizens of Gotham paid
their taxes
Stovicek-*Around*, 198
How the clever father saved his
sons
Amore-*Lustful*, 79–81
How the cow went under the
ground
Faulkner-*Tales*, 152–157
How the dragon was tricked
Lang-*Pink/D*, 6–11
Lang-*Pink/K*, 9–13
How the fire festival came to be
Toth-*Tales*, 31–37
How the first rain came
Radin-*African*, 56–59
How the fox and the elk exchanged
legs
Nagishkin-*Folktales*, 106–
108
How the hare got his split lip
O'Connor-*Tibet*, 1–5
How the hare made a fool of the
wolf
O'Connor-*Tibet*, 60–67
How the hermit helped to win the
king's . . .
Lang-*Pink/D*, 174–183
How the jelly-fish lost its
bones
Piggott-*Japanese*, 123

How the lizard got its hat
Wright-*Gold*, 4–8
How the mason-wasp fetched fire
from god
Radin-*African*, 67–68
How the Mekong River came
to be
Toth-*Tales*, 25–30
How the monkey and goat earned
their reputations
Eels-*Brazil*, 95–102
How the monkey became a
trickster
Eels-*Brazil*, 87–91
How the monkey escaped being
eaten
Eels-*Brazil*, 135–142
How the monkey got a drink when
he was thirsty
Eels-*Brazil*, 105–112
How the monkey got food when he
was hungry
Eels-*Brazil*, 115–119
How the moolah was taught a
lesson
Titiev-*Moolah*, 1–8
How the pigeon became a tame
bird
Eels-*Brazil*, 165–174
How the polar bear became
Royds-*Animal*, 74–79
How the rabbit lost his
tail
Eels-*Brazil*, 15–20
How the rat lost his wings
Wright-*Pigeon*, 24–25
How the raven got fresh
water
Reid-*Myths*, 17–20
How the raven lost his bill
Reid-*Myths*, 29
How the rhinoceros got his saggy,
baby skin
Lewis-*Animal*, 18–19
How the rhinoceros got his skin
Royds-*Animal*, 26–29

How the seven brothers saved their
sister
Haviland-*N. Amer.*, 33–39
How the Shannon got its name
McGarry-*Folk*, 57
How the slaves helped each other
Faulkner-*Tales*, 34–39
How the slaves worshipped
Faulkner-*Tales*, 52–59
How the snake got his rattles
Lester-*Black*, 42–53
How the speckled hen got her
speckles
Eels-*Brazil*, 73–83
How the stars came: Iku's eyes
Radin-*African*, 51–55
How the Summer Queen came to
Canada
Phelps-*Maid*, 129–133
How the sun was made
Parker-*Australian*, 131–132
How the Thai learned to be calm
Toth-*Tales*, 41–48
How the tiger got his stripes
Eels-*Brazil*, 33–44
How the toad got his bruises
Eels-*Brazil*, 23–29
How the turtle got her shell
Stokes-*Turtle*, 37–39
How the world began
Bierhorst-*Hungry*, 115–117,
142
How the world was made
Chalk-*Tales*, unp.
How they got Hairlock home
Booss-*Scand.*, 157–160
How they went to Jotunheim
Crossley-*Legends*, 201–211
How Thomas Connolly met the
banshee
Yeats-*Fairy*, 100–102
How Thor got his hammer
Branston-*Gods*, 101–106
How three serpents carried off
three princesses to the world
to come

Cortes-*Byelorussian*, 36–43
How thunder and lightning came to
be
Toth-*Tales*, 38–40
How to break a bad habit
Macdonald-*Twenty*, 75–78
How to win a prince
Booss-*Scand.*, 151–152
How turtle came
Macmillan-*Canadian* 55–58
How twelve clever brothers got feet
mixed up
Ginsburg-*Twelve*, 82–89
How two brothers improved their luck
Ginsburg-*Twelve*, 36–43
How Wahn became a star
Reed-*Aboriginal*, 139–141
How Wang-Fo was saved
Yourcenar-*Oriental*, 1–20
How women got an excuse
O'Sullivan-*Legends*, 50
HOWLING
Mouse Woman and the Snee-
nee-iq
The wolves of Cernogratz
HUCKSTERS
The goblin and the huckster
HUDDEN
Donald and his neighbours
[Hudden & Dudden]
Hudden and Dudden and Donald
O'Neary
Jacobs-*Celtic*, 35–40
Shah-*World*, 206–210
HUDSON, Henry, d.1611.
Rip Van Winkle
HUGGING
The bear who liked hugging
people
Hughes, Fielden
The mistake
Hughes, Ted
How the polar bear became
HUGHEY, Ralph E.
—Northwest Ark. storyteller
McNeil-*Charm*, 88–100

Hula's dream
    Crouch-*Whole,* 152–155
Huichol Indians. *See under* INDI-
    ANS OF LATIN AMERICA
    (tribes)
HUITZILOPOCHTLI
    The birth of Huitzilopochtli
    Copil's heart
    The eagle on the prickly pear
    The woman of discord
HUITZILOPOCHTLI (subject)
    Nicholson-*Mexican,* 143
    (index)
HUIYUAN the Monk (334–416
    A.D.)
    The monk Huiyuan
Hulama, the royal ball game
    Wright-*Gold,* 24
HULDA
    Mother Hulda
Huldbrand and Undine: a doomed
    alliance of earth and water
    Water Spirits, 126–139
HULDRIES
    An evening in the squire's
    kitchen
HULDUFOLK (HULDRA) (subject)
    Briggs-*Vanish.,* 31, 75–76,
    196
The huluppu-tree
    Wolkstein-*Inanna,* 3–9
Human bait
    Roberts-*Chinese,* 104–105
A human being transformed
    Colombo-*Wind.,* 125–126
Human body. *See* BODY, HUMAN
HUMAN SACRIFICE
    The bare mountains
    Bhima slays the demon [giant,
    man-eating cannibal]
    The Black General
    A dutiful son
    The fifth sun [Nanahuatl]
    Li Chi slays the serpent
    Ludwig and Iskander
    Manora, the bird woman

The milk of death
    Sacrificed by kin, lover brings
    girl back from below
    The seven-headed beast
    Sheena and the water-horse
    When gods and men mingled
Humans. *See* MAN
HUMILITY
    See also MEEKNESS
    King and the wise man
The hummingbird brothers
    Wood-*Spirits,* 121–124
HUMMINGBIRDS
    The children and the
    hummingbird
    The theft of fire
HUMOR
    See also CUMULATIVE
    TALES; TALL TALES
    [Bad news keeps building]
    The barmecide's feast
    Count Dracula [by Woody
    Allen]
    The crooked-mouthed family
    The drovers who lost their feet
    (Mexico)
    Duration of life (Germany)
    The ghost extinguisher
    Goha on the deathbed (Egypt)
    A good thing he wasn't wear-
    ing it!
    The haunted trailer [by R.
    Arthur]
    The imaginary babouche and
    the scorpion
    The mendacious child
    The new bishop
    Noseful of gold
    Now you know
    Numbskull's errand
    Old Dry Frye (rogue preacher)
    The old smith
    One for you, one for me
    Paddock in heaven (England)
    The peasant and his goat
    Peasant priest

Pudding bewitched
Rattlesnake soup
Selfish husband
The squire's bride [a horse]
The storytellers
Talk; everything Ashanti farmer
  contacts starts to talk
Three wishes [of Billy Dawson]
[Tyrannical bull with discon-
  tented lice]
Vhy, vhy, vhy
Vicar of Germsoe [looting
  wrecked ships]
The yellow ribbon [holds wife's
  head on]
—excessive cruelty
  The roots of jealousy
—fool . . . stolen donkey; hit your
  mother again
  The donkey who hit his mother
—jokes about Jews
  Rabbi's donkey falls down a
    well
  The ten commandments
—war and
  The wise old crow
Hump backs. *See* HUNCHBACKS
HUNAIN
  The boots of Hunain
HUNAPU
  Twins of the Popol Vuh
[Hunchback cured by fairies]
  Ratcliff-*Scottish*, 112–116
The hunchbacked old woman
  Raychaudhuri-*Stupid*, 26–29
HUNCHBACKS
  Gesar of Ling
  The legend of Knockgrafton
  The men who wouldn't stay
    dead (France)
  Pepito el corcovado
  The stone frogs, the Youayah
    Mayamah
  Two hunchbacks (condensed)
  The two hunchbacks (Italy)
—removed by fairies

Knockgrafton legend
The hunchback's hump
  Kudian-*More*, 13–14
A hundred times
  Adams-*Iron*, 126–129
The hundredth dove
  Yolen-*Hundreth*, 1–9
HUNGARIAN LANGUAGE
  The gipsy baron
HUNGARY
  Prince of nettles
HUNGER
  See also FOOD RELIEF
  The adventures of Yemima
  All I possess!
  The blind boy and his
    dog
  Boy who was saved by his
    thoughts
  The children and the
    hummingbird
  The corn maidens
  Day of the dead
  Halibut Man and the house on
    the waves
  Heaven and hell [coopera-
    tion]
  How the monkey got food
    when he was hungry
  Juan fetches the devil
  Leppa Polkry and the blue
    cross
  Lioness [protects her cub]
  The master pupil
  Mushkil Gusha: remover of all
    difficulties
  Pussy-Greedyguts
  The ugly duckling
  Upamanyu learns a lesson
    [hermitage school]
  What melody is the sweetest?
  Why the bob-cat stays in the
    woods
  The wonderful little pouch
—spook eats everything
  The owl

264

The hungry peasant, God, and death (Mexico)
  Yolen-*Favorite*, 469–471
The hungry tigress
  Martin-*Hungry*, 123–125
The hungry woman [earth]
  Bierhorst-*Hungry*, 23–25
HUNS
  Walter and Hildegund
The hunted hare
  Phelps-*Tatterhood*, 79–82
The hunter and his greedy wife
  Lang-*Pink/K*, 231–237
Hunter Hailibu's great sacrifice
  Jagendorf-*Magic*, 161–164
The hunter maiden [and Cannibal Demon]
  Phelps-*Maid*, 79–84
The hunter who threw stars
  Reed-*Aboriginal*, 95–97
Hunters
  Weeks-*Pachee*, 1–7
HUNTERS AND HUNTING
  The Angekkok, Oolak, and the Moon-God [spirits]
  Antti and the wizard's prophecy
  Artemis, Orion and the Seven Sisters
  The banyan deer [the Buddha]
  The bat-women of Koitabu
  The blessed gift of joy bestowed upon man
  Boar of Eskdale
  The boy, his sisters, and the magic horse
  The boy who was called Thickhead
  Cannibal
  The chamois-hunter
  Choril and Cholchinay
  Clever Gretchen
  The day Tuk became a hunter
  The deer thief
  The doe, the hunter, and the great stag
  Downfall of the mighty hunter
  The drowned boys
  The duck with red feet
  Ermine and the hunter
  The fairy hunt
  Fated animal does not see the hunter
  The feast of the mountain goats [ancient laws disregarded]
  Glooscap and the wishes
  Goannas and porcupines
  Happy hunter and the skilful fisher
  The hare and the magpie
  Hasjelti's dance
  Herne the hunter
  How panpipes came to be played (Miao)
  How Sainday brought the buffalo
  How the Mekong River came to be
  Juan Oso
  Kate of Ysatter
  Kile Bamba and the Loche bogatyr
  Kitpouseagunow
  Lippo and Tapio
  The magic rattle
  Mouse Woman and the porcupine hunter
  Oden was a Sunday hunter
  Old man and the sun
  Orion (the Hunter)
  Ouyan the curlew
  Peter Gynt
  Pookong kills a bear
  Pumah, the mighty hunter [wanton slaughter]
  Rabbit and the grain buyers
  Redbreasts: the Gwineeboos
  Sable souls
  Sky Elk, the ghost of Whiteface Mountain
  The soldier-bird Deegeenboyah

The stag [saved from the
hunters]
Star Maiden
Stewed, roasted, or live?
The story of Deirdre
The stupid rich man
The summer birds of K'yakime
Sun, night and moon
The swan maiden
The topknot pigeons,
Goolahwilleel
Tortoise, goat and lion: the
price of wisdom
The trolls of Skurugata
Twelve huntsmen [test of
femininity]
The twins
The walker of the snow
The Wasgo and three killer
whales
The Weendigoes
The Weeoombeens and the
Piggiebillah
Wild huntsman
Woman tied behind horse on
her braids
The young hunter [the sun as
enemy]
The young man who refused
to kill
HUNTERS AND HUNTING
(subject)
Briggs-*Vanish.*, 47, 116, 170–
174
The hunter's dilemma
Robinson-*Three*, 7–15
The hunting of the elk
Synge-*Land*, 77–86
The hunting of the hind
McKinley-*Door*, 105–136
HUNTRESSES
The hunter maiden [and Can-
nibal Demon]
The huntsman
Villa-*Armenian*, 159–167, 466–
468

HUON of Bordeaux (subject)
Briggs-*Vanish.*, 141–143
The hurlers
Marshall-*Every.*, 268–270
Hurling
Froud-*Faeries*, unp
HURLING (sport)
Cuchulainn's boyhood
Fairy hurling game: Ireland vs
Scotland
HURLING (subject)
Briggs-*Vanish.*, 49, 175, 178–
180
Husband and wife. *See* HUS-
BANDS; MARRIAGE;
WIVES
Husband and wife should share
equally
MacLean-*Cuentos*, 80–85
The husband who stayed at home
Phelps-*Maid*, 163–166
HUSBANDMEN
The kingdom of beautiful
colors
HUSBANDS
See also WIVES
All I possess!
Back for Christmas
Bluebeard
The brahman in the graveyard
The butcher's bills
The clever old bride [and child-
groom]
Foolish men and scolding
wives
Gifts of the child Christ
How elephant married a Nama
woman and was
deceived . . .
Lai D'Ywenee
The princess, the horse, and
the she-devil
The red stream
Saint Michael wins a soul from
devil
Saxe of Saxeholm

HUSBANDS (continued)
    The spirit of the van
    Wife who ate the wrong
        porridge
    The winding-horn village
    The woman who was saved by
        a miracle
—deceive wives
    The bat-women of Koitabu
—foolish
    Beausoleil
—foolish act: extreme hardship
    Good King Nala's downfall
—good heart: nicest thing in world
    Phra Nang Suwanasopha
—housework attempted by
    The husband who stayed at
        home
—murders wife's family
    The skull in the snow
—trades work with wife
    The nagging husband [Estonia]
—turned into snake by medicine
    Supernatural is not to be
        played with
HUTCHEN
    Heinzelmannchen and
        Hutchen
HUZRUIWUHTI (bride of Tawa)
    Tiyo travels through the
        underworld
HYACINTHS
    Bluebells-hyacinths
—origin of the flower
    Apollo and Hyacinthus
The Hyades
    Gallant-Constel., 133–135
Hyde, Douglas
    The piper and the puca
HYDRA
    The labours of Hercules
    The wonderful lamp [Alad-
        din]
—nine-headed
    The Water Serpent [Heracles
        vs the Hydra]

Hydra: battling a fountain's deadly
        guardian
    Water Spirits, 118
Hydra (the many-headed mon-
        ster)
    Gallant-Constel., 167–169
Hyena and hare search for wealth
    Magel-Gambia, 58–61
Hyena eats the ostrich's eggs
    Magel-Gambia, 134–136
Hyena engages a strange-farmer
    Magel-Gambia, 62–65
The hyena engages the hare as a
        gewel
    Magel-Gambia, 53–57
Hyena ["smell of stale dung"]
    Pitcher-Tokol., 54–57
The hyena wrestles the konder-
        ong. I
    Magel-Gambia, 128–131
The hyena wrestles the konder-
        ong. II
    Magel-Gambia, 132–133
HYENAS
    Dog captures the hyena
    Hare and hyena in the well
    Hare makes hyena his riding
        horse
    Hare saves the hippopotamus
    Hare, the hyena, and the
        lioness's cave
    The lion's treasured goat
    The little hare
    Pilgrimage to Mecca
—eats girl
    City where men are mended
—in form of woman
    Samba's wife
—origin of characteristics
    Hyena ["smell of stale dung"]
HYMNS
    Master Tobacco
HYPNOSIS
    Waxworks
HYPOCRISY
    Beware of hypocrites!

How a poor man made a
　swindler cough up
The three imposters
The two wagoners

I ching: The eight hexagrams
　Sanders-*Dragons*, 131
I know what I have learned
　Lang-*Pink/D*, 148–153
I won't forgive you
　Todd-*Some*, 138–142
Iain Beag MacAindra
　Robertson-*Highland*, 208–209
ICARUS
　Daedalus
ICE
　The coal burner and the troll
　The deacon of Myrka
　The world of ice and fire
ICE CARVING
　The day Tuk became a hunter
Ice castle of Utgard-Loke
　Lee-*Castles*, 47–49
ICE FISHING
　Troll's stone
ICE MOUNTAIN
　Heart of ice [Prince Littleboots]
"ICE PERSON"
　Gluska'be, the Penobscot hero
ICE QUEEN
　Dietrich [of Verona]; castle of
　　the Ice Queen
ICE SKATING
　Far out the long canal
ICELAND
　Autumn and the bear
　The battle of Stamford Bridge
　The bishop and the elves
　The boy who did not know
　　what fear was
　The burning of Bergthorsknoll
　The crossways

The deacon of Myrka
The dead man's nightcap
Door prayer at evening
Erikur rescues a woman from
　the otherworld
The expedition of Thorfin
　Karisefni
The father of eighteen elves
The fisherman of Gotur
Fylgiar
Gellivor
The genesis of the Hid-folk
Gestumblindi's riddles
The ghost and the moneychest
A ghost's vengeance
Girl at the shieling [elf] (Iceland)
The grateful elfwoman
Grimsborg
Gryla
The hauntings at Frodriver
Hildur, the queen of the
　elves
Jora the troll
Katla
Katla's dream
Ketill, the priest of Husavik
The lake monster
The making of the worlds
The man-servant and the wa-
　ter-elves
The man/whale
The merman
Murder will out
Naddi
Nennir, or the one who feels
　inclined
The night-trolls
Olafur and the trolls
The rich farmer and the poor
　farmer
The shepherd of Silfrun-Arstadir
The shepherdess
The skeleton in Holar church
The son of the goblin
The story of Bergthor of Blafell
The story of Jon Asmundsson

268

ICELAND (continued)
Then the merman laughed
(Iceland)
Thordur of Thrastastadir
Thornstein staff-struck
The troll in the Skrudur
Troll's stone
Tungustapi
The two Sigurdurs
Una the elfwoman
Valbjorg the Unelfed
White cap
Who built Reynir church?
The wizards of the Vestmanna
Isles
—origin
[Assipattle vs Stoorworm the
sea-serpent]
ICELAND (subject)
—Irish fairies
Logan-*Old*, 1–2
—land-spirits
Briggs-*Vanish.*, 36–37, 197
Keightley-*World*, 157–162
ICONS
Treasure of the magic icon
IDEALISM
Little Genius
IDEAS
Belling the cat
Identifying a witch [16 legends]
Robe-*Hispanic*, 314–329
The identity of the nightmare
Lindow-*Swedish*, 180–182
Idiots. *See* FOOLS AND
FOOLISHNESS
Idleness. *See* LAZINESS
The idler [a week wasted]
Stuchl-*American*, 111–112
IDOLATRY
Treasure of the magic icon
IDOLS
The fisherman and his soul
"If I had the wings of an angel"
Gorog-*Taste*, 93–104
If the boerboon flowers fall

Poland-*Mantis*, 41–57
Ifrit. *See* JINN
Igaluk: The origin of the winds
Wood-*Spirits*, 25–28
IGNORANCE
The foolish weaver and the
jackal
—taking advantage of
The stupid crocodile
The iguana and the black snake
Parker-*Australian*, 155–159
Iitoi and Coyote: the flood
Dutton-*Navajo*, 15–16
Ikezuki, the horse
Piggott-*Japanese*, 116
Iktomi and the coyote
Zitkala-*Old*, 37–43
Iktomi and the ducks
De Wit-*Talking*, 93–98
Zitkala-*Old*, 3–15
Iktomi and the fawn
Zitkala-*Old*, 47–57
Iktomi and the muskrat
Zitkala-*Old*, 27–33
Iktomi and the red-eyed ducks
Yellow Robe-*Tonweya*, 86–
93
Iktomi and the turtle
Zitkala-*Old*, 103–109
Iktomi's blanket
Zitkala-*Old*, 19–24
IKU-TURSO
The stealing of the sampo
ILLEGITIMACY
Hong Gil-Dong
The three imposters
ILLINOIS
—Galesburg
The third level
ILLITERACY
The dilemma [corpse-pretense]
The false schoolmaster
The illiterate priest
Sheohmelian-*Three*, 132–133
Illness. *See* SICKNESS
ILLUSION(S)

The beggar king [Solomon and
  Asmodeus]
Bremen town musicians
Headman and the magician
How Jack went to seek his
  fortune
A journey into hell
Peter Bull
The white pet
—coyote imagines man with club
Coyote and turkey
The illustrated man
  Hoke-*Horrors,* 117–132
ILMARINEN, the smith
  [Finnish chanters/enchanters]
The forging of the sampo
The maid of the north
  [Kalevala]
The rivals
Vainamoinen's wound
"I'm Tipingee, She's Tipingee,
  we're Tipingee too"
  Wolkstein-*Magic,* 130–134
Images. *See* EFFIGIES; STATUES
Images of the Windigo
  Colombo-*Wind.,* 94–99
The imaginary babouche and the
  scorpion
  Elbaz-*Folktales,* 57
IMAGINATION
  See also ILLUSION
Old people fancies
  [Menominee]
The open window
Travels with Mozart
—figments of
  The country maid and her
  milkpail
—power of
  The waxwork [Murderers' Den,
  by Burrage]
Imagined future evil: The three
  sillies
  Yolen-*Favorite,* 170–173
Imbeciles. *See* FOOLS
IMMIGRANTS

When I first came to this land
The immortal cannibal
  Colombo-*Wind.,* 124–125
The immortal fairy folk
  Haining-*Lepre.,* 29–33
Immortal mountains [Mongolia]
  Magic Knife, 58–65
IMMORTALITY
A boon of immortality
Chang'o and the elixir of
  immortality
[Gilgamesh and Ut-napishtim]
Golden life
The great misfortune of Lay
  Tee-Kwai
Havoc in heaven: Monkey and
  the Jade Emperor
Maui seeking immortality
The Monkey spirit [learning the
  way]
A time for everything
Zhang Daoling
Immortality and the soul
  Nicholson-*Mexican,* 38–41
IMMORTALS
  See also FAIRIES
The faithfull son, Dong Yong
Melmoth the doomed wanderer
Urashima the fisherman
  (Japan)
The wanderer's dream
—a double life
A princess on a swing
—eight
The pointing finger
—heavenly
The peacock's tail
—once-mortals
The stolen princess
The imp cat
  Manning-*Cats,* 16–18
Imp of the perverse
  Baskin-*Imps,* 4–5
IMPATIENCE
  See also PATIENCE
Chitchat turtle and the geese

IMPATIENCE (continued)
The crow and the peacock
Prince Vivien and the Princess
Placida
A time for everything
Why the crow is black
Imperial left-overs
Chalk-*Tales,* unp.
IMPERSONATIONS
The apples of Iduna
Boots and the beasts
Drolmakyid the fairy [Tibetan]
Enchanted ring
Five strange plants
Gioga's son
It happened in a bath
Maid Maleen
Monster with seven heads
Mulha
The parson and the clerk [I]
The parson and the clerk [II]
Puss in Boots
Sedna the sea goddess
Smallhead and the king's son
Star Maiden
Story of the end of trickster
Wihio
The widow's son
Witches on the lake
Wooden horse [mechanical
flight]
—animal
How Sainday brought the buffalo
Masquerading trickster
Why crows are black
—poor brother, as devil
Enchanted castle
—witch takes place of wife of tsar
Sister Alyonushka and Brother
Ivanushka
Imposition: The devoted friend
Wilde-*Fairy,* 42–59
Impossible judgement
Shah-*World,* 204
Impossible tasks. *See* TESTS
(tasks, trials, etc.)

IMPOSTERS
Candida
The case of the royal Arabian
jewels
Doctor Tyl
Don Juan Zurumbete
A false ghost
The false schoolmaster
The great Dreadnought hoax
The hand of glory
The monkey who claimed to
be a gewel
Nails [anatomy]
The police marshall [mass
murder]
The sabio sees a sow
[Servant forces princess into
servitude]
Shooting of the red eagle
The strange history of Pro-
fessor Grasshopper
Turkey Brother and the magic
panther suit
Tyl on a tightrope
Wamundo [punished]
IMPOTENCE
The old man wouldn't take ad-
vice [young wife]
IMPREGNATION
Heaven's reward
—by ball of fire
The tailor (Mikhei) and the
shoemaker
—by blood of slain monster
Aturuarodo and the monster
Butoriku
The Aturuarodo legend
—by feathers
The birth of Huitzilopochtli
—by North Wind
Little Brother of the Winds
—by spirit of dead king
The goblin bride
—by sunbeams
Go Zu-Mong, king of Goguryo
—by urine of horse

Son of the gray horse
—by witchcraft
  Little crop-tailed hen
—magic
  Merirodo and her husband
    Kuieje Kuri
  [Impregnation by earrings] Araruga
    Paru
  Wilbert-*Bororo*, 187–191
The imprisoned princess
  Schwartz-*Elijah*, 254–262
IMPROVIDENCE
  The flies and the bees
  Grasshopper and the ant
  The lazy ducks
  Pepito Conejo: prepare for
    winter
IMPRUDENCE
  Coyote retrieves his brother's
    scalp
  The tortoise and the hare
  [Tyrannical bull with discon-
    tented lice]
IMPS (devils)
  The kingdom of beautiful
    colors
  Story of Ivan the Imbecile
  Tokoloshi [origin of herds and
    flocks]
In a dark, dark room
  Schwartz-*Dark*, 34–41
In a dim room [by Dunsany]
  Hoke-*Horrors*, 49–54
  Schwartz-*Great*, 135–140
In the beginning
  Haviland-*N. Amer.*, 40–43
  Scott-*Fantastic*, 23–36
  Synge-*Land*, 9–12
In the beginning: the Greek panoply
  Lines-*Greek*, 27–41
In the days of the great buffalo
  Jagendorf-*First*, 73–77
In the days of the plentiful
  Highwater-*Anpao*, 15–43
In the graveyard
  Schwartz-*Dark*, 18–23

In the land of the dead
  Crouch-*Whole*, 89–92
In the middle of the night
  And Every., 57–70
INANNA (goddesses)
  Courtship of Inanna and
    Dumuzi
  The huluppu-tree
  Seven hymns to Inanna
INANNA (goddess) (subject)
—Interpretations of
  Wolkstein-*Inanna*, 136–173
—[Queen of Heaven]
  Wolkstein-*Inanna*, xv–xix
Inanna and the god of wisdom
  Wolkstein-*Inanna*, 11–27
INCANTATIONS
  The elephant girls
  How the blackbird went to war
—calls hailstorm on hunters
  Redbreasts: the Gwineeboos
Incas. *See under* INDIANS OF
    LATIN AMERICA (tribes)
INCEST
  Allerleirauh; or, The many-
    furred creature
  Geriguiguiatugo or Toribugo
  The golden box
  [Impregnation by earrings] Ara-
    ruga Paru
  The Seven Sisters
Incommunicability: the butcher's bills
  Macdonald-*Gray*, 131–172
INCUBUS(-BI)
  Adultery with the "demon"
  Folletti and Incubi
INDECISION
  Crane woos the heron
INDESTRUCTIBILITY
  Little Genius
INDIA
  Dialogue with death
  How the blackbird went to war
  Pyoli and Lord Krishna
—Bengal
  The enchanted princess

INDIA—Bengal (continued)
The Gojmati
Golden stick, silver stick
Neelkamal and Lalkamal
The pomegranate prince
India: Uritra
Stallman-*Dragons,* 30–31
The Indian and the hundred cows
Griego-*Cuentos,* 119–121
The Indian Cinderella
Haviland-*N. Amer.,* 94–96
Macmillan-*Canadian,* 76–78
INDIAN GIVING
Iktomi's blanket
Indian legends: Moon Song, Ginger
Blue, and War Eagle
Steele-*Ozark,* 27–33
INDIAN SUMMER
The boy in the Land of
Shadows
Indian time
Nicholson-*Mexican,* 34
INDIANA
Johnny Appleseed
INDIANS OF LATIN AMERICA
—traditions
Uwaboreu: two chiefs with the
same name
INDIANS OF LATIN AMERICA
(subject)
—dwellings
Nicholson-*Mexican,* 143 (index)
INDIANS OF LATIN AMERICA
(tribes)
—Aztecs
Mummies, zombies, and artifi-
cial men
—Huichol
How Jiculi served his tribe
Story of a flood
—Incas
Mummies, zombies, and artifi-
cial men
—Incas: origin
The first Inca: marriage of sun
and moon

—Jivaros-customs
The Tsantsa
—Mayas
Creation of the Mayas
—Suma
A Suma legend
INDIANS OF LATIN AMERICA
(tribes) (subject)
—Aztecs
Nicholson-*Mexican,* 143
(index)
—Bororo
Wilbert-*Bororo,* 1–13
—Mayas
Nicholson-*Mexican,* 143
(index)
INDIANS OF NORTH AMERICA
See also MEDICINE MEN
All that happened must hap-
pen again
Anpao and coyote
Anpao and the animals
Anpao and the magic dogs
Anpao brings the corn
Anpao is born
Bad Indian's ashes [flies tor-
ment people]
Battle [Cheyennes attack
Shoshones]
The battle with the birds
The dawn of the world
Deer woman
The drowned boys
Enchanted youth: Osseo and
Oweenee
The fire plume
The Fishes [Odschig, the chief]
He comes from the east
In the days of the plentiful
The invasion from the sea
The lessons of heaven and
earth
Lox, the mischief maker
Magic moccasins: the Wearer
of the Ball
The magic of the moon

Manabozho and how the diver
[duck] got a flat back
The passing of Glooskap
[whites vs Indians]
The sky beings
The snail and the beaver
Snake boy
Song of the seven herbs [7
legends]
The sorceress
The star and the lily
Star Maiden
The sun journey
Trickster
Ursulo, hijo del oso
The village beneath the water
White Feather and the six
giants
Why dogs sniff each other's
tails
—burial
Powerful medicine
—Canada
The Indian Cinderella
—chants
Bead chant myth
—courtship
Glooskap and the magic gifts
How turtle came
—dances
Hasjelti's dance
Sun dance
—dwellings
Building the ceremonial
house; . . . rain dance
—Five Nations, The
Hiawatha
—health brought to her village
Bending Willow [Indian maid]
—hunters and hunting
Chano's first buffalo hunt
The Eskimo Indian and his fox
wife
Foolish coyote
Pumah, the mighty hunter
Water buffaloes

—maid turns to stone, by choice
The stone maiden
—marriage
How men and women got
together
Rainbow bridge: Buck Ante-
lope and Evening Breeze
—moon-child
Little Brother of the Winds
—Northwest
In the beginning
—Northwest coast
Mouse Woman and the van-
ished princes
Mouse Woman and the tooth
Mouse Woman and the mon-
ster killer whale
Mouse Woman and the Snee-
nee-iq
Mouse Woman and the daugh-
ter of the sun
Mouse Woman and the por-
cupine hunter
Mouse Woman and the wood-
en wife
—personal spirit
Spirit of the bison skull
—powers from animals and birds
The youth and the dog-dance
—Texas
The enchanted mountain
—wars
Se-eh-ha conquers the river
people
—weddings
Tiyo returns home
—women
Life with the wolves
Woman chief
INDIANS OF NORTH AMERICA
(subject)
—[Canada]
De Wit-*Talking*, 181–182
—Coyote stories
Hayes-*Coyote*, 6–7
—The first Americans

INDIANS OF NORTH AMERICA
(subject)—The first Ameri-
cans (continued)
Wood-*Spirits,* 11–15
—Location and historical notes:
Fox, Kiowa, Tewa,
Chiricahua, Menominee;
map
Myles-*Butterflies,* 52–69
—religion-Christ-like prophet ap-
pears among pre-Columbian
tribes
MacLean-*Cuentos,* 121–125
—[Southwest: how their myths
arose]
Dutton-*Navajo,* 3–7
—[Tales: notes and sources for 27
tales]
De Wit-*Talking,* 205–213
INDIANS OF NORTH AMERICA
(tribes)
—Acoma
The crow and the parrot eggs
Meeting the spirit rainmakers
—Afro-Seminoles
The one that got away
—Algonquin
The Algonquin Cinderella
He walked upon the water
[religion]
Honeyed words can't sweeten
evil
How Glooskap found the
summer
South Wind and his golden-
haired love
The Wendigo
Windigo psychosis
—Apache
Coyote fights a lump of pitch
—Biloxi-war with Choctaw
Song that comes from the sea
—Blackfoot
The Blackfoot and the bear
A Blackfoot legend
Napi's wager with rabbit
The orphan boy and the elk dog
Scarface
Star-Boy and the sun dance
Woman chooses death
—Cherokee
Sad marriage of North
—Cheyenne
Behind the waterfall [food]
How the seven brothers saved
their sister
Story of the end of trickster
Wihio
When Plum Bush tricked the
trickster
—Chippewa
The giant sturgeon
Woman in the moon
—Chiricahua
Rising rock [Chiricahua]
—Choctaw-war with Biloxi
Song that comes from the sea
—Comanche
In the days of the great buffalo
—Cree
A cannibal spirit
The existence of the Witigo
Man eaters
Some sort of madness
Stories of the Windigo
—Crow
Masquerading trickster
—Dakota
Why the buzzard's head is
bald
—Delaware
The wampum bird
—Delaware-disappears into river
Mysterious music from the
deep
—Haida
The raven and the first people
—Hopi
Coyote's crying song
Puukonhoya wins a bride
The youth who brought the
corn

—Huron
  The magic snowshoes
—Hurons have Micmac prison
  The magic snowshoes
—Iroquois
  The flying head
  The wampum bird
—Kiowa
  How Sainday brought the
    buffalo
  How Saynday got the sun
  Sky high went the sun
  Sunday and Whirlway maiden
  The twisting tree [Kiowa]
  Why all prairie dogs are brown
  Why crows are black
  Why the bob-cat stays in the
    woods
—Lakota [Canowicake]
  The wicked sister-in-law
—Malecite
  Glooscap, the peacemaker
—Menominee
  Ma'nabus [earth god brings
    fire]
—Mohawk
  The great Penobscot raid
—Mono
  What happened to six wives
    who ate onions
—Montagnais
  The immortal cannial
—Musquakie
  Girls and bears [Musquakie]
  The grey wolf and the orphan
    [Musquakie]
—Naskapi
  The immortal cannibal
—Navajo
  Big long man's corn patch
  Water maiden of the Navajo
—Navajo-holy people
  Hasjelti's dance
—Nimipoo
  Coyote and the swallowing
    monster

—Ojibwa
  The death of Windigo
  How corn came to the Indians
  A human being transformed
  Ithaqua
  A man named Weendigo
  Six traditional tales
  The Snow-Wetigo
  Superstitious belief
  Windagoos! Cannibals!
  Windigo [III]
  The Windigo personality
—Pawnee
  The poor lame horse
  Small Star and the mud pony
—Penobscot
  Glooscap, the peacemaker
  Gluska'be, the Penobscot hero
  The great Penobscot raid
  Kitpouseagunow
—Pima
  The well-baked man
—Ponca
  The flowers' forever land
—Quapaw
  Cranes of the Great Lakes
—Saginaw
  The Weendigoes
—Salinan
  Coyote brings fire to The
    People
  Eagle Woman comes to The
    People
  The Gabilan Mountains [legend]
—Seneca
  The Seneca chief's adventures
  Sky Elk, the ghost of White-
    face Mountain
  The talking stone
—Shoshone
  Hunters
  Reformed Pachee Goyo
  Sun dance
—Sia
  How rabbit got the best of
    coyote

INDIANS OF NORTH AMERICA
(subject) (continued)
—Sioux
End of the world (Sioux tale)
Why the buzzard's head is
bald
—Tarahumara
Kick the wooden ball!
—Tewa
Deer Hunter and White Corn
Maiden
Rising Star finds a wife [dog]
[Tewa]
The Tewa emerge from Sand
Lake
—Tlingit
How mosquitoes came to be
The strong man
—Tuscarora
Great father mosquito [larger
than a bear]
—Ute
Kwi-na the eagle: animal-god
persons
—Wabanaki
The Chenoo who stayed to
dinner
Coolnajoo, the foolish one
Glooscap and the wishes
Glooscap, the great chief
Glooscap, the peacemaker
The great Penobscot raid
How Ableegumooch tracked a
fox
Kespak and the caribou
Kitpouseagunow
Lox and the chief's wife
The magic snowshoes
Pulowech, the partridge
The rabbit makes a match
The strongest boy in the world
Tomik and the magic mat
Wasek and the red giants
Wejosis and the wind giant
The year summer was stolen
—Yuma

The haughty chief
—Zuni
The beginning: Father Sky,
Mother Earth
The beginning of the world
Mud heads and fish men
Poor turkey girl
The spirit-wife
A Zuni creation legend
INDIANS OF NORTH AMERICA
(tribes) (subject)
—Apache
Dutton-*Navajo*, 46–47
—Dakota [Zitkala-Sa tales]
Zitkala-*Old*, xi–xviii
—Haida-[*Raven*, 10 tales]
Reid-*Raven*, 1–91
—Hopi myths
Mullett-*Spiders*, ix–xiv
—Hopi [Pueblos; animals as
people]
Dutton-*Hopi*, 23–24
—Iroquois
De Wit-*Talking*, 3–4
—Lakota-Canowicakte
Yellow Robe-*Tonweya*, 11–18
—Navajo
Dutton-*Navajo*, 24
—Pima-Background: Piman-
speaking Indians
Dutton-*Navajo*, 8–11
Pima legends
Shaw-*Pima*, xi–xv
—Pueblo-[Ruins, beliefs]
Dutton-*Hopi*, 3–4
—Shoshone-Glossary
Weeks-*Pachee*, 100–104
—Shoshone-Indian boy
MacLean-*Cuentos*, 121–125
—Shoshone-Indian boy growing up
Weeks-*Pachee*, vii–x
—Zuni-The Koko-spirit people
Dutton-*Hopi*, 5
INDIC TALES (subject)
—Storytelling in India
Amore-*Lustful*, 3–11

INDIFFERENCE
  The sleepy one: Senor
    Opossum and the rattler
INDISCRETION
  How a peasant cured his wife
    of telling tales
  Now you know
  Three wishes
  —secrets
  Lanval and the Lady Triamor
INDIVIDUATION
  —make friend of the shadow
  Ruckus in the well
INDOLENCE
  Eagle Woman comes to The
    People
INDRA (god)
  Burning of the Khandava forest
  The emerald Buddha
Industriousness: Phoenix fairy
    flower
  Magic Knife, 133–142
INEXHAUSTIBLE SUPPLY
  My lord bag of rice
La infantina
  Keightley-*World*, 459–461
Infants. *See* BABIES
INFATUATION
  The monk and Lady Kiyo
INFIDELITY
  See also FIDELITY
  The artful lad
  The baker's magic wand
  Eagle and the frog
  Frankie and Johnny [song and
    story]
  The honorable wife
  Huldbrand and Undine: a
    doomed alliance . . .
  Magic knife [Uygur]
  The magic ring
  The man who sold his goat
  The mermaid of Duncansby
  Three priests
  Three snake-leaves
  Two unfaithful husbands

What happened to Jadji
Inge of Rantum
  Keightley-*World*, 232–233
INGENUITY
  Stompe Pilt
  Stormalong fights the Kraken
  —necessity mother of invention
  Crow and the pitcher
INGRATITUDE
  See also GRATITUDE
  'Aye, we're flitting'
  Bagged wolf
  Baluan: origin of the island
  The beggar and the gazelle
  Bremen town musicians
  The faithful gazelle
  Good faith
  The heavenly song of the
    green-spotted dove
  Honpain the star-girl
  The nightingale and the rose
  The old woman who lived in a
    vinegar bottle
  The passing of Glooskap
    [whites vs Indians]
  Prince of nettles
  Retribution
  Smith Riechert
  Snow White and Rose Red
  The ungrateful tiger
Ingratitude [king and shephard]
  Villa-*Armenian*, 359–361
The inheritance
  Hoke-*Uncanny*, 56–74
INHERITANCE
  Flying money
  The poor rich man's son gets
    a second chance
INJURIES
  A taste for quiet
INJUSTICE
  See also FALSE
    ACCUSATIONS
  Daniel O'Connell [trickery]
  The eternal lovers
  Flying money

INJUSTICE (continued)
  Glass mountain
  How a poor muzhik looked for
    truth . . .
  Jews of Safi rid . . . antisemitic
    tax-collector
  King and the poor man
  Little Goody Two-Shoes
  "Of course!"
  The rabbi and the inquisitor
  The reward of charity
  The storytellers
  Thieves go free [buyers are
    punished]
  Tortoise and pig: good acts not
    always rewarded
  Two brothers
  Two sisters, Rose and Lotus
  Yeghnig Aghpar
The Inn of the Stone and Spectre
  Manning-*Spooks,* 89–94
Innocent prisoner marries a
    princess
  Elbaz-*Folktales,* 118–119
INNS AND INNKEEPERS
  The lad and the north wind
  The little cattle
  T'ien the brave, hero of the
    Hsia River
INQUISITION
—Spain
  The rabbi and the inquisitor
INSANITY
  See also FOOLS AND
    FOOLISHNESS
  The crossways [madness]
  Duke Magnus and the mermaid
  The Mother Goose madman
  Olafur and the trolls
  Some sort of madness
  A stroke of luck
  The Tsantsa
INSECTS
  Ballad of the boll weevil [song
    and story]
  Little Genius

  Tomorrow's child
  The wonderful plough
—garden bugs
  The rabbits go hunting
INSOMNIA
  The mistake
INSURANCE
  Settlement out of court
INTEGRITY
—rewarded
  Innocent prisoner marries a
    princess
INTELLIGENCE
  Hare seeks endowments from
    Allah
  The leaning silver birch
  A pottle o' brains
  Riquet with the Tuft
  The small, small cat
  Twigmuntus, Cowbelliantus,
    Perchnosius
INTERPERSONAL RELATIONS
  How bear and chipmonk
    stopped . . . friends
The intoxication of the Ulaid
  Gantz-*Early,* 188–218
INTRIGUE
  The bedbug and the flea
The invasion from the sea
  Highwater-*Anpao,* 181–235
Invasion of privacy. *See* PRI-
  VACY—right of
INVENTIONS
  Hermes, the messenger of the
    gods
  Paul Bunyan, the giant logger
Inventiveness. *See* INGENUITY
Investigation of a grotto
  Lindow-*Swedish,* 59–60
INVISIBILITY
  The Algonquin Cinderella
  The fox and the little white hen
  Hinzelmann
  The Indian Cinderella
  Little burnt face
  The magic bonnet

The miller's three sons
Severi and Vappu
The twelve princesses
—cap of
The bird maiden
The dancing princess
Forgetful Fred
The magic cap
Rustam and the iron fortress
The terrible head
—cloak of
The twelve dancing princesses
—coat of
The boy and the robbers' mag-
ical booty
—hat of
Stealing for the trolls
—stone of
The little white stone
INVISIBILITY (subject)
Mckee-*Scottish*, 29
—fairies
Briggs-*Vanish.*, 216 (index)
Inyan: Iktomi's blanket
Zitkala-*Old*, 19–24
Io and Europa
Low-*Greek*, 33–37
IO (priestess)
The children of Io
[Iollan and his fairy mistress]
Spells & Bind, 62–69
IOLOA (Land of the Dead)
How a man found his wife in
the Land of the Dead
The Iparexeba legend
Wilbert-*Bororo*, 120–121
Iphigenia
Stapleton-*Dictionary*, 120–124
The irangiri tree: ugly man seeks a
wife (Africa)
Shelley-*Legends*, 39–44
IRELAND
See also CELTIC MYTHS
The Amadan Mor and the
Gruagach
The ancient spirits of the coast
The beautiful maidens of the
sea
The birth of Cu Chulaind
Boy abducted by fairies
The boyhood dreams of Cu
Chulaind
Branwen, daughter of Llyr
The brewer of egg-shells
Brewery of eggshells
Bricriu's feast
Bridget and the Lurikeen
The cattle raid of Froech
Children of the fairies
Clever Tom and the
leprechauns
Conall Yellowclaw
Conn-eda; or The golden ap-
ples of Lough Erne
Connla and the fairy maiden
The creatures of magic
The dark of the sea
The dead soldier
The death coach
The death of Alfe's only son
The destruction of Da Derga's
hostel
The devil's dark legions
The dream of Oengus
The enchanted island
Eodain the poetess
The evil eye
The exile of the sons of Uisliu
The expedition of Thorfin
Karisefni
The face at the window
Fair, brown, and trembling
The fantasy land of Lord
Dunsany
Far Darrig in Donegal
The fate of the children of Lir
The field of Boliauns
[Finn] Fann Mac Cuil and the
Scotch giant
The great heroes of old
The haunted realm
The horned woman

IRELAND (continued)
  How Cormac MacArt went to
    Faery
  The immortal fairy folk
  The intoxication of the Ulaid
  Jack and his comrades
  Jack and his master
  Jack o' lanterns
  Jemmy Doyle in the fairy
    palace
  John Brodison and the police-
    man (Ireland)
  The King of Ireland's son (Art)
  Labor pains of the Ulaid, and
    twins of Macha
  The lad with the goat-skin
  Lawyer and the devil (Ireland)
  The leeching of Kayn's leg
  The legend of Knockgrafton
  A legend of Knockmany
  The leprechaun in the garden
  Leprechauns
  The little shoe
  Llewellyn and Rhys
    (condensed)
  Lords of the chariot and the
    spear
  The lure of the marsh lights
  Mabinogion (condensed)
  The magic people
  The magician earl
  Man beasts in wolf-land
  The man from the grave
  The man who had no story
  The marvelous shoe-maker
  Melmoth the doomed wanderer
  The merrow and the soul
    cages
  Merrows
  Midnight funeral from America
  The mischievous little drinker
  The nightmare steed
  Paddy O'Kelly and the weasel
  The peistha discomforted
  The phantom islands
  Phooka
  The piper and the puca
  Pixy-led
  The red man's pranks
  The ride of the headless
    phantom
  The Shee and Gannon and the
    Gruagach Gaire
  Smallhead and the king's son
  The spell of the fairy mistress
  The story of Deirdre
  The story-teller at fault
  Sunken palace: King Corc and
    Fior Usga
  Taken [wife taken by fairies]
  The tale of Macc Da Tho's pig
  The terror of the red blood
    sucker
  The three leprechauns
  Tristram and Isolda
  The vision of MacConglinney
  The wailing messenger of
    death
  The wanderer's dream
  Wasting sickness of Cu
    Chulaind, and . . . Emer
  Water beasts and wurrums
  The werewolves of Ossory
  Wildbeam's pranks
  [Witch controls course of ship]
  The witches' excursion
  The Wooing of Etain
—ancient
  [Swan-children of Lir]
—Carnboy
  Melusine: the otherworld wife
—Connacht
  Saint Patrick and Crom Dubh
—Cooley
  Swine-herds: the cattle raid of
    Cooley
—Cork-origin of lake
  Fior Usga [origin of Lough of
    Cork]
—Donegal
  Far Darrig in Donegal
—Dyfed

Manawydan, son of Llyr
—Inner-n-Aillbine
Naming of places
—Killarney Lake
O'Donoghue
—Knockmany
The Knockmany legend
—Tipperary
Willie Brennan [highwayman]
—Ulster
Macha's curse
IRELAND (subject)
Keightley-*World*, 362–383
Ross-*Druids*, 131 (index)
—fairies
Briggs-*Vanish.*, 216 (index)
—history-Invasions: Nemed, Fir
Bolg, Tuatha de Denann,
Sons of Mil
Ross-*Druids*, 14–20
—Irish fairies
Logan-*Old*, 1–2
—Places (origins; nine legends)
O'Sullivan-*Legends*, 147
—Ulster
Ross-*Druids*, 132 (index)
Iris
Ewart-*Lore*, 136
IRISH
Drill, ye tarriers, drill [song and
story]
IRISH FOLKLORE (subject)
—[map and text]
O'Sullivan-*Legends*, 7–14
IRISH TALES (subject)
—Folklore authorities; bibliography
Yeats-*Fairy*, 294, 386–387
—Glossary
Logan-*Old*, 139–143
—Introd.; 17 tales
McGarry-*Folk*, 1–112
—Kiely (Benjamin)
Yeats-*Fairy*, ix–xx, 3–9
—story-tellers
Yeats-*Fairy*, 301–303
IRON

Anpao and the magic dogs
Vainamoinen's wound
The iron wolf
Adams-*Iron*, 100–110
The iron-eating mice
Wood-*Kalila*, 177–182
IRONY
The happy man's shirt (Italy)
The poor man's bowl
The three golden hairs of Old
Man Almanack
IROQUOIS FALSE FACE
SOCIETY
The big turtle
IRRESPONSIBILITY
Frankie and Johnny [song and
story]
Havoc in heaven: Monkey and
the Jade Emperor
Ivan the peasant's son and the
three dragons
IRRIGATION
Gohc Amu and the running
water
Irving, Washington
Adventure of the German stu-
dent [Irving]
Rip Van Winkle
"Is it you?"
Bierhorst-*Hungry*, 108–111,
141
Is much land needed for a man?
Weiss-*Russian*, 139–154
Isaac and the Parson of Brono
Heslewood-*Tales*, 128–135
Isham, James
The devil
Iskandar and the emerald ring
Shah-*Dervishes*, 235–241
The island fish [Sinbad]
Rackham-*Fairy*, 66–70
The island of beautiful women
Hyde-Chambers-*Tibet*, 147–
151
Island of Sanntraigh (condensed)
Briggs-*Vanish.*, 33–34

Island of the Blest: Land of
    Shadows
    Macmillan-*Canadian* 268–272
ISLANDS
    The anglers of Arz
    The dead soldier
    The elf maiden
    Faerie islands
    Finn blood
    The giant eel
    The giant who had no heart
    Glooscap and the wishes
    The golden cradle
    Katla's dream
    Katrineholm Manor
    The night-trolls
    The phantom islands
    Saxe of Saxeholm
    Snipp, Snapp, Snorium
    The troll in the Skrudur
    The tylwyth teg
    Wayland Smith
    Why the sea moans
—floating
    Isles of the blest
—formation of
    The turtle and the island
—phantom
    The enchanted island
ISLANDS (subject)
—magical
    Briggs-*Vanish.*, 216 (index)
The Isle of Man
    Ross-*Druids*, 136–127
ISLE OF MAN
    The brownie
    The fairies' christening
    The fairy banquet [b]
    The fairy chapman
    The fairy hunt
    The fairy whipping
    The fenoderee
    The fiddler and the fairy
    Leanan-Sidhe
    The Moddey Dhoo
    The phynnodderee

    Sleigh Beggey and Tylwyth
        Teg
ISLE OF MAN (subject)
    Briggs-*Vanish.*, 217 (index,
        under Man, Isle of)
    Keightley-*World*, 397–404
ISLE OF ROUE
    The little glass shoe
ISLE OF RUGEN
    Adventures of John Dietrich
    The black dwarfs of Granita
    The lost bell
    The wonderful plough
ISLE OF RUGEN (subject)
    Keightley-*World*, 174–205
Isles of the Blest
    Pinsent-*Greek*, 142
    Sanders-*Dragons*, 18
ISOLDE (ISOLDA, ISOLT)
    Sir Tristram and La Belle
        Isolde
    Tristram and Isolda
[Isolt and Tristram]
    Spells & Bind, 7–14
ISRAEL, Ancient
    The ten plagues of Egypt
    Tobias goes on a journey
—Ephraim
    Aryeh-Ben-Gadi and Fox-of-
        the-Burnt-Tail
It could always be worse (Jewish)
    Yolen-*Favorite*, 408–409
It happened in a bath
    Villa-*Armenian*, 376–379
It started with a thorn
    Villa-*Armenian*, 423–425, 531
ITALIAN TALES (subject)
—folktale as an art
    Fattoross-*Simpleton*, vii–xiv
ITALY
    Caterina the Wise (Sicily)
    Erdluitle
    Fate
    Folletti and Incubi
    Giane
    Lauru

Massarioli
Norggen, Orculli and
  Fankenmannikins
Pamarindo
Servan
Those stubborn souls, the
  Biellese
Wind folletti
—Southern
Monacielli
—Venice
Barabao
ITALY (subject)
  Keightley-*World*, 447–456
Ithaqua
  Colombo-*Wind.*, 150–161
It's a long way to Gamla Uppsala
  Lindow-*Swedish*, 85–86
It's the pichilingis again
  Campos-*Mexican*, 87–90
Ivan and Nastasia [scrubbing off
  sin]
  Cortes-*Byelorussian*, 74–78
Ivan Bear's Ear
  Riordan-*Russia*, 59–62
Ivan Byelarasseiski
  Cortes-*Byelorussian*, 62–74
Ivan the peasant's son and the
  three dragons
  Riordan-*Russia*, 96–105
Ivan the rich and Ivan the poor
  Riordan-Russia, 23–30
Ivan, the Windfall
  Cortes-*Byelorussian*, 16–30
Ivan Tsarevich, the wolf, and the
  firebird
  Bilibin-*Russian*, 7–18
Ivan young in years, old in wisdom
  Riordan-*Russia*, 213–221
Ivanovoushka the simpleton
  Xenophontovna-*Folk*, 77–106
IVY
  The green lady of Caerphilly
The Iwaguddudogue myth
  Wilbert-*Bororo*, 136–137
IXBALANQUE

Twins of the Popol Vuh
Ixtlaccihuatl and Popocatepetl
  Piggott-*Mexican*, 12–21
Iya, the camp-eter
  Zitkala-*Old*, 131–141
IZZARD, Ann
  Lynching a witch [folk-hysteria]

JABIRU STORKS
  The Bakororo and Itubore
    legend
Jack and his comrades
  Jacobs-*Celtic*, 75–80
Jack and his cudgel
  Sampson-*Gypsy*, 45–48
Jack and his magic aids [dish, belt,
    flute]
  Macmillan-*Canadian*, 12–16
Jack and his master
  Jacobs-*Celtic*, 117–122
Jack and his wonderful hen
  Macmillan-*Canadian*, 119–122
Jack and the beanstalk
  Ehrlich-*Random*, 46–57
  Leete-*Golden*, 144–157
  Pierce-*Larousse*, 161–171
  Rackham-*Fairy*, 37–44
  Stovicek-*Around*, 36–39
Jack and the devil's daughter
  Lester-*Black*, 73–90
Jack and the green lady
  Garner-*British*, 16–24
Jack and the robbers
  Macdonald-*Twenty*, 94–103
Jack Frost
  Baskin-*Imps*, 10–11
Jack o' both sides, or The biter bit
  Marshall, *Every.*, 232–235
Jack o' Lantern
  Baskin-*Imps*, 42–43
Jack o' lanterns
  Haining-*Lepre.*, 108–111

Jack o' Legs
    Marshall-*Every.*, 278–282
Jack of Sjoholm and the Gan-Finn
    Booss-*Scand.*, 503–518
Jack the cunning thief
    Jacobs-*Celtic*, 162–170
Jack the Giant Killer
    Lang-*Blue*, 328–336 (notes,
        353, 372)
    Pierce-*Larousse*, 116–128
    Rackham-*Fairy*, 103–119
Jack [the giant-killer] . . . castle of
        Galigantus
    Lee-*Castles*, 171–173
"JACK THE RIPPER"
    A most unusual murder
The jackal inside the elephant
    Raychaudhuri-*Stupid*, 69–71
The jackal, Mpungutye, searches
        for lost mate
    Poland-*Mantis*, 66–79
The jackal, the dove, and the
        panther
    Lang, *Pink/D*, 315–320
JACKALS
    The bedbug and the flea
    The camel, lion, leopard, crow,
        & jackal
    The crocodile's tail
    Fatima and the tiger
    The foolish weaver and the
        jackal
    The fox and the jackal
    The hunchbacked old woman
    Kalila and Dimna
    Lambikin [drumikin]
    The lion and the hare
    Narahari Das
    The scholar jackal
    The stupid crocodile
    The stupid tiger
    The tiger and the jackal
    The tiger and the palanquin
    The tiger-eating jackal cubs
    Uncle tiger and his nephew the
        jackal

The wicked tiger
Jackals and the tiger
    O'Connor-*Tibet*, 76–79
The jackdaw
    Yeats-*Fairy*, 273–275
Jackets. *See under* CLOTHES
Jack-in-irons
    Froud-*Faeries*, unp
"JACK-IN-THE-BOXES"
    Ha, ha, Jack-in-the-box!
JACOB (O.T. patriarch) (subject)
    Patai-*Gates*, 784 (index)
Jacobs, Joseph
    The cat and the mouse
    Childe Rowland
    Cormac MacArt went to Faery
    Deirdre and Naoise
    Fate of the children of Lir
    How Jack went to seek his
        fortune
    Johnny Cake
    The little red hen
    Master of all masters
    The three bears
    The three little pigs
Jacobs, W. W.
    Jerry Bundler
JADE
    Precious Jade
    The Tibetan envoy's mission
Jade leaves
    Roberts-*Chinese*, 30
The jaguar and the cricket
    Wilbert-*Bororo*, 166–167
The jaguar and the lizard [quali-
        ties]
    Wilbert-*Bororo*, 165–166
Jaguar Petronius, a friend of the
        family
    Stuchl-*American*, 246–248
JAGUARS
    Adugo the jaguar and Ruwo
        the snail
    Chief Akaruio Bokodori and
        the jaguars
    The first sun

Juko the monkey and Adugo
the jaguar
Little crab and his magic eyes
Why leaves on trees are differ-
ent colors
—marries daughter of Bororo
The Bakororo and Itubore
legend
—origin of yellow eyes
Adugo the jaguar and Buke
the anteater
—tricked
Monkey, the cavy, and the jaguar
JAM
The goblin and the grocer
The goblin and the huckster
James, Edwin
Cannibals
JAMES, Jesse
Jesse James [song and story]
JAMES I, King (subject)
—fairies and
Briggs-*Vanish.*, 53–54
JAMESON, Raymond de Loy
—[Narratives from legends of New
Mexico collection]
Robe-*Hispanic*, vii–ix, 1–30
Jamie Freel and the young lady
Yeats-*Fairy*, 52–57
Jamie Freel and the young lady
(condensed)
Briggs-*Vanish.*, 105–108
Janet and Tamlin
Phelps-*Tatterhood*, 23–28
JAPAN
Happy hunter and the skilful
fisher
The magic fox
Mirror of Matsuyama
Prince Vamato Take
The rogue of Kachi Kachi
Mountain
Shinansha, or the south-
pointing carriage
Tengu: Japan's winged war
masters

Urashima Taro
Urashima Taro, the fisher lad
Urashima the fisherman
(Japan)
[Urashima: the sea lord on the
ocean floor]
—Inaba
White hare and the crocodiles
—villages
Sumi and the goat and the
Tokyo Express
Japan: dragon kites
Stallman-*Dragons*, 36–37
JAPAN (subject)
—fairies
Briggs-*Vanish.*, 14–15
—The country and its creation
Piggott-*Japanese*, 6–16
JAPANESE MYTHS (subject)
—Historical survey
Piggott-*Japanese*, 17–37
JAPANESE TALES (subject)
—Supernaturals, dieties, ghosts,
and magical animals
Kendall-*Haunting*, 35–38
The jar of tears
Patai-*Gates*, 648–650
JARS
Ares, god of war
—talking (hunger and thirst)
The sky-god: Ratu and the
Dyaks
JASMINE
The elf of the rose
JASON (subject)
Pinsent-*Greek*, 143 (index)
Jason and the golden fleece
Classic Child., 76–83
Gibson-*Gods*, 85–96
Jason: the argonauts
Low-*Greek*, 109–116
JATAKA TALES
[The Buddha's earlier birth;
introd. to twenty sto-
ries]
Martin-*Hungry*, vii–xi

JAYS (birds)
The Chenoo who stayed to
dinner
Pulowech, the partridge
The jealous co-wife
Magel-*Gambia,* 33–36
The jealous shoemaker
Fattoross-*Simpleton,* 73–78
JEALOUSY
See also ENVY
Ant and lizard [origin of en-
mity]
The bald old man
The birch boy
Bird of truth
The Byse
A cure for jealousy
Dead snake and young wife
Deirdre
Dinewan the emu, and the
bustard
Drolmakyid the fairy [Tibetan]
The fairy child
Fat woman who melted away
Gold-tree and Silver-tree
Herne the hunter
How bear and chipmonk
stopped . . . friends
How foolish men are!
How Kwaku Ananse got Aso in
marriage
How turtle came
John and Mary; girl with
chopped-off hands
Lai D'Ywenee
A lesson from a lovelorn cow
Llyr: children of the sea-god
Man's best friend
Medicine is not a plaything
Merchant's daughter and the
slanderer
Nobleman and the slave
The piebald calf
Pretty Goldilocks
Pulowech, the partridge
The roots of jealousy

Snow White and the seven
dwarfs
Supernatural is not to be
played with
Taufatahi and Fakapatu or
Why sharks . . . Moungone
The tinkling laugh
The treachery of Lelewaga
Treasurer under suspicion
Vartiter (Rose-Petal)
The wicked sister-in-law
[Woman with the head of a
horse]
The wondrous fish-hook
Jean Lapin and the foxes
Uttley-*Foxglove,* 94–101
Jean Sotte
Haviland-*N. Amer.,* 134–138
Jeanie, the bogle of Mulgrave
Wood
Marshall-*Every.,* 69–71
Jelly fish and the monkey
Ozaki-*Japanese,* 189–202
Jellyfish. *See under* FISH
Jemmy Doyle in the fairy palace
Haining-*Lepre.,* 31–33
Jenkins, Will F.
Terror
Jenness, Diamond
A human being transformed
Jenny Greenteeth
Froud-*Faeries,* unp
Jerome, Jerome K., 1859–1927.
The haunted mill: or, The
ruined home
Jerry Bundler
Hoke-*Uncanny,* 36–44
"JERSEY DEVIL"
Assorted monsters
JERUSALEM
The six days and the seven
gates
JERUSALEM (subject)
Patai-*Gates,* 785 (index)
—Temple. *See* TEMPLE OF
JERUSALEM

The Jerusalemite's story copied by
  R. Abraham . . .
  Patai-*Gates,* 568–588
Jesse James [song and story]
  Sanders-*Hear,* 139–149
JESUS CHRIST
  See also CHRISTMAS;
    RESURRECTION
  Baboushka, the Wise Men and
    the Prince of Peace
  The Holy Child
  The robin
  The three brothers
  The two wagoners
  The young king
—appearances
  The selfish giant
—crucifixion
  Conor mac Nessa
—grants 3 wishes
  The cobbler and the devil
—invitation to boy
  The straight road: Christmas in
    heaven
—miracles
  The devil's bargain
  How women got an excuse
  The Jews and our Saviour
JESUS CHRIST (subject)
—appearances; pre-Columbian
    Indians
  MacLean-*Cuentos,* 121–
    125
The jewel of the fox's tongue
  Zong-*Korea,* 18–20
JEWELERS
  The wise goldsmith
JEWELRY
  Charge this to the cap
  The golden cradle
  The young lady of Hellerup
—brooches
  Labor pains of the Ulaid, and
    twins of Macha
—designers
  Aphrodite, goddess of love

JEWELS
  See also TURQUOISE
  The black bull of Norroway
  Bolstre Castle
  The diamond
  The Gojmati
  Hansel and Gretel
  King who had no children
  Loki and the dwarf
  The prince who was made of
    precious gems
  The rejected gift
  The reward of charity
  The royal jewel
  Supparaka
  Toller's neighbors
  Upon Jewel Mountain
  The white rooster
—given for poor relief
  The happy prince
—healing
  Son of the Knight of the Green
    Vesture
Jewels of the devil
  Steele-*Ozark,* 56–58
JEWISH TALES (subject)
  Patai-*Gates,* 513–517
  Schwartz-*Elijah,* 1–17
—[Aesthetics; themes]
  Elbaz-*Folktales,* 18–26
—Evolution of Sephardic tales in
    Canada
  Elbaz-*Folktales,* 26–30
—Glossary, bibliography, motifs,
    indexes
  Elbaz-*Folktales,* 163–192
—Legend and myth
  Patai-*Gates,* xvii–li
Jewish-Christian debate: a strange
    contest
  Elbaz-*Folktales,* 58–59
JEWS
  See also ANTI-SEMITISM;
    HANUKKAH; ISRAEL; LOST
    TRIBES OF ISRAEL; RAB-
    BIS; TORAH

JEWS (continued)
   The broken oaths
   A dispute in sign language
   The enchanted journey [time
     warp]
   Golem: a brute born of clay
     (Joseph of Prague)
   It could always be worse
     (Jewish)
   Jha and Jewish cleverness
   King who decreed conversion
   Magic mirror of Rabbi Adam
   Marrano question: Judaism
     kept secret
   The Mazik-ass
   The Moohel
   The two elephants
   Why do Jews rock when
     studying?
—jokes about
   The ten commandments
—music
   Rabbi Eisik of Kalev
—origin: not eating pork
   The Jews and our Saviour
—relations-Moslems
   Magic ring of Rabbi Israel Hacohen
—in Russia
   Hanukkah in the poorhouse
—in Spain
   Flight of the eagle
—Warsaw ghetto (WW II)
   The power of light
—women-comb hair in private
   Envy punished
JEWS (subject)
   Keightley-*World*, 497–511
   Nahman-*Tales*, 331
—miners, ghosts of
   Briggs-*Vanish.*, 84
—Morocco
   Elbaz-*Folktales*, 18–26
The Jews and our Saviour
   O'Sullivan-*Legends*, 42–43
Jews of Safi rid . . . antisemitic tax-
   collector

   Elbaz-*Folktales*, 49–50
Jha and Jewish cleverness
   Elbaz-*Folktales*, 105
Jha and the copper bowl
   Elbaz-*Folktales*, 65
Jha sells beans to the sultan
   Elbaz-*Folktales*, 90
Jha's nail
   Elbaz-*Folktales*, 63
Jimmy Squarefoot
   Froud-*Faeries*, unp
"JIMPLONG"
   The tiger-eating jackal cubs
Jine. *See* JINN
JINN
   See also GENIES;
     KONDERONG
   Adventures of the third dervish
     [b]
   Aisha Kandisha and the
     drunkard
   A baby kidnapped by the jnun
   Bead-seller and the jinn's
     sister
   The beggar, the lion and the
     dog
   A bride kidnapped by the jnun
   The community that was saved
     by a jinn
   The gift of the jnun
   Hassan the brave
   Iskandar and the emerald ring
   The leopard and the Jinn
   The Prince of Nimroz
   Rabbi Haim Pinto orders jinn
     to cure disciple
   Summoning a spirit servant
   Two visits to the jnun
—kidnaps king's son
   Prince Mahsud and King Rat
Jnun. *See* JINN
Joan of Arc
   Stallman-*Witches*, 21–22
Jocoramodogueddu [primeval
    monkey creates races]
   Wilbert-*Bororo*, 77–78

Johan and the trolls
Booss-*Scand.*, 262–264
John and Mary; girl with chopped-
off hands
Thomas-*It's*, 133–138
John Brodison and the policeman
(Ireland)
Yolen-*Favorite*, 156–157
John Connors and the fairies
(condensed)
Briggs-*Vanish.*, 123–125
John Henry [song and story]
Sanders-*Hear*, 88–98
A John o' Groats seal legend
Robertson-*Highland*, 164–165
JOHN the Baptist, Saint
Saint John's Eve bonfires
—head
Waxworks
John the Bear
Thomas-*It's*, 21–28
John Tregeagle
Marshall-*Every.*, 129–136
Johnnie in the cradle
Crossley-*Folk*, 131–132
Johnnie in the cradle (condensed)
Briggs-*Vanish.*, 101–102
Johnny and the three goats [in
turnip field]
dePaola-*Favorite*, 70–74
Johnny Appleseed
Haviland-*N. Amer.*, 196–203
Johnny Appleseed, the appleseed
planter
Lisker-*Tail*, 33–37
Johnny Cake
dePaola-*Favorite*, 11–15
Johnny Chung and the Flying
Figments
Schwartz-*Tales*, 15–18
The Johnson boys [song and story]
Sanders-*Hear*, 159–168
Johnston, Basil
A man named Weendigo
Jokes. *See* HUMOR
JOKWA, Empress

Stones of five colours and the
Empress Jokwa
JONAH (biblical)
The Whale [and Jonah]
Jonah and the whale
Classic Child., 26–31
Jones, Gwyn
Autumn and the bear
Thornstein staff-struck
JONES, John Paul, 1747–1792.
Paul Jones
Jonesboro tornado: folklore, pop.
religion, history . . .
McNeil-*Charm*, 126–138
Jora the troll
Booss-*Scand.*, 633–634
Jorinde and Joringel
Crossley-*Folk.*, 43–46
Lang-*Green*, 311–315
Jorinde and Joringel: Castle of the
Birds
Lee-*Castles*, 162–163
Jose and Princess Florabella
Stovicek-*Around*, 54–57
JOSEPH (biblical, O.T.)
The kindly ghost [Joseph and
his brothers]
JOSEPH (biblical, O.T.) (subject)
—Joseph and his brothers
Shah-*World*, 156
JOSEPH, Saint
How Saint Joseph helped
to win the king's daugh-
ter
JOSEPH of Arimathea
Adventures of Sir Galahad
Joshua and his mother
Patai-*Gates*, 654–656
Jotunheim, land of the giants
Lee-*Castles*, 45–49
JOUKAHAINEN
[Finnish chanters/enchanters]
Joukahainen's revenge
Synge-*Land*, 35–38
A journey into hell
Amore-*Lustful*, 43–45

Journey of dwarfs over the
  mountain
  Keightley-*World*, 223–226
Journey of Nonogo Pori
  Wilbert-*Bororo*, 210–212
Jovita and Mamuelito
  Aiken-*Mexican*, 119–123
JOY
  See also HAPPINESS
  The fish rejoice
  The power of sorrow
  The seven beggars
  The three daughters
Joyce, P. W.
  Air-demons and Fergus
    O'Mara
  Oisin in Tir Nan Og, or last of
    the Fena
"JOYOUS GARD" (castle)
  The passing of Arthur
Juan and the bony one
  Aiken-*Mexican*, 129–134
Juan de Toluca
  Aiken-*Mexican*, 99–103
Juan fetches the devil
  Campos-*Mexican*, 19–23
Juan Oso
  Aiken-*Mexican*, 83–84
Juan Pelon
  Aiken-*Mexican*, 52–54
Juan Soldado
  Aiken-*Mexican*, 94–96
JUDAISM
  The demon princess
  The loss of the princess
Judge true
  Riordan-*Russia*, 195–198
JUDGEMENT DAY
  The nack longs for salvation
Judgements of a magistrate
  Zong-*Korea*, 187–188
JUDGES AND JUSTICE
  See also INJUSTICE;
    RESTITUTION
  As the king, so the kingdom
  Azad Bakht's tale

Catherine, sly country lass
  (Italy)
A clever judge
Clever Manka
The clever wife
Daniel O'Connell [justice,
  cleverness]
The dog goes to court
The fly (as witness)
The gold and the honey
The good sons
Manka and the judge
Old fuddlement
Rabbi Mordekhai Benjio ren-
  ders justice to an Arab
Repaying good with evil
Rich man, poor man ["eats"
  smell of food]
The serpent-slayer
A Solomonic judgment
Story of a gentleman['s wife]
A stroke of luck [wife judged
  as a fool]
Swan [saved by Prince
  Siddhartha]
The thief who kept his hands
  clean
Tight-fisted farmer and clever
  farmhand
Two neighbors
Underground palace [quest for
  lost queen]
A wise judge
The wise little girl
Women and women
—decisions; cases; justice
  The case of the uncooked
    eggs
—humor
  Chelm justice (Jewish)
—solves problems wisely
  Secret royal inspector, Bag
    Mun-Su
—who gets the deer?
  The deer in the dream
Judges: Karakosh and Goha

Mitchnik-*Egyptian*, 109–115
JUDGMENT DAY
The soul-taking angel [Gabriel]
—after death; reprieve
Banshee of the MacCarthys
JUGS
Crow and the jug
The wooden horse and the
painted jug
—water
The widow's son
Juko the monkey and Adugo the
jaguar
Wilbert-*Bororo*, 167–174
Julie of the wolves
And Every., 153–174
Julio
Aiken-*Mexican*, 124–
129
Jump into my sack (Italy)
Yolen-*Favorite*, 451–457
JUMPING
One hairball
The wisdom of the rabbit
JUNIPER (bush)
Butterfly love
The juniper bush
Manning-*Cats*, 83–91
The juniper tree
Crossley-*Folk*, 138–146
JUNIPER TREES
The juniper tree
Jurma and the sea god
Booss-*Scand.*, 554–559
Just married
Hoke-*Uncanny*, 83–86
[Just men (Lamed vav): the thirty-
six]
Schwartz-*Elijah*, 219–226
Justice. *See* JUDGES AND
JUSTICE
JUTLAND
The nis and the boy
The nis stealing corn
The nisses in Vosborg
The penitent nis

Kabbala [Introd. & selections]
Patai-*Gates*, 419–509
KABBALAH (subject)
Nahman-*Tales*, 331
KABOUTERMANNIKINS
Klabautermannikins and
Kaboutermannikins
Kafka's castle
Lee-*Castles*, 182–183
KAHAHANA, King (subject)
—Ivory of Oahu
Westervelt-*Hawaiian*, 114–124
KAHNS
—horns on head of
Tale of the kurai
KAI-ALE-ALE (King of the Sharks)
Punia and the King of the Sharks
Kalele the Bold Wisher
Thompson-*Hawaiian*, 51–57
KALI (goddess)
Good King Nala's downfall
Kali beheaded
Yourcenar-*Oriental*, 117–125
Kalila and Dimna
Wood-*Kalila*, 45–49+
KALIYA (serpent)
The serpent with one hundred
heads [Kaliya]
Kallundborg church
Keightley-*World*, 116–118
KAMA
The destruction of love
The monkey-faced suitor
KAMAKURA (subject)
Piggott-*Japanese*, 143 (index)
Kamala and the seven thieves
Phelps-*Tatterhood*, 55–60
KAMBARA (island)
Tuwara, the cunning one
KA-MEHA-MEHA
Paao from Samoa
Kane, Paul
Superstitious belief
KANGAROO ISLAND
The sacred island, Nar-oong-
owie

KANGAROOS
  Assorted monsters
  The bad kangaroo
  Bohrah the kangaroo and di-
    newan the emu
  Redbreasts: the Gwineeboos
  That wicked crow
  The topknot pigeons,
    Goolahwillel
—enemies of dogs; origin
  The greedy dogs
—learns how to outrun man
  Legs of the kangaroo
KANTELE (harp)
  The first kantele
  The stealing of the sampo
Kappa
  Piggott-*Japanese*, 65–69
Karakosh and Goha: judges
  Mitchnik-*Egyptian*, 109–115
KASSIM
  Slave maiden's eye for evil
Katchen the cat
  Manning-*Cats*, 9–15
Kate Crackernuts
  Garner-*British*, 58–62
  Luri-*Clever*, 66–73
  Phelps-*Tatterhood*, 33–38
Kate of Ysatter
  Booss-*Scand.*, 296–298
Katerina and her destiny
  Lang-*Pink/K*, 118–123
Katla
  Booss-*Scand.*, 634–635
[Katla protects Odd by 'sight
    blinding']
  Seekers Saviors, 13–20
Katla's dream
  Booss-*Scand.*, 606–609
Katrineholm Manor
  Booss-*Scand.*, 257–260
Katsina. *See* MEDICINE MEN
Kaufman, Norman P.
  A sharp loss of weight
KAVIN, Saint
  King O'Toole and his goose

Keary, Annie
  How they went to Jotunheim
KEEL-BOARDS
  Jack of Sjoholm and the Gan-
    Finn
Keep on stepping
  Lester-*Black*, 153–157
Keeping the shirttail in
  Aiken-*Mexican*, 61–63
KEGS
  Death and the doctor
Kelfala's secret something
  Robinson-*Three*, 17–31
KELLY, Edward, 1555–1595.
—Conjurers and the crystal
  Sergeant-*Witches*, 200–227
KELLY, Robert (Robin)
  Giant's stairs [Mahon
    MacMahon]
  Giant's stairs [Ronayne's
    Court]
The kelpie
  Froud-*Faeries*, unp
The kelpie of Corryvreckan
  Robertson-*Highland*, 137–138
KELPIES (subject)
  See also WATER SPIRITS
  Briggs-*Vanish.*, 68–70, 196–
    197
  Mckee-*Scottish*, 9–11
KENDALL, CAROL (subject)
—Biographical note
  Kendall-*Haunting*, 39
Kenkebe
  Radin-*African*, 292–295
Kennedy, Dan
  A near encounter
Kennedy, Patrick
  Kildare pooka
  Lazy beauty and her aunts
  Twelve wild geese
KENYA
  Kelfala's secret something
Kershan (Chadwick), N.
  Gestumblindi's riddles
Kertong

Kendall-*Sweet,* 66–72
Kespak and the caribou
    Hill-*More,* 31–40
Ketill, the priest of Husavik
    Booss-*Scand.,* 644
KETTLES
    The fairies' caldron
    The lost treasure
    The story of Bergthor of Blafell
—copper
    Skotte in the fire
KEVIN, Saint
    King O'Toole and his goose
KEYS
    Bluebeard
    [Bluebeard, Isabelle, the bleed-
      ing key]
    The box with the funny thing in
      it
    The golden key
    The heard boy and the
      dragons
    The Moohel
    Treasure Mountain; a Yao
      folktale
—golden
    Wild Goose Lake
KHANS
    Gulnara the Tartar warrior
    Tiger King's skin cloak
      [Mongolia]
—cruel
    The three talismans
Kick the wooden ball!
    Wright-*Gold,* 32–35
KICKAPOO TALES
    Ua-pa-chi (Kickapoo titles)
Kid Cardula
    Asimov-*Fant.,* 62–75
KIDNAPPING
    A baby kidnapped by the jnun
    How Ableegumooch tracked a
      fox
    Juan and the bony one
    Ljungby horn and pipe
    The outlaw

    Powel and Rhiannon
    Prince Mahsud and King Rat
    Stealing for the trolls
    The stolen princess
    Tibble Castle and Klinta Spring
    Two enemy kings
—fire as ransom
    How raven brought fire to the
      Indians
Kids. *See* GOATS
Kii (subject)
—Sons of Kii
    Westervelt-*Hawaiian,* 47–64
Kildare pooka
    McGarry-*Folk,* 29–32
    Yeats-*Fairy,* 96–98
Kildare pooka (condensed)
    Briggs-*Vanish.,* 56
Kile Bamba and the Loche bogatyr
    Nagishkin-*Folktales,* 210–224
Kille Kopp: The changeling
    speaks . . .
    Lindow-*Swedish,* 92–93
"Killed" person lives on: Anpu and
    Bata
    Shah-*World,* 87–92
KILLER WHALES
    Mouse Woman and the mon-
      ster killer whale
    Nanasimgat [wife abducted by
      killer whale]
    Nanasimgit and his [abducted]
      wife
    The Wasgo and three killer
      whales
The Killiecrankie ghost
    Robertson-*Highland,* 45–46
KILLING
    See also MURDER
    Tiger boys
—hunter's son refuses to kill
      animals
    The boy, his sisters, and the
      magic horse
—wanton
    Downfall of the mighty hunter

KILLING (subject)
—Buddhist stories
  Amore-*Lustful*, 99–100
Killing animals. *See* ANIMALS–
  killing
Killmoulis
  Froud-*Faeries*, unp
The kind man
  Hyde-Chambers-*Tibet*, 101–
  103
Kind word: White dove
  Shub-*About*, 52–53
The kindly ghost [Joseph and his
  brothers]
  Shah-*World*, 156–160
KINDNESS
  See also CRUELTY; GOOD
  DEEDS; GOODNESS
  Ant and the dove
  The baker's daughter
  Beauty and the beast
  The Chenoo who stayed to
    dinner
  Cinderella
  Dame Soasan
  Diamonds and toads
  The dreaded chenoo
  Drinking companions (China)
  Duke Pishposh of Pash
  Eighteen rabbits
  The fairies [jewels or frogs . . .]
  The fairy and the prince
  The fairy grotto
  Flying money
  [Gawain and Dame Ragnell]
  The golden goose
  The grateful elfwoman
  Heaven's reward
  Heimdall in Midgard
  Kespak and the caribou
  The kind man
  Kumba the orphan girl
  The little cattle
  Little crop-tailed hen
  The little mermaid
  The magic mirror
  Maiden Bright-Eye
  Mother Hulda
  Mother of the Waters
  The old witch
  Roly poly rice ball
  The sacred sheet [at
    execution]
  Saint Peter and the two
    women
  Saran and Yumart
  Shoemaker and the elves
  The squirrel wife
  The star dipper [Ursa major]
  Story of Ciccu
  The strongest boy in the world
  Thordur of Thrastastadir
  Tia Miseria's pear tree
  Treasure Mountain; a Yao
    folktale
  Water of life
  Weardale fairies [dislike being
    observed]
  White hare and the crocodiles
  Young boy and the dwarf
—animal helps man
  The Blackfoot and the bear
—breaks witch's spell
  Doll in the grass
—daily food appears
  Metugoe doves and the widow
—death as reward for
  His just reward
—happiness
  Prince Five-Weapons
—not rewarded
  Squirrel, leopard, and goat: do
    it again, then
—rewarded
  The baker's daughter
  The black king, or Fair
    Ferentine
  The brothers and the singing toad
  The golden goose
  Golden rain
  Helping the sjora
    [vantevannen]

How the moolah was taught a
lesson
The Inn of the Stone and
Spectre
Jose and Princess Florabella
The kindly ghost [Joseph and
his brothers]
The little boy Chokcho
The magic coconuts
Mother Holle
A reward for honesty
The talking nightingale
Tiger King's skin cloak
[Mongolia]
Two visits to the jnun
The wizard
Yeghnig Aghpar
[note: kindness is rewarded in
virtually all tales]
—superior to beauty
Cinderella
—to old people
The old man and his grandson
KINDNESS (subject)
—worldwide usage: fairy tales
Lang-*Pink*/*D*, vii–viii
KINDNESS TO CREATURES [animals, birds, etc.]
Baba Yaga
The blacksmith
Boy with the deformed head
Charcoal burner and the bear
The country of the mice
A crippled hero
The deer and the snake
Dragon's eye; jewel as reward
Enchanted watch
First pig and porcupine
The fisherman and his wife
The fisher-prince with the silver apple
The fool and the magic fish
The frog princess
Frog princess: Vassilisa the
Wise
Golden lads

The grey wolf and the orphan
[Musquakie]
Hailibu the hunter
House in the wood
King Eagle
King of the herrings
The magic gifts [dwarf-sorcerer]
Magic pumpkins
Mountain witch and the
Dragon-King
Old man who made withered
trees to flower
Orphan Yan Ran [Kawa]
The pheasants and the bell
Piglet and the cow
Pretty Goldilocks
Prince of nettles
A princess on a swing
Queen bee
Song-bird and the healing
waters
Swan [saved by Prince
Siddhartha]
The talking fish
Thumbelina
The tiger's grave
The turtle friend [freed, carries
sage across . . .]
Two neighbors
Urashima Taro, the fisher lad
Vassilisa [Fair] and Baba Yaga
When the hand rubs the
foot . . .
The white snake
Who is my neighbour?
Woodcutter and the heavenly
maiden
The youth and the eagles
—birds; reward
How three serpents carried
princesses . . .
—fish; reward
The cat and the dog
—no gratitude
Kildare pooka

KINDNESS TO CREATURES
(continued)
—rewarded
The black geese
The doe, the hunter, and the
great stag
A farmer learns a lesson
The great flood [deluge]
Maria Morevna
Sultan's stupid wife and the
jinn-monkey
The Tsarevna frog
[note: kindness is rewarded in
virtually all tales]
—wolf; repaid
Oskus-ool and his wise wife
A king and a dove
Amore-*Lustful*, 60—62
King and the bishop
[Clonmacnoise]
McGarry-*Folk*, 59—68
The king and the emperor
Nahman-*Tales*, 63—78 [notes:
65, 289—291]
King and the poor man
Minford-*Fav.*, 168—172
King and the wise man
Nahman-*Tales*, 113—119
[notes: 115, 301—302]
King Brian Boru the Danish heather
ale
O'Sullivan-*Legends*, 132—133
King Crocodile
Manning-*Marvels*, 58—64
King Dabschelim
Wood-*Kalila*, 3—20
King David and the giant
Schwartz-*Elijah*, 44—46
King David matches wits with An-
gel of Death
Elbaz-*Folktales*, 143—144
King Eagle
Manning-*Kings*, 37—53
King Goldemar
Keightley-*World*, 256—257
King Goodness refuses to fight
Amore-*Lustful*, 102—104
King Gylfi is tricked again
Branston-*Gods*, 151—152
King Josef
Manning-*Kings*, 66—71
King Kojata
Lang-*Green*, 207—220
King Lindorm [a snake]
Lang-*Pink/D*, 301—314
Lang-*Pink/K*, 218—230
King Lion and the beetle, 7
King Matyas and his scholars
(Hungary)
Yolen-*Favorite*, 412
King Miroslav and the proud
princess
Wood-*Palace*, 31—40
The king o' the cats
Crossley-*Folk*, 72—74
The King of Ireland's son (Art)
Yolen-*Favorite*, 248—254
King of Lochlann's three daughters
Lochhead-*Battle*, 37—44
King of snakes
Villa-*Armenian*, 224—229, 484
"KING OF THE FAIRIES" (subject)
Briggs-*Vanish.*, 216 (index)
"KING OF THE FOREST"
The tale of Looseghen
"KING OF THE GOLD MINES"
The yellow dwarf
King of the herrings
Sampson-*Gypsy*, 9—12
King of the pipers and the wonder-
ful tune
Lochhead-*Battle*, 57—60
King of the pomegranate tree
Peacock Maid, 1—11
"KING OF WATERS"
The tale of Looseghen
KING ORFEO (subject)
Briggs-*Vanish.*, 46—47, 115—
116, 171
King O'Toole and his goose
Jacobs-*Celtic*, 63—66
Yeats-*Fairy*, 203—205

[King Shivi] The gift of cows
Amore-*Lustful*, 113–114
King Sivi
Martin-*Hungry*, 115–121
King Solomon and Asmodeus
Schwartz-*Elijah*, 53–58
King Solomon and the winds
Patai-*Gates*, 656–662
The king, the coin, and the
clown
Lewis-*Minute*, 42–43
King the liar and liar the king
Stovicek-*Around*, 130–131
King Thrushbeard
Shub-*About*, 90–95
King who decreed conversion
Nahman-*Tales*, 95–103, [commentary 97, 297–298]
King who fought many wars
Nahman-*Tales*, 121–129
[notes: 303–305]
The king who gave away his
kingdom
Amore-*Lustful*, 116–118
King who had no children
Nahman-*Tales*, 105–111
[notes: 107, 299–300]
The king who would have a beautiful wife
Lang-*Pink/D*, 162–166
Lang-*Pink/K*, 114–117
King Zargand's daughter
Sheohmelian-*Three*, 116–131
The kingdom of beautiful colors
Wyatt-*Princes*, 82–109
Kingdoms of copper, silver, and
gold
Riordan-*Russia*, 264–268
KINGFISHERS
Halcyone: a second life for
love
Locust, ant, and the kingfisher
KINGS AND QUEENS
See also FAIRY KINGS;
PRINCES AND
PRINCESSES

See also titles beginning with
"Queen . . ."
The archer who went I know
not where to fetch . . .
Autumn and the bear
Axad Bakht meets the
dervishes
Azad Bakht's tale
The banyan deer [the Buddha]
Barter
The battle of Stamford Bridge
The battle of the birds
The beggar, the lion and the
dog
Beowulf fights the dragon
Bird of truth
The black colt
The blossom tree
Blue bird [King Charming]
Boots and the beasts
Branwen, daughter of Llyr
Brave Bear, Snake, and Crocodile Killer
Brave little tailor (seven at one
blow)
The broken oaths
Cassiopeia (the Queen)
The castle in the lake
The castle of Melvales
Catherine and her destiny
Catherine, sly country lass
(Italy)
Cepheus (the king)
The charcoal burner
Cinderella [sisters kill/eat
mother]
Clever man and ordinary
Clever woman
Cock with the golden feathers
Conall Yellowclaw
Connla and the fairy maiden
The countess of Hojentorp
The country of the mice
Crab
Crack and crook (Italy)
The desolate island

298

KINGS AND QUEENS (continued)
  Devil with the three golden
    hairs
  Dialogue with death
  Dick Whittington and his cat
  Dietrich of Bern
  The disrespectful son
  Don Juan Zurumbete
  Drakestail [and the king]
  The dwarf-sword tirfing
  Elijah's violin
  Elstorps Woods
  Eodain the poetess
  The eternal lovers
  Faithful John
  Fiery horse
  The flying trunk
  Genius deserves his name
  Genius [more intelligent than
    the king]
  Gesar of Ling
  Gestumblindi's riddles
  The giant who had no heart
  The girl who was already
    queen
  The goblin bride
  Gold Tree and Silver Tree
  The golden feather [talking
    colt]
  The golden goose
  The golden lion
  The golden tree [queen and
    amulet]
  Gold-tree and Silver-tree
  The good sons
  The goose girl
  Grateful animals and the un-
    grateful man
  The great deeds of King Yu
  The greedy youngster
  The Greek princess and the
    young gardener
  Gushtap and the princess of Roum
  Halde hat
  A Hani story: Queen forbids
    servant to eat rice

He who laughs last, laughs
  best
Heart of ice [Prince Littleboots]
The herd-boy
Herne the hunter
How Cormac MacArt went to
  Faery
How Fin went to the kingdom
  of the big men
How the blackbird went to war
How the dragon was tricked
How the speckled hen got her
  speckles
A hundred times
The hyena engages the hare
  as a gewel
Ingratitude [king and shep-
  herd]
Jason and the golden fleece
Jean Sotte
Jelly fish and the monkey
Jovita and Mamuelito
Juan and the bony one
Juan de Toluca
The juniper bush
The king and the emperor
King of Lochlann's three
  daughters
King of the pomegranate tree
The kingdom of beautiful
  colors
"Lars, my lad!"
The leeching of Kayn's leg
Legend of Melusina
Leppa Polkry and the blue
  cross
Liisa and the prince
The little bull calf
The little fox
Little Ida's flowers
Lludd and Llefelys
Llyr: children of the sea-god
The loss of the princess
The magic horse
Maiden Bright-Eye
The making of the worlds

The man who knew how to divide a chicken
The man who wouldn't be king
The master of prayer
The master of Ugerup
Merchant's daughter and the slanderer
Miaoshan-Guanyin, protectress of mortals
Midas, the golden king
Molly Whuppie (England)
Monster with seven heads
Morraha
Mouse's three children [tiger, peacock, boy]
The outlaw
Owney and Owney-na-peak
Padmasambhava and the felicity scarf
Pannu, the marevellous dog
The parson and the clerk [I]
The parson and the sexton
Peik
Phya Paan and the Golden Chedi
Pretty Goldilocks
The prince and his fate
Prince Asraf and the king of the spirits
Prince Meerzat Istvan and the horse of dust . . .
Princess Minon-Minette
The promise of the three sisters
Proud Margaret
Puss in Boots
Queen Pig
The queen's children
Quevedo and the king (Mexico)
Room Bacha and Baki
The ruby ring
Salt above gold
The seven beggars
The seven-day vigil
The shadows

The Shee and Gannon and the Gruagach Gaire
Singard the dragon-slayer
Sir Tristram and La Belle Isolde
Sister Alionushka, Brother Ivanushka
Sleeping Beauty in the woods
Smallhead and the king's son
Snipp, Snapp, Snorium
The snow queen
Snow White and the seven dwarfs
Son of the gray horse
Son of the Mountain
The star child
Story of Ciccu
The story of Deirdre
The story of trembling hood
The story-teller at fault
The sword in the stone
The tailor-bird and the king
The terrible head
Theseus, king of Athens
Thor fights the giant Krangnir
Thor in the giant's stronghold
The three caskets
The three golden hairs of Old Man Almanack
The three heads of the well
The three imposters
Three snake-leaves
Thumbelina
Tibet's first king
The tinder-box
Tom Tit Tot
Treasure Mountain; a Yao folktale
Treasurer under suspicion
The tricking of King Gilfi
The troll's hammer
True and untrue
Twelve dancing daughters
Twelve huntsmen [test of femininity]

KINGS AND QUEENS (continued)
    Twigmuntus, Cowbelliantus,
        Perchnosius
    Two enemy kings
    Underground palace [quest for
        lost queen]
    The unwilling magician
    The Urko of North Wij
    Vaino and the swan princess
    The valiant chanticleer
    Vanooshka
    The vision of MacConglinney
    Walter and Hildegund
    Wayland Smith
    The werewolf
    What happened to Ivan
    The white cat
    Why the executioner is called
        assessor
    Why the sea moans
    The wild swans
    The winding-horn village
    The wise king and the honest
        thief
    The wooden sword
    The wooing of Seppo
        Hmarinen
    The yellow dwarf
    Young Gim and the robbers
    A youth set out to learn what
        fear was
—abdicates
    The cuckoo: its origin and its
        call
—banishes wife and child
    Lion tamer [Tibetan]
—chosen by pigeon
    Shepherd's dream
—coronations
    The young king
—envoys
    The Tibetan envoy's mission
—evil, gets just deserts
    The giant with three golden
        hairs
—evil queen

    Nightingale and the dove
—feared by all, but one
    Sri of Siam
—going blind
    The big bird Katchka
—hoards well-water
    Fior Usga [origin of Lough of
        Cork]
—Ireland
    The fate of the children of Lir
—murders his son
    Ivan Byelarasseiski
—no belief in God: people
        punished
    Town of stone
—of Russia, fooled
    Story of the robbers [master
        thief]
—proud queen
    A dead princess and seven
        giants
—queen an adulteress
    Clever boy
—queen rescues captive husband
    The lute player
—role as protector
    A king and a dove
—sad because of moles on his
        head
    There is no such thing as a
        secret
—seeks reassurance that he is a
        good ruler
    As the king, so the kingdom
—skilled in a craft
    A craft is worth more than gold
—Spain
    The birthday of the Infanta
—wise mediation of dispute
    The day the sun did not rise
KINGS AND QUEENS (subject)
—Hindu stories
    Amore-*Lustful*, 54
—Ka-meha-meha
    Westervelt-*Hawaiian*, 162–175
The king's boatman

Watson-*Thailand*, 18–20
The king's daughter and the pep-
    per man
    Bierhorst-*Hungry*, 45–50, 136
The king's dream
    Schwartz-*Elijah*, 197–202
The king's favorite
    Yolen-*Favorite*, 61
The king's favorite [beauty fades]
    Roberts-*Chinese*, 151
The King's favourite and the beau-
    tiful slave
    Shah-*Afghanistan*, 48–53
The king's kinka [lizard]
    Watson-*Thailand*, 6
The king's rival
    Robinson-*Three*, 33–47
King's son goes bear hunting
    [Finland]
    Yolen-*Favorite*, 155–156
King's/servant's sons switched
    Nahman-*Tales*, 189–209
    [notes: 191, 315–316]
KINKAS
–a kind of lizard
    The king's kinka [lizard]
Kinsman accompany you when he
    asks to go along
    Radin-*African*, 215–217
Kintaro, the golden boy
    Ozaki-*Japanese*, 60–73
Kintu tested before he could marry
    daughter of king of heaven
    Radin-*African*, 69–72
Kipling, Rudyard
    Elephant's child
    How the rhinoceros got his
        skin
KIRK, Robert (subject)
    Briggs-*Vanish.*, 216 (index)
KIROMBO (bird)
    Oh Mister Crocodile
Kirsten's-hill
    Keightley-*World*, 121–122
KISSES
    The promise

The swine herd
    The tinkling laugh
—of death
    The jewel of the fox's tongue
The "Kissing witch"
    Sergeant-*Witches*, 228–250
The kitchen god
    Chalk-*Tales*, unp.
KITCHENS
    An evening in the squire's
        kitchen
    The mountain kitchen
    The young lady of Hellerup
KITES
    The flying kite
    Japan: dragon kites
    The missing treasure
—bigger than house; crashes
    How the Bay of Siam came to
        be
Kitpouseagunow
    Hill-*More*, 41–54
Kitta Gra and the devil
    Lindow-*Swedish*, 174–176
KLABAUTERMAN (sea spirit)
    The kobold and the pirate
Klabautermannikins and
    Kaboutermannikins
    Arrowsmith-*Field*, 152–156
Klis-to E-eki Ta-u-ue-a
    Aiken-*Mexican*, 134–136
KNAPSACKS
—magic
    Juan Soldado
The knight of Ellenholm
    Booss-*Scand.*, 250–251
Knight of the Glens and Bens and
    Passes
    Ratcliff-*Scottish*, 11–18
Knight of the riddles
    Lochhead-*Battle*, 49–54
Knight to knight [the Gogmagog
    hills]
    Marshall-*Every.*, 165–170
Knighting of Cuculain
    Yeats-*Fairy*, 369–372

KNIGHTS AND KNIGHTHOOD
  See also ROUND TABLE
  The black bull of Norroway
  El caballero porfiado
  [Daughters nightly go to under-
    world, engage in dance of
    death]
  Ebbe Skamelson
  Elstorps Woods
  The herd boy and the dragons
  Lai D'Ywenee
  Little weaver of Duleek Gate
  The Longwitton dragon
  Lyulph's tower: Lady
    Greystoke
  Mizilca [woman disguised as
    knight]
  The outlaw
  Philbert the Fearful
  The quest for the Star of the
    Sea
  The red czar and the golden-
    haired Tihota
  Sir Thynne
  Son of the Knight of the Green
    Vesture
—fairy saves
  Lanval and the Lady Triamor
—Heavenly Knight
  The fisher-prince with the sil-
    ver apple
Knights in service of Camelot
  Lehane-*Legends*, 84
The knights of Allaberg
  Booss-*Scand.*, 279
Knights' tales
  Lehane-*Legends*, 100–107
KNITTING
  Duffy and the devil
—pins
  Murder will out
KNIVES
  The elf maiden
  How the rabbit lost his tail
  Magic knife [Uygur]
  A slave's dangerous courtship

  A stork is not always a stork
  The troll's hammer
—as sign of trouble
  The little old man in the tree
Knock! knock!
  Wahl-*Needle*, 35–45
Knock, knock, who's there?
  Ainsworth-*Bear*, 40–46
Knockers
  Arrowsmith-*Field*, 39–42
KNOCKGRAFTON
—legend of
  The legend of Knockgrafton
Knockgrafton legend
  Yeats-*Fairy*, 43–47
The Knockmany legend
  Phelps-*Tatterhood*, 87–92
  Yeats-*Fairy*, 241–251
Knolls (or Knowe) *See* HILLS
KNOTS
  The voyage in a Lapp sled
"KNOTS OF WIND"
  Wind folletti
KNOWALL (giant)
  The giant with three golden
    hairs
Know-All and the cowardly thieves
  Shah-*Afghanistan*, 24–29
KNOWLEDGE
  See also GUESSES
  Aristotle and the bees
  The good scene
  The master pupil
  Mystic knowledge
—accidental possession of
  Home-bred boy dislodges
    spider
  Squirrel and the fox
  The unwilling magician
—conversation overheard
  How foolish men are!
—pretense to have
  The strange history of Pro-
    fessor Grasshopper
—Sionan eats forbidden salmon
  How the Shannon got its name

—supernatural
  Two brothers and the
    magistrate
—whole and parts
  The blind ones and the matter
    of the elephant
Knowledge of future. *See* SECOND
  SIGHT
KNUCKLEBONE (musical
  instrument)
  The boy with the knuckle-
    bones
  The golden knucklebone
Knurre-Murre (condensed)
  Briggs-*Vanish.,* 79
Koala and the rainbow
  Reed-*Aboriginal,* 37–39
KOALAS
—tails
  Why koala has no tail
The kobold and the pirate
  Heslewood-*Tales,* 11–17
Kobolde
  Arrowsmith-*Field,* 135–139
Kobolds
  Froud-*Faeries,* unp
KOBOLDS (fairies)
  Hinzelmann
  Hodeken
  King Goldemar
KOBOLDS (subject)
—house fairies
  Keightley-*World,* 239–258
  Briggs-*Vanish.,* 57–60, 197
KOKLA, Rani
  Her lover's heart
KOKOMO (bird)
  Cassowary [bird] and Kokomo
    [ability to fly]
Kombocke and Hausbocke
  Arrowsmith-*Field,* 204–295
Komodo: the real-life dragon
  Stallman-*Dragons,* 44–45
Komroff, Manuel
  So you won't talk
KONDERONG

The hyena wrestles the kon-
  derong. I
The hyena wrestles the
  kongerong. II
Sidi Ngali and his traveling
  companions
Konderong: The handsome suitor
  Magel-*Gambia,* 45–49
Konyek and his father [Masai]
  Radin-*African,* 174–176
KOOKABURRAS (birds)
  How the sun was made
  The turtle and the turkey
The Koranic teacher
  Magel-*Gambia,* 85–89
KOREA
  Dan-Gun, first king of Korea
  Hong Gil-Dong
  Piglet and the cow
  The toad-bridegroom
KOREAN TALES (subject)
—[Korea: history, neighbors, folk
    beliefs, tale characteristics]
  Zong-*Korea,* xvii–xxviii
KORI (giant bird)
  The birch boy
Koroge tribe defeated by Jerigi
    Otojiwu
  Wilbert-*Bororo,* 221–223
Korred
  Arrowsmith-*Field,* 65–70
KORRED
  The dance and the song of the
    Korred
KORRIGANS
  Fountain women
  Lai D'Ywenee
  Lord Nann and the Korri-
    gans
KORRIGANS (subject)
  Briggs-*Vanish.,* 32, 156–157,
    197
KORSAN, ROCKS OF
  The rocks of Korsan
KOSHCHEY The Deathless
  The frog princess

Kosi, the eagle, and the mountain
lion
Walking-*Song*, 23–28
KOSTSHEI the Deathless
The Tsarevna frog
KOTEI, Emperor
Shinansha, or the south-
pointing carriage
KRAKENS
Stormalong fights the Kraken
Water monsters
Kramer, Samuel Noah
Discovery and decipherment of
"The descent of Inanna"
Sumerian history, culture and
literature
KRIEMHILD, Princess
Siegfried and the Rhine
castles
KRISHNA (god)
Burning of the Khandava for-
est
A handful of rice
Pyoli and Lord Krishna
The serpent with one hundred
heads [Kaliya]
Ku Klux Klansmen and the Pope
McNeil-*Charm*, 95–96
Kuafu chases the sun
Sanders-*Dragons*, 19
The Kuddogo fish
Wilbert-*Bororo*, 144–146
KUI
Gods of the stars: ancient
China
Kullervo
Synge-*Land*, 154–165
Kuma and Aua
Stokes-*Turtle*, 115–118
Kumba the orphan girl
Magel-*Gambia*, 90–95
Kungakhkei: The brave Azmun
Nagishkin-*Folktales*, 13–26
Kupti and Imani
Phelps-Tatterhood, 93–102
KUPUA

Stretching kupua [taller than
40 feet]
The talking spear
KURAI (musical instrument)
Tale of the kurai
Kurreahs. *See* ALLIGATORS AND
CROCODILES
Kwi-na the eagle: animal-god
persons
Jagendorf-*First*, 79–85
Kyang, the fox, the wolf and the
hare
O'Connor-*Tibet*, 43–47
KYOTO (subject)
Piggott-*Japanese*, 143 (index)

Laa-mai-Kahiki from Tahiti
Westervelt-*Hawaiian*, 86–92
Labor. *See* WORK
Labor pains of the Ulaid, and twins
of Macha
Gantz-*Early*, 127–129
The labours of Hercules
Gibson-*Gods*, 62–72
LABYRINTH (mazes)
Wayland Smith
LACE MAKERS
Sister Lace
The lad and the devil
Booss-*Scand.*, 12–13
The lad and the devil (Norway)
Yolen-*Favorite*, 394
The lad and the fox
Booss-*Scand.*, 203
The lad and the north wind
Booss-*Scand.*, 41–44
The lad who went to the north wind
Ross-*Druids*, 65–78
The lad with the goat-skin
Jacobs-*Celtic*, 145–150
Ladder of grass [six races of men]
Dutton-*Hopi*, 9–10

LADDERS
Drakestail [and the king]
LADIES
The stolen lady
—old
Odd jobs
LADY
—green
Jack and the green lady
The lady and the merman
Yolen-*Hundredth*, 59–64
Lady of Gollerus
Yeats-*Fairy*, 328–332
LADY OF THE LAKE
Balin and Balan
Lady Ren: fox spirit
Sanders-*Dragons*, 92–94
Lady White and Shushuan
Sanders-*Dragons*, 87–92
Lady witches [England, history]
Sergeant-*Witches*, 253–269
"LADYDAY" (holiday)
The field of Boliauns
Lai D'Ywenee
Keightley-*World*, 422–433
Laidlaw, G. E.
Six traditional tales
Laidley worm of Spindlestone
Heugh
Marshall-*Every.*, 340–344
Laing, Samuel
The battle of Stamford Bridge
Laird of Duffus (condensed)
Briggs-*Vanish.*, 49, 128–129
Laird of Lorntie (condensed)
Briggs-*Vanish.*, 70–71
The laird's lass and the gobha's
son
Phelps-*Tatterhood*, 65–78
Lake Espantosa, the alligators
Ritchie-*Armadillo*, 38–42
Lake Goldring
Booss-*Scand.*, 307–308
Lake Inchiquin [brings no O'Briens
home]
O'Sullivan-*Legends*, 153

LAKE MAIDENS
Shepherd of Myddvai and the
lake maiden
The lake monster
Booss-*Scand.*, 628
Lake of Zangze
Zong-*Korea*, 45–46
LAKE PEOPLE
The Gwagedd Annwyn
The Gwagedd Annwyn [II]
The shepherd of Myddvai
The lake [personified]
Manning-*Spooks*, 112–114
LAKES
*See also headings begining
with "Lough"*
A bride from the lake
Cannibal Lake
The castle in the lake
The coal burner and the troll
The creation
The daughter of Peter de
Cabinam
The dragon who cried
The fairy's Inquiry
The giant who had no heart
Glashans and Shopiltees
The Gwagedd Annwyn
Hansel and Gretel
Mongolian story of a serf: Ulan
Bator
Opame, Chenrezik, and Dolma
Origin of Tiis Lake
The peistha discomforted
The spirit of the van
Stupid Peikko
The tylwyth teg
The valiant chanticleer
The village beneath the water
The water smith
The white rooster
Wild Goose Lake
—Australia
Origin of the Narran Lake
—honeyed water
Ivan Bear's Ear

LAKES (continued)
—magic
    Search for the magic lake
    Why coyote's coat is the color
        of sand
—moves to get away from people
    The lake [personified]
—origin
    Sunken palace: King Corc and
        Fior Usga
—rope to hang lake from the sky
    Abzelil and the Master of the
        Lake
LAKES (subject)
—[Ireland; origins]
    O'Sullivan-*Legends,* 51
The Lakota woman
    Yellow Robe-*Tonweya,* 94–
        101
La-lee-lu
    Manning-*Spooks,* 15–16
Lam Ku, the basket lady
    Chalk-*Tales,* unp.
LAMAS
    The kind man
—begging priests
    The boy, his sisters, and the
        magic horse
The lama's servant
    O'Connor-*Tibet,* 124–132
LAMB (as food)
—leg of
    Lamb to the slaughter
Lamb to the slaughter
    Hoke-*Demonic,* 3–13
The lamb with the golden fleece
    Shah-*World,* 142–144
Lambikin [drumikin]
    Ross-*Druids,* 37–47
Lambs. *See under* SHEEP
Lamed vav: Prince made of gems
    Schwartz-*Elijah,* 219–226
LAMENESS
    Pixy-vengeance
LAMENTS
    Balder's doom

LAMIGNAK
    Fountain women
LAMPS
    Aladdin and the wonderful
        lamp
    Aladdin, or The wonderful
        lamp
    Photogen and Nycteris; a
        day/night mahrchen
—burns vinegar mistaken for oil
    The miracle of Rabbi David
        Hassine
—magic
    Aladdin and his magic lamp
The lampstand princess
    Vuong-*Brocaded,* 83–100
LANCELOT, Sir
    Castle [Chariot] of Morgan le
        Fay
    La Cote Mal Taile
    Death of King Arthur
    Elaine the Fair Maid of Astolat
    The great king's last battle
    The passing of Arthur
    Quest for the Holy Grail
    Sir Lancelot of the Lake
    Sir Launcelot du Lake
LANCELOT, Sir (subject)
    Briggs-*Vanish.,* 143–144
Lancelot and Guenevere
    Riordan-*Arthur,* 102–113
Lancelot: Castle of Gorre
    Lee-*Castles,* 93–95
Lancelot, the finest of Arthur's
        knights
    Lehane-*Legends,* 88–99
LAND
    Is much land needed for a
        man?
    King O'Toole and his goose
—ownership claimed by bogle
    Farmer and the bogle
Land monsters
    Cohen-*Every.,* 91–99
Land of promise
    Ross-*Druids,* 109–113

"LAND OF SHADOWS"
 The boy in the Land of
  Shadows
"LAND OF THE DEAD" [a lake]
 The spirit-wife
"LAND OF THE YOUNG"
 Oisin
LAND SPIRITS (subject)
—Icelandic
 Briggs-*Vanish.*, 36–37, 197
"LAND UNDERWAVES"
 The black horse
The land where time stood still
 Shah-*World*, 230–232
Landes, Ruth
 The Windigo personality
The landlord and the muzhik
 Cortes-*Byelorussian*, 137–139
LANDLORDS
 How Ivanka freed muzhiks
  from landlord
 A lesson for the landlord
 Little Claus and Big Claus
 Outwitting the landlord
 The tailor (Mikhei) and the
  shoemaker
—cruel
 Rent-day
Landmarks formed by witches
 Robertson-*Highland*, 100–101
Lang, Andrew, 1844–1912.
 Australian legendary tales
 Dick Whittington and his cat
 The gorgon's head
 Three little pigs [houses: mud,
  cabbage, brick]
 To the friendly reader [1892]
  Lang-*Green*, 390–392
LANG, Andrew (subject)
—The "Colour" fairy books
 Lang-*Blue*, 359–363
—More Australian legendary tales
 Parker-*Austral.*, 10
—On the tales in the "Blue"
  collection
 Lang-*Blue*, 349–358

Langland, William
 Belling the cat
LANGUAGE
 See also ANIMAL-HUMAN
  COMMUNICATION
 Periquito, wood dealer
—creation of man
 The golden man and the finger
  men
—of all living things, understood
 Melampus—physician and
  prophet
The language of animals
 Adams-*Iron*, 62–68
The language of flowers
 Ewart-*Lore*, 153–155
Language of the birds
 Xenophontovna-*Folk*, 66–76
Language-of-animals-understood.
 See ANIMAL-HUMAN
  COMMUNICATION
Lanval and the Lady Triamor
 Phelps-*Maid*, 143–148
LAO TZU
 The great misfortune of Lay
  Tee-Kwai
LAPLAND
 The elf maiden
 How some wild animals be-
  came tame ones
 Little Lapp and the Ice King
 The snow queen
 Stars in the snow
The Lapp genesis, or the first of
  mankind
 Booss-*Scand.*, 332–333
The Lapp in magpie form
 Booss-*Scand.*, 326–327
LARES AND PENATES (subject)
 Briggs-*Vanish.*, 54–55
The large gardens and estates
 Ewart-*Lore*, 3–12
Larkin, David, illus.
 Froud-*Faeries*
LARKS
—talking

LARKS—talking (continued)
  The promise of the three
    sisters
The lark's march [contest]
  O'Sullivan-*Legends*, 41–42
"Lars, my lad!"
  Booss-*Scand.*, 169–179
Lasso de la Vega, Luis
  The virgin of Guadalupe
Last laugh: Heifer and the ox
  Williams-*Aesop*, [18–19]
Last laugh: Working the field
  Shannon-*Solve*, 37–40
The last love of Prince Genji
  Yourcenar-*Oriental*, 53–69
The last of the trows
  Robertson-*Highland*, 26–27
Last sacraments. *See* EXTREME
  UNCTION
The last tiger in Haiti
  Wolkstein-*Magic*, 184–187
LAST WISHES
  The passing of Glooskap
    [whites vs Indians]
LATVIA
  The clever fool
  The vain lord
LAUGHTER
  Glooscap and the wishes
  The golden goose
  Hans, who made the princess
    laugh
  The lad with the goat-skin
  The language of animals
  Lazy Jack (England)
  The Shee and Gannon and the
    Gruagach Gaire
  The stone statue
  The tinkling laugh
  The young lady of Hellerup
—the first laugh
  Why raven isn't perfect
Launcelot, Sir. *See* LANCELOT, Sir
Laundresses. *See* WASHING AND
    WASHERWOMEN
Laurel

Ewart-*Lore*, 133
LAURIN, the Dwarf-King
  Dietrich and the dwarf-king's
    castle
Lauru
  Arrowsmith-*Field*, 173–174
Lavender
  Ewart-*Lore*, 113–114
LAVENDER (flower)
  The little white hen and the
    three fox-cubs
LAWS
  There is righteousness
Lawrence, John, illus.
  Lang-*Blue*
Lawyer and the devil (Ireland)
  Yolen-*Favorite*, 375
LAWYERS
  The baker's magic wand
  Daniel O'Connell [justice,
    cleverness]
—honesty
  Coals on the devil's hearth
    (Ireland)
The lay of Thrym
  Crossley-*Legends*, 62–66
LAY TEE-KWAI
  The great misfortune of Lay
    Tee-Kwai
Lay them straight
  Ainsworth-*Phantom*, 139–156
Lazarus and the dragons
  Crouch-*Whole*, 1–6
Laziest man in America
  Stuchl-*American*, 169–174
LAZINESS
  The astonishing brush
  Baluan: origin of the island
  The birch boy
  Buzz-buzz aunty
  The cuckoo's riches
  An empty head
  The fairy child
  Fall of the spider man
  The flies and the bees
  Genie of the mountains

The idler [a week wasted]
Kildare pooka
The little red hen
The magic almond
Mother Holle
Mother Hulda
Prince Vivien and the Princess
   Placida
Rip Van Winkle
Two lazy brothers [under apple
   tree]
A very happy donkey
A well-deserved punishment
Why blackbird has white eyes
Lazy beauty and her aunts
   Yeats-*Fairy*, 259–263
The lazy ducks
   MacLean-*Cuentos*, 149–150
The lazy husband, Ngurmi. [I]
   Magel-*Gambia*, 116–118
The lazy husband, Ngurmi. [II]
   Magel-*Gambia*, 119–122
Lazy Jack (England)
   Yolen-*Favorite*, 174–175
I he lazy miner
   Lewis-*Bedtime*, 44–45
Lazybones [too lazy to eat]
   Zong-*Korea*, 189
Leach, Maria
   Twist-mouth family
LEADERSHIP
   The dove and the mouse
   The meatballs' leader
The leaf
   Roberts-*Chinese*, 66
Leanan-Sidhe
   Froud-*Faeries*, unp
The leaning silver birch
   Riordan-*Tartary*, 129–130
Lear, Edward, 1812–1888.
   The owl and the pussycat
      [poem]
   Seven families of Lake Pipple-
      Popple
Learning about dragons
   Stallman-*Dragons*, 3–11

Learning about witches
   Stallman-*Witches*, 3–13
Leaning to become a witch
   Robe-*Hispanic*, 228–229
LEATHER
—raw hide
   A boom in guarache leather
LEAVES
   Orphan Yan Ran [Kawa]
—color
   Why leaves on trees are differ-
      ent colors
—manmade
   Jade leaves
—origin of autumn color
   Rainbow and the autumn
      leaves
Leaves that hung but never grew
   Sampson-*Gypsy*, 33–36
Leaving home
   Martin-*Hungry*, 127–135
   Reed-*Aboriginal*, 108–113
Lee, Alan, illus.
   Froud-*Faeries*
LEE RIVER
—origin
   Saint Finbar and the River Lee
The leeching of Kayn's leg
   Jacob-*Celtic*, 255–269
Leekley, Thomas B.
   The giant sturgeon
The leeshy cat
   Manning-*Cats*, 37–50
LEGACIES
   Boots and the beasts
   The story of Bergthor of Blafell
Legal judgments. *See*
   JUDGMENTS
Legend of b'ne Moshe
   Patai-*Gates*, 625–628
The legend of Bodedys
   Keightley-*World*, 115–116
The legend of Eagleman
   Shaw-*Pima*, 20–26
The legend of Knockgrafton
   Froud-*Faeries*, unp

The legend of Knockgrafton
(continued)
Jacobs-*Celtic*, 248–251
A legend of Knockmany
Jacobs-*Celtic*, 102–108
Legend of Lilith [Kabbala]
Patai-*Gates*, 453–469
Legend of marshal Gang Gam-
Czan
Zong-*Korea*, 56–58
Legend of Melusina
Keightley-*World*, 480–486
The legend of Puill dugha Ghaunn
Robertson-*Highland*, 205–208
Legend of the old bell-ringer
Weiss-*Russian*, 185–191
Legend of the roadrunner
Shaw-*Pima*, 95–96
Legend of the Russian priest
Weiss-*Russian*, 201–202
Legend of the Virgin Arang
Zong-*Korea*, 121–123
Legendary Lore
Colombo-*Wind.*, 26
LEGENDS
See also AZTEC LEGENDS;
TALES
The blood stain
LEGENDS (subject)
Lindow-*Swedish*, 25–28, 215
Patai-*Gates*, 787 (index)
Legends of the mill
Booss-*Scand.*, 34–41
LEGGINGS
Old man and the sun
Legions of the night
Lehane-*Wizards*, 75–78
LEGS
The Amadan Mor and the
Gruagach
The nis and the boy
The nisses in Vosborg
—bones
Give me my bone
—broken
The leeching of Kayn's leg

The sky beings
Legs of the kangaroo
Reed-*Aboriginal*, 51–52
LEIB SARAH'S, Arye, 1730–1791.
Patai-*Gates*, 701–711
LEISURE
Grave of a faithful dog
LeJeune, Paul
A sort of werewolf
Veritable werewolves
Leland, Charles G.
How Glooskap found the
summer
LEMMINKAINEN
Life songs in the lands of the
dead
Lemminkainen and Kyllikki
Synge-*Land*, 67–76
Lemminkainen's escape
Synge-*Land*, 140–146
LEMONS AND LEMON TREES
The three lemons
Lending. *See* LOANS
LENT
Chisos ghosts
Leo (the Lion)
Gallant-*Constel.*, 162–167
The leopard
And Every., 1–20
The leopard and the Jinn
Shah-*Afghanistan*, 96–102
Leopard, goat, and yam
Yolen-*Favorite*, 44–45
Leopard, the squirrel, and the
tortoise
Radin-*African*, 117–119
LEOPARDS
The camel, lion, leopard, crow,
& jackal
Fated animal does not see the
hunter
Gazelle and the leopard
How hunter obtained money
from friends . . .
How spider obtained the sky
god's stories (Ashanti)

The princess in the ivory tower
Tortoise, goat and leopard:
corpse has few desires
—a bewitched princess
The leopard and the Jinn
—fooled
Squirrel, leopard, and goat: do
it again, then
—lion cub as prey
Lioness [protects her cub]
LEPERS
Master Tobacco
The star child
Leppa Polkry and the blue cross
Booss-*Scand.,* 564–573
Lepracaun, cluricaun, far darrig
Yeats-*Fairy,* 75–76
Lepracaun; or Fairy shoemaker
[poem]
Yeats-*Fairy,* 77–78
The leprechan
Logan-*Old,* 68–73
The leprechaun in the garden
Keightley-*World,* 376–378
Leprechauns
Arrowsmith-*Field,* 231–236
Froud-*Faeries,* unp
LEPRECHAUNS
Clever Tom and the
leprechauns
Cluricaun
Denizens of faerie
The field of Boliauns
Manachar and the leprechaun
The marvelous shoe-maker
The three leprechauns
The leprechaun's trick
Shub-*Seeing,* 6–33
LePrince de Beaumont, Madame
Marie
Beauty and the beast
Leshiye and Lisunki
Arrowsmith-*Field,* 139–144
Lessing, Doris
Amina Shah's Sufi tales
Shah-*Dervishes,* ix–xiv

A lesson for the landlord
Cortes-*Byelorussian,* 116–123
A lesson from a lovelorn cow
Campos-*Mexican,* 122–126
LESSON-LEARNED
The conceited prince
The hill folk
The word the devil made up
("Unh hunh")
The lessons of heaven and earth
Highwater-*Anpao,* 85–179
Let the fire burn, you cannot put it
out
Weiss-*Russian,* 71–87
LETTERS
Graduation
How the speckled hen got her
speckles
The Mother Goose madman
Origin of Tiis Lake
The story of Jon Asmundsson
LETTUCE
How the rabbit lost his tail
Leviathan: spinner of maelstroms
Water Spirits, 64–65
Levitation. *See* FLYING
LEWIS, Shari (subject)
—Biographical note
Lewis-*Animal,* 48
Lewis-*Bedtime,* 48
Lewis-*Minute,* 48
Li Chi slays the serpent
Roberts-*Chinese,* 129–131
Yolen-*Favorite,* 210–211
Li Ching and the rain god
Roberts-*Chinese,* 25–29
The liar
Sheohmelian-*Three,* 93–94
LIARS
See also FALSE ACCUSA-
TIONS; TALL TALES
Best liar in the land
The blue lake
Generosity of Hatim Tai
The golden finger
Helping to lie

LIARS (continued)
How two brothers improved
their luck
The Indian Cinderella
The iron-eating mice
Keeping the shirttail in
King and the wise man
The mendacious child
Pedro de Urdemalas
The shepherd who cried "wolf"
Sultan's stupid wife and the
jinn-monkey
Truthful John
—contests
Aina-kizz and the black-
bearded bai
King the liar and liar the king
—grow "donkey" ears
The boy who told lies
—lying because of fear
The three imposters
—morality of
How the clever father saved
his sons
—punished
The pigeon with nine heads
LIBERTINES
Men accost a woman who is a
skeleton . . .
Liberty. See FREEDOM
Libor and the swan princess
Wood-*Palace*, 95–110
Libra (the Scales)
Gallant-*Constel.*, 85–87
LICE
[Tyrannical bull with discon-
tented lice]
—origin of charcteristics
Bedbug, the louse, and the
flea
Lies. See FALSE ACCUSATIONS;
FALSEHOOD; LIARS
LIFE
See also IMMORTALITY;
WATER OF LIFE
The castle: a parable

Leaving home
The maid who chose a hus-
band [Ghana]
The water of life
—allegory on transitory
The well of life
—elixir of
Bamboo-cutter and the moon-
child
—from death
Coyote's trip to the Land
Above
—length of
How long will you live?
—not a blessing
The well of everlasting life
—precious
Child in the silk-cotton tree
—restoration of
Llyr: children of the sea-god
—sacred
The banyan deer [the Buddha]
Tumani and his mother's
promise
LIFE EXPECTANCY
Duration of life (Germany)
Life of man [stone vs bamboo
cane]
Wilbert-*Bororo*, 80–81
Life songs in the lands of the dead
Lehane-*Wizards*, 11
LIFE SPAN
Life of man [stone vs bamboo
cane]
Life with the wolves
Stuchl-*American*, 38–40
LIGHT
The cleverest son [task: fill a
room]
The eternal light [Solomon &
Benaiah]
The lure of the marsh lights
Raven lets out the daylight
The treasure in Saby Creek
—golden
Gesar of Ling

LIGHTNING
Hob and the storm
Starkad and Bale
Why dogs sniff each other's
tails
—giants and
The old man from Haberg
—origin
How thunder and lightning
came to be
"LIGHTNING-GOD"
Legend of the roadrunner
LIGHTS
The clever fool
Ua-pa-chi (Kickapoo titles)
—phosphorescent
Will-o'-the-wisp
Liisa and the prince
Booss-*Scand.*, 573–579
LILIE-MOUNTAINS
—tops
The werewolf
LILIES
—golden
Golden lads
LILITH (female demon)
Legend of Lilith [Kabbala]
The lily
Ewart-*Lore*, 88–91
Lily-of-the-valley
Ewart-*Lore*, 95–96
LIMBO
Pedro de Ordimalas
LIME TREES
True and untrue
LIMITATIONS
—trying something one is unfit for
The warlike seven
Linchetti
Arrowsmith-*Field*, 187–189
LINCOLN, Abraham
Footprints on the ceiling
LINDEN TREES
The elf of the rose
The three lemons
LINEN

Boots and the beasts
Lini the lost prince
Stovicek-*Around*, 178–179
Link chains as folk art
McNeil-*Charm*, 187–201
LINNETS
The devoted friend
The lion and the hare
Wood-*Kalila*, 90–101
The lion and the mouse
dePaola-*Favorite*, 32–33
Watson-*Aesop*, 16–17
Lion and the mouse [in verse]
Lewis-*Bedtime*, 16–17
The Lion [Heracles]
Lurie-*Heavenly*, 18–20
Lion in love
Williams-*Aesop*, [22–23]
Lion tamer [Tibetan]
Magic Knife, 28–45
LIONEL, Sir
Quest for the Holy Grail
LIONESS
Hare, the hyena, and the lio-
ness's cave
Lioness and the mouse
Royds-*Animal*, 30–34
Lioness [protects her cub]
Pitcher-*Tokol.*, 27–29
LIONS
Aryeh-Ben-Gadi and Fox-of-
the-Burnt-Tail
The bedbug and the flea
The blue lake
Boots and the beasts
The brave lion and the foolish
rabbit
Brer rabbit rescues his children
El caballero porfiado
Cobbler's son and the ser-
pent
A discerning old 'faki'
The ducks and the fox
The faithful lion
The fisher-prince with the sil-
ver apple

LIONS (continued)
    Flying lion of the Rab of
      Tlemcen
    The golden lion
    Grateful animals and the un-
      grateful man
    Juan de Toluca
    Kalila and Dimna
    The labours of Hercules
    Leo (the Lion)
    The little hare
    Manticore and mermecolion
    Marya Morevna
    The monkey's heart
    The prince who had two eyes
    The quest for the Star of the
      Sea
    Rabbi Samuel Benouaich
      tames a lion
    The son of Tata Juan
      Pescador
    The stone lion [vomits gold]
    Tortoise, goat and lion: the
      price of wisdom
    Wine and the devil
    Young man who was carred
      off by a lion
—as adviser (-or)
    Twelve huntsmen [test of
      femininity]
—asks for child in return for help
    Tumani and his mother's
      promise
—Buddha
    Fearless lion, brave elephant,
      merchant's cries
—killed by beggar
    The beggar, the lion and the
      dog
—prince enchanted
    The wounded lion
—rabbi rides on
    Rabbi Ephraim al-Naqawa
      arrives in Tlemcen
—sorcerer in form of
    How Jiculi served his tribe

—starving
    The camel, lion, leopard, crow,
      & jackal
—tricked by rabbit
    Hare and the lions
Lion's milk: the monster's hairs
    Villa-*Armenian*, 202–210, 478–
      480
The lion's treasured goat
    Magel-*Gambia*, 66–69
Lippo and Tapio
    Booss-*Scand.*, 532–536
LIPS
    Loki makes mischief
LIQUOR
    The pulque vendor tricks the
      devil
    Rip Van Winkle
LIR
    Fate of the children of Lir
    [Swan-children of Lir]
Lir, Aoife, and his children
    Ross-*Druids*, 29–41
Lirpa loof!
    Schwartz-*Tales*, 73–75
Lisalill
    Sperry-*Where*, 49–56
LISUNKI
    Leshiye and Lisunki
LITERACY
    Satan and the boy
Literal-minded: Simpleton of Naples
    Fattoross-*Simpleton*, 1–12
Littke, Lael J.
    The Bantam phantom
Little Annie the goose girl
    Crossley-*Folk*, 75–78
LITTLE BEAR (constellation)
—origin
    Zan and the Dactyls in early
      Crete
[Little bird singing: angel of death]
    Yeats-*Fairy*, 200–202
Little boat that could sail on land
    and sea
    Thomas-*It's*, 83–87

The little boy Chokcho
Nagishkin-*Folktales*, 174–181
Little Brother of the Winds
MacLean-*Cuentos*, 129–132
Little brothers: insects, etc.
Berger-*Animalia* [13–15]
The little bull calf
Garner-*British*, 110–114
Little bull with the golden horns
Thomas-*It's*, 56–61
Little burnt face
De Wit-*Talking*, 34–38
The little cattle
Ransome-*War*, 70–74
The little chicken Kluk and his
companions
Booss-*Scand.*, 500
Little cinder girl
Sampson-*Gypsy*, 77–83
Little Claus and Big Claus
Booss-*Scand.*, 402–410
Little crab and his magic eyes
Macdonald-*Twenty*, 24–34
Little crop-tailed hen
Sampson *Gypsy*, 27 32
Little Daylight
Macdonald-*Wise*, 109–130
Little Elga
Nagishkin-*Folktales*, 137–145
Little Finger of the watermelon patch
Vuong-*Brocaded*, 27–43
The little fir tree
Leete-*Golden*, 80–93
The little fox
Garner-*British*, 86–91
Little Freddy with his fiddle
Booss-*Scand.*, 160–164
Little frog repays coyote
Shaw-*Pima*, 79–81
Little Genius
Sperry-*Where*, 17–30
The little girl on the moon
Stovicek-*Around*, 140
The little girl who wanted every-
thing back
Stovicek-*Around*, 80–81

The little glass shoe
Keightley-*World*, 194–197
The little gnome
Baskin-*Imps*, 26–27
The little goddess
Sadler-*Heaven*, 9–14
Little Goody Two-Shoes
Pierce-*Larousse*, 105–110
The little hare
Lang-*Pink/D*, 321–333
Lang-*Pink/K*, 238–246
Little Ida's flowers
Andersen-*Hague*, 95–105
Little John and his animals
Thomas-*It's*, 3–5
Little Lapp and the Ice King
Sperry-*Where*, 80–94
A little love story
Gorog-*Taste*, 75–88
"LITTLE MAN WITH A BIG
BEARD"
John the Bear
Little Masha and Misha the bear
Riordan-*Russia*, 190–193
The little match girl
Andersen-*Hague*, 113–117
"LITTLE MEN"
Elidore
The little mermaid
Anderson-*Hague*, 132–162
Booss-*Scand.*, 377–393
Stovicek-*Around*, 118–123
The little old man in the tree
Manning-*Spooks*, 95–106
Little old women with five cows
Yolen-*Favorite*, 72–79
Little One-Eye, . . . Two-Eyes,
and . . . Three-Eyes
Lang-*Green*, 301–310
LITTLE PEOPLE
See also MANNIKINS; SPRIG-
GANS; Tom Thumb
Boy-man
Cecino the tiny
Coranieid: Lludd and Llefelys
Date stone; a Han story

LITTLE PEOPLE (continued)
  The doll in the grass
  The duck with red feet
  Hop o' My Thumb
  Huia's dream
  Little Finger of the watermelon
    patch
  The little glass shoe
  Lord Nann and the Korrigans
  Mundig [tiny child]
  Thumbelina
  [Thumbling, three inches tall]
  Tikka the tailor
  Tom Thumb
  The tomts
  Twopence Halfpenny
—Irish
  Guleesh
  Seeing is believing
LITTLE PEOPLE, The (subject)
  Marshall-*Every.*, 38–39, 53
The little porridge pot
  Oxenbury-*Nursery*, 19–24
The little red hen
  dePaola-*Favorite*, 16–19
  Oxenbury-*Nursery*, 65–72
Little Red Riding Hood
  Ehrlich-*Random*, 118–125
  Lang-*Blue*, 51–53 (notes, 356,
    365)
  Mulherin-*Favorite*, 24–29; in-
    trod., 22–23
  Oxenbury-*Nursery*, 58–64
  Perrault-*Glass*, 20–24
  Pierce-*Larousse*, 69—75
  Rackham-*Fairy*, 249–252
  Stovicek-*Around*, 110–111
Little Red Riding Hood [in verse]
  Lewis-*Minute*, 28–29
Little rooster and the Turkish sultan
  Macdonald-*Twenty*, 57–67
Little shepherdess and English
    prince
  Stovicek-*Around*, 126–129
The little shoe
  Keightley-*World*, 382–383

Little Sister Fox and Brother Wolf
  Riordan-*Russia*, 20–22
The little soldier
  Lang-*Green*, 166–187
The little talking animal and the
    shining blue fish
  Stovicek-*Around*, 152–153
Little Thumb
  Lang-*Blue*, 236–247 (notes, 370)
  Mulherin-*Favorite*, 84–93, in-
    trod., 82–83
Little Tuk
  Booss-*Scand.*, 468–472
Little weaver of Duleek Gate
  Yeats-*Fairy*, 372–380
The little white hen and the three
    fox-cubs
  Uttley-*Foxglove*, 44–52
The little white stone
  Manning-*Mervels*, 109–117
"Little Wights." *See* WICHTLEIN
The little wise woman
  Radin-*African*, 168–170
Little Wonder [son-changed-to-dog]
  Manning-*Cats*, 65–74
Little Yellow Bird
  Shaw-*Pima*, 32–35
LITTLEBOOTS, Prince
  Heart of ice [Prince Littleboots]
LIU BEI
  Lord Guan: god of martial arts
Liu Yi and the dragon king
  Sanders-*Dragons*, 53–57
LIVERS
—of livestock & humans eaten by
    fox-girl
  Fox-girl and her brother
The living kuan-yin
  Kendall-*Sweet*, 23–29
Living water. *See* WATER OF LIFE
Liza the fox and Catafay the cat
  Riordan-Russia, 91–95
Lizard and crocodile
  Stokes-*Turtle*, 17–18
The lizard who came from nowhere
  Reed-*Aboriginal*, 24–26

LIZARDS
See also MONITOR LIZARDS
Ant and lizard [origin of enmity]
The elfin hill
Green lizard, gray squirrel and
the eagle
The jaguar and the lizard
[qualities]
—origin of bark lizard
The bark lizard, Walloobahl
—origin of characteristics
The Galah, and Oolah the
lizard
—race with deer
How the lizard got its hat
Ljungby horn and pipe
Booss-Scand., 246–248
Lindow-Swedish, 102–103
Llewellyn and Rhys (condensed)
Briggs-Vanish., 18
La llorona
Robe-Hispanic, 92–98
Lludd and Llefelys
Lochhead-Battle, 91–95
Llyr: children of the sea-god
Shelley-Legends, 51–57
LOADS
The tomte carries a single straw
LOANS
See also BORROWING
Drakestail [and the king]
The Hodja and the cauldron
(Turkey)
How hunter obtained money
from friends . . . [no
repayment]
The sausage
Tortoise and pig: good acts not
always rewarded
—business
Graduation
The lobster and the crab
Lobel-Fables, 8
The Loch Ness monster
Robertson-Highland, 124–126
LOCH NESS MONSTER

Water monsters
Lochman Hehkeem, the great
healer
Villa-Armenian, 426–429
LOCKETS
—gold
Nippy and the Yankee Doodle
LOCKSMITHS
The troll's hammer
LOCOFORTO, Ludivico de
Dance of the esqueletons
Locomotive Bill
Stuchl-American, 243–245
Locust, ant, and the kingfisher
Zong-Korea, 35
LOCUSTS
A Navajo story of creation
—leaves rock in empty shell
Coyote and locust
The lodge of the bear [the Great
Mystery]
Yellow Robe-Tonweya, 24–30
Lodging for the night
Hoke-Spirits, 21–32
Loggers. See LUMBERMEN
Logic
Kendall-Sweet, 21–22
LOGS
—wears down to a toothpick
The toothpick [snowed-in]
LOKI
The apples of eternal life
The apples of Iduna
Balder's doom
The building of the wall of
Asgard
The curse of Andvari's ring
The death of Balder
Fenrir the wolf is bound
The gods' revenge
How they went to Jotunheim
How Thor got his hammer
Ice castle of Utgard-Loke
Singard the dragon-slayer
The stealing of Thor's hammer
Thor in the giant's strong-hold

318

LOKI (continued)
   Thor's holiday
   The walls of Asgard
LOKI (subject)
   Scott-*Fantastic*, 96–99
—Myths and legends of the
   Vikings
   Lindow-*Myths*, 6–14, 18–24
Loki and his evil children
   Branston-*Gods*, 48–51
Loki and the dwarf
   Keightley-*World*, 68–70
Loki makes mischief
   Crossley-*Legends*, 48–56
London, Perceval
   Thurnley Abbey
LONDON, England
   Dick Whittington and his cat
   A most unusual murder
LONDON BRIDGE
   Peddler of Swaffham
   (England)
LONELINESS
   Honpain the star-girl
   The old house
LONELY HEARTS CLUB
   Murder and lonely hearts
"LONERS"
   Who knows?
Long ago when the earth was flat
   Luzzatto-*Long*, 8–19
Long Haired Girl
   Minford-*Fav.*, 148–160
Long, Wide and Hawkeye
   Stovicek-*Around*, 168–171
Longevity. See LIFE—length of;
   OLD AGE
The Longwitton dragon
   Yolen-*Favorite*, 218–220
LONO (god)
   The water of life
Look not at strange women
   Patai-*Gates*, 529–530
Looking is free [State Fair]
   Phillips-*Hoity*, 24–31
LOONS

How Glooskap found the
   summer
   Wasek and the red giants
LOOSESTRIFE
—marsh
   Marsh loosestrife, marsh mar-
   igold, mints
Lord Guan: god of martial arts
   Sanders-*Dragons*, 126–127
Lord Nann and the Korrigans
   Keightley-*World*, 433–438
The Lord of Rosendal
   Booss-*Scand.*, 240–242
Lord of the rings
   Lee-*Castles*, 184–189
LORDS
   How grandpa mowed the
   Lord's meadow
   The vain lord
Lords of the chariot and the spear
   Lehane-*Legends*, 6–33
LORD'S PRAYER
   Death and the doctor
   The fairy's inquiry
   Parson could not say "our
   daily bread"
   The soul-taking angel [Gabriel]
   The three old men
LORD'S SUPPER
   Communion wine in the troll
   food
   Girl at the shieling [elf]
   (Iceland)
   Retrieving the cup
Loss of memory
   Roberts-*Chinese*, 85–86
The loss of the princess
   Nahman-*Tales*, 51–61 [notes:
   53, 285–287]
LOST
   The drovers who lost their feet
   (Mexico)
   Home-bred boy finds lost
   turquoise
   Julie of the wolves
   The ruby ring

The unwilling magician
The lost bell
   Keightley-*World*, 200–204
The lost camel
   Griego-*Cuentos*, 83–85
   Shah-*World*, 216–217
Lost child: Frog and Umdhlubu
   Radin-*African*, 106–112
Lost child: The big shaggy dog
   Stuchl-*American*, 193–195
Lost child: The giant's stairs
   Yeats-*Fairy*, 237–241
The lost horse
   Roberts-*Chinese*, 82
The lost horse [blessings and dis-
   asters as interchangeable]
   Yolen-*Favorite*, 407–408
The lost hum
   Blyton-*My*, 6–12
The lost princess
   Macdonald-*Wise*, 1–108
   Patai-*Gates*, 717–725
   Schwartz-*Elijah*, 210–218
Lost sister
   Radin-*African*, 177–178
The lost treasure
   Booss-*Scand.*, 265
LOST TRIBES OF ISRAEL
   The eternal light [Solomon &
     Benaiah]
LOTION
—perfumed
   The Tibetan envoy's mission
LOTTERY
—for self sacrifice
   The lion and the hare
LOTUS
   The Gojmati
   The magic bamboo
   The marsh king's daughter
Lough Corrib and the Aran Islands
   O'Sullivan-*Legends*, 154
Lough Derg
   O'Sullivan-*Legends*, 148
Loughleagh [lake of healing]
   Yeats-*Fairy*, 185–189, 292

LOUHI (sorceress)
   The forging of the sampo
   The maid of the north
     [Kalevala]
   The mistress of Pohja
   Pestilence, darkness and fire
   The stealing of the sampo
Louhi and Vainamoinen
   Lehane-*Wizards*, 27, 30
LOUISIANA
   Bayou tales [five]
Louse. *See* LICE
LOVE
   See also COURTSHIP; MAR-
     RIAGE; POSSESSIVE-
     NESS; SUITORS
   Adventures of the first dervish
   Anpao and the magic dogs
   Aphrodite, goddess of love
   Bagged wolf
   Beautiful lady whose name
     was Ruth
   Beauty and the beast
   The bird maiden
   Blue bird [King Charming]
   Boy with the deformed head
   The bride of heaven
   The broken swords
   Brown Bear of Norway
   Cap o' Rushes
   The cat's elopement
   Choril and Cholchinay
   Cock with the golden feathers
   Cross purposes
   The cruel painter
   The crystal people
   A dead princess and seven
     giants
   Deirdre
   A discerning old 'faki'
   The enchanted orchard
   Enchanted snake
   Enchanted youth: Osseo and
     Oweenee
   The eternal lovers
   Fabiano and Reyes

LOVE (continued
   Fair Magdelon, or the Knight of
     the Keys
   Finn blood
   The fisherman and his soul
   Glooscap and the wishes
   Grania and Diarmid
   The great hunters [animals]
   Guleesh
   Heavenly maiden and the
     wood cutter
   The herd boy and the dragons
   How panpipes came to be
     played (Miao)
   Immortal mountains [Mongolia]
   The jackal, Mpungutye,
     searches for lost mate
   The king's favorite
   A little love story
   Maid Maleen
   The maiden wiser than the
     Tsar
   The marsh king's daughter
   Menashe and Rachel [children
     in love]
   Miraculous flower [stolen by
     prince of ice]
   The nightingale and the rose
   The Northern Lights
   Popocatepetl and Ixtlaccihuatl
   Prince Featherhead and Prin-
     cess Celandine
   The Prince of Nimroz
   Prince Vivien and the Princess
     Placida
   The prize bull
   The red stream
   Rickety Topknot
   Riquet with the Tuft
   Salt above gold
   The snow queen
   The steadfast tin soldier
   The storytellers
   The swan princess
   Tale of the Princess of
     Damascus

   The test [beggar; love]
   Tests of loyalty and love
   The tinkling laugh
   Tomlin [elf-knight]
   Two mothers [one child]
   The village beneath the water
   The waiting maid's parrot
   The weeping woman: the prin-
     ce and the seamstress
   Witch of secret good deeds
     [unloved = sad]
—affection craved
   The cow who tried to act like a
     kitten
—father asks: how much?
   The old flea-bag
—of God
   Birth, dreaming, death: school-
     master's story
—human and animal
   Tayzanne [fish killed, joined by
     girl who loves him]
—its own reward
   The ostrich in love
—lost
   Diarmuid, son of Donn: a spell-
     shackled devotion
—rejected
   Dance of death
—sacrifice
   A tale of love
—sees all as beautiful
   The serpent prince
—stronger than death
   Dialogue with death
—universal
   The north country wolf
—unrequited
   Butterfly love
LOVE (subject)
—Love stories in folklore
   Yolen-*Favorite,* 67
Love and marriage: superstitions
   Steele-*Ozark,* 85–87
The love of a mother
   O'Sullivan-*Legends,* 42

Love of Credhe for Cael
  Logan-*Old,* 59–62
Love: queen and foundling
  Cortes-*Byelorussian,* 81–86
Lover, Samuel
  Devil's mill
  King and the bishop
    [Clonmacnoise]
  King O'Toole and his goose
  Little weaver of Duleek Gate
  The white trout; a legend of
    Cong
The lovers
  Hyde-Chambers-*Tibet,* 164–
    168
LOVERS
  Aphrodissia, the widow
  Burgher and the pauper
  The dwarfs' banquet
  Fenist the bright-eyed falcon
  Gareth and Linet: Castle
    Perilous
  Girl at the shieling [elf]
    (Iceland)
  A girl in green
  Her lover's heart
  Lai D'Ywenee
  Nightingale and the dove
  The Papa-Water and
    Bibaiyibaiyi
  Rainbow bridge: Buck Ante-
    lope and Evening Breeze
  Rapunzel
  Sacrificed by kin, lover
    brings girl back from be-
    low
  The shepherd and the em-
    peror's daughter
  The snake's lover (Peru)
  Springfield Mountain [song and
    story]
  Tanzara and Dyeer
  Tristram and Isolda
  The waiting maid's parrot
    (China)
  Who was most generous?

Wooden horse [mechanical
    flight]
  The Wooing of Etain
  The yellow dwarf
  Young boy and the dwarf
  —reunited
  The two brothers [fire and
    water]
  —waiting for beloved to return
  A tale of love
LOVIATAR
  Pestilence, darkness and fire
Low hurdles
  Gorog-*Taste,* 59–68
Lox and the chief's wife
  Hill-*More,* 113–119
Lox, the mischief maker
  Wade-*Indian,* 89–93
The loyal dog
  Roberts-*Chinese,* 92–93
LOYALTY
  Buying loyalty
  Candida
  [Gawain and Dame Rag-
    nell]
  The hundredth dove
  Look not at strange women
  The snakeman
  Tests of loyalty and love
  [Loyalty: a social network]
    Seekers Saviors, 65
Lu Ban: the Zhaozhou Bridge
  Magic Knife, 125–132
Luch and the sons of Tuirenn
  Ross-*Druids,* 25–29
Lucifer. *See under* DEVIL(S)
LUCK
  See also GUESSES
  Fees
  The force of luck
  The girl who was already
    queen
  Home-bred boy finds lost
    turquoise
  How two brothers improved
    their luck

LUCK (continued)
- The man who did not believe in luck
- Stars in the snow
- The tomts
- The two hunchbacks (Italy)
—accidental hero
- Brave Bear, Snake, and Crocodile Killer
—bad
- Bolstre Castle
- From bad to good to bad to good
- From bad to worse
- When I first came to this land
- Woe Bogotir
—choice: good luck now or later?
- Shepherd's dream
—good
- Destiny
- From bad to good to bad to good
- The jackdaw
- Luck [and Need; personified]
- Nazar the Brave ["kills a thousand with a single blow"]
- The one who would not listen to his own dream
- The robin
- Seven gods of luck
- The unwilling magician
—good-don't count on it
- Lazy beauty and her aunts
—good fortune changes to bad
- Travels of a fox
—good-naivete; tragic
- The doll's house
—good-talking bird
- The jackdaw
LUCK (subject)
—fairies bringing
- Briggs-Vanish., 217 (index)
Luck [and Need; personified]
- Manning-Marvels, 30–36
"LUCK BALLS"
- How ole woodpecker got ole rabbit's conjure bag
Luck in a strange place
- Chalk-Tales, unp.
The luck of Eden Hall
- Keightley-World, 292–293
LUCKY OBJECTS
- The boy who wore turtle shell moccasins
Ludwig and Iskander
- Villa-Armenian, 293–296, 509–511
LUGH
- Gods of the pagan Celts
LUGOSI, Bella
- Mummies, zombies, and artificial men
- Werewolves
LUMBERMEN
- Paul Bunyan, the giant logger
- Red-headed Windego
The lure of the marsh lights
- Haining-Lepre., 107–111
Lure of the pipes [Big John Clachna-Harnich and Black Simon]
- Robertson-Highland, 196–200
The Lurikeen and Bridget
- Yolen-Favorite, 342–343
LUSIGNON, Counts of (subject)
- Briggs-Vanish., 73–74, 147–148
LUST
- The archer who went I know not where to . . .
- Asceticism now, nymphs later!
- Genjias [three with same name]
- Pilar's indiscretion
- Ursulo, hijo del oso
- The vengeance of Oiwa
The lute player
- Phelps-Tatterhood, 103–108
LUTES
- The fox who went to heaven
- The tinkling laugh

Lutey and the mermaid
  Froud-*Faeries*, unp
Lutey and the mermaid
  (condensed)
  Briggs-*Vanish.*, 72
Lutins
  Arrowsmith-*Field*, 128–132
LUXURY
  Sun tribute
LUZ
  The city of Luz [blue dye:
    Tekhelet]
LYCAEON, King of Arcadia
  Werewolves
Lycanthropy. *See* WEREWOLVES
LYDE, Robert
  God on our side
Lying. *See* LIARS
Lynching a witch [folk-hysteria]
  Marshall-*Every.*, 207–212
LYNXES
  Adventures of Ntini, the small
    otter
  Skinkoots steals the springtime
Lyra (the Lyre)
  Gallant-*Constel.*, 58–62
LYRES
  Artemis and Apollo
  Hermes, the messenger of the
    gods
  Lyra (the Lyre)
  The white doe
Lyulph's tower: Lady Greystoke
  Marshall-*Every.*, 170–174

Ma Chung-hsi
  The north country wolf
Mabinogion (condensed)
  Briggs-*Vanish.*, 12–14, 77
The Mabinogion: four branches
  Ross-*Druids*, 65–81
The MacCrimmons of Skye

Robertson-*Highland*, 6–7
MACDONALD, George (subject)
  Macdonald-*Golden*, ix–x
  Macdonald-*Gray*, ix–x
  Macdonald-*Wise*, ix–x
MACE, George
  Phantom coach
MacGovern of Giangevlin; Ighne
  Logan-*Old*, 93–96
Macha's curse
  Ross-*Druids*, 41–43
Mac Iain Direach
  Ratcliff-*Scottish*, 73–83
MACK, Stan, illus. (subject)
  —Biographical note
  Wahl-*Needle*, 56
Maclintock, Letitia
  Jamie Freel and the young lady
Macmillan, Cyrus
  The Indian Cinderella
MACPHERSON, John
  The Black Officer of
    Ballachroan
"MAD GASSER OF MATOON"
  Assorted monsters
Madame rhinoceros and her dress
  Lobel-*Fables*, 26–27
Madness. *See* INSANITY
MADOR, Sir
  Elaine the Fair Maid of Astolat
La madrina muerte
  Aiken-*Mexican*, 76–78
MAEVE, Queen
  Cuchulain's death
Maeve of Connacht
  Lehane-*Legends*, 22–33
MAFU (giant)
  Maui, son of the sun
Magani people: The drum of
  Timpenni
  Stokes-*Turtle*, 136–137
MAGDALENES (islands)
  Mermaid of the Magdalenes
MAGI, THREE
  Baboushka, the Wise Men and
    the Prince of Peace

324

Magic
   Robe-*Hispanic,* 434–454
MAGIC
   See also ENCHANTMENT;
     MAGICIANS; TRANSFOR-
     MATIONS; WITCHES;
     WIZARDS
   See also magical objects:
     RINGS; *etc.*
   The Amadan Mor and the
     Gruagach
   Antti and the wizard's
     prophecy
   The apples of Iduna
   The astonishing brush
   "Binding" and driving off a
     sjora
   The birch boy
   The black horse
   The brook's secret
   Bubbly's trick
   Catherine's fate
   La cenicienta huasteca
   Choril and Cholchinay
   The conjure wives
   The creatures of magic
   The disrespectful son
   The elves' dance
   Finn blood
   The frog
   Glooskap and the giant's frolic
   The golden mountain
   Hagop's wish
   How ole woodpecker got ole
     rabbit's conjure bag
   In the beginning
   Jorinde and Joringel
   Juan de Toluca
   The juniper tree
   Jurma and the sea god
   The kindly ghost [Joseph and
     his brothers]
   King David and the giant
   Leppa Polkry and the blue
     cross
   Liisa and the prince

   Lippo and Tapio
   Mossycoat
   The mouse bride
   Only One, the great shaman
   Pix! Pax! Pox!
   The priest of Hardwork
     mountains
   Queen Pig
   Rabbi Haim Pinto revives the
     dead
   Sedna the sea goddess
   Severi and Vappu
   Something for nothin (a Hui
     story)
   The story-teller at fault
   The strong man
   Susie and her shadow
   Teigneux
   The three wishes
   Thunderbird
   Turkey Brother and the magic
     panther suit
   Una the elfwoman
   Under the wing of magic
   Vaino and the swan princess
   The weathermaker
   Welsh enchanter's fosterling
   White lotus magic
   The wicked stepmother
   Wiley and the hairy man
   Winkle the witch
   The wonderful lamp [Aladdin]
   The wooing of Seppo
     Hmarinen
—black
   Dance of the esqueletons
   Jack of Sjoholm and the Gan-
     Finn
—makes path in sea
   The woman from the sea
—power
   The skilful brothers
–power shared by gods & hermits
   Why the gibbon says "pua"
—sorcerer vs rabbi
   Magic mirror of Rabbi Adam

—wishes fulfilled
   Omelya and the pike
MAGIC
—[Borders of space and time]
   Lehane-*Wizards*, 12
—[healing, horseshoes, devil]
   McKee-*Scottish*, 27–30
—Motif index
   Wilbert-*Bororo*, 301–302
The magic almond
   Stovicek-*Around*, 40–41
The magic bag
   Shah-*World*, 108–109
   Stovicek-*Around*, 106–107
The magic bamboo
   Hyde-Chambers-*Tibet*, 123–143
Magic bird [tells stories]
   Minford-*Fav.*, 67–73
The magic bird-heart
   Villa-*Armenian*, 137–145, 456–458
Magic birds and enchanted animals
   Ross-*Druids*, 104–116
The magic boat
   Jagendorf-*Magic*, 21–31
The magic bonnet
   Sheohmelian-*Three*, 88–92
The magic bow
   Villa-*Armenian*, 217–223, 483–484
Magic brush; a Han folktale
   Sadler-*Treasure*, 48–59
The magic candelabra
   Stovicek-*Around*, 174–177
The magic cap
   Zong-*Korea*, 152–154
Magic carpet: on the wings of wishes
   Spells & Bind, 18–19
Magic carpet. See CARPETS
The magic coconuts
   Stokes-*Turtle*, 77–81
Magic figs
   Villa-*Armenian*, 145–153, 458–460

Magic flute of Asmodeus
   Schwartz-*Elijah*, 94–101
Magic [fourteen legends]
   Robe-*Hispanic*, 434–449
The magic fox
   Macdonald-*Twenty*, 147–180
The magic fruit
   Stovicek-*Around*, 154–155
The magic gifts [dwarf-sorcerer]
   Segovia-*Spanish*, 53–96
The magic horn [flying carriage]
   Lindow-*Swedish*, 168–169
The magic horse
   Villa-*Armenian*, 153–159, 460–466
Magic knife [Uygur]
   Magic Knife, 88–124
Magic mallet
   Seros-*Sun*, 38–45
The magic mirror
   Crouch-*Whole*, 143–151
The magic mirror of Rabbi Adam
   Schwartz-*Elijah*, 187–195
Magic mirror of Rabbi Adam
   Yolen-*Favorite*, 276–282
Magic moccasins: the Wearer of the Ball
   Wade-*Indian*, 67–81
Magic moneybag
   Minford-*Fav.*, 143–147
The magic of the katsinas
   Dutton-*Hopi*, 24–26
The magic of the moon
   Highwater-*Anpao*, 23–43
The magic orange tree [child abuse]
   Wolkstein-*Magic*, 14–21
The magic pear tree
   Roberts-*Chinese*, 51–52
   Sadler-*Heaven*, 26–30
   Yolen-*Favorite*, 286–287
The magic people
   Haining-*Lepre.*, 18–19
Magic plants and waters [condensed]
   Mckee-*Scottish*, 30–31

Magic pumpkins
  Seros-*Sun*, 52–61
The magic rattle
  Stovicek-*Around*, 28–29
The magic ring
  Villa-*Armenian*, 193–197, 473–
  477
Magic ring of Rabbi Israel Hacohen
  Elaz-*Folktales*, 133
The magic shawl and the en-
  chanted trumpet
  Shah-*Afghanistan*, 60–67
The magic snowshoes
  De Wit-*Talking*, 192–197
  Hill-*More*, 150–157
Magic spells. *See*
  ENCHANTMENT;
  TRANSFORMATIONS
The magic turtle [grows/shrinks
  inches each day]
  Schwartz-*Tales*, 5–7
The magician and the bananas
  Watson-*Thailand*, 29–31
The magician earl
  Haining-*Lepre.*, 48–53
MAGICIANS
  Aladdin and the wonderful
  lamp
  El caballero porfiado
  The cat in the sea
  Changeling [exposed with help
  of magician]
  Conflict of the magicians
  The crimson parrot
  Gesar of Ling
  Headman and the magician
  Julio
  Prince Feroz-Shah and the fly-
  ing horse
  Rival magicians
  The star child
  The story of Deirdre
  The ten plagues of Egypt
  The woodpecker
—evil
  The bird maiden

  Caliph Stork
  King Kojata
—Grumedan
  Prince Narcissus and the Prin-
  cess Potentilla
The magician's pupil
  Booss-*Scand.*, 485–488
MAGISTRATES
  A stroke of luck
Magnolia
  Ewart-*Lore*, 74–76
Magnusson, Magnus, and Herman
  Palsson
  The burning of Bergthorsknoll
MAGPIES
  Gooloo the magpie, and the
  Wahroogah
  How Saynday got the sun
  The Lapp in magpie form
  Phoenix fairy flower [Han]
  Sky high went the sun
  Sky-raising magpies
—yelling; cause
  The hare and the magpie
The maguey fence and the rich
  ranchero
  Campos-*Mexican*, 24–27
Mahan, Benton, illus.
  Lewis-*Minute*
Mahosoth [Buddha as wise man]
  Watson-*Thailand*, 4
Maid Maleen
  Lurie-*Clever*, 57–65
Maid of the mill
  Sampson-*Gypsy*, 102–108
The maid of the north [Kalevala]
  Phelps-*Maid*, 1–24
Maid Vae
  Keightley-*World*, 89–90
The maid who chose a husband
  [Ghana]
  Riordan-*Woman*, 53–58
Maiden Bright-Eye
  Lang-*Pink/D*, 289–296
  Lang-*Pink/K*, 206, 212
The maiden made of fire

Yolen-*Hundredth*, 11–17
The maiden wiser than the Tsar
Shah-*World*, 50–52
MAIDENS
Kertong
The serpent-slayer
Maidens (condensed)
Briggs-*Vanish.*, 172–173
Maidens in a mirror
Stovicek-*Around*, 200–203
Maiden's silky winding sheet
Spells & Bind, 44–45
Mail-carriers. *See* POSTMEN
Mair, Charles
A cannibal spirit
Maize. *See* CORN
Majantali Sarkar
Raychaudhuri-*Stupid*, 72–76
The making of the worlds
Crossley-*Legends*, 25–35
Malcolmson, Anne B., and Dell J.
McCormick
Stormalong fights the Kraken
MALIAGAUNT, Sir
Lancelot and Guenevere
Malicious cats
Piggott-*Japanese*, 117–118
MALINALXOCHITL
Copil's heart
The mallet of wealth
Zong-*Korea*, 143–145
MALLETS
Magic mallet
The three sillies [imagined future evils]
Mally Whuppy [sic]
Garner-*British*, 25–31
MALSUM (brother of Gluscap)
Glooskap and Malsum, the wolf
[Glooskap] Gluscap, lord of the north
Mambu the orphan [tyrants' tribute]
Nagishkin-*Folktales*, 182–192
Mammy Yoko: The king's rival
Robinson-*Three*, 33–47

Mamuiauguexeba
Wilbert-*Bororo*, 223
MAN [the human race: mankind]
See also CREATION; RACES
OF MAN; WOMEN
Calabash child [born to First Woman]
Early man
Gift from a star
Life of man [stone vs bamboo cane]
The strongest in the world
Vugiswe: first human child
Who is the mightiest in the world?
Why chief of smiths was unable to create human being
Zeus and the creation of man
—"faithless and dangerous animal"
The tiger and the man
—first
Coyote and his bow
—life expectancy
Duration of life (Germany)
—made from dough; given soul
Nature's ways
—origin
Cosmogony and the origin of man [18 narratives]
Cranes of the Greak Lakes
Creation of the Mayas
Creation story [Pima]
Good and evil: Buri vs Ymir
Jocoramodogueddu [primeval monkey creates races]
A Navajo story of creation
Raven and the first men
—origin of size of
Boy of great strength and the giants
—superior to animals
"Pap God first, man next, tiger last"
MAN (subject)
—origin-Gods from the dawn of time
Sanders-*Dragons*, 13–17

Man and beast
  Roberts-*Chinese*, 121
Man and the snake
  Radin-*African*, 150–152
Man and woman with too many
  children
  Sampson-*Gypsy*, 89–92
Man beasts in wolf-land
  Haining-*Lepre.*, 113–117
Man doomed to die; cow doomed
  to slaughter-house
  Elbaz-*Folktales*, 36
Man eaters
  Colombo-*Wind.*, 10–12
The man from P.I.G.
  Asimov-*Fant.*, 76–105
The man from the grave
  Haining-*Lepre.*, 102–105
The man in the moon
  O'Sullivan-*Legends*, 47
Man into possum [solitary fish thief]
  Reed-*Aboriginal*, 44–47
[Man must praise his maker]
  Nicholson-*Mexican*, 65–66
A man named Weendigo
  Colombo-*Wind.*, 201–203
"MAN OF THE MOUNT"
  Toller's neighbors
Man or beast
  Roberts-*Chinese*, 122–124
"Man overboard"
  Hoke-*Demonic*, 107–110
Man, the burro, and the dog
  Griego-*Cuentos*, 25–27
The man turned into a mule
  Shah-*World*, 233–234
The man/whale
  Booss-*Scand.*, 609–613
The man who buried his money
  Lewis-*Bedtime*, 22–23
The man who couldn't catch a
  ghost
  Roberts-*Chinese*, 173
The man who did not believe in
  luck
  Mitchnik-*Egyptian*, 28–31
The man who didn't notice women
  Amore-*Lustful*, 169–170
The man who drowned in a
  washbasin
  Lindow-*Swedish*, 64
The man who had no story
  Yolen-*Favorite*, 20–23
The man who knew how to divide a
  chicken
  Sheohmelian-*Three*, 1–3
The man who knew the language
  of animals
  Griego-*Cuentos*, 63–75
The man who loved the Nereids
  Yourcenar-*Oriental*, 71–83
The man who never knew fear
  Yeats-*Fairy*, 344–349
The man who never swore
  Patai-*Gates*, 527–529
The man who sat on the tide
  Robinson-*Raven*, 87–100
The man who sold his goat
  Kudian-*More*, 25–30
The man who wanted to bury his
  son
  Zong-*Korea*, 43–44
The man who was going to mind
  the house
  Booss-*Scand.*, 3–4
The man who wouldn't be king
  Amore-*Lustful*, 88
The man with no heart in his body
  Lang-*Pink/K*, 147–153
The man with the wen
  Shah-*World*, 146–149
Man without a heart
  Lang-*Pink/D*, 200–208
MANABOZHO (subject)
  De Wit-*Talking*, 25–26
Manabozho and how the diver
  [duck] got a flat back
  Wade-*Indian*, 171–174
Manabozho and the squirrels
  Wade-*Indian*, 179–181
Manabozho's fishing: the king of
  fishes

Wade-*Indian*, 175–178
Ma'nabus [earth god brings fire]
  Jagendorf-*First,* 17–21
Manachar and the leprechaun
  Smith-*Manachar*, 43–63
Manam Island and the Sepik River
  Stokes-*Turtle*, 84–85
Mananan Mac Lir and Cormac Mac
  Art
  Lehane-*Wizards*, 30–34
MANAWYDDAN
  [Dyfed: under spell . . . Faerie]
Manawyddan, son of Llyr
  Ross-*Druids,* 72–76
  Thomas-*Mabinogion*, 45–62
Manawyddan's castle of skulls
  Lee-*Castles*, 56–57
Mandarin ducks
  Piggott-*Japanese,* 112–114
MANDARINS
  The young head of the family
Mandrake
  Ewart-*Lore*, 137
Mandrake: snaring an earthbound
  demon
  Lehane-*Wizards*, 108
MANDRAKES
  Greek thoughts
Man-Eagle conquered by youth
  Mullett-*Spider*, 78–89
MANGO TREES AND MANGOES
  The bushbabies
  Golden stick, silver stick
  The roots of jealousy
MANGROVE TREES
  The crocodile's tail
MANHOOD
  The story of trembling hood
MANIKINS
  Rumpelstiltskin
MANITOUS (spirits)
  Grasshopper [Indian
    superman]
Manka and the judge
  Lurie-*Clever*, 9–16
MANKIND

—first
  The Lapp genesis, or the first
  of mankind
MANNANAN
  The Isle of Man
MANNANON, Son of Lir (subject)
  Briggs-*Vanish.,* 22–23, 32,
  197
Manners. *See* COURTESY
MANNIKINS
  Changeling [exposed with help
  of magician]
  The hill folk
  Toller's neighbors
Manora, the bird woman
  Toth, *Tales,* 106–115
Man's best friend
  Hoke-*Horrors*, 133–141
The man-servant and the water-
  elves
  Boss-*Scand.*, 624–625
A mansion in heaven
  Amore-*Lustful*, 120–122
MANSIONS
  Ebbe Skamelson
  The young man who refused
  to kill
MANSLAUGHTER
  The piece of straw
Manson, Beverlie, illus.
  Leete-*Golden*
Manstin, the rabbit
  Zitkala-*Old,* 145–155
Manticore and mermecolion
  Magical Beasts, 90–91
Mantis and the All-Devourer
  Radin-*African,* 93–99
The mantis and the moon
  Poland-*Mantis,* 1–5
Mantis creates an eland
  Radin-*African*, 81–84
MANTLES
  The horned woman
Manyi's escape [wife eaten by
  mistake]
  Todd-*Tortoise*, 73–75

MAORIS
  Maui and the islands
  Peodorus Jack
MAPLE TREES
  The red stream
MARA (temptress)
  Enlightenment
  The merchant's walk
March cock banishes the devil
  O'Sullivan-*Legends,* 29–31
MARDUK
  The Dragon [Marduk and
    Tiamat]
Mares. *See* HORSES–mares
MARIA de Agreda, Sr.
  Eagle Woman comes to The
    People
Maria de Atocha: Help for a mule
    caravan
  Campos-*Mexican,* 66–68
Maria Morevna. *See also* MARYA
    MOREVNA
  Phelps-*Maid,* 107–118
  Zvorykin-*Firebird,* 29–47
Marietta's choice
  McCarty-*Skull,* 35–39
Marigold
  Ewart-*Lore,* 150–151
MARIGOLDS
  Marsh loosestrife, marsh mar-
    igold, mints
Marital quarrels. *See*
    QUARRELING
Marjatt
  Synge-*Land,* 217–222
MARK, King of Cornwall
  Sir Tristram and La Belle
    Isolde
  Tristram and Isolda
MARKETS
  Tyndal goes to market
  Zamani goes to market
MARKO KRALJEVIC
  The end of Marko Kraljevic
Marko's [Kraljevic] smile
  Yourcenar-*Oriental,* 21–34

MARKSMANSHIP
  The sure shot
  The tiger and the dwarf
  Zilyan
MAROONED
  Herman the milk bottle
Marrano question: Judaism kept
    secret
  Nahman-*Tales,* 95–103
MARRIAGE
  See also ADULTERY; BE-
    TROTHAL; FIDELITY; HUS-
    BANDS; MATE
    SELECTION; REMAR-
    RIAGE; WEDDINGS;
    WIVES
  Beautiful lady whose name
    was Ruth
  Benten, bringer of happiness
  The butcher's bills
  The costly ring
  The country of the beautiful
    gardens
  Drolmakyid the fairy [Tibetan]
  The fairy grotto
  The fern girl
  Handsome ogre-girl of the pool
  The Jerusalemite's story cop-
    ied by R. Abraham
  The juniper bush
  Just married
  King Thrushbeard
  The laird's lass and the
    gobha's son
  Lake Inchiquin [bring no
    O'Briens home]
  Little old women with five cows
  The maid who chose a hus-
    band [Ghana]
  Pierre, Prince of Murom
  The poet and the peony
  Prince White Hog
  The tale of Looseghen
  The ugly son
  Underworld god of marriage
  Woman in the moon

—animal-human
  Angakok and Mother of Seals
    [sea petrel]
  The bear husband
  Bear Mother and her husband
  The bear mother [human] and
    father
  The dog's fiancee [jinn]
  East o' sun and west o' the
    moon
  The gift of the white cockatoo
  The girl with the large eyes
  The great flood; Jokurugwa or
    Meriri Poro [Bororo]
  The handsome suitor [A]
  Knight of the Glens and Bens
    and Passes
  Panhu, the marvellous dog
  Rising Star finds a wife [dog]
    [Tewa]
  The silkworm [origin: marriage
    of horse & maid]
  The snake bridegroom
  The squirrel wife
  The toad-bridegroom
  The turtle wife
  Ursulo, hijo del oso
—devil sewing discord in
  The old crone who was more
    wily than Iblees
—duck and rat (tribes)
  The platypus Gayardaree
—fidelity
  Look not at strange women
  The master and the serving
    maid
  See also INFIDELITY
—forced
  Girl at the shieling [elf]
    (Iceland)
  Papaya [origin]
  The seven-headed beast
  Thumbelina
—human and an immortal
  Urashima the fisherman
    (Japan)

—husband loses spirit-wife
  Spirit of the Van
—intracaste customs
  The courtship of Yasin
—man and mermaid
  Lady of Gollerus
—mortal and dragon princess
  Liu Yi and the dragon king
—mortal and fairy
  Huldbrand and Undine: a
    doomed alliance . . .
  Prince who married a Peri
—mortal and goddess
  The crane maiden
  The herd boy and the weaving
    girl
—mortal and heavenly maid
  The faithful son, Dong Yong
—mortal & supernatural
  The sultan and the ogress
—peace; devil promotes violence
  The devil and the female
—promises broken
  Lemminkainen and Kyllikki
—rabbi saves
  For domestic peace
—remarriage
  Finist the Falcon
—successful
  Husband and wife should
    share equally
—three sons of tsar
  The frog princess
—traditions not followed
  The young man and the talking
    skull
—waiting for
  Sleeping Beauty in the woods
—who wears the pants
  The man who knew the lan-
    guage of animals
MARRIAGE (subject)
  Zong-*Korea,* 251 (index)
MARRIAGE CUSTOMS
  Gushtap and the princess of
    Roum

MARRIAGE CUSTOMS (continued)
How Kwaku Ananse got Aso in
marriage
Kelfala's secret something
The tall maiden, Untombinde
Why a girl should marry him to
whom she is given
Wonder-worker of the plains
—ask the father
The hemp smoker, Zimwa-
mbanje
Marriage customs among Missouri
Low Germans
McNeil-*Charm*, 159–168
Marriage of Sir Gawaine
Marshall-*Every.*, 375–384
Marriage of two masters of Wolof.
[A]
Magel-*Gambia*, 163–167
Marriage of two masters of Wolof.
[B]
Magel-*Gambia*, 168–171
Marriages are made in heaven
Elbaz-*Folktales*, 71–72
Marriott, Alice
How Saynday got the sun
Marsh, Joyce
Tomorrow's child
MARSH GAS
—origin
Wicked John and the devil
The marsh king's daughter
Booss-*Scand.*, 426–454
Marsh loosestrife, marsh marigold,
mints
Ewart-*Lore*, 157–158
MARSH WOMEN
The girl who trod on the loaf
MARTENS
Mouse Woman and the mon-
ster killer whale
Nanasimgat [wife abducted by
killer whale]
—origin of "sables"
Heart of ice [Prince Littleboots]
Martha and Mary

Weiss-*Russian*, 197–200
MARTIAL ARTS
Lord Guan: god of martial arts
Martin, Frances
In the beginning
Raven lets out the daylight
MARTIN, Saint
Saint Martin's Eve [a]
Saint Martin's Eve [b]
MARTINEZ, Chico
El caballo negro muy
magnifico
Martyrdom of Solika Hatsadika
Elbaz-*Folktales*, 99–101, 156–
162
MARTYRS
England's first martyr
Marvelous creatures [motif index]
Wilbert-*Bororo*, 252–254
The marvelous shoe-maker
Haining-*Lepre.*, 71–75
MARY, Virgin
A boy and his dog
The devil in guise of the
Blessed Virgin
The love of a mother
Our-Lady-of-the-Swallows
The plague of Moscow
[Varvarka]
The virgin of Guadalupe
The woman in blue
Marya Morevna
Bilibin-*Russian*, 37–50
Phelps-*Maid*, 107–118
Riordan-*Russia*, 148–160
Zvorykin-*Firebird*, 29–47
Mary's little lamb: further adven-
tures [verse]
Lewis-*Animal*, 14–15
MASAUWUH (god of death)
Tiyo rejoins his clan
The youth who brought the
corn
The mask that wore the man
Roberts-*Jung*, 34–41
MASKS

—devil
A boom in guarache leather
MASON-WASPS
How the mason-wasp fetched
fire from god
MASONS
The walls of Asgard
Masquerading trickster
Anderson-*Trick.*, 72–75
Mass. *See under* CATHOLICISM
Mass murder. *See under* MURDER
MASSACRES
Sturt's desert pea, the blood
flower
Massarioli
Arrowsmith-*Field*, 267–269
The mast of sand ["impossible"
task]
Zong-*Korea*, 77–78
Master and man
Yeats-*Fairy*, 79–84
Master and pupil
Lang-*Pink/D*, 220–222
Lang-*Pink/K*, 163–165
The master and the serving maid
Roberts-*Chinese*, 137–139
The master and the worker
Sheohmelian-*Three*, 60–65
The master cat. *See* Puss in Boots
Master Frog
Vuong-*Brocaded*, 65–82
Master James' nightmare
Shepard-*Conjure*, 43–58
Master Log
Bierhorst-*Hungry*, 52–55, 137
Master of all masters
dePaola-*Favorite*, 84–85
The master of prayer
Nahman-*Tales*, 211–250
[notes: 213, 317–319]
The master of Ugerup
Booss-*Scand.*, 242–244
The master pupil
Stovicek-*Around*, 34–35
Master rabbit [tries to do what oth-
er species do]

Wade-*Indian*, 59–65
Master tailor
Lofgren-*Boy*, 25–28
The master thief
Thomas-*It's*, 181–185
Wolkstein-*Magic*, 136–141
Yolen-*Favorite*, 138–144
Master Tobacco
Booss-*Scand.*, 141–144
The mastermaid
Lang-*Blue*, 130–147 (notes,
350, 367)
Lurie-*Clever*, 35–44
Phelps-*Tatterhood*, 149–155
Shah-*World*, 34–44
Masters of forbidden arts
Lehane-*Wizards*, 56–87
MATCHMAN, Gervase
Truth, and murder, will out
MATCHES
February dragon
The flying trunk
The little match girl
Sally Simple's matches
Matching wits [two robbers have
same wife]
Villa-*Armenian*, 383–388
MATCHMAKERS
Ivan Byelarasseiski
Rubizal and the miller's
daughter
The waiting maid's parrot
(China)
MATE SELECTION
Samba's wife
—advice to women
Donkeys of Jolof
MATH (person)
Welsh enchanter's fosterling
Math, son of Mathonwy
Ross-*Druids*, 77–81
Thomas-*Mabinogion*, 63–85
MATHEMATICS
—puzzles
Dividing the horses
Fishing [two fathers, two sons]

MATHEMATICS—puzzles
(continued)
Getting older and older faster
and faster
Stories to solve; 14 folktales
Matheson, Richard Christian
Graduation
Mathey Trewella
Marshall-*Every.*, 344–348
MATS
—magic animal
Tomik and the magic mat
MATTRESSES
The real princess
T'ien the brave, hero of the
Hsia River
MATTSSON, Sten
The devil as the fourth wheel
Matupit: The tumarang's revenge
Stokes-*Turtle,* 88–90
Maugham, Somerset
Her lover's heart
MAUI
Maui and the islands
MAUI (subject)
—Alapa regiment
Westervelt-*Hawaiian,* 125–142
Maui and the islands
Heslewood-*Tales,* 116–121
Maui seeking immortality
Westervelt-*Hawaiian,* 19–23
Maui slows down the sun
Hadley-*Legends,* 20–21
Maui, son of the sun
Wright-*Pigeon,* 18–22
Maui the Polynesian
Westervelt-*Hawaiian,* 13–18
Maupassant, Guy de
Who knows?
The Mauritanian and his wealth
Magel-*Gambia,* 126–127
MAXIMS
—never leave the old for the new
Andrew and King Solomon [in
2 parts]
MAY BASKETS
Death out of season
MAY DAY
Oisin
MAY DAY EVE
Death out of season
Maya parallels with the Nahua
gods
Nicholson-*Mexican,* 123–131
The Mayamah: enemies turned to
stones
Parker-*Australian,* 50
Mayas. *See under* INDIANS OF
LATIN AMERICA (tribes)
MAYBUGS
Thumbelina
MAYORS
The pied piper of Hamelin
She was good for nothing
MAYPOLES
The dance of the spectres
The maze, or Se-eh-ha's house
Shaw-*Pima,* 15–16
The Mazik-ass
Keightley-*World,* 510–511
MAZIKEEEN
The Mazik-ass
McCaffrey, Ann
The smallest dragonboy
McCormick, Dell J., jt. auth.
Stormalong fights the Kraken
The McDonnell headstone
O'Sullivan-*Legends,* 123
ME (Sumerian attributes) (subject)
Wolkstein-*Inanna,* 224 (index)
MEADOWS
How grandpa mowed the
Lord's meadow
—enchanted
The herd boy and the dragons
Meadows and pastures
Ewart-*Lore,* 102–109
MEALS
The cat and his visions
—tricked peasant eats his own
wife
Slaying of the Tanuki

Appearance of the spirits Meri
and Ari
Death and revival of Meri
First death of Ari and his
resurrection
Heron gives Meri power over
the night
Meri and Ari ascend to the sky
Wilbert-*Bororo*, 43–46
Meri and Ari, sun and moon: death
of Meri
Wilbert-*Bororo*, 30–32
Meri and Ari take revenge
Wilbert-*Bororo*, 32–34
Meri and the woodpeckers
Wilbert-*Bororo*, 159–160
Meri avenges his brother Ari
Wilbert-*Bororo*, 36–38
Meri improves beaks of birds &
gives Bororo teeth
Wilbert-*Bororo*, 155–157
Meri seizes the Iakomea ornament
Wilbert-*Bororo*, 160–161
Meri steals a bow
Wilbert-*Bororo*, 157–158
Meri steals an ax
Wilbert-*Bororo*, 158–159
Meri takes a rig from his brother Ari
Wilbert-*Bororo*, 41–42
Meri, the creator-traveler
Wilbert-*Bororo*, 56
Merirodo and her husband Kuieje
Kuri
Wilbert-*Bororo*, 102–106
MERIT
The Buddhist Job
—transferred to ghost
The woman who cursed
herself
MERLIN
The castle and the dragons
Childe Rowland
The coming of Arthur
Coming of King Arthur
The Round Table
Sir Lancelot of the Lake

The sword in the stone
Tom Thumb
Vivien: the lady of the lake
Merlin and Britanny
Lehane-*Wizards*, 34–39
Merlin and the Tower of Air
Lee-*Castles*, 106–107
The mermaid and the Lord of
Colonsay
Robertson-*Highland*, 161–164
The mermaid of Cromarty Firth
Robertson-*Highland*, 153–155
The mermaid of Duncansby
Robertson-*Highland*, 157–158
The mermaid of Kessock
Robertson-*Highland*, 156–157
The mermaid of Mackay
Robertson-*Highland*, 151–153
Mermaid of the Magdalenes
Macmillan-*Canadian*, 20–23
[Mermaid rewards Cornishman with
magic powers]
Water Spirits, 6–11
The mermaid wife
Keightley-*World*, 169–171
Mermaids
Froud-*Faeries*, unp
MERMAIDS
See also FAIRIES—sea;
MERROWS
The angry merwife of
Nordstrand
Bride from the sea: the mer-
maid's cap
The dead soldier
Duke Magnus and the
mermaid
The fisherman and his soul
Golden mermaid [theft of gold-
en apples]
Hans, the mermaid's son
Laird of Lorntie (condensed)
The little mermaid
Lutey and the mermaid
Lutey and the mermaid
(condensed)

MERMAIDS (continued)
  Mathey Trewella
  Mer-women
  Miranda and the mermaid
  Old man of Cury (condensed)
  Pergrin and the mermaid
    (Wales)
  Ponam Island [first people on]
  [Selkies, seal-maidens, and
    mermaids]
  The three wishes
  The woman from the sea
  The yellow dwarf
—desire for human soul
  The little mermaid
—saves boy
  Finn magic
—sea princess
  King of the pipers and the
    wonderful tune
MERMAIDS (subject)
  Briggs-*Vanish.*, 70–73, 88–89,
    197
  Keightley-*World*, 147–155
  Mckee-*Scottish*, 23–24
  Scott-*Fantastic*, 135–148
The mermaid's grave
  Robertson-*Highland*, 150–151
The merman
  Booss-*Scand.*, 626–627
Mer-men
  Arrowsmith-*Field*, 118–120
MERMEN
  Finn blood
  Finn magic
  Handout for the merman
  The lady and the merman
  The merrow and the soul
    cages
  The seal fisher and the Roane
  Then the merman laughed
    (Iceland)
—home at bottom of sea
  Soul cages
MERMEN (subject)
  Keightley-*World*, 147–155

The merrow and the soul cages
  Heslewood-*Tales*, 98–103
Merrow [Irish for 'mermaid']
  Yeats-*Fairy*, 60
Merrows
  Froud-*Faeries*, unp
MERROWS
  See also MERMAIDS
  The beautiful maidens of the
    sea
  The dead soldier
  Lady of Gollerus
MERROWS (subject)
  Briggs-*Vanish.*, 81, 88
A merry prank of Pa-leng-ts'
    ang
  Jagendorf-*Magic*, 159–160
The merry widow
  Elbaz-*Folktales*, 33
The merry wives
  Lang-*Pink/D*, 297–300
  Lang-*Pink/K*, 213–217
Meru the stingray
  Wilbert-*Bororo*, 153–155
Mer-women
  Arrowsmith-*Field*, 114–118
A message for the cat
  Lindow-*Swedish*, 101
MESSAGES
  The Pan legend
MESSENGERS
  Hermes, the messenger of the
    gods
The Messiah [Midrash]
  Patai-*Gates*, 410–418
MESSIAH
  Burgher and the pauper
  The rabbi's son [in disguise]
MESSIAH (subject)
  Patai-*Gates*, 789 (index)
MESSIANIC ERA (Judaism)
  The lost princess
Meteor showers
  Gallant-*Constel.*, 183–185
METEORS
  Fall of the spider man

MEXICO (continued)
—Tula
    The fall of Tula
    Quetzalcoatl in Tula
MEXICO (subject)
—Cycles of history
    Bierhorst-*Hungry*, 5–7
—Guerrero
    Ritchie-*Armadillo*, 1–5
MEXICO CITY
    Copil's heart
    "Is it you?"
"MHORAG"
    Water monsters
Miaoshan-Guanyin, protectress of
    mortals
    Sanders-*Dragons*, 61–64
MICE
    See also titles beginning with
      "Mouse . . ."
    Adventures of Ntini, the small
      otter
    Back of the moon
    Battle of the birds
    A bell for the cat
    The blue lake
    The bronze ring
    The cat and mouse in
      partnership
    The cat and the mice
    Cinderella
    City mouse and country mouse
    The clever mice
    Country mouse and city mouse
    The cows who came to tea
    Dance in a buffalo skull
    Dick Whittington and his cat
    The dove and the mouse
    [Dyfed: under spell . . . [Faerie]
    The faithful trio [shelter in
      house]
    The fir tree
    The fleetest of foot
    Frog went a-courting [song
      and story]
    Graduation
    Grateful animals and the un-
      grateful man
    The hoity-toity mouse
    The honest penny
    How they got Hairlock home
    The iron-eating mice
    The juniper bush
    Lion and the mouse [in verse]
    Lioness and the mouse
    The little red hen
    Looking is free [State Fair]
    The magic mirror
    Prince Miaow
    Roly poly rice ball
    The sleepy one: Senor
      Opossum and the rattler
    Soup from a sausage skewer
    Titty Mouse and Tatty Mouse
    Toad's wedding [to Miss
      Mouse] [in verse]
    Town mouse and country
      mouse
    Two bad mice
    Two weak ones against one
      strong one
    The war of the birds and the
      beasts
    Wicked girl and her
      punishment
—disrupt invading army
    The country of the mice
—field
    Slip root, catch Reynard's foot
    Thumbelina
—hanging mouse, as thief
    Manawydan, son of Llyr
—make coyote laugh
    Coyote and the mice
—makes hut out of mitten
    The squeaking mouse
—mouse frees lion from net
    Lion and the mouse
—origin of size and color
    The mouse and the sun
—snake eats mouse
    A faithful mouse

—as tailors
The tailor of Gloucester
—tails
The cat and the mouse
Soup from a sausage skewer
—turns tables on weasel
The rock and the weasel
—why cats eat mice
Carlotta the Italian cat
—Mice in the corn
Adams-*Iron*, 26–34
Mice women who turned into
dingoes
Reed-*Aboriginal*, 52–54
MICHAEL, Saint
Saint Michael wins a soul from
devil
MICHAELMANS
Sunflower, Michaelmas, daisy,
dahlia
MICHIGAN
—Detroit (subject) Delray and its
people
Villa-*Armenian*,
Midas, the golden king
Gibson-*Gods*, 126–128
Midas, with the ass's ears
Magical Beasts, 25, 28–29
MIDDLE-AGE ROMANCE (subject)
Keightley-*World*, 28–43
"MIDDLE EARTH"
The building of the wall of
Asgard
Middleton, Richard, 1882–1911.
The ghost ship
MIDDLEWEST
Johnny Appleseed
MIDGARD
Heimdall in Midgard
Midnight funeral from America
O'Sullivan-*Legends*, 64–66
Midrash [Introd. and selections]
Patai-*Gates*, 257–418
MIDSUMMER DAY
The Cormorants of Andvaer
Midwife fox [steals honey]

Riordan-*Russia*, 179–180
MIDWIVES
The fairy lalour
The fary-labour
The golden haired twins
The nix-labour
The rejected gift
Teapot spout: Mother Han-
nah's story
Troll labour (condensed)
Wild Darrell
MIDWIVES (subject)
Briggs-*Vanish.*, 93–100, 116
Might. *See* POWER
Mighty bear has problems
MacLean-*Cuentos*, 167–169
MIGRANT FARMERS
Hare makes hyena his riding
horse
Hyena engages a strange-
farmer
Migration (birds). *See* BIRDS—
migration.
Migration separates lovers; A tale
of birds
Campos-*Mexican*, 127–130
Mikolaycak, Charles, illus.
Ginsburg-*Twelve*
MILESIANS
The magic people
MILITARY SERVICE
King Josef
MILK
Bird that made milk
The cat and the mouse
The grateful elfwoman
The hand of glory
Milkmaid and the bucket of milk
Munachar and Manachar
Munachar and the raspberries
Old woman who stole milk
—cream
Back of the moon
MILK (subject)
–Tribute to the Good People
Logan-*Old*, 123–124

MILK BOTTLES
  Herman the milk bottle
The milk of death
  Yourcenar-*Oriental*, 35–51
Milking others' cows
  Lindow-*Swedish*, 170–172
Milkmaid and the bucket of milk
  Ross-*Druids*, 34–36
Milkmaid and the pail
  Williams-*Aesop*, [27–29]
MILKMAIDS AND MILKMEN
  The vatt's storehouse
MILKY WAY (galaxy)
—origin
  The herd boy and the weaving
    girl
The Milky Way [Wahn (crow) &
    Baripa (cat)]
  Reed-*Aboriginal*, 102–104
The mill spirit
  Lindow-*Swedish*, 124–126
Miller, Mitchell, illus.
  Perrault-*Glass*
The miller and the fox
  Villa-*Armenian*, 127–133,
    455
The miller, his son, and their
    donkey
  dePaola-*Favorite*, 96–98
MILLERS
  The devoted friend
  The golden thumb [witch
    claims first-born]
  How some wild animals be-
    came tame ones
  Munachar and Manachar
  Munachar and the raspberries
  Prince of nettles
  Snipp, Snapp, Snorium
  Stupid Peikko
  The sun princess
  Urisk
  The water sprite and the bear
  Wise sayings for a thousand
    dinars each
—son wins princess

  The princess in the ivory tower
The miller's three sons
  Manning-*Marvels*, 7–18
MILLS
  Klabautermannikins and
    Kaboutermannikins
  The water nymph
MILLSTONES
  The hill folk
  The juniper tree
—ring of destiny
  The princess in the ivory tower
MIMICRY
  Leaving home
MIND-READING
  Julio
Mind your own business: Words of
    wisdom
  Griego-*Cuentos*, 87–91
MINERAL SPRINGS
—origin
  Song-bird and the healing
    waters
—sulphurous
  Mighty bear has problems
MINERS
—Old Mines, Missouri: the
    community
  Thomas-*It's*, 212–220
MINES AND MINING
  The changeling [b]
  Knockers
  The lazy miner
—flooded
  When they gave out wisdom,
    H. queued up twice
MINES AND MINING (subject)
—fairies in
  Briggs-*Vanish.*, 82–84, 122–
    123
—elementals
  Briggs-*Vanish.*, 37, 82–84
Miniature people. *See* LITTLE
    PEOPLE
Ministers. *See* CLERGYMEN
MINNESOTA

The frozen logger [song and
story]
Minnie
Gorog-*Taste*, 89–92
Minotaur
Low-*Greek*, 131–139
Magical Beasts, 8–12
MINOTAUR
Theseus, king of Athens
[Theseus vs the Minotaur]
MINOTAUR (subject)
Lloyd-*Mythical*, 31–38
Pinsent-*Greek*, 143 (index)
MINSTRELS
The men who wouldn't stay
dead (France)
MINTS
Marsh loosestrife, marsh mar-
igold, mints
A miracle in Montreal
Elbaz-*Folktales*, 54
The miracle of Rabbi David
Hassine
Elbaz-*Folktales*, 44
Miracle of the sailing ship
Patai-*Gates*, 645–648
MIRACLES
See also JESUS CHRIST–
miracles
The cripple and Senor San
Antonio
Devil's armful [Canterbury]
Flying lion of the Rab of
Tlemcen
The footprint of Buddha
Help for a mule caravan
King O'Toole and his goose
The magic pear tree
A mother saved by her son's
grave
Saint Colmkille's well
Saint Eustace's well
The Santo Nino [de Atocha]
visits a prison
The squire
The sultan and the psalms

The virgin of Guadalupe
—body incorrupt
Edmund the holy
—leprosy cured by "Act of Truth"
The radiant Sambula
The miraculous catch
Elbaz-*Folktales*, 127
A miraculous cure
Elbaz-*Folktales*, 91
Miraculous flower [stolen by prince
of ice]
Weiss-*Russian*, 171–183
Miraculous spring of Rabbi
Aharone Abehsera
Elbaz-*Folktales*, 134
MIRAGE (personified)
The great hunters [animals]
The mirage maker Beereeun
Parker-*Australian*, 112–118
Miranda and the mermaid
Ainsworth-*Bear*, 34–39
Mirror of Matsuyama
Ozaki-*Japanese*, 119–139
MIRRORS
Clod's comb
Maidens in a mirror
The silver whistle
The snow queen: an adventure
in seven stories
—distorted
The snow queen
—magic
The enchantress Medusa
The leeshy cat
The magic mirror
Magic mirror of Rabbi Adam
Snow White and the seven
dwarfs
—of wisdom
The fisherman and his soul
MIRRORS (subject)
Piggott-*Japanese*, 143 (index)
Mischance. *See* ERROR;
MISFORTUNE
MISCHIEF AND MISCHIEF-
MAKERS

MISCHIEF AND MISCHIEF-
  MAKERS (continued)
  See also TRICKERY
  Barabao
  Duende
  Follets
  Grasshopper [Indian
    superman]
  Lox, the mischief maker
  Lutins
  Mouse Woman and the por-
    cupine hunter
  Mouse Woman and the van-
    ished princes
  The nis and the boy
  Salvanelli
  Servan
  The spook and the beer barrel
  Tom Thumb
  Vily
"MISCHIEF MAKER"
  The apples of eternal life
The mischief maker, Lox, and the
    three fires
  Wade-*Indian,* 95–99
The mischievous little drinker
  Haining-*Lepre.,* 25–27
Miser and the fairy Gump
    (condensed)
  Briggs-*Vanish.,* 84, 122
The miser on the faerie gump
  Froud-*Faeries,* unp
The miser who swallowed his
    pearls
  Patai-*Gates,* 607–608
MISERS
  See also GREED
  Aldar-Kose and Shigai-Bai
  Ali Baba and the forty theives
  All I possess!
  Charity saves from death
  Death of a miser (Russia)
  The ghost and the moneychest
  The giant's daughter
  Gold colt and the fire dragon
    shirt
  'Gold, Ezekiel! Gold'
  One who deserved the money
  The parson and the clerk [II]
  Saran and Yumart
  Tight-fisted farmer and clever
    farmhand
  The treasure in Saby Creek
  —heaven's gates shut against
  The black spectre
  —outwitted
  The pilgrim from paradise
MISERY
  The enchanted apple tree
  Pulga
  The ugly duckling
  The young king
MISFORTUNE
  See also DISASTERS;
    LUCK—bad
  Beauty and the beast
  The beduin's gazelle (Saudi
    Arabia)
  The death of little Kiko
  Katrineholm Manor
  The lampstand princess
  The weathermaker
Misplaced trust: The poor man . . .
  Riordan-*Tartary,* 125–128
Miss Peggy Top
  Ainsworth-*Bear,* 90
"MISS PRIMROSE"'
  Goosey Goosey Gander
The missing axe
  Roberts-*Chinese,* 58
  Yolen-*Favorite,* 412–413
The missing butter
  Lindow-*Swedish,* 141–142
The missing treasure
  Hyde-Chambers-*Tibet,* 144–
    146
MISSIONARIES
  Windagoos! Cannibals!
  —Christian
  Rain for Bongi
  The rain that came too late
MISSIONS

—California
Eagle Woman comes to The
People
MISSISSIPPI RIVER
Gold treasure of Mississippi
MISSOURI
Attitudes toward Missouri
speech
Marriage customs among Mis-
souri Low Germans
Social customs and usages in
Mo. [19th cent.]
MISSOURI (subject)
—the Old Mines community
Thomas-*It's*, 212–220
MIST (personified)
The great hunters [animals]
The mistake
Hoke-*Demonic*, 119–124
A mistaken gift
Amore-*Lustful*, 114–115
MISTAKES
—learning from
There'll always be a tomorrow
Mister Fox [suitor/murderer]
Garner-*British*, 115–118
Macdonald-*Twenty*, 154–162
Yolen-*Favorite*, 87–90
Mister Jeremy Fisher
Phelps-*Tatterhood*, 83–92
Mister Miacca
Crossley-*Folk*, 121–122
Mister Raccoon realizes that winter
is coming
McCarthy-*Raccoon*, 1–9
Mister Velvet's bad deeds
Ainsworth-*Bear*, 63–68
Mister Vinegar
Wahl-*Needle*, 1–10
Mistletoe
Ewart-*Lore*, 170–172
MISTLETOE
Balder's doom
—Nature lore
Steele-*Ozark*, 60–61
The mistress of Pohja

Synge-*Land*, 39–44
MISTRESSES
The bald old man
The centipede girl
Fairy queens and mistresses
[condensed]
MISTS
—green
The green mist
MIXTECS (subject)
Nicholson-*Mexican*, 143
(index)
Mizilca [woman disguised as
knight]
Lurie-*Clever*, 23–29
MOAR
The hunter and his greedy wife
MOCCASINS
The boy and the dragon
The boy who wore turtle shell
moccasins
The great Penobscot raid
Magic moccasins: the Wearer
of the Ball
Mockery of fairies punished
O'Sullivan-*Legends*, 75–76
The mocking bird, Weedah
Parker-*Australian*, 37–39
MOCKINGBIRDS
Brer rabbit goes a courting
Wine and the devil
—origin
The mocking bird, Weedah
The Moddey Dhoo
Adams-*Iron*, 35–41
MODESTY
The good girl and the bad girl
The sheep butcher and his
king
—of girl become sun
The sun and the moon
Moerae
Arrowsmith-*Field*, 206–
210
Moi-Keha, the restless
Westervelt-*Hawaiian*, 79–85

346

MOLDAVIA
Tyndal and the priest
Tyndal goes to market
MOLES
The antelope maid
The competitive tiger
How raven brought fire to the
Indians
Mister Velvet's bad deeds
Rooting out bad feelings
Thumbelina
—origin
The children with one eye
Molly Whuppie
Lurie-*Clever*, 45–52
Yolen-*Favorite*, 228–231
"MO-MO" (Missouri Monster)
Wild men
Momotaro, or the son of a peach
Ozaki-*Japanese*, 244–261
Monacielli
Arrowsmith-*Field*, 239–242
MONASTERIES
Elidore
MONEY
Katla's dream
Looking is free [State Fair]
The two Sigurdurs
—hidden
The bold soldier of Antwerp
The ghost and the moneychest
—worship of
The master of prayer
MONEY (subject)
—fairy
Briggs-*Vanish.*, 62, 99–100
"MONEY TREES"
A true money tree
MONEYBAGS
Magic moneybag
MONGOLIA
Tiger King's skin cloak
[Mongolia]
Mongolian story of a serf: Ulan
Bator
Seven Sisters, 16–30

MONGOLS
A great misfortune
Unofficial history of the Confu-
cian Academy
MONGOOSES
The brahmin's wife and the
mongoose
Fudo and the prickly pear
thieves
MONITOR LIZARDS
Adventures of Ntini, the small
otter
The monk and Lady Kiyo
Kendall-*Haunting*, 22–25
The monk and the bird
O'Sullivan-*Legends*, 55–56
The monk and the drunk
Kendall-*Sweet*, 106–107
The monk from Everclear
Roberts-*Chinese*, 165–167
The monk Huiyuan
Sanders-*Dragons*, 70–71
Monkey and dog court the same
girl
Magel-*Gambia*, 75–77
Monkey and the cheese
Lewis-*Animal*, 46–47
Monkey and the crocodile (India)
Yolen-*Favorite*, 151–152
Monkey god: epic battle for earthly
supremacy
Magical Beasts, 44–55
Monkey keeper
Roberts-*Chinese*, 120
The Monkey spirit
Sanders-*Dragons*, 96–97
Monkey, the cavy, and the jaguar
Wilbert-*Bororo*, 127–130
The monkey who asked for misery
Wolkstein-*Magic*, 114–116
The monkey who claimed to be a
gewel
Magel-*Gambia*, 196–198
The monkey-faced suitor
Amore-*Lustful*, 82–84
Monkeys

Hoke-*Spirits,* 85–102
MONKEYS
See also APES
Brer rabbit dances for a wife
Dog and monkey build a town
Duration of life (Germany)
The elephant girls
The enchanted princess
Enmity between monkeys and
  crabs
The great battle between the
  grasshoppers and . . .
Havoc in heaven: Monkey and
  the Jade Emperor
How Aisu found the happy
  land
How night came
How the monkey and goat
  earned their reputations
How the monkey became a
  trickster
How the monkey escaped
  being eaten
How the monkey got a drink
  when he was thirsty
How the monkey got food
  when he was hungry
How the tiger got his stripes
Jackals and the tiger
Kintaro, the golden boy
Momotaro, or the son of a
  peach
The peacock's tail
Pierre Brassau ["non-objective"
  painting by monkey]
Quarrel of the monkey and the
  crab
The rabbit and the well
Sagacious monkey and the
  boar
Smart head better than sharp
  teeth
Tale of the golden vase and
  the . . .
The tar baby
The tiger-eating jackal cubs

Tripitaka: quest of the Buddhist
  scriptures
Two neighbors
The umbrella tree
The water nick
[White man created by Juko,
  the monkey]
Why the bananas belong to
  the monkey
—female outsmarts shark
  The monkey's heart
—heart
  Monkey and the crocodile
  (India)
—jinn
  Sultan's stupid wife and the
  jinn-monkey
—liver of
  Jelly fish and the monkey
—outsmarts jaguar
  Juko the monkey and Adugo
  the jaguar
—outsmarts tortoise
  The tortoise and the monkey
—scratching
  How to break a bad habit
—tails
  Why the monkey still has a
  tail
The monkeys and the moon
  Hyde-Chambers-*Tibet,* 96
The monkey's heart
  Martin-*Hungry,* 37–43
  Phelps-*Maid,* 45–50
Monkeys, turkeys, and fish
  [creation]
  Bierhorst-*Hungry,* 27–29,
  134
MONKS
  Black monk's curse
  The golden legend
  (condensed)
  [Little bird singing: angel of
  death]
  The missing treasure
  Monacielli

MONKS (continued)
O horrid dede! [monk murdered for stealing pig's head]
Old Nick is a gentleman
Our-Lady-of-the-Swallows
Sea friend: otter saves monk's lost book
Servant in the monastery
Super rat and the monks
Tungustapi
The young man who refused to kill
—Buddhist
The ascetic who visited home
Asceticism now, nymphs later!
Goblin of Adachigahara
The governor and the Buddhist
The monk Huiyuan
The only child who left home
The prostitute who lost her charm
—Buddhist (subject)-[Values]
Amore-*Lustful*, 145–146
—England: rivals in collecting relics
Ednoth's relics, and Thurkill's beard
—St Hilda's monastery
Boar of Eskdale
The monk's sins
Roberts-*Chinese*, 168–169
The monster of Poot Holler
Hoke-*Spirits*, 109–114
The monster of Strathhalladale
Robertson-*Highland*, 129–130
Monster with seven heads
Manning-*Kings*, 54–65
The monster-killers
Pinsent-*Greek*, 61–67
Monsters [tales]
Robertson-*Highland*, 121–146
MONSTERS
See also DRAGONS; SEA MONSTERS; SNAKES
The antelope maid

[Assipattle vs Stoorworm the sea-serpent]
The beastly creature and the magical flower
Beauty and the beast
The bird of happiness
The Botticelli horror
Cannibal
Coyote and the swallowing monster
The death of the Chimaera
The Dragon [Marduk and Tiamat]
The dreaded chenoo
The early heroes: Yi, the ten suns, the monsters
The flying head
How Aisu found the happy land
How panpipes came to be played (Miao)
Hydra (the many-headed monster)
King Zargand's daughter
The little hare
The magic bonnet
Man-Eagle conquered by youth
Monster with seven heads
Nennir, or the one who feels inclined
The peistha discomforted
Peter Gynt
Predators from the primal world
Prince Five-Weapons
Prince Vamato Take
The red stream
The sea maiden
The seven-headed beast
Sikulume and the seven brothers
Son of the Mountain
The sprightly tailor
The twins of Paikala Mountain
Twins visit Tawa

The vision of MacConglinney
Water beasts and wurrums
The world of the gods
The Yellow Emperor: war
    against Chitou
Youth without age and life
    without death (Turkey)
—answer questions or else . . .
The talking fish
—assorted
Assorted monsters
—cannibal
Aturuarodo and the monster
    Butoriku
—land
Land monsters
—nine-headed
"Black Horse," the third Broth-
    er Zhang (Tu)
—seven-headed
The blue lake
—winged
The story of trembling hood
MONSTERS (subject)
Briggs-*Vanish.,* 152
—Fairyland
Briggs-*Vanish.,* 16, 22, 76,
    172–174
—[Greek myths; six tales]
Wise-*Monster,* 7–48
The monster's hairs
Villa-*Armenian,* 202–210, 478–
    480
Monstrous birth. See BIRTH—
    monstrous.
MONTEZUMA, Aztec Emperor,
    d.1520
Calling the ghost of
    Montezuma
Eight omens
"Is it you?"
The return of Quetzalcoatl
The talking stone
Montezuma's wound
Bierhorst-*Hungry,* 93–98
The Moohel

Keightley-*World,* 506–510
MOON
All that happened must hap-
    pen again
The apprentice [rabbit as
    painter]
Back of the moon
Bamboo-cutter and the moon-
    child
The battle with the birds
Chang'o and the elixir of
    immorality
Daughter of the moon
The dog that ran to the moon
The fifth and final sun
The first Inca: marriage of sun
    and moon
Gumiya; a Blang story:
    origins . . .
The hare in the moon
The hares and the elephants
The hare's sacrifice
How spider read the sky-god's
    thoughts
Klis-to E-eki Ta-u-ue-a
Leppa Polkry and the blue
    cross
Little Daylight
The little girl on the moon
The magic of the moon
Maidens in a mirror
The Morning Star
Night and day
Nourie Hadig [a "Snow White"
    type]
Origin of death [Hottentot]
The palace of the moon
Photogen and Nycteris; a
    day/night mahrchen
Powdered blondie and three-
    haired blondie
The priest of Hardwork
    mountains
The rabbit and the two coyote
Raven lets out the daylight
The Rikubugu myth

MOON (continued)
  Sea, sun and moon [visit; leap
    to sky to avoid drowning]
  Snuff-box [wishes-come-true]
  Son of Kimanaueze and
    daughter of sun and moon
  Star-Boy and the sun dance
  Stones of five colours and the
    Empress Jokwa
  The sun journey
  Sun, night and moon
  The three sillies [imagined fu-
    ture evils]
  Woman in the moon
  The woman in the moon
  The young girl and the moon
—beginnings
  Sea, sun and moon [visit; sun
    and moon leap to sky]
—capturing the
  The mantis and the moon
—changes places with sun
  The moon and his frog-wife
—full
  The island of beautiful women
—half
  Nippy and the Yankee Doodle
—Igaluk (spirit)
  The origin of the winds
—leaves earth
  Sun, moon, and water
—leaves earth for the sky
  Anansi's six sons
—lonesome for female companions
  The fat moon
—man in the
  Daniel O'Rourke [makes D. fall
    off]
  The man in the moon
  Rabbit and the moon-man
—mothers coyote
  Coyote and Iitoi: the flood
—once harmful to earth (heat)
  Shooting the moon; a Yao
    folktale
—origin

  Aztec sun goddess
  Mantis creates an eland
  Meri and Ari ascend to the sky
  Raven steals the light
  Sun and moon
  Sun and sago
  The sun and the moon
—origin of eclipse
  Rahou [origin of eclipses]
—origin of image of archer and
    wife
  Shooting the moon; a Yao
    folktale
—origin of phases
  The moon and his frog-wife
  Orphan Yan Ran [Kawa]
—origin of splotches on
  Rabbit and the moon-man
—origin: rabbit markings
  The fifth and final sun
—personified, on earth
  Brothers (Sun and Moon) and
    the pretty girl
—reflection
  The monkeys and the moon
—talisman
  Golden chisel and the stone
    ram
—transformed, pursues sun
  The cruel stepmother
—visited by water (personified)
  Why the sun and the moon
    live in the sky
MOON (subject)
–Legends
  Hadley-Legends, [4]
—[astrology]
  Lehane-Wizards, 91
The moon and his frog-wife
  Macmillan-Canadian, 64–66
Moon and Morning Star
  Reed-Aboriginal, 104–107
The moon god [how moon got up
    in sky]
  Reed-Aboriginal, 138–139
Moon signs

Steele-*Ozark,* 89–90
The moon walk
Ainsworth-*Bear,* 75–83
MOONBEAMS
Back of the moon
MOON-CAKES
The clever sewing-maid
Moon-child and the bamboo-cutter
Ozaki-*Japanese,* 98–118
Moonflower
Walking-*Song,* 45–50
The Moon-God, the Angekkok, and the Oolak
Shelley-*Legends,* 63–69
MOONLIGHT
Asrai
The extra days: Ra, Thoth, and Nut
Raccoon's tale
The moon's apparent motion
Gallant-*Constel.,* 12
Mooregoo the mopoke, and bahloo the moon
Parker-*Australian,* 61
MOORS
Tom Hickathrift and the old giant
MOOSE
Lippo and Tapio
—personified
Strange tale of caribou and moose
The mopoke, and the mosquito bird
Parker-*Australian,* 73–75
Moral legends [twenty-three]
Rope-*Hispanic,* 498–510
MORDRED, Sir
Death of King Arthur
The great king's last battle
The passing of Arthur
MOREA (island)
The giant eel
Morenus, Richard
Restless souls
Morgan le Fay
Spells & Bind, 60
MORGAN le Fay
Castle [Chariot] of Morgan le Fay
Coming of King Arthur
MORGIANA (servant/heroine)
Ali Baba and the forty thieves
Slave maiden's eye for evil
MORGUES
Drawer 14
'Morning, alligator!
Stuchl-*American,* 48–49
The Morning Star
Wood-*Spirits,* 81–84
MORNING STAR
The battle with the birds
The rain bulls
Scar Face and the sun dance
Star-Boy and the sun dance
The sun journey
—brother made into woman
Moon and Morning Star
—origin
Mullyangah the morning star
Sky Elk, the ghost of White-face Mountain
Morning Star and Meteor
Shaw-*Pima,* 107–111
MOROCCO
Martyrdom of Solika Hatsadika
MOROKY, Saint
Three wishes [of Billy Dawson]
Morraha
Jacobs-*Celtic,* 203–212
[The Morrigan, Goll, and Finn MacCumal]
Seekers Saviors, 73–77
Morris, William
How Sigourd awoke Brynhild upon Hindfell
Morrisseau, Norval
The death of Windigo
The mortal
Manley-*Fun,* 179–182
The mortal lord
Roberts-*Chinese,* 218–219

MORTARS
    Girl who stayed in fork of a
      tree
    Treasure Mountain; a Yao
      folktale
—golden
    Catherine, sly country lass
      (Italy)
Moscow. *See under* RUSSIA
MOSES (biblical)
    Princess and the slave
    The ten plagues of Egypt
—impersonated
    Sidna Mussa
MOSES (biblical) (subject)
    Patai-*Gates*, 790–791 (index)
Moses faces the angels
    Patai-*Gates*, 402–405
Moses king of Ethiopia
    Patai-*Gates*, 615–625
MOSLEMS
    Azad Bakht's tale
    Magic ring of Rabbi Israel
      Hacohen
The mosquito bird and the mopoke
    Parker-*Australian*, 73–75
Mosquito [origin of its buzz]
    Pitcher-*Tokol.*, 36–39
MOSQUITOES
    The great flood [deluge]
    The great Penobscot raid
    Tuwara, the cunning one
    Wooing of Pumei; and Oroqen
      story
—origin
    The first mosquito
    Great father mosquito [larger
      than a bear]
    How mosquitoes came to be
—origin of characteristics
    Mosquito [origin of its buzz]
MOSS
    Jack o' lanterns
Moss people
    Arrowsmith-*Field*, 178–180
MOSS PEOPLE (subject)

Briggs-*Vanish.*, 76, 197
Mossycoat
    Garner-*British*, 47–57
"MOST AWFUL OF NAMES"
    (book)
    The Prince of Nimroz
A most unusual murder
    Hoke-*Spirits*, 115–129
Mother confessor fox
    Riordan-*Russia*, 127–128
MOTHER EARTH
    The world of the gods
Mother Earth and her children
    Low-*Greek*, 3–10
The Mother Goose madman
    Hoke-*Horrors*, 78–88
Mother Holle
    Lurie-*Clever*, 97–103
    Seekers Saviors, 106–107
Mother Hulda
    Tudor-*Bedtime*, [18–19]
Mother of the Waters
    Wolkstein-*Magic*, 152–156
A mother saved by her son's grave
    Elbaz-*Folktales*, 110
Mother Shipton and Cardinal
      Wolsey
    Marshall-*Every.*, 292–295
MOTHERS
    See also STEPMOTHERS
    Birth, dreaming, death: school-
      master's story
    Child in the silk-cotton tree
    City where men are mended
    The curse [elk takes liver of
      new mother]
    The devoted son
    Discontented Lado
    Elidore
    The eye can deceive
    The festival of the seven
      maidens
    The frog
    Gertrude and Rosy
    Gooloo the magpie, and the
      Wahroogah

Heavenly maiden and the
wood cutter
The iron wolf
Lemminkainen's escape
Leopard, the squirrel, and the
tortoise
Lioness [protects her cub]
Love: queen and foundling
Nourie Hadig [a "Snow White"
type]
She was good for nothing
Sister Becky's child
Solomon the wise
The star child
The stone frogs, the Youayah
Mayamah
A story about death
The swan of Tuonela
The tears of blood
That wicked crow
The toad and the boy
Tortoise and his mother: eye
not always accurate
Tushcoon Eigna
Two mothers [one child]
The wonderful Chuang
brocade
—abandon babies
The Bunbundoolooeys
—beats dullard-son to death
Ghost of Lady Hobby
—buried alive, nurses baby after
"death"
The milk of death
—cared for, though unworthy
"One, my darling, come to
mamma"
—courage
Fair exchange
—dying, sends for daughters
The three daughters
—eaten
O no, not my mother!
—forced to cut off head of
daughter
The roots of jealousy
—killed
Fox and the wolf
—kills her children
The weeping woman: forever
without rest
—neglected, until death . . .
The cuckoo
—rash promise: give child to lion
Tumani and his mother's
promise
—reincarnated as dog
Grave of a faithful dog
—seven loves for sons
The love of a mother
—survival skills taught by
A mother's yarn
—transformed to animal . . .
That her children might be fed
MOTHERS-IN-LAW
Lam Ku, the baskey lady
The Wasgo and three killer
whales
—evil
The bird wife
MOTHER'S MILK
Tale of the kurai
A mother's yarn
Riordan-*Woman*, 7–14
MOTHS
—silver-spotted ghost moth
The season of the stubby
caterpillar
Motif index
Briggs-*Vanish.*, 209–213
Motif indices
Wilbert-*Bororo*, 225–334
MOTIFS (subject)
—Index: Stith Thompson, with
adaptations
Villa-*Armenian*, 538–593
—[Register; Stith Thompson]
Robe-*Hispanic*, 535–548
Motions in the sky
Gallant-*Constel.*, 10–12
MOTIVATION
Aesop's dog [chasing rabbit]

MOUND BUILDERS
—origin
    The turtle and the turkey
Mound folk
    Arrowsmith-*Field*, 109–114
MOUNDS
    The girl clad in mouseskin
    Katla's dream
    Toller's neighbors
MOUNT FOLK
    Toller's neighbors
The mountain and the rivers
    Zong-*Korea*, 14–15
MOUNTAIN GOATS
—revenge
    The feast of the mountain
        goats
The mountain kitchen
    Booss-*Scand.*, 290–292
MOUNTAIN LIONS
    The great hunters [animals]
    Kosi, the eagle, and the moun-
        tain lion
—origin of ring mark on head
    Coyote retrieves his brother's
        scalp
Mountain of jade
    Shah-*Dervishes*, 149–153
"MOUNTAIN OF QWARK"
    Mouse Woman and the mon-
        ster killer whale
Mountain witch and the Dragon-
    King
    Zong-*Korea*, 169–171
MOUNTAINS
    *See also names of particular
        mountains*
    The creation
    The daughter of Peter de
        Cabinam
    Erh-lang and the suns
    The giant maiden in Boraserod
        mountain
    The giant puke
    The great battle between the
        grasshoppers and monkeys

The great deeds of King Yu
Halde hat
Journey of dwarfs over the
    mountain
The knights of Allaberg
The lost treasure
Mongolian story of a serf: Ulan
    Bator
The red stream
Taufatahi and Fakapatu or
    Why sharks . . . Moungone
The three billy goats Gruff
Three sisters were entrapped
    into a mountain
Tibble Castle and Klinta Spring
Toller's neighbors
Treasure Mountain; a Yao
    folktale
The Urko of North Wij
The Vatters
The white rooster
—giant's
    The giant and Johannes
        Blossom
—glass
    Glass mountain
—origin
    Long ago when the earth was
        flat
—origin of bare tops
    The bare mountains
—spirits
    The white-hair waterfall
MOUNTAINS (subject)
—spirits
    Briggs-*Vanish.*, 66–67, 84,
        172–173
MOURNERS
    Origin of gourd trumpet, me-
        mento of the dead
Mouse
    Hoke-*Spirits*, 41–53
The mouse and the rooster
    Fattoross-*Simpleton*, 79–82
The mouse and the sun
    Macmillan-*Canadian*, 30–33

The mouse at the seashore
Lobel-*Fables*, 40–41
The mouse bride
Booss-*Scand.*, 541–547
MOUSE PIE
The pie and the patty-pan
MOUSE WOMAN
Bear Mother and her husband
Mouse Woman and the daughter of
the sun
Harris-*Mouse*, 91–105
Mouse Woman and the monster
killer whale
Harris-*Mouse*, 68–90
Mouse Woman and the porcupine
hunter
Harris-*Mouse*, 5–20
Mouse Woman and the Snee-
nee-iq
Harris-*Mouse*, 39–53
Mouse Woman and the tooth
Harris-*Mouse*, 106–114
Mouse Woman and the vanished
princes
Harris-*Mouse*, 21–38
Mouse Woman and the wooden
wife
Harris-*Mouse*, 54–67
Mouse's three children [tiger, pea-
cock, boy]
O'Connor-*Tibet*, 68–75
A mouse's wedding [who is the
most powerful?]
Lewis-*Bedtime*, 26–27
MOUSESKINS
The girl clad in mouseskin
MOUSE-ORGAN MUSIC
Snake with an ear for music
MOUTHS
—in armpit
Cunning mouth
—twisted
Twist-mouth family
MOVING
The nis removing
MOVING (subject)

—fairies move buildings
Briggs-*Vanish.*, 129–130
MOWERS
Why mowers are poor
Moya [child of Wind; returns to
place-of-stars]
Pitcher-*Tokol*, 40–42
Moytura: the second battle
Ross-*Druids*, 21–24
Mrs. Sadili and the sesame seeds
Wood-*Kalila*, 219–225
MUBARAK
Adventures of the third dervish
[b]
Mud heads and fish men
Dutton-*Hopi*, 43–47
"MUDDLEHEADS"
Old fuddlement
MUDHENS
—origins of bald heads
Maui the Polynesian
Mud-snail fairy
Zong-*Korea*, 29–31
MUIYINWUH (god of growing
things)
The children and the
hummingbird
MULBERRY TREES
The betrothal
—leaves
The chao ku bird
—shade sold
Under the shade of the mul-
berry tree
Mule lore: "mule eggs"
Steele-*Ozark*, 75–77
MULES
The biter bit
Conjurer's revenge [slave
changed into mule]
The Mazik-ass
Rooting out bad feelings
—excrement = gold coins
Story of Campriano (Italy)
—groom trades places with
The enchanted mule

MULES (continued)
—transformation to, at will
    Husband and wife should
      share equally
Mulha
    Phelps-*Maid,* 91–96
Mulien rescues his mother
    Sanders-*Dragons,* 64–70
Mullyangah the morning star
    Parker-*Australian,* 57–58
MULTIPLE BIRTHS
    The seven churches
    Twelve children on a platter
—tsar's wife
    Darakhvei, the great oak
Mummies, zombies, and artificial
    men
    Cohen-*Every.,* 37–52
MUMPS
    Hob and Mump
Munachar and Manachar
    Jacobs-*Celtic,* 57–59
    Yeats-*Fairy,* 267–270
Munachar and the raspberries
    Smith-*Manachar,* 6–42
Munchausen and the bear
    Lewis-*Animal,* 24–25
Munchausen and the buck
    Lewis-*Animal,* 38–39
Mundig [tiny child]
    Villa-*Armenian,* 235–240, 488
Munro, H. H. *See* Saki (pseud.
    of . . .)
Munuck
    Villa-*Armenian,* 425–426
MURDER
    See also EUTHANASIA;
      FRATRICIDE; HOMICIDE
    Aphrodissia, the widow
    Babes in the wood
    Back for Christmas
    Bad Indian's ashes [flies tor-
      ment people]
    Blue Beard
    [Bluebeard, Isabelle, the bleed-
      ing key]

    The brocaded slipper
    Captain Murderer and the de-
      vil's bargain [by Dickens]
    The confession of Charles
      Linkworth
    Death out of season
    Deer woman
    The dog goes to court
    Ebbe Skamelson
    The elf of the rose
    Erigone and her dog
    The flying childer
    The ghost at Fjelkinge
    Goonur, the woman-doctor
    The guardian sheep
    Helle and Phrixus
    Hildur, the queen of the elves
    The illustrated man
    Jerry Bundler
    Katla
    King Goldemar
    The Koranic teacher
    Lamb to the slaughter
    The little wise woman
    The lovers
    Master Frog
    The Metronome
    Mister Fox
    A most unusual murder
    Murder will out
    O horrid dede! [monk mur-
      dered: stealing pig's head]
    One word solves a mystery
    The police marshall [mass
      murder]
    Quarrel of the monkey and the
      crab
    The rose tree
    Rosy apple and the golden
      bowl
    The Santo Nino [de Atocha]
      saves a friendship
    The secret of the growing gold
      [by Stoker]
    Settlement out of court
    The singing bone

Slave girl tried to kill her
  mistress
Smallhead and the king's son
Soul-taker
The story of Zibong
The swordmaker's son: King-
  don of Chu
Tanzara and Dyeer
The tell-tale heart [by Poe]
Terror
There is righteousness
Truth, and murder, will out
Unborn child avenged its
  mother's death
Wamundo
The waxwork [Murderers' Den,
  by Burrage]
Waxworks
The weeping woman: the
  prince and the seamstress
White lotus magic
The wicked stepmother
Witches of Tring [killed by
  Colley]
Woman who killed her co-wife
The woman who was saved by
  a miracle
—attempted
  Emperor's lesson
  The wicked sister-in-law
—attempted, to avoid fate
  Underworld god of marriage
—avoided by chance
  Three evil wives punished
—exposed
  Legend of the Virgin Arang
—filicide attempted
  Shun, the wise emperor
—of Gunda
  Yorkshire giant [Penhill]
—king covets Deirdre
  Deirdre and Naoise
—mass murder
  Fishing of the women [adultery
    with otters]
—origin

The child and the eagle
—by poison
  [Impregnation by earrings] Ara-
    ruga Paru
—revealed by whistle
  The rose of Peppermette
—saved from
  The three golden hairs of Old
    Man Almanack
—skull of murdered man
  Dick o' Tunstead
—by starvation
  Parson could not say "our
    daily bread"
Murder and lonely hearts
  Hoke-*Demonic*, 51–67
Murder will out
  Booss-*Scand.*, 643–644
MURDERERS
—caught
  One word solves a mystery
MURRAY, Margaret Alice
  Sergeant-*Witches*, 288 (index)
MUSES
  Low hurdles
MUSEUMS
  Waxworks
Mushkil Gusha: remover of all
  difficulties
  Shah-*World*, 130–134
MUSHROOMS
  Fairie ring mushroom
  How salt was discovered
MUSIC
  Artemis and Apollo
  Fairy music
  The lark's march [contest]
  The origin of music
  Orpheus and Eurydice
—effect of
  The traveller and the
    innkeeper
—gift of
  The white gander
—heavenly
  The King or Ireland's son (Art)

MUSIC (continued)
—magic
   The stealing of the sampo
—Mexican
   La cucaracha
—talent given by pooka
   The piper and the puca
MUSIC (subject)
—fairies
   Briggs-*Vanish.*, 217 (index)
MUSICAL INSTRUMENTS
   Origin of the poari
   What melody is the sweetest?
MUSIC-BOXES
   The nightingale
MUSICIANS
   See also FLUTES AND FLUT-
   ISTS; PIPERS
   The Bremen town musicians
   Orpheus and Eurdice
Musicians of Bremen. *See* Bremen
   town musicians
MUSKRATS
   Iktomi and the muskrat
MUSLIN
   The white cat
MUSSELS
   How mussels were brought to
   the creeks
The mute prince [kingship rejected]
   Amore-*Lustful*, 151–153
The mute princess
   Schwartz-*Elijah*, 148–154
MUTES
   Guleesh
   The living kuan-yin
MUTTON
   The crossways
—bones
   Una the elfwoman
The muzhik, the wolf, and the fox
   Cortes-*Byelorussian*, 14
My displaced ghosts
   Manley-*Fun*, 15–33
My godmother's story of buried
   treasure

Campos-*Mexican*, 95–98
My Lady Greensleeves
   Robertson-*Highland*, 62–64
My lord bag of rice
   Ozaki-*Japanese*, 1–11
My mother warned me . . .
   Todd-*Some*, 144–150
My shadow [poem]
   dePaola-*Favorite*, 40–41
MYRTLE TREES
   The bottle-neck
The mysterious of Eden
   Patai-*Gates*, 432–439
Mysterious cannon ball
   Marshall-*Every.*, 109–112
Mysterious music from the deep
   Stuchl-*American*, 203–204
Mysterious palace [Solomon &
   Ramirat]
   Schwartz-*Elijah*, 77–81
The mystery of Sandwood
   Robertson-*Highland*, 40–43
Mystic knowledge
   Elbaz-*Folktales*, 115–116
MYTH (subject)
—Motif index
   Wilbert-*Bororo*, 227
Mythical animals. *See* ANIMALS—
   mythical

Na Sithichean
   Robertson-*Highland*, 2–3
Nachman of Bratslav. *See* Nahman
   of Bratslav
NACK (subject)
   Lindow-*Swedish*, 38–39, 216
The nack longs for salvation
   Lindow-*Swedish*, 123–124
The nack pulls the plow
   Lindow-*Swedish*, 119–120
The nack's reel
   Lindow-*Swedish*, 117–119

NACKS (water horses)
    Riding the backahast
Naddi
    Booss-*Scand.*, 629
NAGGENEENS
    Wildbeam's pranks
The nagging husband [Estonia]
    Riordan-*Woman*, 15–19
NAGUI
    Degei and his sons
Nahman of Bratslav, 1772–1811
    The lost princess
    The pirate princess
    The prince who was made of
      precious gems
    The water palace
NAHMAN of Bratslav (subject)
    The golden bird
—Biography
    Nahman-*Tales*, 9–25
NAHUAS (subject)
    Nicholson-*Mexican*, 143
      (index)
NAHUATL LEGENDS (subject)
—Myths and legends
    Bierhorst-*Hungry*, 3–18
Nail soup (Sweden)
    Yolen-*Favorite*, 187–191
NAILS
    The old woman and the tramp
Nails [anatomy]
    Zong-*Korea*, 37–38
Nair. *See* OTTERS
NALA
    An act of truth
The name [girl must learn employ-
    er's name, or not eat]
    Wolkstein-*Magic*, 118–122
NAMES
    Inge of Rantum
    The living kuan-yin
    Mouse Woman and the por-
      cupine hunter
    The Pleiades
    Tom Tit Tot
    Who built Reynir church?

—babies'
    What shall baby's name be?
—guessing
    Duffy and the devil
    Peerifool [secret name of fairy]
    Rival kempers
    Rumpelstiltskin
    Tom Tit Tot
    Whuppity Stoorie
—nonsensical
    Master of all masters
—secret (personal names)
    Tom Tit Tot
Names of fairies: importance
    Ratcliff-*Scottish*, 84–96
NAMES, Place
—origin
    Baitogogo names the hill
    Kudorori
NAMESAKES
    The rich farmer and the poor
      farmer
Naming of places
    Ross-*Druids*, 123–124
NANAHUAZTZIN
    Aztec sun goddess
Nanasimgat [wife abducted by killer
    whale]
    Reid-*Myths*, 30–36
Nanasimgit and his [abducted] wife
    Reid-*Raven*, 61–67
NANDI BEARS
    Assorted monsters
NAOISE
    Deirdre and Naoise
NAPI (Old Man of the Dawn)
    The serach for the buffalo
Napi's wager with rabbit
    Anderson-*Trick.*, 16–20
NAPKINS
—magic
    Old Man Le Feve
    [bumblebees]
NARA (subject)
    Piggott-*Japanese*, 144 (in-
    dex)

NARADA
The monkey-faced suitor
Narahari Das
Raychaudhuri-*Stupid*, 12–15
Narcissus
Low-*Greek*, 57–59
NARCISSUS
Echo and Narcissus
NARNAUKS
Mouse Woman and the daughter of the sun
Mouse Woman and the monster killer whale
Mouse Woman and the porcupine hunter
Mouse Woman and the Snee-nee-iq
Mouse Woman and the tooth
Mouse Woman and the vanished princes
Mouse Woman and the wooden wife
The Narran Lake [origin]
Parker-*Australian*, 24–26
NARWHALS
Land monsters
Nash, Ogden
The Wendigo
Nasr-ed-Din Hodja in the pulpit (Turkey)
Yolen-*Favorite*, 173–174
NASTASIA
Tremsin and the maid of the sea
Nasturtium, stock, thrift
Ewart-*Lore*, 122–125
Natural phenomena
Robe-*Hispanic*, 426–433
Nature
Roberts-*Chinese*, 248
NATURE
Man and beast
[Secret life: nature charged with intelligence]
The stone maiden
The strongest in the world

We give thanks
NATURE (subject)
—Friendship between the earthly and the heavenly
Luzzatto-*Long*, 44
Nature lore
Steele-*Ozark*, 56–64
NATURE SPIRITS (subject)
See also FERTILITY
Briggs-*Vanish.*, 66–80
Nature's ways
Villa-*Armenian*, 338–340, 519
A Navajo story of creation
Dutton-*Navajo*, 25–34
NAVAL BATTLES
Sir Andrew Barton [ballad]
NAVELS
Luck in a strange place
Nazar the Brave ["kills a thousand with a single blow"]
Sheohmelian-*Three*, 44–51
A near encounter
Colombo-*Wind.*, 200–201
NECESSITIES
—given
A wonderful bird
"NECK" (subject)
Briggs-*Vanish.*, 72–73
Necklace of life: the fairy child
Villa-*Armenian*, 91–96, 445
NECKLACES
The lampstand princess
The roots of jealousy
—eagle detects theft of
Battle [Cheyennes attack Shoshones]
NECKLETS
I won't forgive you
"NECKS"
Power of the harp
NECKS (subject)
Keightley-*World*, 147–155
"NEED"
Luck [and Need; personified]
Needle and Noodle
Wahl-*Needle*, 17–28

NEEDLES
Spindle, shuttle, and needle
Neelkamal and Lalkamal
Bang-*Five*, 21–34
Negro slaves. *See* SLAVES AND
SLAVERY
Negroes. *See* BLACKS
NEIGHBORS
The leprechaun in the garden
Let the fire burn, you cannot
put it out
The rich farmer and the poor
farmer
Toller's neighbors
Who is my neighbour?
—good
Fir Bolg
—one rich, one poor
Two neighbors
NEIGHBORS (subject)
—good
Briggs-*Vanish.*, 216 (index, un-
der Good . . .)
Nennir, or the one who feels
inclined
Booss-*Scand.*, 628
Nera and the Otherworld
Ross-*Druids*, 44–45
Nereides
Arrowsmith-*Field*, 269–273
NEREIDS
The man who loved the
Nereids
Odd jobs
NEREUS
Peleus and Thetis [marriage]
NETHERLANDS
Stormalong fights the Kraken
Tyl on a tightrope
—history: Spanish wars of
independence
The Christmas thief
—Wierum
Far out the long canal
Netherworld. *See* UNDERWORLD
NETS

—introduced to New Zealand
Huia's dream
NETTLES
The wild swans
Nevins, J. B.
A tale of the Windego
The new bishop
Griego-*Cuentos*, 93–95
NEW BRITAIN (New Guinea)
Five strange plants
New clothes for the tomte
Lindow-*Swedish*, 139–140
The new gods-Zeus and Hera
Gibson-*Gods*, 14–20
New Guinea. *See* PAPUA NEW
GUINEA
The new hand [old man made
young again]
Shah-*World*, 32–33
NEW IRELAND
The turtle wife
NEW MEXICO (subject)
—[Narratives from the R. D.
Jameson collection]
Robe-*Hispanic*, vii–xi, 1–30
NEW ORLEANS
Hoodoo [voodoo]
The new people and their food
Piggott-*Mexican*, 101–106
NEW YEAR'S
The clever sewing-maid
Coffin cash
Draw the curtains
The Gwagedd Annwyn [II]
The kitchen god
The little match girl
The spirit of the van
Ten jugs of wine
Tungustapi
The wizards of the Vestmanna
Isles
NEW YEAR'S EVE
La Guillonnee: French holidays
in Miss. Valley
NEW YORK
"Bye-bye" (Haiti)

NEW YORK CITY
–Grand Central Station
    The third level
NEW ZEALAND
    Huia's dream
    Pedorous Jack
–origin
    The wondrous fish-hook
Newman, Dora Lee
    The tar baby
NEWS
–broadcasters
    A little love story
–supernatural, transoceanic
    knowledge of
    Boy abducted by fairies
Next life. *See* FUTURE LIFE;
    OTHERWORLD
NIAGARA FALLS
    Bending Willow [Indian maid]
NIBELUNGS
    Treachery of the Nibelungs
NICHOLAS, Saint
    The little cattle
    Saint Nicholas and the children
Nidhoggr [Scandinavia]
    Stallman-*Dragons,* 16–17
Nielsen, Helen
    Murder and lonely hearts
Niggardliness. *See* STINGINESS
NIGHT
    See also DARKNESS
    Bohrah the kangaroo and di-
      newan the emu
    Gumiya; a Blang story:
      origins . . .
    Heron gives Meri power over
      the night
    How night came
    How spider read the sky-god's
      thoughts
    Linchetti
    Visitors from the realm of
      shadow
    [Wayfarers: dangers at night]
–darkness

Photogen and Nycteris; a
    day/night mahrchen
–origin
    Sun, night and moon
NIGHT (subject)
    Zong-*Korea,* 254 (index)
Night and day
    Branston-*Gods,* 24–28
The night bird
    Sanders-*Dragons,* 86
The night it rained [hitchhiker]
    Schwartz-*Dark,* 42–49
NIGHT RIDERS
    Simon and the pater-rollers
The night the ghost got in
    Manley-*Fun,* 101–107
The night trolls
    Booss-*Scand.,* 642
NIGHTCAPS
    The dead man's nightcap
NIGHTHAWKS
    The mopoke, and the mosquito
      bird
The nightingale
    Adams-*Iron,* 111–115
    Booss-*Scand.,* 415–422
Nightingale and the dove
    Schwartz-*Elijah,* 122–126
The nightingale and the hawk
    Lewis-*Minute,* 40–41
The nightingale and the rose
    Wilde-*Fairy,* 83–92
NIGHTINGALES
    Duet: song
    The hawk and the nightingale
    Jorinde and Joringel
    Mister Miacca
    The swine herd
    The talking nightingale
–bewitched prince
    The princess and the bulbul
–tongues-gold
    The nightingale
The nightingale's song [escape]
    Riordan-*Tartary,* 33–36
The nightmare steed

Haining-*Lepre.*, 87–89
NIGHTMARES
    Elves, night
    Linchetti
NIGHTMARES (spirits)
    Farm hand tied scythes over
      horse's back
    The identity of the nightmare
    Werewolf and nightmare
Nightstalker of Groglin Grange
    Night Creatures, 98–107
NIMNE, Lady
    Sir Lancelot of the Lake
The nine-headed giant
    Seros-*Sun*, 24–31
    Zong-*Korea*, 166–169
NINEPINS
    Rip Van Winkle
    The youth who went forth to
      learn what fear was
The nine-seeded apple
    Villa-*Armenian*, 229–232, 486
The nine-tailed fox
    Zong-*Korea*, 38
NINEVEH
    Jonah and the whale
Niobe
    Low-*Greek*, 49–52
Nippy and the Yankee Doodle
    Haviland-*N. Amer.*, 155–159
The nis and the boy
    Keightley-*World*, 142–143
The nis and the mare
    Keightley-*World*, 144–145
The nis removing
    Keightley-*World*, 140–141
The nis riding
    Keightley-*World*, 145
The nis stealing corn
    Keightley-*World*, 143
NISSE (evil spirits)
    Exorcising the tomte
    The penitent nis
NISSE (subject)
    Keightley, *World*, 139–145
Nissen and Tomtra

Arrowsmith-*Field*, 165–169
The nisses in Vosburg
    Keightley-*World*, 146–147
Nivkhs: The brave Azmun
    Nagishkin-*Folktales*, 13–26
[The nix and her mortal lover]
    Water Spirits, 116–119
The nix-labour
    Keightley-*World*, 261–263
Nix nought nothing (condensed)
    Briggs-*Vanish.*, 39–40
Nixen and river men
    Arrowsmith-*Field*, 101–104
NIXIES
    Henizelmanchen
    [Houaru and the nix's spell]
    The nix-labour
    The peasant and the
      waterman
    The water nick
    The water smith
    The working waterman
NIXIES (subject)
    Briggs-*Vanish.*, 61–63, 73, 197
    Keightley-*World*, 258–263
The N'jenge and M'wambia [myth-
    ical animals]
    Radin-*African*, 254–257
No pity in women
    Patai-*Gates*, 602–605
No pooch 'em
    Aiken-*Mexican*, 92–94
NOAH (biblical)
    The real daughter of Noah
Noah and Satan [wine: proper
    amount]
    Patai-*Gates*, 518–519
NOAH'S ARK
    It's the pichilingis again
Nobleman and the slave
    Shah-*Dervishes*, 221–226
NOBLEMEN
    Hinzelmann
    The magic bamboo
Noblest quest of all
    Lehane-*Legends*, 108–131

The Nomad
  Hyde-Chambers-*Tibet,* 163
Non-aging. *See* TIME—illusion . . .
NONCONFORMITY
  Tatterhood
—older women
  Bucca Dhu and Bucca Gwidden
NON-COOPERATION
  Why the hare runs away
"NONDESCRIPT"
  Wild men
NONSENSE
  See also WORDS—nonsensical
  Apple pie
NONVIOLENCE
—rewarded
  King Goodness refuses to fight
The noodle
  Kendall-*Sweet,* 100–105
NOON WOMEN
  Poleviki and Poludnitsy
Norggen, Orculli and
  Fankenmannikins
  Arrowsmith-*Field,* 92–97
The Norns
  Branston-*Gods,* 46–47
NORSE MYTHS
  The apples of eternal life
  The apples of Iduna
  Balder's doom
  The building of the wall of
    Asgard
  The creation of the world
  The death of Balder
  Fenrir the wolf is bound
  The first humans
  The gods return
  The gods' revenge
  The golden age in Asgard
  Heimdall in Midgard
  How they went to Jotunheim
  How Thor got his hammer
  King Gylfi is tricked again
  The lay of Thrym
  Loki and his evil children
  Loki makes mischief

The making of the worlds
Night and day
The Norns
Odin prepares for the
  Ragnarok
Ragnarok
The Ragnarok, doom of the
  gods
Singard the dragon-slayer
The stealing of Thor's hammer
The story of trembling hood
Symbols in the Nordic myths
Thor fights the giant Krangnir
Thor goes fishing
Thor goes fishing with Hymir
Thor in the giant's strong-hold
Thor's holiday
The tricking of King Gilfi
The walls of Asgard
War in heaven
The world of ice and fire
Yggdrasill, the world ash
NORSE TALES (subject)
—Myths and legends of the
  Vikings
  Lindow-*Myths,* 1–48
Norsemen: Scourges of the North
  Water Spirits, 28–35
The north country wolf
  Roberts-*Chinese,* 111–118
NORTH DAKOTA
  Paul Bunyan, the giant logger
North polar sky
  Gallant-*Constel.,* 21–24
NORTH POLE
  How the polar bear became
NORTH SEA
  The skipper and old Nick
NORTH STAR
  Gods of the stars: ancient
    China
NORTH WALES
  The castle of Melvales
NORTHERN
  Annie Norn and the fin folk
  The apples of Iduna

Autumn and the bear
Balder's doom
The battle of Stamford Bridge
Beowulf fights the dragon
The black bull of Norroway
The bold soldier of Antwerp
Bremen town musicians
The building of the wall of
    Asgard
The burning of Bergthorsknoll
The curse of Andvari's ring
The dead man's nightcap
Door prayer at evening
The elf maiden
The enchanted apple tree
Erikur rescues a woman from
    the otherworld
The expedition of Thorfin
    Karisefni
Gestumblindi's riddles
The ghost and the moneychest
The hauntings at Frodriver
The herd-boy and the giant
How some wild animals be-
    came tame ones
How they went to Jotunheim
Johnnie in the cradle
Jorinde and Joringel
The juniper tree
The king o' the cats
The lay of Thrym
Little Annie the goose girl
The making of the worlds
Mister Miacca
The old troll of Big Mountain
Peter Bull
The Pleiades
Ragnarok
The rich farmer and the poor
    farmer
Snipp, Snapp, Snorium
A stork is not always a stork
Thornstein staff-struck
The three heads of the well
Three sisters were entrapped
    into a mountain

Toller's neighbors
Tom Tit Tot
The troll ride
True and untrue
Walter and Hildegund
The water sprite and the bear
Wayland Smith
Why the sea is salt
The wizards of the Vestmanna
    Isles
The woman of the sea
Yallery Brown
NORTHERN CROSS
    Corona Borealis (the Northern
    Crown)
NORTHERN CROWN
    Corona Borealis (the Northern
    Crown)
NORTHERN ISLANDS (subject)
    Keightley-*World*, 156–
The Northern Lights
    Macmillan-*Canadian*, 85–90
NORTHERN LIGHTS (subject)
    Briggs-*Vanish.*, 91
Norhtwest Pacific coast tribal
    [commentary]
    Robinson-*Raven*, 9–12
NORWAY
    Ashiepattle who made the prin-
    cess tell . . .
    Boots and the beasts
    The box with the funny thing in
    it
    Bruin and Reynard partners
    Castle in the air: Odainsaker
    The charcoal burner
    The companion
    Death and the doctor
    The death of Chanticleer
    The dwarfs' banquet
    East of the sun and west of
    the moon
    The elfin hill
    An evening in the squire's
    kitchen
    Finn blood

NORWAY (continued)
The fisherman and the draug
Foolish men and scolding wives
Fylgiar
The giant and Johannes
Blessom
The giant who had no heart
The greedy youngster
Hans, who made the princess
laugh
Hello, Aurora
The honest penny
How they got Hairlock home
How to win a prince
The lad and the devil
The lad and the north wind
Legends of the mill
Little Annie the goose girl
Little Freddy with his fiddle
The making of the worlds
The man who was going to
mind the house
Master Tobacco
The pancake
The parson and the clerk [I]
Peik
Peter Gynt
Pork and honey
Pussy-Greedyguts
Reynard and Chanticleer
The seven fathers in the house
The skipper and old Nick
Slip root, catch Reynard's foot
The smith and the devil
A summer night in a Nor-
wegian forest
The three billy goats Gruff
The three billy-goats who
went . . . to get fat
The three lemons
Three sisters were entrapped
into a mountain
The trolls in Hedale Wood
True and untrue
The way of the world
Why the sea is salt

The widow's son
The witch
NORWAY (subject)
—fairies
Briggs-*Vanish.*, 151–152
Noseful of gold
Stuchl-*American*, 205–207
NOSES
Prince Dorus
The sausage
—cut off
The dervish and the thief
—as punishment, stretched to
seven feet
The candy man; a Han folktale
—as test of truth (tip soft = telling
truth)
King the liar and liar the king
NOSINESS
The woodpecker
Nostradamus: the Provencal
prophet
Lehane-*Wizards*, 64
Not snow nor rain
Hoke-*Spirits*, 5–20
The not-really-a-dragon dragon
Stallman-*Dragons*, 40–41
Nourie Hadig [a "Snow White"
type]
Villa-*Armenian*, 84–91, 442–
445
Nova Scotia. *See under* CANADA
Now you know
Todd-*Tortoise*, 118–120
Nuckelavee
Froud-*Faeries*, unp
NUCKELAVEE (subject)
Briggs-*Vanish.*, 76, 197–198
Nuckelavee the monster
Ratcliff-*Scottish*, 138–140
Nuckelavee: The water folk
Scott-*Fantastic*, 141
NUCLEAR WAR
—afterwards
A little love story
—result

Tomorrow's child
"A nude horse is a rude horse"
  Schwartz-*Tales*, 26–32
NUDITY
  The emperor's new clothes
NUMBER(S) (subject)
  Zong-*Korea*, 256 (index)
Numbskull's errand
  Marshall-*Every.*, 359–362
Numenos: In the beginning
  Scott-*Fantastic*, 23–36
NUMEUK
  Pursuit of Numeuk the hunter
Nunneries. *See* CONVENTS
NURSES AND NURSING
  Drawer 14
  The fairies' nurse
  Shurik: A story of the siege of
    Leningrad
  The sunset call
NURSES AND NURSING (subject)
  Briggs-*Vanish.*, 93–94
NUTCRACKERS
  Little Ida's flowers
NUTS AND NUT TREES
  The apples of Iduna
  Hazel
  Kate Crackernuts
  King Lindorm [a snake]
  The lad and the devil
  The lost hum
NUWA (subject)
—Gods from the dawn of time
  Sanders-*Dragons*, 13–17
NYAMATSANE (a monster)
  The hunter and his greedy wife
  The little hare
NYCTERIS
  Photogen and Nycteris: a
    day/night mahrchen
NYMPHS
  Echo and Narcissus
  Nereides
  Our-Lady-of-the-Swallows
  Pan and Dionysus, the wild gods
—wood

The polite coal burner
Nyx, the night goddess
  Night Creatures, 13–15

O horrid dede! [monk murdered:
    stealing pig's head]
  Marshall-*Every.*, 240–242
"O luck of the ugly . . ."
  Mitchnik-*Egyptian*, 22–27
O no, not my mother!
  Todd-*Tortoise*, 48–52
OAHU (subject)
—Ivory of Oahu: King Kahahana
  Westervelt-*Hawaiian*, 114–
    124
OAK TREES
  The giant of Skalunda
  Oaks
  Soup from a sausage skewer
—brothers take refuge in
  Darakhvei, the great oak
OAK TREES (subject)
  Briggs-*Vanish.*, 74
OAKMEN
  Oaks
Oaks
  Froud-*Faeries*, unp
OATHS
  The broken oaths
  [Servant forces princess into
    servitude]
—false
  Retribution
—violation of
  The Jerusalemite's story cop-
    ied by R. Abraham
OATMEAL
  The fairy borrowing oatmeal
  The lad who went to the north
    wind
Obdurman the clever huntsman
  Riordan-*Tartary*, 136–143

368

OBEDIENCE
See also DISOBEDIENCE
Adventures of the first dervish
Julio
Upamanyu learns a lesson
[hermitage school]
The wise woman, or The lost
princess
—literal
A test for a disciple
Oberon (subject)
Briggs-Vanish., 142–143, 198
Oberon and Titania
Baskin-Imps, 12–13
Oberon: castles of Alberich
Lee-Castles, 146–147
OBESITY
Pamarindo
OBSESSION
—get one more whale, even
though no room
Greenland whale fishery [song
and story]
Obsidian arrow points
Weeks-Pachee, 25–31
Obstacles: The maze, or Se-eh-
ha's house
Shaw-Pima, 15–16
Occasion [death trapped in bottle]
Shah-World, 258
OCCUPATIONS
See also TRADES
also names of particular
occupations
Master Thief
The Pleiades
OCEAN
See also SEA
The creation of the world
Mer-men
Mer-women
Odd jobs
Poseidon's ocean kingdom
Sea, sun and moon [visiting;
sun and moon . . .
—food from

The man who sat on the tide
OCEAN LIFE
A visit from Mister Sea
—origin of sea animals
Sedna (Eskimo)
O'CONNELL, Daniel, 1775–1847
Daniel O'Connell [justice,
cleverness]
Daniel O'Connell [trickery]
OCTOPUS
—why o. hates rats
The rat and the octopus
Odd by 'sight-blinding': Katla
Seekers Saviors, 13–20
Odd jobs
Gorog-Taste, 43–57
O'Dell, Scott
The black pearl
Oden was a Sunday hunter
Lindow-Swedish, 114–115
ODIN
The apples of eternal life
Asgard: war of the gods and
giants
Balder's doom
The building of the wall of
Asgard
The creation of the world
The curse of Andvari's ring
The death of Balder
Fenrir the wolf is bound
The first humans
The gods' revenge
The golden age in Asgard
Good and evil: Buri vs Ymir
Heimdall in Midgard
How Thor got his hammer
King Gylfi is tricked again
Ragnarok
The Ragnarok, doom of the
gods
Singard the dragon-slayer
Thor fights the giant Krangnir
The walls of Asgard
War in heaven
Yggdrasill, the world ash

ODIN (subject)
—Myths and legends of the
Vikings
Lindow-*Myths*, 6–14
Odin prepares for the Ragnarok
Branston-*Gods*, 72–77
O'Donoghue
Froud-*Faeries*, unp
The O'Donoghue legend
Yeats-*Fairy*, 181–182
ODORS
Odd jobs
ODSHIG
The Fishes [Odschig, the chief]
Odysseus
Stapleton-*Dictionary*, 147–148
ODYSSEUS
Voyage of Odysseus
The wanderings of Odysseus
ODYSSEUS (subject)
Pinsent-*Greek*, 143 (index)
Odysseus and Circe
Lines-*Greek*, 210–216
[Odysseus and Poseidon]
Water Spirits, 45–59
Odysseus: the Trojan War
Low-*Greek*, 146–153
[Odysseus vs Polyphemus]
Wise-*Monster*, 38–45
Oedipus
Low-*Greek*, 70–74
Stapleton-*Dictionary*, 158–164
OEDIPUS
The house of Thebes
Oedipus (subject)
Lloyd-*Mythical*, 57–65
Oedipus: inexorable workings of
man's fate
Lehane-*Legends*, 46–47
"OENNEREESKE" (dwarfs)
The changeling [b]
"Of course!"
Minford-*Fav.*, 61–66
OFFERINGS (subject)
—made to fairies
Briggs-*Vanish.*, 217 (index)

OGIER, the Dane
Charlemagne and Ogier, the
Dane
"OGOPOGO"
Water monsters
O'Grady, Stanish
Knighting of Cuculain
Ogre of Rashomon
Ozaki-*Japanese*, 262–272
The ogre with no soul
Thomas-*It's*, 34–39
OGRES AND OGRESSES
See also HILL OGRES;
TITANS
Abzelil and the Master of the
Lake
The enchanted orchard
The ghoul and the youth of
Ispahan
The gorgon's head
Handsome ogre-girl of the pool
Hop o' My Thumb
Liisa and the prince
Lini the lost prince
Little Thumb
Prince of nettles
The promise of the three
sisters
Puss in Boots
The radiant Sambula
Room Bacha and Baki
Sikulume and the seven
brothers
The sultan and the ogress
—cannibals
Aisha Kandisha and the
drunkard
The grave-yard mule
—disobey: eats hearts
Prince and the ogre's castle
—forces girl to exchange clothes
Mulha
—Oni
The old woman and the rice
cakes
—queen-mother

OGRES AND OGRESSES queen-
mother (continued)
Sleeping Beauty in the wood
—transformed to mouse, eaten by
cat
Puss in Boots
—tricked by child
Man and woman with too
many children
—wants to eat son's wife
Abo Beckeer
OGRES AND OGRESSES
(subject)
—Motif index
Wilbert-*Bororo*, 255–256, 306
The ogre's soul
Villa-*Armenian*, 77–84, 438–
442
Oh Mister Crocodile
Manning-*Cats*, 51–57
O'HANLON, Redmond, d.1681
Redmond O'Hanlon
OHIO
Johnny Appleseed
Johnny Appleseed, the ap-
pleseed planter
OINTMENT
The fary-labour
OINTMENT (subject)
—magic
Briggs-*Vanish.*, 217 (index)
Oisin
Froud-*Faeries*, unp
OISIN (subject)
Briggs-*Vanish.*, 21–22
Oisin in Tir Nan og, or last of the
Fena
McGarry-*Folk*, 87-95
Ojeeg, the hunter, and the Ice Man
De Wit-*Talking*, 39-43
Okiku and the saucers
Kendall-*Haunting*, 12–15
OKLAHOMA
The Johnson boys [song and
story]
Olafur and the trolls

Booss-*Scand.*, 635–636
OLD AGE
Bagged wolf
The creation
Glooscap and the wishes
The golden key
How long will you live?
The hunchbacked old woman
The land where time stood still
The lazy ducks
Legend of the old bell-ringer
A little love story
The lost bell
Man, the burro, and the dog
The new hand [old man made
young again]
The old house
The old man wouldn't take ad-
vice [young wife]
Old people fancies
[Menominee]
Sagacious monkey and the
boar
Seventh father of the house
Ten jugs of wine
War of the wolf and the fox
The werewolf
The wisdom of a child
Youth without age and life
without death (Turkey)
—care
If the boerboon flowers fall
—care of the aged
The aged father
—diversion in
King O'Toole and his goose
—great, great, great grandfathers
The King of Ireland's son (Art)
—kahn kills all old people
The golden vase
—woman supported by tiger that
ate her son
The repentant tiger of
Chaoch'eng
—women's behavior
Bucca Dhu and Bucca Gwidden

"OLD BONES" (devil)
The blacksmith
Ivan, the Windfall
"OLD BONES THE IMMORTAL"
Frog princess: Vassilisa the
Wise
Marya Morevna
—[Folk villain]
Riordan-*Russia*, 280
The old crone who was more wily
than Iblees
Mitchnik-*Egyptian*, 39–46
Old Dry Frye (rogue preacher)
Yolen-*Favorite*, 191–194
Old Erik in the mill
Lindow-*Swedish*, 161–163
Old fire dragaman
Haviland-*N. Amer.*, 160–166
The old flea-bag
Lang-*Green*, 160–165
The old fort [door will not open]
Villa-*Armenian*, 413–414
Old fuddlement
Kendall-*Sweet*, 45–48
The old hag
Sheohmelian-*Three*, 7–10
The old hag and the devil
Stovicek-*Around*, 52–53
The old house
Booss-*Scand.*, 356–362
OLD MAN ALMANACK (the sun)
The three golden hairs of Old
Man Almanack
The old man and his grandson
Yolen-*Favorite*, 62–63
Old man and the sun
Hadley-*Legends*, 10–11
The old man and woman who
switched jobs
Yolen-*Favorite*, 178–180
The old man from Haberg
Lindow-*Swedish*, 88–89
Old Man La Feve [bumblebees]
Thomas-*It's*, 127–128
Old man of Cury (condensed)
Briggs-*Vanish.*, 71–72

The old man of the sea [Sinbad]
Rackham-*Fairy*, 88–93
Old Man of the Sea;-Earth;-
Fire: . . . golden key
Macdonald-*Golden*, 1–35
Old man who made withered trees
to flower
Ozaki-*Japanese*, 177–188
The old man wouldn't take advice
[young wife]
Lester-*Black*, 139–146
Old man Zackery and the cranes
Manning-*Cats*, 92–96
Old Mother Shipton
Marshall-*Every.*, 288–295
"OLD NICK"
The skipper and old Nick
Old Nick and the girl
Booss-*Scand.*, 203–206
Old Nick and the pedlar
Booss-*Scand.*, 224–229
Old Nick is a gentleman
Marshall-*Every.*, 99–103
Old One Eye [robbers foiled]
Macdonald-*Twenty*, 43–51
Old people fancies [Menomi-
nee]
Myles-*Butterflies*, 47–50
"OLD SAND SPIRIT"
The fire plume
The old smith
Sampson-*Gypsy*, 49–54
The old tiger and the hare
Zong-*Korea*, 157–160
Old Tommy and the spectre
Manning-*Spooks*, 9–14
The old troll of Big Mountain
Crossley-*Folk*, 38–42
Old troll tricked into revealing his
treasure
Lindow-*Swedish*, 75–76
[The old, vagrant woman and] The
three bears
Rackham-*Fairy*, 188–191
The old witch
Garner-*British*, 92–96

The old woman and El Senor
 Campos-*Mexican,* 73–76
The old woman and her pig
 Ross-*Druids,* 1–9
The old woman and her rice
 Raychaudhuri-*Stupid,* 30–32
Old woman and the doctor
 Williams-*Aesop,* [14–15]
The old woman and the rice
 cakes
 Phelps-*Maid,* 59–63
The old woman and the tramp
 Booss-*Scand.,* 182–186
The old woman who lived in a vin-
 egar bottle
 Yolen-*Favorite,* 283–285
Old woman who stole milk
 Radin-*African,* 279–283
Old woman's faith overcomes devil
 O'Sullivan-*Legends,* 27–29
The old woman's prayer
 O'Sullivan-*Legends,* 97
The Oldenburg horn
 Keightley-*World,* 273–238
The oldest: deer, hare, and toad
 Zong-*Korea,* 33–34
O'Leary, Ellen
—A legend of Tyrone [poem]
 Yeats-*Fairy,* 121–122
Olga and the brown cow
 Riordan-*Russia,* 238–240
Oliver, Tony, illus.
 Stokes-*Turtle*
Olli the terrible
 Crouch-*Whole,* 11–19
OLYMPUS
 The new gods-*Zeus and Hera*
O'MALLEY, Grace, *ca.*1530–
 *ca.*1600.
 Grace O'Malley [a & b]
Omelya and the pike
 Ransome-*War,* 35–39
Omens
 Robe-*Hispanic,* 51–54
OMENS
 Folk beliefs about portents

—flight of birds
 Zan and the Dactyls in early
 Crete
Omens: the owl; the cuckoo
 Magical Beasts, 81
The Omokoy: children of the tribe
 Stokes-*Turtle,* 26–28
On naming a son [Joseph]
 Lewis-*Bedtime,* 40–41
On top of Old Smoky [song and
 story]
 Sanders-*Hear,* 59–70
Onaouientagos
 Colombo-*Wind.,* 8
Onassis, Jacqueline
—Zvorykin and Russian tales
 Zvorykin-*Firebird,* 6–8
Once a good man [eat with arms
 chained]
 Yolen-*Hundredth,* 53–57
One for you, one for me
 Stuchl-*American,* 59–60
One hairball
 Kendall-*Sweet,* 73–77
One member of a family fated to
 die
 O'Sullivan-*Legends,* 20
"One, my darling, come to mama"
 Wolkstein-*Magic,* 16–170
One night in Paradise (Italy)
 Yolen-*Favorite,* 428–430
One particular small, smart boy
 Lewis-*Minute,* 16–17
The one that got away
 Ritchie-*Armadillo,* 50–55
One who deserved the money
 Kudian-*More,* 65–67
"ONE WHO KNOWS"
 Tiyo travels through the
 underworld
The one who would not listen to his
 own dream
 Wolkstein-*Magic,* 72–74
One word solves a mystery
 Roberts-*Chinese,* 220–221
 Shannon-*Solve,* 48–50

ONEATA (island)
  Tuwara, the cunning one
Oni
  Piggott-*Japanese*, 61–65
ONION PATCH
  The rabbit and the two coyote
Onions, Oliver
  The mortal
Onions
  Zong-*Korea*, 20–21
ONIONS
  King Lindorm [a snake]
  What happened to six wives
    who ate onions
—wild
  What happened to six wives
    who ate onions
Onions [keg of "powder"]
  Schwartz-*Tales*, 11–12
Only a dream
  Hoke-*Spirits*, 55–62
The only child who left home
  Amore-*Lustful*, 48–49
Only One, the great shaman
  Wood-*Spirits*, 58–63
Oolak, the Moon-God, and the
    Angekkok
  Shelley-*Legends*, 63–69
Oona and the giant Cuchulain
  Riordan-*Woman*, 35–41
OONAGH
—saves Finn by her cleverness
  Knockmany legend
Oonagh and the giants
  McCarty-*Skull*, 7–13
Oongnairwah and Guinarey
  Parker-*Australian*, 53
Opame, Chenrezik, and Dolma
  Hyde-Chambers-*Tibet*, 5–6
Opele-of-the-Long-Sleeps
  Thompson-*Hawaiian*, 43–50
"OPEN SESAME"
  Ali Baba and the forty thieves
The open window [by Saki]
  Manley-*Fun*, 123–127
  Schwartz-*Great*, 39–41

Ophiuchus (the Serpent Holder)
  Gallant-*Constel.*, 78–82
OPIUM-EATERS
  Lam Ku, the basket lady
OPOSSUMS
  Brer possum and brer snake
  The dog and the possum [origin of enmity]
  The sleepy one: Senor
    Opossum and the rattler
  Why the opossum's tail is bare
  Wiley and the hairy man
—origin
  Man into possum [solitary fish thief]
—why no hair on tail
  The witches' fire
Oppression: The Amir who was a
    beggar
  Shah-*Afghanistan*, 108–113
ORACLES
  The adventure of Perseus
  The house of Thebes
—shaman
  The yes-no-yes-no spirit
ORAL TALES (subject)
  Thomas-*It's*, 208–211
ORANGE TREES
  The magic orange tree [child abuse]
  Selim and the snake queen
ORCHARDS
  See also TREES
  The three sons
—cherry
  The enchanted orchard
Orchids
  Ewart-*Lore*, 130–132
ORCHIDS
  Green thoughts
ORCULLI
  Norggen, Orculli and
    Fankenmannikins
ORDER
—excessive
  The crocodile in the bedroom

ORDERLINESS
The crocodile in the bedroom
ORDERS
"Lars, my lad!"
Oresteia (Aeschylus)
Stapleton-*Dictionary*, 164–166
ORESTES (subject)
Pinsent-*Greek*, 143 (index)
Orestes: the violent creed of
vengeance
Lehane-*Legends*, 50
The organ that brayed like a
donkey
Schwartz-*Tales*, 19–22
ORIANDE la Fee (subject)
Briggs-*Vanish.*, 145, 198
ORIENTAL ROMANCES (subject)
—Arabian romance
Keightley-*World*, 24–28
—Persian romance
Keightley-*World*, 14–20
Origin of certain fish [from flowers,
palm-leaf, &]
Wilbert-*Bororo*, 149–150
Origin of certain necklaces and
plants
Wilbert-*Bororo*, 132–135
Origin of death [Hottentot]
Radin-*African*, 63
Origin of death: Krachi
Radin-*African*, 60–61
Origin of dogs
Wilbert-*Bororo*, 147–148
Origin of gourd trumpet, memento
of the dead
Wilbert-*Bororo*, 125–126
The origin of music
Bierhorst-*Hungry*, 37–38, 135
Origin of sickness
Wilbert-*Bororo*, 81–86
Origin of sun shield and joints of
bamboo
Wilbert-*Bororo*, 130–132
Origin of the Acuma leaf headdress
Wilbert-*Bororo*, 107–109
Origin of the aige

Wilbert-*Bororo*, 119–120
Origin of the house of Haro
Keightley-*World*, 458–459
Origin of the name "Bokodori
Exerae"
Wilbert-*Bororo*, 92–93
Origin of the names of some stars
Wilbert-*Bororo*, 51–55
Origin of the Narran Lake
Parker-*Australian*, 24–26
Origin of the poari
Wilbert-*Bororo*, 126–127
Origin of the stars and of certain
animals
Wilbert-*Bororo*, 47–51
The origin of the winds
Wood-*Spirits*, 25–28
Origin of Tiis Lake
Keightley-*World*, 111–112
[Origin of tobacco] The Kuddogo
fish
Wilbert-*Bororo*, 144–146
ORIGINS
See also titles beginning with
"How . . .", "Origin . . ."
"Where . . .", "Why . . ."
See also subhead—origin un-
der particular topics:
MOON; SUN; etc.
—multiple
Gumiya; a Blang story
The sky-god: Ratu and the
Dyaks
ORIGINS (subject)
—Motif index
Wilbert-*Bororo*, 307
Origins of the world
Pinsent-*Greek*, 10–18
ORIOLES
Why the sun rises when the
rooster crows
ORION (constellation)
Artemis, Orion and the Seven
Sisters
The Scorpion [Orion, the
Hunter]

The Seven Sisters
Orion (the Hunter)
Gallant-*Constel.*, 121–125
ORKNEY ISLANDS
Annie Norn and the fin folk
Glashans and Shopiltees
Selkies
ORKNEY ISLANDS (subject)
Keightley-*World*, 171–174
ORLANDO(S) (subject)
—age of fantasy.
Lee-*Castles*, 137–145
ORNAMENTS
The golden tree [queen and
amulet]
Orobas: demon
Lehane-*Wizards*, 77
The orphan boy and the elk dog
Yolen-*Favorite*, 220–227
Orphan Yan Ran [Kawa]
Magic Knife, 66–79
ORPHANS
The Angekkok, Oolak, and the
Moon-God
Julio
King Zargand's daughter
Little Goody Two-Shoes
Magic brush; a Han folktale
Olga and the brown cow
The phantom carousel
Spindle, shuttle, and needle
The strongest boy in the world
—war
Shurik: A story of the siege of
Leningrad
Orpheus
Low-*Greek*, 66–70
ORPHEUS (subject)
Briggs-*Vanish.*, 46–47, 115–
116
Orpheus and Eurydice
Gibson-*Gods*, 113–118
Nye-*Out*, 31–43
Yolen-*Favorite*, 422–423
O'SHEA, Kathleen
Countess Kathleen O'Shea

OSKOREI (subject)
Briggs-*Vanish.*, 151–152
Oskus-ool and his wise wife
Titiev-*Moolah*, 36–53
OSONG BUWON-GUN, General
The tiger priest
Ossian. *See* OISIN
The ostler and the grave robbers
(Scotland)
Yolen-*Favorite*, 444
The ostrich in love
Lobel-*Fables*, 20–21
OSTRICHES
Hyena eats the ostrich's eggs
The other Celia
Hoke-*Horrors*, 142–163
OTHERWORLD
Erikur rescues a woman from
the otherworld
How three serpents carried
princesses . . .
Nera and the Otherworld
Rainbow bridge: Buck Ante-
lope and Evening Breeze
—next life experience
One night in Paradise (Italy)
OTOTACHIBANA, Princess
Prince Vamato Take
OTTERS
Adventures of Ntini, the small
otter
The curse of Andvari's ring
Fishing of the women [adultery
with otters]
Fudo and the prickly pear
thieves
Hare and otter
Master rabbit [tries to do what
other species do]
The rabbit makes a match
Sea friend: otter saves monk's
lost book
Singard the dragon-slayer
Swarthy Smith of the Socks
The toad and the fire
—called "nair" or "water-cat"

OTTERS—called "nair" or "water-
cat" (continued)
The golden knucklebone
—white, sea
Mouse Woman and the mon-
ster killer whale
—why it has small eyes
[Origin of tobacco] The Kud-
dogo fish
OUD (musical instrument)
The golden mountain
Our-Lady-of-the-Swallows
Yourcenar-*Oriental,* 85–99
The outlaw
Booss-*Scand.,* 496–499
Outlaw stories: Belle Starr, H.
Starr, F. Edings, James
brothers
Steele-*Ozark,* 45–55
OUTLAWS
Bad Indian's ashes [flies tor-
ment people]
Outwitting giants
Villa-*Armenian,* 361–364, 523
Outwitting the devil
Lindow-*Swedish,* 158–159
Outwitting the landlord
Peacock Maid, 134–141
Ouyan the curlew
Parker-*Australian,* 62–63
OVENS
The old witch
Overcrowdedness: Big family in the
little house
Lewis-*Bedtime,* 36–37
Overdoing it
Roberts-*Chinese,* 59
OVEREATING
The hippopotamus at dinner
OVERLAND JOURNEYS TO THE
PACIFIC
Sweet Betsy from Pike [song
and story]
OVID
[World-devastating flood in-
flicted by Zeus]

Owen, Mary Alicia, 1850–1935.
How ole woodpecker got ole
rabbit's conjure bag
Social customs and usages in
Mo. [19th cent.]
The owl
Manning-*Spooks,* 39–42
The owl [14 legends]
Robe-*Hispanic,* 348–355
The owl and the pussycat
dePaola-*Favorite,* 68–69
Tudor-*Bedtime,* [36–37]
Owl [ashamed of his face]
Wolkstein-*Magic,* 30–36
"OWL-MAN"
The spirit-wife
Owl with the face of a woman
Ritchie-*Armadillo,* 25–29
Owl with the great head and eyes
Macmillan-*Canadian* 214–
219
OWLS
Adventures of Ntini, the small
otter
The baker's daughter
Caliph Stork
The conjure wives
Cross purposes
Eerin, the small grey owl
The enchanted princess
No pooch 'em
El pajaro cu
Pretty Goldilocks
Seven families of Lake Pipple-
Popple
The small, small cat
The tale of Squirrel Nutkin
The Wooing of Olwen
—cry "Pu-nin-ga"
Little Elga
—hoot
Who got brer Gilyard's
treasure?
—monster
Water buffaloes
—origin of characteristics

Owl with the great head and
     eyes
—punished
The girl who always cried
—war with crows
The wise old crow
—wise
Pepito Conejo: prepare for
     winter
—women transformed into
The dance of the owls
OWNERSHIP
The girl who was already
     queen
Owney and Owney-na-peak
     Yeats-*Fairy*, 356–366
"OX STAR"
The herd boy and the weaving
     girl
OXEN
Animals in winter
The apples of Iduna
The farmer who listened to his
     livestock
The fool and the birch
The frog and the ox
Great Joy, the self-respecting
     ox
How the tiger got his stripes
How they got Hairlock home
Man without a heart
The nis riding
The stolen ox
The straw ox
Svend Faelling
The tricking of King Gilfi
—blue
Babe the blue ox
—origin of characteristics
Bao Luotuo the sage
—yokes
How they got Hairlock home
Oxen and the creaky wheels
     Williams-*Aesop*, [17]
OYSTERS
—shells

The black pearl
Ozark Mountain riddles
     McNeil-*Charm*, 59–68

Paao from Samoa
     Westervelt-*Hawaiian*, 65–78
Pablito prays for El Senor Diablo
     MacLean-*Cuentos*, 160–162
The Paddo
     Garner-*British*, 119–122
Paddock in heaven (England)
     Yolen-*Favorite*, 472
Paddy Corcoran's wife
     Yeats-*Fairy*, 35–37
Paddy O'Kelly and the weasel
     Jacobs-*Celtic*, 183–188
Padilla, Stan, illus.
     Walking-*Song*
Padmasambhava and the felicity
     scarf
     Hyde-Chambers-*Tibet*, 21–23
PAGODAS
Prince Nocha
PAIN
The night bird
Paintbrush. *See* BRUSHES
PAINTERS AND PAINTING
The apprentice [rabbit as
     painter]
The cruel painter
The god of faces
How Wang-Fo was saved
Magic brush; a Han folktale
Pierre Brassau ["non-objective"
     painting by monkey]
The sadness of Cornelius Berg
Unofficial history of the Confu-
     cian Academy
The wonderful Chuang
     brocade
A pair of skinnies
     Crouch-*Whole*, 20–25

PAISLEY
 Pixy-gratitude
PAITATUMA (Bringer of Dawn)
 The corn maidens
El pajaro cu
 Aiken-*Mexican,* 4–6
Palace of Oblivion
 Lee-*Castles,* 144–145
The palace of the moon
 Wood-*Palace,* 9–23
PALACES
 The daughter of Peter de
  Cabinam
 Fairies, English
 The herd-boy
 Hildur, the queen of the elves
 Hodeken
 "Lars, my lad!"
 Mysterious palace [Solomon &
  Ramirat]
 The nightingale
 Prince Meerzat Istvan and the
  horse of dust . . .
 Sunken palace: King Corc and
  Fior Usga
 The water palace [boat and
  feathers]
—magic
 The war of the birds and the
  beasts
—in the sky
 Wooden horse [mechanical
  flight]
—underwater
 The peasant and the
  waterman
PALANQUIN
 The tiger and the palanquin
Paleschuk and the devil
 Cortes-*Byelorussian,* 130–
  136
PALESTINE
—Ashkelon
 Witches of Ashkelon
"Pallas-Athene." *See* ATHENE
Palmer, Francis L.

How Jack went to seek his
 fortune
Palsson, Herman, jt. author
 The burning of Bergthorsknoll
PALULKON (Great Plumed
 Serpent)
 The youth who brought the
  corn
Pamarindo
 Arrowsmith-*Field,* 150–151
PAN (god)
 Midas, the golden king
 The Sea Goat [Pan vs Typhon]
Pan and Dionysus, the wild gods
 Gibson-*Gods,* 60–61
Pan and Satyr (condensed)
 Lloyd-*Mythical,* 43–49
Pan is dead
 O'Sullivan-*Legends,* 54–55
The Pan legend
 Lindow-*Swedish,* 99–101
Pan, the goat-god
 Magical Beasts, 32–35
The pancake
 Booss-*Scand.,* 10–12
PANCAKES
 The unwilling magician
Pandora
 Low-*Greek,* 26–29
PANDORA'S BOX
 Prometheus and Pandora
 [Pandora's box: evils/hope]
 Spells & Bind, 58–61
PANGU (subject)
—Gods from the dawn of time
 (China)
 Sanders-*Dragons,* 13–17
Panhu, the marvelous dog
 Sanders-*Dragons,* 38–39
PANPIPES
 How panpipes came to be
  played (Miao)
Pansies
 Ewart-*Lore,* 42–45
Pansy
 Froud-*Faeries,* unp.

PANTHERS
    The jackal, the dove, and the
      panther
PAPA GOD
    Cat and dog and return of the
      dead
    A very happy donkey
    Papa God and General Death
      Wolkstein-*Magic*, 76–78
    "Papa God first, man next, tiger last"
      Wolkstein-*Magic*, 178–181
    Papa God sends turtle doves
      Wolkstein-*Magic*, 88–90
    The Papa-Water and Bibaiyibaiyi
      Todd-*Some*, 160–169
PAPAW TREES
    —origin
      Papaya
    Papaya [origin]
      Stokes-*Turtle*, 97–99
PAPUA NEW GUINEA
    How a man found his wife in
      the Land of the Dead
    In the land of the dead
    —origin
    The turtle and the island
PAPUA NEW GUINEA TALES
    (subject)
    —[Creative writing effort of Univ.
      students]
      Stokes-*Turtle*, 6–8
    —[Map showing locations]
PARADISE
    See also GARDEN OF EDEN;
      HEAVEN
    Connla and the fairy-maiden
    La cucaracha
    The golden age in Asgard
    One night in Paradise (Italy)
    The pilgrim from paradise
    Prospectors in Paradise
    —not for those who have "everlast-
      ing life"
    The well of everlasting life
    The parakeet named Dreidel
      Singer-*Power*, 17–22

PARAKEETS
    —once man-eating
    The Bakororo and Itubore
      legend
PARENT AND CHILD
    See also FILIAL PIETY
    The boy and his grandfather
    Hansel and Gretel
    Journey of Nonogo Pori
    The magic shawl and the en-
      chanted trumpet
    The reason for turtles
    [Search for parents] Pari Ao
    —bad behavior reflects parents
    The bad kangaroo
PARENTS
    See also CHILDREN; FA-
      THERS; MOTHERS;
      STEPMOTHERS
    Eye will see what it is destined
      to see
    Powdered blondie and three-
      haired blondie
    The three brothers
    —foster
    Fairest of all others
Parents and children. *See* PAR-
    ENT AND CHILD
PARIS (god)
    The apple of discord
    Helen of Troy
Parker, Agnes Miller, illus.
    Sampson-*Gypsy*
Parkman, Francis
    Legendary Lore
Parler, Mary Celestia
    Folklore from the campus
Parley Garfield and the frogs
    Macdonald-*Twenty*, 52–56
The parrot tale-teller
    Aiken-*Mexican*, 32–37
Parrot that says, "Kra, Kra,
    Kra"
    Wilbert-*Bororo*, 151
The parrot who bought firewood
    Griego-*Cuentos*, 111–113

PARROTS
Brave little parrot and the eagle's tears
The Gojmati
How the Brazilian beetles got their . . . coats
No pooch 'em
"Of course!"
Periquito, wood dealer
Seven families of Lake Pipple-Popple
The steadfast parrot and his tree
Tales of a parrot
Who is my neighbour?
—crimson
The crimson parrot
—matchmaker
The waiting maid's parrot (China)
—origin
The greedy boy
—origin of Acuma crests
Origin of the Acuma leaf headdress
—red breast, origin
The witches' fire
—talking
Parselina [marriage to evil dwarf]
The waiting maid's parrot
Parselina [marriage to evil dwarf]
Fattoross-*Simpleton,* 47–51
PARSLEY
Death out of season
Puddocky
The parson and the clerk [I]
Booss-*Scand.,* 52–53
The parson and the clerk [II]
Booss-*Scand.,* 232–237
Parson and the clerk [island in Devon]
Marshall-*Every.,* 270–274
The parson and the sexton
Yolen-*Favorite,* 29–30

Parson could not say "our daily bread"
Lindow-*Swedish,* 187
PARSONAGES
The giant and Johannes Blessom
Parsons. *See* CLERGYMEN
PARTIES
How the toad got his bruises
The spook's party
The parting song
Stuchl-*American,* 251–252
PARTNERS
The cat and mouse in partnership
Partnership with Asmodeus
Schwartz-*Elijah,* 101–106
The partridge and his drum
Macmillan-*Canadian* 44–49
PARTRIDGES
Gumiya; origins of characteristics
Pulowech, the partridge
The party
McCarthy-*Raccoon,* 11–21
PASCAGOULA BAY
Song that comes from the sea
PASQUE FLOWER
Anemone and pasque flower
Passage of time. *See* TIME — passage of
The passing of Arthur
Malory-*King,* 243–282
The passing of Glooskap [whites vs Indians]
Macmillan-*Canadian* 69–75
Passion flower
Ewart-*Lore,* 120
The passion of the gewel
Magel-*Gambia,* 50–52
PASSION(S)
The monk and Lady Kiyo
The apes and the busybody bird
The destruction of love
—conquest of, exposed

The monkey-faced suitor
Passover soup
  Elbaz-*Folktales*, 140
PASTURES
  Meadows and pastures
PATERNITY TESTS
  Merirodo and her husband
  Kuieje Kuri
  The three stars
PATER-ROLLERS
  Simon and the pater-rollers
PATIENCE
  See also IMPATIENCE
  The fairy and the prince
  The giant maiden in Boraserod
  mountain
  The goose with the golden
  feathers
  Kupti and Imani
  Patient Griselda
  Sleeping Beauty in the woods
  The spirit-wife
  Story of Ivan and Imbecile
Patience of Hillel
  Patai-*Gates*, 223–224
Patience overcomes fate [piast]
  O'Sullivan-*Legends*, 18–19
Patient Griselda
  Shah-*World*, 73–74
The patient suitor
  Villa-*Armenian*, 175–180,
  469
PATRICIDE
  Toribugu: legend of the hero
PATRICK, Saint
  The cat and the dog
  Conversion of King Laoghair's
  daughters
  The golden idol
  Lough Derg
  Oisin
  Oisin in Tir Nan Og, or last of
  the Fena
  The plaice and the salmon
  Saint Patrick and Crom Dubh
  Saint Patrick curses Ireland

The tavern-woman and St.
  Patrick
  —Celtic magic
  Lochhead-*Battle*, ix
PATROCLUS
  Achilles and the death of
  Hector
Patterns in the sky
  Gallant-*Constel.*, 3–18
Paudyeen O'Kelly and the weasel
  (condensed)
  Briggs-*Vanish.*, 175–180
Paul Bunyan
  Lewis-*Bedtime*, 34–35
Paul Bunyan, the giant logger
  Lisker-*Tall*, 22–32
Paul Jones
  O'Sullivan-*Legends*, 145–146
PAVEMENTS
  The winding-horn village
Pawpaw. *See* PAPAW TREES
PAYMENTS
  The walls of Asgard
PAYUPKI (Indian village)
  Foot racers of Payupki
PEACE
  The first Inca: marriage of sun
  and moon
  Glooscap, the peacemaker
  The good sons
  How the Thai learned to be
  calm
  Opame, Chenrezik, and Dolma
  People of peace
  Quiet folk
  —psychology
  The eternal light [Solomon &
  Benaiah]
Peace in the grave
  Lindow-*Swedish*, 188–189
"PEACE STEAD"
  Balder's doom
The peach thief
  Roberts-*Chinese*, 45–48
PEACHES
  —son born from

Dumplings in the river
The giant maiden in Boraserod
  mountain
The golden cradle
Halde hat
A hundred times
Is much land needed for a
  man?
The knights of Allaberg
The magician's pupil
The man/whale
Outwitting the landlord
Peter Bull
Seven Simeons
The shepherd and the em-
  peror's daughter
Stan Bolovan and the dragon
Sun tribute
Tibet's first king
The troll's hammer
The water nymph
The witch
The wonderful little pouch
—and rulers
Unofficial history of the Confu-
  cian Academy
—tricked by fox
Little Sister Fox and Brother
  Wolf
PEBBLES
Hansel and Gretel
The little hare
Performing stick
Pecos Bill and the cyclone
Lisker-*Tall*, 10–21
Pecos Bill becomes a coyote
Haviland-*N. Amer.*, 169–174
Peddler of Swaffham (England)
Yolen-*Favorite*, 414–415
PEDDLERS
Mice in the corn
Old Nick and the pedlar
On top of Old Smoky [song
  and story]
Pedorus Jack
Heslewood-*Tales*, 83–87

Pedro de Ordimalas
Griego-*Cuentos*, 161–171
Pedro de Ordinales goes to heaven
Campos-*Mexican*, 51–54
Pedro de Urdemalas
Aiken-*Mexican*, 55–61
Peerifool [secret name of fairy]
Ratcliff-*Scottish*, 88–92
PEG O'NELL (subject)
Briggs-*Vanish.*, 68–70, 81, 198
Peg Powler
Froud-*Faeries*, unp
PEG POWLER (subject)
Briggs-*Vanish.*, 68, 81, 198
Pegasus
Magical Beasts, 57–65
PEGASUS
The death of the Chimaera
The phantom carousel
Prince Bellerophon and
  Pegasus
PEGASUS (subject)
Lloyd-*Mythical*, 39–42
Pegasus (the Winged Horse)
Gallant-*Constel.*, 105–106
Peik
Booss-*Scand.*, 44–49
Yolen-*Favorite*, 144–150
The peistha discomforted
Haining-*Lepre.*, 84–85
PELEUS (subject)
Pinsent-*Greek*, 144 (index)
Peleus and Thetis [marriage]
Lines-*Greek*, 129–145
The pelican and the crane
Lobel-*Fables*, 34–35
Pelican babies
Reed-*Aboriginal*, 123–127
The pelican Goolayyahlee
Parker-*Australian*, 152–154
PELICANS
The wicked crow
PELIOS, King
Jason and the golden fleece
PELLAM, King
Noblest quest of all

PELLINOR, Sir
  Sir Pellinor's adventure
Pelops
  Stapleton-*Dictionary*, 173–174
PENATES AND LARES (subject)
  Briggs-*Vanish.*, 54–55
PENITENCE
  Angel of death
  Banshee of the MacCarthys
  Black monk's curse
  Child's soul in a tree
  The fisher-prince with the silver apple
  Ghost of Lady Hobby
  The magic mirror of Rabbi Adam
  The missing butter
  Prince Asraf and the king of the spirits
  The Santo Nino [de Atocha] saves a friendship
  Treasure of the magic icon
  White trout: a legend of Cong
  The wife from heaven
—rewarded
  Desecrators of Rabbi Haim Messas' tomb
The penitent nis
  Keightley-*World*, 141
Penney, Grace Jackson
  How the seven brothers saved their sister
PENNSYLVANIA
  Johnny Appleseed
PENOBSCOT RIVER
—origin
  Gluska'be, the Penobscot hero
Pentecost castle [submerged]
  Lee-*Castles*, 68–69
PEONIES
  The poet and the peony
Peony
  Ewart-*Lore*, 118–120
People. *See* MAN
People and other creatures formed [Sun-father]

Dutton-*Hopi*, 8
People of peace
  Arrowsmith-*Field*, 144–148
PEOPLE OF PEACE (subject)
  Briggs-*Vanish.*, 7, 33–34, 50–51
People who could fly
  Lester-*Black*, 147–152
Pepito Conejo: prepare for winter
  MacLean-*Cuentos*, 146–147
Pepito el corcovado
  Keightley-*World*, 461–464
PERCIVAL, Sir
  Castle of the Maimed King
  Knights' tales
  Noblest quest of all
  Quest for the Holy Grail
PERFECTION
  Kali beheaded
Perfidy. *See* BETRAYAL; DISHONESTY; TREACHERY
Performing stick
  Kudian-*More*, 48–57
PERFUME
  Pervasive perfume of las zorrillas the skunk
  Strewing, perfumes, pomanders, pot-pourri
Pergrin and the mermaid (Wales)
  Yolen-*Favorite*, 347–348
PERI (subject)
  Keightley-*World*, 22–23
Peril. *See* DANGER
Perilous borderlands
  Water Spirits, 100–125
Perilous paths through the dark
  Night Creatures, 7–37
Periquita
  MacLean-*Cuentos*, 158–159
Periquito, wood dealer
  Aiken-*Mexican*, 90–92
The peri-wife
  Keightley-*World*, 20–22
Perrault, Charles
  Bluebeard
  Cinderella

385

Hop o' My Thumb
Little Red Riding Hood
Puss in Boots
Riquet with the Tuft
Sleeping Beauty in the woods
PERRAULT, Charles (subject)
Quiller-*Sleeping*, 9–14
—[Comment on the tales/Bierhorst]
Perrault-*Glass*, 97–105
—Life and work
Mulherin-*Favorite*, 6–10
PERSECUTION
The deacon of Myrka
The ruse of Rabbi Reuben
Estrogli
—of Jews
Martyrdom of Solika Hatsad-
ika
Persephone
Lines-*Greek*, 42–49
Low-*Greek*, 38–45
PERSEPHONE (subject)
Pinsent-*Greek*, 144 (index)
Persephone among the dead
Gibson-*Gods*, 25–28
Perseus
Gallant-*Constel.*, 125–126
Low-*Greek*, 84–87
Stapleton-*Dictionary*, 175–
177
PERSEUS
The adventures of Perseus
The youngest god [Dionysius]
PERSEUS (subject)
—Gorgon
Lloyd-*Mythical*, 17–23
[Perseus vs Medusa]
Wise-*Monster*, 12–17
PERSEVERANCE
The black lady
The cock who wanted to be
shah
Crow and the jug
The merchant's walk
Tortoise and the hare
Wise frog and foolish frog

—against great odds
Brave little parrot and the ea-
gle's tears
—bird will fill up the sea
The bird and the sea: Jingwei
—slow but sure
Hare and the tortoise [the true
story]
PERSIA
The peri-wife
Prince Feroz-Shah and the fly-
ing horse
Rustam and the iron fortress
PERSIA (subject)
Keightley-*World*, 22–23
PERSIMMONS
—seeds
Quarrel of the monkey and the
crab
Persistence. *See*
PERSEVERANCE
PERSONALITY
—changed by wearing mask
The mask that wore the man
Pervasive perfume of las zorrillas
the skunk
MacLean-*Cuentos*, 145–146
Perversity. *See* STUBBORNNESS
The peryton
Magical Beasts, 98–99
PESTILENCE
The blind boy and his dog
Pestilence, darkness and fire
Synge-*Land*, 204–216
PESTLES
The night bird
The pet of a prince
Wood-*Kalila*, 250–253
PETER, Saint
La cucaracha
The fox who went to heaven
Paddock in heaven (England)
Pedro de Ordinales goes to
heaven
Prospectors in Paradise
Wicked John and the devil

386

PETER, Saint (continued)
—guard at heaven's gate
  The devil's bargain
Peter and the wolf
  Lewis-*Animal*, 34–35
Peter Bull
  Crossley-*Folk*, 133–137
  Lang-*Pink/D*, 126–131
  Lang-*Pink/K*, 80–85
Peter Gynt
  Booss-*Scand.*, 30–34
Peter Rabbit
  Lewis-*Animal*, 40–41
PETER RABBIT
  The tale of Benjamin Bunny
  The tale of Peter Rabbit
PETRELS
  Sedna the sea goddess
PETRIFACTION
—people petrified
  Town of stone
Petronella [sorcerer]
  Williams-*Practical*, 65–80
PETS
  Beaver Tail and the Indians
  February dragon
Petty bargaining
  Elbaz-*Folktales*, 93
PEYOTE
—origin
  How Jiculi served his tribe
Phaethon
  Low-*Greek*, 60–65
PHAETHON
  The chariot of the sun
  The Swan [Phaethon and
    Cygnus]
Phaethon and the sun-horses
  Mayo-*Book*, 98–102
Phantom army of Flowers Barrow
  Marshall-*Every.*, 163–165
The phantom card players
  Robertson-*Highland*, 187–188
The phantom carousel
  Ainsworth-*Phantom*, 7–21
Phantom coach

  Marshall-*Every.*, 106–109
The phantom herd
  MacLean-*Cuentos*, 53–56
The phantom islands
  Haining-*Lepre.*, 95–97
Phantom isle (Giraldus
    Cambrensis)
  Yeats-*Fairy*, 191
Phantoms. *See* GHOSTS
PHARAOHS
  Anpu and Bata
  The ten plagues of Egypt
PHEASANTS
  Momotaro, or the son of a
    peach
—white; wearing feathers of
  How panpipes came to be
    played (Miao)
The pheasants and the bell
  Zong-*Korea*, 96–97
The pheasants, the dove, the mag-
    pie, and the rat
  Zong-*Korea*, 32
Phikool Thong
  Toth-*Tales*, 66–72
Philbert the Fearful
  Williams-*Practical*, 81–99
PHILEMON
  Tree-guardians for a temple:
    Philemon and Baucis
PHILOSOPHERS
  Dream: the philosopher and
    the butterfly
  The great misfortune of Lay
    Tee-Kwai
PHILOSOPHY OF LIFE
  Graduation
PHOENIX (bird)
  Double-headed phoenix
  A fine phoenix
  How salt was discovered
  Son of the Mountain
Phoenix fairy flower [Han]
  Magic Knife, 133–142
Phoenix of Arabia
  Magical Beasts, 82–84

Phooka
    Froud-*Faeries,* unp
PHOOKA (subject)
    Briggs-*Vanish.,* 198
Photogen and Nycteris; a day/night
    mahrchen
    Macdonald-*Golden,* 36–86
Phoukas. *See* POOKAS
Phra Nang Suwanasopha
    Watson-*Thailand,* 43–46
Phya Paan and the Golden Chedi
    Toth-*Tales,* 133–140
PHYA TAN (god)
    How the fire festival came to
    be
The phynnodderee
    Keightley-*World,* 402–403
PHYNNODHEREE (subject)
    Briggs-*Vanish.,* 49, 57, 196
PHYSICIANS
    See also SURGEONS
    Back for Christmas
    The confession of Charles
        Linkworth
    Godfather death (Germany)
    Lochman Hehkeem, the great
        healer
    Melampus—physician and
        prophet
    Partnership with Asmodeus
    The shepherd of Myddvai
    Waxworks
    —Death transforms wood-carrier
    Donald of the Burthens
Picard, Barbara Leonie
    Dietrich of Bern
Pichilingis: It's the mischief-
    makers . . .
    Campos-*Mexican,* 87–90
PICKPOCKETS
    The two pickpockets
PICNICS
    George's picnic
Picotte, Agnes M.
    [Zitkala-Sa and Dakota/Sioux
    legends]

PICTS (subject)
    Briggs-*Vanish.,* 33, 35
PIDGIN ENGLISH (subject)
    Todd-*Some,* 5–16, 179–
    184
The pie and the patty-pan
    Phelps-*Tatterhood,* 71–82
The piebald calf
    Kendall—Sweet, 92–97
The piece of straw
    Lindow-*Swedish,* 66–67
Piece of Zhuang brocade
    Peacock Maid, 54–67
The pied piper of Hamelin
    Classic Child., 40–46
Pierre Brassau ["non-objective"
    painting by monkey]
    Schwartz-*Tales,* 46–47
Pierre, Prince of Murom
    Weiss-*Russian,* 155–166
PIES
    Tom Tit Tot
PIETY
    See also FILIAL PIETY
    —rewarded
    The sultan and the psalms
The pig at the candy store
    Lobel-*Fables,* 30–31
The pig builds the house on the
    hill
    dePaola-*Favorite,* 122–127
The pig who made a hog of him-
    self
    MacLean-*Cuentos,* 148–149
The pigeon with nine heads
    Wright-*Pigeon,* 6–10
PIGEONS
    "Bye-bye" [Haiti]
    Cat lying on velvet cushion,
        while dog sleeps
    How the pigeon became a
        tame bird
    Wise Pigeon
    Zirac and friends
    —golden
    The battle of the birds

PIGEONS (continued)
—rock
    A well-deserved punishment
Piggiebillah the porcupine
    Parker-*Australian*, 138–139
The pig-headed wife
    Booss-*Scand.*, 579–581
Piglet and the cow
    Crouch-*Whole*, 51–58
Pigmies. *See* PYGMIES
Pigs. *See* HOGS
Pigs into pythons
    Stokes-*Turtle*, 103–105
Pikes. *See* FISH—pike
Pikuwa and his wives
    Reed-*Aboriginal*, 69–70
Pilar's indiscretion
    MacLean-*Cuentos*, 102–109
The pilgrim from paradise
    Shah-*World*, 82–83
Pilgrimage to Mecca
    Magel-*Gambia*, 192–195
Pilgrimages to tomb of Rabbi
    Amram Ben Diouane
    Elbaz-*Folktales*, 92
PILGRIMS AND PILGRIMAGES
    Aztec's journey to Anahuac
—Croagh Patrick
    The white gander
—gold cross, silver shrine
    Martha and Mary
PILI
    Paao from Samoa
Pilkington, Simon
    The inheritance
PILLAGE
    The badger and the bear
    The golden cradle
PILLAGE (subject)
—Hawaii: Law
    Westervelt-*Hawaiian*, 162–
    175
Pinders. *See* PEANUTS
PINE GUM FACES
    Big long man's corn patch
PINE TREES

    The crooked pine
—resin
    The troll ride
—roots
    Slip root, catch Reynard's foot
Pinkey, Jerry, illus.
    Wise-*Monster*
Pinks and carnations
    Ewart-*Lore*, 92–95
PINS
    Odd jobs
Pint of flax seeds
    Minford-*Fav.*, 49–60
PIONEERS
    The green prairie
    When I first came to this land
Pious bride and the angel of death
    Patai-*Gates*, 563–565
The pious cow
    Patai-*Gates*, 597–598
PIPE SMOKING
    Why Bootup, the whale,
      smokes a pipe
The piper and the puca
    Haining-*Lepre.*, 88–89
    Yeats-*Fairy*, 88–90
PIPERS
    Finder lock (condensed)
    [Hameln: punishment for not
      keeping bargain]
    King of the pipers and the
      wonderful tune
    The lark's march [contest]
    The white gander
    Why the fairies are vindictive
—a fairy child
    The young piper
PIPES (medicine)
    All that happened must hap-
      pen again
    Anpao is born
    The magic of the moon
PIPES (musical)
    The herd-boy
    Ljungby horn and pipe
    Midas, the golden king

Odd jobs
Pan and Dionysus, the wild
  gods
Rosy apple and the golden
  bowl
Temptations
—compels dancing
Golden reed pipe
The pirate
  Schwartz-*Dark*, 50–59
The pirate princess
  Schwartz-*Elijah*, 237–245
PIRATES
God on our side
The kobold and the pirate
PIRILI (star)
The hunter who threw stars
Pisces (the Fishes)
  Gallant-*Constel.*, 106–108
Piscis Australis (the Southern Fish)
  Gallant-*Constel.*, 116
Piskies in the cellar (condensed)
  Briggs-*Vanish*, 47–48
Piskies or Pisgies. *See* PIXIES
Pisky mischief
  Shub-*Seeing*, 34–63
Pistoleer Mike Fink
  Stuchl-*American*, 73–75
Pitacochi (birds); A tale of love
  Campos-*Mexican*, 127–130
PITCH
—man (trap)
  Coyote fights a lump of pitch
Pitcher and the fox
  Riordan-*Russia*, 194
PITCHERS
The field of Boliauns
—never empty
  Pyoli and Lord Krishna
PITCHFORKS
Simon challenges the
  McCrackens
PITS
The troll shoes
Pitted loquats
  Roberts-*Chinese*, 77

PITY
Jonah and the whale
No pity in women
Pix! Pax! Pox!
  Ainsworth-*Bear*, 84–89
Pixies
  Arrowsmith-*Field*, 132–135
  Froud-*Faeries*, unp
PIXIES
Pisky mischief
The squirrel and the pixie
Susie and her shadow
—water
  Bubbly's trick
PIXIES (subject)
  Briggs-*Vanish.*, 198, 217
  (index)
Pixy-gratitude
  Keightley-*World*, 304–305
The pixy-labour
  Keightley-*World*, 301–303
Pixy-led
  Froud-*Faeries*, unp
Pixy-vengeance
  Keightley-*World*, 303–304
Place memory
  Marshall-*Every.*, 155
Place-names. *See* NAMES, Place
Places and historical traditions
  Robe-*Hispanic*, 486–497
Placido, Francisco, 16th century
How the world began
PLAGIARISM
Low hurdles
The plague of Moscow [Varvarka]
  Weiss-*Russian*, 21–33
Plague omens
  Lindow-*Swedish*, 71–72
Plague victims dig their own
  graves
  Lindow-*Swedish*, 74
PLAGUES
See also BLACK DEATH
Buried alive to stop the
  plague
Lludd and Llefelys

PLAGUES (continued)
Pestilence, darkness and fire
Poe [E. A.] and the castle of
the Red Death
Song-bird and the healing
waters
The ten plagues of Egypt
The plaice and the salmon
O'Sullivan-*Legends*, 39–40
PLAIN OF ASPHODEL
Hades, lord of the underworld
Plant life: True corn; origin
Bierhorst-*Hungry*, 32–33, 135
The plant of gold
Walking-*Song*, 11–14
PLANT RHYS DWYFEN (subject)
Briggs-*Vanish.*, 81, 159–161,
198
PLANTAIN (tree)
—Watcher of the road
Spells & Bind, 40–41
PLANTERS
Wamundo
PLANTS AND PLANTING
Green thoughts
—grow from ashes of slain
monster
Aturuarodo and the monster
Butoriku
—healing
The magic boat
—magic
The seven rats
PLAQUES
Princes and the donkey
The platypus Gayardaree
Parker-*Australian*, 140–142
PLAY
—vs work
Simangolo and the akara
PLAYS [theater]
The walking shadow
PLEASING
—everybody
The miller, his son, and their
donkey

Pleasing everybody: That's no way
to do it!
Lewis-*Bedtime*, 10–11
The Pleiades
Crossley-*Folk*, 13–15
Gallant-*Constel.*, 129–133
PLEIADES (constellation)
How the seven brothers saved
their sister
The seven sisters
Wurrunna and the Seven Sisters
—origin
Meamei the seven sisters
Where the frost comes from
Artemis, Orion and the Seven
Sisters
The crystal sisters
What happened to six wives
who ate onions
The plot to kidnap the Queen
[Salamasina]
Wright-*Pigeon*, 32–37
PLOUGHMEN
Clod's comb
PLOUGHS AND PLOUGHING
The farmer of Liddesdale
Little Claus and Big Claus
The little glass shoe
The nack pulls the plow
The tricking of King Gilfi
The wonderful plough
The wooing of Seppo
Hmarinen
PLUME (feather)
The spirit-wife
PLUMS
The black bull of Norroway
The fiery dragon
When Plum Bush tricked the
trickster
Plunder. *See* PILLAGE
Poe, Edgar Allan
The tell-tale heart [by Poe]
Poe [E. A.] and the castle of the
Red Death
Lee-*Castles*, 180/181

Poe [E. A.] and the house of Usher
  Lee-*Castles*, 179
The poet and the peony
  Sadler-*Heaven*, 15–20
POETICAL
  See also NONSENSE; RE-
    PETITIVE RHYMES AND
    STORIES; RHYMES
  Beowulf fights the dragon
  The clever mice
  Deer and Vila
  Duke Magnus and the
    mermaid
  The elf-woman and Sir Olof
  Escape at bedtime [poem]
  The exile of the sons of Uisliu
  Favorite verses, proverbs, and
    riddles
  Gertrude and Rosy
  The goblin and the huckster
  Goldilocks [in verse]
  The goose girl
  How Sigourd awoke Brynhild
    upon Hindfell
  La infantina
  Lai D'Ywenee
  The lay of Thrym
  Lion and the mouse [in verse]
  Little Red Riding Hood [in
    verse]
  Lord Nann and the Korrigans
  The Nomad
  The noodle
  The owl and the pussycat
  Power of the harp
  Proud Margaret
  Puck
  Shingebiss: the wild duck
  Sir Olof in the elve-dance
  Sir Thynne
  Sugar-plum tree [poem]
  Suit of white feathers
    (Dongxiang)
  Toad's wedding [to Miss
    Mouse] [in verse]
  Vilas
  The walker of the snow
  Wasting sickness of Cu
    Chulaind, and . . . Emer
  The Wendigo
  The Windigo [I]
  Windigo [II]
  The young swain and the
    elves
POETS AND POETRY
  The dance of the thirteen
    skeletons
  Eodain the poetess
  Leanan-Sidhe
  A princess on a swing
  Seanchan the Bard and the
    king of the cats
  Waxworks
  —prayer ends drought
  Princess Hase
POHJA (or Pohjola)
  The mistress of Pohja
  The rivals
The pointing finger
  Kendall-*Sweet*, 60–62
Pointing the bone: Spooks
  a-hunting
  Manning-*Spooks*, 24–27
POISON
  Clever Daniel
  Death out of season
  Ditch-digger falls into his own
    ditch
  Gold-tree and Silver-tree
  The riddle
  The ridere of riddles
  The sorceress
  A stepchild that was treated
    mighty bad
  The world of ice and fire
"POISON BAG"
  The iguana and the black
    snake
Poisonous persimmons
  Zong-*Korea*, 188–189
POLAND
  Domoviye

POLAND (continued)
Moss people
Rusalky
—Warsaw
The power of light
POLAR BEARS
The day Tuk became a hunter
How the polar bear became
Polaris (the Pole Star)
Gallant-*Constel.*, 24–28
Pole Star. *See* NORTH STAR
Polecats. *See* SKUNKS
Poleviki and Poludnitsy
Arrowsmith-*Field*, 242–245
POLGRAINS, Sarah
Yorkshire Jack and Sarah
Polgrains
POLICE
Why wolves fear the bell
The police marshall [mass murder]
Zong-*Korea*, 129–136
The polite coal burner
Booss-*Scand.*, 293
Politeness. *See* COURTESY
POLITICAL ETHICS
Underworld justice
POLITICAL SATIRE
—on greed
Liza the fox and Catafay the
cat
POLITICIANS
—buying offices
The scholar's concubine
—gifts from
Hearsay
POLITICS
Jack o' lanterns
Polly MacGarry, the Co. Leitrim
witch
Logan-*Old*, 91–92
POLTERGEISTS (subject)
Briggs-*Vanish.*, 57–58, 127
Poltersprites
Arrowsmith-*Field*, 222–225
POLUDNITSY
Poleviki and Poludnitsy

POLYANDRY
Matching wits [two robbers
have same wife]
POLYGAMY
Caterina the Wise (Sicily)
The dreamer and his dream
Manyi's escape [wife eaten by
mistake]
POLYNESIA
The giant eel
Maui and the islands
Taufatahi and Fakapatu or
Why sharks . . . Moungone
POLYNESIANS (subject)
—Legendary home
Westervelt-*Hawaiian*, 41–46
[Polyphemus vs Odysseus]
Wise-*Monster*, 38–45
POMANDER BALL
[Well at the World's End]
POMANDERS
Strewing, perfumes, po-
manders, pot-pourri
The pomegranate prince
Bang-*Five*, 64–78
POMEGRANATE TREES
King of the pomegranate tree
Pom-Pom the clown
Ainsworth-*Bear*, 69–74
Ponam Island [first people on]
Stokes-*Turtle*, 93–95
PONDS
—reflects stars
The stars in the sky
Ponds. *See* POOLS
Ponies. *See* HORSES—ponies
Pooka [or puca]
Yeats-*Fairy*, 87
POOKAS
The cold iron spurs
Crookened back [pooka]
Kildare pooka
The nightmare steed
The piper and the puca
The white gander
—ass: housework as punishment

Kildare pooka
Pookong kills a bear
  Dutton-*Hopi*, 27–28
A pool of bright water
  Manning-*Cats*, 58–64
POOLS
  Asrai
  Urisk
  The wooing of Seppo
    Hmarinen
—for bathing
  Tortoise and hare: a dying
    wish
—reflections
  Echo and Narcissus
The poor lame horse
  Mayo-*Book*, 81–89
The poor man and his thousand
    tanga
  Riordan-*Tartary*, 125–128
The poor man Monokto
  Nagishkin-*Folktales*, 80–86
Poor man of Peatlaw (condensed)
  Briggs-*Vanish.*, 49
The poor man's bowl
  Mitchnik-*Egyptian*, 31–37
The poor old dog
  Lobel-*Fables*, 24–25
The poor rich man's son gets a
    second chance
  Campos-*Mexican*, 111–114
Poor Sandy [conjure woman]
  Shepard-*Conjure*, 1–12
Poor. *See* POVERTY
Poor turkey girl
  Haviland-*N. Amer.*, 76–82
POORHOUSES
  Hanukkah in the poorhouse
POPES
  The fisherman and his wife
  Ku Klux Klansmen and the
    Pope
POPLAR TREES
  The chariot of the sun
Popocatepetl and Ixtlaccihuatl
  Piggott-*Mexican*, 12–21

Poppy
  Ewart-*Lore*, 96–101
PORCUPINES
  Goannas and porcupines
  The heavenly song of the
    green-spotted dove
  Mouse Woman and the por-
    cupine hunter
—origin
  The Weeoombeens and the
    Piggiebillah
  First pig and porcupine
—origin: flat nose
  How turtle came
—origin of quills
  Piggiebillah the porcupine
—quills
  End of the world (Sioux tale)
Pork and honey
  Booss-*Scand.*, 138–139
PORPOISES
  Pikuwa and his wives
  The porpoises of Koromira
  Stokes-*Turtle*, 128–129
PORRIDGE
  Axe porridge
—oatmeal
  How porridge was cooked in
    Gotham
Porridge pot [magic]
  Lewis-*Minute*, 36–37
Portent from the Nissar
  Lindow-*Swedish*, 71
Portents. *See* OMENS
PORTRAITS
—ugly (on purpose)
  King Miroslav and the proud
    princess
PORTUGAL
  The dancing princess
  Duende
Portunes
  Arrowsmith-*Field*, 230–231
  Keightley-*World*, 285–286
POSEIDON
  Mother Earth and her children

POSEIDON (continued)
   Peleus and Thetis [marriage]
POSEIDON (subject)
   Pinsent-*Greek*, 144 (index)
[Poseidon and Odysseus]
   Water Spirits, 45–59
Poseidon's ocean kingdom
   Gibson-*Gods*, 29–32
Possessed by devil [daughters of J
   Baldwin]
   Marshall-*Every.*, 212–215
POSSESSIONS
   All I possess!
   The happiest man in the world
POSSESSIVENESS
   Nature's ways
Possums. *See* OPOSSUMS
Posting the dragon tablet
   Magic Knife, 80–88
POSTMEN
   Not snow nor rain
POTATO CAKES
   In the middle of the night
POTATOES
   Anpao is born
   The bride of heaven
   King Josef
   The stupid crocodile
POTEEN (whiskey)
   Soul cages
POT-POURRI
   Strewing, perfumes, po-
      manders, pot-pourri
POTS AND PANS
   The father of eighteen elves
   The flying trunk
   The peasant and the
      waterman
   Peik
   Porridge pot [magic]
   The sausage
   Smartest man in the
      countryside
   The werewolf
—boils without fire
   Story of Campriano (Italy)

—"has a baby"
   The witty joker
—magic
   Cook, pit, cook!
—magic; thieves
   The providential pot
—musical
   The swine herd
—pot had child and died
   Jha and the copper bowl
Pots for hire [Dankuro]
   Piggott-*Japanese*, 116
A potsherd speaks
   Shaw-*Pima*, 29–31
POTTER, Beatrix (subject)
   Potter-*Peter*, 5–6
POTTERS AND POTTERY
   Honpain the star-girl
—broken
   A potsherd speaks
A pottle o' brains
   Riordan-*Woman*, 47–52
POUCHES
   The frog
   The wonderful little pouch
—magic
   The hawk and the rattlesnake
Pouka. *See* POOKAS (imaginary
   animals)
POVERTY
   See also WEALTH
   Aid and punishment
   Babes in the wood
   Beauty and the beast
   Bride-price: a woman for a
      hundred cattle
   [Brindled cat and the miller's
      son]
   The cat and the dog
   Destiny
   The devil as a cat
   The diamond
   Different times have different
      'adans'
   Dividing the goose
   Dona Sebastiana

Emperor's lesson
Fairy greyhound
Frankie and Johnny [song and story]
The gingerbread house [Hansel and Gretel]
The godfather
The guardian dragon's magic pearl
Hansel and Gretel
The happy prince
Hop o' My Thumb
It could always be worse (Jewish)
The jar of tears
King Josef
The lake monster
Little Thumb
[Man must praise his maker]
Miracle of the sailing ship
Pablito prays for El Senor Diablo
Phoenix fairy flower [Han]
Piece of Zhuang brocade
The poor man Monokto
The poor old dog
Rich man, poor man ["eats" smell of food]
Roly poly rice ball
The squire
Stan Bolovan and the dragon
The story of Jon Asmundsson
The straw ox
That her children might be fed
Tia Miseria's pear tree
The tiger's grave
Treasure Mountain; a Yao folktale
The vengeance of Oiwa
Who is my neighbour?
Why mowers are poor
Why the sea is salt
The widow's son
Woe [personified]
The young king
—daughter marries bear for riches

East of the sun, west of the moon
—escape from
Tokarsberget's treasure
—sell souls to devil
Countess Kathleen O'Shea
—to wealth
The centipede girl
POWDER
White powder (condensed)
Powdered blondie and three-haired blondie
Ritchie-*Armadillo,* 20–24
Powel and Rhiannon
Lochhead-*Battle,* 96–106
Powel, Prince of Dyfed. *See* Pwyll, Prince of Dyfed
Powell, Talmage
Drawer 14
POWER
The cripple
King who decreed conversion
The lion and the mouse
Mouse Woman and the Snee-nee-iq
A mouse's wedding [who is the most powerful?]
Stonemason: a T'ung folktale
Who is the mightiest in the world?
—corrupts
Enchanted ring
—might makes right
Jack o' Legs
POWER (subject)
—Motif index
Wilbert-*Bororo,* 310
The power of a lie
Amore-*Lustful,* 134–136
The power of light
Singer-*Power,* 41–48
The power of sorrow
Lindow-*Swedish,* 190–191
Power of the harp
Keightley-*World,* 150–152

Powerful medicine
  Weeks-*Pachee*, 65–73
PRACTICAL JOKERS
  The witty joker
The practical princess
  Williams-*Practical*, 1–16
Practicality: The heavenly flute
    player
  Seven Sisters, 119–122
PRAIRIE DOGS
  Coyote's rain song
  The twisting tree [Kiowa]
  Why all prairie dogs are brown
PRAIRIES AND PLAINS
—Canadian
  The thing that walked on the
    wind
PRAISE
  The golden man and the finger
    men
The prayer that was answered
  Hyde-Chambers-*Tibet*, 152–
    155
Prayer that was answered (Tibet)
  Yolen-*Favorite*, 79–82
PRAYER(S)
  Bearskin (Germany)
  Door prayer at evening
  Goosey Goosey Gander
  The little goddess
  Possessed by devil [daughters
    of J Baldwin]
  Rabbi David Hassine feasted
    his family
  The stone statue
  Value of a Pater and a Creed
—defense against spooks
  The owl
—force of
  A false ghost
—of intercession
  The cripple and Senor San
    Antonio
—miraculous power
  A mellah defended by its dead
—not helped by

  The two wagoners
—protective power
  The old woman's prayer
—tames wild animal
  Rabbi Samuel Benouasich
    tames a lion
—unheard: despair
  Dead mother/children come for
    dying father
PRAYING
—deception
  The rock and the weasel
Praying for rain: beginning of rain
    dance
  Dutton-*Navajo*, 17–19
PRAYING MANTIS
—origin
  The mantis and the moon
PREACHERS
  See also CLERGYMEN
  Nasr-ed-Din Hodja in the pulpit
    (Turkey)
PRECAUTION
  The three fish [wise; clever;
    stupid]
Precious gems. *See* JEWELS
Precious Jade
  McCarty-*Skull*, 18–24
PRECIPICES
  Hildur, the queen of the elves
  Naddi
PRECOGNITION. *See* FORE-
    KNOWLEDGE; SECOND
    SIGHT
Predators from the primal world
  Water Spirits, 60–67
PREGNANCY
  See also IMPREGNATION
  Girl at the shieling [elf]
    (Iceland)
  The snake's lover (Peru)
—bayberry causes
  Golden reed pipe
—magic
  Two sisters, Rose and Lotus
—unmarried woman

Banshee of the MacCarthys
The pregnant priest
  Riordan-*Russia*, 211–212
PREHISTORIC PEOPLES (subject)
  Briggs-*Vanish.*, 33–35
PREJUDICE
  If the boerboon flowers fall
  The missing axe
Prelutsky, Jack
  The dance of the thirteen
    skeletons
Presidio Monclova Viejo
  Ritchie-*Armadillo*, 7–10
PRESUMPTION
  The country maid and her
    milkpail
  Don't count your chickens . . .
  Periquito, wood dealer
  Tortoise and the hare
Presumption, False. *See* ERRORS
PRETENSE
  See also DEATH—pretense;
    IMPOSTERS
  Andrew and King Solomon [in
    2 parts]
  The barmecide's feast
  Brave little tailor (seven at one
    blow)
  [Brindled cat and the miller's
    son]
  Cat of Catton [princess and
    pea story]
  Caterpillar and the wild
    animals
  Home-bred boy finds lost
    turquoise
  The honorable wife
  Lazy beauty and her aunts
  Love: queen and foundling
  Monkey and dog court the
    same girl
  Mother confessor fox
  Nazar the Brave ["kills a thou-
    sand with a single blow"]
  Puss in Boots
  Valiant John

  What happened to Ivan
  Wolf in sheep's clothing
  —be yourself
  The cow who tried to act like a
    kitten
A pretty girl in the road
  Yolen-*Favorite*, 430–432
Pretty Goldilocks
  Lang-*Blue*, 202–216 (notes,
    369)
PREY
  The sleepy one: Senor
    Opossum and the rattler
PRIAM, King
  Achilles and the death of
    Hector
Price, Nick, illus.
  Watson-*Aesop*
PRICKLY PEAR
  The eagle on the prickly pear
  Fudo and the prickly pear
    thieves
PRIDE
  See also BRAGGARTS;
    VANITY
  Banshee of the MacCarthys
  Bear Mother and her husband
  The blue-tail fly [song and
    story]
  The cock and the crested hen
  The conceited prince
  Coyote and the water serpent
  Cross purposes
  Echo and Narcissus
  The fairy and the prince
  The haughty chief
  Havoc in heaven: Monkey and
    the Jade Emperor
  Honpain the star-girl
  King Miroslav and the proud
    princess
  King Thrushbeard
  The king's kinka [lizard]
  Kuma and Aua
  The monkey-faced suitor
  Montezuma's wound

PRIDE (continued)
The old woman who lived in a vinegar bottle
Periquito, wood dealer
The priest goes down to hell
Priest's soul
Prince Narcissus and the Princess Potentilla
The remarkable rocket
Seanchan the Bard and the king of the cats
Simmer Water
Snow White and the seven dwarfs
The star child
The talking stone
The tragic story of Antigone
Woman chief
—lion's defeat
Hare and the lions
—made humble
Haughty princess
Pride goeth before a fall
Amore-*Lustful*, 139–141
A priest and his servant Balda
Pushkin-*Fairy*, 82–86
The priest goes down to hell
Campos-*Mexican*, 35–44
The priest of Hardwork mountains
Roberts-*Chinese*, 39–41
"PRIEST-HOLES"
Through the door
PRIESTS
El borracho del bahio
The boy who drew cats [by Hearn]
A dispute in sign language
Erikur rescues a woman from the otherworld
The fisherman and his soul
The golden cradle
Guleesh
Honor [fidelity]
How Ivan frightened away the robbers
The illiterate priest
The Indian and the hundred cows
The iron wolf
Juan Pelon
Ketill, the priest of Husavik
Lake Goldring
The Lord of Rosendal
The magic bag
The magic pear tree
The man from the grave
The man who had no story
The man/whale
The marsh king's daughter
Mice in the corn
Murder will out
Peasant priest (humor)
The pregnant priest
The Shrove Tuesday visitor
The son of the goblin
The Spanish sailor
The story of Jon Asmundsson
Taken [wife taken by fairies]
Tale of Elidurus
Three priests [infidelity]
Troll's stone
The two Sigurdurs
Tyndal and the priest
Valbjorg the Unelfed
The water nymph
The werewolves of Ossory
—chooses poverty
The devil as a cat
—elfin
Tungustapi
—healing power
One member of a family fated to die
—illiterate
The dilemma [corpse-pretense]
—immoral
Soot
—money overrules church laws
Lady of Gollerus
Priest's soul
Yeats-*Fairy*, 195–199
Priest's supper

Yeats-*Fairy*, 18–21
[Primal waters, magic powers]
Water Spirits, 12–14
The prime minister's coachman
Roberts-*Chinese*, 201
Primrose
Ewart-*Lore*, 53–57
Primroses
Froud-*Faeries*, unp
PRIMROSES
Weardale fairies [dislike being
observed]
Primulas
Ewart-*Lore*, 19
The prince and his fate
Crouch-*Whole*, 44–50
Prince and the ogre's castle
O'Connor-*Tibet*, 103–115
The prince and the three fates
Phelps-*Tatterhood*, 17–22
Prince Asraf and the king of the
spirits
Stovicek-*Around*, 142–145
Prince Bellerophon and Pegasus
Mayo-*Book*, 72–80
Prince Dorus
Lang-*Blue*, 227–235 (notes,
369–370)
Prince Featherhead and Princess
Celandine
Lang-*Green*, 97–113
Prince Feroz-Shah and the flying
horse
Shah-*Dervishes*, 246–258
Prince Fickle and fair Helena
Lang-*Green*, 221–227
Prince Five-*Weapons*
Martin-*Hungry*, 53–61
Prince Green Serpent and La
Valeur
Thomas-*It's*, 118–122
Prince Mahsud and King Rat
Shah-*Afghanistan*, 103–107
Prince Meerzat Istvan and the
horse of dust . . .
Adams-*Iron*, 134–142

Prince Miaow
Stovicek-*Around*, 17–19
Prince Mirko
Mayo-*Book*, 48–59
Prince Narcissus and the Princess
Potentilla
Lang-*Green*, 79–96
Prince Nocha
Sanders-*Dragons*, 74–76
Prince of ice: The miraculous
flower
Weiss-*Russian*, 171–183
Prince of nettles
Crouch-*Whole*, 36–43
The Prince of Nimroz
Shah-*Dervishes*, 47–54
Prince Vamato Take
Ozaki-*Japanese*, 224–243
Prince Vivien and the Princess
Placida
Lang-*Green*, 242–268
Prince White Hog
Thomas-*It's*, 66–75
The prince who had two eyes
Wyatt-*Princes*, 132–167
Prince who married a Peri
Shah-*Dervishes*, 174–179
The prince who was made of pre-
cious gems
Schwartz-*Elijah*, 219–226
PRINCES AND PRINCESSES
See also KINGS AND
QUEENS
Adventures of the third dervish
[a]
Aladdin and the wonderful
lamp
Allerleirauh; or, The many-
furred creature
Ash lad who made princess
say "You're a liar!"
Ashiepattle who made the prin-
cess tell . . .
Bamboo-cutter and the moon-
child
The battle of the birds

400

PRINCES AND PRINCESSES
  (continued)
  Beauty and the beast
  The bird 'Grip'
  The birthday of the Infanta
  The black colt
  The black fox
  The black horse
  The blacksmith
  Boots and the beasts
  Brier Rose
  The brocaded slipper
  The bronze ring
  Brown Bear of Norway
  El caballero porfiado
  The castle of Melvales
  Caterina the Wise (Sicily)
  The cat's elopement
  La cenicienta huasteca
  Charcoal burner and the bear
  Chestnut grey
  Cinderella
  The clever little tailor
  Cock with the golden feathers
  The companion
  The country of the beautiful
    gardens
  The crimson parrot
  The dancing princess
  Death and the doctor
  The Dervish and the fakir
  The devil and the old hag
  Don Giovanni de la Fortuna
  Doves [caught in net, then
    freed]
  Drolmakyid the fairy [Tibetan]
  Duke Pishposh of Pash
  East of the sun and west of
    the moon
  The enchanted princess
  Enchanted snake
  Enchanted watch
  The enchantress Medusa
  The exiled princess
  Fair, brown, and trembling
  The fairy and the prince

Far have I sought ye: Red Bull
  or Norroway
Farmer's son and the geni
The fire bird and Ryska and
  vixen
Firebird's powers
The fisher-prince with the sil-
  ver apple
Flying horse [wooden]
The flying trunk
Foolish Vanya and Princess
  Helena the Fair
Frog and Umdhlubu
The frog prince
Frog princess: Vassilisa the Wise
Frog who became an emperor
The giant who had no heart
The giant-slayer
Girl who had seven divs for
  brothers
Girl with the golden hair
The gizzard [riches for the one
  who eats it]
Gold Tree and Silver Tree
The golden cockerel
The golden goose
The golden lion
The golden mountain
Golden pears
Golden stick, silver stick
Gold-tree and Silver-tree
The goose girl
The Greek princess and the
  young gardener
Guleesh
Halva-maker
Hans my Hedgehog
Hans, who made the princess
  laugh
Haughty princess
The hawk and the rattlesnake
Helpful spirit
The herd-boy
A horse called Terror
How three serpents carried
  princesses to world to come

How to win a prince
The hunting of the hind
The huntsman
The imprisoned princess
Ivan and Nastasia [scrubbing
 off sin]
Ivan Byelarasseiski
Jack the Giant Killer
John the Bear
Juan and the bony one
Juan de Toluca
Julio
Kate Crackernuts
King Miroslav and the proud
 princess
The kingdom of beautiful
 colors
The lad with the goat-skin
The lampstand princess
"Lars, my lad!
The leeshy cat
Leppa Polkry and the blue
 cross
Liisa and the prince
Lini the lost prince
Little Annie the goose girl
Little Daylight
Little Finger of the watermelon
 patch
The little fox
The little mermaid
Little shepherdess and English
 prince
Long, Wide and Hawkeye
The loss of the princess
The lost princess
Love: queen and foundling
Ludwig and Iskander
The magic boat
The magic fruit
The magic gifts [dwarf-
 sorcerer]
Magic knife [Uygur]
Maid Maleen
Marietta's choice
The mastermaid

The miller's three sons
Mongolian story of a serf: Ulan
 Bator
Mouse Woman and the van-
 ished princes
Mouse Woman and the wood-
 en wife
The mute prince [kingship
 rejected]
The mute princess
Neelkamal and Lalkamal
Nightingale and the dove
Nobleman and the slave
Nourie Hadig [a "Snow White"
 type]
The old flea-bag
Olga and the brown cow
The palace of the moon
The parrot tale-teller
Peerifool [secret name of fairy]
The pet of a prince
Petronella [sorcerer]
Pierre, Prince of Murom
The pirate princess
The Pleiades
The pomegranate prince
Powel and Rhiannon
The practical princess
Prince and the ogre's castle
Prince Feroz-Shah and the fly-
 ing horse
Prince Meerzat Istvan and the
 horse of dust . . .
Prince of nettles
The princess and the bulbul
A princess on a swing
The princess on the glass hill
Puddocky
[Pwyll] Powell, Prince of Dyfed
Rapunzel
The real princess [pea-under-
 mattress test]
The red cow [a Cinderella-type
 story]
The rich boy and the poor boy
The rocks of Korsan

402

—married to frog
Master Frog
—mute, 3 days to make her speak
The wise goldsmith
—never laughs
The golden goose
—pledged, at birth, to enchanter
King Kojata
—princess bewitched
The travelling companion
—princess in stone
Elijah's violin
—promise to marry king's choice
The twelve huntsmen
—proud
The three wishes
—rescued
Little Wonder [son-changed-to-dog]
Water carrier's fabulous sons
—rescued from tower
The turner and the goldsmith
—sleeping spell
Three musicians [princess under spell]
—spell broken
The King of Ireland's son (Art)
—statue
The happy prince
—sweetest and fairest
A dead princess and seven giants
—task: make her talk
Phra Nang Suwanasopha
—test of "real" princess
Cat of Catton [princess and pea story]
—trans. into poor mare
The conceited prince
—under spell
The twelve dancing princesses
—under spell as cat
The cat Johann
—wear out shoes every night dancing
The twelve princesses

—will marry if she can be made to talk
Tale of the ricebirds
—with head of a serpent
The serpent prince
The princess and the bulbul
Shah-*Afghanistan*, 54–59
Princess and the donkey
Shah-*Dervishes*, 203–206
The princess and the frog
McKinley-*Door*, 79–103
The princess and the pea
dePaola-*Favorite*, 64–67
Ehrlich-*Random*, 126–129
Pierce-*Larousse*, 76–78
Rackham-*Fairy*, 132–134
Stovicek-*Around*, 167
Tudor-*Bedtime*, [24–25]
Princess and the slave
Schwartz-*Elijah*, 36–43
Princess Hase
Ozaki-*Japanese*, 74–86
Princess in the chest [coffin]
Lang-*Pink/D*, 57–72
Lang-*Pink/K*, 53–65
The princess in the ivory tower
Wyatt-*Princes*, 11–28
Princess in the tower
Schwartz-*Elijah*, 47–52
Princess [Libane] at the well
Lee-*Castles*, 70–71
Princess Minon-Minette
Lang-*Pink/D*, 274–288
A princess on a swing
Crouch-*Whole*, 126–135
Princess on the glass hill
Lang-*Blue*, 317–327 (notes, 372)
The princess on the glass hill
Yolen-*Favorite*, 260–267
Princess on the glass mountain
Schwartz-*Elijah*, 155–161
The princess, the horse, and the she-devil
Mayo-*Book*, 12–20

Princess with the golden hair
  Schwartz-*Elijah,* 169–180
PRISONS AND PRISONERS
  The confession of Charles
    Linkworth
  The great Penobscot raid
  Lai D'Ywenee
  The master of Ugerup
  The monk and the drunk
  Princess in the tower
  The Santo Nino [de Atocha]
    visits a prison
  A sharp loss of weight
  Soup from a sausage skewer
  The tinder-box
PRIVACY
  Death out of season
—right of
  Goldilocks and the three bears
  [The old, vagrant woman and]
    The three bears
Private parts: Quevedo and the
    king
  Yolen-*Favorite,* 131–132
The prize bull
  Villa-*Armenian,* 418–419
PROCESSIONS
  The fairy rade
  Hans, who made the princess
    laugh
PROCRASTINATION
  South Wind and his golden-
    haired love
  Why blackbird has white eyes
PRODIGALITY
  See also SPENDTHRIFTS
  Banshee of the MacCarthys
  Frankie and Johnny [song and
    story]
  The poor rich man's son gets
    a second chance
  What happened to Ivan
  The wizard's lesson
PRODUCTIVITY
  Demon of energy
PROFANITY

The dwarfs borrowing bread
PROFESSOR GRASSHOPPER
  The strange history of Pro-
    fessor Grasshopper
PROFESSORS
  Twigmuntus, Cowbelliantus,
    Perchnosius
  Projection psychology: The crystal
    people
  Roberts-*Jung,* 63–66
PROMETHEUS
  Mummies, zombies, and artifi-
    cial men
  Prometheus and his gift to man
    Low-*Greek,* 22–26
  Prometheus and Pandora
    Gibson-*Gods,* 33–36
PROMISCUITY
  Bokodori Ecerae chief and
    clan customs
  Men accost a woman who is a
    skeleton or has head of
    horse [9 legends]
  The promise
    Yolen-*Hundredth,* 39–50
  The promise of the three sisters
    Yolen-*Favorite,* 268–276
PROMISES
  The battle of the birds
  The frog prince
  Golden apple and his
    stepmother
  King's son goes bear hunting
    (Finland)
  The Paddo
  [Well at the World's End]
  The white dove [princess un-
    der spell]
  The yellow dwarf
—baby as pledge
  Rumpelstiltskin
—prince and fiancee
  The twelve huntsmen
—rash
  Phaethon and the sun-horses
—to God, not kept

Retribution
—wolf will eat kyang
Kyang, the fox, the wolf and
the hare
The proper way to make sago
Stokes-*Turtles*, 113–114
PROPERTY
The Chuang brocade
A prophecy of war
Robertson-*Highland*, 189–190
Prophecy: Wan and the Great Wall
of China
Sanders-*Dragons*, 109–114
PROPHETS AND PROPHECY
See also SECOND-SIGHT
The adventures of Perseus
Antti and the wizard's
prophecy
The charcoal burner
Deirdre
Frog who became an emperor
Gesar of Ling
Ghost: the radiant boy
The gods return
The governor and the Buddhist
Hinzelmann
Melampus—physician and
prophet
Mother Shipton and Cardinal
Wolsey
Old Mother Shipton
The prince and his fate
Ragnarok
The sod of death
The talking stone
—king to be killed by grandson
The terrible head
—son will kill his father
Phya Paan and the Golden
Chedi
PROPRIETY
—"eyes that see more than they
should"
Spooks a-hunting
Prospectors in Paradise
Aiken-*Mexican*, 113–115

PROSPERITY
Husband and wife should
share equally
Luck [and Need; personified]
Precious Jade
Witches on the lake
The young head of the family
—comes by money or by luck?
The force of luck
PROSPERO, Prince
Poe [E. A.] and the castle of
the Red Death
Prosser, Bill, illus.
Hoke-*Horrors*
The prostitute who lost her charm
Amore-*Lustful*, 39
PROSTITUTES
Kali beheaded
Two sisters and a harlot
PROSTITUTION
The rabbi and the harlot
PROTECTION
—against magic
Pigs into pythons
Protection against black witchcraft
Lehane-*Wizards*, 100–103
Protection against faeries
Froud-*Faeries*, unp
PROTESTS
Brer rabbit's protest meeting
Proud Ilbatyr in the land of Cathay
Riordan-*Tartary*, 154–160
Proud Margaret
Keightley-*World*, 103–108
PROUT, G. Clifford
"A nude horse is a rude
horse"
PROVERBS
See also SAYINGS
Favorite verses, proverbs, and
riddles
PROVIDENCE
—divine
Birth, dreaming, death: school-
master's story
Flying money

PROVIDENCE—divine (continued)
   The hermit [paradoxical
      behavior]
   Marriages are made in heaven
   Princess in the tower
The providential pot
   Elbaz-*Folktales,* 83
PRUDENCE
   Grasshopper and the ant
—dividing food
   Tortoise, goat and leopard:
      corpse has few desires
PRYDERI
   [Dyfed: under spell . . . Faerie]
   Manawydan, son of Llyr
   Math, son of Mathonwy
Pryderi and Gwydion
   Lehane-*Wizards,* 25–27
PSALMS
   The fiddler and the fairy
   The seven penitential psalms
   The sultan and the psalms
PSYCHE
   Cupid and Psyche
   Eros and Psyche
Psyche and Eros
   Spells & Bind, 103–108
PSYCHICS
   The elemental
PSYCHOLOGICAL
   Wasting sickness of Cu
      Chulaind and . . . Emer
Pu, Sung-Ling, 1640–1715
   The poet and the peony
PUBS (saloons)
   The Moddey Dhoo
The puca
   Logan-*Old,* 63–68
Pucas. *See* POOKAS (imaginary
   animals)
Puck
   Froud-*Faeries,* unp
   Keightley-*World,* 314–349
PUCK (subject)
   Briggs-*Vanish.,* 122, 199
Pudding bewitched

Yeats-*Fairy,* 166–177
PUDDINGS
   The changeling [a]
PUDDLEFOOT (subject)
   Briggs-*Vanish.,* 55
Puddocky
   Lang-*Green,* 228–235
"PUKS"
   Inge of Rantum
Pulga
   And Every., 205–233
Pulowech, the partridge
   Hill-*More,* 158–167
The pulque vendor tricks the devil
   Campos-*Mexican,* 31–34
Pumah, the mighty hunter
   MacLean-*Cuentos,* 132–138
PUMAS
—origin
   Pumah, the mighty hunter
PUMPKINS
   Cinderella
   General Pumpkin
   Jonah and the whale
   Magic pumpkins
   Meng Chiang and the Great
      Wall of China
PUMPS
   The skipper and old Nick
PUNGALUNG (giant)
   Mice women who turned into
      dingoes
Punia and the King of the Sharks
   Macdonald-*Twenty,* 163–173
PUNISHMENT
   See also REVENGE; RE-
      WARDS; TRANSFORMA-
      TIONS
   Baucis and Philemon
   Beebyeebyee and the water-
      god
   Bubbly's trick
   Dance of death
   Ebbe Skamelson
   Erigone and her dog
   The fairy and the prince

Fall of the spider man
First pig and porcupine
Flying money
Frankie and Johnny [song and
story]
The giant eel
Girls and bears [Musquakie]
God's court, no appeal
Good and evil
Good done to you, do good in
return
Greed of the old man and his
wife
How Thor got his hammer
Hyena engages a strange-
farmer
The king's favorite [beauty
fades]
Klis-to-E-eki Ta-u-ue-a
Lake of Zangze
The Lord of Rosendal
The man/whale
Math, son of Mathonwy
Meri and Ari ascend to the sky
Meri avenges his brother Ari
The monk's sins
Moral legends [twenty-three]
The old woman and her rice
The peasant and the fiend
Pedro de Ordinales goes to
heaven
[Pwyll] Powel, Prince of Dyfed
Rapunzel
Raven and the big fisherman
The reason for turtles
The sad tale of the rabbit's
tail
Seven days and nights
The seven penitential psalms
The sky-god: Ratu and the
Dyaks
Spirit Burekoibo (Meri) pun-
ishes the Bororo
The stone lion [vomits gold]
Thief girl: no appeal in God's
court

Thieves go free [buyers are
punished]
Three snake-leaves
Tushcoon Eigna
Two lovers punished
Vassilisa [Fair] and Baba Yaga
The weeping woman: forever
without rest
A well-deserved punishment
Whipping children: how it
came about
The wicked sister-in-law
Woodpecker and bluejay: a
sad tale
Yorkshire giant [Penhill]
—blinded
The mantis and the moon
—for cursing the sun
The sunset lad [giantess]
—eternal-male hunter, female
quarry
Woman tied behind horse on
her braids
The man in the moon
—of false bride
The goose girl
—harsh (wives & children
executed)
The soldier-bird
Deegeenboyah
—man to snake, woman to
centipede
The centipede girl
—offense against church
The man turned into a mule
—sinfulness of mankind
How the fire festival came to
be
—sons taken to Milky Way
The mopoke, and the mosquito
bird
—for stealing
Jack and his wonderful hen
PUNISHMENT (subject)
—fairies
Briggs-*Vanish.*, 217 (index)

PUNISHMENT (subject)
  (continued)
—Motif index
  Wilbert-*Bororo,* 312
PUNS
  Aldar-Kose and Shigai-Bai
  Welcome to Canada
PURGATORY
  Pedro de Ordimalas
  'Twixt saddle and ground
—years inside a tree
  Child's soul in a tree
PURITY
  Asceticism now, nymphs later!
  The brahman and the sacred
    river [purification]
  The monk from Everclear
  The priest of Hardwork
    mountains
PURSES
  The smith and the devil
  The tale of Ivan
—magic-gives gold
  The three talismans
—never empty; never failing
  Don Giovanni de la Fortuna
  The miller's three sons
  Pablito prays for El Senor Diablo
PURSUIT
  The doctor and his pupil
—of lost husband
  Knight of the Glens and Bens
    and Passes
Pursuit of Numeuk the hunter
  Reed-*Aboriginal,* 74–86
Pushkin, Alexander
  At river's bend (poem)
    Riordan-*Russia,* 9–10
PUSHKIN, Aleksandr (subject)
  Pushkin-*Fairy,* 7–12
Puss in Boots
  Ehrlich-*Random,* 74–81
  Lang-*Blue,* 154–160 (notes,
    368)
  Mulherin-*Favorite,* 42–51; in-
    trod., ii, 40–41

Perrault-*Glass,* 36–45
Pierce-*Larousse,* 27–35
Rackham-*Fairy,* 217–223
Schindler-*Golden,* 15–28
Stovicek-*Around,* 136–139
Tarrant-*Fairy,* 51–67
Pussy Cat Twinkle
  Manning-*Cats,* 19–28
Pussy-Greedyguts
  Crouch-*Whole,* 121–125
Put that man to bed
  Wolkstein-*Magic,* 38–42
Puukonhoya wins a bride
  Mullett-*Spider,* 62–77
PUZZLES
  See also MATHEMATICS
    [puzzles]; RIDDLES
  Odd jobs
PWCA (subject)
  Briggs-*Vanish.,* 199
PWYLL
  The Mabinogion: four branches
  Pwyll and Rhiannon
    Spells & Bind, 20–33
  [Pwyll] Powel, Prince of Dyfed
    Jacobs-*Celtic,* 171–182
  Pwyll, Prince of Dyfed
    Thomas-*Mabinogion,* 10–28
Pygmalion
  Lines-*Greek,* 98–100
  Low-*Greek,* 52–54
  Spells & Bind, 14–17
Pygmalion's statue
  Gibson-*Gods,* 122–123
PYGMIES
  Pigs into pythons
  Tale of Elidurus
PYGMIES (subject)
  Briggs-*Vanish.,* 15–17, 158,
    215 (index)
Pyoli and Lord Krishna
  Shelley-*Legends,* 30–34
PYRENEES (mountains)
  Fountain women
Pyrrha and Deucalion and the
  great flood

Low-*Greek*, 26–29
Pythons. *See under* SNAKES

QUACKERY
Medical techniques
The quail clan punishes coyote
Shaw-*Pima*, 76–78
QUAIL
The falcon and the quail
[cleverness]
—pull hair from coyote's tail
Coyote and the quail
—trick coyote
Coyote eats his own fat
QUAKERS
Wildbeam's pranks
Quarrel of the monkey and the
crab
Ozaki-*Japanese*, 203–213
QUARRELING
The devil and Kitta Gra
Dividing the axe
Foolish men and scolding
wives
Lini the lost prince
Monkey and the cheese
On naming a son [Joseph]
Stewed, roasted, or live?
The storytellers
Vaino and the swan princess
Wise men three
—married couple
A sure sign
El que canta sus males espanta
Aiken-*Mexican*, 86–90
Queen bee
Shub-*About*, 55–57
QUEEN CHARLOTTE ISLANDS
The flood
Raven and the beavers
QUEEN OF LONELINESS
Melusine: the otherworld wife

Queen Pig
Gorog-*Taste*, 27–42
The queen who cried rape
Amore-*Lustful*, 36–38
The queen's children
Manning-*Kings*, 19–31
Queen's County witch
Yeats-*Fairy*, 138–141
Queens. *See* KINGS AND
QUEENS
QUERNS (grinders)
Why the sea is salt
Quest for the Holy Grail
Riordan-*Arthur*, 90–101
The quest for the Star of the Sea
Wyatt-*Princes*, 168–187
Quest of the Fair Unknown
Seekers Saviors, 122–139
Quest of the white hart
Riordan-*Arthur*, 26–33
Quest to the castle of the cauldron
Lee-*Castles*, 58–59
QUESTIONS AND ANSWERS
See also GUESSES;
RIDDLES
Antti and the wizard's
prophecy
The fairy's inquiry
The living kuan-yin
The parson and the clerk [I]
The talking fish
Twigmuntus, Cowbelliantus,
Perchnosius
—accidentally correct
Home-bred boy dislodges
spider
QUESTS
Adventures of the third dervish
[b]
The bird maiden
Bird of happiness
Bird of truth
The boy and the robbers' mag-
ical booty
The city of Luz [blue dye:
Tekhelet]

QUESTS (continued)
The costly ring
The country of the beautiful
gardens
East of the sun, west of the
moon
The enchanted forest
The eternal light [Solomon &
Benaiah]
Fenist the bright-eyed falcon
The fire bird and Ryska and
vixen
The first kantele
The four rings
Frog princess: Vassilisa the
Wise
Girl with the golden hair
Gold treasure of Mississippi
The golden bird
Golden blackbird
Heart of ice [Prince Littleboots]
How raven brought the salmon
Huia's dream
The hunting of the hind
Juan fetches the devil
King Zargand's daughter
Long, Wide and Hawkeye
The lost princess
Marya Morevna
The ogre with no soul
Opele-of-the-Long-Sleeps
Philbert the Fearful
Prince Mirko
Search for the magic lake
The stars in the sky
The stolen princess
Stupid Marco
The tinkling laugh
Tiyo's story
Tripitaka: quest of the Buddhist
scriptures
The twelve dancing princesses
Underground palace [quest for
lost queen]
Water carrier's fabulous sons
The water of life

The white doe
—bitter fruit of satisfaction
Forgetful Fred
—find and abduct the Princess
Helena
Seven Simeons
—for rain
Tiyo travels through the
underworld
—rescue the three princesses
Twilight, Midnight, and Dawn
—wear out three pairs of iron
shoes
Finist the Falcon
QUESTS (subject)
—Motif index
Wilbert-*Bororo*, 313
QUETZALCOATL
The fifth and final sun
The flight of Quetzalcoatl
Monkey, turkeys, and fish
[creation]
The new people and their food
The return of Quetzalcoatl
QUETZALCOATL (subject)
—Four aspects of nature
Nicholson-*Mexican*, 95–111,
144 (index)
Quetzalcoatl in Tula
Bierhorst-*Hungry*, 39–41
The Quetzalcoatl myth
Nicholson-*Mexican*, 77–94
Quevedo and the king (Mexico)
Yolen-*Favorite*, 131–132
Quick-witted [boy outsmarts evil
dervish]
Villa-*Armenian*, 379–383, 525
QUIET
A taste for quiet
Quiet folk
Arrowsmith-*Field*, 54–60
Quiet folk chagelings
Arrowsmith-*Field*, 61–65
Quiller-Couch, Arthur
The Cabinet des Fees, of M.
Cuchet

Quiller-*Sleeping,* 9–14
QUILTS
    Stretch out your leg to the
        length of your quilt

RA
    A rude awakening
RA (god)
    The extra days: Ra, Thoth,
        and Nut
The ra helps a charcoal-burner
    Lindow-*Swedish,* 107–109
Rabbi Akiba and the sinner
    Patai-*Gates,* 538–539
The rabbi and the harlot
    Patai-*Gates,* 540–541
The rabbi and the inquisitor
    Yolen-*Favorite,* 157–158
Rabbi David Ben Baruk, candle-
    salesman
    Elbaz-*Folktales,* 120
Rabbi David Bussidan prevented
    sale of synagogue
    Elbaz-*Folktales,* 37
Rabbi David Hassine feasted his
    family
    Elbaz-*Folktales,* 45–46
Rabbi Eisik of Kalev
    Patai-*Gates,* 732–734
Rabbi Ephraim al-Naqawa arrives
    in Tlemcen
    Patai-*Gates,* 642–643
Rabbi Haim Pinto and the London
    Stock Exchange
    Elbaz-*Folktales,* 125
Rabbi Haim Pinto, detective
    Elbaz-*Folktales,* 47–48
Rabbi Haim Pinto orders jinn to
    cure disciple
    Elbaz-*Folktales,* 135
Rabbi Haim Pinto predicts a man's
    death

Elbaz-*Folktales,* 56
Rabbi Haim Pinto revives the dead
    Elbaz-*Folktales,* 75
Rabbi Loew and the Golem
    Patai-*Gates,* 636–639
Rabbi Makhluf consults the jnun
    Elbaz-*Folktales,* 138
Rabbi Mordekhai Benjio renders
    justice to an Arab
    Elbaz-*Folktales,* 61–62
Rabbi Samuel Benouaich tames a
    lion
    Elbaz-*Folktales,* 154
RABBIS
—saving a marriage
    For domestic peace
Rabbi's donkey falls down a well
    Elbaz-*Folktales,* 141
The rabbi's son [in disguise]
    Nahman-*Tales,* 131–138
    [notes: 307–308]
Rabbit and the berries
    Radin-*African,* 129–132
Rabbit and the grain buyers
    Macmillan-*Canadian,* 147–152
Rabbit and the gum-baby
    Crouch-*Whole,* 32–35
Rabbit and the Indian chief
    Macmillan-*Canadian* 171–177
Rabbit and the moon-man
    Macmillan-*Canadian* 229–232
The rabbit and the two coyote
    Piggott-*Mexican,* 58–73
The rabbit and the well
    Macdonald-*Twenty,* 126–141
The rabbit makes a match
    Hill-*More,* 10–20
Rabbit shoots the sun
    Wood-*Spirits,* 112–113
RABBITS
    See also "Peter Rabbit . . ."
    See also titles beginning with
        "hare"
    The adventures of Iktomi
    Aesop's dog [chasing rabbit]
    Anizu's magic wonder flute

412

RABBITS (continued)
The ants and the hare
The badger and the rabbit
B'er rabbit is an uncle
Big brother: man; Little brother: rabbit
The blown away rabbit
The brave lion and the foolish rabbit
Brer bear gets a taste of man
Brer fox meets Mister Trouble
Brer fox tries farming, too
Brer possum and brer snake
Brer rabbit and brer cooter race
Brer rabbit and his riding horse
Brer rabbit dances for a wife
Brer rabbit goes a courting
Brer rabbit keeps his word
Brer rabbit rescues his children
Brer rabbit's protest meeting
Brer tiger and the big wind
Brer wolf and brer fox get a big surprise
Brer wolf plants pinders
Brer wolf wants the honey
Brer wolf's magic gate
The bun [personified]
Cottontail plays a trick on coyote
Coyote and rabbit
Farmer and the badger
First pig and porcupine
The fleetest of foot
The fox and the little white hen
Golden blackbird
Gray Arrow learns a lesson
Hare and otter
The hare and the magpie
Hare and the tortoise [the true story]
The hare, Nwashisisana
Hare saves the hippopotamus
The hare's hut [fox chased out]
House of ice and house of wood

How Ableegumooch tracked a fox
How ole woodpecker got ole rabbit's conjure bag
How rabbit deceived fox
How rabbit got the best of coyote
How sly-fox was fooled
How the cow went under the ground
How the hare made a fool of the wolf
How the tiger got his stripes
The hunted hare
Hyena and hare search for wealth
Hyena engages a strange-farmer
The hyena engages the hare as a gewel
Ivan Bear's Ear
Kintaro, the golden boy
The lion and the hare
The little hare
The magician's pupil
The monkey's heart
Napi's wager with rabbit
The old tiger and the hare
The pig builds the house on the hill
A pool of bright water
Run brer gator, run!
Severi and Vappu
The Shee and Gannon and the Gruagach Gaire
Sheep, lamb, wolf, and the hare
Sister hare [rescues lost girl]
The skunk and the frogs
Skunk's tale
Slaying of the Tanuki
Smart head better than sharp teeth
The star child
The story-teller at fault
The tar baby

The tar baby tricks brer rabbit
Temptations
The theft of fire
Thieves go free [buyers are
  punished]
Tiger and the rabbit
Tortoise and hare: intelligence
  beats speed
Tortoise and hare: intelligence
  beats strength
The tortoise and the hare
The troll's daughter
True and untrue
The two compadres
Ua-pa-chi (Kickapoo titles)
White hare and the crocodiles
White hare of Oki
Who got brer Gilyard's
  treasure?
Who stole brer Gilyard's
  sheep?
Why the monkey still has a tail
Why the opossum's tail is bare
The wisdom of the rabbit
—caught by tar
Tortoise and hare: a dying
  wish
—gets revenge
The rogue of Kachi Kachi
  Mountain
—herding
Eighteen rabbits
—lips
The weathermaker
—in the moon?
The hares and the elephants
—origin of characteristics
Rabbit and the moon-man
Why the hare runs away
—origin of characteristics-cleft lip
The apprentice [rabbit as
  painter]
How the hare got his split
  lip
—origin of characteristics-diet
Rabbit and the Indian chief

—origin of characteristics-split/slit
  nose
Crocodile and hare
Origin of death [Hottentot]
—origin of characteristics-tail
The rabbit's [short] tail
Why the hare has a short tail
—origin of characteristics-tail, legs,
  split lip
How rabbit lost his tail
—origin of characteristics-wall-eyed
The braggart
—outwits tiger
Good faith
—saves the kyang [wild ass]
Kyang, the fox, the wolf and
  the hare
—shoes for
Slipper slopper
—tails
How the rabbit lost his tail
The sad tale of the rabbit's tail
—trickery
Jean Lapin and the foxes
—tricks ape
Ape [why it has no tail]
—tricks hyena
Hyena ["smell of stale dung"]
—tricks wolf
Owl with the great head and
  eyes
—twitching
How to break a bad habit
—why they cannot sing
Why a rabbit hides in a burrow
—witch in form of
Bewitched butter [Queen's
  County]
The rabbits go hunting
Uttley-*Foxglove*, 67–72
The rabbit's tail
Watson-*Thailand*, 1
RACCOONS
The adventures of Iktomi
[The fox with the purple
  umbrella]

RACCOONS (continued)
   Lox and the chief's wife
   Mister Raccoon realizes that
     winter is coming
   Skunk's tale
Raccoon's tale
   Tompert-*Three*, 15–32
Race between toad and donkey
   Yolen-*Favorite*, 152–154
RACE HORSES
   Sister Becky's child
—reads news; speaks
   Horace the horse
RACE RELATIONS
   The green prairie
RACES
   Smart head better than sharp
     teeth
—athletic
   Atalanta [and Hippomenes]
   Brer rabbit and brer cooter
     race
   Coyote and skunk
   The fleetest of foot
   Foot racers of Payupki
   Fox and the ant [race]
   Glooskap and the magic gifts
   Great Heart and the three
     tests
   Hare and the tortoise [the true
     story]
   Horse and toad
   How the Brazilian beetles got
     their . . . coats
   How the lizard got its hat
   How they went to Jotunheim
   Iktomi and the muskrat
   Old Nick and the girl
   The Seneca chief's adventures
   The slowest may win the race
   Thor in the giant's strong-hold
   Tortoise and hare: intelligence
     beats speed
   Tortoise and hare: intelligence
     beats strength
   The tortoise and the hare

   White Feather and the six
     giants
   Why the lamb is meek
RACES OF MAN
   Early man
   Jocoramodogueddu [primeval
     monkey creates races]
   The well-baked man
Rackham, Arthur, 1867–1939.
   On fairy tales
   Rackham-*Fairy*, 3–4
RADCLIFFE, Charles
   Causes celebres, high and
     low: C. Radcliffe
RADES
   Faerie rades
RADES (subject)
—cavalcades
   Briggs-*Vanish.*, 216 (index)
The radiant Sambula
   Amore-*Lustful*, 34–36
RADISHES
   The white-hair waterfall
RAFTS
   The heavenly song of the
     green-spotted dove
   Kitpouseagunow
"RAGINOHART"
   The fox who went to heaven
Ragnarok
   Crossley-*Legends*, 224–228
The Ragnarok, doom of the gods
   Branston-*Gods*, 144–148
RAGNELL, Lady
   Gawain and the Lady Ragnell
RAGWEED
   Clever Tom and the
     leprechauns
Ragwort
   Froud-*Faeries*, unp
Rahou [origin of eclipses]
   Watson-*Thailand*, 36–38
RAIDS
   The great Penobscot raid
RAILROADS
   Casey Jones [song and story]

Drill, ye tarriers, drill [song and story]
John Henry [song and story]
RAIN
  See also FLOODS
  Anpao brings the corn
  The creation
  The jar of tears
  Odd jobs
  Sacrificed by kin, lover brings girl back from below
  The simpleton makes rain fall
  Sparrow's search for rain
  A tale of the Grand Jardin
—excessive, punishment for blasphemy
  The old woman and El Senor
—origin
  The first rain [war of two villages in Papua]
  How the first rain came
—personified as blind
  A potsherd speaks
  weaving-girl's tears
  The herd boy and the weaving girl
The rain bird Bougoodoogahdah
  Parker-*Australian,* 76–78
The rain bulls
  Poland-*Mantis,* 115–120
RAIN DANCES
  Building the ceremonial house; . . . rain dance
  Praying for rain: beginning of rain dance
—origin
  Water maiden of the Navajo
Rain for Bongi
  Todd-*Some,* 170–176
The rain that came too late
  Todd-*Tortoise,* 54–56
Rainbow and the autumn leaves
  Macmillan-*Canadian* 224–228
Rainbow bridge: Buck Antelope and Evening Breeze
  MacLean-*Cuentos,* 125–129

Rainbow [Nvelingange relieves drought]
  Pitcher-*Tokol.,* 18–20
RAINBOWS
  The flowers' forever land
  The frogs at the rainbow's end
  Gesar of Ling
  Heavenly maiden and the wood cutter
  Koala and the rainbow
  Sam Pig seeks his fortune
  Sister Lace
  The talking spear
—keeping bright
  The kingdom of beautiful colors
—origin
  The wagtail Deereeree, and the rainbow
  Woodcutter and the heavenly maiden
—stairs-without-steps
  The stars in the sky
Rain-cloak: The heavenly flute player
  Seven Sisters, 119–122
The rainmaker Wirreenun
  Parker-*Australian,* 95–98
RAINMAKERS
  Coyote's rain song
  Honi the rainmaker
  Li Ching and the rain god
  The stone frogs, the Youayah Mayamah
  The Yellow Emperor: war against Chitou
The rain-makers, the dragon-palace, and Ling mountains
  Shelley-*Legends,* 24–29
RAJAHS
  The enchanted princess
  The Gojmati
  Neelkamal and Lalkamal
RAKHOSHES (demons)
  Golden stick, silver stick
  Neelkamal and Lalkamal

RAKHOSHES (demons)
(continued)
The pomegranate prince
RALPH of Coggeshall (subject)
Briggs-*Vanish.*, 100, 109
The Ram [devil as creator]
Lurie-*Heavenly*, 35–37
RAM (mountain goat)
Boy-who-snared-the-wind and
shaman's daughter
The ram of Derby [song and story]
Sanders-*Hear*, 37–46
RAMIRAT (demon prince)
Mysterious palace [Solomon &
Ramirat]
RAMPARTS
The walls of Asgard
Rams. *See* SHEEP–rams
RANCHES
Babe the blue ox
Roam the wild country
RANIS
The enchanted princess
Neelkamal and Lalkamal
RANLS
The Gojmati
RANSOM
The nightingale and the
hawk
—son promised as
Two enemy kings
RANSOME, Arthur (subject)
—collects Russian folk-tales
Ransome-*War*, 9–11
RAPHAEL (Saint, Archangel)
Tobias goes on a journey
Rapunzel
Ehrlich-*Random*, 26–33
Lewis-*Minute*, 30–31
Shub-*About*, 38–43
Stallman-*Witches*, 33–35
Rapunzel: golden maid in a stony
cage
Lehane-*Wizards*, 103–104
A rare bargain
Kendall-*Sweet*, 13

A rare horse [catches rabbits &
fish]
Stuchl-*American*, 145–146
RASALU, Raja
Her lover's heart
RASCALS
Duke Pishposh of Pash
Puss in Boots
RASH ACTIONS, JUDGMENTS,
etc.
Gray Arrow learns a lesson
Maiden's silky winding sheet
The Swan [Phaethon and
Cygnus]
Tortoise and his mother: eye
not always accurate
Rash promises. *See* PROMISES—
rash.
Rashness of the young and wis-
dom of the old
Mitchnik-*Egyptian*, 54–61
Rasmussen, Knud
The blessed gift of joy be-
stowed upon man
RASPBERRIES
Munachar and Manachar
Munachar and the raspber-
ries
RASTEKAIS (Mount)
Little Lapp and the Ice King
The rat and the octopus
Wright-*Pigeon*, 42–47
RAT-CATCHERS
The pied piper of Hamelin
Rathlin (island): Fair Head
O'Sullivan-*Legends*, 149
RATS
See also MICE
The boy who drew cats [by
Hearn]
Captain Murderer and the dev-
il's bargain [by Dickens]
The cat and the dog
Cinderella
Dick Whittington and his cat
Endless story (Japan)

The faithful trio [shelter in
house]
Frog went a-courting [song
and story]
The game of rat and dragon
[Hameln: punishment for not
keeping bargain . . .]
How the Brazilian beetles got
their . . . coats
The kindly ghost [Joseph and
his brothers]
The pied piper of Hamelin
The platypus Gayardaree
The steadfast tin soldier
Super rat and the monks
Water-rat and fire
Zirac and friends
—driven out by St Nicholas
The little cattle
—escape
The seven rats
—famine
If the boerboon flowers fall
—kindness repaid: rescues kid-
napped son
Prince Mahsud and King Rat
—origin of characteristics
How the rat lost his wings
—origins
The pheasants, the dove, the
magpie, and the rat
—sandhill
Bilber and Mayrah
—takes form of man, moves into
his house
Nails [anatomy]
—water
The devoted friend
Rat's bridegroom
Zong-*Korea*, 184–186
Rats cut their throats
O'Sullivan-*Legends*, 88–89
RATTLES
—musical
The swine herd
The rattlesnake receives his fangs

Shaw-*Pima*, 17–19
Rattlesnake soup [humor]
Schwartz-*Tales*, 13–14
Rattlesnakes. *See* SNAKES—
rattlesnakes.
RAVANA, King
Monkey god: epic battle for
earthly supremacy
The raven and the ball of light
Reid-*Myths*, 25–27
Raven and the beavers
Wood-*Spirits*, 53–57
Raven and the big fisherman
Reid-*Raven*, 31–39
Raven and the first men
Reid-*Raven*, 25–30
The raven and the first people
Reid-*Myths*, 3–11
[Raven and the fisherman's wife]
Reid-*Myths*, 37
Raven and the fox
Royds-*Animal*, 72–73
Raven and the north lands
Robinson-*Raven*, 47–55
Raven and the nose of the
Gonaqadet
De Wit-*Talking*, 142–149
The raven and the salmon
Reid-*Myths*, 20–23
Raven brings fire
Robinson-*Raven*, 13–20
Raven lets out the daylight
Haviland-*N. Amer.*, 44–51
Raven steals the light
Reid-*Raven*, 11–17
Raven steals the salmon from the
beaver house
Reid-*Raven*, 19–23
Raven with the broken beak
Reid-*Raven*, 41–48
Ravens
Magical Beasts, 74, 79–81
RAVENS
Anpao and the animals
The battle of the birds
Big long man's corn patch

RAVENS (continued)
Cannibal
Corvus (the raven)
The Dove [Noah and the
Flood]
Eagle and the frog
The giant who had no heart
The great hunters [animals]
Halibut Man and the house on
the waves
How the raven lost his bill
In the beginning
The language of animals
The man who sat on the
tide
Pretty Goldilocks
Raven lets out the daylight
The riddle
The troll's daughter
Water lily: the gold spinners
The white snake
The yes-no-yes-no spirit
—beak
Raven and the nose of the
Gonaqadet
—as bridegroom
Marya Morevna
—conversation overheard
Home-bred boy dislodges
spider
—as creator
The coming of Raven
How raven brought the salmon
Northwest Pacific coast tribal
[commentary]
Raven brings fire
Sila [human female born to be
a sea-being]
Why raven is no longer
Why raven isn't perfect
—feathers
Scarface
—language
The princess in the ivory tower
—origin of characteristics
Giant with the grey feathers

—origin of characteristics-
blackness
How the raven got fresh water
—prince under spell
Battle of the birds
—sharp dealer
How raven brought fire to the
Indians
—speech of birds
Trusty John
RAVENS (subject)
—[Haida mythology]
Reid-Myths, 2–3
RAVINES
The monster of Poot Holler
RAYCHAUDHURI, Upendrakishore,
1863–1915
Raychaudhuri-Stupid, 85–86
RAYMOND de Lusignon (subject)
Briggs-Vanish., 147–148
Read, Allen Walker
Attitudes toward Missouri
speech
Reading. See BOOKS AND
READING
The real daughter of Noah
Patai-Gates, 652–654
The real princess. See The prin-
cess and the pea
The realm of faerie
Froud-Faeries, unp
REAPING
Earwig in sickle
The reason for turtles
Campos-Mexican, 91–94
Rebellions. See REVOLUTIONS
Rebirth. See REINCARNATION
Recitatives. See REPETITIVE
RHYMES AND STORIES
Reckoning with the Fianna's an-
cient bane
Night Creatures, 30–37
Red and black flying foxes
Reed-Aboriginal, 47–49
Red caps
Arrowsmith-Field, 47

"RED COD PEOPLE"
  Mouse Woman and the mon-
    ster killer whale
The red cow [a Cinderella-type
    story]
  Sheohmelian-*Three*, 52–59
The red czar and the golden-haired
    Tihota
  Stovicek-*Around*, 42–45
The Red Etin
  Lang-*Blue*, 337–343 (notes,
    352, 373)
The red man's pranks
  Haining-*Lepre.*, 43–45
"RED PLUME"
  Coming of the corn
Red Riding Hood. *See* Little Red
    Riding Hood
The red room [by Wells]
  Schwartz-*Great*, 67–79
RED SEA
  "Man overboard"
The red stream
  Jagendorf-*Magic*, 39–45
Redbirds. *See* CARDINALS
Redbreasts: the Gwineeboos
  Parker-*Australian*, 40–42
Redcap
  Froud-*Faeries*, unp
REDEMPTION
  The cripple
  The king and the emperor
  The loss of the princess
REDEMPTION (subject)
  Nahman-*Tales*, 333
Red-headed Windego
  Colombo-*Wind.*, 36–43
Redmond O'Hanlon
  O'Sullivan-*Legends*, 136–
    138
REEDS
  King Matyas and his scholars
    (Hungary)
REFLECTION
—in water
  The cormorant and the star

The dog and his shadow
Dog and the bone
  Greed can cause one's
    downfall
  Hare and the lions
Reformed Pachee Goyo
  Weeks-*Pachee*, 91–98
REGRET
  See also PENITENCE
  The penitent nis
REINCARNATION
  The great misfortune of Lay
    Tee-Kwai
  Prince Nocha
  Ragnarok
—as deer
  The ascetic and the deer
—as dog
  Mulien rescues his mother
—as ghost
  The woman who cursed
    herself
—as horse, dog, snake (seriatim)
  Three former lives
—as princess
  Zo Han-Zun who became a
    stone Buddha
REINDEER
  How a bear kept reindeer
  The snow queen
  The snow queen: an adventure
    in seven stories
—with golden horns
  Little Lapp and the Ice King
—skins
  Jack of Sjoholm and the Gan-
    Finn
The rejected gift
  Keightley-*World*, 275–276
REJUVENATION
  See also YOUTH—restored
  Goophered grapevine
RELATIVES (kin)
  The slowest may win the race
RELATIVITY (in life)
  Big family in the little house

RELATIVITY (in life) (continued)
Different times have different
'adans'
The fox and the grapes
It could always be worse
(Jewish)
The king's favorite
The missing axe
—importance
Sidi Ngali and his traveling
companions
RELICS
—monks, rivals in collecting
Ednoth's relics, and Thurkill's
beard
RELIEF WORK
Eye will see what it is destined
to see
RELIGION
See also GODS AND
GODDESSES
Jonesboro tornado: folklore,
pop. religion, history . . .
[Man must praise his maker]
Peasant priest (humor)
—religious when young; a devil
when old
Old woman's faith overcomes
devil
Religious legends
O'Sullivan-*Legends*, 91
Robe-*Hispanic*, 510–533
The reluctant dragon
Stallman-*Dragons*, 42–43
The remarkable rocket
Wilde-*Fairy*, 62–79
REMARRIAGE
—socially unacceptable
The young widow
"REMOLINO de la MANO"
The hand and the whirlpool
Remorse. *See* PENITENCE
RENCOROSA
The enchanted forest
Rendezvous with a death ship
Water Spirits, 92–99

RENT
The greedy youngster
Value of a Pater and a Creed
Rent-day
Yeats-*Fairy*, 183–185
REPAIRMEN
About Abner the tinker
Repaying good with evil
Aiken-*Mexican*, 23–26
Repentance. *See* PENITENCE
Repentance: The star-child
Wilde-*Fairy*, 149–172
The repentant tiger of Chaoch'eng
Roberts-*Chinese*, 100–101
REPETITIVE RHYMES AND
STORIES
See also CUMULATIVE
TALES
Coyote's crying song
Coyote's rain song
Drakestail [and the king]
The fisherman and his wife
The gingerbread boy
Girl who stayed in fork of a
tree
Groundhog dance
The gunny wolf
Hic! Hic! Hic!
Jack and the robbers
Knock! knock!
Little rooster and the Turkish
sultan
Monster with seven heads
Munachar and the raspberries
The old woman who lived in a
vinegar bottle
Parley Garfield and the frogs
Punia and the King of the
Sharks
The rabbit and the well
Roly poly rice ball
Sody sallytytus
Udala tree
A whale of a tale
Reptile people [seven tales]
Reed-*Aboriginal*, 9–28

REPUTATION
    Mysterious palace [Solomon &
        Ramirat]
REQUESTS
    The young lady of Hellerup
RESCUES
    See also QUESTS
    Adventures of Ntini, the small
        otter
    Anansi's six sons
    Ant and the dove
    Badger rents a house
    The black geese
    The blind boy and his dog
    The blue lake
    The boy and the robbers' mag-
        ical booty
    Brer rabbit rescues his children
    The bride from Bird Island
    [Burd Helen, Childe Rowland,
        and Elf King]
    [Caoilte rescues Finn
        MacCumal]
    Castles of the wizard and the
        hippogriff
    Coyote and the swallowing
        monster
    Drakestail [and the king]
    The dwarf in search of lodging
        [deliverance]
    The early heroes: Yi, the ten
        suns, the monsters
    The enchanted forest
    An eventful pilgrimage
    The faithful lion
    Finn blood
    The fisher-prince with the sil-
        ver apple
    Giant's stairs [Ronayne's
        Court]
    Golden reed pipe
    How the seven brothers saved
        their sister
    How three serpents carried
        princesses to the world to
        come
    The hummingbird brothers
    Iskandar and the emerald ring
    The jealous shoemaker
    John the Bear
    Jorinde and Joringel
    King David and the giant
    King of Lochlann's three
        daughters
    The language of animals
    The little bull calf
    The little red hen
    The magic boat
    The magic bonnet
    Magic mirror of Rabbi Adam
    The magic snowshoes
    Maria (or Marya) Morevna
    Mountain of jade
    Nanasimgat [wife abducted by
        killer whale]
    Nanasimgit and his [abducted]
        wife
    Nine-headed giant
    The palace of the moon
    Peter and the wolf
    Phikool Thong
    The prince and his fate
    Prince Feroz-Shah and the fly-
        ing horse
    Proud Ilbatyr in the land of
        Cathay
    Roly Poly
    Rustam and the iron fortress
    The skilful brothers
    The snow queen
    Stretching kupua [taller than
        40 feet]
    The swan geese
    Thorston and the dwarf
    Three dogs [named Salt, Pep-
        per, Mustard]
    Three heroes [and the
        3-headed boa]
    Thumbelina
    Tiger King's skin cloak
        [Mongolia]
    Tonweya and the eagles

RESCUES (continued)
    Two brothers [and seven-
      headed monster]
    Unanana and the elephant
    Vassilissa the valiant
    Water lily: the gold spinners
    Why Bootup, the whale,
      smokes a pipe
    The young gentleman and the
      tiger
—children saved from bear after
    praying . . .
    The lodge of the bear [the
      Great Mystery]
—Elder Brother kills Eagleman
    The legend of Eagleman
—maidens-turned-to-stone
    Elsa and the evil wizard
—marooned person
    Herman the milk bottle
from spells
    La Bel Inconnu and the castle
      of Senaudon
—what was most important?
    Zilyan
RESIN
    How the monkey got a drink
      when he was thirsty
RESISTANCE
    How the animals stopped the
      freeway
RESPECT
    The tomte carries a single
      straw
    Why the executioner is called
      assessor
—for elders
    Owl with the face of a woman
RESPONSIBILITY
    Cat lying on velvet cushion,
      while dog sleeps
    Lisalill
—rewarded
    Origin of the Acuma leaf
      headdress
RESTING

    The tomte learns to rest
RESTITUTION
    The beggar, the lion and the
      dog
    The herd boy and the dragons
    The repentant tiger of
      Chaoch'eng
Restless souls
    Colombo-*Wind.*, 162
A resumed identity
    Hoke-*Demonic*, 15–21
RESURRECTION, The
    Legend of the old bell-ringer
RESUSCITATION
    Ari, his third death and his
      resurrection
    Dismembered body: The
      peach thief
    The eagle [Aquila vs
      Aesculapius]
    The firebird
    First death of Ari and his
      resurrection
    Girl who stayed in fork of a
      tree
    Glooskap and the giant's frolic
    Golden mermaid [theft of gold-
      en apples]
    Goonur, the woman-doctor
    Grasshopper [Indian
      superman]
    Handsome ogre-girl of the pool
    Man and the snake
    Origin of death: Krachi
    Second death of Ari and his
      new resurrection
    Snow White and the seven
      dwarfs
    Three snake-leaves
    The water of life
    The white duck
    Wicked girl and her
      punishment
    Yoni and her stepmother
—dead maiden brought back to life
    The brahman in the graveyard

—deception
   The ostler and the grave rob-
   bers (Scotland)
—failed
   Swarthy Smith of the Socks
—feigned
   Story of Campriano (Italy)
—of girl eaten by hyena
   City where men are mended
RESUSCITATION (subject)
—Motif index
   Wilbert-*Bororo*, 251, 314
Retaliation. *See* REVENGE
RETIREMENT
   Not snow or rain
Retribution
   Lindow-*Swedish*, 67–68
   Villa-*Armenian*, 413
Retrieving the cup
   Lindow-*Swedish*, 103–104
The return of Quetzalcoatl
   Bierhorst-*Hungry*, 99–108
Reuter, Frank
   Link chains as folk art
Revenants. *See* GHOSTS
REVENGE
   All I possess!
   Aniz the shepherd
   Baitogogo and Aroia Kurireu
      fight the Kaiamo-Doge
   Bishop Svedberg and the
      devil
   Bobburr the giant brown and
      yellow snake
   The burning of Bergthorsknoll
   Captain Murderer and the dev-
      il's bargain [by Dickens]
   The crane and the crab
   Death to the giant snake
   Dinewan the emu, and Wahn
      the crow
   The eagle hawk
   Farmer and the badger
   The feast of the mountain
      goats
   The fox and the stork

Genjias [three with same
   name]
A ghost's vengeance
Gold colt and the fire dragon
   shirt
The golden mountain
Grania and Diarmid
Gray wolf's haint
How the Beldys stopped
   fighting
The hunter's dilemma
The iron-eating mice
Kullervo
Kuma and Aua
A lesson for the landlord
The little boy Chokcho
Luch and the sons of Tuirenn
Magic moccasins: the Wearer
   of the Ball
Mambu the orphan [tyrants'
   tribute]
Mongolian story of a serf: Ulan
   Bator
The mopoke, and the mosquito
   bird
The nis riding
The nisses in Vosborg
The Papa-Water and
   Bibaiyibaiyi
Pixy-vengeance
Prince Green Serpent and La
   Valeur
Pursuit of Numeuk the hunter
Quarrel of the monkey and the
   crab
The rabbit and the two coyote
The rain bird Bougoodoo-
   gahdah
Rooster/Brother
The roots of jealousy
The secret of the growing gold
   [by Stoker]
A sharp loss of weight
The skull in the snow
Slaying of the Tanuki
Snuff-box [wishes-come-true]

REVENGE (continued)
    The son of the goblin
    The story of Deirdre
    The swordmaker's son: King-
        don of Chu
    The tiger and the palanquin
    Tungustapi
    Two weak ones against one
        strong one
    Udala tree
    Ulster woman's magic
    Upon Jewel Mountain
    Young Gim and the robbers
—by devils
    The blind man and the devils
—for father's death
    The tiger and the dwarf
Revenge of Joaquina
    MacLean-*Cuentos,* 156
REVIVALS
    How the slaves worshipped
Revivication. *See*
    RESUSCITATION
REVOLUTIONS
—horse crushes enemies of prince
    A horse called Terror
REWARD
    Saran and Yumart
A reward for honesty
    Campos-*Mexican,* 115–118
The reward of charity
    Patai-*Gates,* 554–558
Reward of study
    Patai-*Gates,* 533–536
REWARDS
    See also KINDNESS; KIND-
        NESS TO CREATURES;
        PUNISHMENT; TESTS
    Crab
    Dead snake and young wife
    The fairy Ialour
    The good girl and the bad girl
    Heaven's reward
    Knock, knock, who's there?
    The language of animals
    The little white stone

    The merman
    My lord bag of rice
    Patient Griselda
    The pied piper of Hamelin
    Prince Asraf and the king of
        the spirits
    Saint Peter and the two
        women
    Savatri and the god of death
    The sheep butcher and his
        king
    Thorston and the dwarf
    Treasure of the magic icon
    The trolls of Skurugata
—for lost and found
    The poor old dog
—life restored
    Death's substitute
REWARDS (subject)
—fairies give
    Briggs-*Vanish.,* 217 (index)
Rewards and punishments [motif
    index]
    Wilbert-*Bororo,* 267–269, 312,
        315
Reynard and Chanticleer
    Boose-*Scand.,* 124
RHIANNON
    [Dyfed: under spell . . . Faerie]
    Manawydan, son of Llyr
    Pwyll, Prince of Dyfed
Rhiannon and Pwyll
    Spells & Bind, 20–33
Rhine castles
    Lee-*Castles,* 128–136
RHINOCEROS
    Madame rhinoceros and her
        dress
—origin of skin
    How the rhinoceros got his
        saggy, baby skin
    How the rhinoceros got his
        skin
RHODES (island)
    Moerae
RHYMES

See also POETICAL; REPETI-
TIVE RHYMES AND
STORIES
The bun [personified]
The fool and the magic fish
House in the wood
The magic gifts [dwarf-
sorcerer]
Rhys at the fairy-dance
Keightley-*World*, 415–416
Rhythms. *See* REPETITIVE
RHYMES AND STORIES
RIBBONS
The yellow ribbon [holds wife's
head on]
—holds girl's head on
The green ribbon
RICE
My lord bag of rice
The old woman and her rice
Roly poly rice ball
Thievery
—"bones"
A Hani story: Queen forbids
servant to eat rice
RICE CAKES
The old woman and the rice
cakes
RICEBIRDS
—reincarnated as prince &
princess
Tale of the ricebirds
Rich. *See* WEALTH
The rich boy and the poor boy
Villa-*Armenian*, 309–315, 512–
514
The rich farmer and the poor
farmer
Crossley-*Folk*, 147–149
Rich man of Sung
Roberts-*Chinese*, 68
Rich man, poor man ["eats" smell
of food]
Yolen-*Favorite*, 406–407
Rich man: Under the shade of the
mulberry tree

Peacock Maid, 119–121
The rich ranchero's maguey fence
Campos-*Mexican*, 24–27
Riches. *See* WEALTH
Rickety Topknot
Perrault-*Glass*, 69–79
Ricky of the Tuft
Mulherin-*Favorite*, 74–81; in-
trod., 72
RIDDANCE
The nis removing
The riddle
Lang-*Green*, 347–351
A riddle for freedom
Faulkner-*Tales*, 66–70
The riddles
Shah-*World*, 65–67
Villa-*Armenian*, 189–193
RIDDLES
See also PUZZLES;
QUESTIONS
The clever little tailor
Clever Manka
The clever sewing-maid
Crossing the river [man, wolf,
goat, cabbage]
The daughter and the helper
The dreamer and his dream
Farmer who found his match in
daughter-in-law
Favorite verses, proverbs, and
riddles
Fisherman and the prince
The fly (as witness)
The four rings
Gawain and the Lady Ragnell
Gestumblindi's riddles
The golden neckband
A hundred times
Jean Sotte
Knight of the riddles
Leopard, goat, and yam
Manka and the judge
Owney and Owney-na-peak
Ozark Mountain riddles
The parson and the sexton

RIDDLES (continued)
  Phra Nang Suwanasopha
  A pottle o' brains
  Precious Jade
  Princess and the slave
  El que canta sus males
    espanta
  The ridere of riddles
  The shepherd boy
  Stories to solve; 14 folktales
  The sultan and the cobbler
  The tale of Squirrel Nutkin
  A Tartar riddle: Which is
    biggest?
  Three challenges for King
    Solomon
  Three corpses, money, and a
    wine-bottle
  The troll's daughter
  Two brothers
  The wise goldsmith
  The wise little girl
  The woodsman's riddle
  The young head of the family
—answers sold to merchants
  Clever answers (Russia)
The ride of the headless phantom
  Haining-*Lepre.*, 39–41
Rider acquired by horseman or
  driver [8 legends]
  Robe-*Hispanic*, 126–134
The ridere of riddles
  Jacobs-*Celtic*, 279–282
Riders of the wind [flying creatures]
  Magical Beasts, 56–99
RIDES
  A ghost gets a free ride
  Giving the devil a ride
RIDICULE
  He who laughs last, laughs
    best
  King Matyas and his scholars
    (Hungary)
  The swine herd
  Tortoise and hawk: never
    laugh at friends

Riding. *See* FAIRY RADE—flying
Riding the backahast
  Lindow-*Swedish*, 120–121
RIGHT . . .
  Country mouse and city mouse
  The real princess [pea-under-
    mattress test]
RIGHT AND WRONG
  The spook and the beer barrel
RIGHTEOUSNESS
  Eagle Woman comes to The
    People
  There is righteousness
—Buddhism
  A deer king offers his life
RIGHTEOUSNESS (subject)
—Buddhist stories
  Amore-*Lustful*, 63
RIGIDITY (psychology)
  The man who sat on the tide
The Rikubugu myth
  Wilbert-*Bororo*, 95–97
Rin Jin: The jelly fish and the
  monkey
  Ozaki-*Japanese*, 189–202
Ringdove's taming voice
  Magical Beasts, 124
RINGS
  Aladdin, or The wonderful
    lamp
  The black horse
  The bronze ring
  Cat lying on velvet cushion,
    while dog sleeps
  The cattle raid of Froech
  The charcoal burner
  The costly ring
  Crab
  The curse of Andvari's ring
  Enchanted ring
  The four rings
  The ghost at Fjelkinge
  The girl clad in mouseskin
  How Sigourd awoke Brynhild
    upon Hindfell
  How Thor got his hammer

Iskandar and the emerald
    ring
Jack and the green lady
Juan and the bony one
Lake Goldring
Liisa and the prince
Loki makes mischief
The magic ring
Magic ring of Rabbi Israel
    Hacohen
Master Tobacco
The old flea-bag
The seawife and the crone
The shepherd of Silfrun-
    Arstadir
Singard the dragon-slayer
The squirrel wife
Wayland Smith
Why the sea moans
—arm
    Wayland Smith
—causes sleep
    Nourie Hadig [a "Snow White"
    type]
—diamond
    Truthful John
—lost, swallowed by fish, fish
    taken to castle
The ruby ring
—magic
    Aladdin and his magic lamp
    Old fire dragaman
    Scabby: beauty is only skin
        deep
    The scabby child
    Star Maiden
—red lion
    The dwarf's feast
—wedding
    Just married
—when rubbed, lady appears
    Enchanted castle
—wishes granted
    Goggle eyes
RINGS (subject)
—fairy rings

Briggs-*Vanish.*, 11, 18, 49, 82,
    165
RIO GRANDE
    The hand and the whirlpool
Rip Van Winkle
    Lewis-*Bedtime*, 14–15
    Rackham-*Fairy*, 230–249
RIP VAN WINKLE STORIES
    (subject)
    Briggs-*Vanish.*, 24–25
Riquet with the Tuft
    Shah-*World*, 211–215
Rising rock [Chiricahua]
    Myles-*Butterflies*, 21–28
Rising Star finds a wife [dog]
    [Tewa]
    Myles-*Butterflies*, 41–45
RISK
    The fox and the drum
Ritchie, Jack
    Kid Cardula
Rival kempers
    Yeats-*Fairy*, 308–313
Rival magicians
    Zong-*Korea*, 70–71
The rival twins
    Gibson-*Gods*, 80–84
RIVALRY
    The wood and sea nymphs
The rivals
    Synge-*Land*, 114–126
River claims a victim
    O'Sullivan-*Legends*, 16–17
RIVER MEN
    Nixen and river men
RIVER SPIRITS
    River women
RIVER SPIRITS (subject)
    Briggs-*Vanish.*, 68–70
River women
    Arrowsmith-*Field*, 98–101
RIVERS
    The bushbabies
    Chiefs make the rivers
        beautiful
    The creation of the world

RIVERS (continued)
   The cuckoo: its origin and its
      call
   Drakestail [and the king]
   Eridanus (the River)
   The great deeds of King Yu
   How porridge was cooked in
      Gotham
   How the speckled hen got her
      speckles
   In the beginning
   Tibet's first king
   Tiyo's story
—bride transformed into
   Give me something you
      have . . . unawares
—how five in Siam got named
   How the Mekong River came
      to be
ROADRUNNERS
   El pajaro cu
—steals fire for Indians
   Legend of the roadrunner
ROADS
—proposed highway haunted
   My displaced ghosts
Roam the wild country
   And Every., 21–42
ROANE
   The seal fisher and the Roane
   Seal people: Sea trows and
      Roane
Roast duckling [to cover guilt]
   Stuchl-*American,* 183–184
Robbers. *See* BANDITS; OUT-
     LAWS; THIEVES AND
     THIEVERY
Roberts, Leonard
   Nippy and the Yankee Doodle
The robin
   Adams-*Iron,* 130–133
ROBIN GOODFELLOWS (subject)
   Briggs-*Vanish.*, 53–54, 59, 199
ROBINS
—origin of red breast
   Echidna's spines

How raven brought fire to the
   Indians
Piggiebillah the porcupine
Robinson, Gail, and Douglas Hill
   How coyote stole fire
Roc. *See* ROCS
The rock and the weasel
   Watson-*Thailand,* 21–24
Rock-a-bye baby
   Ainsworth-*Phantom,* 64–76
ROCKS AND STONES
   The bearded rock
   The bridge over Kalmarsound
   The deacon of Myrka
   The dwarfs on the tree
   The giant puke
   The giant who had no heart
   Girl swallowed up by the stone
   The guilty stone
   The hill man at the dance
   The honest penny
   Hunter Hailibu's great sacrifice
   Little Annie the goose girl
   The little white stone
   Ljungby horn and pipe
   The Mayamah: enemies turned
      to stones
   The night-trolls
   Thy phynnodderee
   The pied piper of Hamelin
   Rising rock [Chiricahua]
   The snake people of Ayers
      Rock
   Stupid Peikko
   The sword in the stone
   The talking stone
   Thorston and the dwarf
   Town of stone
   Two hunting dogs [Burra-
      jahnee and Inneroogun]
   The Ulfgryt stones
   Vaino and the swan princess
   Wasek and the red giants
   The wild swans
   Yallery Brown
—chases coyote

Coyote and the rock
—dancers turned to stone
Wedding at Stanton Drew
—human thoughts, feelings, etc.
The grey stone [fossil
personified]
—magic transport
Son of the Knight of the Green
Vesture
—speaks, "not going anywhere"
The rock and the weasel
—talking
When rocks rolled crackling
wisdom
—throwing
Thordur of Thrastastadir
—whispers advice
Squirrel and the fox
The rocks of Korsan
Adams-*Iron*, 93–99
ROCS (birds)
The bird maiden
Land monsters
Rocs [Ruc, or Rukh] the behemoth
bird
Magical Beasts, 70
Rod: Munachar and the raspberries
Smith-*Manichar*, 6–42
[Roger Bacon foils Satan]
Lehane-*Wizards*, 74
ROGERO, Sir
Bloody castle of Altaripa
Castles of the wizard and the
hippogriff
The rogue of Kachi Kachi Mountain
Kendall-*Haunting*, 7–11
Rogues, cheats, and tricksters
Yolen-*Favorite*, 125–166
Rogues. *See* RASCALS
Roland: a choice of death before
dishonor
Lehane-*Legends*, 48
Role reversal: The daughter and
the helper
Timpanelli-*Tales*, 15–27
ROLLER BIRD

—saves girl
Oh Mister Crocodile
ROLLING
The pancake
The rollright stones
Marshall-*Every.*, 265–267
ROLLRIGHT STONES (subject)
Briggs-*Vanish.*, 7, 74–75, 88
ROLSTONA
Three heroes [and the
3-headed boa]
Roly Poly
Stovicek-*Around*, 194–197
Roly poly rice ball
Macdonald-*Twenty*, 104–114
ROMANCE
Moerae
ROMANIA
Rusalky
ROME
The founding of Rome
Gods and goddesses, Greek
and Roman
—ancient
Dream of Macsen
ROMULUS
The founding of Rome
RONAYNE, Philip
Giant's stairs [Mahon
MacMahon]
Giant's stars [Ronayne's Court]
Ronwe: demon
Lehane-*Wizards*, 76
ROOFERS
Chelm justice (Jewish)
ROOFS
Lippo and Tapio
Room Bacha and Baki
O'Connor-*Tibet*, 147–157
ROOMING HOUSES
The other Celia
ROOMS
—secret
Jurma and the sea god
Severi and Vappu
The widow's son

Rooster/Brother
  Villa-*Armenian,* 393–396, 527
Roosters. *See* CHICKENS—
  roosters
Rooster's advice [beat your wife]
  Villa-*Armenian,* 401
Roosters, snakes and basiliscs
  Arrowsmith-*Field,* 174–178
Rooting out bad feelings
  Phillips-*Hoity,* 32–37
The roots of jealousy
  Todd-*Tortoise,* 33–35
ROPE(S)
  Anpao is born
  The confession of Charles
    Linkworth
  How they got Hairlock home
—to hang lake from the sky
  Abzelil and the Master of the
    Lake
—magic
  The peach thief
  What happened to six wives
    who ate onions
The rose of Peppermette
  Thomas-*It's,* 157–160
The rose tree
  Garner-*British,* 82–85
ROSEBUSHES
  Three rosebushes
Rosemary
  Ewart-*Lore,* 120–121
ROSEMARY
  Sprig of rosemary
Roses
  Ewart-*Lore,* 79–87
ROSES
  Beauty and the beast
  The elf of the rose
  The rose of Peppermette
  The snow queen
  Snow White and Rose Red
  The swine herd
  The wild swans
—berries
  Moonflower

—red
  The nightingale and the rose
—white
  The white rose
Rosy apple and the golden bowl
  Riordan-*Russia,* 138–143
The Round Table
  Riordan-*Arthur,* 24–25
ROUND TABLE (Camelot; King
    Arthur)
  Brotherhood of the Round
    Table
  The coming of Arthur
  Elaine the Fair Maid of Astolat
  Jack the Giant Killer
  Siege of Joyous Garde
  Sir Gareth of Orkney
  Sir Launcelot du Lake
ROUNDUPS
  The parting song
ROW BOATS
—wrecked
  Severi and Vappu
Rowan
  Froud-*Faeries,* unp
ROWAN TREES
  Laidley worm of Spindlestone
    Heugh
  Weardale fairies [dislike being
    observed]
The royal detectives
  Shah-*World,* 184
The royal jewel
  Roberts-*Chinese,* 202–205
Royal pillow-talk: Medb and Ailill
  Ross-*Druids,* 46–47
RUAD
  Naming of places
RUBEZAHL
  Hey-hey men
RUBIES
  Azad Bakht's tale
Rubizal and the miller's daughter
  Manning-*Spooks,* 51–61
The ruby ring
  Shah-*Afghanistan,* 71–75

Ruc. *See* ROCS
Ruckus in the well
  Roberts-*Jung,* 19–27
A rude awakening
  Lindow-*Swedish,* 112–113
Rudeness. *See* DISCOURTESY
RUG, Peter
  The ghost rider
Rugs. *See* CARPETS
Rukhs. *See* ROCS
RULERS
  See also EMPERORS;
    KHANS; KINGS AND
    QUEENS; SULTANS;
    TSARS; TYRANTS
  The Amir who was a beggar
  Buying loyalty
  Dreams
  The golden cockerel
  the master of prayer
—and subjects
  The Amir who became a
    weaver
Rules for living. *See* CONDUCT
  OF LIFE
RUMANIA
  Stan Bolovan and the dragon
RUMORS
  Chicken Licken
Rumpelstiltskin
  dePaola-*Favorite,* 46–52
  Ehrlich-*Random,* 166–173
  Lang-*Blue,* 103–107 (notes,
    367)
  Leete-*Golden,* 48–57
  Lewis-*Bedtime,* 8–9
  Shub-*About,* 76–79
RUMPLESTILTSKIN-TYPE
  STORIES
  Duffy and the devil
  Tom Tit Tot
RUMPELSTILTSKIN-TYPE STO-
  RIES (subject)
  Shah-*World,* 120
Run brer gator, run!
  Faulkner-*Tales,* 128–131

RUNNERS AND RUNNING
  Johnny Cake
  The little chicken Kluk and his
    companions
  Silbado
Rural women. *See* FARM GIRLS
Rusalky
  Arrowsmith-*Field,* 189–192
The ruse of Rabbi Reuben Estrogli
  Elbaz-*Folktales,* 145–146
Ruslan and Chernomor
  Weiss-*Russian,* 49–52
The russet dog
  Jacobs-*Celtic,* 230–235
RUSSIA
  Baboushka, the Wise Men and
    the Prince of Peace
  Barter
  Domoviye
  The fool and the birch
  Half-ram leaves home
  How a poor muzhik looked for
    truth and found it
  Leshiye and Lisunkl
  Poleviki and Poludnitsy
  Roosters, snakes and basiliscs
  Rusalky
  Vodyaniye
  Wizard of Kiev
—Leningrad
  Shurik: A story of the seige of
    Leningrad
—Moscow
  The plague of Moscow
    [Varvarka]
—Murom
  Pierre, Prince of Murom
RUSSIA (subject)
—Lands of old Rus (map)
  Riordan-*Russia,* 6
RUSSIAN TALES (subject)
  Riordan-*Russia,* 269–286
—[Forty-eight tales]
  Riordan-*Russia,* 1–286
—[Nine folk tales]
  Xenophontovna-*Folk,* 1–151

RUSSIAN TALES
   (subject)(continued)
—[Seven tales, Bilibin]
   Bilibin-*Russian,* 1–77
—[Zvorykin, Diaghilev, Afanas'ev]
   Zvorykin-*Firebird,* 6–8
Rustam and Tahmina
   Shah-*Dervishes,* 207–211
Rustam and the iron fortress
   Shah-*Dervishes,* 154–158
RYSKA
   The fire bird and Ryska and
      vixen
Ryugu: Urashima Taro
   Nye-*Out,* 45–59

SABBATH
   See also SUNDAY
   Fisherman's dream
   Flying lion of the Rab of
      Tlemcen
   The pious cow
—breaking
   Wedding at Stanton Drew
   Why mowers are poor
—working on
   Girls at parsonage get help
      sewing crinoline
SABBATH (subject)
   Patai-*Gates,* 796 (index)
SABBATS (subject)
—Fancy and fact
   Sergeant-*Witches,* 29–35
The sabio sees a sow
   Campos-*Mexican,* 134–136
Sable souls
   Nagishkin-*Folktales,* 99–105
SABLES
—master of
   Sable souls
SABOTAGE
   How the animals stopped the
      freeway

SACKS
   Bagged wolf
   Death and the soldier
   Jump into my sack (Italy)
   The magic bag
   [Pwyll] Powel, Prince of Dyfed
   The soldier and death
   Wiley and the hairy man
—magic bag
   The queen's children
—never filled
   Pwyll, Prince of Dyfed
"SACRED BIRD"
   Poor turkey girl
The sacred honey bees
   Lines-*Greek,* 107–110
The sacred island, Nar-oong-owie
   Parker-*Australian,* 181–182
SACRED PLACES
—desecrated
   Assaraf baths closed
The sacred sheet [at execution]
   Villa-*Armenian,* 419–420
SACRIFICE
   See also HUMAN SACRIFICE
   Anpao brings the corn
   Hunter Hailibu's great sacrifice
   The little mermaid
   The serpent-slayer
—of animals
   The goat who laughed and
      cried
Sacrificed by kin, lover brings girl
      back from below
   Radin-*African,* 272–273
SACRILEGE
   Legend of the Russian priest
The sad end of Wu-Lung-Tru
   Jagendorf-*Magic,* 19–20
Sad fate of Pikuwa
   Reed-*Aboriginal,* 70–73
Sad marriage of North
   Jagendorf-*First,* 27–29
The sad tale of the rabbit's tail
   Jagendorf-*Magic,* 33–34
SADDLE BAGS

Wali and the magic saddle-bag
SADDLES AND SADDLERS
    Guleesh
    Libor and the swan princess
    Silbado
—magic
    The magic fruit
SADNESS
    The bird of happiness
    Hob and the Sad
    Tearless woman cries on
        seeing the devil
The sadness of Cornelius Berg
    Yourcenar-*Oriental*, 134–141
Saga of Santiago Sanchez
    MacLean-*Cuentos*, 189–195
Sagacious monkey and the boar
    Ozaki-*Japanese*, 148–152
SAGAS (subject)
    Keightley-*World*, 60–75
Sagittarius (the Archer)
    Gallant-*Constel.*, 87–91
SAGO (food)
    The proper way to make sago
    Sun and sago
SAILORS
    The bottle-neck
    The fairy hunt
    Give me my bone
    God on our side
    The lady and the merman
    Soul cages (condensed)
    The wind cap
—song of mermaids and
    The little mermaid
Saint Brigid's cloak
    McGarry-*Folk*, 96–97
Saint Colmkille's well
    O'Sullivan-*Legends*, 108–109
Saint Conall's stone
    O'Sullivan-*Legends*, 82–83
Saint Eustace's well
    Marshall-*Every.*, 189–191
Saint Finbar and the River Lee
    O'Sullivan-*Legends*, 152–153
Saint George

Stallman-*Dragons*, 22–23
SAINT JOHN'S DAY
    Adventures of John Dietrich
SAINT JOHN'S EVE
    The princess on the glass hill
Saint John's Eve bonfires
    O'Sullivan-*Legends*, 51
SAINT JOHN'S NIGHT
    The sleeping prince
Saint John's wort
    Froud-*Faeries*, unp
Saint Martin's Eve [a]
    O'Sullivan-*Legends*, 114–115
Saint Martin's Eve [b]
    O'Sullivan-*Legends*, 115–116
Saint Michael wins a soul from
        devil
    O'Sullivan-*Legends*, 33–34
Saint Nicholas and the children
    Macmillan-*Canadian* 153–159
Saint Patrick and Crom Dubh
    O'Sullivan-*Legends*, 109–112
Saint Patrick curses Ireland
    O'Sullivan-*Legends*, 113
Saint Peter and the two women
    Booss-*Scand.*, 190–194
Saint Sebastian
    Griego-*Cuentos*, 123–125
Saint snakes
    Villa-*Armenian*, 356–357
SAINTS
    See also MARTYRS
    The smith and the devil
    Treason in saints
SAINTS (subject)
    Marshal-*Every.*, 44, 177
Saints Colmkille and Edna
    O'Sullivan-*Legends*, 106–108
SAKE (rice wine)
    The eight-forked serpent
Saki [pseud. of H. H. Munro, 1870–
        1916]
    The open window
    The wolves of Cernogratz
SAKKA (god)
    The Buddhist Job

SAKKA (god) (continued)
  The hare in the moon
  How a youth lost his virtue
  The radiant Sambula
Sakka: The eye restored
  Amore-*Lustful*, 136–137
SALAMANDER
  The dwarf's feast
SALAMASINA, Queen of Samoa
  The plot to kidnap the Queen
    [Salamasina]
Salary. *See* WAGES
Salem [witchcraft, ca. 1692]
  Sergeant-*Witches*, 115–175
SALESMEN AND SALESMANSHIP
  Lodging for the night
  Mossycoat
SALIVA
  The truth about ghosts
Sally Simple's matches
  Blyton-*My*, 38–42
Salmon. *See under* FISH
SALMON RIVER
—Idaho
  Coyote and the swallowing
    monster
SALOME
  Waxworks
Saloons. *See* PUBS (saloons)
SALT
  Ali Baba and the forty thieves
  The blind sea captain
  The butterflies carried him
    home [Tewa]
  Cap o' Rushes
  Hic! Hic! Hic!
  How black became white
  How salt was discovered
  Kertong
  The lady and the merman
  The old flea-bag
  The story of the Salt Mother
  Why the sea is salt
Salt above gold
  Wood-*Palace*, 59–71
SALT LAKES

Sturt's desert pea, the blood
    flower
SALTWATER
  Wurrunnah's trip to the sea
Salvanelli
  Arrowsmith-*Field*, 258–261
Salvani and Aguane
  Arrowsmith-*Field*, 156–159
SALVATION
  The bundle of straw
  The three brothers
  The three old men
Sam Pig seeks his fortune
  Uttley-*Foxglove*, 11–19
Samba the Satan and Omadi the
    Righteous
  Magel-*Gambia*, 104–106
Samba's wife
  Magel-*Gambia*, 159–162
SAMBATYON (legendary river)
  The eternal light [Solomon &
    Benaiah]
SAMOA
  The creation of Samoa
  How Samoa was named
  Maui, son of the sun
  Paao from Samoa
  The plot to kidnap the Queen
    [Salamasina]
—overthrows Tongan conquerers
  Brave warrior, Malietoa!
SAMOA (subject)
—[History, customs, legends]
  Wright-*Pigeon*, 4–5
—Legendary home
  Westervelt-*Hawaiian*, 41–46
SAMOYEDS
  The girl with the silver voice
SAMPHIRES
  Sea bindweed, sea holly, sea
    pea, samphire
SAMPO (magic mill)
  The forging of the sampo
  The maid of the north
    [Kalevala]
  The mistress of Pohja

The stealing of the sampo
SAMURAI
    Kintaro, the golden boy
    Okiku and the saucers
    The vengeance of Oiwa
SAMURAI (subject)
    Piggott-*Japanese,* 144
The San Francisco earthquake
    O'Sullivan-*Legends,* 66–67
SANCTUARY
    —boar seeks to escape hunters
    Boar of Eskdale
SAND
    The scabby child
Sand as fertiliser
    O'Sullivan-*Legends,* 49–50
SAND HILLS
    The fire plume
SAND LAKE, N.M.
    The Tewa emerge from Sand
    Lake
Sandoz, Maurice
    The Tsantsa
SANDPAINTINGS (subject)
    —The how and why of . . .
    Dutton-*Navajo,* 35
The sandpipers and the sea
    Wood-*Kalila,* 147, 151–153
SANDSTORMS
    A potsherd speaks
SANDWOOD COTTAGE
    The mystery of Sandwood
Sandy Harg's wife (condensed)
    Briggs-*Vanish.,* 108–109
SANNTRAIGH, Isle of
    Island of Sanntraigh
    (condensed)
The Santa Lucias [demon-
    foundling; legend]
    MacLean-*Cuentos,* 179–
    184
Santo Nino de Atocha: Help for a
    mule caravan
    Campos-*Mexican,* 66–68
The Santo Nino [de Atocha] saves
    a friendship

    Campos-*Mexican,* 77–79
The Santo Nino [de Atocha] visits a
    prison
    Campos-*Mexican,* 80–83
Saran and Yumart
    Riordan-*Tartary,* 95–99
SARCASM
    Coyote and the rattlesnake
    The tomte carries a single
    straw
SARDINES
    Mermaid of the Magdalenes
SARDINIA
    Monacielli
SARKIS, Saint
    Tushcoon Eigna
Sarrantonio, Al
    Haunting of [computer] Y-12
"SASQUATCH"
    Wild men
Satan. *See* DEVIL(S)
Satan and the boy
    Aiken-*Mexican,* 145–146
SATANISM
    The dance of the owls
SATI
    A goddess is born
SATIRE
    Goat's funeral [religious satire]
    High John the conqueror
Satyr and Pan (condensed)
    Lloyd-*Mythical,* 43–49
SATYRS
    Goat people
    Midas, the golden king
    Pan and Dionysus, the wild
    gods
SATYRS (subject)
    Scott-*Fantastic,* 111–120
Satyrs, with Ariadne
    Magical Beasts, 14–15
SAUCERS
    Okiku and the saucers
SAUL, King
    Fortune-teller recognizes King
    Saul

The sausage
    Booss-*Scand.*, 179–182
The sausage: stuck on wife's nose
    Yolen-*Favorite*, 185–187
SAUSAGES
—skewers
    Soup from a sausage skewer
Savatri and the god of death
    Amore-*Lustful*, 28–33
Save it for tomorrow
    Lindow-*Swedish*, 82
SAVEA, King of Samoa
    Brave warrior, Malietoa!
SAVES
    The dwarfs' banquet
SAWMILLS
    Legends of the mill
    The new hand [old man made
        young again]
Saxe of Saxeholm
    Booss-*Scand.*, 292–293
SAYINGS
    Wise sayings for a thousand
        dinars each
Sayre, Craig
    Flight over XP-637
Scabby: beauty is only skin deep
    Todd-*Tortoise*, 85–98
The scabby child
    Todd-*Some*, 102–117
SCALES
    Catherine and her destiny
    Libra (the Scales)
SCALPELS
    A most unusual murder
SCANDINAVIA
    The altar-cup in Angerup
    The changeling [a]
    Departure of the trolls from
        Vendsyssel
    Drakes [house spirits]
    The elf-woman and Sir Olof
    The elle-maid near Ebeltoft
    The elle-maids
    A farmer tricks a troll
    The girl at the troll-dance

Hans Puntleder
The hill men invited to the
    christening
The hill smith
Kallundborg church
Kirsten's-hill
The legend of Bodedys
Maid Vae
Mer-men
Mound folk
Nissen and Tomtra
Origin of Tiis Lake
Proud Margaret
Sir Olof in the elve-dance
Sir Thynne
Skotte in the fire
Stormalong fights the Kraken
Svend Faelling
Svend Faelling and the elle-
    maid
The tile-stove jumping over the
    brook
The troll labour
Troll labour (condensed)
The troll turned cat
The troll wife
Why the sea is salt
The young swain and the
    elves
SCANDINAVIA (subject)
    Keightley-*World*, 76–78
—fairies
    Briggs-*Vanish.*, 218 (index)
Scarface
    Haviland-*N. Amer.*, 83–93
Scar Face and the sun dance
    Wood-*Spirits*, 85–89
SCARS
    The battle with the birds
    The sun journey
SCARVES
    Padmasambhava and the felic-
        ity scarf
Scary dragons
    Stallman-*Dragons*, 12–27
SCATHACH (a woman-warrior)

A champion's schooling in another world
A scattering of seeds
  Ewart-*Lore*, 164–167
Scepticism. *See* SKEPTICISM
Scheherazade
  Lewis-*Minute*, 22–23
Scheherazade retold
  Phelps-*Maid*, 167–173
The scholar jackal
  Raychaudhuri-*Stupid*, 60–64
SCHOLARS
  Unofficial history of the Confucian Academy
  The vision of MacConglinney
The scholar's concubine
  Roberts-*Chinese*, 157–161
SCHOLARSHIP
—unending learning
  The master pupil
Scholarship is the best merchandise
  Patai-*Gates*, 630–631
SCHOOL CHILDREN
  Pyoli and Lord Krishna
School teachers. *See* TEACHERS
Schoolcraft, Henry Rowe
  The Weendigoes
SCHOOLMASTERS
  See also TEACHERS
  Birth, dreaming, death: schoolmaster's story
Schools. *See* EDUCATION
Schwarz, Herbert T.
  Windigo [III]
SCIENCE
  So you won't talk
SCIENTISTS
  The anglers of Arz
SCISSORS
—golden
  The companion
Scold (wife). *See* SHREWS
The Scorpion [Orion, the Hunter]
  Lurie-*Heavenly*, 28–30
SCORPIONS

Princess with the golden hair
Scorpius (the Scorpion)
Scorpius (the Scorpion)
  Gallant-*Constel.*, 82–85
SCOT, Reginald (subject)
  Briggs-*Vanish.*, 50, 55–56
SCOTLAND
  Beth Gellert
  The black bull of Norroway
  The boy of the red twilight sky
  The brownies
  Cassley: Cnoc na Cnoimn
  The fachan
  The farmer of Liddesdale
  Glashans and Shopiltees
  Goodwife of Laggan: enemy of the sisterhood
  Johnnie in the cradle
  The kelpie
  Laird of Duffus (condensed)
  The laird's lass and the gobha's son
  Mer-men
  Nuckelavee
  People of peace
  Red caps
  The ridere of riddles
  Saints Colmkille and Edna
  The seal fisher and the Roane
  The seal maiden
  Shellycoat
  Sluagh (condensed)
  The sprightly tailor
  The sunset call
  Undying guardianship: Rashin Coatie
  The unseelie court
  Urisk
—Carterhaugh
  Janet and Tamlin
  Tomlin [elf-knight]
—Highlands
  The brownies
  The changeling [c]
  The fairy borrowing oatmeal
  The fairy gift

SCOTLAND—Highlands
  (continued)
  The fairy lalour
  The fairy's inquiry
  The stolen lady
  The stolen ox
  The two fiddlers
  Urisk
  The wounded seal
  The young man in the shian
—Lowlands
  The changeling [d]
  Departure of the fairies
  The fairies' nurse
  The fairy rade
—Mull
  Treasure island: Tobermory
    argosy
—Norroway
  Far have I sought ye: Red Bull
    of Norroway
—Ruthven
  The wow o'Rivven; the bell
SCOTLAND (subject)
  Ross-*Druids,* 132 (index)
—Bibliography
  McKee-*Scottish,* 45
—fairies
  Briggs-*Vanish.,* 218 (index)
—Highlands
  Keightley-*World,* 384–396
—Lowlands
  Keightley-*World,* 350–361
—[Supernormal contacts]
  Robertson-*Highland,* vii–viii
Scott, Walter
  The hauntings of Frodriver
SCOTTISH TALES (subject)
  Lochhead-*Battle,* 1
—[Characteristics]
  Ratcliff-*Scottish,* 7–10
The Scottish thistle
  Ewart-*Lore,* 126–128
SCULPTORS AND SCULPTURES
  Pygmalion's statue
The scythe bitten by a snake

Stuchl-*American,* 142
SCYTHES
  The cat, the cock and the
    scythe
SEA
  See also BOATS; OCEAN;
    SHIPS AND SHIPBUILDING
  The angry merwife of
    Nordstrand
  The black dragon of the Sea of
    Dunting
  The boy of the red twilight sky
  The Cormorants of Andvaer
  Duke Magnus and the
    mermaid
  The enchanted fisherman
  Fairest of all others
  The guardian cock
  The invasion from the sea
  Isaac and the Parson of Brono
  The kobold and the pirate
  Maui and the islands
  The merrow and the soul
    cages
  Pedorus Jack
  The sea captain and the
    serpent
  The seal fisher and the Roane
  The seal maiden
  Taufatahi and Fakapatu or
    Why sharks . . . Moungone
  Urashima Taro
  Why the sea is salt
—cruel
  The bird and the sea: Jingwei
—moaning
  Why the sea moans
—surface
  The little mermaid
—visits sun (then on earth)
  A visit from Mister Sea
SEA ANIMALS
  Sedna the sea goddess
Sea battles. *See* NAVAL BATTLES
Sea beings: Sila [human female]
  Robinson-*Raven,* 101–113

Sea bindweed, sea holly, sea pea, samphire
  Ewart-*Lore,* 161–162
The sea captain and the serpent
  Heslewood-*Tales,* 108–115
SEA CAPTAINS
  The captain's cabin
  Greenland whale fishery [song and story]
  Orpheus and Eurdice
  The ship without a captain
  Supparaka
SEA CREATURES
  See also SJORA
  The cat in the sea
SEA DRAUGS (subject)
  Briggs-*Vanish.,* 151
SEA EAGLES
  Vaino and the Swan princess
The sea fairies [Na Buctogai]
  Logan-*Old,* 81–84
Sea fairies. *See* FAIRIES—sea; MERMAIDS
SEA FOLK
  The fiddler and the sea nymph
  The fisherman and his soul
  Funeral of Flory Cantillon
  The great flood
  Huldbrand and Undine: a doomed alliance of earth and water
  Nuckelavee
  Soul cages (condensed)
  The woman of the sea
  The wood and sea nymphs
Sea folk: The water folk
  Scott-*Fantastic,* 135–148
Sea friend: otter saves monk's lost book
  Berger-*Animalia* [41–43]
Sea ghosts. *See* GHOSTS
Sea girl: Wild goose lake
  Sadler-*Heaven,* 31–37
The Sea Goat [Pan vs Typhon]
  Lurie-*Heavenly,* 56–58
SEA GODDESSES

Sedna the sea goddess
SEA GODS
  Jurma and the sea god
The sea gods' realm
  Water Spirits, 37–44
Sea gods: The water folk
  Scott-*Fantastic,* 135–148
SEA GULLS
  The giant sturgeon
  The girl who trod on the loaf
  How mussels were brought to the creeks
  Manabozho's fishing: the king of fishes
—brother trans. into
  Galo and Vasiri
—keeps daylight in box
  How raven brought fire to the Indians
SEA HORSES
  Nennir, or the one who feels inclined
SEA KINGS
  The little mermaid
Sea kupua: the talking spear
  Thompson-*Hawaiian,* 29–42
Sea life. *See* OCEAN LIFE
SEA LORE
  The tales of Rabba bar Hana
The sea maiden
  Jacobs-*Celtic,* 95–101
Sea maidens. *See* MERMAIDS; MERROWS; SEA FOLK
SEA MONSTERS
  [Assipattle vs Stoorworm the sea-serpent]
  The black pearl
  The lake monster
  The merman
  Mouse Woman and the vanished princes
  Naddi
  Raven and the nose of the Gonaqadet
  Thor goes fishing
  Water monsters

The sea nymph
    Booss-*Scand.,* 268–269
Sea nymphs. *See* SEA FOLK; WA-
    TER NYMPHS; names of
    sea nymphs
SEA PALACES
    Jurma and the sea god
SEA PEAS
    Sea bindweed, sea holly, sea
    pea, samphire
Sea people. *See* SEA FOLK
Sea prince
    Roberts-*Chinese,* 15–16
SEA PRINCESSES
    The little mermaid
    Uraschimataro and the turtle
    Urashima
Sea serpents. *See* SEA
    MONSTERS
Sea shells. *See* SHELLS
SEA SLOTHS
    Assorted monsters
SEA SPIRITS
    Sedna, the witch under the
    sea
SEA SPIRITS (subject)
    Briggs-*Vanish.,*73, 81, 88–89
Sea, sun and moon [visiting; sun
    and moon leap to sky . . .]
    Pitcher-*Tokol.,* 33–35
SEA TROWS
    Gioga's son
    Seal people: Sea trows and
    Roane
SEA TURTLES
    The turtle and the island
"SEA WOMEN"
    Mer-women
SEAFARING LIFE
    Wraiths of wind and wave
The seal fisher and the Roane
    Heslewood-*Tales,* 51–55
SEAL-HUNTERS
    The wounded sea
The seal maiden
    Heslewood-*Tales,* 136–140

SEAL MAIDENS
    [Selkies, seal-maidens, and
    mermaids]
    The white seal maid
Seal maidens and fairy seals
    [condensed]
    Mckee-*Scottish,* 21–23
Seal people: Sea trows and Roane
    Arrowsmith-*Field,* 170–173
Seal people: The water folk
    Scott-*Fantastic,* 144
SEALS (animals)
    The fisherman and the draug
    Gioga's son
    The grey selchie of Sule
    Skerrie
    A John o' Groats seal legend
    The mermaid wife
    Sedna the sea goddess
    The woman of the sea
    The wounded seal (Scotland)
—origin
    Angakok and Mother of Seals
    [sea petrel]
    Sedna (Eskimo)
    Sedna, the witch under the
    sea
—skins
    Gioga's son
    The mermaid wife
    The woman of the sea
—wife; resumes skin, returns to
    sea
    The seal's skin (Iceland)
SEALS (animals) (subject)
—fairies in form of
    Briggs-*Vanish.,* 39, 77, 81,
    162
The seal's skin (Iceland)
    Yolen-*Favorite,* 310–311
SEAMEN
    Stormalong fights the Kraken
SEAMSTRESSES
    The clever sewing-maid
    Vasilisa the Beautiful
    The young seamstress

Seanchan the Bard and the king of
the cats
Yeats-*Fairy*, 353–356
Search for a friend
Magel-*Gambia*, 175–178
[Search for parents] Pari Ao
Wilbert-*Bororo*, 212–213
The search for the buffalo
Wood-*Spirits*, 92–96
Search for the magic lake
Phelps-*Tatterhood*, 121–128
SEASHORES
The mouse at the seashore
The season of the stubby
caterpillar
Poland-*Mantis*, 80–88
SEASONS
*See also names of seasons,
e.g.* SUMMER
Cause of the seasons
The green mist
How summer [personified]
came to Canada
The seawife and the crone
Garner-*British*, 97–109
SEBASTIAN, Saint
Saint Sebastian
Second death of Ari and his new
resurrection
Wilbert-*Bororo*, 24–28
SECOND SIGHT
See also FOREKNOWLEDGE
Cat in the box
Clever boy
The Highland vision [23 tales]
Portent from the Nissar
Wise man and the apprentice
"SECOND SIGHT" (subject)
Mckee-*Scottish*, 33–37
[Secret life: nature charged with
intelligence]
Seekers Saviors, 21
The secret of the growing gold [by
Stoker]
Schwartz-*Great*, 21–37
The secret of Tomuni

Walking-*Song*, 31–36
The secret ones
Hoke-*Horrors*, 172–177
Secret races: In the beginning
Scott-*Fantastic*, 23–36
Secret royal inspector, Bag Mun-Su
Zong-*Korea*, 54–55
Secret sins: A teacher's tricky test
Amore-*Lustful*, 78
SECRETS
The green ribbon
Katrineholm Manor
Kertong
The language of animals
Lanval and the Lady Triamor
The lost treasure
The magic mirror
There is no such thing as a
secret
The treasure seekers
The white-hair waterfall
The yellow ribbon [holds wife's
head on]
SECURITY
The three little pigs
Wolf who traded his freedom
for security
—in society
The handsome suitor [A]
Sedna (Eskimo)
Yolen-*Favorite*, 105–107
SEDNA
—mother of seals
Angakok and Mother of Seals
[sea petrel]
Sedna the sea goddess
Haviland-*N. Amer.*, 60–64
Sedna, the witch under the sea
Wood-*Spirits*, 21–24
SEDUCTION
Bride-price: a woman for a
hundred cattle
Castle of an enchantress
Gawain and the Green Knight
King of the pipers and the
wonderful tune

SEDUCTION (continued)
  The queen who cried rape
  Sad fate of Pikuwa
  Wise sayings for a thousand
    dinars each
—attempted
  The man who didn't notice
    women
SEED(S)
  The bone garden
  Pint of flax seeds
  A scattering of seeds
—magic
  Little Yellow Bird
The seed's secret
  Roberts-*Jung*, 45–47
Se-eh-ha conquers the river people
  Shaw-*Pima*, 8–14
Seein' snakes
  Aiken-*Mexican*, 136–138
SEEING
—only some can see the grand
    estate
  The Chuang brocade
Seeing is believing
  Marshall-*Every.*, 53–58
SEEKERS (birds)
  Suit of white feathers
    (Dongxiang)
SEERS
—divination
  The sabio sees a sow
Seithenin the Drunkard
  Lee-*Castles*, 64
SELCHIES
  The white seal maid
SELF
  The dream castle
  The seed's secret
SELF CONFIDENCE
  The miller and the fox
SELF CONTROL
  The arising of Bodhi
  The blue lake
  The mute prince [kingship
    rejected]

  The servant who tested her
    mistress
SELF DEFENSE
  Glooskap and the turtle
SELF DENIAL
  Bagged wolf
Self effacement: The mask that
    wore the man
  Roberts-*Jung*, 34–41
SELF IMAGE
  Ruckus in the well
  The wolf and the cub
—negative
  The broken swords
SELF INDULGENCE
  The kingdom of beautiful
    colors
  The wizard's lesson
SELF LOVE
  Echo and Narcissus
  Prince Dorus
SELF MUTILATION
  Ouyan the curlew
SELF PITY
  Fleas and cockleburrs
SELF PRESERVATION
  Tortoise, goat and lion: the
    price of wisdom
SELF RELIANCE
  Kupti and Imani
SELF RIGHTEOUSNESS
  The devoted friend
SELF SACRIFICE
  The banyan deer [the Buddha]
  The boy who laughed at death
  Death's substitute
  The doe, the hunter, and the
    great stag
  Faithful John
  Generosity of Hatim Tai
  The governor and the Buddhist
  Hailibu the hunter
  The hare in the moon
  The hungry tigress
  King Sivi
  The lion and the hare

Lioness [protects her cub]
Long Haired Girl
Ludwig and Iskander
The nightingale and the rose
The pearl that shown by night
The pheasants and the bell
Prince Nocha
The swordmaker's son: King-
don of Chu
A tale of love
The tiger girl
Trusty John
Twelve wild geese
—Princess Ototachibana
Prince Vamato Take
—rewarded
A deer king offers his life
A king and a dove
SELF-SACRIFICE (subject)
—Buddhist stories
Amore-*Lustful*, 128
—Hindu stories
Amore-*Lustful*, 122
The selfish giant
Wild-*Fairy*, 29–39
Selfish husband
Zong-*Korea*, 191
SELFISHNESS
Anizu's magic wonder flute
Chang'o and the elixir of
immortality
The devoted friend
Discontented Lado
Dog in the manger
The greedy father
He comes from the east
The little girl who wanted ev-
erything back
The mopoke, and the mosquito
bird
The mortal lord
Once a good man [eat with
arms chained]
The pearl that shown by night
Pilgrimage to Mecca
The remarkable rocket

Saint Peter and the two
women
Seven sisters; a Miao story
The trolls in Resslared
Wisdom belongs to everyone
The wise woman, or The lost
princess
—looking out for self
O no, not my mother!
—punished
The wizard
Seligen Fraulein
Arrowsmith-*Field*, 212–217
Selim and the snake queen
Manning-*Kings*, 7–18
Selkies
Froud-*Faeries*, unp
[Selkies, seal-maidens, and
mermaids]
Water Spirits, 109–111
SEMELE
The youngest god [Dionysius]
Semi-humans
Scott-*Fantastic*, 111–120
The Seneca chief's adventures
Jagendorf-*First*, 31–37
Senor San Antonio retrieves an
axe
Campos-*Mexican*, 47–50
Separation of god from man
Radin-*African*, 28–32
SEPIK RIVER
Sun and sago
Sepik River and the island
Stokes-*Turtles*, 84–85
SERBIA
Marko's [Kraljevic] smile
SERMONS
The charcoal burner
Serpens (the Serpent)
Gallant-*Constel.*, 78–82
The serpent prince
Fattoross-*Simpleton*, 57–
61
The serpent-slayer
Kendall-*Sweet*, 33–38

Serpent spirits: Sea prince
    Roberts-*Chinese*, 15–16
The serpent [trust betrayed]
    Shah-*World*, 170
The serpent with one hundred
    heads [Kaliya]
    Amore-*Lustful*, 54–57
The serpent-woman (Spain)
    Yolen-*Favorite*, 315–323
Serpents. *See* SNAKES
Servan
    Arrowsmith-*Field*, 162–164
[Servant forces princess into
    servitude]
    Seekers Saviors, 24–31
Servant in the monastery
    Villa-*Armenian*, 420–422
The servant who tested her
    mistress
    Amore-*Lustful*, 154
SERVANTS
    Adventures of John Dietrich
    The artful lad
    The bishop and the elves
    The cat palace
    The cauld lad of Hilton
    The charcoal burner
    Crab
    The daughter and the helper
    Don Juan Zurumbete
    Dreams
    Elves ask a servant girl to be
        godmother
    The elves' dance
    Faithful John
    The giant's daughter
    Gifts of the child Christ
    Hagop's wish
    How Wang-Fo was saved
    Johan and the trolls
    Jovita and Manuelito
    The man-servant and the
        water-elves
    Monster with seven heads
    The nis riding
    Pixy-vengeance
    A priest and his servant Balda
    Rhys at the fairy-dance
    She was good for nothing
    The skeleton in Holar church
    Snipp, Snapp, Snorium
    Solomon the wise
    Toller's neighbors
    The triumph of death
    Trusty John
    Una the elfwoman
    Why the sea moans
    The wine bibber
    —forces princess to change places
        The goose girl
    —saves life of master
        Story-spirits [confined in bag;
        plan revenge]
    —treated badly
        Rahou [origin of eclipses]
    —usurps place of princess
        The goose girl
SERVICE
    Herman the milk bottle
SESAME SEEDS
    —transformed into soldiers
        Servant in the monastery
    Settlement out of court
        Hoke-*Horrors*, 105–116
Settlers. *See* PIONEERS
The seven against Thebes
    Pinsent-*Greek*, 82–84
The seven beggars
    Nahman-*Tales*, 251–282
    [notes: 253, 321–324]
The seven churches
    O'Sullivan-*Legends*, 148–149
Seven days and nights
    Shelley-*Legends*, 35–38
Seven families of Lake Pipple-
    Popple
    Royds-*Animal*, 15–25
The seven fathers in the house
    Booss-*Scand.*, 22–24
Seven fears
    Nagishkin-*Folktales*, 65–76
The seven foals

Mayo-*Book*, 103–109
The seven giant brothers
Villa-*Armenian*, 113–119, 451
Seven gods of luck
Piggott-*Japanese*, 55–60
The seven-headed beast
Thomas-*It's*, 8–15
Seven hymns to Inanna
Wolstein-*Inanna*, 91–110
The seven penitential psalms
O'Sullivan-*Legends*, 43–44
The seven rats
Stokes-*Turtle*, 19–21
Seven Simeons [brothers]
Riordan-*Russia*, 199–206
Xenophontovna-*Folk*, 27–65
The Seven Sisters
Reed-*Aboriginal*, 91–95
Wood-*Spirits*, 39–43
Seven Sisters; a Miao story
Seven Sisters, 31–37
Seven Sisters [subject]. *See*
PLEIADES
The seven stars
Villa-*Armenian*, 429–430
The seven stars of the north
Zong-*Korea*, 12
The seven-day vigil
Rungachary-*Tales*, 18–31
Seventh father of the house
Yolen-*Favorite*, 59–60
The seventh son
O'Sullivan-*Legends*, 80–81
Severi and Vappu
Booss-*Scand.*, 559–564
SEWING
Girls at parsonage get help
sewing crinoline
SEX
Courtship of Inanna and
Dumuzi
The devil and the female
El Diablo, el chivo, y Senor
Bonifacio
Folletti and Incubi
How a youth lost his virtue

How men and women got
together
Nature's way
Put that man to bed
[Woman with the head of a
horse]
—origin
Raven and the first men
—taboo broken
Origin of certain necklaces and
plants
SEX (subject)
—Motif index
Wilbert-*Bororo*, 271–273
SEX DIFFERENCES
Werewolf and nightmare [spirit,
not dream]
SEXES
—battle of the
Sweet Betsy from Pike [song
and story]
The young seamstress
—contests; V. can beat any
man
Vassilissa the valiant
—female cat saves husband
Pussy Cat Twinkle
—superiority
Why women are like cats
—women vs men
woman chief
SEXES (subject)
—[Status in tales]
Riordan-*Woman*, vii–viii
SEXTONS
Little Claus and Big Claus
The parson and the sexton
SEXUAL BEHAVIOR
Men accost a woman who is a
skeleton . . .
SEXUAL ETHICS
Ivan and Nastasia [scrubbing
off sin]
SEXUAL HARASSMENT
The fat moon
Honor [fidelity]

SHADE
    Under the shade of the mul-
        berry tree
"Shades" *See* DEAD
SHADOW PEOPLE
    The walker of the snow
The shadows
    Macdonald-*Golden*, 87–124
SHADOWS
    Donkey's shadow
    The golden key
    Susie and her shadow
—acoustic
    A resumed identity
—body of the soul
    The fisherman and his soul
—Jungian
    Ruckus in the well
SHAH, Amina (subject)
—Doris Lessing on
    Shah-*Dervishes*, ix–xv
Shaitan the devil and his forty
        daughters
    Riordan-*Tartary*, 60–69
SHAKESPEARE, William
—horror
    The walking shadow
SHAKESPEARE, William (sub-
        ject)
    Briggs-*Vanish.*, 67, 122–123
SHAKRA (god)
    The hare's sacrifice
    King Sivi
SHAMAN(S)
    Boy-who-snared-the-wind and
        shaman's daughter
    The golden neckband
    A great misfortune
    Only One, the great shaman
—evil
    Choril and Cholchinay
—never wrong
    The yes-no-yes-no spirit
SHAME
—shamelessness
    The lazy husband, Ngurmi. [I]

SHAMIR (precious stone)
    King Solomon and Asmodeus
The shamrock
    Ewart-*Lore*, 91–92
SHAMROCKS
    Four-leafed shamrock
SHANGHAIING
    Paul Jones
Shanly, C. D.
    The walker of the snow
SHANNON RIVER
    How the Shannon got its name
The Shannon: the two birds
    Ross-*Druids*, 125
SHAPE
    Man or beast
SHAPE-SHIFTERS
    See also
        TRANSFORMATIONS
    Badger and the green giant
    Glooskap and the three
        seekers
    Grasshopper [Indian
        superman]
    Ogre of Rashomon
    Shaitan the devil and his forty
        daughters
    Sinbad and the genie
    Slave maiden's eye for evil
—man to bull, at will
    And they wondered
—man to stud bull
    Saga of Santiago Sanchez
—transform at will
    Locomotive Bill
Shape-shifters [commentary]
    Yolen-*Favorite*, 299–300
SHAPE-SHIFTERS (subject)
    Briggs-*Vanish.*, 218 (index)
—[Illustrations]
    Scott-*Fantastic*, 95–108
Shapiro, Irwin
    Strong but Quirky
Shard: A potsherd speaks
    Shaw-*Pima*, 29–31
SHARING

See also CHARITY;
GENEROSITY
Beebyeebyee and the water-
god
The children with one eye
Golden chisel and the stone
ram
How the Mekong River came
to be
The hungry peasant, God, and
death (Mexico)
Husband and wife should
share equally
The jaguar and the lizard
[qualities]
King of Lochlann's three
daughters
Raven brings fire
Redbreasts: the Gwineeboos
Sunken palace: King Corc and
Fior Usga
—food
Iktomi and the muskrat
—food with god = no
Day of the dead
—food with starving man = yes
Day of the dead
—a social value
Hyena and hare search for
wealth
The shark and the turtle
Wright-*Pigeon*, 38–41
Shark man: The flying war club
Thompson-*Hawaiian*, 19–28
SHARKS
"Man overboard"
The monkey's heart
Punia and the King of the
Sharks
A sharp loss of weight
Hoke-*Horrors*, 24–29
Sharp sword
Roberts-*Chinese*, 195
SHAWLS
The magic shawl and the en-
chanted trumpet

She was good for nothing
Booss-*Scand.*, 472–478
SHEA (surname)
The wave of Toime
The Shee and Gannon and the
Gruagach Gaire
Jacobs-*Celtic*, 81–86
SHEEHOGUES (little people)
Guleesh
Sheena and the water-horse
Mayo-*Book*, 42–46
"SHEE-NEE-IQ"
Mouse Woman and the Snee-
nee-iq
SHEEP
The foolish young Mussulman
Liu Yi and the dragon king
The pig builds the house on
the hill
The shepherd of Silfrun-
Arstadir
Valbjorg the Unelfed
—"cattle plague"
Pistoleer Mike Fink
—ewes
The eternal lovers
—head of, on girl
Kate Crackernuts
—lamb runs out of luck
Lambikin [drumikin]
—lambs
La cenicienta huasteca
The herd-boy
Mary's little lamb: further ad-
ventures [verse]
Sheep, lamb, wolf, and the
hare
The vegetable lamb
Why the lamb is meek
—origin of stumpy tail
The Ram [devil as creator]
—prophecies
When the hand rubs the
foot . . .
—rams
Animals in winter

SHEEP—rams (continued)
  Aries (the Ram)
  Frightened wolves [wolf head]
  Half-ram leaves home
  Helle and Phrixus
  Jason and the golden fleece
  Stumpy
—rams-*in belly of king*
  The eternal lovers
—rams-*stone*
  Golden chisel and the stone
    ram
—saves shepherd boy
  The guardian sheep
—tails
  The tail
—The sheep butcher and his king
  Roberts-*Chinese,* 199–200
SHEEP DOGS
—killer of sheep
  T'girt dog of Ennerdale
The sheep is the cousin of the ox
  Zong-*Korea,* 31–32
Sheep, lamb, wolf, and the hare
  O'Connor-*Tibet,* 56–59
SHEETS
  The sacred sheet [at
    execution]
She-ghoul: The beduin's gazelle
  Yolen-*Favorite,* 415–416
SHEIKS
  The honorable wife
SHELLS (conch)
  Boy-who-snared-the-wind and
    shaman's daughter
  The gift of the white cockatoo
  The golden mountain
—baby found in
  Boy of the red twilight sky
—magic
  Urashima
—why have to dive for
  The treachery of Lelewaga
Shellycoat
  Froud-*Faeries,* unp
Shephard, Esther

Babe the blue ox
The shepherd and the emperor's
  daughter
  Chalk-*Tales,* unp.
The shepherd boy
  Rose-*Druids,* 82–87
Shepherd Boy and Suola: Immortal
  mountains
  Magic Knife, 58–65
The shepherd of Myddvai
  Jacobs-*Celtic,* 41–43
Shepherd of Myddvai and the lake
  maiden
  Phelps-*Tatterhood,* 115–120
The shepherd of Silfrun-Arstadir
  Booss-*Scand.,* 638–642
The shepherd who cried "wolf"
  dePaola-*Favorite,* 117
The shepherdess
  Booss-*Scand.,* 633
SHEPHERDS AND
    SHEPHERDESSES
  Anizu's magic wonder flute
  The complacent one; sheep to
    be slaughtered
  Curiosity punished
  The dwarf in search of lodging
  The herd-boy
  Hildur, the queen of the elves
  Ingratitude [king and shepherd]
  King Zargand's daughter
  The lamb with the golden
    fleece
  The language of animals
  Little shepherdess and English
    prince
  The little white stone
  The lost bell
  The magician's pupil
  Selim and the snake queen
  The shepherd of Silfrun-
    Arstadir
  Three dogs [named Salt, Pep-
    per, Mustard]
  Valbjorg the Unelfed
Shepherd's dream

Villa-Armenian, 340–344
SHERIFFS
Little Freddy with his fiddle
SHETLAND ISLES
Gioga's son
Glashans and Shopiltees
The gray wolf
The mermaid wife
Seal people: Sea trows and
Roane
Selkies
Trows
The woman of the sea
SHETLAND ISLES (subject)
Briggs-*Vanish.*, 77, 161
Keightley-*World*, 164–171
SHIANS
The fairy lalour
The two fiddlers
The young man in the shian
SHIELDS AND SHIELD-MAKERS
The unanswerable
Shinansha, or the south-pointing
carriage
Ozaki-*Japanese*, 54–59
Shingebiss: the wild duck
Tudor-*Bedtime*, [12–13]
SHINTO (subject)
Piggott-*Japanese*,144 (index)
Shinto and Buddhism
Piggott-*Japanese*, 39–40
The ship without a captain
Ainsworth-*Bear*, 58–62
SHIPS AND SHIPBUILDING
See also BOATS
Annie Norn and the fin folk
Balder's doom
The bronze ring
The expedition of Thorfin
Karisefni
Flying ship
The golden cradle
How the hermit helped to win
the king's . . .
Jason and the golden fleece
Jonah and the whale

The little mermaid
Loki makes mischief
"Man overboard"
Miracle of the sailing ship
Rats cut their throats
Stormalong fights the Kraken
Supparaka
The tail
Theseus, king of Athens
The wanderings of Odysseus
Why the sea moans
—cargos
Dick Whittington and his cat
—cargos-*salt*
The blind sea captain
—phantom
The kobold and the pirate
SHIPS' FIGUREHEADS
Klabautermannikins and
Kaboutermannikins
SHIPS-IN-BOTTLE
Gives me my bone
A ship's tomte
Lindow-*Swedish*, 144–145
SHIPTON, Ursula
Old Mother Shipton
SHIPWRECKS
The bottle-neck
The island of beautiful women
The lampstand princess
The little mermaid
The lobster and the crab
Vicar of Germsoe [looting
wrecked ships]
The shirt collar
Lang-*Pink/D*, 54–56
Shirts. *See under* CLOTHES
SHIVA (Hindu god; also SIVA;
sometimes "King")
Arjuna's penance
The destruction of love
The eye restored
The eye transplant
A king and a dove
Shoemaker and the elves
Tudor-*Bedtime*, [32–33]

SHOEMAKERS
  The battle of the birds
  The boots of Hunain
  Chelm justice (Jewish)
  The elves and the shoemaker
  Elves and the shoemaker
    whose work they did
  The hawk and the rattlesnake
  Lazarus and the dragons
  Leprechauns
  The marvelous shoe-maker
  Old Nick is a gentleman
  The sultan and the cobbler
  The three heads of the well
  The wooden sword
—old, ugly
  The jealous shoemaker
SHOES
  Katla
  Little Goody Two-Shoes
  The little shoe
  Stupid Peikko
  The Ulfgryt stones
—birch
  Jurma and the sea god
—boots
  The dancing princess
  Isaac and the Parson of Brono
—boots-*magic*
  Hop o' My Thumb
—boots, seven-league
  Little Thumb
—on fire
  The elephant and his son
—glass
  The herd-boy
  The little glass shoe
—leather
  Old Nick and the girl
—magic
  The boy and the robbers' mag-
    ical booty
—red
  The juniper tree
—sandals
  Jason and the golden fleece

  Theseus, king of Athens
—slippers
  Cinderella
  Fair, brown, and trembling
  Liisa and the prince
  Little cinder girl
  Mossycoat
—of swiftness
  The terrible head
—three gold coins
  Andromeda dances
—unsatisfactory for rabbits
  Slipper slopper
—witches'
  The troll shoes
SHONKES, Piers
  The devil's own [dragon]
"SHOOPILTEE" (water spirits)
  The mermaid wife
Shooting of the red eagle
  Zitkala-*Old*, 93–99
Shooting the moon; a Yao folktale
  Sadler-*Treasure*, 39–47
Shooting the skogsra
  Lindow-*Swedish*, 111–112
Shooting-stars. *See* METEORS
SHOPILTEES
  Glashans and Shopiltees
SHOPLIFTING
  Corpse of the cat
[Shore creatures: crane and turtle]
  Water Spirits, 108–109
Short people. *See* LITTLE
    PEOPLE
SHOVELS
  The mastermaid
  Plague omens
The shrew
  Sheohmelian-*Three*, 84–87
SHREWS
  Sparrow with the slit-tongue
SHRIMP
  Tale of the shrimp and the
    earthworm
The shrinking hat
  Schwartz-*Tales*, 8–10

The Shrove Tuesday visitor
Macmillan-*Canadian*, 108–111
"SHUDDERING"
The youth who went forth to
learn what fear was
Shun, the wise emperor
Sanders-*Dragons*, 35–36
Shuralee the wood demon
Riordan-*Tartary*, 21–24
Shurik: A story of the siege of
Leningrad
And Every., 71–100
SHUTTLECOCKS
The magic bamboo
SHUTTLES
Spindle, shuttle, and needle
SHYNESS
The ostrich in love
Siam. *See* THAILAND
SIBERIA
—Yakut
Little old women with five cows
SICK
Tend the sick
SICKLES
Earwig in sickle
SICKNESS
Origin of sickness
Wasting sickness of Cu
Chulaind, and . . . Emer
The witch
—monkey's heart as cure
The tortoise and the monkey
—origin
How sickness came
—punishment by fairies
Paddy Corcoran's wife
SICKNESS (subject)
—fairies as cause
Briggs-*Vanish.*, 218 (index)
SIDDHARTHA
Leaving home
SIDH (subject)
Briggs-*Vanish.*, 28, 30, 36, 199
Sidhe
Arrowsmith-*Field*, 20–23

Sidhean. *See* SIDH
Sidi Ngali and his traveling
companions
Magel-*Gambia*, 100–103
Sidna Mussa
Elbaz-*Folktales*, 51–52
Siege of Joyous Garde
Lee-*Castles*, 114–117
Sieges. *See* WAR—sieges
SIEGFRIED (or Sigurd)
The curse of Andvari's ring
How Sigourd awoke Brynhild
upon Hindfell
Treachery of the Nibelungs
SIEGFRIED (or Sigurd) (subject)
—Myths and legends
Lindow-*Myths*, 30–40
Siegfried and the Rhine castles
Lee-*Castles*, 130–131
Sierra Leone. *See under* AFRICA
SIEVES
Munachar and the raspberries
—water
The horned woman
Sight. *See* EYESIGHT
Sight-blinding: Katla protects Odd
Seekers Saviors, 13–20
SIGHTSEEING
Grave of a faithful dog
SIGN LANGUAGE
—symbolism
A dispute in sign language
[Sign language mutually
misunderstood]
Elbaz-*Folktales*, 58–59
SIGN OF THE CROSS
The fisherman and his soul
Sigourd, or Sigurd. *See*
SIEGFRIED
SIGURD the Dragonslayer
Valkyrie's tower
Sikulume and the seven brothers
Stovicek-*Around*, 184–185
Sila [human female born to be a
sea-being]
Robinson-*Raven*, 101–113

Silbado
    Aiken-*Mexican,* 142–145
SILENCE
    The boy in the Land of
      Shadows
    The bride who would not
      speak
    Selfish husband
    Sir Launval (condensed)
    [Sister saves six brothers cast
      into swan-form]
    The story of Jon Asmundsson
—boy under spell: speechless
    The promise
—vow of
    The seven-day vigil
    The wizard's lesson
—of wife
    The white seal maid
The silent couple
    Shah-*World,* 124
SILK
    Catherine and her destiny
The silkworm [origin: marriage of
    horse & maid]
    Sanders-*Dragons,* 45–46
SILKWORMS
    The betrothal
—origin
    Maiden's silky winding sheet
Silliness. *See* FOOLS AND
    FOOLISHNESS
SILVER
    Big brother: man; Little brother:
      rabbit
    Coffin cash
    Conall Yellowclaw
    The cunning Lapp
    The dwarfs' banquet
    The fairy banquet [b]
    The frog
    The honest penny
    The mountain kitchen
    Odd jobs
    The Oldenburg horn
    The seawife and the crone

Stupid Peikko
Supparaka
    Three sisters were entrapped
      into a mountain
    Twilight, Midnight, and Dawn
    The Vatters
    The winding-horn village
SILVER LAKE SEA SERPENT
    Water monsters
The silver mountain
    Lindow-*Swedish,* 97–98
The silver swindle
    Roberts-*Chinese,* 61–63
The silver whistle
    Williams-*Practical,* 35–52
SILVERSMITHS
    The shepherd of Silfrun-
      Arstadir
SILVERWARE
    Mother of the Waters
Simangolo and the akara
    Todd-*Tortoise,* 79–83
Simmer Water
    Marshall-*Every.,* 367–370
Simon and the pater-rollers
    Faulkner-*Tales,* 29–33
Simon challenges the McCrackens
    Faulkner-*Tales,* 21–25
Simon marries Ellen
    Faulkner-*Tales,* 17–20
Simon sees a ghost
    Faulkner-*Tales,* 40–45
SIMPLE LIFE
    Town mouse and country
      mouse
The simpleton makes rain fall
    Patai-*Gates,* 735–738
Simpleton of Naples [in two parts]
    Fattoross-*Simpleton,* 1–12
Simpletons. *See* FOOLS AND
    FOOLISHNESS; STUPIDITY
SIMU (serpent)
    The birch boy
SIMURG (magic bird)
    Rustam and the iron fortress
Simurg, protector of princes

Magical Beasts, 66, 67
SIN(S)
  Dance of the esqueletons
  Devil's armful [Canterbury]
  Ivan and Nastasia [scrubbing
    off sin]
  Master Log
  Mulien rescues his mother
  Rabbi Akiba and the sinner
  —relativism of degree
  Legend of the Russian priest
  —secret, do not exist
  A teacher's tricky test
SIN(S) (subject)
  Patai-*Gates,* 799–800 (index)
Sinbad and the genie
  Lewis-*Bedtime,* 38–39
Sinbad the sailor [1st–7th voyages]
  Rackham-*Fairy,* 65–102
SINEW STRINGS
  The blessed gift of joy be-
    stowed upon man
Singard the dragon-slayer
  Branston-*Gods,* 78–88
SINGERS AND SINGING
  The blessed gift of joy be-
    stowed upon man
  The dance and the song of the
    Korred
  The dwarf husband
  The fairy gift
  The fate of the children of Lir
  The first kantele
  The girl with the silver voice
  The gunny wolf
  Love: queen and foundling
  The magic of the moon
  Mathey Trewella
  Orpheus and Eurydice
  Pepito el corcovado
  Sirens
  The tar baby
  Wild Goose Lake
  The wooing of Seppo
    Hmarinen
  —magic

The contest
SINGERS AND SINGING (subject)
  —fairies
    Briggs-*Vanish.,* 218 (index)
  Singers at the world's dawn
    Lehane-*Wizards,* 6–39
  The singing birds
    Shelley-*Legends,* 70–71
  The singing bone
    Wolkstein-*Magic,* 92–97
  The singing frog
    Reed–Aboriginal, 127–
      131
SINGLE-PARENT FAMILIES
  The disobedient sun-child
SINGLE WOMEN
  —by choice
    Woman in the moon
  The sinner and his wife
    Patai-*Gates,* 548—552
  Sinners: The harga-dance
    Lindow-*Swedish,* 148–150
  Sir Andrew Barton [ballad]
    Marshall-*Every.,* 303–313
  Sir Galahad and the quest of the
    Holy Grail
    Malory-*King,* 169–202
  Sir Gareth of Orkney
    Malory-*King,* 61–97
  Sir Gawain. *See* GAWAIN, SIR
  Sir Lancelot of the Lake
    Riordan-*Arthur,* 68–79
  Sir Launcelot du Lake
    Malory-*King,* 19–59
  Sir Launval (condensed)
    Briggs-*Vanish.,* 150
  Sir Olof in the elve-dance
    Keightley-*World,* 82–83
  Sir Pellinor's adventure
    Riordan-*Arthur,* 32–33
  Sir Thynne
    Keightley-*World,* 97–103
  Sir Tor's adventure
    Riordan-*Arthur,* 30–31
  Sir Tristram and La Belle Isolde
    Malory-*King,* 121–167

Sirens
  Arrowsmith-*Field*, 237–2381
SIRENS
  The wanderings of Odysseus
SIRENS (subject)
  Lloyd-*Mythical*, 51–56
Sis, Peter, illus.
  Shannon-*Solve*
Sister Alyonushka and Brother
  Ivanushka
  Bilibin-*Russian*, 19–24
  Riordan-*Russia*, 107–111
  Yolen-*Favorite*, 305–308
Sister Becky's child
  Shepard-*Conjure*, 87–99
Sister Fox and Brother Coyote
  Aiken-*Mexican*, 6–11
Sister hare [rescues lost girl]
  Berger-*Animalia* [33–35]
Sister Lace
  Minford-*Fav.*, 122–128
[Sister saves six brothers cast into
  swan-form]
  Seekers Saviors, 49–56
SISTERS
  Altynchech and the padishah's
    wife
  Bird of truth
  The bridal present
  The chao ku bird
  Diamonds and toads
  Eros and Psyche
  The golden ball
  The golden fish, the wicked
    sisters, and good Forgetta
  The good girl and the bad girl
  Hassan the physician
  How the seven brothers saved
    their sister
  Kate Crackernuts
  The king who would have a
    beautiful wife
  Little cinder girl
  Little One-Eye, . . . Two-Eyes,
    and . . . Three-Eyes
  Lost sister

  The magic bamboo
  Martha and Mary
  Merchant's daughter and the
    slanderer
  The Norns
  The old witch
  The promise of the three
    sisters
  Seven sisters; a Miao story
  Smallhead and the king's son
  Snow white and Rose red
  The strongest boy in the world
  The three daughters and the
    lost cow
  Three sisters
  Three sisters were entrapped
    into a mountain
  The tinkling laugh
  Toads and diamonds
  The wild swans
  Wurrunna and the Seven
    Sisters
—beautiful/stupid; ugly/wise
  Rickety Topknot
—dies, goes to Land of Shadows
  The boy in the Land of
    Shadows
—jealousy
  Finist the Falcon
—marry: 1)eagle 2)falcon 3)raven
  Marya Morevna
—tries to kill brother
  Clever Daniel
SITA (wife of Prince Rama)
  Monkey god: epic battle for
    earthly supremacy
Sith [condensed]
  Mckee-*Scottish*, 17–18
SITTING
  The smith and the devil
Siva (Hindu god). *See* SHIVA (Hin-
    du god) . . .)
The six days and the seven gates
  Patai-*Gates*, ix–xv
The six fools
  Stovicek-*Around*, 46–47

Six swans
  Shub-*About,* 82–87
Six traditional tales
  Colombo-*Wind.,* 119–123
SIZE
  Date stone; a Han story
  The dwarf who wanted to
    grow
  Goldilocks and the three bears
  Grasshopper [Indian
    superman]
  The great bronze Buddha and
    the whale
  The lion and the mouse
  Lion and the mouse [in verse]
  Lioness and the mouse
  [The old, vagrant woman and]
    The three bears
  Tortoise and elephant: small-
    ness not an illness
—of humans; origin
  Boy of great strength and the
    giants
—tall tale
  A Tartar riddle: Which is
    biggest?
—wanting to be big
  The small, small cat
SJORA
  "Binding" and driving off a
    sjora
  The blind sea captain
The sjora in Helgasjon
  Lindow-*Swedish,* 127–128
The sjora warns of an impending
    storm
  Lindow-*Swedish,* 126
"SKELETON ETERNAL"
    (magician)
  Czarina frog
The skeleton in Holar church
  Booss-*Scand.,* 665–666
SKELETONS
  See also BONES; SKULLS
  Curse of the devil's gold
  Dance of the esqueletons

The dance of the thirteen
    skeletons
  Vaino and the swan princess
  Waxworks
—gives directions, smokes pipe
  The boy in the Land of
    Shadows
SKEPTICISM
  The hen and the apple tree
SKIING
  Lipo and Tapio
—flying skies
  The little boy Chokcho
The skilful brothers
  Shah—*World,* 150–151
SKILLS
  The man who had no story
SKILLYWIDDEN (subject)
  Briggs—*Vanish.,* 88, 199
SKIN
  Jack and his master
  The other Celia
  Snake [steals skin of everlast-
    ing life]
—green
  The green children
—snakes
  The serpent-woman (Spain)
Skinkoots steals the springtime
  De Wit—*Talking,* 113—117
The skipper and old Nick
  Boos—*Scand.,* 150–151
SKOGSRA
  Encounters with the skogsra
    [woman-front, hollow-tree
    back]
  Garlic and tar [Tibastsagnen]
  Shooting the skogsra
  Tibast and vandelrot
  Tricking a Christian
SKOGSRA (subject)
  Lindow-*Swedish,* 36–38, 217
Skogsra or wood trolls
  Arrowsmith-*Field,* 198–203
Skotte in the fire
  Keightley-*World,* 113–114

The skull
  Roberts-*Chinese*, 196
The skull in the snow
  McCarty-*Skull*, 76–82
SKULLS
  The castle [five live in empty
    horse-skull]
  Dance in a buffalo skull
  Dancing in Dalarna
  Haunter of the birch forest
  Manawyddan's castle of skulls
  Murder will out
  Only a dream
—burns up stepmother &
    stepsisters
  Vasilisa the Beautiful
—devil
  The young man and the talking
    skull
—laughs
  March cock banishes the devil
—refuses to stay buried
  Dick o' Tunstead
—talking
  Now you know
The skunk and the frogs
  Stuchl-*American*, 63–64
"SKUNK APE"
  Wild men
SKUNKS
  Adventures of Ntini, the small
    otter
  Big long man's corn patch
  [The fox with the purple
    umbrella]
  Kitpouseagunow
  The skunk and the frogs
—"Cibet"
  The little talking animal and
    the shining blue fish
—origin of their "perfume"
  Pervasive perfume of las zor-
    rillas the skunk
—outsmarts coyote
  Coyote and skunk
—scent routs dogs

Badger rents a house
Skunk's tale
  Tompert-*Three*, 33–48
SKY
  The creation of the world
  Gods and demons
  Long ago when the earth was
    flat
  Motions in the sky
  Patterns in the sky
—a "great hole"
  Dinosaurs of the sky
—autumn
  The autumn sky
—country
  Fall of the spider man
—falling
  Chicken Licken
—as food
  Why men have to work
—North Polar
  North polar sky
—raised up off the earth
  Maui the Polynesian
—space between earth and sky
  Baiame: in the beginning
—spring
  The spring sky
—summer
  Summer sky
—winter
  The winter sky
The sky beings
  Highwater-*Anpao*, 87–101
Sky Elk, the ghost of Whiteface
    Mountain
  De Wit-*Talking*, 9–12
SKY GOD
  How spider obtained the sky-
    god's stories
  How spider read the sky-god's
    thoughts
The sky-god: Ratu and the Dyaks
  Shelley-*Legends*, 17–19
Sky high went the sun
  Anderson-*Trick.*, 63–71

"SKY HOLDER" (Indian Great
    Father)
    Great father mosquito [larger
        than a bear]
The sky is falling
    Lewis-*Minute*, 44–45
SKY-PEOPLE
    Klis-to E-eki Ta-u-ue-a
Sky-raising magpies
    Reed-*Aboriginal*, 87–89
SKY WOMAN
    The big turtle
SKYLARKS
    Why the sun rises when the
        rooster crows
SLAUGHTERING
    The complacent one; sheep to
        be slaughtered
Slave girl: The ruby ring
    Shah-*Afghanistan*, 71–75
Slave girl tried to kill her mistress
    Radin-*African*, 193–196
Slave maiden's eye for evil
    Seekers Saviors, 78–95
SLAVES AND SLAVERY
    The barn is burning
    The blue-tail fly [song and
        story]
    The bushbabies
    Cat in the box
    Conjurer's revenge [slave
        changed into mule]
    Deer and Vila
    Fishing with bare hands
    High John the conqueror
    Hot-foot Hannibal
    How night came
    How the slaves helped each
        other
    How the slaves worshipped
    John Henry [song and story]
    Keep on stepping
    Kullervo
    Nobleman and the slave
    Poor Sandy [conjure woman]
    Princess and the slave

A riddle for freedom
Simon and the pater-rollers
Simon challenges the
    McCrackens
Simon marries Ellen
Simon sees a ghost
A slave's dangerous courtship
Tall tales (Burma)
The ten plagues of Egypt
Vilas
The wager: clever slave wins
    freedom
The ways of a witch
—alligator speaks to
    'Morning, alligator!
—fly home to Africa
    People who could fly
—forgot they had wings
    Wings
—Morgiana
    Ali Baba and the forty thieves
—mother traded for race horse
    Sister Becky's child
—treatment of
    Master James' nightmare
SLAVES AND SLAVERY (subject)
    Keightley-*World*, 490–494
A slave's dangerous courtship
    Faulkner-*Tales*, 10–16
A slave's escape
    Faulkner-*Tales*, 60–65
Slaying of the Tanuki
    Lang-*Pink/D*, 33–39
    Lang-*Pink/K*, 20–24
SLEDS AND SLED RACES
    The giant and Johannes
        Blessom
    The snow queen
—Lapp
    The voyage in a Lapp sled
SLEEP
    Bohrah the kangaroo and di-
        newan the emu
    The butterflies carried him
        home [Tewa]
    Eros and Psyche

SLEEP (continued)
  Hob and Sleepyhead
  Katla's dream
  The knight of Ellenholm
  Leppa Polkry and the blue
    cross
  Napi's wager with rabbit
  Rip Van Winkle
  Why the bob-cat stays in the
    woods
—forbidden
  Town where none might go to
    sleep
Sleeping Beauty in the wood
  Ehrlich-*Random,* 10–21
  Lang-*Blue,* 54–65 (notes,
    366)
  Leete-*Golden,* 94–107
  Lewis-*Minute,* 8–9
  Mulherin-*Favorite,* 14–21, in-
    trod., 12–13
  Perrault-*Glass,* 3–19
  Pierce-*Larousse,* 36–50
  Pollack-*Moonbeam,* 22–29
  Quiller-*Sleeping,* 17–48
  Rackham-*Fairy,* 172–177
  Stovicek-*Around,* 160–163
  Tarrant-*Fairy,* 20–33
Sleeping-mat confidences not to be
    repeated
  Radin-*African,* 212–214
The sleeping prince
  Lurie-*Clever,* 74–83
SLEEPING SICKNESS
  Opele-of-the-Long-Sleeps
SLEEPING SPELLS
  Brier Rose
  [Burd Helen, Childe Rowland,
    and Elf King]
  Castle of Melvales
  Curse: an embowered sleep
    [one hundred years]
  The enchanted orchard
  The merchant's fortune
  Sleeping Beauty in the wood
  The sleeping prince

Sleeping warrior [fear: to return to
    life]
  O'Sullivan-*Legends,* 56–57
The sleepy one: Senor Opossum
    and the rattler
  Ritchie-*Armadillo,* 30–33
SLEEVES
  Djuha's sleeve (Syria)
  Sleigh Beggey and Tylwyth Teg
    Arrowsmith-*Field,* 88–92
Slip root, catch Reynard's foot
  Booss-*Scand.,* 139
Slipper slopper
  Uttley-*Foxglove,* 81–86
Slippers. *See under* SHOES
The slit-tongue sparrow. *See* The
    sparrow with the slit-tongue
SLOTH [vice]
  The grasshopper and the ant
SLOTHS
—giant
  Assorted monsters
The slowest may win the race
  Shah-*World,* 252
Sluagh (condensed)
  Briggs-*Vanish.,* 218
SLUGS
—lettuces eaten by
  The rabbits go hunting
The sly devil
  Baskin-*Imps,* 38–39
SMAALAND
  Duke Magnus and the
    mermaid
A small favor
  Roberts-*Chinese,* 74–76
Small people. *See* LITTLE PEO-
    PLE; SIZE
The small, small cat
  Manning-*Cats,* 126–127
Small Star and the mud pony
  De Wit-*Talking,* 99–107
Smallboy and his halfpenny wife
  Todd-*Tortoise,* 68–71
The smallest dragonboy
  Asimov-*Fant.,* 5–19

Smallhead and the king's son
  Jacobs-*Celtic*, 236–247
SMALL-MINDEDNESS
—repaid
  The roots of jealousy
SMALLPOX
  He comes from the east
  Smart head better than sharp teeth
  Jagendorf-*Magic*, 145–147
Smart man and the fool
  Radin-*African*, 197–198
Smartest man in the countryside
  Lewis-*Bedtime*, 42–43
SMELL, Sense of
  Rich man, poor man ["eats"
    smell of food]
  Zilyan
Smith, Cordwainer
  The game of rat and dragon
SMITH, Riley K. (subject)
—Biographical note
  Smith-*Manachar*, 64
The smith and the devil
  Booss-*Scand.*, 24–29
The smith and the fairies
    (condensed)
  Briggs-*Vanish.*, 102–103
The smith and the fairies
  [MacEachern]
  Lochhead-*Battle*, 30–32
Smith Riechert
  Keightley-*World*, 221–222
Smiths. *See* BLACKSMITHS
SMOKE
  The iron wolf
  The story of the house
SMOKING
—dying for a smoke
  Saint Colmkille's well
SMUGGLERS AND SMUGGLING
  Bury me in England [fake-
    dying wish; humor]
  Faeries on the eastern green
  Jack o' both sides, or The biter
    bit
Smuggler's bride [ballad]

Marshall-*Every.*, 231–232
The snail and the beaver
  Wade-*Indian*, 53–58
SNAIL-COLLECTORS
  The snail-watcher
SNAILS
  The competitive tiger
  Those three wishes
—origin of furrows on shell
  Adugo the jaguar and Ruwo
    the snail
—spirits
  Kertong
The snail-watcher
  Hoke-*Uncanny*, 75–82
Snake and goat: tomorrow is an-
    other day
  Todd-*Tortoise*, 21
Snake boy
  Highwater-*Anpao*, 102–112
The snake bridegroom
  Stokes-*Turtle*, 131–133
"SNAKE CHILDREN"
  Tiyo rejoins his clan
SNAKE MOUNTAIN
  The birth of Huitzilopochtli
The snake of Rabbi Daoud
  Elbaz-*Folktales*, 153
The snake people of Ayers Rock
  Reed-*Aboriginal*, 10–12
Snake [steals skin of everlasting
    life]
  Pitcher-*Tokol.*, 61–64
Snake with an ear for music
  Stuchl-*American*, 82–86
The snakeman
  Roberts-*Chinese*, 107–110
SNAKES
  The anglers of Arz
  The Bakororo and Itubore
    legend
  Bobburr the giant brown and
    yellow snake
  The boy and the dragon
  Brer possum and brer snake
  Brer rabbit rescues his children

SNAKES (continued)
    Castle of the serpent
    The cat's elopement
    Coyote and the water serpent
    Day the sun rose in the west
    Dead snake and young wife
    The deer and the snake
    Dietrich of Bern
    Elephant's child
    Fair Margaret
    Fearless lion, brave elephant,
      merchant's cries
    The four rings
    The frogs at the rainbow's
      end
    The gods' revenge
    Grateful animals and the un-
      grateful man
    The great deeds of King Yu
    The heavenly song of the
      green-spotted dove
    His just reward
    How night came
    Jason and the golden fleece
    King Lindorm [a snake]
    The language of animals
    Leppa Polkry and the blue
      cross
    The living kuan-yin
    Lochman Hehkeem, the great
      healer
    Loki and his evil children
    The magic boat
    The magic mirror
    Man and the snake
    The man who knew the lan-
      guage of animals
    Melampus—physician and
      prophet
    The mountain kitchen
    Orpheus and Eurdice
    Patience overcomes fate
      [piast]
    The pomegranate prince
    The prince and his fate
    Repaying good with evil
    Rooster's advice [beat your
      wife]
    Roosters, snakes and basiliscs
    The scythe bitten by a snake
    The sea captain and the
      serpent
    Seein' snakes
    Selim and the snake queen
    Serpens (the Serpent)
    The serpent-slayer
    The serpent-woman (Spain)
    Snake boy
    Thor goes fishing with Hymir
    Tiyo appears before Snake
      Mana
    Tiyo returns home
    Turkey Brother and the magic
      panther suit
    Two brothers [and seven-
      headed monster]
    Why the sea moans
    The wooing of Seppo
      Hmarinen
—"Angel of Death"
    Charity saves from death
—blacksnakes
    The sleepy one: Senor
      Opossum and the rattler
—boa constrictors
    There'll always be a tomorrow
    Three heroes [and the 3-head-
      ed boa]
—"childless" couple has son
    King of snakes
—cobras
    The brahmin's wife and the
      mongoose
—embryo killed/burnt; plants from
      ashes
    The Aturuarodo legend
—giant
    Li Chi slays the serpent
—giant; driven away
    Saint Finbar and the River Lee
—girl under spell
    Cobbler's son and the serpent

—grows in woman's stomach
The seven giant brothers
—holders
Ophiuchus (the Serpent
Holder)
—impersonates voice of
grandfather
The centipede girl
—inside princess
Helpful spirit
—kills bride-to-be
Death to the giant snake
—kings
The language of animals
—man-eating serpent killed
Chavalai: taboos and
deception
—origin of characteristics
How the snake got his rattles
—poisonous; origin
The iguana and the black
snake
Snakes and turtles [exchange
heads]
—rattlesnakes
Cherokees fight king of
rattlesnakes
Coyote and the rattlesnake
The hawk and the rattlesnake
Pecos Bill and the cyclone
The sleepy one: Senor
Opossum and the rattler
Snake with an ear for music
Springfield Mountain [song and
story]
—rattlesnakes-flat head
Coyote and the swallowing
monster
—rattlesnakes-witch lives in skin of
Kwi-na the eagle: animal-god
persons
—saved
Hailibu the hunter
—secret husband
Cibairago and her husband
Jure [snake]

—Takshaka, King of Serpents
The seven-day vigil
—teeth
The house of Thebes
—trained
The snakeman
—trans. into man; marries
The handsome suitor [A]
—transformed to girl
The pheasants and the bell
—"Tree of the Serpent"
The prince who had two eyes
—twelve-headed serpent killed
A crippled hero
—visits earth, first time
First Man and First Woman
—white
Hunter Hailibu's great sacrifice
SNAKES (subject)
Briggs-*Vanish.*, 73–74, 146–
148
Snakes and turtles [exchange
heads]
Reed-*Aboriginal*, 12–15
The snake's lover (Peru)
Yolen-*Favorite*, 323–328
"SNARE" (a thief)
Crack and crook (Italy)
Snaring a witch [9 legends]
Robe-*Hispanic*, 328–336
Sneaky, straight, and the tree
Wood-*Kalila*, 164–171
SNEEZES (-ING)
Master and man
Plague victims dig their own
graves
The sparrows and the tiger
The unforgetable sneeze
The snipe
Booss-*Scand.*, 300
Snipp, Snapp, Snorium
Crossley-*Folk*, 54–57
SNOBS
Paddock in heaven (England)
Snouters
Schwartz-*Tales*, 48–55

SNOW
  The dawn of the world
  Mary's little lamb: further adventures [verse]
  The walker of the snow
SNOW LIONS
  The umbrella tree
The snow maiden
  Riordan-*Russia*, 53–55
  Zvorykin-*Firebird*, 49–61
The snow queen
  Andersen-*Hague*, 1–43
  Ehrlich-*Random*, 174–193
  Lang-*Pink/D*, 76–101
  Lang-*Pink/K*, 275–177
The snow queen: an adventure in seven stories
  Lang-*Pink/K*, 275–310
The snow storm
  Stuchl-*American*, 151–152
Snow White
  Ehrlich-*Random*, 58–73
Snow-White and Rose-Red
  Lang-*Blue*, 269–277 (notes, 371)
  Leete-*Golden*, 16–31
SNOW-WHITE AND ROSE-RED (subject)
  A stepchild that was treated mighty bad
Snow White and the seven dwarfs
  Lewis-*Minute*, 46–47
  Stovicek-*Around*, 100–105
  Tudor-*Bedtime*, [10–11]
SNOW-WHITE-TYPE STORIES
  A dead princess and seven giants
  Nourie Hadig [a "Snow White" type]
Snowdrops and crocuses
  Ewart-*Lore*, 20–25
Snowflake [snowchild comes to life]
  Lang-*Pink/D*, 143–147
  Lang-*Pink/K*, 96–100
SNOWFLAKES
  The snow queen

The snow-man [the dog and the sun]
  Lang-*Pink/D*, 47–53
  Lang-*Pink/K*, 39–45
SNOWSHOES
  Jack of Sjoholm and the Gan-Finn
  The magic snowshoes
The Snow-Wetigo
  Colombo-*Wind.*, 51–58
Snubby's tail
  Blyton-*My*, 43–51
Snuff-box [wishes-come-true]
  Lang-*Green*, 72–78
So you won't talk
  Hoke-*Demonic*, 111–118
SOAP
  Stormalong fights the Kraken
SOCIAL ACTIVISTS
  How the animals stopped the freeway
  Zon U-Czi
SOCIAL CLASSES
  —why some are ministers, others boatmen
  The king's boatman
SOCIAL CONDITIONS
  The first Inca: marriage of sun and moon
Social connections
  Roberts-*Chinese*, 70–73
Social customs and usages in Mo. [19th cent.]
  McNeil-*Charm*, 139–149
SOCIAL EVOLUTION
  Bao Luotuo the sage
SOCIAL ROLE
  The man who knew how to divide a chicken
SOCIETY FOR INDECENCY TO ANIMALS (SINA)
  "A nude horse is a rude horse"
The sod of death
  O'Sullivan-*Legends*, 17
Soderstrom, Sven
  The blind sea captain

Sody sallytytus
    Macdonald-*Twenty*, 79–89
SOIL
    How salt was discovered
The soldier and death
    Ransome-*War*, 85–104
The soldier-bird Deegeenboyah
    Parker-*Australian*, 87–91
SOLDIERS
    See also WARRIORS
    The broken swords
    Bull-calf goes to school
    Clever answers (Russia)
    The crimson parrot
    Dame Soasan
    The dancing princess
    The dead soldier
    Juan Soldado
    The Moddey Dhoo
    Prince Green Serpent and La
      Valeur
    Story of Ivan the Imbecile
    The tinder-box
    The treasure seekers
    What happened to Ivan
—Confederate (U.S.)
    Ghost of the radar base
—discharged
    Bearskin (Germany)
—officers
    Honor [fidelity]
—retired
    The twelve dancing princesses
—"The Warrior"
    The master of prayer
—tin
    The old house
—tin; one leg
    The steadfast tin soldier
—tricks demons
    Death and the soldier
SOLIKA HATSADIKA, 1820–1834.
    Martyrdom of Solika Hatsadika
Solitary fairies
    Yeats-*Fairy*, 75–115, 289
SOLITUDE

Unwelcome neighbour
Solomon, Ashmodai, and the
    Shamir
    Patai-*Gates*, 185–188
SOLOMON, King
    Andrew and King Solomon [in
      2 parts]
    The beggar king [Solomon and
      Asmodeus]
    The eternal light [Solomon &
      Benaiah]
    King Solomon and Asmodeus
    King Solomon and the winds
    Marriages are made in hea-
      ven
    Mysterious palace [Solomon &
      Ramirat]
    No pity in women
    Princess in the tower
    A time for everything
    Which flower?
—death of
    Three challenges for King
      Solomon
SOLOMON, King (subject)
    Patai-*Gates*, 800 (index)
Solomon the wise
    Aiken-*Mexican*, 146–148
A Solomonic judgment
    Patai-*Gates*, 628–630
Solomon's throne
    Patai-*Gates*, 355–338
Some sort of madness
    Colombo-*Wind.*, 29
SOMERIA
    Enter the Sumerians
Something for nothin (a Hui story)
    Seven Sisters, 6–15
Son of Kimanaueze and daughter
    of sun and moon
    Radin-*African*, 73–78
Son of Kim-ana-u-eze and daugh-
    ter of sun/moon
    Lester-*Black*, 62–72
The son of Tata Juan Pescador
    Aiken-*Mexican*, 17–22

464

The son of the goblin
Booss-*Scand.*, 655–656
Son of the gray horse
Villa-*Armenian*, 273–290, 506
Son of the Knight of the Green
Vesture
Ratcliff-*Scottish*, 19–39
Son of the Mountain
Peacock Maid, 122–133
Son of the Strong Man of the
Wood
Ratcliff-*Scottish*, 57–72
Son of the wind [was once a man]
Radin-*African*, 49–50
Song of the seven herbs [7
legends]
Walking-*Song*, 4–60
Song that comes from the sea
Jagendorf-*First*, 39–41
Song-bird and the healing waters
Macmillan-*Canadian* 250–252
SONGS
The wooing of Seppo
Hmarinen
—Jewish
Rabbi Eisik of Kalev
—taboo
Ananse: origin, big hinder part;
small head
Songs in English and Creole
Wolkstein-*Magic*, 195–209
SONS
Anansi's six sons
Anizu's magic wonder flute
Ash lad who had an eating
match with the troll
The black horse
The brahman in the graveyard
The clever fool
The clever sewing-maid
Conall Yellowclaw
The death of Alfe's only son
The disrespectful son
Glass mountain
A goddess is born
The good sons

Heavenly maiden and the
wood cutter
How the pigeon became a
tame bird
How they got Hairlock home
Ivan and Nastasia [scrubbing
off sin]
Ivan Tsarevich, the wolf, and
the firebird
Jack and his cudgel
Jack and his master
The legend of Bodedys
The mouse bride
The outlaw
Piece of Zhuang brocade
The Pleiades
Prince Mirko
The ridere of riddles
She was good for nothing
The shepherd of Myddvai
Sikulume and the seven
brothers
The story of the McAndrew
family
Tiger boys
Tomik and the magic mat
Ursulo, hijo del oso
Why the flat fish is flat
The widow's son
The wonderful Chuang
brocade
The young man who refused
to kill
The youth who went forth to
learn what fear was
—eaten by she-ghoul
The beduin's gazelle (Saudi
Arabia)
—golden
Golden lads
—hides his father
The golden vase
—sold to devil, before birth
Give me something you
have . . . unawares
—thirty-three, from bird's eggs

Ivan young in years, old in
wisdom
—tokens inherited from father
The three sons
—youngest derided
The doll in the grass
Soot
Cortes-*Byelorussian,* 127–128
SOOT
The thief who kept his hands
clean
Sorach of Glenane [rob rich, give
poor]
O'Sullivan-*Legends,* 141–143
Sorcerer from Loudon Hill
Stuchl-*American,* 234–235
SORCERERS
See also MAGICIANS
Aladdin, or The wonderful
lamp
The blue lake
The flight of Quetzalcoatl
Foot racers of Payupki
[Hameln: punishment for not
keeping bargain with piper]
How Jiculi served his tribe
Iskandar and the emerald ring
King who had no children
The magic gifts [dwarf-
sorcerer]
The magic mirror of Rabbi
Adam
Master Log
Petronella [sorcerer]
Philbert the Fearful
Pigs into pythons
The promise
Ruslan and Chernomor
—eats wife of partridge
The partridge and his drum
Sorcerer's apprentice
Lewis-*Bedtime,* 24–25
Tudor-*Bedtime,* [14–15]
The sorcerer's dance
Bierhorst-*Hungry,* 51–52
The sorceress

Highwater-*Anpao,* 113–124
Sorceress: bewitched butter
Yeats-*Fairy,* 142–150
Sorceress. *See* WITCHES
Sorcery. *See* MAGIC
SORROW
The beduin's gazelle (Saudi
Arabia)
Donkeys of Jolof
Katla's dream
Sorrows of storytelling [Celtic]
Ross-*Druids,* 25–29
A sort of werewolf
Colombo-*Wind.,* 7
Soul cages
Yeats-*Fairy,* 61–71
Soul cages (condensed)
Briggs-*Vanish.,* 73, 88
The soul-eater
Todd-*Tortoise,* 65–66
SOUL(S)
Anpu and Bata
Filial piety [souls of parents in
butterflies]
The fisherman and his soul
The great misfortune of Lay
Tee-Kwai
The greedy youngster
Hassan the brave
Immortality and the soul
King who fought many wars
The little mermaid
The monk from Everclear
The ogre with no soul
The ogre's soul
The peasant and the
waterman
Priest's soul
—external
The sultan and the ogress
—of giant
The boy and the robbers' mag-
ical booty
—hidden
Ivan, the Windfall
—immortal

466

SOUL(S)—immortal (continued)
The little mermaid
—restless
Restless souls
—restored to dead girl
The three sons
—selling to devil. *See* DEVIL(S)—
selling soul to
Soul-taker
Villa-*Armenian,* 344–345
The soul-taking angel [Gabriel]
Villa-*Armenian,* 323–327, 515
Sounding at Vassdal
Lindow-*Swedish,* 60–61
SOUP
Allerleirauh; or, The many-
furred creature
The old woman and the tramp
—ladles
The valiant chanticleer
Soup from a sausage skewer
Booss-*Scand.,* 367–377
SOUTH CAROLINA
Brer rabbit's protest meeting
South Wind and his golden-haired
love
Jagendorf-*First,* 93–94
SOUTHEIL, Agatha
Breakfast party [witch]
SOUTHERN CROWN
Corona Australis (the Southern
Crown)
Southesk, Earl of
Some sort of madness
Southey, Robert
The three bears [the first
printed version]
SOWS
The sabio sees a sow
—cured by witch
Whuppity Stoorie
SPACE TRAVEL
Heaven's reward
SPACESHIPS
Mouse
SPAIN

The birthday of the Infanta
The daughter of Peter de
Cabinam
Duende
Follets
La infantina
Origin of the house of Haro
Pepito el corcovado
—Toledo
The tinker and the ghost
SPAIN (subject)
Keightley-*World,* 456–464
SPANISH LANGUAGE (subject)
—Words and phrases
MacLean-*Cuentos,* 199–205
The Spanish sailor
O'Sullivan-*Legends,* 101–102
SPANISH TALES (subject)
—California
MacLean-*Cuentos,* ix–xiii
The sparrow and the crow
Raychaudhuri-*Stupid,* 33–36
The sparrow with the slit-tongue
Kendall-*Haunting,* 30–34
Lang-*Pink/D,* 334–338
Lang-*Pink/K,* 247–252
Ozaki-*Japanese,* 12–25
Piggott-*Japanese,* 110
SPARROW-HAWKS
Suit of white feathers
(Dongxiang)
SPARROWS
The sparrow and the crow
The war of the birds and the
beasts
Why the cat washes after
meals
—fairy
The sparrow with the slit-
tongue
—healed
Who is my neighbour?
—protected by Indians
Sparrow's search for rain
The sparrows and the tiger
Raychaudhuri-*Stupid,* 37–39

Sparrow's search for rain
   Macmillan-*Canadian* 263–267
SPEAKERS
   The fairies [jewels or
      frogs . . .]
Spearfinger, the witch
   De Wit-*Talking,* 52–56
SPEARGUNS
—fishing
   The bushbabies
SPEARS
   Champion spearsman
   Loki makes mischief
   The talking spear
   The unanswerable
Special powers
   O'Sullivan-*Legends,* 79
Speck, Frank G.
   The immortal cannibal
A speckled hen
   Cortes-*Byelorussian,* 5–11
The spectre wolf
   Manning-*Spooks,* 86–88
Spectres. *See* APPARITIONS;
   GHOSTS
Spectres and spooks
   Manning-*Spooks,* 7–8
SPEECH
   See also TALK
   Diamonds and toads
—dog, tree, chair: all speak
   Chit-chat [African tale]
—good word vs. evil tongue
   Toads and diamonds
Speech of the pioneers
   McNeil-*Charm,* 48–58
SPEED
   Caoilte the swift
   Casey Jones [song and story]
   The voyage in a Lapp sled
The spell of the fairy mistress
   Haining-*Lepre.,* 91–93
Spells. *See* ENCHANTMENT;
   MAGIC; TRANSFORMA-
   TIONS
Spenceley, Annabel, illus.

Royds-*Animal*
SPENDTHRIFTS
   The flying trunk
   Frankie and Johnny [song and
      story]
   The jackdaw
   Lanval and the Lady Triamor
   "Lars, my lad!"
SPENSER, Edmund
   Faerie queene
SPHINX
   The house of Thebes
SPHINX (subject)
   Lloyd-*Mythical,* 57–65
   Scott-*Fantastic,* 111–120
Spider Grandmother: Foot racers of
      Payupki
   De Wit-*Talking,* 63–75
SPIDER WOMAN
   Man-Eagle conquered by
      youth
   Puukonhoya wins a bride
   Tiyo appears before Snake
      Mana
   Tiyo meets Spider Woman
   The youth and the eagles
SPIDERS
   See also ANANSI STORIES
   See also titles beginning with
      "Anansi . . ."
   Anpao is born
   Arachne
   Arachne: price of a weaver's
      pride
   Athene, goddess of wisdom
   Brer rabbit rescues his children
   Gift from a star
   Hare saves the hippopotamus
   The Mother Goose madman
   The princess in the ivory tower
   The season of the stubby
      caterpillar
   The tale of the magic green
      water-pearl
   Turkey Brother and the magic
      panther suit

SPIDERS (continued)
  Ways of providence are
    inscrutable
  Why crows are black
—and fly
  King who fought many wars
—origin: 8 legs, etc.
  Fall of the spider man
—tricked to come out of lady's
    ear
  Home-bred boy dislodges
    spider
—webs
  Tom Thumb
SPIES
  All I possess!
Spindle, shuttle, and needle
  Lang-*Green*, 329–332
SPINDLES
  Curse: an embowered sleep
    [one hundred years]
  Sleeping Beauty in the wood
SPINES
  Echidna's spines
SPINNING
  Bead-seller and the jinn's
    sister
  The betrothal
  Dame Soasan
  Duffy and the devil
  Giane
  Habetrot [name of fairy]
  Haunter of the birch forest
  Peerifool [secret name of fairy]
  The princess in the ivory tower
  Tom Tit Tot
  Water lily: the gold spinners
—contests
  Rival kempers
SPINNING WHEELS
—golden
  East of the sun and west of
    the moon
Spirit Burekoibo (Meri) punishes
    the Bororo
  Wilbert-*Bororo*, 86–88

Spirit helpers: Turkey Brother and
    magic suit
  De Wit-*Talking*, 13–21
The spirit multitude [brought by
    West Wind]
  Robertson-*Highland*, 194
Spirit of the bison skull
  Stuchl-*American*, 20–21
The spirit of the spring
  Sheohmelian-*Three*, 19–24
The spirit of the van
  Keightley-*World*, 409–415
  Yolen-*Favorite*, 110–112
The spirit-wife
  Yolen-*Favorite*, 423–427
SPIRITS
  See also ANIMALS—spirits;
    BANSHEES; DEMONS;
    GHOSTS; JINN; POL-
    TERGEISTS; WATER SPIR-
    ITS; WOOD SPIRITS
  Boy of the red twilight sky
  Creatures and spirits
  Deer Hunter and White Corn
    Maiden
  The fire plume
  The genesis of the Hid-folk
  The goblin bride
  Helpful spirit
  Hinzelmann
  [Impregnation by earings] Ara-
    ruga Paru
  Lady Ren: fox spirit
  The origin of music
  The orphan boy and the elk
    dog
  Poor Sandy [conjure woman]
  Prince Asraf and the king of
    the spirits
  Rip Van Winkle
  Time to think [crossroads: fatal
    accidents]
  The yes-no-yes-no spirit
  The youth who went forth to
    learn what fear was
—of ancestors

Baluan: origin of the island
—dream
The dancing bird Bralgah
—evil
The elemental
The enchanted mountain
Enchanted youth: Osseo and
Oweenee
Good and evil
The lost treasure
—flower by day, woman by night
The poet and the peony
—the four points of the earth
Manabozho and how the diver
[duck] got a flat back
—good
The enchanted mountain
Enchanted youth: Osseo and
Oweenee
—good vs bad
The bride from Bird Island
—"Great Spirit"
Cranes of the Great Lakes
How Hoof Lake got its name
Iktomi's blanket
In the days of the great buffalo
The singing birds
The snail and the beaver
Thunderbird
—hairy
Urisk
—household
Hob and Eggy Palmer
Hob and Hinky Punk
Hob and Sootkin
Hob and the storm
Hob stories [five]
Kildare pooka (condensed)
Pepito el corcovado
The tomte's favorite horse
See also BROWNIES
—Manitos
Grasshopper [Indian
superman]
—offended, punishes by damaging
corn crop

Spirit Burekoibo (Meri) pun-
ishes the Bororo
—sea
The kobold and the pirate
Sirens
—the "Wordless Voice"
The timid frogs
—wounded, takes revenge
The great flood; Jokurugwa or
Meriri Poro
SPIRITS (subject)
Zong-*Korea*, 250 (index)
—household
Briggs-*Vanish.*, 53–65
—household; Heinzelmanchen
Briggs-*Vanish.*, 60, 196
—Motif index
Wilbert-*Bororo*, 318
Spirits and demons
Sanders-*Dragons*, 83–84
SPIRITUAL LIFE
The man who wouldn't be king
SPITTING
The truth about ghosts
—forbidden
Town where none might go to
sleep
—in face of rabbi
For domestic peace
SPITTLE
Bewitched cow
Dame Soasan
SPLINTERS
—of glass
The snow queen: an adventure
in seven stories
The split dog
Yolen-*Favorite*, 295
Spoiled children. See BEHAVIOR
PROBLEMS
The spook and the beer barrel
Manning-*Spooks*, 62–64
The spook and the pigs
Manning-*Spooks*, 83–85
SPOOKS
Heaven forbid!

SPOOKS (continued)
—huge man with head of owl
    The owl
—in form of bird
    Ha! Ha! Ha!
—steal haystacks
    Tangletop: the haystacks
—throws out pieces of gold
    The lake [personified]
–trans. into geese
    La-lee-lu
—turned to stone
    Dilly-dilly-doh!
Spooks a-hunting
    Manning-*Spooks*, 24–27
The spook's party
    Manning-*Spooks*, 22–23
SPOOKS (subject)
    Manning-*Spooks*, 7–9
SPOONS
—silver
    The Finn messenger (Norway)
—wooden
    The curse [elk takes liver of
      new mother]
SPORTS (subject)
    See also ATHLETICS
—fairies
    Briggs-*Vanish.*, 39–40, 162–
      180
SPRATS (a small fish)
    The great bronze Buddha and
      the whale
Sprig of rosemary
    Ainsworth-*Phantom*, 22–35
    Lang-*Pink/D*, 230–237
    Lang-*Pink/K*, 166–172
Spriggans
    Froud-*Faeries*, unp
SPRIGGANS
    Faeries on the eastern green
    Miser and the fairy Gump
      (condensed)
SPRIGGANS (subject)
    Briggs-*Vanish.*, 45, 54, 199
The sprightly tailor

Jacobs-*Celtic*, 44–45
SPRING
    The green mist
    The rain bulls
    The selfish giant
    Skinkoots steals the spring-
      time
    Wind that blows the winter
      away: Mayrah
    Winter's end (personified)
—origin
    Persephone
Spring flowers
    Ewart-*Lore*, 17
The spring sky
    Gallant-*Constel.*, 148–181
Springfield Mountain [song and
    story]
    Sanders-*Hear*, 12–18
SPRINGS (water)
    The giant of Skalunda
    Golden chisel and the stone
      ram
    In the beginning
    The rocks of Korsan
    Tibble Castle and Klinta Spring
    The umbrella tree
    The white-hair waterfall
—magic (Ohai)
    The spirit of the spring
SPRITES
    Heinzelmannchen and
      Hutchen
—house
    Kobolde
    Nissen and Tomtra
    Poltersprites
    Witchtln
—jungle
    The bushbabies
—Norwegian
    Ellefolk
The spunkies
    Robertson-*Highland*, 8–9
SPUNKIES (subject)
    Briggs-*Vanish.*, 81, 120, 199

SPURS
—overcome pooka
The cold iron spurs
SPURWINGED PLOVERS
Snakes and turtles [exchange heads]
The squeaking mouse
Cortes-*Byelorussian,* 5
The squire
Singer-*Power,* 33–40
SQUIRES
An evening in the squire's kitchen
The fiery dragon
The squire's bride [a horse]
Phelps-*Tatterhood,* 129–132
Riordan-*Woman,* 75–79
Squirrel and the fox
Sampson-*Gypsy,* 59–65
The squirrel and the pixie
Blyton-*My,* 66–72
Squirrel, leopard, and goat: do it again, then
Todd-*Tortoise,* 26–28
The squirrel wife
Royds-*Animal,* 80–92
SQUIRRELS
Fated animal does not see the hunter
George's picnic
The giant sturgeon
Green lizard, gray squirrel and the eagle
How coyote stole fire
Leopard, the squirrel, and the tortoise
The lost hum
Sody sallytytus
The squirrel and the pixie
The tale of Squirrel Nutkin
—origin of characteristics
Manabozho and the squirrels
SQUONKS
Assorted monsters
Sri of Siam

Toth-*Tales,* 73–79
Sri Thanonchai
Watson-*Thailand,* 14–15
The stag [saved from the hunters]
Berger-*Animalia* [49–51]
Stagolee
Lester-*Black,* 113–135
Stags. *See* DEER
STAMFORD BRIDGE
The battle of Stamford Bridge
STAMP-COLLECTING
The third level
Stan Bolovan and the dragon
Adams-*Iron,* 69–85
The star and the lily
Wade-*Indian,* 21–26
"STAR BEINGS"
The prince who had two eyes
Star-Boy and the sun dance
Macmillan-*Canadian* 7–11
The star child
Wilde-*Fairy,* 149–172
The star dipper [Ursa major]
Tudor-*Bedtime,* [20–21]
STAR EYES
Stars in the snow
Star-jackal: Mpungutye
Poland-*Mantis,* 66–79
Star Maiden
Haviland-*N. Amer.,* 97–100
"STAR OF THE SEA"
The quest for the Star of the Sea
Star people [seven tales]
Reed-*Aboriginal,* 87–107
STARING
Fairy bride
Starkad and Bale
Booss-*Scand.,* 328–330
STARKIE FAMILY (16th century)
The "Kissing witch"
STARR, Henry
—Ozark's last horseback outlaw
Steele-*Ozark,* 47–50

STARS
   See also CONSTELLATIONS;
      METEORS
   See also names of stars, e.g.
      MORNING STAR; NORTH
      STAR; etc.
   Andromeda dances
   The apples of eternal life
   The beginning: Father Sky,
      Mother Earth
   The bride of heaven
   La cenicienta huasteca
   Escape at bedtime [poem]
   Heaven's reward
   The magic of the moon
   Meteor showers
   A Navajo story of creation
   Polaris (the Pole Star)
   Raven lets out the daylight
—Aswins
   Upamanyu learns a lesson
      [hermitage school]
—Gidgereegah and Quarrian
   Redbreast: the Gwineeboos
—names
   Origin of the names of some
      stars
—origin
   Deer Hunter and White Corn
      Maiden
   How the stars came: Iku's
      eyes
   Morning Star and Meteor
   Origin of the stars and of cer-
      tain animals
   The raven and the ball of light
   Raven steals the light
   The seven stars
—origin of Gwaibillah, the red star
   Goonur, the woman-doctor
—source of fire
   Gift from a star
—as spirits
   Enchanted youth: Osseo and
      Oweenee
—Vespa and Aquila

   The herd boy and the weaving
      girl
STARS (subject)
—Myths
   Lines-Greek, 267
Stars, brightest [a title]
   Gallant-Constel., 187
The stars in the sky
   Phelps-Maid, 135–141
Stars in the snow
   Sperry-Where, 69–79
STARVATION
   Lam Ku, the basket lady
   The new people and their food
State fairs. See FAIRS
State flowers of the U.S.A.
   Ewart-Lore, 181
STATUES
   The happy prince
   The old woman and El Senor
   Pygmalion
   Pygmalion's statue
   Saint Sebastian
   The stone statue
   Treason in saints
   The white-hair waterfall
—put in place of girl
   Long Haired Girl
—wax
   Waxworks
STATUS
   Havoc in heaven: Monkey and
      the Jade Emperor
The steadfast parrot and his tree
   Martin-Hungry, 15–18
The steadfast tin soldier
   Ehrlich-Random, 130–137
Stealing. See THIEVES AND
      THIEVERY
Stealing for the trolls
   Lindow-Swedish, 98–99
The stealing of the sampo
   Synge-Land, 187–196
The stealing of Thor's hammer
   Branston-Gods, 130–133
STEEL

The Vatters
Stein Veg of Tarbert
 Robertson-*Highland*, 97–98
A stepchild that was treated mighty
 bad
 Haviland-*N. Amer.*, 147–157
STEPFATHERS
 The little bull calf
 Shun, the wise emperor
—evil
 The leeshy cat
STEPMOTHERS
 Baba Yaga
 The black colt
 Cinderella
 The cruel stepmother
 East of the sun and west of
  the moon
 Ednoth's relics, and Thurkill's
  beard
 The fate of the children of Lir
 Father Frost
 [Ghost of mother protects her
  children]
 Golden apple and his
  stepmother
 Grandfather Frost
 Hansel and Gretel
 Haunter of the birch forest
 The herd-boy
 The juniper tree
 King Lindorm [a snake]
 Knight of the riddles
 Lir, Aoife, and his children
 Little Elga
 The magic orange tree [child
  abuse]
 Maiden Bright-Eye
 Mirror of Matsuyama
 Mother Holle
 Mother Hulda
 Piglet and the cow
 Prince who married a Peri
 Princess Hase
 The red cow [a Cinderella-type
  story]

The ridere of riddles
 The rose tree
 The singing bone
 [Sister saves six brothers cast
  into swan-form]
 Six swans
 Snow White and the seven
  dwarfs
 A stepchild that was treated
  mighty bad
 Suit of white feathers
  (Dongxiang)
 A true money tree
 Twelve wild geese
 Two sisters, Rose and Lotus
 Udala tree
 Undying guardianship: Rashin
  Coatie
 Vasilisa the Beautiful
 The werewolf
 The wicked stepmother
 The wild swans
 Yeghnig Aghpar
 Yoni and her stepmother
—cruel
 The brothers Samba
—cruelty punished
 "I'm Tipingee, She's Tipingee,
  we're Tipingee, too"
—cuts child's hand off
 Story of Miriam
—greedy
 Kumba the orphan girl
—kills wife and child
 Story of Miriam
—tries to kill stepson
 The guardian sheep
 The jealous co-wife
—by usurpation
 A mother's yarn
—a witch
 Little Wonder [son-changed-to-
  dog]
 The queen's children
Stepmother's head
 Manning-*Marvels*, 19–29

STEPSISTERS
 The brocaded slipper
 Cinderella
 Father Frost
 Little crop-tailed hen
 Vassilisa [Fair] and Baba Yaga
STEPSONS
 Little Wonder [son-changed-to-
  dog]
 The Metronome
Stevens, James R.
 Stories of the Windigo
Stevenson, Robert Louis, 1850–
  1894.
 Escape at bedtime [poem]
 My shadow [poem]
Stevenson, William
 The bushbabies
Stewed, roasted, or live?
 Kendall-*Sweet,* 98–99
STICKING
 The baker's magic wand
 The rabbit and the well
—touch, and stuck-together
 The lamb with the golden
  fleece
STICKS
 Golden stick, silver stick
 Jack and his cudgel
 The lad and the north wind
 Man and woman with too
  many children
 Munachar and Manachar
 Performing stick
—magic
 The disrespectful son
 The lad who went to the north
  wind
 The lost bell
—magic, witch rides on
 Esben and the witch
—white
 Bokodori Ecerae chief and
  clan customs
The sticks of truth
 Shannon-*Solve,* 26–29

STILES
 The old woman and her pig
Stillson's leap: a jataka
 Martin-*Hungry,* 147–153
Sting: The glass diamond
 Watson-*Thailand,* 39–41
STINGINESS
 See also GREED; MISERS
 All I possess!
 Axe porridge
 Betty Booker's bridle
 Ivan the rich and Ivan the poor
 The magic pear tree
 Saint Brigid's cloak
 The spook and the pigs
—punished
 Swarthy Smith of the Socks
STINGING NETTLE
 The plant of gold
Stingray: legend of the Meru
 Wilbert-*Bororo,* 152–155
STIPULATIONS
 See also DISOBEDIENCE;
  TABOOS
 A bride from the lake
 Don Giovanni de la Fortuna
 The kingdom of beautiful
  colors
 The princess in the ivory tower
 Treasure hunt
—condition(s) not observed
 Iktomi and the fawn
—foolish
 The handsome suitor [A]
—name not to be mentioned
 Lanval and the Lady Triamor
—violated
 Heavenly maiden and the
  wood cutter
Stobbs, William, illus.
 Crouch-*Whole*
STOCK (flower)
 Nasturtium, stock, thrift
STOCKADES
 How the tiger got his stripes
STOCKS (subject)

Briggs-*Vanish.*, 93, 106, 108–
   109, 112–113
Stockton, Frank R., 1834–1902.
   The transferred ghost
Stoker, Bram
   The secret of the growing gold
Stolen children. *See* CHILDREN—
   stolen
The stolen lady
   Keightley-*World*, 391–392
The stolen ox
   Keightley-*World*, 390–391
The stolen princess
   McKinley-*Door*, 1–77
STOMACH
   La cenicienta huasteca
—cat rests in s. of farmer
   The cow who tried to act like a
      kitten
Stompe Pilt
   Booss-*Scand.*, 239–240
STONE CARVING
   The talking stone
The stone frogs, the Youayah
   Mayamah
   Parker-*Australian*, 168–170
The stone lion [vomits gold]
   O'Connor-*Tibet*, 116–123
The stone maiden
   Stuchl-*American*, 155–157
Stone memorial to a dog
   Zong-*Korea*, 93–94
Stone of patience: Nourie Hadig;
      truth
   Villa-*Armenian*, 84–91, 442–
      445
The stone statue
   Booss-*Scand.*, 206–208
STONECHAT (bird)
   Adventures of Ntini, the small
      otter
Stonemason: a T'ung folktale
   Sadler-*Treasure*, 60–66
STONEMASONS
   The building of the wall of
      Asgard

Golden chisel and the stone
   ram
Stones. *See* ROCKS AND
   STONES
Stones of five colours and the Em-
   press Jokwa
   Ozaki-*Japanese*, 283–296
Stories of the Windigo
   Colombo-*Wind.*, 193–200
Stories to solve; 14 folktales
   Shannon-*Solve*, 7–55
A stork is not always a stork
   Crossley-*Folk*, 47–48
STORKS
   See also JOBIRU STORK
   Caliph Stork
   The fairy and the prince
   The fox and the stork
   The marsh king's daughter
   The rocks of Korsan
   Seven families of Lake Pipple-
      Popple
STORM PETRELS
   Sedna, the witch under the
      sea
Storm witches . . . control the
      weather
   Robertson-*Highland*, 90–91
Stormalong fights the Kraken
   Haviland-*N. Amer.*, 184–191
STORMMAKER
   The ghost rider
STORMS
   See also LIGHTNING; RAIN;
      THUNDER
   The antelope maid
   The black dwarfs of Granita
   The bottle-neck
   The crimson parrot
   The dwarf in search of lodging
   The fisherman and the draug
   The fisherman of Gotur
   Gioga's son
   The gray wolf
   Jack of Sjoholm and the Gan-
      Finn

STORMS (continued)
    Jonah and the whale
    The little mermaid
    The story of the house
    A tale of the Grand Jardin
    The voyage in a Lapp sled
—at sea
    Boy of the red twilight sky
    The sjora warns of an impend-
      ing storm
    Three evil wives punished
      [magic]
—severe; mistake
    Sorcerer from Loudon Hill
A story about death
    Gorog-*Taste*, 9–16
STORY (literary form)
    Where stories grow
Story of a flood
    Piggott-*Mexican*, 74–83
Story of a gentleman['s wife]
    Zong-*Korea*, 123–126
The story of Bergthor of Blafell
    Booss-*Scand.*, 642–643
Story of Campriano (Italy)
    Yolen-*Favorite*, 163–166
Story of Ciccu
    Lang-*Pink/D*, 339–355
    Lang-*Pink/K*, 253–268
The story of Deirdre
    Jacobs-*Celtic*, 46–56
Story of Ivan the Imbecile
    Weiss-*Russian*, 89–116
The story of Jon Asmundsson
    Booss-*Scand.*, 657–665
Story of Miriam
    Villa-*Armenian*, 253–255, 495
Story of the end of trickster Wihio
    Anderson-*Trick.*, 86
The story of the house
    Jagendorf-*Magic*, 109–111
The story of the McAndrew family
    Jacobs-*Celtic*, 213–218
Story of the robbers [master thief]
    Villa-*Armenian*, 388–390, 526
The story of the Salt Mother

    Dutton-*Hopi*, 19–20
The story of trembling hood
    Branston-*Gods*, 89–96
The story of Zibong
    Zong-*Korea*, 103–105
Story-spirits [confined in bag; plan
    revenge]
    Zong-*Korea*, 154–157
The story-teller at fault
    Jacobs-*Celtic*, 87–94
The storytellers
    Gorg-*Taste*, 69–73
STORYTELLERS AND STORY-
    TELLING
    Adventures of John Dietrich
    Andrew Coffey
    The blossom tree
    Critch
    The elfin hill
    An evening in the squire's
      kitchen
    Far Darrig in Donegal
    The flying trunk
    [Haitian storytelling
      (commentary)]
    In a dim room
    The man who had no story
    The parrot tale-teller
    Scheherazade
    Scheherazade retold
    Seein' snakes
    Story-sprints [confined in bag;
      plan revenge]
    A summer night in a Nor-
      wegian forest
STORYTELLERS AND STORY-
    TELLING (subject)
    Griego-*Cuentos*, 7–9
    Thomas-*It's*, 237–242
    Yolen-*Favorite*, 1–16
—Audience participation
    Macdonald-*Twenty*, 190–191
—Finding, learning and telling tales
    Macdonald-*Twenty*, 181–190
—Note to the teacher
    Macdonald-*Twenty*, xv–xvi

—Tell, don't sell
Lewis-*Animal,* 6–7
—Telling styles
Macdonald-*Twenty,* 195–197
—Why tell one-minute fairy tales?
Lewis-*Minute,* 6–7
STOVES
The death of Chanticleer
STOWAWAYS
The secret ones
The straight road: Christmas in
heaven
O'Sullivan-*Legends,* 103–104
Strand-ghosts
Lindow-*Swedish,* 185–186
The strange history of Professor
Grasshopper
Wood-*Spirits,* 87–94
Strange tale of caribou and moose
Macmillan-*Canadian,* 115–118
Strange visitors
Manning-*Spooks,* 115–117
A stranger comes to Leon
Campos-*Mexican,* 62–65
STRANGERS
Anpao and the animals
Strangers (condensed)
Briggs-*Vanish.,* 154–156
Strategy
Roberts-*Chinese,* 207–208
STRATEGY
Glooscap, the peacemaker
Strathardle water bulls
Robertson-*Highland,* 144–146
STRAW
Munachar and Manachar
Munachar and the raspberries
The piece of straw
Story of Compriano (Italy)
—as "load"
The tomte carries a single
straw
—task: turn to gold
Rumpelstiltskin
The straw ox
dePaola-*Favorite,* 75–82

STRAWBERRY TREES
Clematis and Arbutus (the
strawberry tree)
STRAWS (subject)
—flying on
Briggs-*Vanish.,* 25
Stray sod
Foud-*Faeries,* unp
STRENGTH
The bishop and the elves
Boy of great strength and the
giants
The boy who ate more than
the giant
Clever Daniel
The cunning Lapp
Degei and his sons
Devil's tale
Erh-lang and the suns
The flying war club
Four sworn brothers
The ghoul and the youth of
Ispahan
Glooskap and the fairy
Grasshopper [Indian
superman]
Great Heart and the three
tests
Hans, the mermaid's son
John Henry [song and story]
John the Bear
Kintaro, the golden boy
A legend of Knockmany
Leppa Polkry and the blue
cross
The master of Ugerup
Mouse Woman and the van-
ished princes
Nine-headed giant
The Northern Lights
One particular small, smart
boy
Oona and the giant Cuchulain
Oonagh and the giants
Pedro de Urdemalas
Sable souls

STRENGTH (continued)
  Son of the gray horse
  Son of the Strong Man of the
    Wood
  Stormalong fights the Kraken
  The story of Jon Asmundsson
  The strongest boy in the
    world
  The strongest in the world
  Stupid Peikko
  Svend Faelling
  Theseus, king of Athens
  Three heroes [and the 3-head-
    ed boa]
  Tom Hickathrift and the old
    giant
  Valiant John
  Water carrier's fabulous sons
  Zilyan
—in Cucullan's finger
  Knockmany legend
—cumulative tale
  God is stronger
—cured by magic water
  A crippled hero
—fabulous
  The blacksmith
  Kile Bamba and the Loche
    bogatyr
  The tailor (Mikhei) and the
    shoemaker
—fabulous (four Hercules's)
  Ivan, the Windfall
—false pretense
  Francis and the giant
—fantastic
  Three strong women
—hyperbole
  The ant, the elephant, and the
    brahmin's servant
—tall tales
  Three strong women: Forever
    Mountain [Japan]
—tests of
  The herd-boy and the giant
—training in secret

  The strong man
Stretch out your leg to the length of
  your quilt
  Sheohmelian-*Three*, 95–96
Stretch your legs according to your
  quilt
  Kudian-*More*, 40–41
Stretching kupua [taller than 40
  feet]
  Thompson-*Hawaiian*, 11–18
Strewing, perfumes, pomanders,
  pot-pourri
  Ewart-*Lore*, 28–30
STRIKING
  The spirit of the van
Striking taboo: A bride from the
  lake
  Crouch-*Whole*, 75–81
A stroke of luck
  Yolen-*Favorite*, 183–185
The stromkarl at Garphytte
  Lindow-*Swedish*, 121–122
Strong arms, sturdy hearts
  Seekers Saviors, 96–121
Strong but Quirky
  Haviland-*N. Amer.*, 192–195
The strong man
  Wood-*Spirits*, 64–67
The strongest boy in the world
  Hill-*More*, 140–149
The strongest in the world
  Nagishkin-*Folktales*, 57–60
Stuart, Dee
  Man's best friend
STUBBORNNESS
  Adventures of John Dietrich
  The hunchback's hump
  The pig-headed wife
  Pikuwa and his wives
  Those stubborn souls, the
    Biellese
Stubbornness causes trouble
  Todd-*Tortoise*, 77
Stubbornness does not pay
  Todd-*Some*, 64–65
Stubbs, Jean

The walking shadow
STUD ANIMALS
  The complacent one; sheep to
    be slaughtered
  El Diablo, el chivo, y Senor
    Bonifacio
STUDENTS
  The goblin and the huckster
  The nightingale and the rose
  The parrot tale-teller
—dullard-son beaten to death
  Ghost of Lady Hobby
—hunger vs learning
  The master pupil
Stumpy
  Stovicek-*Around*, 70–71
The stupid boy and the wand
  Macmillan-*Canadian*, 126–129
The stupid crocodile
  Raychaudhuri-*Stupid*, 58–59
The stupid fox [and trapped tiger]
  Wheeler-*Fox*, 39–56
Stupid Marco
  Williams-*Practical*, 17–34
Stupid Peikko
  Booss-*Scand.*, 581–588
The stupid rich man
  Nagishkin-*Folktales*, 156–
    161
The stupid tiger
  Raychaudhuri-*Stupid*, 53–57
STUPIDITY
  See also FOOLS AND
    FOOLISHNESS
  *See also as subhead under
    topics, e.g.* GIANTS—
    stupidity
  The cat, the cock and the
    scythe
  Fated animal does not see the
    hunter
  The golden neckband
  Hare and hyena in the well
  Hare, the hyena, and the
    lioness's cave
  "Lars, my lad!"

Little Sister Fox and Brother
  Wolf
Old fuddlement
Rickety Topknot
The scholar jackal
The six fools
The story of the McAndrew
  family
Tuwara, the cunning one
Ukrainian tale [grief: imagined
  future woes]
Uncle tiger and his nephew the
  jackal
Who was the stupidest
The wolf and the fox
Sturgeon, Theodore
  The other Celia
Sturt's desert pea, the blood flower
  Parker-*Australian*, 133–137
STYX RIVER
  Hades, lord of the underworld
SUBARCTIC
—Canadian
  Restless souls
SUBMARINES, ca. 1598
  Admiral Yi
SUBMISSIVENESS
  Kyang, the fox, the wolf and
    the hare
  Sheep, lamb, wolf, and the hare
SUBSTITUTION
  The daughter and the helper
  The girl with the silver voice
  How the fox and the elk ex-
    changed legs
  Who is my neighbour?
—sexton takes parson's place
  The parson and the sexton
—wife of troll eaten
  Olli the terrible
—wolf for bride
  Wolfskin's bride
SUCCESS
  See also FAILURE; LUCK
  The man who did not believe
    in luck

SUCCESS (continued)
The young rooster
—accidental
Enchanted castle
Home-bred boy defeats the
enemy
Home-bred boy finds lost
turquoise
Know-All and the cowardly
thieves
Old One Eye [robbers foiled]
The strange history of Pro-
fessor Grasshopper
The transferred ghost
The unwilling magician
Succession myth
Pinsent-*Greek*, 144
SUDANESE TALES (subject)
—Introduction: 17 tales
Mitchnik-*Egyptian*, vii–x
SUFFERING
Brown Bear of Norway
Catherine and her destiny
The creation
The cruel painter
Opame, Chenrezik, and Dolma
—world of sin and sorrow
Spirit of the Van
SUFI TALES (subject)
—Amina Shah's . . .
Shah-*Dervishes*, ix–xiv
SUGAR CANE
—origin
The snake bridegroom
Sugar-plum tree [poem]
Tudor-*Bedtime*, [34–35]
SUICIDE
The devil advises suicide
The hanged man seeks his
pine tree
Herne the hunter
Rainbow bridge: Buck Ante-
lope and Evening Breeze
Tanzara and Dyeer
The tiger priest
Two sisters, Rose and Lotus

The weeping woman: the
prince and the seamstress
—attempted
The centipede girl
The poor rich man's son gets
a second chance
—life restored
The wife from heaven
Suit of white feathers (Dongxiang)
Seven Sisters, 71–79
The suitable husband
Amore-*Lustful*, 107–108
Suited to be a fish [eaten by
colleagues]
Roberts-*Chinese*, 20–24
SUITORS
See also COURTSHIP
An act of truth
Bamboo-cutter and the moon-
child
Beautiful girl who had no teeth
Boy-who-snared-the-wind and
shaman's daughter
Ebbe Skamelson
The frozen logger [song and
story]
Genie of the mountains
Great Heart and the three
tests
Horse and toad
King Miroslav and the proud
princess
Kuma and Aua
The maid of the north
[Kalevala]
Marriage of two masters of
Wolof. [B]
Mister Fox [suitor/murderer]
"O luck of the ugly . . ."
On top of Old Smoky [song
and story]
Prince Narcissus and the Prin-
cess Potentilla
The riddle
Riddles
Scarface

The suitable husband
The tail of the squire's bride
Tikka the tailor
To-Dola
The transferred ghost
Twigmuntus, Cowbelliantus,
    Perchnosius
Twins Akaruio Bokodori and
    Mamuiawuge Eceba
What shall baby's name be?
The white doe
The white snake
Woman in the moon
The yellow dwarf
—all with "scars" rejected
The handsome suitor [A]
—deceiver punished
    Prayer that was answered
    (Tibet)
—disposed of, by spook
    Rubizal and the miller's
    daughter
—old magician/young princess
    Flying horse [wooden]
—rejected
    The three wishes
    The toad-bridegroom
—rejected as small-minded
    Sparrow's search for rain
SULIMAN, Son of David
    Iskandar and the emerald ring
    Water carrier's fabulous sons
Sulphur water: El Paso de los
    Robles
    MacLean-*Cuentos*, 49–53
The sultan and the cobbler
    Mitchnik-*Egyptian*, 14–20
The sultan and the ogress
    Elbaz-*Folktales*, 87–89
The sultan and the psalms
    Elbaz-*Folktales*, 102–103
SULTANS
    Aladdin and the wonderful
    lamp
    Aladdin, or The wonderful
    lamp

Bead-seller and the jinn's
    sister
The crimson parrot
The leopard and the Jinn
Little rooster and the Turkish
    sultan
Sultan's stupid wife and the jinn-
    monkey
    Elbaz-*Folktales*, 84–85
A Suma legend
    Gallant-*Constel.*, 17–18
SUMERIA
    The Zodiac
Sumerian history, culture and
    literature
    Wolkstein-*Inanna*, 115–126
SUMERIANS (subject)
    Wolkstein-*Inanna*, 226 (index)
Sumi and the goat and the Tokyo
    Express
    And Every., 235–251
SUMMER
    Gluska'be, the Penobscot hero
    How Glooskap found the
    summer
    The year summer was stolen
—daughters: sunshine, light,
    flowers
    How the Summer Queen came
    to Canada
—fairy queen
    How summer [personified]
    came to Canada
—origin
    The Fishes [Odschig, the chief]
The summer birds of K'yakime
    De Wit-*Talking*, 80–87
Summer in winter
    Ewart-*Lore*, 146–149
A summer night in a Norwegian
    forest
    Booss-*Scand.*, 89–99
SUMMER QUEEN
—overpowers Winter Giant
    How the Summer Queen came
    to Canada

482

Summer sky
  Gallant-*Constel.*, 48–97
Summoning a spirit servant
  Spells & Bind, 21
The sun
  Roberts-*Chinese*, 87
SUN
  Anpao is born
  The bonfire
  The building of the wall of
    Asgard
  The chariot of the sun
  The creation
  Creation story [Pima]
  The day the sun did not rise
  Day the sun rose in the west
  The disobedient sun-child
  The early heroes: Yi, the ten
    suns, the monsters
  The fifth and final sun
  The fifth sun
  The fifth sun [Nanahuatl]
  The first Inca: marriage of sun
    and moon
  Frost, Sun, and Wind
  Gumiya; a Blang story: origins
    of characteristics
  How Saynday got the sun
  Ivan the rich and Ivan the poor
  Kuafu chases the sun
  Lepa Polkry and the blue cross
  The little girl on the moon
  Little Lapp and the Ice King
  Logic
  The magic of the moon
  Maui and the islands
  Maui slows down the sun
  Monkeys, turkeys, and fish
    [creation]
  The Morning Star
  A Navajo story of creation
  Night and day
  Old man and the sun
  The palace of the moon
  Phaethon and the sun-horses
  Rabbit shoots the sun

  Raven lets out the daylight
  The Rikubugu myth
  Sad marriage of North
  Scarface
  Sea, sun and moon [leap to
    sky to avoid drowning]
  The seed's secret
  The seven sisters
  Sky high went the sun
  The snow-man [the dog and
    the sun]
  Snuff-box [wishes-come-true]
  Son of Kimanaueze and
    daughter of sun and moon
  The sorceress
  Star-Boy and the sun dance
  Stones of five colours and the
    Empress Jokwa
  The sun's daughter
  The Swan [Phaethon and
    Cygnus]
  The village beneath the water
  Why the bananas belong to
    the monkey
  Why the sun rises when the
    rooster crows
  The young rooster
—bad temper
  The young hunter
—beginnings
  Sea, sun and moon [visiting;
    sun and moon . . .
—captured
  Pestilence, darkness and fire
—changes places with moon
  The moon and his frog-wife
—creation
  The first sun
—daughter of
  Mouse Woman and the daugh-
    ter of the sun
—distance from earth, dawn/noon
  The sun
—fifth and final
  Aztec sun goddess
—hunts the morning star

The rain bulls
—leaves earth
   Sun, moon, and water
—leaves earth, to live in sky
   Sea, sun and moon
   A visit from Mister Sea
—mother of the
   The sunset lad [giantess]
—multiple suns; hunter kills
   Sun, night and moon
—Nardu and Sun Goddess
   The Seven Sisters
—Old Man Almanack
   The three golden hairs of Old
     Man Almanack
—origin
   How spider read the sky-god's
     thoughts
   How the sun was made
   Meri and Ari ascend to the sky
   The raven and the ball of light
   Raven steals the light
   Sun and moon
   The sun and the moon
—origin of eclipse
   Rahou [origin of eclipses]
—origin of place in the sky
   Sun and the children
—personified, on earth
   Brothers (Sun and Moon) and
     the pretty girl
—"sap" of the
   The fisher-prince with the sil-
     ver apple
—seven suns
   Erh-lang and the suns
—talisman
   Golden chisel and the stone
     ram
—transformed
   The cruel stepmother
—trapped with a snare
   The mouse and the sun
visited by water (personified)
   Why the sun and the moon
     live in the sky

—Yhi, the sun maiden
   The crystal sisters
SUN (subject)
—[astrology]
   Lehane-*Wizards,* 90
—Legend of the five suns
   Nicholson-*Mexican,* 53–54
—Legends
   Hadley-*Legends,* [4]
Sun and moon
   Seros-*Und,* 8–15
Sun and sago
   Stokes-*Turtle,* 34–36
Sun and the children
   Radin-*African,* 42–44
The sun and the moon
   Zong-*Korea,* 7–10
Sun dance
   Weeks-*Pachee,* 45–64
The sun dance and Scar Face
   Wood-*Spirits,* 85–89
The sun journey
   Highwater-*Anpao,* 183–193
Sun, moon, and water
   Hadley-*Legends,* 12–13
Sun, night and moon
   Todd-*Some,* 88–92
Sun people: The hummingbird
   brothers
   Wood-*Spirits,* 121–124
The sun princess
   Lochhead-*Battle,* 120–131
Sun tribute
   Roberts-*Chinese,* 226–227
SUNBEAMS
—clothes hung on
   Cian of the golden ears
SUNDAY
   See also SABBATH
   The hurlers
—"breaking the Sabbath"
   Oden was a Sunday hunter
—not observing
   Fate of Frank M'Kenna
Sunday and Whirlway maiden
   Anderson-*Trick.,* 47–51

Sunflower, Michaelmas, daisy,
dahlia
Ewart-*Lore,* 144–146
SUNFLOWERS
Baba Yaga and the hedgehog
Bright Light
[Clytie the water nymph & the
Greek sunflower]
—how they became abundant on
prairie
Cowboy Billy Coyote
Sun Ting-po catches a ghost
Roberts-*Chinese,* 171–172
Sunken palace: King Corc and Fior
Usga
Lochhead-*Battle,* 82–83
SUNLIGHT
Raccoon's tale
The sun's apparent motion
Gallant-*Constel.,* 12–14
The sun's daughter
Hadley-*Legends,* 14–15
SUNSET
Boy of the red twilight sky
The sunset call
Ainsworth-*Phantom,* 95–104
The sunset lad [giantess]
Villa-*Armenian,* 430–433, 532–
534
SUNSHADES
—visor
Origin of sun shield and joints
of bamboo
SUNSHINE
—the first
Sky-raising magpies
"SUN-SONS"
The battle with the birds
The sun journey
Super rat and the monks
Wood-*Kalila,* 212–218
SUPERMEN
Stagolee
SUPERNATURAL
Mouse Woman and the Snee-
nee-iq

Tales of the supernatural; five
Ozark legends
—powers
Legend of marshal Gang Gam-
Czan
Supernatural beings and forces
[legends]
Robe-*Hispanic,* 50–485
Supernatural creatures
Colombo-*Wind.,* 162
Supernatural is not to be played
with
Todd-*Some,* 124–126
Supernaturals and fairies
[condensed]
Mckee-*Scottish,* 9–24
Superstitions
Steele-*Ozark,* 79–96
SUPERSTITIONS
Folklore from the campus
Love and marriage:
superstitions
SUPERSTITIONS (subject)
—Scottish daily life
McKee-*Scottish,* 24–27
Superstitious belief
Colombo-*Wind.,* 21–22
SUPERVISORS
Drill, ye tarriers, drill [song and
story]
Supparaka
Hyde-Chambers-*Tibet,* 14–18
The sure shot
Booss-*Scand.,* 238–239
A sure sign
Nagishkin-*Folktales,* 151–155
SURGEONS
Monkeys
SURGERY
The man who had no story
SURPRISES
The box marked secret
SURVIVAL
—skills
A mother's yarn
The survivors

Lindow-*Swedish,* 74–75
SUSA-NO-O, Prince
  The eight-forked serpent
Susie and her shadow
  Blyton-*My,*52–58
SUSPICION
—ruins friendship
  Double-headed phoenix
SUTHON, Prince
  Manora, the bird woman
SUTRAS
  Tripitaka: quest of the Buddhist
    scriptures
Svend Faelling
  Keightley-*World,* 127–128
Svend Faelling and the elle-maid
  Keightley-*World,* 88
SWALLOWED-ALIVE
  Beginning of the Narran Lake
  Boy-man
  Elephant and the tortoise
  The eternal lovers
  First Woman and Elephant
  Frog went a-courting [song
    and story]
  The giant caterpillar
  Manabozho's fishing: the king
    of fishes
  Mantis and the All-Devourer
  Monkey, the cavy, and the
    jaguar
  Monster with seven heads
  Origin of the Narran Lake
  Punia and the King of the
    Sharks
  Pussy-Greedyguts
  Sody sallytytus
  The tiger and the dwarf
  Unanana and the elephant
  Wolf and the seven kids
  Yeghnig Aghpar
  Ygnacio y el toro gigantesco
SWALLOWS
  The happy prince
  Mouse Woman and the mon-
    ster killer whale

Our-Lady-of-the-Swallows
  A tale of love
  Thumbelina
—apparently dead
  Thumbelina
—healed
  Thumbelina
—injured
  Magic pumpkins
SWAMPS
  The lure of the marsh lights
SWAN BEDS
  Lini the lost prince
[Swan-children of Lir]
  Spells & Bind, 51–58
The swan geese
  Riordan-*Russia,* 175–178
The swan maiden (Sweden)
  Booss-*Scand.,* 248–250
  Yolen-*Favorite,* 303–304
SWAN MAIDENS
  Wayland Smith
SWAN MAIDENS (subject)
  Briggs-*Vanish.,* 24, 39–40,
    199–200
The swan of Tuonela
  Synge-*Land,* 91–102
The Swan [Phaethon and
  Cygnus]
  Lurie-*Heavenly,* 38–41
The swan princess
  Ransome-*War,* 26–34
SWAN PRINCESS
  Libor and the swan princess
Swan [saved by Prince Siddhartha]
  Berger-*Animalia* [53–55]
SWANS
  The black swans
  The castle of Melvales
  Cygnus (the Swan)
  Discontented Lado
  The dream of Oengus
  The fate of the children of Lir
  Jack and the green lady
  Lir, Aoife, and his children
  The magic of the moon

SWANS (continued)
  Nix nought nothing
    (condensed)
  Scarface
  Shaitan the devil and his forty
    daughters
  [Sister saves six brothers cast
    into swan-form]
  Six swans
  Tsar Saltan
  The ugly duckling
  Vaino and the swan princess
  The wild swans
—feathers
  The marsh king's daughter
  The swan maiden
Swapping. See TRADERS AND
    TRADING
Swarthy Smith of the Socks
  Ratcliff-Scottish, 40–48
SWEARING
  The man who never swore
  No pooch 'em
  The two wagoners
SWEATERS
  The night it rained [hitchhiker]
SWEDEN
  All I possess!
  The artful lad
  Church grims
  The cock and the crested hen
  Ellefolk
  The herd-boy and the giant
  King Gylfi is tricked again
  The lad and the fox
  The Lapp genesis, or the first
    of mankind
  "Lars, my lad!"
  Old Nick and the girl
  Old Nick and the pedlar
  The old troll of Big Mountain
  The old woman and the tramp
  The parson and the clerk [II]
  Poleviki and Poludnitsy
  River women
  Saint Peter and the two women
  The sausage
  Skogsra or wood trolls
  Snipp, Snapp, Snorium
  The stone statue
  The tricking of King Gilfi
  The troll ride
  Twigmuntus, Cowbelliantus,
    Perchnosius
  The valiant chanticleer
  What shall baby's name be?
  Why the executioner is called
    assessor
—Blekinge
  The knight of Ellenholm
  The swan maiden
—Bohuslan
  The bridal present
  The giant maiden in Boraserod
    mountain
  The golden cradle
  Halde hat
—Bro
  Retrieving the cup
—Dal
  The mountain kitchen
  The wood and sea nymphs
—Dalarna
  Dancing in Dalarna
—Dalarne
  The Lapp in magpie form
  The treasure seekers
  The water nymph
—Gestrikland
  The Vatters
—Gotland
  The Byse
  The sea nymph
  The ten fairy servants
—Halland
  Elstorps Woods
  The young lady of Hellerup
—Herjedalen
  The vatt's storehouse
—Lappland
  The cunning Lapp
  The giant's bride

The Lapp genesis, or the first
of mankind
—Ljunga
Captain Eli
—Medelpad
Starkad and Bale
—Narike
The elves' dance
The fiddler and the sea nymph
Kate of Ysatter
The Ulfgryt stones
—Oland
The bridge over Kalmarsound
—Ostergotland
The tomts
The troll shoes
The Urko of North Wij
—Skane
The ghost at Fjelkinge
Ljungby horn and pipe
The Lord of Rosendal
The master of Ugerup
Stompe Pilt
The sure shot
—Smaland
Dame Soasan
Ebbe Skamelson
The giant puke
Johan and the trolls
Katrineholm Manor
The lost treasure
The trolls of Skurugata
—Sodermanland
The changelings
Lake Goldring
The troll's garden at
Stallsbacke
—Upland
The herd-boy
The werewolf
—Vermland
The harvesters
The polite coal burner
Saxe of Saxeholm
—Vesterbotten
The voyage in a Lapp sled

—Vestergotland
Bishop Svedberg and the devil
The countess of Hojentorp
The giant of Skalunda
The knights of Allaberg
The treasure in Saby Creek
The trolls in Resslared
—Vestermanland
Bostre Castle
The coal burner and the troll
The snipe
Tibble Castle and Klinta Spring
SWEDEN (subject)
—fairies
Briggs-*Vanish.*, 63, 72–73
—Legends, etc.
Lindow-*Swedish,* 1–56
SWEDES
—in North Dakota
Paul Bunyan, the giant logger
SWEDISH TALES (subject)
—[Three folktales]
Lofgren-*Boy,* 1–32
Sweet Betsy from Pike [song and
story]
Sanders-*Hear,* 192–202
Sweet dung, cake-tree, and the bu-
gle of life
Zong-*Korea,* 178–180
SWEET MEDICINE (Cheyenne
Indian)
Behind the waterfall
Sweet pea
Ewart-*Lore,* 150–152
SWEET POTATOES
Chit-chat [African tale]
Sweet violet
Ewart-*Lore,* 26–28
SWIMMING
The rabbit makes a match
SWINDLERS
Buffalo skinners [song and
story]
The emperor's new clothes
The haunted well
The pilgrim from paradise

SWINDLERS (continued)
Sweet dung, cake-tree, and
the bugle of life
—swindled
Clever Yaro
The swine herd
Booss-*Scand.*, 398–402
SWINEHERDS
The magic fruit
The squirrel wife
Yorkshire giant [Penhill]
Swine-herds: the cattle raid of
Cooley
Ross-*Druids*, 43
SWITZERLAND
Aid and punishment
The chamois-hunter
Curiosity punished
The dwarf in search of lodging
The dwarfs on the tree
Erdluitle
Follets
Gertrude and Rosy
Lutins
The rejected gift
Servan
Witchtin
The wonderful little pouch
SWITZERLAND (subject)
Keightley-*World*, 264–266
The sword Excalibur
Ross-*Druids*, 89–92
The sword in the stone
Classic Child., 47–53
Ross-*Druids*, 85–89
"SWORD OF MURAKUMO"
Prince Vamato Take
The swordmaker's son: Kingdom of
Chu
Sanders-*Dragons*, 116–119
SWORDS
See also ARTHUR, King —
sword (Excalibur)
Adventures of Sir Galahad
Boots and the beasts
Childe Rowland

Dietrich of Bern
The dwarf's feast
The dwarf-sword tirfing
Helpful spirit
The herd boy and the dragons
The magic bamboo
Master Tobacco
Morraha
Performing stick
Pierre, Prince of Murom
The sea maiden
Sharp sword
Singard the dragon-slayer
The swordmaker's son: King-
dom of Chu
The terrible head
Theseus, king of Athens
Thornstein staff-struck
The troll's hammer
War in heaven
Water of life
The wooden sword
—broken
The broken swords
—magic
The boy and the robbers' mag-
ical booty
The red czar and the golden-
haired Tihota
—magic, destroys distance
General Gim Dog-Nyong
SYCAMORE TREES
The woman and the children of
the sycamore
Symbols in the Greek myths
Gibson-*Gods*, 154
Symbols in the Nordic myths
Branston-*Gods*, 156
SYMPATHY
Minnie
SYNAGOGUES
Rabbi David Bussidan pre-
vented sale of synagogue
Synge, Ursula
The building of the wall of
Asgard

SYRIA
   When one man has two wives

TABLECLOTHS
   Master Tobacco
—magic
   The lad and the north wind
   The lad who went to the north
      wind [food]
   The spirit of the spring
Tables-turned. *See* FORTUNE —
   reversal of
TABOOS
   The bearded rock
   Diarmuid and Grainne
   How the Shannon got its name
   Sir Launval (condensed)
   Whipping children: how it
      came about
—book not to be opened
   Chavalai: taboos and
      deception
—box not to be opened
   Urashima Taro, the fisher lad
—broken
   Marya Morevna [evil results]
   Princess in the chest [coffin]
   Sister Alyonushka and Brother
      Ivanushka
   Why coyote's coat is the color
      of sand
—broken-wife/children disappear
   Melusine: the otherworld wife
—kissing
   The hawk and the rattlesnake
—laugh; death
   The Bakororo and Itubore
      legend
   Twins Akaruio Bokodori and
      Mamuiawuge Eceba
—marriage
   Chavalai: taboos and
      deception

   Lake Ichiquin [bring no
      O'Briens home]
—meat of large animals
   Blue-jay who married daughter
      of god
—midwife: don't take any pay
   Teapot spout: Mother Han-
      nah's story
—origins not to be revealed
   Why one does not reveal the
      origin of another
—revealing name of husband
   Knight of the Glens and Bens
      and Passes
—sadness = death
   Tearless woman cries on
      seeing the devil
—sex
   Adultery with the "demon"
—songs
   Ananse: origin, big hinder part;
      small head
—thirteenth chamber not to be
      entered
   The golden finger
—tree and fairies
   Fly together, chips and
      shavings!
—violated: head cut off
   Metugoe doves and the Indian
      Magurereu
—wait to eat the fruit
   Atam and Im
TABOOS (subject)
—fairy
   Briggs-*Vanish.*, 218 (index)
—Motif index
   Wilbert-*Bororo*, 228, 244–245,
      321
TACITURNITY
   The Johnson boys [song and
      story]
Tacksman of Auchriachan
   (condensed)
   Briggs-*Vanish.*, 125–126,
      137

[Tadaka] The brahman and the
demons
Amore-*Lustful*, 71—73
TADPOLES
—spirit
Baitogogo takes possession of
Aije spirit
TAHITI
Laa-mai-Kahiki from Tahiti
TAHITI (subject)
—Sons of Kii
Westervelt-*Hawaiian*, 47—64
Tahmina and Rustam
Shah-*Dervishes*, 207—211
The tail
Jacobs-*Celtic*, 283
The tail of the squire's bride
McCarty-*Skull*, 66—69
The tailor and the deev
Shah-*Afghanistan*, 15—23
The tailor-bird and the barber
Raychaudhrui-*Stupid*, 3—6
The tailor-bird and the cat
Raychaudhuri-*Stupid*, 1—2
The tailor-bird and the king
Raychaudhrui-*Stupid*, 7—11
The tailor (Mikhei) and the
shoemaker
Cortes-*Byelorussian*, 110—114
The tailor of Gloucester
Phelps-*Tatterhood*, 17—30
TAILORS
The brave clever tailor
Brave little tailor (seven at one
blow)
The clever little tailor
Crystal coffin
The devil and his
entanglements
The fox who went to heaven
Heinzelmanchen
How three serpents carried
princesses off to world to
come
Johnnie in the cradle
Legends of the mill

Master tailor
The sprightly tailor
Stretch out your leg to the
length of your quilt
Stretch your legs according to
your quilt
The tailor and the deev [ex-
changes soul for rescue]
Tikka the tailor
The vain lord
The white doe
The wolf and the tailor
The tailor's sleeve
Patai-*Gates*, 740—743
TAILS
*See also as subhead under
particular animals, birds,
etc.*
Anpao brings the corn
One hairball
Why the opossum's tail is bare
TAIRA (subject)
Piggot-*Japanese*, 144 (index)
Tait, Douglas, illus.
Harris-*Mouse*
Take by force. *See* PLUNDER
Taken [wife taken by fairies]
Yolen-*Favorite*, 115—116
Takshaka (prince of serpents):
brahman's curse
Amore-*Lustful*, 74—75
Tale of a she-bear
Pushkin-*Fairy*, 30—33
The tale of Benjamin Bunny
Potter-*Peter*, 41—50
Tale of Elidurus
Keightley-*World*, 404—407
The tale of Ivan
Jacobs-*Celtic*, 125—128
The tale of Looseghen
Sheohmelian-*Three*, 97—103
A tale of love
Campos-*Mexican*, 127—130
Sheohmelian-*Three*, 66—68
The tale of Macc Da Tho's pig
Gantz-*Early*, 179—187

The tale of Mrs Tiggy-Winkle
Potter-*Peter*, 17–30
The tale of Peter Rabbit
Potter-*Peter*, 7–16
The tale of Squirrel Nutkin
Potter-*Peter*, 31–40
Tale of the golden vase and the
bright monkeys
Jagendorf-*Magic*, 49–52
A tale of the Grand Jardin
Colombo-*Wind.*, 113–118
Tale of the kurai
Riordan-*Tartary*, 46–49
The tale of the magic green water-
pearl
Jagendorf-*Magic*, 113–117
Tale of the Princess of Damascus
Shah-*Dervishes*, 25–28
Tale of the ricebirds
Toth-*Tales*, 91–96
Tale of the shrimp and the
earthworm
Jagendorf-*Magic*, 17–18
The tale of the trusty tiger
Roberts-*Chinese*, 97–99
A tale of the Windego
Colombo-*Wind.*, 22–25
TALENTS
Rickety Topknot
TALES
See also AFRICAN TALES;
AMERICAN TALES; ARME-
NIAN TALES; AZTEC
TALES; BENGALI TALES;
BIDPAI TALES;
CAMEROON TALES;
CANADIAN TALES;
CHINESE TALES; ESKIMO
TALES; FAIRY TALES;
GAMBIAN WOLOF TALES;
HAITIAN TALES; HASIDIC
TALES; HINDU TALES; IN-
DIC TALES; IRISH TALES;
ITALIAN TALES; JA-
PANESE TALES; JATAKA
TALES; JEWISH TALES;
LEGENDS; MEXICAN
TALES; NORSE TALES;
PAPUA NEW GUINEA
TALES; RUSSIAN TALES;
SCOTTISH TALES;
SUDANESE TALES; TAR-
TAR TALES; TIBETAN
TALES; WELSH TALES
TALES (subject)
—Bratslav theory of the sacred tale
Nahman-*Tales*, 27–39
—Origins of the folktale
Macdonald-*Twenty*, 192–194
—Researching tale variants
Macdonald-*Twenty*, 198–199
Tales of a parrot
Shah-*World*, 2–11
Tales of the supernatural; five
Ozark legends
Steele-*Ozark*, 17–27
Taliesin and Ceridwen
Lehane-*Wizards*, 13–20
TALISMANS
—sun & moon
Golden chisel and the stone
ram
TALISMANS (subject)
—Black magic
MacLean-*Cuentos*, 70
Talismans: a cache of charms
Lehane-*Wizards*, 120
TALK
Chitchat turtle and the geese
—beheading as result
Now you know
—evil tongue
Mother of the Waters
—flowers fall from lips of princess
Phikool Thong
—good sister/bad sister
Toads and diamonds
—opens mouth, falls into sea
"Bye-bye" (Haiti)
—uncontrollable speech
Lanval and the Lady Triamor
—uncontrolled speech

TALK—uncontrolled speech
(continued)
Garrulousness: Hyena wrestles
konderong
Talk; everything Ashanti farmer
contacts starts to talk
Yolen-*Favorite*, 246–248
A talkative old woman
Zong-*Korea*, 192
Talkative wife
Villa-*Armenian*, 402–403
TALKATIVENESS
How a peasant cured his wife
of telling tales
The talking fish
Kudian-*More*, 9–12
Sheohmelian-*Three*, 15–18
The talking goat
Todd-*Tortoise*, 114–116
The talking nightingale
Elbaz-*Folktales*, 94–97
The talking spear
Thompson-*Hawaiian*, 29–42
The talking stone
Bierhorst-*Hungry*, 87–92, 140
De Wit-*Talking*, 5–9
The tall maiden, Untombinde
Radin-*African*, 221–225
TALL TALES
See also STRENGTH; SWAL-
LOWED-ALIVE
Ash lad who made princess
say "You're a liar!"
Babe the blue ox
Believe it or not
Billy-goat and the handkerchief
Cowboy Billy Coyote
Davy Crockett, king of the old
wild west
Finn MacCumhail and the son
of the king of Alba
Five million ducks
Flying ship
Frosty [and five with superhu-
man powers]
Hound-dog stories (four tall tales)

How El Bizarron fooled the
devil
Johnny Appleseed
Laziest man in America
Little cinder girl
Munchausen and the bear
Old Dry Frye (rogue preacher)
Oona and the giant Cuchulain
Paul Bunyan
Paul Bunyan, the giant logger
Pecos Bill and the cyclone
Pecos Bill becomes a coyote
The ram of Derby [song and
story]
The scythe bitten by a snake
Son of the Strong Man of the
Wood
Stormalong fights the Kraken
Strong but Quirky
Sun dance [big lie contests]
A Tartar riddle: Which is
biggest?
Three strong women: Forever
Mountain [Japan]
The toothpick [snowed-in]
Unanana and the elephant
A whale of a tale
Yerensay's forty fables
TALL TALES (subject)
Lisker-*Tall*, 5–9
Tall tales (Burma)
Yolen-*Favorite*, 30–32
Tall tales of Rabba bar Hana
Patai-*Gates*, 173–177
Talmud [Introd. and selections]
Patai-*Gates*, 159–256
The tam and the hakham
Nahman-*Tales*, 139–161
Tam Lin
Froud-*Faeries*, unp
Tametomo and his dog
Piggott-*Japanese*, 116
Tamlane (condensed)
Briggs-*Vanish.*, 113
Tamlin and Janet
Phelps-*Tatterhood*, 23–28

TAMOANCHAN (meeting place of
    gods)
    The new people and their food
TANGALOA (god)
    The creation of Samoa
    How Samoa was named
Tangletop: the cave at the world's
    end
    Manning-*Spooks*, 77–82
Tangletop: the haystacks
    Manning-*Spooks*, 71–76
TANUKI
    Slaying of the Tanuki
Tanzara and Dyeer
    Villa-*Armenian*, 232–234, 487
TAOISM
    The god behind the curtain
    The priest of Hardwork
        mountains
    Zhang Daoling
TAOISM (subject)
—Taoist tales of magic and fantasy
    Sanders-*Dragons*, 73–74
TAPESTRIES
    The archer who went I know
        not where to . . .
    Athene, goddess of wisdom
    The triumph of death
—magic
    The fox who went to heaven
TAPIO (god of the forests)
    Lippo and Tapio
TAR
    Jurma and the sea god
    Stupid Peikko
    The werewolf
TAR BABIES
    The tar baby tricks Brer Rabbit
The tar baby
    Haviland-*N. Amer.*, 109–114
The tar baby tricks Brer Rabbit
    Faulkner-*Tales*, 122–127
TAR MEN
    The tar baby
TARANS (subject)
    Briggs-*Vanish.*, 81, 200

"TARBABY"
    The rabbit and the well
Tarot: taletelling cards
    Lehane-*Wizards*, 67–69
A Tartar riddle: which is big-
    gest?
    Riordan-*Tartary*, 79–82
TARTAR TALES (subject)
—Commentary
    Riordan-*Tartary*, 163–171
TARTARS (or TATARS)
    The crooked pine
    Gulnara the Tartar warrior
    Walter and Hildegund
    Wizard of Kiev
TARTARUS
    Hades, lord of the underworld
    Orpheus and Eurydice
TARTS
—blackberry
    Blackberry tart
TASH
    The haunted realm
Tasks. *See* TESTS
A taste for quiet
    Gorog-*Taste*, 21–26
Tatars. *See* TARTARS (or
    TATARS).
TATLERA the Loon
    How the Summer Queen came
        to Canada
Tatterhood
    Phelps-*Tatterhood*, 1–6
TATTOOS
    The clever Nikorima
    The illustrated man
Taufatahi and Fakapatu or Why
    sharks . . . Moungone
    Heslewood-*Tales*, 56–59
TAULIL PEOPLE
—origin
    The giant eel
TAURUS (constellation)
—origin
    What happened to six wives
        who ate onions

Taurus (the Bull)
Gallant-*Constel.*, 126–129
The tavern-woman and St Patrick
O'Sullivan-*Legends,* 112
TAWA (sun god)
First tale: In the beginning . . .
Tiyo travels through the
underworld
Twins visit Tawa
TAX COLLECTORS
Date stone; a Han story
Jews of Safi rid themselves of
antisemitic tax-collector
The tax officials and Gohc Amu
Villa-*Armenian,* 405–406
TAXATION
Dumplings in the river
How the citizens of Gotham
paid their taxes
Taylor, Paul B., and W. H. Auden
The lay of Thrym
Tayrnadz: [The Old Man of the
Sea]
Nagishkin-*Folktales,* 13–26
Tayzanne [fish killed, joined by girl
who loves him]
Wolkstein-*Magic,* 58–63
TEA
—Tibetan
The lovers
Tea and camellias
Ewart-*Lore,* 57–63
TEACHERS
See also SCHOOLMASTERS
The false schoolmaster
Little Goody Two-Shoes
Padmasambhava and the felic-
ity scarf
—murders his pupils
The Koranic teacher
A teacher's tricky test
Amore-*Lustful,* 78
TEAMWORK
The dove and the mouse
The young gentleman and the
tiger

Teapot spout: Mother Hannah's
story
Manning-*Kings,* 120–126
Tearless woman cries on seeing
the devil
O'Sullivan-*Legends,* 26–27
TEARS
See also CRYING
The diamond
The frog
The happy prince
The jar of tears
The nightingale
—magic
The golden fish, the wicked
sisters, and good Forgetta
—relief from
The little mermaid
The tears of blood
Chalk-*Tales,* unp.
Tebbetts, Diane
Fishing on the Arkansas: Earl
Ott
TECUCIZTECATL
Aztec sun goddess
The fifth sun
TEDDY-BEARS
Ha, ha, Jack-in-the-box!
Teepees. *See* TIPIS.
The teeth
Schwartz-*Dark,* 10–17
TEETH
The baby with the fangs [13
legends]
Beautiful girl who had no teeth
Meri improves beaks of birds &
gives Bororo teeth
Mouse Woman and the tooth
The wonderful Chuang
brocade
—golden
The tooth of gold
Teicher, Morton L.
Windigo psychosis
Teig O'Kane and the corpse
Yeats-*Fairy,* 23–35

Teigneux
Thomas-*It's*, 43–50
Teigue of the Lee
Yeats-*Fairy*, 320–325
Tekhelet: The city of Luz
Schwartz-*Elijah*, 279–293
TELEPHONES
Alex and Avery [dogs exercised by telephone]
TELL, William (subject)
Shah-*World*, 222
The tell-tale heart [by Poe]
Schwartz-*Great*, 3–10
TEMBLOR MOUNTAINS (subject)
—Origin of name
MacLean-*Cuentos*, 45–46
TEMPER
Dame Soasan
The devil's hide
Jora the troll
Katla
The marsh king's daughter
Prince Nocha
The tears of blood
The three counsels
—overcoming
Hob and the Temper
—violent
The fairy and the prince
The temple ghost and Ai Tzu
Roberts-*Chinese*, 174
TEMPLE OF JERUSALEM
(subject)
Patai-*Gates*, 801–802 (index)
TEMPLES
The god of faces
Prince Nocha
—Buddhist
The magic fox
TEMPTATION
The ascetic who visited home
The devil advises suicide
The fisherman and his soul
Look not at strange women
—overcome by chance
The pig at the candy store

Temptations
Booss-*Scand.*, 488–493
The ten commandments
Elbaz-*Folktales*, 60
TEN COMMANDMENTS
Death out of season
The ten fairy servants
Booss-*Scand.*, 265–268
Ten jugs of wine
Kendall-*Sweet*, 18–20
The ten plagues of Egypt
Classic Child., 68–75
Ten white doves
Mitchnik-*Egyptian*, 85–93
Tend the sick
Amore-*Lustful*, 176–177
Tenderfoot: The dying cowboy
Sanders-*Hear*, 181–191
Tengu: Japan's winged war
masters
Magical Beasts, 75–78
Tepoztecatl [swallowed by giant;
escapes]
Piggot-*Mexican*, 118–128
The terrible head
Lang-*Blue*, 190–201 (notes,
353, 368)
"TERRIBLE WILD MONSTER"
Assorted monsters
Terror
Hoke-*Uncanny*, 1–14
The terror of the red blood sucker
Haining-*Lepre.*, 99–105
The test [beggar; love]
Villa-*Armenian*, 348–350
A test for a disciple
Elbaz-*Folktales*, 117
Test of conviction
Roberts-*Chinese*, 176–177
Test of femininity: Twelve huntsmen
Lang-*Green*, 324–328
A test of fire
Amore-*Lustful*, 105–106
TESTS (tasks, trials, etc.)
See also QUESTIONS;
RIDDLES

TESTS (tasks, trials, etc.)
(continued)
Altynchech and the padishah's
wife
The archer who went I know
not where to . . .
[Assipattle vs Stoorworm the
sea-serpent]
Bamboo-cutter and the moon-
child
Battle of the birds
Bead-seller and the jinn's
sister
Bear cub [and six companions]
Bhima slays the demon [giant,
man-eating cannibal]
The birch boy
Bird from the golden land
The bird 'Grip'
The black king, or Fair
Ferentine
The blind man and the devils
A boy and his dog
The boy and his three helpers
Boy-who-snared-the-wind and
shaman's daughter
Brave little tailor (seven at one
blow)
Buzz-buzz aunty
Caoilte the swift
The castle of the Melvales
Cat lying on velvet cushion,
while dog sleeps
The cave of emeralds
Chilbik and the greedy czar
Childe Rowland
The choosy maid of Yen-Pien
Choril and Cholchinay
The Chuang brocade
The clever wife
The cleverest son [task: fill a
room]
Cobbler's son and the serpent
Conall Yellowclaw
Conn-eda; or The golden ap-
ples of Lough Erne

The crimson parrot
Cupid and Psyche
The dancing princess
Death's substitute
Devil with the three golden
hairs
Devil's tale
The dewdrop tiara
Diarmuid, son of Donn: a spell-
shackled devotion
Disappearing apples [of
immortality]
A discerning old 'faki'
Doll in the grass
The dreamer and his dream
Eighteen rabbits
The eight-forked serpent
Enchanted castle
Enchanted snake
Eros and Psyche
Esben and the witch
Faithful John
Fiery horse
The fire bird and Ryska and
vixen
The firebird
The fisher-prince with the sil-
ver apple
Four hairs from the beard of
the devil
Frosty [and five with superhu-
man powers]
Gawain and the Green Knight
Genie of the mountains
Genius deserves his name
The giant with three golden
hairs
Goggle eyes
The golden goose
Golden mermaid [theft of gold-
en apples]
Golden rain
The gorgon's head
Great Heart and the three tests
Green lizard, gray squirrel and
the eagle

Green Man of No Man's Land
Gulnara the Tartar warrior
Hassan the brave
Haunter of the birch forest
Hiisi's horse
How spider obtained the sky
    god's stories (Ashanti)
How the dragon was tricked
How the hermit helped to win
    the king's . . .
The huntsman
Ivan the peasant's son and the
    three dragons
Ivan Tsarevich, the wolf, and
    the firebrid
Ivanovoushka the simpleton
Jack and his cudgel
Jack and the devil's daughter
Jack the Giant Killer
Jason and the golden fleece
King of Lochlann's three
    daughters
King of the herrings
King O'Toole and his goose
King the liar and liar the king
The king's dream
Kintu tested before he could
    marry daughter of king of
    heaven
The labours of Hercules
Leaves that hung but never
    grew
Libor and the swan princess
Lion tamer [Tibetan]
Little boat that could sail on
    land and sea
Little burnt face
Little cinder girl
Little Elga
Little Finger of the watermelon
    patch
The lost princess
Mac Iain Direach
The magic boat
The magic box
The magic coconuts

The magic horse
Magic knife [Uygur]
The maid of the north
    [Kalevala]
The maiden wiser than the
    Tsar
The man who had no story
Man-Eagle conquered by
    youth
Manora, the bird woman
March cock banishes the devil
Marya Morevna
The mast of sand ["impossible"
    task]
The master thief
The mastermaid
Miraculous flower [stolen by
    prince of ice]
Molly Whuppie (England)
Mouse Woman and the daugh-
    ter of the sun
The mute princess
Nails [anatomy]
Odd jobs
The ogre's soul
The old smith
Old troll tricked into revealing
    his treasure
Olga and the brown cow
The orphan boy and the elk
    dog
The palace of the moon
Patient Griselda
The patient suitor
The pearl that shown by night
Petronella [sorcerer]
Phikool Thong
Piece of Zhuang brocade
Posting the dragon tablet
Pretty Goldilocks
A priest and his servant Balda
Prince and the ogre's castle
Prince Asraf and the king of
    the spirits
Prince Bellerophon and
    Pegasus

TESTS (tasks, trials, etc.)
  (continued)
  Prince Fickle and fair Helena
  Prince Miaow
  Princess on the glass hill
  Princess with the golden hair
  Puddocky
  Queen bee
  The real princess [pea-under-
    mattress test]
  The red czar and the golden-
    haired Tihota
  The riddles
  The rivals
  Roly Poly
  Rumpelstiltskin
  Scabby: beauty is only skin
    deep
  Separation of god from man
  The seven foals
  Seven Simeons [brothers]
  Shaitan the devil and his forty
    daughters
  Shooting the moon; a Yao
    folktale
  The silver whistle
  The sleeping prince
  Son of Kimanaueze and
    daughter of sun and moon
  Son of the gray horse
  Son of the Mountain
  Story of Ciccu
  The sunset lad [giantess]
  The tale of Looseghen
  The talking nightingale
  A teacher's tricky test
  The terrible head
  The three brothers
  The three caskets
  The three feathers
  The three golden hairs of Old
    Man Almanack
  Three rosebushes
  Three thieves [eggs, shoe
    soles, food]
  The Tibetan envoy's mission
  Tiger King's skin cloak
    [Mongolia]
  Tikka the tailor
  Tom Tit Tot
  Tomlin [elf-knight]
  Tremsin and the maid of the
    sea
  The troll's daughter
  The Tsarevna frog
  Turtle skin
  Twelve wild geese
  Twins visit Tawa
  Two enemy kings
  Two mothers [one child]
  Twopence Halfpenny
  Vainamoinen's wound
  Vassilisa [Fair] and Baba Yaga
  The water palace [boat of
    feathers]
  Weardale fairies [dislike being
    observed]
  Which flower?
  The white cat
  The white doe
  The white snake
  Who was most generous?
  Wild goose lake
  The wizard's lesson
  The wonderful Chuang
    brocade
  Wonderful healing leaves
  The wooing of Seppo
    Hmarinen
  Working the field
  The world below
  Young boy and the dwarf
  The young head of the family
  Yvon and Finette
—death
  The sultan and the ogress
—devotion to Shiva
  Arjuna's penance
—done only with help of giant's
    daughter
  The hawk and the rattlesnake
—done with the help of Velena

King Kojata
—father uses, to try to kill son
  Toribugu: legend of the hero
—"fear is still ahead"
  Seven fears
—feed elephant
  The two elephants
—feel pea through 20 mattresses
  The real princess
—find hidden person, or lose wife
  Oskus-ool and his wise wife
—find 8-legged dog
  Golden apple and his
  stepmother
—gelding a colt
  Ivan Byelarasseiski
—of generosity
  The king who gave away his
  kingdom
—get harp, goose, cat
  Ivan young in years, old in
  wisdom
—get magic perfume to free
  woman
  The widow's son and the fig-
  pecker
—get magic powder to break spell
  The princess and the bulbul
—heroine assists
  The mastermaid
—hide; if found = beheaded
  The black fox
—identify the princess
  The golden lion
—impossible
  Flying ship
—impossible; devil's daughter
  helps
  Give me something you
  have . . . unawares
—kill dragon
  Glooskap and the magic gifts
—king rule with justice
  As the king, so the kingdom
—make carpet
  The frog princess

—make princess talk
  Phra Nang Suwanasopha
—move mountain, etc.
  The boy and the dancing fairy
—questions and answers
  The talking fish
—set by king
  Mouse's three children [tiger,
  peacock, boy]
—source of heavenly music
  The King of Ireland's son (Art)
—spin, weave, sew shirt overnight
  The doll in the grass
—straw
  Rumpelstiltskin
—of three brides
  Czarina frog
—trick plus apology
  Quevedo and the king
  (Mexico)
—trolls fail; beggar lass passes
  East of the sun, west of the
  moon
—of virtue
  The hare in the moon
—water & firewood for three year
  Ivan, the Windfall
—woman helps man succeed
  The mastermaid
—of wrong ambition
  Nobleman and the slave
Tests of loyalty and love
  Seekers Saviors, 49–77
Tests of prowess [motif index]
  Wilbert-Bororo, 257–258
The Tewa emerge from Sand Lake
  Dutton-Hopi, 37–41
TEXAS
  Ballad of the boll weevil [song
  and story]
  Cowboy Billy Coyote
  Head devil in Texas [satire]
  Snake with an ear for music
—El Estero
  Lake Espantosa, the
  alligators?

TEXAS (subject)
—Four cultures: the Texas Middle
    Corridor (map)
    Ritchie-*Armadillo*, vii–ix
TEZCATLIPOCA
    The fifth and final sun
    The first sun
    The king's daughter and the
        pepper man
    Monkeys, turkeys, and fish
        [creation]
TEZCATLIPOCA (subject)
    Nicholson-*Mexican*, 144
        (index)
—Four aspects of nature
    Nicholson-*Mexican*, 95–111
T'girt dog of Ennerdale
    Marshall-*Every*, 314–319
THAILAND
    How the Bay of Siam came to
        be
    Phya Paan and the Golden
        Chedi
THAILAND (subject)
—folktales and Thai culture
    Toth-*Tales*, 153–168
—Religious influences in Thailand
    Toth-*Tales*, 169–179
—Salute to the kings of old Siam
    Toth-*Tales*, 143–152
Thanet, Octave [pseud of Alice
        French], 1850–1934
    Folklore in Arkansas
Thanksgiving. *See* GRATITUDE
That her children might be fed
    MacLean-*Cuentos*, 156–157
That wicked crow
    Crouch-*Whole*, 82–88
That's no way to do it!
    Lewis-*Bedtime*, 10–11
THEATER
    The walking shadow
THEBES
    The house of Thebes
    The seven against Thebes
    The theft of fire

De Wit-*Talking*, 49–51
Wood-*Spirits*, 114–120
Theft. *See* THIEVES AND
    THIEVERY
THEMIS
    Peleus and Thetis [marriage]
Then the merman laughed
    (Iceland)
    Yolen-*Favorite*, 346–347
There is no such thing as a secret
    Toth-*Tales*, 80–84
There is righteousness
    Villa-*Armenian*, 345–348
There'll always be a tomorrow
    Todd-*Some*, 68–70
Theseus
    Pinsent-*Greek*, 106–112
    Stapleton-*Dictionary*, 199–202
Theseus and Ariadne
    Magical Beasts, 12–16
Theseus, king of Athens
    Gilbert-*Gods*, 103–112
Theseus: the banquet, the mino-
    taur
    Low-*Greek*, 127–139
Theseus vs the Minotaur]
    Wise-*Monster*, 26–33
THETIS
    The childhood of Achilles
    Peleus and thetis [marriage]
THETIS (subject)
    Pinsent-*Greek*, 144 (index)
THEVSHI
    The haunted realm
Thief girl: no appeal in God's court
    Todd-*Tortoise*, 61–62
The thief: neighbor steals farmer's
    corn
    Stuchl-*American*, 153–154
The thief who kept his hands clean
    Kendall-*Sweet*, 30–32
Thiele, Colin
    February dragon
Thievery
    Kendall-*Sweet*, 78–79
THIEVES AND THIEVERY

See also BANDITS;
  CHEATING
Aladdin and the wonderful
  lamp
Ali Baba and the forty thieves
The bark lizard, Walloobahl
Battle [Cheyennes attack
  Shoshones]
Beware of the bull
The Bremen town musicians
The bride of heaven
The bundle of straw
The charcoal burner
Child's soul in a tree
The countess of Hojentorp
Country of thieves
Crack and crook (Italy)
Cunning mouth
The cunning shoemaker
The deer thief
Dwarfs stealing corn
The enchanted apple tree
The fairy thieves
Fairy thieves (condensed)
Flying money
General Pumpkin
The giant eel
God's court, no appeal
Golden life
Golden pears
Half-ram leaves home
The hand of glory
The honorable wife
How honey-guide came to
  have authority
How Jack went to seek his
  fortune
How the rat lost his wings
Hudden and Dudden and Do-
  nald O'Neary
The hunter's dilemma
The Inn of the Stone and
  Spectre
The iron-eating mice
Ivan the rich and Ivan the poor
Jack and his comrades

Jack and the beanstalk
Jack and the robbers
Jack o' both sides, or The biter
  bit
Jack the cunning thief
Jesse James [song and story]
Johan and the trolls
Journey of dwarfs over the
  mountain
Julio
Kamala and the seven thieves
Know-All and the cowardly
  thieves
The lad and the north wind
The lama's servant
The leopard
Little John and his animals
The little white stone
The lizard who came from
  nowhere
The man in the moon
Man into possum [solitary fish
  thief]
The marsh king's daughter
The master thief
Matching wits [two robbers
  have same wife]
Meri takes a ring from his
  brother Ari
Mister Vinegar
The mountain kitchen
The nis stealing corn
O horrid dede! [monk mur-
  dered: stealing]
Old One Eye [robbers foiled]
The old woman and her rice
Old woman and the doctor
Old woman who stole milk
The ostler and the grave rob-
  bers (Scotland)
A pair of skinnies
The Pleiades
The poor man and his thou-
  sand tanga
Rabbi Haim Pinto, detective
The rival twins

502

THIEVES AND THIEVERY
(continued)
The royal detectives
Sandy Harg's wife
(condensed)
Senor San Antonio retrieves
an axe
Sister Fox and Brother Coyote
Slave maiden's eye for evil
Sleigh Beggey and Tylwyth
Teg
Sneaky, straight, and the tree
Sorach of Glenane [rob rich,
give poor]
The stolen lady
The stolen ox
Story of a gentleman['s wife]
Story of the robbers [master
thief]
Tale of Elidurus
A teacher's tricky test
The thief who kept his hands
clean
Three corpses, money, and a
wine-bottle
Three thieves [eggs, shoe
soles, food]
T'ien the brave, hero of the
Hsia River
Tom Thumb
Treason in saints
Tremsin and the maid of the
sea
Two neighbors
The tylwyth teg
The wager: clever slave wins
freedom
The white pet
Who is my neighbour?
Why the executioner is called
assessor
The wise king and the honest
thief
—caught
Fudo and the prickly pear
thieves

The guilty stone
The sticks of truth
—exposed
Smartest man in the
countryside
—foiled by servant girl
Hand of glory [severed hand of
hanged man]
—foolish attempt
Whose horse is it?
—frightened by "dead" man in
coffin
Giufo's debts
—gander stolen
The piper and the puca
—harrassed by boy-victim
Rooster/Brother
—punishment harsh
The soldier-bird
Deegeenboyah
—robber-girl
The snow queen: an adventure
in seven stories
—robbers tricked
The biter bit
—tricked
The man who buried his
money
Thieves go free [buyers are
punished]
Lewis-*Animal*, 36–37
The thing that walked on the wind
Colombo-*Wind.*, 139–149
Thinking. See THOUGHT(S)
THINNESS
A pair of skinnies
The third level
Hoke-*Spirits*, 131–136
THIRST
Glooskap and the monster
bullfrog
How the monkey got a drink
when he was thirsty
The hunter and his greedy wife
King Matyas and his scholars
(Hungary)

Leppa Polkry and the blue
cross
Why the hare runs away
"THISTIMELASTYEAR"
Shuralee the wood demon
THISTLES
The Scottish thistle
Thomas, Edward
The making of the worlds
THOMAS BECKET, Saint
Devil's armful [Canterbury]
Thomas of Ercildoun. See ERCIL-
DOUN, Thomas of
Thomas, Rosemary Hyde
La Guillonnee: French holidays
in Miss. Valley
Thomas the rhymer
Froud-*Faeries*, unp
Thomas the Rhymer. See ERCIL-
DOUN, Thomas of
THOMAS, Vivia, *d.*1870
—Legend of Vivia
Steele-*Ozark*, 65–69
Thompson, David
Man eaters
Thomson, E. W.
Red-headed Windego
THOR
The golden age in Asgard
How they went to Jotunheim
How Thor got his hammer
Ice castle of Utgard-Loke
The lay of thrym
Loki makes mischief
The Ragnarok, doom of the
gods
The stealing of Thor's hammer
—hammer
Loki and the dwarf
THOR (subject)
—Myths and legends of the
Vikings
Lindow-*Myths*, 15–18
Thor fights the giant Krangnir
Branston-*Gods,* 107–111
Thor goes fishing

Branston-*Gods,* 112–115
Thor goes fishing with Hymir
Crossley-*Legends,* 212–214
Thor in the giant's strong-hold
Branston-*Gods,* 116–123
Thordur of Thrastastadir
Booss-*Scand.,* 600–601
THORKILL
City of the Not-Dead
THORNS
It started with a thorn
The robin
Thornstein staff-struck
Crossley-*Legends,* 155–163
THOROUGHNESS
The king's boatman
Thor's holiday
Branston-*Gods,* 124–129
Thorston and the dwarf
Keightley-*World* 70–71
Those stubborn souls, the Biellese
Yolen-*Favorite,* 176–177
Those three wishes
Gorog-*Taste,* 17–20
THOUGHT(S)
The elephant and his son
Four ages of thought
—eternal
Boy who was saved by his
thoughts
Thoughtlessness: "Bye-bye"
Wolkstein-*Magic,* 190–193
THRALLS
Heimdall in Midgard
THREAD
Princess Minon-Minette
—ball of
The son of the goblin
The story of Jon Asmundsson
The three bears. See Goldilocks
and the three bears
The three bears [the first printed
version]
Lang-*Green,* 236–241
Three billy goats Bruse [sic]
Lofgren-*Boy,* 29–31

The three billy goats Gruff
  Baskin-*Imps*, 34–35
  Classic Child., 55–59
  dePaola-*Favorite*, 42–45
  Oxenbury-*Nursery*, 54–57
  Tudor-*Bedtime*, [16–17]
The three billy-goats who
    went . . . to get fat
  Booss-*Scand.*, 29–30
The three brothers
  Griego-*Cuentos*, 97–109
The three brothers [camel stolen &
    butchered]
  Schwartz-*Elijah*, 4–6
Three brothers [craft contest]
  Lang-*Pink/D*, 73–75
  Lang-*Pink/K*, 50–52
The three caskets
  Shah-*World*, 226–229
Three challenges for King Solomon
  Campos-*Mexican*, 99–103
Three corpses, money, and a wine-
    bottle
  Zong-*Korea*, 186
The three counsels
  Aiken-*Mexican*, 26–29
The three daughters
  Riordan-*Tartary*, 104–105
The three daughters and the lost
    cow
  Hyde-Chambers-*Tibet*,104–
    106
Three dogs [named Salt, Pepper,
    Mustard]
  Lang-*Green*, 294–300
Three evil wives punished
  O'Sullivan-*Legends*, 84–85
"THREE FATES"
  Moerae
The three feathers
  Shub-*About*, 58–61
The three fish [wise; clever; stupid]
  Wood-*Kalila*, 102–108
Three foolish brides
  Zong-*Korea*, 194
Three former lives

Roberts-*Chinese*, 162–164
The three golden hairs of Old Man
    Almanack
  Wood-*Palace*, 45–56
The three heads of the well
  Crossley-*Folk*, 20–24
Three heroes [and the 3-headed
    boa]
  Minford-*Fav.*, 180–194
The three imposters
  Shah-*World*, 254–256
The three lemons
  Booss-*Scand.*, 144–148
The three leprechauns
  Keightley-*World*, 379–382
The three little pigs
  dePaola-*Favorite*, 34–39
  Lang-*Green*, 147–151
  Oxenbury-*Nursery*, 25–31
  Pierce-*Larousse*, 103–104
Three little pigs [houses: mud, cab-
    bage, brick]
  Lang-*Green*, 393–397
Three musicians [princess under
    spell]
  Lang-*Green*, 286–293
The three old men
  Weiss-*Russian*, 131–138
Three priests
  Sampson-*Gypsy*, 41–43
Three rosebushes
  Shannon-*Solve*, 30–33
The three sillies [imagined future
    evils]
  Ross-*Druids*, 10–22
  Yolen-*Favorite*, 170–173
Three sisters
  Sampson-*Gypsy*, 24–26
Three sisters were entrapped into a
    mountain
  Crossley-*Folk*, 123–127
Three snake-leaves
  Lang-*Green*, 341–346
The three sons
  Patai-*Gates*, 542–548
  Zong-*Korea*, 146–149

The three stars
Zong-*Korea*, 13–14
Three strong women: Forever
Mountain [Japan]
Phelps-*Tatterhood*, 39–48
Riordan-*Woman*, 59–68
Three suitors for a wooden statue
Elbaz-*Folktales*, 123–124
The three talismans
Riordan-*Tartary*, 83–93
Three thieves [eggs, shoe soles,
food]
O'Connor-*Tibet*, 80–91
Three unmarried ministers
Zong-*Korea*, 106–110
The three wishes
Fattoross-*Simpleton*, 67–72
Robertson-*Highland*, 160–161
Tudor-*Bedtime*, [8–9]
Three wishes [of Billy Dawson]
Yeats-*Fairy*, 214–233
The three witches of Kintail
Robertson-*Highland*, 92–96
THRESHERS AND THRESHING
Dream of Owen O'Mulready
Munachar and Manachar
THRIFT
The foolish jackal
A rare bargain
THRIFT (flower)
Nasturtium, stock, thrift
Through the door
Ainsworth-*Phantom*, 157–176
THRUSHES
Why the sun rises when the
rooster crows
Thumbelina
Andersen-*Hague*, 67–82
Ehrlich-*Random*, 194–205
Lewis-*Minute*, 20–21
Pierce-*Larousse*, 144–156
"THUMBELINA" STORIES
Little Finger of the watermelon
patch
[Thumbling, three inches tall]
Seekers Saviors, 103–105

THUMBS
—thumb-sucking
Oona and the giant Cuchulain
THUNDER
The sky beings
Ua-pa-chi (Kickapoo titles)
A well-deserved punishment
—"Mother Thunder"
Hob and the storm
—origin
How thunder and lightning
came to be
"THUNDER GOD"
Gods of the elements
How Aisu found the happy
land
Thunderbird
De Wit-*Talking*, 27–33
THUNDERBIRDS
Big bird of south Texas
Thurber, James, 1894–1962
The night the ghost got in
Thurkill's beard
Marshall-*Every.*, 191–200
Thurnley Abbey
Hoke-*Spirits*, 67–84
THURSDAY
—magic
The nack's reel
Tia Miseria's pear tree
McCarty-*Skull*, 70–75
TIAMAT
The Dragon [Marduk and
Tiamat]
TIANDI (god)
The giant without a head
Isles of the blest
Yu controls the flood
TIARAS
The dewdrop tiara
Tibast and vandelrot
Lindow-*Swedish*, 109–110
Tibble Castle and Klinta Spring
Booss-*Scand.*, 300–302
TIBET
The bird of happiness

TIBET (continued)
The blossom tree
The castle in the lake
The clever mice
The creation
The disrespectful son
Favorite verses, proverbs, and riddles
The frog
Gesar of Ling
How Asanga came to see the future Buddha
The island of beautiful women
The kind man
The lovers
The magic bamboo
The missing treasure
The monkeys and the moon
The Nomad
One hairball
Opame, Chenrezik, and Dolma
Padmasambhava and the felicity scarf
The prayer that was answered
Supparaka
Tale of the golden vase and the . . .
The three daughters and the lost cow
The Tibetan envoy's mission
Tibet's first king
The umbrella tree
The weathermaker
The white rooster
Who is my neighbour?
The young man who refused to kill
The Tibetan envoy's mission
Jagendorf-*Magic*, 57–60
TIBETAN TALES (subject)
—[People, places, culture]
Timpanelli-*Tales*, vii–x
—[Twenty-two stories]
O'Connor-*Tibet*, 1–176
Tibet's first king
Hyde-Chambers-*Tibet*, 19–20

Tiburon: a pelagic scavenger
Water Spirits, 62–63
TICKING
The Metronome
TIDES
Fairest of all others
The man who sat on the tide
—control of
Happy hunter and the skilful fisher
Tidings of the heavens
Lehane-*Wizards*, 88–95
T'ien the brave, hero of the Hsia River
Jagendorf-*Magic*, 83–86
"TIENS-BON-LA"
The baker's magic wand
The tiger and the dwarf
Zong-*Korea*, 78–81
The tiger and the jackal
Phelps-*Maid*, 65–68
The tiger and the man
O'Connor-*Tibet*, 6–11
The tiger and the palanquin
Raychaudhuri-*Stupid*, 44–46
The tiger and the persimmon
Zong-*Korea*, 184
Tiger and the rabbit
Seros-*Sun*, 46–51
The tiger behind the fox
Roberts-*Chinese*, 67
Tiger boys
Roberts-*Chinese*, 102–103
The tiger-eating jackal cubs
Raychaudhuri-*Stupid*, 65–68
The tiger girl
Zong-*Korea*, 88–89
Tiger King's skin cloak [Mongolia]
Magic Knife, 46–57
The tiger priest
Zong-*Korea*, 90–92
TIGERS
The boarded window [by Bierce]
Brer tiger and the big wind
Buddhur Bap

The competitive tiger
Father Wren and King Tiger
Fatima and the tiger
Hong Do-Ryong, the filial tiger
How the monkey and goat
    earned their reputations
How the monkey got a drink
    when he was thirsty
How the monkey got food
    when he was hungry
Human bait
In a dim room [by Dunsany]
The last tiger in Haiti
Majantali Sarkar
Mouse's three children [tiger,
    peacock, boy]
Narahari Das
Nazar the Brave ["kills a thou-
    sand with a single blow"]
The old tiger and the hare
One hairball
"Papa God first, man next, ti-
    ger last"
The red stream
The repentant tiger of
    Chaoch'eng
Shooting the moon; a Yao
    folktale
The sparrows and the tiger
The story of the house
The stupid tiger
Sun and moon
The tale of the trusty tiger
Tall tales (Burma)
Traveller, the fox and the tiger
The umbrella tree
Uncle tiger and his nephew the
    jackal
Who got brer Gilyard's
    treasure?
Why the tiger and the stag fear
    each other
Why tigers have stripes
The wicked tiger
The young gentleman and the
    tiger
—dancing
    The three sons
—eats (human) mother, bit by bit
    The sun and the moon
—foolish
    Good faith
    How the hare got his split
        lip
—killed by housewife
    The white-eared tiger
—loved by man, so must die
    The tiger girl
—man-eating
    Curse on the only son
    Little Elga
—origin of spots; fear of man
    How Aisu found the happy
        land
—origin of stripes
    How the tiger got his stripes
    Why the tiger is striped
—outsmarted
    The stupid fox [and trapped
        tiger]
—raising human children
    Greedy Kanchuga
—tricked by farmer's wife
    The tiger and the jackal
—tricked by jackals
    Jackals and the tiger
—tricked/fooled
    The ungrateful tiger
—warned not to hunt man
    The tiger and the man
Tigers forever
    Royds-*Animals*, 35–55
The tiger's grave
    Zong-*Korea*, 82–84
TIGGY-WINKLE, Mrs.
    The tale of Mrs Tiggy-Winkle
Tight-fisted farmer and clever
    farmhand
    Stuchl-*American*, 125–130
TIGHTROPES
—walking
    Tyl on a tightrope

TIGRESSES
    The hungry tigress
Tikka the tailor
    Sperry-*Where*, 31–44
The tile-stove jumping over the
        brook
    Keightley-*World*, 127
Till Eulenspiegel. *See* EU-
        LENSPIEGEL, Till
TIME
    The dawn of the world
    The dead bridegroom
    Maui slows down the sun
    The Norns
    The orge's soul
    The stolen princess
    A tale of love
    Urashima
    Urashima Taro
—Buddhism
    The world in a pillow
—in fairy land
    The fairy grotto
—illusion (non-aging, non-passage,
        time warps, &)
    The beggar king [Solomon and
        Asmodeus]
    The dragon-king's palace:
        Urashima Taro
    Elves ask a servant girl to be
        godmother
    The land where time stood still
    The enchanted journey [time
        warp]
    [Little bird singing: angel of
        death]
    One night in Paradise [300
        years pass unnoticed] (Italy)
    A princess on a swing
    Uraschimataro and the turtle
—lapses
    A resumed identity
—lapses (subject) - [supernatural]
    Briggs-*Vanish.*, 11–26
—non-aging in
    See above under—illusion

Time and eternity
    Nicholson-*Mexican*, 19–35
A time for everything
    Aiken-*Mexican*, 3–4
TIME MACHINES
    A most unusual murder
Time-lapse. *See* TIME—lapses.
Time to think [crossroads: fatal
        accidents]
    Marshall-*Every.*, 155–163
Time warps. *See* TIME—illusion.
The timid frogs
    Reed-*Aboriginal*, 30–33
TIMIDITY
    Valiant John
The tinder-box
    Booss-*Scand.*, 454–460
    Pierce-*Larousse*, 19–26
The tinker and the ghost
    Yolen-*Favorite*, 435–438
Tinkerbell
    Baskin-*Imps*, 32–33
TINKERS
    About Abner the tinker
    Far Darrig in Donegal
The tinkling laugh
    Segovia-*Spanish*, 137–187
Tiny people. *See* LITTLE PEOPLE
TIPIS (WIGWAMS)
    Anpao is born
—dew cloth (inner lining)
    The wicked sister-in-law
Ti-Ra-Wa (god)
    The poor lame horse
TIR-NAN-OG
    The enchanted island
    Oisin in Tir Nan Og, or last of
        the Fena
    The phantom islands
TIR NAN OG (subject)
    Briggs-*Vanish.*, 22, 36
Tir-na-n-Og [youth]
    Yeats-*Fairy*, 179–191, 291
Tismila wanders through the forest
    Stuchl-*American*, 161
Titania and Oberon

Baskin-*Imps*, 12–13
TITANS
    The new gods-*Zeus and Hera*
TITANS (subject)
    Pinsent-*Greek*, 144 (index)
    Scott-*Fantastic*, 39–60
TITMOUSE (bird)
    Lippo and Tapio
    Two weak ones against one
        strong one
—short tongue
    Spearfinger, the witch
Titty Mouse and Tatty Mouse
    Royds-*Animal*, 56–59
Tiyo appears before Snake Mana
    Mullett-*Spider*, 29–33
Tiyo meets Spider Woman
    Mullett-*Spider*, 15–21
Tiyo rejoins his clan
    Mullett-*Spider*, 37–43
Tiyo returns home
    Mullett-*Spider*, 33–37
Tiyo travels through the underworld
    Mullett-*Spider*, 21–28
Tiyo's story
    Mullett-*Spider*, 7–14
TLALOC
    The fifth and final sun
Tloque Nahuaque
    Nicholson-*Mexican*, 116–119
To kill Windigo
    Colombo-*Wind.*, 123
To starch a spook [deghosting a
    house]
    Manley-*Fun*, 159–177
The toad and the boy
    Zitkala-*Old*, 119–127
The toad and the fire
    Wilbert-*Bororo*, 23–24
The toad-bridegroom
    Seros-*Sun*, 32–37
    Yolen-*Favorite*, 112–115
    Zong-*Korea*, 175–178
TOADS
    Adventures of John Dietrich
    The big turtle

    The brothers and the singing
        toad
    Fairy frog (condensed)
    [Glooskap] Gluscap, lord of the
        north
    The hill folk
    Horse and toad
    How the toad got his bruises
    Race between toad and
        donkey
    The Seneca chief's adventures
    Thumbelina
    The ungrateful tiger
    Why the lamb is meek
—as migrant labor
    Hyena engages a strange-
        farmer
—origin: flat nose
    How turtle came
TOADS (subject)
    Briggs-*Vanish.*, 77–78, 99–100
Toads and diamonds [from speech]
    Lang-*Blue*, 286–289 (notes,
        371)
    Mulherin-*Favorite*, 54–59; in-
        trod., 52
    Rackham-*Fairy*, 184–186
Toads: belled and beribboned
    dancers
    Lehane-*Wizards*, 119
Toad's wedding [to Miss Mouse] [in
    verse]
    Wahl-*Needle*, 11–16
Toadstools
    Froud-*Faeries*, unp
TOBACCO
    The Aturuarodo legend
    The fire plume
    Master Tobacco
—found in stomach of fish
    [Origin of tobacco] The Kud-
        dogo fish
Tobacco fairy from the Blue Hills
    Macmillan-*Canadian* 220–223
Tobias goes on a journey
    Crouch-*Whole*, 101–108

Today's laughter, tomorrow's
	sadness
	Villa-*Armenian,*403–405
Todhunter, J.
	How Thomas Connolly met the
	banshee
To-Dola
	Stokes-*Turtle,* 107–109
Todzi-touega
	Walking-*Song,* 17–20
Tokanao: the first coconut
	Stokes-*Turtle,* 15–16
Tokarsberget's treasure
	Lindow-*Swedish,* 76–77
TOKOLOSHI
	Calabash child [born to First
	Woman]
Tokoloshi [origin of herds and
	flocks]
	Pitcher-*Tokol.,* 10–13
TOLAI (people)
	Five strange plants
TOLKIEN, J. R. R.
	Lord of the rings
Toller's neighbors
	Booss-*Scand.,* 479–482
	Crossley-*Folk,* 150–153
Tolstoy, Leo
	Let the fire burn, you cannot
	put it out
	The three old men
	Where love is, God is
TOLTECS
	Quetzalcoatl in Tula
TOLTECS (subject)
	Nicholson-*Mexican,* 144
	(index)
Tom Hickathrift and the old giant
	Classic Child., 12–17
Tom Thumb
	Classic Child., 33–39
	Stovicek-*Around,* 48–51
	Tarrant-*Fairy,* 34–50
TOM THUMB (subject)
	Shah-*World,* 21
Tom Tit Tot

Crossley-*Folk,* 49–53
Garner-*British,* 9–15
Shah-*World,* 120–123
Tomik and the magic mat
	Hill-*More,* 75–85
Tomlin [elf-knight]
	Lurie-*Clever,* 104–110
Tommy the faithful trout
	Stuchl-*American,* 227–229
Tomorrow's child
	Hoke-*Horrors,* 55–62
TOMTE [Tomte = plural; Tomtar =
	singular]
	Encounters with tomtar
	Exorcising the tomte
	The missing butter
	New clothes for the tomte
—friendly, at sea
	A ship's tomte
TOMTE (subject)
	Briggs-*Vanish.,* 63, 200
	Lindow-*Swedish,* 40–42, 218
The tomte carries a single straw
	Lindow-*Swedish,* 138–139
The tomte learns to rest
	Lindow-*Swedish,* 140–141
The tomte's favorite horse
	Lindow-*Swedish,* 142–143
TOMTRA
	Nissen and Tomtra
The tomts
	Booss-*Scand.,* 285
TONGA
	The plot to kidnap the Queen
	[Salamasina]
—conquest of Samoa
	Brave warrior, Malietoa!
The tongue-cut sparrow
	See The sparrow with the slit-
	tongue
TONGUE(S)
	The goblin and the grocer
	The goblin and the huckster
	The little mermaid
—made 100 feet long
	Magic mallet

The mallet of wealth
Tonweya and the eagles
  Yellow Robe-*Tonweya*, 102–114
TOOLS
—magic: knife, flint, spear
  The poor man Monokto
TOOTH FAIRIES
  Hob and Tooth Fairy
  The tooth fairy
    Baskin-*Imps*, 16–17
  The tooth of gold
    Alken-*Mexican*, 72–76
  The toothpick [snowed-in]
    Stuchl-*American*, 41–44
TOOTHPICKS
  The golden toothpick
  The topknot pigeons, Goolahwilleel
    Parker-*Australian*, 65–66
TOPS
—humming
  The lost hum
TOR, Sir
  Sir Tor's adventure
TORAH
  Innocent prisoner marries a
    princess
  King David matches wits with
    Angel of Death
  King who fought many wars
  Legend of b'ne Moshe
  Reward of study
  Why do Jews rock when
    studying
—studying, in heaven
  The extinguished lights
TORAH (subject)
  Nahman-*Tales*, 334
Toribugu: legend of the hero
  Wilbert-*Bororo*, 198–210
Tortoise and elephant: smallness
  not an illness
  Todd-*Some*, 30–34
Tortoise and hare: a dying wish
  Todd-*Tortoise*, 17–19
Tortoise and hare: intelligence
  beats speed

Todd-*Tortoise*, 14–15
Tortoise and hare: intelligence
  beats strength
  Todd-*Some*, 36–39
Tortoise and hawk: never laugh at
  friends
  Todd-*Some*, 18–21
  Todd-*Tortoise*, 3–5
Tortoise and his mother: eye not
  always accurate
  Todd-*Some*, 48–49
Tortoise and his mother: wise man
  dies, . . . buries him
  Todd-*Some*, 52–59
Tortoise and pig: good acts not al-
  ways rewarded
  Todd-*Some*, 24–28
  Todd-*Tortoise*, 7–9
Tortoise and the elephants: fine
  goods often come in small
  packages
  Todd-*Tortoise*, 11–12
The tortoise and the hare
  dePaola-*Favorite*, 112–113
  Ross-*Druids*, 48–51
  Watson-*Aesop*, 2–3
The tortoise and the monkey
  O'Connor-*Tibet*, 141–146
Tortoise, goat and leopard: corpse
  has few desires
  Todd-*Some*, 44–47
Tortoise, goat and lion: the price of
  wisdom
  Todd-*Tortoise*, 23–24
TORTOISES
  See also TURTLES
  Elephant and the tortoise
  Fudo and the prickly pear
    thieves
  Hare and the tortoise [the true
    story]
  Isles of the blest
  Leopard, the squirrel, and the
    tortoise
  The slowest may win the race
  Urashima

TORTOISES (continued)
—hoarding wisdom
    Wisdom belongs to everyone
—kills mother
    The eye can deceive
—origin of characteristics
    Why the cracks in tortoise's shell
—protects his mother
    O no, not my mother!
TORTURE
    Marko's [Kraljevic] smile
    The triumph of death
TOTEMS
    The singing frog
    The stone frogs, the Youayah
      Mayamah
Touch not a married woman
    Patai-*Gates*, 530–533
TOURNAMENTS
    The princess, the horse, and
      the she-devil
Tower of Babel
    Patai-*Gates*, 519–522
TOWERS
    Legend of Melusina
    Mice in the corn
—prison
    Maid Maleen
    The prince and his fate
    The princess in the ivory tower
    Princess in the tower
    The quest for the Star of the
      Sea
Town mouse and country mouse
    Watson-*Aesop*, 10–13
Town of stone
    Villa-*Armenian*, 411–412, 529
Town where none might go to
    sleep
    Radin-*African*, 247–249
TOWNS
    Little Tuk
A toy for the giant
    Lindow-*Swedish*, 80–81
TOYS AND TOY SHOPS
    The flying kite

    Ha, ha, Jack-in-the-box!
    Little Elga
    The lost hum
TRADE(S)
    The Pleiades
—value in having alternative trade
    The Amir who became a
      weaver
TRADERS AND TRADING
    The stolen lady
    What the old man does is al-
      ways right
—foolish
    Mister Vinegar
—for profit
    Smallboy and his halfpenny
      wife
TRAGEDY
    The farmer of Liddesdale
    Grania and Diarmid
The tragic story of Antigone
    Lines-*Greek*, 111–121
TRAILER(S)
    The haunted trailer [by R.
      Arthur]
TRAIN ROBBERIES
    Locomotive Bill
TRAINS
—passengers
    Thurnley Abbey
—"Tokyo Express"
    Sumi and the goat and the
      Tokyo Express
TRAMPS
    Lodging for the night
    Nail soup (Sweden)
    [The old, vagrant woman and]
      The three bears
    The old woman and the tramp
    The parson and the clerk [II]
The transferred ghost
    Manley-*Fun*, 129–143
Transformation [motif index]
    Wilbert-*Bororo*, 246–248, 322–
    323
TRANSFORMATIONS

See also CONJURING; CON-
STELLATIONS; DIS-
GUISES; ENCHANTMENT;
EVIL EYE; SHAPE-
SHIFTERS
Abo Beckeer
Animals transformed into
humans
The apples of eternal life
The archer who went I know
not where to . . .
Artemis and Apollo
Bear cub [and six companions]
Beauty and the beast
The blue lake
The boy and the dragon
Boy of the red twilight sky
The castle in the lake
The cat woman (France)
Cinderella
Conflict of the magicians
Conn-eda; or The golden ap-
ples of Lough Erne
The Cormorants of Andvaer
The cricket
Crystal coffin
Daughter of the stars
The destruction of Da Derga's
hostel
El Diablo, el chivo, y Senor
Bonifacio
The doctor and his pupil
Downfall of the mighty hunter
The dragon who cried
The dream of Oengus
Drolmakyid the fairy [Tibetan]
East of the sun and west of
the moon
The enchanted buck
The enchanted fountain
Enchanted youth: Osseo and
Oweenee
The Eskimo Indian and his fox
wife
The everlasting frogs [daugh-
ters turned to]

The fairy and the prince
The flies and the bees
Foolish Vanya and Princess
Helena the Fair
The frog
Galo and Vasiri
Genie of the mountains
Giant with the grey feathers
A girl in green
The girl who always cried
The goddess who drank blood
Gulnara the Tartar warrior
Halva-maker
The handsome suitor. [B]
The Hedley Kow
The herd-boy
Hong Do-Ryong, the filial tiger
How Jiculi served his tribe
How the pigeon became a
tame bird
How the seven brothers saved
their sister
Husband and wife should
share equally
Iktomi and the fawn
The iron wolf
Ivan the peasant's son and the
three dragons
Janet and Tamlin
Journey of Nonogo Pori
[Katla protects Odd by 'sight
blinding']
Kertong
King Sivi
King Zargand's daughter
The king's daughter and the
pepper man
Lady White and Shushuan
Leaves that hung but never
grew
Libor and the swan princess
The little wise woman
The lost bell
Love: queen and foundling
Luch and the sons of Tuirenn
The magic fruit

514

—bear/prince into human
Ursulo, hijo del oso
—beaver to men
Raven steals the salmon from
the beaver house
—birds
Jorinde and Joringel: Castle of
the Birds
—blackened face, to whiteness
The cave of emeralds
—bone to girl to fox
The nine-tailed fox
—Bororo into woodpecker
Meri steals an ax
—boy into ant
The giant with three golden
hairs
—boy into carp
The promise
—boy into giant
The lizard who came from
nowhere
—boy (swallows pearl) to dragon
The guardian dragon's magic
pearl
—boy to bird
Meru the stingray
—bride-to-be into salmon
The fate of Aino
—brother into bluejay
Woodpecker and bluejay: a
sad tale
—brother into kid (goat)
Sister Alyonushka and Brother
Ivanushka
—brother into stag
Yeghnig Aghpar
—bug into birds, for arrow feathers
Baitogogo and the arrows
—bushpigs into people
Why one does not reveal the
origin of another
—butterfly into man
The woman and the butterflies
—caliph into stork
Caliph Stork

—cat into stallion
The cat Johann
—chicken into turtle
The reason for turtles
—children into flying foxes
The children of the Omokoy
tribe
—children into porpoises
The porpoises of Koromira
—children into swans
Fate of the children of Lir
—crocodile into king
King Crocodile
—cruel mothers into animals
Origin of the stars and of certain animals
—cruel sisters into aspens
The Indian Cinderella
—daughter into owl
Owl with the face of a woman
—daughter to frogs to stones
The stone frogs, the Youayah
Mayamah
—devil into boar
The devil invented alcoholic
drink
—devil into mouse, then eaten by
cat
The tailor and the deev
—dog into Indian maid
Rising Star finds a wife [dog]
[Tewa]
—dog into woman
Story of a flood
—donkey into man
Donkeys of Jolof
—donkeys into humans
The two donkeys
—doves into girls
Metugoe doves and the widow
—doves into women
Metugoe doves and the Indian
Magurereu
—drowned girl into small bird
The bird and the sea: Jingwei
—effected by Great Spirit

516

TRANSFORMATIONS—effected
    by Great Spirit (continued)
    The snail and the beaver
—farmer into frog
    Those stubborn souls, the
    Biellese
—father into whirlwind
    The mopoke, and the mosquito
    bird
—father into stingray
    Meru the stingray
—fear makes permanent
    Enchantment of Earl Gerald
—fisherman into kingfisher
    Meri steals a bow
—fool into prince
    Chestnut grey
—frog into lady
    The frog princess
—frog into princess
    Frog princess: Vassilisa the
    Wise
—frog to man
    Frog who became an emperor
—fur pelts from ear tips
    The woman and the giant
—ghost into sheep
    Sung Ting-po catches a ghost
—giant into foundling
    Iya, the camp-eater
—giant into mountain
    Kuafu chases the sun
—girl into dog
    The laird's lass and the
    gobha's son
—girl into dove
    Suit of white feathers
    (Dongxiang)
—girl into duck
    Maiden Bright-Eye
—girl into goose
    Ayoga
—girl into gull
    The bird-bride
—girl into toad
    Puddocky

—girl (spoiled) turns self into swan
    Discontented Lado
—girls into elephants
    The elephant girls
—girls into stone
    Kuma and Aua
    Three sisters
—gold into pastry
    Rent-day
—hedgehog into boy
    Baba Yaga and the hedgehog
—hibernating bear into prince
    The fox who went to heaven
—horse into fox
    The golden knucklebone
—horse into woman
    The black mare
—horse's skin into palace
    The boy, his sisters, and the
    magic horse
—human into parrot
    The greedy boy
—human into toad
    The toad-bridegroom
—hunters into stars
    Redbreasts: the Gwineeboos
—husband into bird
    The magic box
—husband into snake
    Medicine is not a plaything
—husband kills self, becomes
    bluebird
    Mud-snail fairy
—Indian hunter into puma
    Pumah, the mighty hunter
—Indian into eagle
    The legend of Eagleman
—Indian into fly
    The legend of Eagleman
—Indian maid into stone
    The stone maiden
—Indian to beaver, to elk, to brant
    Grasshopper [Indian
    superman]
—king into blue bird
    Blue bird [King Charming]

—leaves into birds
  How Glooskap made the birds
—loaves into dogs
  Chavalai: taboos and
    deception
—loon in form of man
  Sedna (Eskimo)
—maiden to waterlily
  Water lily: the gold spinners
—man in form of dog
  Knight of the Glens and Bens
    and Passes
—man into bear
  Choril and Cholchinay
—man into eagle-hawk
  The eagle hawk
—man into fish
  Suited to be a fish [eaten by
    colleagues]
—man into hog, by day
  Prince White Hog
—man into macaw, to provide ar-
    row feathers
  Butoreagaddu legend
—man into monkey
  Donkeys of Jolof
—man into mule
  The man turned into mule
—man into snake
  King of snakes
—man into stone
  Hailibu the hunter
  Pedro de Ordinales goes to
    heaven
—man into tiger
  The censor and the tiger
—man into white crow
  Leaving home
—man (ox) eats onions, returns to
    human form
  Onions
—man to vegetable
  The witch and the cabbage
—men into hawks
  Cibairago and her husband
  Jure [snake]

—men into wild boars
  Fishing of the women [adultery
    with otters]
—men to birds
  Zan and the Dactyls in early
    Crete
—multiple
  Chavalai: taboos and
    deception
  Give me something you
    have . . . unawares
  Sorcerer's apprentice
—nag into ship
  King of the herrings
—ogre into old woman
  Ogre of Rashomon
—old man into nag
  King of the herrings
—people into donkeys
  The magic bird-heart
—prince into bear
  East o' sun and west o' the
    moon
—prince into falcon
  Finist the Falcon
—prince into fly/spy
  Darakhvei, the great oak
—prince into kid (goat)
  Sister Alionushka, Brother
    Ivanushka
—prince into mare
  The conceited prince
—prince into snake
  Enchanted snake
—prince into turtle
  Immortal mountains [Mon-
    golia]
—prince to crab
  Water lily: the gold spinners
—prince to frog
  The frog prince
—princes into foals
  The seven foals
—prince/sons [12] into geese
  Twelve wild geese
—princess into dove

TRANSFORMATIONS—princess
  into dove (continued)
    The white dove [princess un-
      der spell]
—princess into milestone
    King Kojata
—princess into owl
    Caliph Stork
—princess into serpent
    The little soldier
—princess to ducks
    King Kojata
—as punishment
    Math, son of Mathonwy
—as punishment: devil transforms
  man into horse
    The peasant and the fiend
—queen into ugly old woman
    He who laughs last, laughs
      best
—Queen to doe
    The white doe
—rabbit, to raven, to fish
    The troll's daughter
—rattlesnake into woman
    Stepmother's head
—raven into deer
    Raven brings fire
—raven into human fetus
    The raven and the ball of light
—raven to fisherman
    Raven and the big fisherman
—raven to human fetus
    Raven steals the light
—red bird into Indian
    The boy who wore turtle shell
      moccasins
—rich boy to donkey
    Servant in the monastery
—river god to sea serpent
    When gods and men mingled
—ruler into ox
    When gods and men mingled
—sea petrel in human form
    Angakok and Mother of Seals
      [sea petrel]
—servant into stone
    Faithful John
—Shun to dragon
    Shun, the wise emperor
—sister into woodpecker
    Woodpecker and bluejay: a
      sad tale
—slave into wolf
    Gray wolf's haint
—slave/husband into pine tree
    Poor Sandy [conjure woman]
—slaveowner into slave
    Master James' nightmare
—snail into woman
    Mud-snail fairy
—snake to worm
    The seven-day vigil
—son to part-hedgehog
    Hans my Hedgehog
—sons into doves
    Papa God sends turtle doves
—sorcerer into wolf
    Chavalai: taboos and
      deception
—sparrow/princess
    Sparrow with the slit-tongue
—squirrel to woman
    The squirrel wife
—statue comes to life
    Three suitors for a wooden
      statue
—stepchildren into swans
    Lir, Aoife, and his children
—stepdaughter under witch's spell
    Laidley worm of Spindlestone
      Heugh
—stepfather into elephant
    Shun, the wise emperor
—stepmother into vampire bat
    Fate of the children of Lir
—storm petrel as man
    Sedna, the witch under the
      sea
—stump into elk
    The hunting of the elk
—swan into princess

The swan princess
—swan to woman
 The swan maiden (Sweden)
—sycamore fruit into children
 The woman and the children of
  the sycamore
—three daughters into swans
 Green Man of No Man's Land
—"tiger man" - *multiple*
 Greedy Kanchuga
—tigers in form of humans
 Four sworn brothers
—turtle into woman
 The turtle wife
—turtle into princess
 The dragon-king's palace:
  Urashima Taro
—unkind girl into goat
 The baker's daughter
—vulture into man
 Phikool Thong
—wife into hound
 [Iollan and his fairy mistress]
—wife into Sheldrake duck
 The duck with red feet
—wife into sow
 Little cinder girl
—wife to heifer, by choice
 Pilar's indiscretion
—witch rides man t'd into horse
 The blacksmith's wife of Yarrowfoot (Scotland)
—witch to weasel
 Revenge of Joaquina
—witch transforms princess into
  duck
 The white duck
—wives leave husbands, become
  bats
 The bat-women of Koitabu
—wolf into form of girl
 The gray wolf
—wolf into princess
 The firebird
 Ivan Tsarevich, the wolf, and
  the firebird

—woman executed, turns into rain
  bird
 The rain bird
 Bougoodoogahdah
—woman in form of owl
 Stepmother's head
—woman into bluebird
 Bird from the golden land
—woman into cat
 The white cat
—woman into deer
 The hunting of the hind
—woman into fish
 Fisherman and the prince
—woman into mouse
 Manawydan, son of Llyr
—woman into spider
 Arachne
—woman into trout
 White trout: a legend of Cong
 The white trout; a legend of
  Cong
—woman into turtle
 Turtle skin
—woman to sow
 The bell-shaped pendant
—women (abducted) into goldfish
 Ruslan and Chernomor
—women into owls
 The dance of the owls
—women into rosebushes
 Three rosebushes
—worm, to dog, to man
 Panhu, the marvellous dog
TRANSFORMATIONS (subject)
—fairy
 Briggs-*Vanish.*, 218 (index)
TRANSMIGRATION
 The monk from Everclear
TRANSPLANTATION OF
  ORGANS
 Miaoshan-Guanyin, protectress
  of mortals
TRANSPORTATION
 Spirits and demons
 White cap

TRANSPORTATION (continued)
—magic
  Son of the Knight of the Green
    Vesture
—while asleep
  The butterflies carried him
    home [Tewa]
TRANSVESTISM
  Billy the milkmaid
TRANSYLVANIA
  [Count Dracula's castle]
TRAP-DOORS
  Three sisters were entrapped
    into a mountain
TRAPS
  The tiger and the palanquin
  Wise pigeon
—animal
  Smart head better than sharp
    teeth
—clever animal escapes
  Squirrel, leopard, and goat: do
    it again, then
TRAVEL
—magic
  Midnight funeral from America
—outside the body
  The Finn messenger (Norway)
Traveling musicians of Bremen
  Tudo-*Bedtime,* [30–31]
  See also The Bremen town
    musicians
The traveller and the innkeeper
  Stuchl-*American,* 50–54
Traveller, the fox, and the tiger
  Zong-*Korea,* 174–175
TRAVELLERS
  The Byse
  The companion
  The genesis of the Hid-folk
  Melmoth the doomed wanderer
  The seven fathers in the house
  Soup from a sausage skewer
  Stan Bolovan and the dragon
  A stork is not always a stork
  The umbrella tree

  The witches' excursion
The travelling companion
  Shah-*World,* 54–64
Travels of a fox
  Ross-*Druids,* 23–33
Travels with Mozart
  Roberts-*Jung,* 53–59
TREACHERY
  See also STEPMOTHERS;
    WITCHES
  Aladdin and the wonderful lamp
  Ali Baba and the forty thieves
  Azad Bakht's tale
  The badger and the rabbit
  The baker's magic wand
  Bird from the golden land
  The camel, lion, leopard, crow,
    & jackal
  The cat and the mice
  Cibairago and her husband
    Jure [snake]
  Cock with the golden feathers
  The crane and the crab
  Creator Nyame and his four
    wives
  The daughter and the helper
  Degei and his sons
  Disappearing apples [of
    immortality]
  The exile of the sons of Uisliu
  Fair Margaret
  The fire bird and Ryska and
    vixen
  The firebird
  The first mosquito
  First pig and porcupine
  Fishing of the women [adultery
    with otters]
  Fox and the wolf
  Fudo and the prickly pear
    thieves
  Gheeger Gheeger the cold
    west wing
  The gift of the white cockatoo
  Glooskap and Malsum, the
    wolf

Golden blackbird
Gooloo the magpie, and the
Wahroogah
The goose girl
The great flood [deluge]
The guardian dragon's magic
pearl
Happy hunter and the skilful
fisher
How Aisu found the happy
land
The irangiri tree: ugly man
seeks a wife (Africa)
Ivan Tsarevich, the wolf, and
the firebird
Jesse James [song and story]
King Lindorm [a snake]
Kingdoms of copper, silver,
and gold
Leaves that hung but never
grew
Little Red Riding Hood
Llyr: children of the sea-god
The magic boat
Magic mirror of Rabbi Adam
Maid Maleen
Manora, the bird woman
The merchant's fortune
The Northern Lights
Orphan Yan Ran [Kawa]
Prince Feroz-Shah and the fly-
ing horse
The prince who had two eyes
The promise of the three
sisters
Quarrel of the monkey and the
crab
The queen's children
The rich boy and the poor
boy
Rising rock [Chiricahua]
Scabby: beauty is only skin
deep
The scabby child
Seven Simeons [brothers]
Shun, the wise emperor

Sister Alyonushka and Brother
Ivanushka
Snow White and the seven
dwarfs
Snuff-box [wishes-come-true]
Son of the gray horse
Story of Miriam
Strange tale of caribou and
moose
Three dogs [named Salt, Pep-
per, Mustard]
The tiger's grave
The tinkling laugh
Two brothers [and seven-
headed monster]
Water of life
Welsh enchanter's fosterling
The woman of discord
The wondrous fish-hook
The world below
—murder attempted
The golden haired twins
—servant-treated-as-son
An eventful pilgrimage
The treachery of Lelewaga
Stokes-*Turtle*, 73–75
Treachery of the Nibelungs
Lehane-*Legends*, 64–75
Treason in saints
Aiken-*Mexican*, 50–51
TREASURE
See also GOLD; JEWELS
Ali Baba and the forty thieves
The altar-cup in Angerup
Coffin cash
The enchanted forest
Fairy greyhound
The fisherman and his soul
Galveston Island: the treasure
Gesar of Ling
The giant maiden in Boraserod
mountain
Gold treasure of Mississippi
The haunted mill: or, The
ruined home
How Thor got his hammer

TREASURE (continued)
Katrineholm Manor
King Dabschelim [rules for governing]
The language of animals
The legend of Puill dugha Ghaunn
The living kuan-yin
The lost treasure
The magic candelabra
The man who knew the language of animals
The man-servant and the water-elves
Monacielli
My grandmother's story of buried treasure
Mysterious palace [Solomon & Ramirat]
Old troll tricked into revealing his treasure
Orpheus and Eurdice
Peddler of Swaffham (England)
Saxe of Saxeholm
The shepherd of Silfrun-Arstadir
The three daughters and the lost cow
Three musicians [princess under spell]
The tinker and the ghost
Tokarsberget's treasure
Value of a treasure house
Who got brer Gilyard's treasure?
—buried
Chisos ghosts
Curse of the devil's gold
—gold
How evil produces evil
—money found
A stroke of luck
—red garter on field of ragweed, to hide . . .
The leprechaun's trick

Treasure hunt
Villa-*Armenian*, 351–352
The treasure in Saby Creek
Booss-*Scand.*, 284–285
Treasure island: Tobermory argosy
Robertson-*Highland*, 105–108
Treasure Mountain; a Yao folktale
Sadler-*Treasure*, 3–15
Treasure of the magic icon
Elbaz-*Folktales*, 130–132
The treasure seekers
Booss-*Scand.*, 324–326
Treasure tales [six]
Steele-*Ozark*, 34–44
The treasure wrecks [Sinbad]
Rackham-*Fairy*, 93–97
Treasurer under suspicion
Villa-*Armenian*, 414–417
Treasures
Robe-*Hispanic*, 470–485
"TREE"
—spinning
The Norns
The tree-bound
Zitkala-*Old*, 77–89
Tree-guardians for a temple: Philemon and Baucis
Spells & Bind, 38–39
TREE-KANGAROOS
Why koala has no tail
TREE OF LIFE
The golden feather [talking colt]
Severi and Vappu
Tree people [four tales]
Reed-*Aboriginal*, 37–49
TREE PEOPLE (subject)
Scott-*Fantastic*, 151–164
TREE SPIRITS (subject)
Briggs-*Vanish.*, 74–76
Tree worship
Logan-*Old*, 18–19
TREES
See also names of particular species

See also FRUIT; ORCHARDS
—fruit
Alder
Ash
Bagged wolf
Child in the silk-cotton tree
The dwarfs on the tree
Faerie trees
Farmers three
The giant sturgeon
The golden tree [queen and
    amulet]
Leprechauns
Little One-Eye, . . . Two-Eyes,
    and . . . Three-Eyes
The mouse bride
The nine-seeded apple
Old man who made withered
    trees to flower
Pork and honey
Rowan
Sugar-plum tree [poem]
The tinder-box
Twigmuntus, Cowbelliantus,
    Perchnosius
Unantishee
Vily
Wejosis and the wind giant
Whitethorn
—blossom
The blossom tree
—chopping
Jack and the green lady
—crotches
Antti and the wizard's
    prophecy
—falling
The wolves of Cernogratz
—as father of boy
The great flood [deluge]
—fruit
How the monkey became a
    trickster
—Indian hunter held by
The twisting tree [Kiowa]
—limbs

The first humans
—magic growth
Udala tree
—magic, saves girl
To-Dola
—origin
Five strange plants
—sing to Lisalill
Lisalill
—spirits
The blossom tree
—stumps
The umbrella tree
—taboo
Fly together, chips and shav-
    ings!
—talks/helps deer
Good faith
—trunks
The Tibetan envoy's mission
—watering
The cripple
Tremsin and the maid of the sea
    May-Book, 1–11
TRESPASS
Goldilocks and the three
    bears
Trial and error creation
    Wright-Gold, 10–16
TRIALS (judicial)
—ghost testifies
John Tregeagle
Trials (tasks). See TESTS
TRIAMOR, Lady (fairy)
Lanval and the Lady Triamor
TRIANGLES
Triangulum (the Triangle)
Triangulum (the Triangle)
    Gallant-Constel., 102–103
TRIBAL GOVERNMENT
—justice
The bat Narahdarn
—leadership
Baitogogo and Akaruio Boroge
    renounce their powers
—teaching ways of

TRIBAL GOVERNMENT—teaching ways of (continued)
Uaboreu's journey in region of the Poxereu
Tribes. *See* INDIANS . . .
TRIBUTE
Mambu the orphan [tyrants' tribute]
The twins
TRICKERY
See also CLEVERNESS; DECEPTION; ESCAPES; HOAXES; IMPOSTERS; PRETENSE
The adventures of Iktomi
Adventures of Ntini, the small otter
The adventures of Yemima
Ash lad who had an eating match with the troll
The ashman's money
Axe porridge
The badger and the rabbit
B'er rabbit is an uncle
Big long man's corn patch
The biter bit
A boom in guarache leather
The boots of Hunain
Boy who overcame the giants
Boy-man
The brave clever tailor
Brave little tailor (seven at one blow)
The Bremen town musicians
Brer wolf's second pinder patch
Bridget and the Lurikeen
A broomstick trick [make glass of water stick to ceiling]
Bruin and Reynard partners
Bubbly's trick
Buddhur Bap
The building of the wall of Asgard
Bury me in England [fake-dying wish; humor]

Buzz-buzz aunty
Cannibal
Charge this to the cap
Chilbik and the greedy czar
The Christmas thief
The clever little tailor
Clever Tom and the leprechauns
Clever Yaro
The coal burner and the troll
Cottontail plays a trick on coyote
Coyote and skunk
Coyote and the quail
Coyote and turkey
Coyote's crying song
Crack and crook (Italy)
Crane, kangaroo rat, fire makers
The crooked pine
Cross purposes
The crow's call
The cruel painter
La cucaracha
The cunning Lapp
The cunning shoemaker
The dahut [hunting prohibited]
Daniel O'Connell [trickery]
Death and the soldier
The devil and his entanglements
Devil with the three golden hairs
The devil's bargain
The devil's yellehr [sic]
The doctor and his pupil
The dog and the possum [origin of enmity]
Dog captures the hyena
Donald and his neighbours [Hudden & Dudden]
Dream bread
Eagle hawk again
False witnesses
Far Darrig in Donegal
A farmer tricks a troll

Farmer who found his match in daughter-in-law
The field of Boliauns
Five strange plants
The flowers' forever land
The food balls [Kiowa]
Fox and the ant [race]
The fox and the Barkantz
Fox and the stork
The fox who went to heaven
The giant sturgeon
The giant's bride
The giant-slayer
The gingerbread boy
The gipsy baron
The girl who always cried
Goannas and porcupines
Gray wolf's haint
Half-ram leaves home
Hansel and Gretel
Hare and otter
Hare and the lions
Hare makes hyena his riding horse
Hare, the hyena, and the lioness's cave
The hares and the elephants
He comes from the east
The hen and the apple tree
Hermes, messenger of the gods
Honeyed words can't sweeten evil
Hot-foot Hannibal
How coyote stole fire
How hunter obtained money from friends . . .
How Ivan frightened away the robbers
How Ivanka freed muzhiks from landlord
How rabbit deceived fox
How rabbit got the best of coyote
How raven brought fire to the Indians
How Sainday brought the buffalo
How Saynday got the sun
How spider obtained the sky-god's stories
How the dragon was tricked
How the hare got his split lip
How the hare made a fool of the wolf
How the monkey and goat earned their reputations
How the monkey became a trickster
How the monkey escaped being eaten
How the monkey got a drink when he was thirsty
How the turtle got her shell
How to break a bad habit
Hudden and Dudden and Donald O'Neary
The hyena engages the hare as a gewel
Iain Beag MacAindra
The iguana and the black snake
Iktomi and the ducks
Iktomi and the muskrat
"I'm Tipingee, she's Tipingee, we're Tipingee, too"
Jack the giant-killer
The jackal, the dove, and the panther
Jean Sotte
Jews of Safi rid . . . antisemitic tax-collector
John Connors and the fairies (condensed)
Johnny Cake
Jurma and the sea god
Kelfala's secret something
The king and the emperor
King Gylfi is tricked again
Knockmany legend
The Koranic teacher
The lama's servant

526

TRICKERY (continued)
The lay of Thrym
Lazarus and the dragons
The leaning silver birch
Leaving home
The leprechaun's trick
The lion's treasured goat
Little bull with the golden horns
The little chicken Kluk and his
  companions
Little crab and his magic eyes
The little hare
Little Sister Fox and Brother
  Wolf
Liza the fox and Catafay the
  cat
Loki makes mischief
The magic fox
The magic turtle
  [grows/shrinks inches each
  day]
The man turned into a mule
Manachar and the leprechaun
Masquerading trickster
The master thief
A merry prank of Pa-leng-ts'
  ang
Midwife fox [steals honey]
The mischievous little drinker
Molly Whuppie (England)
Monkey and the crocodile
  (India)
The moon god [how moon got
  up in sky]
The muzhik, the wolf, and the
  fox
Napi's wager with rabbit
The nightingale's song
  [escape]
Obdurman the clever
  huntsman
The ogre's soul
The old hag
Old Man La Feve
  [bumblebees]
Old Nick and the pedlar

The old tiger and the hare
Old woman and the doctor
Olli the terrible
One particular small, smart
  boy
Onions [keg of "powder"]
Oona and the giant Cuchulain
The organ that brayed like a
  donkey
Outwitting the devil
The peasant and the devil
Pedro de Urdemalas
Peerifool [secret name of fairy]
Peik
Peter Bull
Pierre Brassau ["non-objective"
  painting by monkey]
The quail clan punishes coyote
Rabbit and the gum-baby
Rabbit and the Indian chief
The rabbit and the two coyote
The rabbit and the well
Race between toad and
  donkey
Rashness of the young and
  wisdom of the old
Raven and the beavers
Raven with the broken beak
The red man's pranks
Red-headed Windego
The rich ranchero's maguey
  fence
The rogue of Kachi Kachi
  Mountain
The russet dog
Satan and the boy
Sedna the sea goddess
Selim and the snake queen
Separation of god from man
The shepherd who cried "wolf"
The shrinking hat
Shuralee the wood demon
The silver swindle
Sister Fox and Brother Coyote
The skunk and the frogs
Skunk's tale

TRICKERY—backfires (continued)
  Iktomi and the turtle
—farmer buys his own pigs
  The spook and the pigs
—Indian carries coyote supposedly
    dead
  Iktomi and the coyote
—prince uses ventriloquism
  Tale of the ricebirds
—rock in empty locust skin
  Coyote and locust
—tortoise "flies" to visit hawk
  Tortoise and hawk: never
    laugh at friends
TRICKERY (subject)
—Bald-headed whizzers [introd. to
    22 tales]
  Schwartz-*Tales*, 3–4, 77–84
Tricking a Christian
  Lindow-*Swedish*, 113–114
The tricking of King Gilfi
  Branston-*Gods*, 11–14
Trickster
  Anderson-*Trick.*, 11–15
Trickster tales of the Pacific North-
    west tribes . . .
  Robinson-*Raven*, 9–12
[Tricksters found in every folk
    tradition]
  Yolen-*Favorite*, 127–128
Tricksters, rogues, and cheats
  Yolen-*Favorite*, 125–126
Tripitaka: quest of the Buddhist
    scriptures
  Sanders-*Dragons*, 100–108
TRIPLETS
  The three stars
Triplets [Light Foot, Skilful Hand,
    Keen Eye]
  Weiss-*Russian*, 61–69
TRISTRAM, Sir
  Sir Tristram and La Belle
    Isolde
Tristram and Isolda
  Riordan-*Arthur*, 44–53
[Tristram and Isolt]

Spells & Bind, 7–14
TRITONS (subject)
  Scott-*Fantastic*, 135–148
—[Old Man of the Sea]
  Lloyd-*Mythical*, 67–70
The triumph of death
  Hoke-*Uncanny*, 103–119
"TROJAN HORSE"
  The fall of Troy
The Trojan War
  Pinsent-*Greek*, 113–130
TROJAN WAR
  Achilles and the death of
    Hector
  Helen of Troy
Trojan women (Euripides)
  Stapleton-*Dictionary*, 203–205
The troll in the Skrudur
  Booss-*Scand.*, 636–637
The troll labour
  Keightley-*World*, 122–123
Troll labour (condensed)
  Briggs-*Vanish.*, 98–99
The troll ride
  Crossley-*Folk*, 79–84
The troll shoes
  Booss-*Scand.*, 289–291
The troll turned cat
  Keightley-*World*, 120–121
The troll wife
  Keightley-*World*, 108–109
TROLLS
  The altar-cup in Angerup
  Ash lad who had an eating
    match with the trolls
  The bear trainer and the trolls
  Beating the changeling
  Bergtagen
  The Black Bull of Norroway
  Bolstre Castle
  The bridal present
  The changeling speaks on the
    way to baptism
  The coal burner and the troll
  Communion wine in the troll
    food

The companion
Dame Soasan
Departure of the trolls from
    Vendsyssel
East o' sun and west o' the
    moon
Erikur rescues a woman from
    the otherworld
A farmer tricks a troll
Gellivor
The girl at the troll-dance
The greedy youngster
Grettir, the troll
Gryla
I know what I have learned
Investigation of a grotto
Johan and the trolls
Jora the troll
Kallundborg church
Katla
Katrineholm Manor
Knurre-Murre (condensed)
The Lapp in magpie form
The last of the trows
The legend of Bodedys
Ljungby horn and pipe
The magician's pupil
Mound folk
The night-trolls
Olafur and the trolls
The old troll of Big Mountain
Old troll tricked into revealing
    his treasure
Olli the terrible
Origin of Tiis Lake
The outlaw
Peter Gynt
Retrieving the cup
The shepherd of Silfrun-
    Arstadir
The shepherdess
The sjora in Helgasjon
Skotte in the fire
Stealing for the trolls
The story of Bergthor of Blafell
Svend Faelling

Tatterhood
Three billy goats Bruse [sic]
The three billy goats Gruff
The three billy-goats who
    went . . . to get fat
The three lemons
Three sisters were entrapped
    into a mountain
The tile-stove jumping over the
    brook
Toller's neighbors
The travelling companion
The troll in the Skrudur
The Urko of North Wij
The voyage in a Lapp sled
The widow's son
The witch at Tadas
—Christianity
    Trolls take over the farm
—church bells
    The silver mountain
—have prince under spell
    East of the sun, west of the
        moon
—tails
    The polite coal burner
—wood
    Skogsra or wood trolls
TROLLS (subject)
    Briggs-*Vanish*, 51, 98–99, 161,
        170, 200 ("Trows")
    Keightley-*World*, 94–96
    Lindow-*Swedish*, 33–35,
        218
    Scott-*Fantastic*, 63–74
—[illustrations]
    Scott-*Fantastic*, 63–74
—Irish fairies
    Logan-*Old*, 1–2
The troll's daughter
    Lang-*Pink/D*, 247–257
    Lang-*Pink/K*, 181–190
The troll's garden at Stallsbacke
    Booss-*Scand.*, 309
The troll's hammer
    Booss-*Scand.*, 482–485

The trolls in Hedale Wood
  Booss-*Scand.*, 149–150
The trolls in Resslared
  Booss-*Scand.*, 282–283
The trolls of Skurugata
  Booss-*Scand.*, 251–253
Troll's stone
  Booss-*Scand.*, 629–630
Trolls take over the farm
  Lindow-*Swedish*, 89–90
Trooping fairies [17 tales]
  Yeats-*Fairy*, 11–74, 287
Trooping fairies. *See* FAIRIES —
  trooping; FAIRY RADE;
  HOSTS; SLUAGH
TROUBLE(S)
  Brer fox meets Mister Trouble
  Imp of the perverse
—foolish worry
  Don't beat your children before
  they're born
TROUBLEMAKER(S)
  The devil and Kitta Gra
  Pedro de Ordimalas
Trout. *See under* FISH
Trows
  Froud-*Faeries*, unp
Trows. *See* TROLLS
The trows of Papa Stour
  Robertson-*Highland*, 24–25
TROY, Hugh
  The organ that brayed like a
  donkey
TROY
  The fall of Troy
TRUCKS
  Pulga
True and untrue
  Crossley-*Folk*, 61–66
True corn [origin of plant life]
  Bierhorst-*Hungry*, 32–33, 135
A true money tree
  Jagendorf-*Magic*, 35–38
True Thomas [Thomas the
  Rhymer]
  Nye-*Out*, 13–29

True Thomas. *See* ERCILDOUN,
  Thomas of
True to your nature: Master Rabbit
  Wade-*Indian*, 59–65
TRUMPETS
  The magic shawl and the en-
  chanted trumpet
TRUNKS
  The prayer that was answered
—flying
  The flying trunk
TRUST
  See also FAITH; LOYALTY
  The missing treasure
  The serpent [trust betrayed]
—betrayed
  Story of a gentleman['s wife]
TRUST IN GOD
  The wooden sword
Trusty John
  Lang-*Blue*, 297–305
TRUTH
  Ashiepattle who made the prin-
  cess tell . . .
  Bird of truth
  The eye restored
  How a poor muzhik looked for
  truth
  King and the wise man
  Pride goeth before a fall
  Tale of Elidurus
—"Crystal of Truth"
  The fox who went to heaven
The truth about ghosts
  Roberts-*Chinese*, 170
Truth and falsehood [personified]
  Cortes-*Byelorussian*, 148–150
  Yolen-*Favorite*, 403–404
Truth, and murder, will out
  Marshall-*Every.*, 257–262
[Truth revealed by stone of
  patience]
  Villa-*Armenian*, 84–91, 442–
  445
Truthful John
  Aiken-*Mexican*, 45–47

TRUTHFULNESS
—credibility lost
    Gohc Amu and the matzoon
TRUTHFULNESS (subject)
—Hindu stories
    Amore-*Lustful*, 132
The Tsantsa
    Hoke-*Demonic*, 69–105
Tsar Saltan
    Pushkin-*Fairy*, 34–53
The Tsarevna frog
    Xenophontovna-*Folk*, 13–26
TSARS
    Chilbik and the greedy czar
    Clever answers (Russia)
    The frog princess
    Green lizard, gray squirrel and
      the eagle
    Haunter of the birch forest
    The maiden wiser than the
      Tsar
    The red czar and the golden-
      haired Tihota
    Seven Simeons
    The soldier and death
    The wise little girl
—marries Vasilisa
    Vasilisa the Beautiful
Tuatha de Danann
    Froud-*Faeries*, unp
Tuatha de Danaan. *See* DANA,
    PEOPLE OF
TUCKONIES
    Pelican babies
TUG-O-WAR
    Tortoise and elephant: small-
      ness not an illness
    Tortoise and the elephants:
      fine goods often come in
      small packages
TUIREN
    [Iollan and his fairy mistress]
Tulips
    Ewart-*Lore*, 30–33
TULIPS
    Pixy-*gratitude*

Tumani and his mother's promise
    Magel-*Gambia*, 25–27
The tumarang's revenge
    Stokes-*Turtle*, 88–90
Tummeldink
    Manning-*Spooks*, 65–70
Tungustapi
    Booss-*Scand.*, 595–597
TUNNELS
    The skeleton in Holar church
TUNTUNIR BAI (subject)
    Raychaudhuri-*Stupid*, 85–86
TUONELA (underworld)
    The maid of the north
    [Kalevala]
    Vainamoinen's boat building
TURF
    The sod of death
TURKEY [country]
    The flying trunk
    The magic mirror
Turkey Brother and the magic pan-
    ther suit
    De Wit-*Talking*, 13–21
Turkey tale [drawing while telling]
    Macdonald-*Twenty*, 90–93
The turkey wench
    Stuchl-*American*, 102–103
TURKEYS
    Crab
    Poor turkey girl
    The turtle and the turkey
—the evil Wurrun
    The crystal sisters
—outsmarts coyote
    Coyote Bun and the turkey
—stupid
    Coyote and turkey
TURNAROUND
—failure to success
    The boy, the crow and the
      sesame seeds
    The turner and the goldsmith
    Cortes-*Byelorussian*, 78–81
TURNERS
    The turner and the goldsmith

The turnip [huge; many help in
pulling]
Oxenbury-*Nursery*, 13–18
TURNIPS
The Morning Star
—taboo: don't pull up
Star-Boy and the sun dance
TURPENTINE
February dragon
TURQUOISE
The frog
The girl who was already
queen
Home-bred boy finds lost
turquoise
The turtle and the island
Stokes-*Turtle*, 13–14
The turtle and the turkey
Parker-*Australian*, 160–163
[Turtle-boat, world's first
submarine]
Zong-*Korea*, 77
Turtle feeds his children
Shaw-*Pima*, 73f–75
The turtle [freed, carries sage
across . . .]
Berger-*Animalia* [57–59]
Turtle skin
Villa-*Armenian*, 210–216, 480–
482
The turtle wife
Stokes-*Turtle*, 65–68
TURTLEDOVES
—sons transformed into
Papa God sends turtle doves
TURTLES
See also TORTOISES
Brer rabbit and brer cooter race
Brer rabbit dances for a wife
"Bye-bye" (Haiti)
Chitchat turtle and the geese
Coyote and turtle
The drowned boys
Fishing with bare hands
Gumiya; a Blang story: origins
of characteristics
Iktomi and the turtle
The magic turtle
[grows/shrinks inches each
day]
The sad tale of the rabbit's tail
[Shore creatures; crane and
turtle]
Uraschimataro and the turtle
Urashima Taro
The warlike seven
Zirac and friends
—dragon king
Mountain witch and the Drag-
on-King
—eggs
Snakes and turtles [exchange
heads]
—fairy
The wind cap
—goes to live in sky
Rainbow and the autumn
leaves
—Letuli transformed into
The shark and the turtle
—origin
Wayambeh the turtle
How turtle came
—origin of characteristics
Glooskap and the turtle
—rescued
The dragon-king's palace:
Urashima Taro
—sea
The cat in the sea
—shell
How the turtle got her shell
—as supreme animal
The big turtle
Tushcoon Eigna
Villa-*Armenian*, 302–308
Tuwara, the cunning one
Shelley-*Legends*, 82–88
Twain, Mark
A ghost story [by Mark Twain]
The twelfth man
Marshall-*Every.*, 357–358

Twelve children on a platter
   Lindow-*Swedish*, 65
The twelve clever brothers go to
      town
   Ginsburg-*Twelve*, 12–19
Twelve dancing daughters
   Lewis-*Minute*, 38–39
The twelve dancing princesses
   Ehrlich-*Random*, 34–45
   McKinley-*Door*, 137–216
Twelve huntsmen [test of femininity]
   Lang-*Green*, 324–328
   Phelps-*Maid*, 51–58
The twelve princesses
   Stovicek-*Around*, 10–13
Twelve wild geese
   Yeats-*Fairy*, 255–259
"TWENTY AT ONE BLOW"
   The brave clever tailor
Twigmuntus, Cowbelliantus,
      Perchnosius
   Booss-*Scand.*, 199–203
Twilight, Midnight, and Dawn
   Riordan-*Russia*, 227–232
Twin brothers
   Radin-*African*, 289–291
The twins
   Nagishkin-*Folktales*, 199–204
TWINS
   All that happened must hap-
      pen again
   Anpao is born
   Artemis and Apollo
   The baker's daughter
   Brewery of eggshells
   The dawn of the world
   Gemini (the Twins)
   Glooscap, the great chief
   Golden rain
   How the Beldys stopped
      fighting
   [Impregnation by earrings] Ara-
      ruga Paru
   In the days of the plentiful
   The Johnson boys [song and
      story]
   The magic of the moon
   Odd jobs
   Old Nick and the girl
   Peik (Norway)
   The rival twins
   Tatterhood
   —sisters
   The stolen princess
   —subdue man-eating animals
   The Bakororo and Itubore
      legend
   Twins Akaruio Bokodori and
      Mamuiawuge Eceba
Twins Akaruio Bokodori and
      Mamuiawuge Eceba
   Wilbert-*Bororo*, 174–179
The twins of Paikala Mountain
   Jagendorf-*Magic*, 169–174
Twins of the Popol Vuh
   Nicholson-*Mexican*, 55–64
Twins visit Tawa
   Mullett-*Spider*, 54–61
The twisting tree [Kiowa]
   Myles-*Butterflies*, 9–13
Twist-mouth family
   Haviland-*N. Amer.*, 144–146
'Twixt saddle and ground
   O'Sullivan-*Legends*, 99–100
Two bad mice
   Phelps-*Tatterhood*, 51–60
Two badgers
   Riordan-*Tartary*, 115
The two blind men [thieves]
   Weiss-*Russian*, 193–196
Two brothers
   Cortes-*Byelorussian*, 100–
      107
   Ransome-*War*, 105–112
Two brothers [and seven-headed
      monster]
   Land-*Pink/D*, 209–219
   Lang-*Pink/K*, 154–162
Two brothers and the magistrate
   Zong-*Korea*, 101–103
The two brothers [fire and water]
   Elbaz-*Folktales*, 68–70

The two compadres
Aiken-*Mexican*, 37–42
The two donkeys
Wolkstein-*Magic*, 24–28
The two elephants
Elbaz-*Folktales*, 53
Two enemy kings
Manning-*Kings*, 91–108
The two fiddlers
Deightley-*World*, 387–388
Two fiddlers (condensed)
Briggs-*Vanish.*, 20–21
The two friends [die for each other]
Patai-*Gates*, 552–554
Two Hasidim visit Hell
Patai-*Gates*, 726–728
Two hunchbacks (condensed)
Briggs-*Vanish.*, 40–43
The two hunchbacks (Italy)
Yolen-*Favorite*, 343–345
Two hunting dogs [Burrajahnee
and Inneroogun]
Reed-*Aboriginal*, 55–56
Two lazy brothers [under apple
tree]
Riordan-*Tartary*, 94
Two lies
Zong-*Korea*, 195
The two little cottages
Stovicek-*Around*, 172
Two lovers punished
Magel-*Gambia*, 107–108
Two mothers [one child]
Shannon-*Solve*, 14–16
Two neighbors
O'Connor-*Tibet*, 20–25
The two old women and the boast-
ful fish
Stovicek-*Around*, 141
The two old women's bet
Yolen-*Favorite*, 181–183
The two pickpockets
Yolen-*Favorite*, 58
The two Sigurdurs
Booss-*Scand.*, 651–652
Two sisters and a harlot

Campos-*Mexican*, 131–133
Two sisters, Rose and Lotus
Zong-*Korea*, 201–207
The two travellers [evil man
blinded]
Shah-*World*, 198
Two true friends
Elbaz-*Folktales*, 150–151
Two unfaithful husbands
Zong-*Korea*, 197
Two visits to the jnun
Elbaz-*Folktales*, 80–81
The two wagoners
Griego-*Cuentos*, 153–155
Two weak ones against one strong
one
Nagishkin-*Folktales*, 162–166
Twopence Halfpenny
Sampson-*Gypsy*, 37–40
Tyl Eulenspiegel. *See* EU-
LENSPIEGEL, Till
Tyl on a tightrope
Williams-*Wicked*, 1–13
Tyll Ulenspiegel's merry prank
Yolen-*Favorite*, 128–129
The tylwyth teg
Keightley-*World*, 408–409
TYLWYTH TEG
Sleigh Beggey and Tylwyth
Teg
TYLWYTH TEG (subject)
Briggs-*Vanish.*, 98, 159, 200
Tyndal and the priest
Ginsburg-*Twelve*, 52–55
Tyndal goes to market
Ginsburg-*Twelve*, 56–59
TYPHON
The Sea Goat [Pan vs Typhon]
[Tyrannical bull with discontented
lice]
MacLean-*Cuentos*, 176–179
TYRANTS
—deceive, steal, punish
The three talismans
—harsh rulers
The king's rival

—sultan tamed
   Scheherazade retold

Uaboreu's journey in region of the
   Poxereu
   Wilbert-*Bororo,* 123–125
Ua-pa-chi (Kickapoo titles)
   Aiken-*Mexican,* 85–86
Uath the Stranger [a giant]
   Lehane-*Legends,* 7–11
Uchida, Yoshiko
   Sumi and the goat and the
   Tokyo Express
Udala tree
   Macdonald-*Twenty,* 115–125
Udege: A great misfortune
   Nagishkin-*Folktales,* 32–38
UGLINESS
   Beauty and the beast
   The birthday of the Infanta
   The Chinese bride
   City where men are mended
   The costly ring
   Gods of the stars: ancient
      China
   Golden apple and his
      stepmother
   The irangiri tree: ugly man
      seeks a wife (Africa)
   The lady and the merman
   Little crop-tailed hen
   The men who wouldn't stay
      dead (France)
   "O luck of the ugly . . ."
   Rickety Topknot
   Riquet with the Tuft
   Scar Face and the sun dance
   The season of the stubby
      caterpillar
   The ugly dog
   The ugly duckling
—appearances deceiving

   Beauty and the beast
—changed by girl's love &
   constancy
   Ricky of the Tuft
—elongated lips
   Habetrot [name of fairy]
—repulsiveness
   The serpent prince
—woman under spell; love
   Gawain and the Lady Ragnell
The ugly dog
   Stuchl-*American,* 98–101
The ugly duckling
   Andersen-*Hague,* 118–131
   Booss-*Scand.,* 339–345
   Leete-*Golden,* 58–73
   Rackham-*Fairy,* 120–131
The ugly girl
   Patai-*Gates,* 560–563
The ugly son
   Yolen-*Favorite,* 158–160
The ugly son-in-law
   Chalk-*Tales,* unp.
UKKA
   Pestilence, darkness and fire
Ukrainian tale [grief: imagined fu-
   ture woes]
   Weiss-*Russian,* 35–39
ULCHES (people)
   Mambu the orphan [tyrants'
      tribute]
Ulenspiegel. *See* EULENSPIEGEL,
   Till
The Ulfgryt stones
   Booss-*Scand.,* 294–296
ULSTER CYCLE STORIES
   Bricriu's feast
   The cattle raid of Froech
   The tale of Macc Da Tho's pig
Ulster woman's magic
   O'Sullivan-*Legends,* 83–84
The umbrella tree
   Hyde-Chambers-*Tibet,* 156–
      162
UMBRELLAS
   The baboon's umbrella

UMBRELLAS (continued)
The black umbrella
The blown away rabbit
[The fox with the purple
umbrella]
Umfreville, Edward
An evil being
Una the elfwoman
Booss-*Scand.*, 617
Unanana and the elephant
Phelps-*Tatterhood*, 7–12
The unanswerable
Kendall-*Sweet*, 63–65
Unantishee
Froud-*Faeries*, unp
Unbelief. *See* BELIEF AND
DOUBT
Unborn child avenged its mother's
death
Radin-*African*, 186–189
The unbroken web
Adams-*Iron*, 8–11
Uncle Cornelius, his story
Macdonald-*Gray*, 101–130
Uncle tiger and his nephew the
jackal
Raychaudhuri-*Stupid*, 16–18
UNCLES
Aladdin, or The wonderful
lamp
Coolnajoo, the foolish one
The strongest boy in the world
UNCONSCIOUS, The
The dream castle
Under the shade of the mulberry tree
Peacock Maid, 119–121
Under the wing of magic
Seekers Saviors, 6–31
UNDERGROUND
Fairies, English
Monacielli
UNDERGROUND (subject)
—Fairyland; hills
Briggs-*Vanish.*, 218 (index)
Underground palace [quest for lost
queen]

Schwartz-*Elijah*, 270–278
UNDERSEAS (Underwater)
Glashans and Shopiltees
King Crocodile
—deep
Asrai
—palaces
The dragon-king's palace:
Urashima Taro
Urashima Taro, the fisher lad
UNDERSEAS (underwater)
(subject)
—Fairyland
Briggs-*Vanish.*, 218 (index)
UNDERWATER BEASTS
Stormalong fights the Kraken
Underwater kingdom: Urashima
Stovicek-*Around*, 20–23
UNDERWEAR
—long
The lazy miner
UNDERWORLD
See also HELL; TUONELA
The archer who went I know
not where to . . .
[Daughters nightly go to under-
world; dance of death]
The descent of Inanna
Hades, lord of the underworld
Havoc in heaven: Monkey and
the Jade Emperor
Headman and the magician
The labours of Hercules
The little goddess
Mullien rescues his mother
Orpheus and Eurydice
Persephone among the dead
Sacrificed by kin, lover brings
girl back
The story of Jon Asmundsson
Tiyo's story
Twins of the Popol Vuh
Yggdrasill, the world ash
Underworld god of marriage
Sanders-*Dragons*, 127–129
Underworld justice

Roberts-*Chinese*, 188–194
Undine and Huldbrand: a doomed
  alliance . . .
  Water Spirits, 126–139
Undying guardianship: Rashin
  Coatie
  Seekers Saviors, 32–47
Unfaithfulness. *See* INFIDELITY
The unforgetable sneeze
  Shah-*Afghanistan*, 7–9
UNFORGIVENESS
  The enchantress Medusa
  The everlasting frogs [daugh-
    ters turned to]
  I won't forgive you
  —bad incident not forgotten
  The unforgetable sneeze
Ungenerosity. *See* STINGINESS
The ungrateful tiger
  Zong-*Korea*, 183
"UNH HUNH"
  The word the devil made up
    ("Unh hunh")
Unicorn: paragon of purity
  Magical Beasts, 100–139
Unicorn: peerless mount for
  Alexander
  Magical Beasts, 130–139
UNICORNS
  Brave little tailor (seven at one
    blow)
  Land monsters
UNITED STATES
  —history—revolution
  Rip Van Winkle
  Yankee Doodle [song and
    story]
UNIVERSE
  How the world was made
Universe and its beginnings [21
  tales]
  Radin-*African*, 23–89
UNKINDNESS
  —punished
  Half-chick [Medio Pollito]
  The unmarried girl's grave

Zong-*Korea*, 39–40
Unofficial history of the Confucian
  Academy
  Roberts-*Chinese*, 229–247
Unquiet spirits and spectral beasts
  Marshall-*Every.*, 129–142
The unseelie court
  Froud-*Faeries*, unp
UNTRUSTWORTHINESS
  —in verbal agreements
  Hare saves the hippopot-
    amus
Unusual animals [14 legends]
  Robe-*Hispanic*, 418–425
Unwelcome neighbour
  Stuchl-*American*, 76–79
The unwilling magician
  Timpanelli-*Tales*, 29–41
Up from the Dead Land
  Bierhorst-*Hungry*, 29–32
Upamanyu learns a lesson [her-
  mitage school]
  Rungachary-*Tales*, 32–42
Upon Jewel Mountain
  Riordan-*Tartary*, 131–135
Uraschimataro and the turtle
  Lang-*Pink/D*, 25–32
  Lang-*Pink/K*, 14–19
Urashima
  Piggott-*Japanese*, 126–129
  Stovicek-*Around*, 20–23
Urashima Taro
  Heslewood-*Tales*, 64–71
  Nye-*Out*, 45–59
URASHIMA TARO (subject)
  Briggs-*Vanish.*, 14–15
Urashima Taro, the fisher lad
  Ozaki-*Japanese*, 26–42
Urashima the fisherman (Japan)
  Yolen-*Favorite*, 107–110
[Urashima: the sea lord on the
  ocean floor]
  Water Spirits, 103–109
URINATION
  —on white bones
  The nine-tailed fox

Urisk
  Froud-*Faeries,* unp
  Keightley-*World,* 396
The urisk of Sgurr-a-Chaorainn
  Robertson-*Highland,* 21
URISKS (subject)
  Mckee-*Scottish,* 19
The Urko of North Wij
  Booss-*Scand.,* 286–289
Ursa Major (the Great Bear)
  Gallant-*Constel.,* 28–33
  See also BIG DIPPER;
    GREAT BEAR
Ursa Minor (the Lesser Bear)
  Gallant-*Constel.,* 28–33
Ursulo, hijo del oso
  MacLean-*Cuentos,* 85–93
USEFULNESS
  A potsherd speaks
USHER, House of
  Poe [E. A.] and the house of
    Usher
Usurpation. *See* FORCIBLE
    ENTRY
USURY
  The fly (as witness)
UTHER, King of Britain
  The sword in the stone
[Ut-napishtim and Gilgamesh]
  Water Spirits, 20–27
Uwaboreu: two chiefs with the
    same name
  Wilbert-*Bororo,* 121–123

VAAGE (people)
  The giant and Johannes
    Blessom
Vagrants. *See* TRAMPS
The vain bear
  Booss-*Scand.,* 591
The vain lord
  Ginsburg-*Twelve,* 64–67

VAINAMOINEN (the Wise Singer)
  [Finnish chanters/enchanters]
  In the beginning
  The maid of the north
    [Kalevala]
  —final disappearance of
    Marjatt
Vainamoinen's boat building
  Synge-*Land,* 103–113
Vainamoinen's wound
  Synge-*Land,* 45–54
Vainglory. *See* PRIDE; VANITY
Vaino and the swan princess
  Booss-*Scand.,* 528–532
VAIRIES
  Pixy-gratitude
Valbjorg the Unelfed
  Booss-*Scand.,* 612–617
"VALE OF COMPLAINT"
  Youth without age and life
    without death (Turkey)
Valerian
  Ewart-*Lore,* 160
VALHALLA
  Odin prepares for the
    Ragnarok
The valiant chanticleer
  Booss-*Scand.,* 194–199
Valiant John
  Thomas-*It's,* 201–203
The valiant little tailor
  Ehrlich-*Random,* 102–117
Valkyrie's tower
  Lee-*Castles,* 32–33
"VALKYRIES" (women warriors)
  Odin prepares for the
    Ragnarok
  Singard the dragon-slayer
Valley of the diamonds [Sinbad]
  Rackham-*Fairy,* 70–76
VALLEYS
  —silent
  Gesar of Ling
Vall-Lisbet's mother: peace in the
    grave
  Lindow-*Swedish,* 188–189

Value of a Pater and a Creed
O'Sullivan-*Legends,* 95–96
Value of a treasure house
Shah-*World,* 70
VALUES
Boy who was saved by his
thoughts
City mouse and country mouse
The fisherman and his soul
The goblin and the grocer
The gold piece
The Great Dog [Yudistira and
Svana]
Little Genius
Manka and the judge
The mendacious child
The three sons
Wagging my tail in the mud
The vampire of Fealaar
Robertson-*Highland,* 64–65
Vampires
Cohen-*Every.,* 1–21
VAMPIRES
Blood feasts of the damned
The cruel painter
The elemental
Kid Cardula
Leanan-Sidhe
The man from the grave
Nightstalker of Groglin Grange
The terror of the red blood
sucker
Vampires, ghosts, and ghouls
Scott-*Fantastic,* 123–132
Van de Voort, Donnell
Wiley and the hairy man
Van Iterson, Siny Rose
Pulga
Vandelrot and tibast
Lindow-*Swedish,* 109–110
Vandersteene, Roger
The existence of the Witigo
VANIR
War in heaven
VANITY
See also PRIDE

Ayoga
The blue-tail fly [song and
story]
The cave of emeralds
Coyote's vanity
The dewdrop tiara
The dog and the possum [ori-
gin of enmity]
The ducks and the fox
The emperor's new clothes
An empty head
Genie of the mountains
How the polar bear became
Madame rhinoceros and her
dress
Mouse Woman and the daugh-
ter of the sun
Powdered blondie and three-
haired blondie
Raven and the fox
The tooth of gold
The vain lord
Why the opossum's tail is bare
—spoiled girl cured
Prince Featherhead and Prin-
cess Celandine
Vanooshka
Manning-*Kings,* 72–90
Vartiter (Rose-Petal)
Sheohmelian-*Three,* 104–115
VASES
—gold
The golden vase
Tale of the golden vase and
the bright monkeys
VASSDAL, Lake
Sounding at Vassdal
VASSILISA [spellings vary]
Haunter of the birch forest
Vassilisa [fair] and Baba Yaga
Riordan-*Russia,* 11–19
Vassilisa the Beautiful
Bilibin-*Russian,* 57–68
Yolen-*Favorite,* 335–342
Vassilisa the Fair
Zvorykin-*Firebird,* 63–78

Vassilisa the valiant
    McCarty-*Skull*, 40–46
Vassilisa the Wise: the frog
    princess
    Riordan-*Russia*, 129–137
Vattar: Retrieving the cup
    Lindow-*Swedish*, 103–104
The Vatters
    Booss-*Scand.*, 327–329
The vatt's storehouse
    Booss-*Scand.*, 330–331
Vazili, Bagany and Banniki
    Arrowsmith-*Field*, 81–83
VEDS TALES
    The twelve clever brothers go
    to town
Vega: The three stars
    Zong-*Korea*, 13–14
The vegetable lamb
    Magical Beasts, 92–93
VEGETABLES
    Imperial left-overs
—less volume when cooked
    The eye can deceive
VENGATIVO
    The enchanted forest
The vengeance of Oiwa
    Kendall-*Haunting*, 26–29
Vengeance. *See* REVENGE
VENTRILOQUISM
    The singing frog
    Tale of the ricebirds
VENUS
    The Botticelli horror
—the laughing star
    Where the frost comes from
VEPS TALES
    How twelve clever brothers got
    feet mixed up
The Veracruz maize legend
    Nicholson-*Mexican*, 61–64
Veritable werewolves
    Colombo-*Wind.*, 7–8
A very happy donkey
    Wolkstein-*Magic*, 158–163
Vestiges of the elder days

    Magical Beasts, 6–55
Vestly, Anne-Cath.
    Hello, Aurora
VESTMANNA ISLANDS
    Erikur rescues a woman from
    the otherworld
    The wizards of the Vestmanna
    Isles
VETERANS
—disabled
    The girl with the silver voice
Vhy, vhy, vhy [humor]
    Villa-*Armenian*, 364–369
Vicar of Germsoe [looting wrecked
    ships]
    Marshall-*Every.*, 216–217
VICTIMS
—innocent
    The soldier-bird
    Deegeenboyah
Victory over Butoriku, the dragon
    Wilbert-*Bororo*, 137–138
VIETNAM
    The wonderful peal [Vietnam]
VIETNAM (subject)
—notes on culture, customs, tradi-
    tions; five tales
    Vuong-*Brocaded*,101–108
Viking of the Pacific
    Westervelt-*Hawaiian*, 35–40
VIKINGS
    The apples of eternal life
    The creation of the world
    The death of Balder
    Fenrir the wolf is bound
    The first humans
    The gods return
    The gods' revenge
    The golden age in Asgard
    Heimdall in Midgard
    How Thor got his hammer
    King Gylfi is tricked again
    Loki and his evil children
    The marsh king's daughter
    Night and day
    The Norns

Odin prepares for the
Ragnarok
The Ragnarok, doom of the
gods
Singard the dragon-slayer
The stealing of Thor's hammer
The story of trembling hood
Symbols in the Nordic myths
Thor fights the giant Krangnir
Thor goes fishing
Thor in the giant's strong-hold
Thor's holiday
The tricking of King Gilfi
The walls of Asgard
War in heaven
The world of ice and fire
Yggdrasill, the world ash
VIKINGS (subject)
—Myths and legends
Lindow-*Myths*, 1–48
Vilas
Keightley-*World*, 492
VILAS
Deer and Vila
VILLA, Pancho
Gold of the gods
The village beneath the water
Highwater-*Anpao*, 227–235
VILLAGES
Anpao is born
He comes from the east
The twelve clever brothers go
to town
—drowned
The village beneath the water
VILLAINS
Three wishes [of Billy Dawson]
Villeneuve, Madame de
Beauty and the Beast
VILLENEUVE, Madame de
Quiller-*Sleeping*, 9–14
Vily
Arrowsmith-*Field*, 225–230
VINEGAR
Mister Vinegar
A rare bargain

VIOLENCE
Red caps
VIOLENT DEATH
—foretold
Ghost: the radiant boy
VIOLETS
The secret of Tomuni
Sweet violet
VIOLINISTS AND VIOLINS
Elijah's violin
The fiddler and the fairy
The fiddler and the sea nymph
How the toad got his bruises
The two fiddlers
Two fiddlers (condensed)
The water nymph
VIRGIL (subject)
—Aeneid, Books I–XII (summary)
Stapleton-*Dictionary*, 13–19
VIRGIN BIRTH (myth)
The flower child
The virgin of Guadalupe
Bierhorst-*Hungry*, 119–127, 142
VIRGINIA CREEPER
Cyclamen, Delphinium, Virginia
creeper
VIRGINS
Virgo (the virgin)
Virgo (the virgin)
Gallant-*Constel.*, 154–161
VIRTUE(S)
See also GOODNESS
See also names of virtues and
vices: GENEROSITY; HU-
MILITY; PRIDE; PRU-
DENCE; etc
Little shepherdess and English
prince
—rewarded
The radiant Sambula
VISHNU (god)
A boon of immortality
The emerald Buddha
[Vishvamitra] The brahman and the
demons
Amore-*Lustful*, 71–73

542

The vision of MacConglinney
  Jacobs-*Celtic*, 195–199
Vision (sight) *See* EYESIGHT
VISIONS
  The enchanted journey [time
    warp]
  Portent from the Nissar
  The troll's garden at
    Stallsbacke
Visions of fairies [sightings, funeral,
  etc.]
  Marshall-*Every.*, 71–74
A visit from Mister Sea
  Luzzatto-*Long*, 20–35
VISITING
  Heimdall in Midgard
VISITORS
—taboo against
  Melusine: the otherworld wife
Visitors from the realm of shadow
  Night Creatures, 39–61
Vivien: the lady of the lake
  Lee-*Castles*, 104–107
VIVISECTION
  Coyote eats his own fat
  Monkeys
VIXENS (female fox)
  The fire bird and Ryska and
    vixen
VIZIERS
—steals fine money of beggar's
    wife
  The beggar, the lion and the
    dog
VLAD IV (dracul)
  Vampires
VOCATION
  The gypsy and Saint George
—divine
  Birth, dreaming, death: school-
    master's story
Vodyaniye
  Arrowsmith-*Field*, 183–186
VOICES
  The little mermaid
VOLCANOES

  Katla
Popocatepetl and Ixtlaccihuatl
—Matupit-*origin*
  The tumarang's revenge
VOLGA VSESLAVICH
  Wizard of Kiev
VOLSUNG, King
  Branstock: the hall of the
    Volsungs
VOLSUNGA SAGA
  How Sigourd awoke Brynhild
    upon Hindfell
Voltaire, F. M. A. de
  The hermit [paradoxical
    behavior]
VOODOO
  Mummies, zombies, and artifi-
    cial men
VORTIGERN, King
  The castle and the dragons
VOWS
  Princess with the golden hair
—broken
  The demon princess
The voyage in a Lapp sled
  Booss-*Scand.*, 332
Voyage of Odysseus
  Low-*Greek*, 153–169
Vugiswe: first human child
  Pitcher-*Tokol.*, 24–26
VULGARITY
  Quevedo and the king
    (Mexico)
Vulnerable spot
  Minford-*Fav.*, 129–132
VULTURES
  Little crab and his magic eyes
  The white does
  Why the cracks in tortoise's
    shell
—eats boy's buttocks
  Toribugu: legend of the hero
—insulted by princess; marries her
  Phikool Thong
Vuyu gods: Degei and his sons
  Shelley-*Legends*, 78–81

The wager: clever slave wins
   freedom
   Stuchl-*American,* 93–94
WAGERS (bets)
   Candida
   Chicoria [invited to eat at
     rancher's table]
   Day the sun rose in the west
   Great Joy, the self-respect-
     ing ox [pull 100 carts of
     stone]
   Napi's wager with rabbit
   The parrot tale-teller
   Selim and the snake queen
   The sure shot
   Temptations
   Truthful John
   The two old women's bet
   What the old man does is al-
     ways right
   The wisdom of the rabbit
   The witty joker
WAGES
   A hundred times
   The tale of Ivan
   Tight-fisted farmer and clever
     farmhand
   The walls of Asgard
—how to divide money each month
   The woodsman's riddle
Wagging my tail in the mud
   Roberts-*Chinese, 126*
   Yolen-*Favorite,* 61–62
WAGONERS
   The two wagoners
The wagtail Deereeree, and the
   rainbow
   Parker-*Australian,* 71–72
WAHL, JAN (subject)
—Biographical note
   Wahl-*Needle,* 56
The wailing messenger of death
   Haining-*Lepre.,* 11–13
The waiting maid's parrot (China)
   Roberts-*Chinese,* 9–14
   Yolen-*Favorite,* 90–94

Waiting: The Sleeping Beauty
   Perrault-*Glass,* 3–19
WAKE, William
   William Wake of Wareham
Wakefield, H. Russell
   The triumph of death
WAKES
   Funeral of Flory Cantillon
   The man who had no story
WAK-WAK ISLANDS
   The bird maiden
WALES
   Le Bel Inconnu and the castle
     of Senaudon
   Brewery of eggshells
   A bride from the lake
   The brownie
   The Bwca (booka)
   Bwciod
   Coblynau
   The fairies banished
   Gitto Bach
   Glashans and Shopiltees
   The Gwagedd Annwyn
   The Gwagedd Annwyn [II]
   Gwyllion
   Mice in the corn
   Oisin
   Pergrin and the mermaid
     (Wales)
   Powel and Rhiannon
   Rhys at the fairy-dance
   The shepherd of Myddvai
   Sleigh Beggey and Tylwyth
     Teg
   The spirit of the van
   Tale of Elidurus
   The tylwyth teg
   The water leaper
WALES (subject)
   Keightley-*World,* 361, 404–
     419
—Carmarthanshire
   Briggs-*Vanish.,* 19
—fairies
   Briggs-*Vanish.,* 218 (index)

WALES (subject) (continued)
—[Gypsy tales; introd. and 21
    folktales]
    Sampson-*Gypsy*, vii–ix, 1–108
Wali and the magic saddle-bag
    Shah-*Dervishes*, 185–190
The walker of the snow
    Colombo-*Wind.*, 27–29
The walking shadow
    Hoke-*Horrors*, 63–77
WALKING-STICKS
    Lay them straight
Wall of thorn: Curse: an embow-
    ered sleep
    Spells & Bind, 74–87
Wallabies. *See* KANGAROOS
Wallflowers
    Ewart-*Lore*, 1–3
WALLPAPER
    The crocodile in the bedroom
WALLS
    The building of the wall of
        Asgard
    The selfish giant
—Chinese
    Meng Chiang and the Great
        Wall of China
The walls of Asgard
    Branston-*Gods*, 60–64
WALNUT TREES AND WALNUTS
    The nightingale and the hawk
    Water carrier's fabulous sons
    The white cat
WALRUS TOOTH
    The skull in the snow
WALRUSES
—origin
    Sedna, (Eskimo)
    Sedna, the witch under the
        sea
Walter and Hildegund
    Crossley-*Legends*, 78–91
WAMPUM
—origin
    The wampum bird
The wampum bird

Wood-*Spirits*, 73–76
Wamundo
    Stokes-*Turtle*, 53–56
The wanderer's dream
    Haining-*Lepre.*, 68–69
The wanderings of Aeneas
    Lines-*Greek*, 217–231
The wanderings of Odysseus
    Gilbert-*Gods*, 144–152
WANDS
    Man without a heart
    The stupid boy and the wand
—magic
    The baker's magic wand
    The magic bonnet
    Math, son of Mathonwy
WAR(S)
    See also BATTLES; SIEGES
    Ares, god of war
    Asgard: war of the gods and
        giants
    The bat [war of birds and
        animals]
    The country of the mice
    The eagle on the prickly pear
    The first rain [war of two vil-
        lages in Papua]
    The golden cockerel
    Home-bred boy defeats the
        enemy
    How the blackbird went to war
    How the Thai learned to be
        calm
    The intoxication of the Ulaid
    The Ragnarok, doom of the gods
    Shinansha, or the south-
        pointing carriage
    Shurik: A story of the siege of
        Leningrad
    Song that comes from the sea
    The ugly son-in-law
    Walter and Hildegund
    William Wake of Wareham
    The woman of discord
    The Yellow Emperor: war
        against Chitou

—dead girl comes back as yellow
    handkerchief
The tiger priest
—not won with weapons alone;
    need wit to win
The wise old crow
—sieges
    Frog who became an emperor
    Panhu, the marvelous dog
War in heaven
    Branston-*Gods*, 52–59
The war of the birds and the
    beasts
    Ransome-*War*, 13–25
War of the wolf and the fox
    Lang-*Green*, 280–285
War with the Kaiamodogue
    Wilbert-*Bororo*, 213–218
WAREHOUSES
    Thordur of Thrastastadir
WARFARE (subject)
—fairies
    Briggs-*Vanish.*, 218 index)
The warlike seven
    Zitkala-*Old*, 159–165
WARNING(S)
    The fairy banquet [b]
    The grant
    The village beneath the water
—saves fisherman
    Pergrin and the mermaid
    (Wales)
WARRIORS
    Beowulf fights the dragon
    The boy who did not know
        what fear was
    Bricriu's feast
    The cattle raid on Froech
    The clever Nikorima
    Dietrich of Bern
    Gesar of Ling
    The house of Thebes
    Odin prepares for the
        Ragnarok
    Perseus
    Prince Vamato Take

    Rustam and Tahmina
    The smallest dragonboy
    Starkad and Bale
    The story of trembling hood
    Wayland Smith
—duty: to protect
    The serpent with one hundred
        heads [Kaliya]
—women
    Gulnara the Tartar warrior
The warrior's death
    Amore-*Lustful*, 94–96
Warsaw. *See under* POLAND
"WASCO"
    Mouse Woman and the van-
        ished princes
Wasek and the red giants
    Hill-*More*, 55–64
The Wasgo and three killer
    wales
    Reid-*Raven*, 69–74
WASHERS (game)
    The game of washers
WASHING AND WASHERWOMEN
    The bean-nighe
    The black bull of Norroway
    East of the sun and west of
        the moon
    Little Tuk
    She was good for nothing
    The tale of Mrs Tiggy-Winkle
WASPS
    Drakestail [and the king]
    Jack and his magic aids [dish,
        belt, flute]
    Pork and honey
WASTE
    The mischief maker, Lox, and
        the three fires
    Why men have to work
Wastewin and the beaver
    Yellow Robe-*Tonweya*, 52–58
Wasting sickness of Cu Chulaind,
    and . . . Emer
    Gantz-*Early*, 153–178
Wastrels. *See* SPENDTHRIFTS

A wastrel's three wishes
   Yeats-*Fairy,* 214–233
WATCHES
   Charge this to the cap
   Enchanted watch
WATER
   See also SPRINGS
   The dawn of the world
   Elephant and the tortoise
   Fountain women
   The four elements
   Good and evil
   How the pigeon became a
      tame bird
   How the raven got fresh water
   King Matyas and his scholars
      (Hungary)
   Kitpouseagunow
   Leppa Polkry and the blue
      cross
   Munachar and Manachar
   Munachar and the raspberries
   A pool of bright water
   [Primal waters, magic powers]
   Rusalky
   The sun journey
   Ten jugs of wine
—for drinking
   Glooskap and the monster
      bullfrog
from goolahgool tree
   Cookooburrahs and the
      Goolahgool
—magic
   Ivan, the Windfall
   The soldier and death
—origin
   The Baitogogo legend
—personified
   Why the sun and the moon
      live in the sky
—pumping of
   Saint Peter and the two
      women
—red
   The red stream

—scarce
   Papa God and General Death
—singing
   The promise of the three
      sisters
—visits sun & moon (on earth)
   Sun, moon, and water
WATER BARRELS
   Kertong
Water beasts and wurrums
   Haining-*Lepre.,* 81–85
"WATER BUFFALO" ("The Holy
      One")
   Water maiden of the Navajo
Water buffaloes
   Weeks-*Pachee,* 75–89
WATER BUFFALOES
   The winding-horn village
WATER CARRIERS
   Aguarius (the Water-Carrier)
Water carrier's fabulous sons
   Shah-*Afghanistan,* 83–89
Water cats. *See* OTTERS
WATER CATTLE (subject)
   Briggs-*Vanish.,* 35, 74, 76, 81,
      89
"WATER DEVIL"
   The platypus Gayardaree
Water faeries
   Froud-*Faeries,* unp
The water folk
   Scott-*Fantastic,* 135–148
Water folk. *See* SEA FOLK
Water games: football on a lake
   Manning-*Spooks,* 17–21
The water ghost: Harrowby Hall
   Manley-*Fun,* 41–49
Water girls: The Seven Sisters
   Reed-*Aboriginal,* 91–95
WATER GODS
—killed and eaten
   Beebyeebyee and the water-
      god
WATER HOLES
   The drowned boys
WATER HORSES

—annual human victim
  Sheena and the water-horse
WATER JARS
  Tumani and his mother's
    promise
Water-kelpies
  Robertson-*Highland*, 141–142
The water leaper
  Froud-*Faeries*, unp
Water life. *See* AQUATIC LIFE
WATER LILIES
  The girl with large eyes
  The star and the lily
Water lily
  Ewart-*Lore*, 110–111
Water lily: the gold spinners
  Lang-*Blue*, 180–189 (notes,
    268)
Water maiden of the Navajo
  Jagendorf-*First*, 87–91
Water monsters
  Cohen-*Every.*, 67–89
The water nick
  Manning-*Cats*, 97–100
The water nymph
  Booss-*Scand.*, 324–325
[The water nymph and Colville]
  Water Spirits, 111–115
WATER NYMPHS
  Holecek and the water nymph
  The partridge and his drum
WATER OF DEATH
  Jurma and the sea god
  The rocks of Korsan
The water of life
  Lang-*Pink/D*, 184–190
  Lang-*Pink/K*, 133–139
  Shah-*World*, 164–168
  Shub-*About*, 65–73
  Westervelt-*Hawaiian*, 24–34
WATER OF LIFE [restores the
    dead to life]
  The blacksmith
  The fisher-prince with the sil-
    ver apple
  Juan and the bony one

  Jurma and the sea god
  The rocks of Korsan
WATER OGRES
  The seawife and the crone
  The water palace [boat of feathers]
    Schwartz-*Elijah*, 227–236
WATER PEOPLE
  The dawn of the world
Water pixies. *See* PIXIES —water
WATER POLLUTION
  Bending Willow [Indian maid]
Water-rat and fire
  Reed-*Aboriginal*, 56–60
Water rats. *See* RATS—water
The Water Serpent [Heracles vs
    the Hydra]
  Lurie-*Heavenly*, 21–23
WATER SHEERIE
  Jack o' lanterns
  The lure of the marsh lights
The water smith
  Keightley-*World*, 260–261
"WATER SPIRIT"
  The wonderful pearl [Vietnam]
WATER SPIRITS
  See also FAIRIES —water
  Fate
  Hour is come but not the man
    (condensed)
  The mermaid wife
  River women
  [Urashima: the sea lord on the
    ocean floor
WATER SPIRITS (subject)
  Briggs-*Vanish.*, 68–74, 81, 88–
    89, 146
The water sprite and the bear
  Crossley-*Folk*, 112–117
WATER SUPPLY
  Gaoliang bridge [Peking]; wa-
    ter supply
WATERFALLS
  Behind the waterfall
  Kombocke and Hausbocke
  Long Haired Girl
  Nixen and river men

WATERFALLS (continued)
    The white-hair waterfall
"WATERLEAF PLANT"
    Erh-lang and the suns
WATERMELONS
    Little Finger of the watermelon
        patch
WATERMEN
    The peasant and the waterman
    The working waterman
Waters and plants: magic
        [condensed]
    Mckee-*Scottish*, 30–31
The wave of Toime
    O'Sullivan-*Legends*, 69
Waves save the saintly
    Patai-*Gates*, 540
WAX
    Why the bananas belong to
        the monkey
WAX-FIGURES
    Sister Fox and Brother Coyote
The waxwork [Murderers' Den, by
        Burrage]
    Schwartz-*Great*, 141–157
Waxworks
    Hoke-*Demonic*, 23–49
Way of the werebeast
    Night Creatures, 108–131
The way of the world
    Booss-*Scand.*, 136–138
Wayambeh the turtle
    Parker-*Australian*, 93–94
[Wayfarers: dangers at night]
    Night Creatures, 15–19
Wayland Smith
    Crossley-*Legends*, 108–120
Wayne, Kyra Petrovskya
    Shurik: A story of the siege of
        Leningrad
The ways of a witch
    Faulkner-*Tales*, 46–51
Ways of providence are inscrutable
    Elbaz-*Folktales*, 76–77
WAZAR, The
    The silver whistle

We give thanks
    Walking-*Song*, 8–9
Weak character: Woe Bogotir
    Xenophontovna-*Folk*, 107–117
WEALTH
    See also GREED; LUXURY;
        POVERTY; PROSPERITY;
        TREASURE
    Aid and punishment
    Aina-kizz and the black-
        bearded bai
    All I possess!
    The broken oaths
    The Chinese bride
    The companion
    The cuckoo's riches
    Day the sun rose in the west
    The deer and the snake
    Dick Whittington and his cat
    The flying trunk
    The gizzard [riches for the one
        who eats it]
    The gold harvest
    Juan Soldado
    Katla's dream
    Lake Goldring
    The magic bamboo
    The man who never knew fear
    The Moohel
    The penitent nis
    The story of the McAndrew
        family
    The tinder-box
    The treasure in Saby Creek
    Treasurer under suspicion
    The two compadres
    Who is my neighbour?
    Woe [personified]
    Words of wisdom
    The young man who refused
        to kill
—appearance of, honored
    A stranger comes to Leon
—desire for
    The frogs at the rainbow's end
—dream of

Don't count your chickens . . .
—lost by frivolous behavior
   The passion of the gewel
—the rich take by force
   Phoenix fairy flower [Han]
—wit superior to
   Puss in Boots
—work, not magic
   The magician and the bananas
"WEALTHSOUND"
   Eagle and the frog
WEAPONS
   The sun journey
Weardale fairies [dislike being
   observed]
   Marshall-*Every.*, 74–80
The Wearer of the Ball: magic
   moccasins
   Wade-*Indian*, 67–81
The weasel and the well
   Patai-*Gates*, 536–538
WEASELS
   Honeyed words can't sweeten
     evil
   Paddy O'Kelly and the weasel
   Paudyeen O'Kelly and the
     weasel (condensed)
—praying/deception/eats mice
   The rock and the weasel
—war over
   How the Beldys stopped
     fighting
WEATHER
   See also COLD; WIND
   Boy of the red twilight sky
   Graduation
   Mer-men
   Mer-women
—sun's emotions and The sun's
     daughter
Weather signs
   Steele-*Ozark*, 91–93
WEATHERCOCKS
—origin
   Half-chick [Medio Pollito]

The weathermaker
   Hyde-Chambers-*Tibet,* 107–
     111
WEAVER-BIRD
   Origin of death: chameleon
WEAVERS AND WEAVING
   See also BLANKET WEAVING
   Athene, goddess of wisdom
   The Chuang brocade
   The foolish weaver and the
     jackal
   The herd boy and the weaving
     girl
   Little weaver of Duleek Gate
   Mouse Woman and the wooden wife
   The three imposters
   The wonderful Chuang
     brocade
—Amir saves his own life
   The Amir who became a
     weaver
WEBS
   The unbroken web
Webs of enchantment
   Spells & Bind, 50–87
Wedding at Stanton Drew
   Marshall-*Every.*, 274–277
The wedding feast at Pohja
   Synge-*Land*, 127–131
Wedding feast of the little people
   Keightley-*World*, 220–221
WEDDING FEASTS
   The seven beggars
WEDDINGS
   The battle of the birds
   The bottle-neck
   Brer rabbit dances for a wife
   Dead couple marry after death
   The exiled princess
   The giant who had no heart
   Halde hat
   How some wild animals became tame ones
   The iron wolf
   "Lars, my lad!"

WEDDINGS (continued)
The mastermaid
The owl and the pussycat
[poem]
Simon marries Ellen
Stupid Peikko
Toad's wedding [to Miss
Mouse] [in verse]
Vhy, vhy, vhy [humor]
Walter and Hildegund
The wild swans
The young lady of Hellerup
—dead man as best man
One night in Paradise (Italy)
—gifts
Maid Vae
The troll wife
—trolls
Bergtagen
The wee folk [17 tales]
Ratcliff-*Scottish*, 97–125
Wee folk [condensed]
Mckee-*Scottish*, 19–20
Wee folk. *See* FAIRIES; LITTLE
PEOPLE—Irish
WEEKS, Rupert
—[The man and his stories]
Weeks-*Pachee*, 105–106
WEEKS
The idler [a week wasted]
The Weendigoes
Colombo-*Wind.*, 14–20
The Weeoombeens and the
Piggiebillah
Parker-*Australian*, 30–32
The weeping woman: Cortes and
Malintzin
Bierhorst-*Hungry*, 129–130
The weeping woman: forever with-
out rest
Bierhorst-*Hungry*, 130–131
The weeping woman: the prince
and the seamstress
Bierhorst-*Hungry*, 127–129,
142
A Weetigo in the woods

Colombo-*Wind.*, 59–64
WEIGELA
Amaranth, Weigela
WEIGHT
A sharp loss of weight
—getting heavier
A ghost gets a free ride
Wejosis and the wind giant
Hill-*More*, 21–30
Welcome to Canada
Elbaz-*Folktales*, 55
[Well at the World's End]
Spells & Bind, 89–93
The well of everlasting life
Shah-*Afghanistan*, 68–70
The well of life
Amore-*Lustful*, 166–168
The well-baked man
Yolen-*Favorite*, 331–333
A well-deserved punishment
Jagendorf-*Magic*, 69–70
The well-digger and the deev
Shah-*Afghanistan*, 42–47
Wells, H. G.
The red room [by Wells]
WELLS
The black horse
Cormac MacArt went to Faery
Fior Usga [origin of Lough of
Cork]
The four rings
The giant who had no heart
The Longwitton dragon
The luck of Eden Hall
Man's best friend
The monkeys and the moon
The Norns
The rabbit and the well
Ruckus in the well
The shrew
Talkative wife
The tar baby
The tar baby tricks brer rabbit
Why a rabbit hides in a burrow
Yggdrasill, the world ash
—fairy

Janet and Tamlin
—magic
   The wine well
—pure spring water
   Sunken palace: King Corc and
   Fior Usga
—spirit of
   The honored woman
Wellspring of the universe
   Water Spirits, 6–27
Welsh enchanter's fosterling
   Lehane-*Wizards,* 40–55
WELSH NAMES (subject)
—glossary
   Thomas-*Mabinogion,* 87–88
WELSH TALES (subject)
—The Mabinogion
   Thomas-*Mabinogion,* 5
WELSHMEN (subject)
   Keightley-*World,* 361–442
The Wendigo
   Colombo-*Wind.,* 127
WENDIGO
   Another being
   Cannibal Lake
   A cannibal spirit
   Cannibals
   The death of Windigo
   The devil
   An evil being
   The existence of the Witigo
   Giant cannibals
   Guilty of murder
   A human being transformed
   The immortal cannibal
   Ithaqua
   Legendary Lore
   Man eaters
   A man named Weendigo
   A near encounter
   Onaouientagos
   Red-headed Windego
   Restless souls
   Six traditional tales
   The Snow-Wetigo
   Some sort of madness

   A sort of werewolf
   Stories of the Windigo
   Supernatural creatures
   Superstitious belief
   A tale of the Grand Jardin
   A tale of the Windego
   The thing that walked on the
   wind
   To kill Windigo
   Veritable werewolves
   The walker of the snow
   The Weendigoes
   A Weetigo in the woods
   The Wendigo
   The Wendigo (I–IX)
   Windagoos! Cannibals!
   The Windigo [I]
   Windigo [II]
   Windigo [III]
   The Windigo personality
   Windigo psychosis
—drawings
   Images of the Windigo
The Wendigo (I–IX)
   Colombo-*Wind.,* 65–112
WENS (deformity)
   How an old man lost his
   wen
   The man with the wen
   Woodcutters' wens
The werewolf
   Booss-*Scand.,* 309–316
Werewolf and nightmare [spirit, not
   dream]
   Lindow-*Swedish,* 176–179
Werewolves
   Cohen-*Every.,* 23–36
WEREWOLVES
   Becoming a werewolf
   Man beasts in wolf-land
   Shape-shifters [commentary]
   A sort of werewolf
   The troll's hammer
   Way of the werebeast
The werewolves of Ossory
   Haining-*Lepre.,* 116–117

Wesolego Alleluja = Happy Easter
  McNeil-*Charm.*, 169–172
West, John (pseud. of Robert
  Arthur)
  My displaced ghosts
WESTERN STORIES
  The dying cowboy [song and
    story]
WEST-HIGHLANDS
  Mally Whuppy
Westwood, Jennifer
  Walter and Hildegund
Wetigo. *See* WENDIGO
The Whale [and Jonah]
  Lurie-*Heavenly*, 42–44
A whale of a tale
  Macdonald-*Twenty*, 1–9
WHALES
  See also KILLER WHALES
  Animals in different parts of
    Australia
  The brave Azmun
  Cetus (the Whale)
  Fair, brown, and trembling
  The first mosquito
  Glooskap and the giant's frolic
  Glooskap and the whale
  The great bronze Buddha and
    the whale
  Greenland whale fishery [song
    and story]
  Grimsborg
  How Glooskap found the
    summer
  Jonah and the whale
  Kitpouseagunow
  The man/whale
  Raven with the broken beak
  Why Bootup, the whale,
    smokes a pipe
—origin
  Sedna (Eskimo)
  Sedna, the witch under the
    sea
—swallows pregnant woman
  Yeghnig Aghpar

—swallows princess
  The three caskets
What a fish!
  Villa-*Armenian*, 355–356
What happened to Ivan
  Manning-*Kings*, 109–119
What happened to Jadji
  Yolen-*Favorite*, 85–87
What happened to six wives who
  ate onions
  De Wit-*Talking*, 117–121
  Phelps-*Tatterhood*, 29–32
What melody is the sweetest?
  Yolen-*Favorite*, 413
What shall baby's name be?
  Booss-*Scand.*, 186–190
What the old man does is always
  right
  Rackham-*Fairy*, 262–271
WHEAT
  Silbado
WHEELBARROWS
  The devoted friend
WHEELS
  Bishop Svedberg and the
    devil
  Oxen and the creaky wheels
—cart
  The devil as the fourth wheel
When gods and men mingled
  Sanders-*Dragons*, 37–38
When I first came to this land
  Sanders-*Hear*, 1–11
When one man has two wives
  Yolen-*Favorite*, 62
When Plum Bush tricked the
  trickster
  Anderson-*Trick.*, 83–85
When rocks rolled crackling
  wisdom
  Jagendorf-*Magic*, 71–74
When the hand rubs the foot . . .
  Todd-*Some*, 78–82
"WHEN THE SAINTS GO
  MARCHIN' IN"
  Snake with an ear for music

When they gave out wisdom, H.
    queued up twice
    Stuchl-*American*, 70–72
Where love is, God is
    Weiss-*Russian*, 117–129
Where stories grow
    Sperry-*Where*, 1–5
Where the frost comes from
    Parker-*Australian*, 164–165
Which flower?
    Shannon-*Solve*, 20–22
Whipping children: how it came
    about
    Radin-*African*, 209–211
WHIPS AND WHIPPING
    The fairy whipping
    Maid Vae
    Maidens in a mirror
—bravery tested
    The youth who brought the
    corn
WHIRLPOOLS
    The hand and the whirlpool
    The inheritance
    Supparaka
WHIRLWINDS
    The dancing bird Bralgah
    The devil and his
    entanglements
    Little Yellow Bird
    The mopoke, and the mosquito
    bird
—banished, rain goes too
    Sparrow's search for rain
—personified
    Morning Star and Meteor
WHIRLWINDS (subject)
    Briggs-*Vanish.*, 129
WHISKEY
    See also POTEEN
    King of the pipers and the
    wonderful tune
WHISTLE-BLOWING (public
    interest)
    Doctor Bidpai
    The goose girl

When the hand rubs the foot
WHISTLES
    The rose of Peppermette
    Saint Nicholas and the chil-
    dren
    The silver whistle
    The white butterfly
    Piggott-*Japanese*, 138–139
White cap
    Booss-*Scand.*, 644–645
    Marshall-*Every.*, 80–86
The white cat
    Lang-*Blue*, 161–179 (notes,
    368)
    Yolen-*Favorite*, 95–105
WHITE CLIFFS OF DOVER
    Stormalong fights the Kraken
The white doe
    Wyatt-*Princes*, 56–81
White dove
    Shub-*About*, 52–53
The white dove [princess under
    spell]
    Lang-*Pink/D*, 238–246
    Lang-*Pink/K*, 173–180
The white duck
    Bilibin-*Russian*, 51–56
The white-eared tiger
    Zong-*Korea*, 86–88
White Feather and the six giants
    Wade-*Indian*, 27–41
The white fox
    Yellow Robe-*Tonweya*, 42–
    51
The white gander
    O'Sullivan-*Legends*, 76–78
The white-hair waterfall
    Jagendorf-*Magic*, 101–107
White hair and the crocodiles
    Ozaki-*Japanese*, 214–223
White hare of Oki
    Piggott-*Japanese*, 109–110
White ladies
    Arrowsmith-*Field*, 30–32
White lotus magic
    Roberts-*Chinese*, 42–44

[White man created by Juko, the monkey]
Wilbert-*Bororo*, 78–80

The white pet
Lochhead-*Battle*, 33–36

The white pony
Ainsworth-*Phantom*, 125–138

White powder (condensed)
Briggs-*Vanish.*, 135–136

The white rabbit
Marshall-*Every.*, 138–142

The white rooster
Hyde-Chambers-*Tibet*, 83–93

The white rose
Ewart-*Lore*, 87–88

The white seal maid
Yolen-*Hundredth*, 29–37

The white snake
Lang-*Green*, 360–365

The white stallion
Stuchl-*American*, 253–254

White trout: a legend of Cong
McGarry-*Folk*, 21–24
Yeats-*Fairy*, 38–40

Whitethorn
Froud-*Faeries*, unp

WHITTINGTON, Dick
Dick Whittington and his cat

Whittington and . . . *See* Dick Whittington and . . .

Who built Reynir church?
Booss-*Scand.*, 605–606

Who got brer Gilyard's treasure?
Faulkner-*Tales*, 178–185

Who is my neighbour?
Crouch-*Whole*, 26–31

Who is the mightiest in the world?
Riordan-*Tartary*, 122–124

Who? [Joseph David Oznot]
Schwartz-*Tales*, 68–70

Who knows?
Hoke-*Horrors*, 89–104

Who stole brer Gilyard's sheep?
Faulkner-*Tales*, 158–163

Who was most generous?
Shah-*World*, 176–177

Who was the stupidest
Wood-*Palace*, 41–44

Whose horse is it?
Wheeler-*Fox*, 9–23

Whuppity Stoorie
Ratcliff-*Scottish*, 92–96

WHUPPITY-STOORIE (subject)
Briggs-*Vanish.*, 64, 200

Why a girl should marry him to whom she is given in marriage
Radin-*African*, 207–208

Why a rabbit hides in a burrow
Stuchl-*American*, 29–32

Why all prairie dogs are brown
Anderson-*Trick.*, 52–55

Why apes look like people
Lester-*Black*, 21–37

Why blackbird has white eyes
De Wit-*Talking*, 75–79

Why Bootup, the whale, smokes a pipe
De Wit-*Talking*, 188–191

Why chief of smiths was unable to create human beings
Radin-*African*, 85–86

Why coyote's coat is the color of sand
Shaw-*Pima*, 70–72

Why crows are black
Anderson-*Trick.*, 56–62

Why do Jews rock when studying?
Patai-*Gates*, 496–497

Why dogs sniff each others tails
Lewis-*Animal*, 20–21

Why koala has no tail
Reed-*Aboriginal*, 40–44

Why leaves on trees are different colors
Wilbert-*Bororo*, 111–112

Why men have to work
Lester-*Black*, 38–41

Why mowers are poor
O'Sullivan-*Legends*, 48–49

Why one does not reveal the origin of another

Radin-*African*, 204–206
Why raven is no longer
Robinson-*Raven*, 115–125
Why raven isn't perfect
Robinson-*Raven*, 37–45
Why sharks never attack . . . *See*
Taufatahi and Fakapatu . . .
Why some animals are
domesticated
Radin-*African*, 143
Why stems of arrows have joints
Wilbert-*Bororo*, 131–132
Why the bananas belong to the
monkey
Eels-*Brazil*, 123–131
Why the bob-cat stays in the
woods
Anderson-*Trick.*, 32–38
Why the buzzard's head is bald
Anderson-*Trick.*, 79–82
Why the cat washes after meals
Lewis-*Bedtime*, 20–21
Why the cracks in tortoise's shell
Radin-*African*, 141–142
Why the crow is black
Toth-*Tales*, 116–120
Why the executioner is called
assessor
Booss-*Scand.*, 229–232
Why the fairies are vindictive
O'Sullivan-*Legends*, 45–47
Why the flat fish is flat
Chalk-*Tales*, unp
Why the gibbon says "pua"
Toth-*Tales*, 95–105
Why the hare has a short tail
Robe-*Hispanic*, 48–49
Why the hare runs away
Yolen-*Favorite*, 132–133
Why the lamb is meek
Eels-*Brazil*, 47–57
Why the monkey still has a tail
Eels-*Brazil*, 145–151
Why the opossum's tail is bare
Wood-*Spirits*, 77–80
Why the sea is salt

Crossley-*Folk*, 25–28
Heslewood-*Tales*, 31–44
Lang-*Blue* 148–153 (notes, 367)
Why the sea moans
Eels-*Brazil*, 177–197
Heslewood-*Tales*, 72–82
Why the sun and the moon live in the sky
Radin-*African*, 41
Why the sun rises when the rooster crows
Jagendorf-*Magic*, 87–91
Why the tiger and the stag fear each other
Eels-*Brazil*, 61–69
Why the tiger is striped
Toth-*Tales*, 85–90
Why there is death [Nikoduma]
Stokes-*Turtle*, 23–25
Why tigers have stripes
Watson-*Thailand*, 8–9
Why wolves fear the bell
Cortes-*Byelorussian*, 13
Why women are like cats
Aiken-*Mexican*, 111–113
Wichtlein
Froud-*Faeries*, unp
"WICHTLEIN" ("Little Wights")
The changeling [b]
Wicked girl and her punishment
Radin-*African*, 274–278
Wicked John and the devil
Yolen-*Favorite*, 359–366
The wicked Lord of Melgund
Robertson-*Highland*, 178–179
The wicked sister-in-law
Yellow Robe-*Tonweya*, 66–85
The wicked stepmother
Fattoross-*Simpleton*, 13–23
The wicked tiger
Raychaudhuri-*Stupid*, 40–43
The Wicked Witch of the West
Baskin-*Imps*, 6–7
Wickes, Frances G.
The conjure wives

WIDE (personification)
    Long, Wide and Hawkeye
WIDOWS
    Butterflies
    The frog
    Lox and the chief's wife
    Martha and Mary
    The merry widow
    Vhy, vhy, vhy [humor]
    Why the flat fish is flat
A widow's curse
    O'Sullivan-*Legends*, 81–82
The widow's son
    Booss-*Scand.*, 56–63
The widow's son and the fig-pecker
    Shah-*Afghanistan*, 30–41
Wife. *See* WIVES
WIFE ABUSE
    A bride from the lake
The wife from heaven
    Zong-*Korea*, 136–139
Wife who ate the wrong porridge
    Radin-*African*, 285–288
WIGS
—moss
    The widow's son
Wild children. *See* FERAL
    CHILDREN
Wild Darrell
    Marshall-*Every.*, 370–374
WILD EDRIC (subject)
    Briggs-*Vanish.*, 39
Wild Goose Lake
    Phelps-*Tatterhood*, 133–138
    Sadler-*Heaven*, 31–37
WILD HUNT (subject)
    Briggs-*Vanish.*, 218 (index)
Wild huntsman
    Marshall-*Every.*, 104–106
"WILD HUNTSMEN"
    The changeling [b]
Wild men
    Cohen-*Every.*, 53–66
The wild swans
    Andersen-*Hague*, 44–66
    Booss-*Scand.*, 345–356

    Robertson-*Highland*, 194
Wild thyme
    Froud-*Faeries*, unp
"WILD WOMEN"
    The Oldenburg horn
"WILD WOMEN" (subject)
—Germany
    Keightley-*World*, 234–238
"WILD, WOOD, TIMBER, AND
    MOSS PEOPLE"
    The changeling [b]
Wildbeam's pranks
    Haining-*Lepre.*, 26–27
WILDCATS
    The food balls [Kiowa]
Wilde, Lady
    Priest's soul
    Seanchan the Bard and the
        king of the cats
Wilde, Oscar, 1854–1900
    The Canterville ghost
WILDE, Oscar (subject)
—Life and work, by Naomi Lewis
    Wilde-*Fairy*, 7–12
Wiley and the hairy man
    Haviland-*N. Amer.*, 126–133
    Yolen-*Favorite*, 395–400
WILL
    The seed's secret
William Wake of Wareham
    Marshall-*Every.*, 282–287
Willie Brennan [highwayman]
    O'Sullivan-*Legends*, 139–141
Will-o'-the-wisp
    Arrowsmith-*Field*, 34–36
    Froud-*Faeries*, unp
WILL-O-THE-WISP (subject)
    Briggs-*Vanish.*, 120, 200
Willow-trees
    Froud-*Faeries*, unp
WILLOW TREES
    Temptations
—twigs
    Stupid Peikko
WILLOW TREES (subject)
    Briggs-*Vanish.*, 74

WILLS
  Story of Ciccu
Wilson, Gahan
  Yesterday's witch [Miss
    Marble]
WIND
  Bilber and Mayrah
  Brer tiger and the big wind
  The clever sewing-maid
  The Dragon [Marduk and
    Tiamat]
  The drowned boys
  The early heroes: Yi, the ten
    suns, the monsters
  East of the sun and west of
    the moon
  The four elements
  Frost, Sun, and Wind
  Gift from a star
  Gluska'be, the Penobscot hero
  Jack of Sjoholm and the Gan-
    Finn
  King Solomon and the winds
  The lost princess
  The magic bag
  Moya [child of Wind; returns to
    place-of-stars]
  The origin of the winds
  The palace of the moon
  The prince who had two eyes
  The sleeping prince
  Snuff-box [wishes-come-true]
  Son of the wind [was once a
    man]
  Sprig of rosemary
  The yes-no-yes-no spirit
  —east
  The merchant's fortune
  —four winds; North especially
    East of the sun, west of the
      moon
  —herder
    The rain bulls
  —magic cloth
    Ivan the rich and Ivan the poor
  —north

  Boy-who-snared-the-wind and
    shaman's daughter
  The lad and the north wind
  The lad who went to the north
    wind
  Sad marriage of North
  Shingebiss: the wild duck
  Wejosis and the wind giant
  —north; impregnates Indian maid
  Little Brother of the Winds
  —obeys
    The goose girl
  —rid tribe of fox
    The white fox
  —south
    The dandelion [beloved of the
      South Wind]
    South Wind and his golden-
      haired love
  —spirits
    The fire plume
  —west
    Gheeger Gheeger the cold
      west wind
    Mighty bear has problems
    Tungustapi
  The wind cap
    Yolen-*Hundredth*, 19–27
  Wind folletti
    Arrowsmith-*Field*, 28–29
  Wind that blows the winter away:
    Mayrah
    Parker-*Australian*, 92
  Windagoos! Cannibals!
    Colombo-*Wind.*, 32–35
  The Windigo [I]
    Colombo-*Wind.*, 44–50
  Windigo [II]
    Colombo-*Wind.*, 187–191
  Windigo [III]
    Colombo-*Wind.*, 191–193
  The Windigo personality
    Colombo-*Wind.*, 128–138
  Windigo psychosis
    Colombo-*Wind.*, 164–186
  Windigo . . . *See also* Wendigo . . .

The winding-horn village
  Jagendorf-*Magic,* 75–81
WINDOWS
  Raccoon's tale
WINE
  El borracho del bahio
  King and the bishop
    [Clonmacnoise]
  Leppa Polkry and the blue
    cross
  The monk and the drunk
  Noah and Satan [wine: proper
    amount]
  A rare bargain
  Ten jugs of wine
  The youngest god [Dionysius]
—bottle never empties
  Gift of Elijah
—Greeks introduced to
  Erigone and her dog
—magic
  Girl with the golden hair
Wine and the devil
  Aiken-*Mexican,* 63
The wine bibber
  Kendall-*Sweet,* 42–44
The wine well
  Roberts-*Chinese,* 53–54
Wings
  Stuchl-*American,* 230–233
WINGS
  The apples of Iduna
  Wayland Smith
Winkle the witch
  Ainsworth-*Bear,* 53–57
Winning: The bat: war of
    birds/animals
  Lewis-*Animal,* 44–45
"WINPE"
  Glooskap and the witch
    maidens
WINTER
  See also COLD
  Coming of spring
  How Glooskap found the
    summer

Ojeeg, the hunter, and the Ice
    Man
Pepito Conejo: prepare for
    winter
The selfish giant
Shurik: A story of the siege of
    Leningrad
The squirrel and the pixie
Summer in winter
Wind that blows the winter
    away: Mayrah
—giant
  How summer [personified]
    came to Canada
—origin
  The Fishes [Odschig, the chief]
  Persephone
—preparation for
  Mister Raccoon realizes that
    winter is coming
WINTER GIANT
—freezing all life in Canada
  How the Summer Queen came
    to Canada
The winter sky
  Gallant-*Constel.,* 116–147
Winter's end (personified)
  Crouch-*Whole,* 72–74
WIRE
  The monster of Poot Holler
Wirinum: the everlasting frogs
  Reed-*Aboriginal,* 33–36
Wirreenun: The stone frogs
  Parker-*Australian,* 168–170
WISDOM
  Anpao is born
  Athene, goddess of wisdom
  The clever brothers
  Glooscap and the wishes
  The kind man
  King's/servant's sons switched
  Manka and the judge
  Peddler of Swaffham
    (England)
  Prince Asraf and the king of
    the spirits

Rickety Topknot
The sleepy one: Senor
  Opossum and the rattler
Supparaka
The three sons
When rocks rolled crackling
  wisdom
Words of wisdom
—of the aged
The golden vase
—children
The twins
—of earth, but not of heaven
The jewel of the fox's tongue
—heed advice of elders
The lazy ducks
—infinity of
Wisdom belongs to everyone
—youth and age
A great misfortune
WISDOM (subject)
—[The literati and the folk]
  Yolen-*Favorite*, 403
Wisdom belongs to everyone
  Todd-*Some*, 84–86
  Todd-*Tortoise*, 30–31
The wisdom of a child
  Amore-*Lustful*, 23–25
Wisdom of Senor Zorro
  MacLean-*Cuentos*, 141–142
The wisdom of the rabbit
  Booss-*Scand.*, 592
Wise and unwise conduct [motif
  index]
  Wilbert-*Bororo*, 259
Wise frog and foolish frog
  Riordan-*Russia*, 241–242
The wise goldsmith
  Wood-*Palace*, 80–86
A wise judge
  Roberts-*Chinese*, 222–223
The wise king and the honest thief
  Stovicek-*Around*, 204–205
The wise little girl
  Yolen-*Favorite*, 38–40
Wise Ma Zai

Peacock Maid, 106–118
Wise man and the apprentice
  Shah-*Dervishes*, 171–173
WISE MEN
Hiawatha
Mahosoth [Buddah as wise
  man]
On naming a son [Joseph]
Prince Meerzat Istvan and the
  horse of dust . . .
Wise men three
  Marshall-*Every.*, 355–357
The wise old crow
  Amore-*Lustful*, 57–60
Wise pigeon
  Kudian-*More*, 57–58
The wise quail and the foolish quail
  Martin-*Hungry*, 45–52
Wise sayings for a thousand dinars
  each
  Mitchnik-*Egyptian*, 46–53
Wise woman: Mastermaid
  Phelps-*Tatterhood*, 149–155
The wise woman, or The lost
  princess
  Macdonald-*Wise*, 1–108
Wisely spent
  Villa-*Armenian*, 109–113, 449–
  451
WISHES
  See also COVETING; DESIRE
Aladdin and the wonderful
  lamp
Boots and the beasts
The boy and the dancing fairy
La cenicienta huasteca
The enchanted apple tree
Farmer's son and the geni
Glooscap and the wishes
Gods of the stars: ancient
  China
Hagop's wish
The herd-boy
Kalele the Bold Wisher
Little Freddy with his fiddle
Midas, the golden king

WISHES (continued)
Mossycoat
The sausage
The sausage: stuck on wife's
nose
The snow-man [the dog and
the sun]
Stonemason: a T'ung folktale
The tinder-box
Tyll Ulenspiegel's merry prank
Wali and the magic saddle-bag
Wicked John and the devil
—come true
The magic shawl and the en-
chanted trumpet
The poor old dog
Snuff-box [wishes-come-true]
—foolish
The frog and the ox
The small, small cat
—granted
Little cinder girl
—magically fulfilled
Omelya and the pike
—three
Glooskap and the three
seekers
The smith and the devil
Those three wishes
Three wishes
WISHING-WELLS
Snubby's tail
Wit. *See* CLEVERNESS; HUMOR;
INTELLIGENCE
The witch
Booss-*Scand.,* 99–106
The witch and the boy Israel
Schwartz-*Elijah,* 203–209
The witch and the cabbage
Robe-*Hispanic,* 293–294
[Witch, as hare, takes milk from cows]
Lehane-*Wizards,* 97–99
The witch at Tadas
Lindow-*Swedish,* 165–168
[Witch controls course of ship]
Lehane-*Wizards,* 104–106

WITCH DOCTORS
The irangiri tree: ugly man
seeks a wife (Africa)
People who could fly
Witch hare
Yeats-*Fairy,* 141
Witch hunters: Lancashire, Essex,
and Salem
Sergeant-*Witches,* 55–175
Witch of dark adventures
Baskin-*Imps,* 28–29
Witch of secret good deeds [un-
loved = sad]
Baskin-*Imps,* 40–41
The witch of Strathardle
Robertson-*Highland,* 102–104
Witchcraft
Robe-*Hispanic,* 219–413
[collection]
Robertson-*Highland,* 87–120
[collection]
WITCHCRAFT
Anpao brings the corn
The conjure wives
The golden ass
Katla
[Katla protects Odd by 'sight
blinding']
The magician's pupil
The marsh king's daughter
Milking others' cows
Protection against black
witchcraft
The witch
—in house with caged fairy
The fairy in the cage
WITCHCRAFT (subject)
Marshall-*Every.,* 44–45, 201
—Fancy and fact; history
Sergeant-*Witches,* 19–43
—[Nomenclature]
Sergeant-*Witches,* 11–12
—Scottish history
McKee-*Scottish,* 5–9
—Short way with witches
Sergeant-*Witches,* 44–51

WITCHES (continued)
The palace of the moon
Photogen and Nycteris; a
    day/night mahrchen
Pix! Pax! Pox!
Prince Meerzat Istvan and the
    horse of dust . . .
Prince Mirko
Princess on the glass
    mountain
The princess, the horse, and
    the she-devil
Rapunzel
Revenge of Joaquina
The rollright stones
The Santa Lucias [demon-
    foundling; legend]
The seawife and the crone
The serpent-slayer
The silver whistle
Sister Alionushka, Brother
    Ivanushka
Smallhead and the king's son
The snow queen
The snow queen: an adventure
    in seven stories
The sorceress
Stars in the snow
The sun princess
Ten white doves
That her children might be
    fed
The three daughters and the
    lost cow
The three witches of Kintail
The tinder-box
The tinkling laugh
The troll shoes
Two brothers [and seven-
    headed monster]
Vaino and the swan princess
Vulnerable spot
War in heaven
Water lily: the gold spinners
Waxworks
The ways of a witch

The white dove [princess un-
    der spell]
The white duck
The Wicked Witch of the West
Winkle the witch
The witches' excursion
With her godmother to
    Josefsdal
Wolfskin's bride
Yesterday's witch [Miss
    Marble]
Yvon and Finette
—beheaded by soldier
The tinder-box
—child turned into
The land where time stood still
—crone is Princess of the side, un-
    der spell
Diarmuid, son of Donn: a spell-
    shackled devotion
—cures fisherman
Betty Booker's bridle
—eats human livers
Spearfinger, the witch
—Gheonoea and Scorpia
Youth without age and life
    without death (Turkey)
—gives legs, takes away voice
The little mermaid
—gives power to change shape
Husband and wife should
    share equally
—horned
The horned woman
—Ino
Helle and Phrixus
—kills woman and takes her place
Sister Alyonushka and Brother
    Ivanushka
—Laplander
The mouse bride
—maidens turned into caged birds
The enchanted forest
—plans to feast on rats
The seven rats
—Princess of the Side, under spell

Diarmuid, son of Donn
—punishes Omokoy tribe
The children of the Omokoy
tribe
—screams; bursts
A pool of bright water
—sorceress turned into mosquito
The first mosquito
—steals milk from cows
Queen's County witch
—Ublyane
Sleeping Beauty in the wood
WITCHES (subject)
Briggs-*Vanish.*, 127–128, 135–
136
Lindow-*Swedish*, 48–52
Scott-*Fantastic*, 167–176
Sergeant-*Witches*, 290 (index)
Stallman-*Witches*, 47 (index)
—brujas
MacLean-*Cuentos*, 70
—Fairy doctors
Yeats-*Fairy*, 133–135, 290
—Shadowy sisterhood
Lehane-*Wizards*, 96–121
[Witches appear to be ordinary folk]
Lehane-*Wizards*, 103–104
The witches' excursion
Haining-*Lepre.*, 120–123
Witches' excursion
Yeats-*Fairy*, 152–154
The witches' fire
Stokes-*Turtle*, 111–112
Witches from history
Stallman-*Witches*, 14–27
Witches in stories [7 tales]
Stallman-*Witches*, 28–43
Witches of Ashkelon
Schwartz–Elijah, 25–28
Witches of today
Stallman-*Witches*, 44–46
Witches of Tring [killed by Colley]
Marshall-*Every.*, 201–206
Witches on the lake
Manning-*Marvels*, 102–106
Witches: raging revelries, frightful rites

Lehane-*Wizards*, 116–117
Witches' Sabbath [commentary]
Robe-*Hispanic*, 390–400
Witches: Satanic master
Lehane-*Wizards*, 112–113
Witches: secret of flight
Lehane-*Wizards*, 112
The witch's cat
Ainsworth-*Bear*, 12–25
Witch's child: Ursula Southeil
Marshall-*Every.*, 291–292
Witch's garden
Lehane-*Wizards*, 110–111
Witchtln
Arrowsmith-*Field*, 49–52
With her godmother to Josefsdal
Lindow-*Swedish*, 164–165
The witty joker
Stovicek-*Around*, 86–87
WIVES
See also BRIDES; HOME-
MAKERS; HUSBANDS;
SHREWS; STEPMOTHERS
Ahmad and the nagging wife
All I possess!
Back for Christmas
The bad wife [in bottomless
pit] (Russia)
Birth, dreaming, death: school-
master's story
Bluebeard
Brer rabbit dances for a wife
The brothers and the singing
toad
Buzz-buzz aunty
The cat woman (France)
The clever sewing-maid
The clever wife
Creator Nyame and his four
wives
A cure for jealousy
Easter-hag put a water-trough
in her place
The faithful son, Dong Yong
Foolish men and scolding
wives

WIVES (continued)
  Gifts of the child Christ
  Hodeken
  How a peasant cured his wife
    of telling tales
  How elephant married a Nama
    woman and was deceived
  The husband who stayed at
    home
  Katla's dream
  Kirsten's-hill
  Lady Ren: fox spirit
  Lai D'Ywenee
  The language of animals
  A legend of Knockmany
  Matching wits [two robbers
    have same wife]
  The men who wouldn't stay
    dead (France)
  The mermaid wife
  The merry wives
  Nanasimgit and his [abducted]
    wife
  The old man wouldn't take ad-
    vice [young wife]
  The peri-wife
  The piebald calf
  The pig-headed wife
  Pilar's indiscretion
  A pottle o' brains
  The prayer that was answered
  Sandy Harg's wife
    (condensed)
  Saxe of Saxeholm
  Scheherazade
  The secret of the growing gold
    [by Stoker]
  Slaying of the Tanuki
  Smallboy and his halfpenny
    wife
  The spirit of the van
  Story of a gentleman['s wife]
  A stroke of luck [tricked: judg-
    ed as fool]
  A tale of the Windego
  Talkative wife
  The ten fairy servants
  Three evil wives punished
  Three unmarried ministers
  The troll wife
  What happened to six wives
    who ate onions
  Who was most generous?
  Who was the stupidest
  Witches on the lake
  The woman in the moon
  The woman who was saved by
    a miracle
—adultery
  The carpenter's wife
—as enemy
  The woodsman's riddle
—attitude toward husband
  What the old man does is al-
    ways right
—badger makes, into soup
  Farmer and the badger
—beaten; to make her obey
  Rooster's advice [beat your
    wife]
—builder of the house
  Wisely spent
—burns that by which husband
    turns back from tiger . . .
  Hong Do-Ryong, the filial tiger
—clever; outwits husband
  Marietta's choice
—cleverness
  The Knockmany legend
—dead
  In the land of the dead
—faithful, saves husband
  Good King Nala's downfall
—faithful to leprous husband
  The radiant Sambula
—false pretenses
  Andrew and King Solomon [in
    2 parts]
—falsely accused
  [Woman with the head of a
    horse]
—fidelity

Prophecy: Wan and the Great
Wall of China
—foolish
The spirit of the spring
Today's laughter, tomorrow's
sadness
—ghost of wife gains revenge
The vengeance of Oiwa
—greedy
The cobbler who became an
astrologer
The fisherman and his wife
—greedy; never satisfied
A fisherman and a golden fish
—helps find devil's soul
Ivan, the Windfall
—humor
Goha on the deathbed (Egypt)
The headstrong woman
–husband-killers
Goonur, the woman-doctor
—kills tiger that killed her husband
The white-eared tiger
—lost, by disobedience
Urashima the fisherman
(Japan)
—more important than husband
The fairy child
—multiple
Pikuwa and his wives
—one old, one young
When one man has two wives
—Oonagh saves Finn
Knockmany legend
—outsmarts tiger
Fatima and the tiger
—princess "sells" her husband for
a night
Finist the Falcon
—quest for a wife
Tangletop: the cave at the
world's end
—returned to parents
Fat woman who melted away
—saves Finn McCool
Oonagh and the giants

—saves foolish husband
Beausoleil
The foolish young Mussulman
—saves husband by loyalty, courage, cleverness
Savatri and the god of death
—saves husband jailed for infidelity
What happened to Jadji
—saves Shun
Shun, the wise emperor
—search for a wife
Kingdoms of copper, silver,
and gold
—shrewish
The devil and the farmer's wife
—stronger than fate
The prince and the three fates
—subject to husbands
Rashness of the young and
wisdom of the old
—superior intelligence
Dialogue with death
—taming
The devil and the old hag
—taming a cruel woman
Ivan Byelarasseiski
—termagant
Rip Van Winkle
—transformed into men
Seven sisters; a Miao story
—treachery
The irangiri tree: ugly man
seeks a wife (Africa)
—tricks giant-killer-husband
Bolster and Jecholiah
—vicious
The magic bag
—virtuous
Envy punished
—wicked, persuades husband to
kill his senile father
The wisdom of a child
—Wife murdered by badger
The rogue of Kachi Kachi
Mountain
—wife would kill husband

566

WIVES—wife would kill husband
(continued)
Three snake-leaves
—wooden
Mouse Woman and the wood-
en wife
—young, beautiful, prisoner
The jealous shoemaker
WIVES (subject)
—fairy
Briggs-*Vanish.*, 218 (index)
The wizard
Sheohmelian-*Three*, 74–76
[Wizard, enchanter, sorcerer, magi-
cian: terms]
Lehane-*Wizards*, 10
"WIZARD OF FINLAND"
Water lily: the gold spinners
Wizard of Kiev
Lehane-*Wizards*, 21–25
WIZARDS
Antti and the wizard's
prophecy
The astonishing brush
Bubbly's trick
The creatures of magic
Elsa and the evil wizard
How Ableegumooch tracked a
fox
The hunting of the hind
Kespak and the caribou
Kitpouseagunow
Leppa Polkry and the blue
cross
Long, Wide and Hawkeye
The magician's pupil
Maria Morevna
Master and pupil
Mice in the corn
The Pleiades
Pussy Cat Twinkle
Stones of five colours and the
Empress Jokwa
The wizards of the Vestmanna
Isles
—takes Ilbatyr prisoner

Proud Ilbatyr in the land of
Cathay
—Win-pe
Why Bootup, the wale, smokes
a pipe
—Wirreenun
The stone frogs, the Youayah
Mayamah
The wizard's lesson
Roberts-Chinese, 31–38
The wizards of the Vestmanna
Isles
Crossley-*Folk*, 34–37
WODEN (subject)
Briggs-*Vanish.*, 7
Woe Bogotir
Xenophontovna-*Folk*, 107–117
Woe [personified]
Riordan-*Tartary*, 54–58
The wolf and the cub
Stuchl-*American*, 138–141
The wolf and the fox
Fattoross-*Simpleton*, 53–55
Wolf and the seven kids
Shub-*About*, 17–19
The wolf and the tailor
Riordan-*Tartary*, 59
The wolf cub
Ginsburg-*Twelve*, 68–71
Wolf in sheep's clothing
Williams-*Aesop*, [8–9]
Wolf, John Q.
Country dance in the Ozarks in
1874
The wolf [Noah's Ark]
Lurie-*Heavenly*, 53–55
Wolf who traded his freedom for
security
MacLean-*Cuentos*, 152–154
The wolf who wished to hoard
Wood-Kalila, 220–222
Wolfskin's bride
Crouch-*Whole*, 59–65
WOLOF LANGUAGE
Marriage of two masters of
Wolof [A]

Wolof tales. *See* GAMBIAN
WOLOF TALES
WOLSEY, Thomas, Cardinal,
1495–1530
Mother Shipton and Cardinal
Wolsey
WOLVES
See also WEREWOLVES
The adventures of Yemima
Animals in winter
Bagged wolf
B'er rabbit is an uncle
Beth Gellert
The boy who cried wolf
Brer fox tries farming, too
Brer rabbit and his riding horse
Brer wolf and brer fox get a
big surprise
Brer wolf plants pinders
Brer wolf wants the honey
Brer wolf's magic gate
Brer wolf's second pinder
patch
The bun [personified]
Counselor to the wolves
Dog and the wolf [dog chained
by-day]
The end of the world
Farmers three
Fenrir the wolf is bound
Foolish wife
Fox and the wolf
Frightened wolves [wolf head]
The giant who had no heart
Gray wolf's haint
Half-ram leaves home
The hen and the apple tree
Honeyed words can't sweeten
evil
How the hare made a fool of
the wolf
How they got Hairlock home
Ivan Bear's Ear
Ivan Tsarevich, the wolf, and
the firebird
Julie of the wolves

Kyang, the fox, the wolf and
the hare
The lad with the goat-skin
The language of animals
Little Brother of the Winds
Little Red Riding Hood
Little Red Riding Hood [in
verse]
Little Sister Fox and Brother
Wolf
Lox, the mischief maker
Midwife fox [steals honey]
The mischief maker, Lox, and
the three fires
Mouse Woman and the van-
ished princes
The muzhik, the wolf, and the
fox
The north country wolf
Obsidian arrow points
Oskus-ool and his wise wife
Peter and the wolf
A pool of bright water
Rainbow and the autumn
leaves
The russet dog
Sheep, lamb, wolf, and the
hare
The shepherd who cried "wolf"
Skunk's tale
Smart head better than sharp
teeth
The spectre wolf
Stars in the snow
The straw ox
The tar baby tricks brer rabbit
The theft of fire
The three little pigs
Three little pigs [houses: mud,
cabbage, brick]
True and untrue
The valiant chanticleer
War of the wolf and the fox
The weathermaker
Who stole brer Gilyard's
sheep?

WOLVES (continued)
Why wolves fear the bell
The wolf cub
Wolfskin's bride
—enchanter in form of
Golden mermaid [theft of golden apples]
—fairy in form of
Twelve wild geese
—Indian spirit
The grey wolf and the orphan [Musquakie]
—Indian woman befriended by wolves
Life with the wolves
—iron
The iron wolf
—save Indian brave
The wicked sister-in-law
—tricked
Groundhog dance
—tricked by rabbit
Owl with the great head and eyes
The wolves of Cernogratz
Hoke-*Spirits*, 103–108
The woman and the butterflies
Wood-*Spirits*, 125–128
The woman and the children of the sycamore tree
Radin-*African*, 179–180
The woman and the giant
Wood-*Spirits*, 29–33
Woman chief
McCarty-*Skull*, 1–6
Woman chooses death
Yolen-*Favorite*, 449–450
The woman from the sea
Stokes-*Turtle*, 123–127
The woman in blue
Villa-*Armenian*, 417–418
The woman in the moon
Hadley-*Legends*, 22–23
Woman in the moon
Riordan-*Woman*, 1–6
The woman of discord

Bierhorst-*Hungry*, 75–79, 139
The woman of the sea
Crossley-*Folk*, 128–130
[Woman: the mother goddess's mystery]
Seekers Saviors, 13
Woman tied behind horse on her braids
Lindow-*Swedish*, 115–117
The woman who chose her brother
O'Sullivan-*Legends*, 124
The woman who cursed herself
Amore-*Lustful*, 138–139
Woman who killed her co-wife
Radin-*African*, 190–192
The woman who was saved by a miracle
Campos-*Mexican*, 58–61
[Woman with the head of a horse]
MacLean-*Cuentos*, 73–80
WOMANIZERS
Men accost a woman who is a skeleton or has head of a horse [9 legends]
WOMEN
See also BRIDES; MAIDENS; MARRIAGE; MATE SELECTION; SEXES; SINGLE WOMEN; WARRIORS— women; WIVES
See also titles beginning with "Woman . . ."
Fishing of the woman [adultery with otters]
How men and women got together
The island of beautiful women
The maid who chose a husband [Ghana]
Mice women who turned into dingoes
No pity in women
Solomon the wise
Test of femininity: Twelve huntsmen
Why women are like cats

—athletes
Foot racers of Payupki
—beautiful/cruel
The cat palace
—chained
Andromeda (the Chained
Woman)
—creation of
Moon and Morning Star
—dying without having known a
man
The unmarried girl's grave
—equality
Three strong women
—escapes from ogres
The old woman and the rice
cakes
—excuses: origin
How women got an excuse
—Greek religion
The youngest god [Dionysius]
—head of the household
Precious Jade
—helps suitor with tasks
The maid of the north
[Kalevala]
—heroines
Two enemy kings
—a matriarchic society
A princess on a swing
—old age; behavior
Bucca Dhu and Bucca
Gwidden
—old lady, a heroine
Old One Eye [robbers foiled]
—outsmarts old suitor
The tail of the squire's bride
—sexual advances by
Mountain witch and the
Dragon-King
—sexually insatiable
The queen who cried rape
—sorrow for, as war victims
The first rain [war of two vil-
lages in Papua]
—statue comes to life

Pygmalion
—strength abides where?
The devil and the female
—talkativeness
Three suitors for a wooden
statue
—tricks tiger
The tiger and the jackal
—what w. want most: free will
Gawain and the Lady Rag-
nell
—what women most desire: sov-
ereignty over men
[Gawain and Dame Ragnell]
WOMEN (subject)
Phelps-*Tatterhood*, xv–xxi
—Heroines in fairy tales
Lurie-*Clever*, xi–xiii
—Highlanders, ancient
McKee-*Scottish*, 3–5
—Hindu stories
Amore-*Lustful*, 26–27
—[Status in tales]
Riordan-*Woman*, vii–viii
—[Stories about 14 winners]
McCarty-*Skull*, v–vi
Women and women
Sheohmelian-*Three*, 69–72
Women vs men. See SEXES–
battle of the
The wonder voyage [Sinbad]
Rackham-*Fairy*, 76–83
A wonderful bird
Manning-*Cats*, 101–106
The wonderful Chuang brocade
Jagendorf-*Magic*, 119–124
The wonderful head: Celtic
myths
Ross-*Druids*, 128–129
Wonderful healing leaves
Schwartz-*Elijah*, 163–168
The wonderful horse [head where
tail should be]
Schwartz-*Tales*, 38–39
The wonderful lamp [Aladdin]
Shah-*World*, 172–174

The wonderful little pouch
  Keightley-*World*, 276–277
The wonderful pearl [Vietnam]
  Riordan-*Woman*, 69–74
The wonderful plough
  Keightley-*World*, 197–200
Wonder-worker of the plains
  Radin-*African*, 229–234
The wondrous fish-hook
  Shelley-*Legends*, 89–96
WOOD
  How coyote stole fire
—carrying of
  Big long man's corn patch
—firewood
  The parrot who bought
    firewood
  Periquito, wood dealer
—magic
  How black became white
The wood and sea nymphs
  Booss-*Scand.*, 290
WOOD-CARVERS AND
    WOODCARVING
  Mouse Woman and the wood-
    en wife
Wood demons. *See* DEMONS
WOOD FAIRIES (subject)
  Briggs-*Vanish.*, 75–76, 200–
    201
WOOD MAIDENS
  The wood and sea nymphs
WOOD NYMPHS
  Three wishes
WOOD SPIRITS
  Fate
  Giane
  Moss people
  Skogsra or wood trolls
WOODCHUCKS
  Mister Raccoon realizes that
    winter is coming
—origin of short tail
  Groundhog dance
Woodcutter and the fountain of
  youth

Piggott-*Japanese*, 129
Woodcutter and the heavenly
    maiden
  Seros-*Sun*, 16–23
WOODCUTTERS
  Hansel and Gretel
  Juan de Toluca
  The magic boat
  Mushkil Gusha: remover of all
    difficulties
  The rogue of Kachi Kachi
    Mountain
  The star child
  A summer night in a Nor-
    wegian forest
  Tom Thumb
  When rocks rolled crackling
    wisdom
Woodcutters' wens
  Piggott-*Japanese*, 134
The wooden horse and the painted
    jug
  Stovicek-*Around*, 164–166
Wooden horse [mechanical flight]
  Minford-*Fav.*, 10–121
The wooden sword
  Patai-*Gates*, 631–634
  Schwartz-*Elijah*, 89–93
The woodpecker
  Adams-*Iron*, 42–46
Woodpecker and bluejay: a sad
    tale
  Macmillan-*Canadian*, 123–125
WOODPECKERS
  How ole woodpecker got ole
    rabbit's conjure bag
  Master rabbit [tries to do what
    other species do]
  Meri and the woodpeckers
  That wicked crow
  The wagtail Deereeree, and
    the rainbow
—origin of red head
  The mouse and the sun
Woods. *See* FORESTS; TREES
The woodsman's riddle

Watson-*Thailand*, 32–35
WOODSMEN
    The kingdom of beautiful
        colors
—rescued by tiger
    The tale of the trusty tiger
The Wooing of Etain
    Gantz-*Early*, 37–59
The Wooing of Olwen
    Jacobs-*Celtic*, 67–74
Wooing of Pumei; an Oroqen story
    Seven Sisters, 92–107
The wooing of Seppo Hmarinen
    Booss-*Scand.*, 536–541
"WORD PEOPLE"
    Mambu the orphan [tyrants'
        tribute]
The word the devil made up ("Unh
    hunh")
    Yolen-*Favorite*, 471
"WORDLESS VOICE"
    The timid frogs
WORDS
    Vainamoinen's boat building
—nonsensical
    Master of all masters
Words of wisdom
    Griego-*Cuentos*, 87–91
WORK
    The cuckoo's riches
    The food of Paradise
    The girl who was already
        queen
    The husband who stayed at
        home
    Lazy beauty and her aunts
    The magician and the bananas
    The maid who chose a hus-
        band [Ghana]
    Spindle, shuttle, and needle
    Story of Ivan the Imbecile
    Sun tribute
    There is righteousness
    Why men have to work
    Yallery Brown
—play vs

    Simangolo and the akara
—rewarded by spirits of an-
        cestors
    Baluan: origin of the island
Work of the genii
    Villa-*Armenian*, 133–137
Working for the Bergfolk
    (condensed)
    Briggs-*Vanish.*, 116
Working the field
    Shannon-*Solve*, 37–40
The working waterman
    Keightley-*World*, 261
WORKS OF MERCY
    The kingdom of beautiful
        colors
WORLD
—end of. *See* END OF THE
    WORLD
—Upper, Lower, and Middle
    Bao Luotuo the sage
The world below
    Villa-*Armenian*, 266–273, 500–
        505
The world beyond: The rainbow
        bridge
    MacLean-*Cuentos*, 125–
        129
World calamities [motif index]
    Wilbert-*Boror*, 235–236
The world in a pillow
    Sanders-*Dragon*, 71–72
The world of ice and fire
    Branston-*Gods*, 15–19
The world of the gods
    Gibson-*Gods*, 15–19
"WORLD SERPENT"
    Thor goes fishing
WORLD WAR II
    A prophecy of war
—JEWS - Warsaw ghetto
    The power of light
[World-devastating flood inflicted by
        Zeus]
    Water Spirits, 14–20
"WORLDS OF WONDER"

The fantasy land of Lord
Dunsany
WORMS
The flying childer
How Asanga came to see the
future Buddha
Rabbit and the grain buyers
[earth worms]
The serpent-slayer
Tale of the shrimp and the
earthworm
Worship of the devil
Robe-*Hispanic,* 20–205
Worshippers: The devil in the
church
Lindow-*Swedish,* 159–161
The wounded lion
Lang-*Pink/D,* 191–199
Lang-*Pink/K,* 140–146
The wounded seal
Keightley-*World,* 394–395
Yolen-*Favorite,* 311–312
The wow o'Rivven; the bell
Macdonald-*Gray,* 82–100
Wraiths of wind and wave
Water Spirits, 68–91
Wrath. *See* ANGER
Wrecker of Sennen Cove
Marshall-*Every.,* 217–221
Wren: filled with goodness
Magical Beasts, 81–83
WRENS
That wicked crow
—"scares off" tiger
Father Wren and King Tiger
WRESTLERS AND WRESTLING
Coming of the corn
The king's rival
Kintaro, the golden boy
Thor in the giant's strong-hold
Three strong women: Forever
Mountain [Japan]
Wright, Betty Ren
The Mother Goose madman
WRITERS
Low hurdles

WRITING
Winkle the witch
Wu Ching-tzu
Unofficial history of the Confu-
cian Academy
WULBARI (god)
Separation of god from man
WURRUMS
Water beasts and wurrums
Wurrunna and the Seven Sisters
Reed-*Aboriginal,* 97–102
Wurrunnah's trip to the sea
Parker-*Australian,* 16–149
WYND, Childre
Laidley worm of Spindlestone
Heugh

XOCHICALCATL (cannibal-giant)
Tepoztecatl [swallowed by
giant; escapes]

YAKS
Gesar of Ling
The Nomad
The white rooster
Yallery Brown
Crossley-*Folk,* 97–101
Garner-*British,* 32–40
YAMA, King of the Underworld
Mulien rescues his mother
Savatri and the god of death
Yamamoto, Fumiko Y.
Japanese supernaturals, de-
ities, ghosts . . .
Kendall-*Haunting,* 35–38
YAMS
Talk; everything Ashanti farmer
contacts starts talking

Yamstick: Moon and Morning Star
Reed-*Aboriginal*, 104–107
YANGTZE RIVER
When gods and men mingled
Yankee Doodle [song and story]
Sanders-*Hear*, 19–27
"YANKEE DOODLES"
Nippy and the Yankee Doodle
YARN
The companion
Maidens in a mirror
—of fate
The imprisoned princess
YARROW (herb)
Todzi-touega
Yawayawa and crow
Stokes-*Turtle*, 134–135
YAWNING
Old One Eye [robbers foiled]
Yder challenged by Eric
Lehane-*Legends*, 74–79
YEAR
—number of day in
The extra days: Ra, Thoth,
and Nut
The year summer was stolen
Hill-*More*, 65–74
Yeats, W. B.
Priest of Coloony [poem]
Yeats-*Fairy*, 199–200, 293
Stolen child [poem]
Yeats-*Fairy*, 57–59
Yeghnig Aghpar
Villa-*Armenian*, 255–266, 496–
500
YELLOW BIRDS
How the seven brothers saved
their sister
The yellow dwarf
Lang-*Blue*, 27–50 (notes 354,
365
The Yellow Emperor: war against
Chitou
Sanders-*Dragons*,20–21
The yellow ribbon [holds wife's
head on]

Stuchl-*American*, 143–144
YELLOW RIVER
Golden chisel and the stone
ram
Yerensay's forty fables
Riordan-*Tartary*, 13–20
The yes-no-yes-no spirit
Robinson-*Raven*, 57–69
Yesterday's witch [Miss Marble]
Schwartz-*Great*, 81–91
YETI
Wild men
Yggdrasill, the world ash
Branston-*Gods*, 31–36
Ygnacio y el toro gigantesco
MacLean-*Cuentos*, 142–143
YI (a god)
Chang'o and the elixir of
immortality
Yi Chang and the spectres
Manning-*spooks*, 28–35
YITZHAQ, Rabbi, 1745–1815
—Seer of Lublin
Patai-*Gates*, 711–716
The Yom Kippur flutist
Patai-*Gates*, 671–672
Yoni and her stepmother
Zong-*Korea*, 46–48
YORIMITSU (subject)
Piggott-*Japanese*, 144 (index)
Yorkshire giant [Penhill]
Marshall-*Every.*, 143–151
Yorkshire Jack and Sarah
Polgrains
Water Spirits, 86–87
YOSHITSUNE (subject)
Piggott-*Japanese*, 144 (index)
Young, Egerton Ryerson
Windagoos! Cannibals!
Young boy and the dwarf
Todd-*Some*, 152–158
The young gentleman and the
tiger
Zong-*Korea*, 160–162
Young Gim and the robbers
Zong-*Korea*, 62–66

The young girl and the moon
  Weiss-*Russian*, 167–170
The young head of the family
  Phelps-*Tatterhood*, 83–86
The young hunter
  Hadley-*Legends*, 18–19
The young king
  Wilde-*Fairy*, 95–115
The young lady of Hellerup
  Booss-*Scand.*, 271–272
The young man and the priest
  Zong-*Korea*, 73–75
The young man and the talking
    skull
  Magel-*Gambia*, 81–84
The young man in the shian
  Keightley-*World*, 386–387
The young man who refused to kill
  Hyde-Chambers-*Tibet*, 76–82
Young man who was carried off by
    a lion
  Radin-*African*, 161–164
The young piper
  Yeats-*Fairy*, 313–319
The young rooster
  Lobel-*Fables*, 36–37
The young seamstress
  Sheohmelian-*Three*, 73–83
The young swain and the elves
  Keightley-*World*, 86–87
The young widow
  Zong-*Korea*, 110–120
The youngest god [Dionysius]
  Lines-*Greek*, 81–88
YOUTH
  See also GROWTH;
    REJUVENATION
  "If I had the wings of an
    angel"
  Youth without age and life
    without death (Turkey)
  —apples of
  The apples of Iduna
  —cannot return to
  The boy and the dancing fairy
  —eternal

Oisin in Tir Nan Og, or last of
    the Fena
  Prince Meerzat Istvan and the
    horse of dust . . .
  —fountain of
  See FOUNTAIN OF YOUTH
  —golden apples of
  The apples of eternal life
  —restored
  The king who would have a
    beautiful wife
  The new hand [old man made
    young again]
  Princess and the slave
The youth and the dog-dance
  Macmillan-*Canadian*, 258–262
The youth and the eagles
  Mullett-*Spider*, 90–107
A youth set out to learn what fear
    was
  Lang-*Blue*, 92–102 notes, 353,
    367
The youth who brought the corn
  Mullett-*Spider*, 44–53
The youth who went forth to learn
    what fear was
  Yolen-*Favorite*, 235–242
Youth without age and life without
    death (Turkey)
  Yolen-*Favorite*, 457–465
Y's: the city of the depths
  Lee-*Castles*, 66–67
Yu controls the flood
  Sanders-*Dragons*, 32–33
YUCCA
  The drowned boys
YUGOSLAVIA
  Vodyaniye
  —ballads
  See BALLADS – Yugoslavia
Yule. *See* CHRISTMAS
Yvon and Finette
  Lochhead-*Battle*, 132–147

ZADIK
King who had no children
ZADIK (subject)
Nahman-*Tales*, 335
ZAIRE
A pair of skinnies
Zamani goes to market
And Every., 253–264
Zan and the Dactyls in early Crete
Shelley-*Legends*, 48–50
Zeal
Our-Lady-of-the-Swallows
ZEELAND
The tricking of King Gilfi
ZEUS
Artemis and Apollo
Athene, goddess of wisdom
Baucis and Philemon
Gods and goddesses of Mount
Olympus
The Great Bear [Callisto and
Arcas]
In the beginning: the Greek
panoply
Mother Earth and her children
The new gods - Zeus and
Hera
Peleus and Thetis [marriage]
Prometheus and Pandora
[World-devastating flood in-
flicted by Zeus]
The youngest god [Dionysius]
ZEUS (subject)
Pinsent-*Greek*, 144 (index)
—Myths
Lines-*Greek*, 268 (index)
Zeus and the creation of man
Low-*Greek*, 22–32
Zhang Daoling
Sanders-*Dragons*, 76–80
Zhaozhou Bridge [Han]

Magic Knife, 125–132
Zhong Jingwen
Chinese tales
Minford-*Fav.*, 5–16
Zilyan
Riordan-*Tartary*, 150–153
Zimmer, Dirk, illus.
Schwartz-*Dark*
Zirac and friends
Wood-*Kalila*, 185–256
[Zitkala-Sa and Dakota/Sioux
legends]
Zitkala-*Old*, xi–xviii
ZITKALA-SA (subject)
—[Dakota legends]
Zitkala-*Old*, xi–xviii
"ZIUSDRA"
Seven days and nights
Zo Han-Zun who became a stone
Buddha
Zong-*Korea*, 75–77
ZOBOPS
Mummies, zombies, and artifi-
cial men
The Zodiac
Gallant-*Constel.*, 173–181
ZODIAC
Tidings of the heavens
The Zodiac, in time and space
Gallant-*Constel.*, 173–178
The Zodiac, precession of the
Equinoxes
Gallant-*Constel*, 178–181
ZOMBIES
Mummies, zombies, and artifi-
cial men
Zon U-Czi
Zong-*Korea*, 224–234
Zulus. *See under* AFRICA—tribes
Zuni creation legend
Gallant-*Constel.*, 16–17